the
War
on
Sex

David M. Halperin and Trevor Hoppe | *editors*

the

War

on

Sex

Duke University Press | Durham and London | 2017

© 2017 Duke University Press
All rights reserved
Printed in the United States of America on acid-free paper ∞
Text designed by Mindy Basinger Hill
Cover designed by Matthew Tauch
Typeset in Arno Pro by Westchester Publishing Services

Library of Congress Cataloging-in-Publication Data
Names: Halperin, David M., [date] editor. | Hoppe, Trevor, [date] editor.
Title: The war on sex / David M. Halperin and Trevor Hoppe, eds.
Description: Durham : Duke University Press, 2017. | Includes
bibliographical references and index.
Identifiers: LCCN 2016045797 (print)
LCCN 2016047432 (ebook)
ISBN 9780822363514 (hardcover : alk. paper)
ISBN 9780822363675 (pbk. : alk. paper)
ISBN 9780822373148 (ebook)
Subjects: LCSH: Sexual minorities—Legal status, laws, etc.—United
States. | Sexual minorities—Civil rights—United States. | Sex
discrimination in criminal justice administration—United States. |
Sex offenders—Legal status, laws, etc.—United States.
Classification: LCC KF4754.5 .W37 2017 (print) | LCC KF4754.5 (ebook) |
DDC 345.73/0253—dc23
LC record available at https://lccn.loc.gov/2016045797

Contents

Foreword: Thinking Sex and Justice
TREVOR HOPPE | *ix*

Introduction: The War on Sex
DAVID M. HALPERIN | *1*

PART I The Politics of Sex

1. The New Pariahs: Sex, Crime, and Punishment in America
ROGER N. LANCASTER | *65*

2. Sympathy for the Devil: Why Progressives Haven't Helped the Sex
Offender, Why They Should, and How They Can
JUDITH LEVINE | *126*

3. Queer Disavowal: "Controversial Crimes" and Building Abolition
OWEN DANIEL-MCCARTER, ERICA R. MEINERS, AND R. NOLL | *174*

4. A New Iron Closet: Failing to Extend the Spirit
of *Lawrence v. Texas* to Prisons and Prisoners
J. WALLACE BORCHERT | *191*

5. Seeing the Sex and Justice Landscape through the Vatican's Eyes:
The War on Gender and the Seamless Garment of Sexual Rights
MARY ANNE CASE | *211*

PART II The Invention of the Sex Offender

6. Sex Panic, Psychiatry, and the Expansion of the Carceral State
REGINA KUNZEL | *229*

7. The Creation of the Modern Sex Offender
SCOTT DE ORIO | *247*

8. For What They Might Do:
A Sex Offender Exception to the Constitution
LAURA MANSNERUS | 268

PART III   Sex Work and the Trouble with Trafficking

9. The "Hooker Teacher" Tells All
MELISSA PETRO | 291

10. Carceral Politics as Gender Justice? The "Traffic in Women"
and Neoliberal Circuits of Crime, Sex, and Rights
ELIZABETH BERNSTEIN | 297

11. California's Proposition 35 and the Trouble with Trafficking
CAROL QUEEN AND PENELOPE SAUNDERS | 323

PART IV   Making HIV a Crime

12. HIV: Prosecution or Prevention? HIV Is Not a Crime
SEAN STRUB | 347

13. HIV Monsters: Gay Men, Criminal Law, and the
New Political Economy of HIV
GREGORY TOMSO | 353

14. HIV Care as Social Rehabilitation: Medical Governance,
the AIDS Surveillance Industry,
and Therapeutic Citizenship in Neoliberal Taiwan
HANS TAO-MING HUANG | 378

PART V   Resistance

15. The New War on Sex: A Report from the Global Front Lines
MAURICE TOMLINSON | 409

16. Building a Movement for Justice: *Doe v. Jindal* and
the Campaign against Louisiana's Crime Against Nature Statute
ALEXIS AGATHOCLEOUS | 429

17. Bringing Sex to the Table of Justice
AMBER HOLLIBAUGH | 454

Afterword: How You Can Get Involved

TREVOR HOPPE | 461

Contributors | 465

Index | 469

TREVOR HOPPE

Foreword

Thinking Sex and Justice

When Gayle Rubin declared in her now-famous 1984 essay, "Thinking Sex," that sex "has its own internal politics, inequities, and modes of oppression," she was highlighting the urgent need for a coherent analysis of sex on its own terms.[1] Reacting against an analysis of sex couched solely in terms of gender, she proposed that scholars and activists needed to come up with new terms for understanding how sex becomes an important site of social control, adjudication, and — ultimately — oppression.

Much has changed since 1984. Gay men, lesbians, and transgender people have made important strides in achieving legal and social equality as sexual identity and, more recently, gender identity have become widely recognized as illegitimate bases for discrimination. At the same time, HIV/AIDS has claimed millions of lives and created new fears about sex, adding fuel to long-standing public debates over sexual morality. Yet, despite these shifts, very little has been done to realize Rubin's vision for analyzing and politicizing sex in its own terms — both within and outside of the academy.

Outside of academia, social movement organizations such as the New York–based group Sex Panic! or the sexuality-focused Woodhull Sexual Freedom Alliance are rare. Many of them have typically focused on sexual health and do not generally frame their work in terms of social justice or civil rights. This is changing, as the groundbreaking activism highlighted in the pages that follow demonstrates. But there is much work that remains to be done.

Within academia, scholars studying relevant issues tend to work within disciplinary and professional boundaries. The tendency and academic pressure to publish in disciplinary journals in many fields means that their work is not often read by scholars outside their immediate field. Conferences also tend to be organized within disciplinary boundaries, further compounding the problem.

Despite these trends, the politics of sex remains a rich site for academic inquiry and political action. News headlines from across the country reveal that sex remains a politically salient category worthy of attention. Accusations of sexual misconduct were a central issue in the public case against WikiLeaks founder Julian Assange. Efforts to pass legislation in Uganda that would have made sex for HIV-positive people a crime punishable by death were linked to American evangelical organizations. A teacher in New Jersey was fired from her job when her employers discovered her earlier career in pornography, while a teacher in California was fired for seeking consensual sex online. Sex offender registries have exploded in both scope and use nationwide with little resistance or debate.

These events are both troubling and deserving of critical examination, and yet they are just pieces of a much larger puzzle comprising legal, social, and economic systems that do not readily seem to fit together. Without a coherent analysis of sex and its relationship to social justice to make sense of how sex is mobilized legally, politically, and socially, it becomes impossible to think critically about these cases — and the countless others like them — as a whole. By bringing together academics, legal experts, and activists invested in these issues, *The War on Sex* aims to lay the foundation necessary to analyze how sex is intertwined with justice.

The volume emerged from a conference on "Sex and Justice" held in October 2012 at the University of Michigan, organized by the coeditors of this book and hosted by the University of Michigan's Institute for Research on Women and Gender. Invited scholars from a range of disciplinary approaches — from the humanities to the social sciences to law — spoke alongside legal experts and activists. Hundreds of attendees came to the three-day event, reaffirming our belief that the gathering was sorely needed.

We are grateful to the many faculty members at the University of Michigan who served as faculty advisors, including Elizabeth Armstrong, David Caron, Jarrod Hayes, Anna Kirkland, Sara McClelland, Mark Padilla, JJ Prescott, Gayle Rubin, Scott Spector, Valerie Traub, Elizabeth Wingrove, and Robert Wyrod. In addition, several Michigan faculty and graduate students volunteered to assist in various ways, including Rostom Mesli, Charles Gueboguo, and Frieda Ekotto.

We also must thank Catherine Hanssens from the Center for HIV Law and Policy, and longtime LGBT activist Amber Hollibaugh, who both took time out of their busy schedules to serve as external advisors for the event.

We are especially grateful to our many funders on campus, including the College of Literature, Science, and the Arts, the Institute for Humanities (especially then-director Daniel Herwitz), the Lesbian-Gay-Queer Research Initiative (a program area at the Institute for Research on Women and Gender), the Office of the Vice President for Research, the Rackham Graduate School, and the following academic departments: Communications, Comparative Literature, English, History, Law, Political Science, Public Health, Romance Languages, Sociology, and Women's Studies.

Many of the panelists from the conference are included in this volume, although we were unable to include everyone. We would like to thank those speakers whose work is not represented in these pages: Barry Adam, Naomi Akers, Sienna Baskin, Eli Braun, Bill Dobbs, Kenyon Farrow, Joseph Fischel, David John Frank, Carol Galletly, Catherine Hanssens, Deon Haywood, Todd Heywood, Nan Hunter, Janice Irvine, Gabriele Koch, Greggor Mattson, Jeff Montgomery, Eric Mykhalovskiy, Alice N'Kom, Gayle Rubin, Yolanda Simon, Robert Suttle, Matthew Weait, and Corey Yung.

Without the tireless work of these individuals and institutions, this volume would not have been possible. We are grateful for their contributions.

NOTE

1. Gayle Rubin, "Thinking Sex: Notes for a Radical Theory of the Politics of Sexuality," in *Pleasure and Danger: Exploring Female Sexuality*, 2nd ed., ed. Carole S. Vance (London: Pandora, 1992), 267–319.

DAVID M. HALPERIN

Introduction

The War on Sex

I

The world is waging a war on sex.

It is a quiet war. It is often an undercover war. It has gone unnoticed, for the most part, except by those who have been affected by it, directly or indirectly.

And yet it is hardly an unpopular war. Many people, when asked to endorse it, do so enthusiastically. It has aroused little indignation, opposition, or resistance. It is painfully difficult to contest. It relies on a mainstream consensus — if not exactly in its favor, at least in support of the general principles in whose name it is fought.

It is also a terribly destructive war. It has devastated civil liberties. It has had grave consequences for the autonomy and agency of women, young people, the disadvantaged, and the vulnerable. It has ruined many, many lives. It has had a particularly violent impact on those who are socially marginalized, socially stigmatized, or racially marked, or who cherish nonstandard sexual practices. Sexual freedom has lost significant ground to it — ground that will take a very long time to recover.

Costly for some, the war on sex has turned out to be immensely profitable and useful for others — not only for politicians and academics, therapists and police officers, journalists and moralists, but also for a multitude of interested parties. It is not about to end any time soon. And, as in most wars, fog and shadows, propaganda and disinformation conceal the contours of events. So we need to understand what is going on in order to confront it and to challenge it. And we need to do that now.

"We have heard a great deal of overblown rhetoric during the sixties in which the word 'war' has perhaps too often been used — the war on poverty, the war on misery, the war on disease, the war on hunger." So Richard Nixon remarked on January 22, 1970, in his first Annual Message to the Congress on the State of the Union, no doubt with a backward glance at his predecessor, President Lyndon Johnson. "But if there is one area where the word 'war' is appropriate," Nixon continued, "it is in the fight against crime. We must declare and win the war against the criminal elements which increasingly threaten our cities, our homes, and our lives."[1] In addition to launching what became known as the War on Crime, Nixon reportedly called for a War on Drugs when, a year and a half later, on June 17, 1971, he issued a "Special Message to the Congress on Drug Abuse Prevention and Control." In fact, that White House statement spoke only of a "war against heroin addiction" and the "threat of narcotics"; it proposed "a full-scale attack on the problem of drug abuse in America." It did not employ the phrase "war on drugs," but Nixon's earlier declaration of a "war against crime" provided a model for the formula by which his drug policy, and its successors, became known.[2]

Is the word "war" actually appropriate to designate the sharp rise in the limitations placed on sexual freedom in the United States and elsewhere since the 1970s? Some readers may greet these opening paragraphs — and the title of this book itself — with a measure of Nixon's skepticism about overblown rhetoric. The war on sex is not, admittedly, a single, integrated phenomenon, nor does it appear to be a deliberate strategic plan coordinated at some high level of centralized authority: it is rather the cumulative effect of many independent, though interrelated, initiatives. No one in power in the U.S. government has formally declared a war on sex as a matter of public policy. On the contrary, the last fifty years are conventionally understood to have witnessed an inexorable expansion of sexual liberties in the United States — if not exactly a sexual revolution, then at least a slow extension into law, policy, and social practice of the revolutionary changes in sexual life associated with the upheavals and counterculture of the 1960s.

The essays collected in this volume tell a very different story, a story quite unlike that conventional tale of progress — though thoroughly cognizant of the standard progress narrative they challenge. It is a story that runs counter to many received ideas about recent history and sexual politics. It focuses on the United States but it also glances elsewhere — at the Caribbean, at Asia, and at Europe (which is particularly affected). The war on sex is a global phenomenon, and the work assembled here offers a narrow glimpse of its global dimensions. But the war on sex is also an American export, and the contributors to this collection pay particular attention to the United States because its influence, both through government programs and policies and through U.S. funding of international nongovernmental organizations (NGOs), has had a worldwide impact.

It may not in fact be a gross exaggeration to call the current rollback of sexual freedom a war. Although it is not a conventional armed conflict, the state is deeply involved in waging it, and it does so to the full extent of its might. In the United States, for example, no fewer than two federal agencies, the Department of Justice (DOJ) and the Department of Homeland Security, and one municipal agency, the New York Police Department (NYPD), combined on August 25, 2015, to launch a massive raid on the Manhattan offices of Rentboy.com, an entirely aboveground, two-decades-old online clearinghouse for advertisements by gay male escorts. At the same time, officers armed with guns and vests appeared without warning at the homes of the organization's staffers and arrested them, though six months later the feds quietly dropped all charges against everyone but the CEO. What made this organization so dangerous, so deserving of an armed response, and its employees such a threat to national security? The most serious crime of which the latter stood accused was "conspiring to violate the Travel Act by promoting prostitution"; there were no allegations of trafficking, pimping, exploiting minors, creating a public nuisance, using force or coercion, or victimizing anyone (the 1961 Travel Act merely forbids interstate commerce that promotes illegal activities).[3] Sex itself was the enemy — nonstandard forms of it in particular, such as gay sex and commercial sex. Many government agencies, including the police, the FBI, and the Immigration and Customs Enforcement (ICE, a branch of the Department of Homeland Security), are routinely engaged in sexual surveillance, and they do not hesitate to pursue even noncontact crimes of a sexual nature with disproportionate deployments of militarized force.[4]

As this example shows, the war on sex should not be confused with a heightened awareness of sexual violence, rape, and the sexual abuse of children along with a greater determination to do something about them by means of law and social policy. There is nothing wrong with using legal and moral pressure to reduce the incidence of sexual assault, forced prostitution, and child pornography featuring real children subjected to sexual mistreatment: those are all instances of grievous personal harm, which must be prevented, if possible, and, if not, must be met with a firm, appropriate response.

The war on sex, however, cannot be reduced to an enlightened effort to prevent and punish sexual harm, though it often camouflages itself as such. It is rather a war against sex itself — in many cases, against sex that does no harm but that arouses disapproval on moral, aesthetic, political, or religious grounds. Those grounds provide an acceptable and politically palatable cover for a war on the kinds of sex that are disreputable or that many people already happen to dislike.

Let me be very clear on this point. There is no denying that sex can be a vehicle for harm, sometimes very serious harm. It is not only legitimate but indeed imperative to stop people from using sex to harm one another. Sexual freedom is not a license to abuse others for one's own pleasure. But preventing sexual abuse should not furnish a pretext for an all-out war on sex that permanently identifies sex itself with danger and with potential or actual harm. Nor should it provide a justification for dispensing with all measure and proportion in deterrence and punishment.

The view that sex *in itself* is bad or harmful is rarely articulated or argued. But it is powerfully if wordlessly expressed in the tendency to punish sexual crimes much more harshly than other serious crimes, even the most destructive and violent crimes. It is also present in hyperbolic condemnations of the kinds of sex that are admittedly unsavory, disgusting, or selfish: those judgments easily slide into portraying disapproved sex as inappropriate or undesirable sex, then as objectifying or exploitative sex, and finally as genuinely abusive, violent, or harmful sex.

Under that cover, and in the guise of a campaign against sexual violence or abuse, the war on sex offers a noble cause and an effective rallying point for people located on every part of the political spectrum. It unites feminists and evangelicals, liberals and radicals, politicians and activists, intellectuals and populists, Left and Right. That is what makes it so hard to critique and to challenge. But that is also what makes it so important to address.

The purpose of this book is to document, to describe, and to oppose the war on sex.

In the United States today, it is common to believe that we live in an era of sexual emancipation. And there are good reasons for thinking so. Within the span of a single lifetime, within the memory of many people who are alive today, sexual attitudes in the United States have undergone major transformations. A series of judicial and legislative decisions have permitted certain sexual freedoms that, just a short time before, would have seemed unthinkable. The U.S. Supreme Court has enshrined many sexual freedoms in constitutional law. Let us recall a few of the major legal milestones.

For most of U.S. history, it was constitutionally permissible for individual states to criminalize the distribution and use of contraception. Only in 1965 did the Supreme Court guarantee a right of access to contraception — for husbands and wives only, not for unmarried partners or anyone else. The Court went further in 1972, when it struck down laws that restricted the availability of contraceptives to married couples. In 1977, it went further still, prohibiting states from limiting the sale or distribution of contraceptives to people sixteen and older, thereby permitting adolescents to purchase condoms and other contraceptive products.[5] To be sure, the battle over contraception is not yet over. There are ongoing social conflicts today over a series of policy questions relating to contraception: whether the U.S. military should provide it to service members, whether private insurance companies can be required by the federal government to cover its costs, whether employers can be required to offer such coverage, whether certain kinds of pharmaceutical contraceptives should be available without a doctor's prescription, and whether there should be age restrictions on obtaining them over the counter. But the legality of contraception itself and its availability for general sale are no longer contested.

Abortion has been legal since 1973, though it is often unobtainable in practice, especially by poor women, in many parts of the United States. Obscenity, whether verbal or pictorial, is rarely prosecuted, except in reference to child pornography: books with four-letter words in them cannot be banned from publication (though they may be removed from libraries and schools). Since 1969, it has been legal to possess pornography and to view it in one's home (as long as the individuals who figure in it and who view it are at least eighteen years of age: pornography depicting minors, which was once illegal only to produce, is now also illegal to possess). It took the Supreme Court longer to legalize non-heterosexual and non-genital sex, but in 2003 it vacated state laws that criminalized anal, oral, and manual sex between consenting adults performed in private for noncommercial purposes.[6] Women can no longer be prohibited by the states from serving on juries; other restrictions, both formal and informal, on the access of women to employment, education, athletics, and care for their young children have been lifted, thereby guaranteeing women a degree of social autonomy without which real sexual autonomy is not possible. Marriage has finally ceased to be a license to rape: spousal rape has been illegal in all fifty states since the early 1990s. In at least twenty-two states homosexuality is no longer a legally permissible ground for denial of access to employment, housing, and public accommodation, and marriage between two people of the same sex is now legal nationwide. The rights of transgender people are slowly gaining official recognition.

How is it possible, in the context of such broad and far-reaching progressive reforms, to speak of a war on sex?

This volume does not ignore or attempt to play down these historical changes. The work collected here acknowledges that in many respects the last fifty years have witnessed a significant expansion of sexual freedoms — at least, of certain sexual freedoms. That expansion represents an important historical development. It also represents a positive development, since sexual freedom is a good in itself. The contributors to this volume seek neither to minimize nor to deny these striking changes.

But the progressive liberalization of sex in the United States over the last fifty years is not the whole story. Outside the privileged domain of certain approved, legally permitted, and constitutionally protected sexual practices, sexual freedom has come under sustained attack. There has been a war, in short, on the kinds of sex that are morally disapproved, or that are stigmatized, or that simply fall outside the range of practices currently sanctified by legal guarantees.

New restrictions, both formal and informal, are being placed on commercial sex and sexual services, public sexual expression and publicly visible sexual representation, sex in publicly accessible venues, nonmarital sex and sex outside the context of the couple, sex online, sex in the workplace, HIV-positive sex, pornography, gay sex, sex in schools and prisons, sex between adults and minors, and sex among minors.

It would be impossible to produce an exhaustive list of the complex ways in which sexual freedom is currently under siege in the United States. But the last fifty years, especially the last two and a half decades, have witnessed a series of ominous developments that can be enumerated easily enough. There have been, for example:

- a gradual restriction of public access to contraception and abortion, including a nationwide campaign against Planned Parenthood;

- a widening and diversifying opposition to sex education in public schools;

- a multiplication of attacks on sex research and sex-related scholarship;

- a series of panics over sex crimes and sexual predators that have eventuated in new waves of repressive legislation;

- an expansion of sex offender registries and of the categories of sex crimes for which registration is mandatory;

- an accelerating drive to protect children and adolescents from dangers of all kinds, including sexual danger, which has had the effect of curtailing the sexual agency of minors and young adults;

- the emergence of a new consensus and political infrastructure opposed to human trafficking, which has often targeted all forms of commercial sex instead of focusing on forced prostitution, labor exploitation, coerced work, and other nonsexual forms of trafficking;

- an attack on online advertising for sexual services, as part of the campaign against trafficking;

- new restrictions on access to pornography, which the state of Utah, in a piece of non-binding legislation passed in 2016, went so far as to declare a "public health crisis";[7]

- a growing concern for the rights of victims at the expense of the civil liberties of the accused and due process for the accused;

- a continuing crackdown on sex in publicly accessible venues;

- a mounting tendency to treat sex itself as a danger or threat;

- an intensifying urgency to protect people from sex;

- an increasing regulation and criminalization of sex;

- an imposition of ever-narrowing legal and administrative definitions of who is entitled to engage in sex;

- an expansion of the populations whose sexual behavior falls under state or bureaucratic control;

- a striking upsurge in the severity of the punishments meted out to those who commit sex offenses, even those convicted of relatively minor infractions: for example, the proportion of sex offenders subject to federal mandatory minimum sentences has skyrocketed (from 5 percent in 2001 to 51 percent in 2010);[8] and

- an explosion in the number of registered sex offenders, with a 35 percent increase from 2005 to 2013, by a conservative measure.[9]

In comparing rates of sex offender registration against general trends in American correctional supervision, Trevor Hoppe, one of the editors of this volume, has found that sex offender registration rates have spiked in recent years, even as trends in corrections have plateaued (see figure Intro1).[10]

In the light of these developments, there is reason to temper the optimism that has greeted the dramatic success of the lesbian/gay/bisexual/transgender (LGBT) rights movement in decriminalizing private, consensual, noncommercial adult sex and in legalizing gay marriage. Recent victories for LGBT rights at the U.S. Supreme Court and in federal policy have induced a false sense of complacency among many people on the progressive end of the political spectrum. The resulting faith in the ongoing enlargement of sexual freedom has blocked an awareness of what the essays assembled in this collection show: that sex has increasingly become a distinct target of contemporary policing, punishment, and bureaucratic management. In fact, during the same period that has witnessed the progress of LGBT rights, a complex array of both governmental and nongovernmental institutions — such as sex offender registries and the anti-prostitution industry — has emerged and expanded. Sexual and racial minorities, along with immigrants and the poor, are often

FIGURE INTRO1. Change in rates of sex offender
registration vs. corrections, 2005–2013

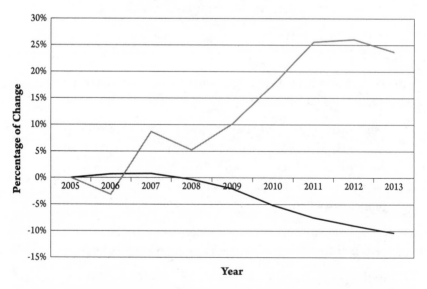

Cumulative change in corrections supervision rate per 100K adult population (50 States & DC)
Cumulative change in sex offenders rate per 100K adult population (50 States & DC)

vulnerable to their effects, but White heterosexual couples and children do not escape them either. And "outside of the global north," as Maurice Tomlinson reminds us in his contribution to this collection, "the ongoing struggle for securing basic legal protections for LGBTI [lesbian, gay, bisexual, Trans*, and intersex] people . . . remains a pressing issue."

In short, the familiar stories we have been telling ourselves about the sexual revolution, the rise of sexual permissiveness, the collapse of old-fashioned sexual morality, the change in sexual attitudes, the progress of women's rights and gay rights, the decriminalization of sodomy, and the legalization of gay marriage have all diverted attention from a less familiar but equally important story about the new war on sex, a war that in recent years has intensified in scope and cruelty. One aim of this volume, then, is to tell at least some parts of that neglected story — and to document the increasing restriction and regulation of sex in an era otherwise characterized by sexual liberalization.

The proliferating restrictions placed on sex in recent decades should not be seen as mere bumps on the road to greater sexual tolerance or the last gasps of Victorian prohibitions — residual formations or dwindling pockets of reaction, destined to be swept away by the rising tide of progress and enlightenment. On the contrary, many of these phenomena represent emergent formations: new developments that point to urgent problems of justice. They demand to be addressed. They call in particular for a reconsideration not just of specific tactics but also of broad political strategies on the part of feminist, LGBT, and other progressive forces. They require new mobilizations of political resistance in the name of sexual freedom itself. For sexual freedom, as Amber Hollibaugh writes in her contribution to this volume, "is a fundamental, an essential, freedom, and, oddly enough, the ultimate protector of human privacy, vulnerability, autonomy." Moreover, since the war on sex is entwined with racism, sexism, social inequality, and homophobia — though, as I shall argue, it is also distinct and independent from them — it demands a coalitional response that can bring together a range of social movements.

Recently, a number of mainstream political and civil stakeholders have contested some of the extreme consequences of the ominous developments just mentioned. So there are real and significant opportunities for new alliances along the front lines of certain battles in the intensifying war on sex. All of these developments point to the need for a fresh historical vision of how we got into our present situation and for an enhanced understanding of the embattled terrain on which we now find ourselves.

That, in sum, is what this volume aims to provide. The essays collected here document what some of the authors (and others) do not scruple to call "The War on Sex" — the manifold ways in which sexual freedom and sexual expression have in recent decades come under attack from both government and civil society. The contributors trace the history of how progressive political movements came to abandon the cause of human rights pertaining to sex. They also examine how kinds of sexual conduct as well as kinds of sexually defined individuals are currently being hemmed in by new sorts of formal regulation, social disqualification, policing, hypercriminalization, and administrative management in a period of otherwise expanding sexual liberties.

The recent decades have been marked in both Europe and the United States by an expansion of what legal scholar Bernard Harcourt calls "neoliberal penality." Harcourt understands something quite precise by this term. He uses it to refer to "a form of rationality in which the penal sphere is pushed outside political economy and serves the function of a boundary: the penal sanction is marked off from the dominant logic of classical economics as the only space where order is legitimately enforced by the State." As the state retreats from regulation of the market, it vastly expands into other realms of regulation, control, and punishment, "passing new criminal statutes and wielding the penal sanction more liberally *because that is where administration is necessary, that is where the State can legitimately act, that is the proper sphere of governing.*"[11] In the case of sex, neoliberal penality has conduced to an intensification of criminal and regulatory social-control programs affecting ever-widening spheres of human behavior.

Particularly in the last fifty years, as Roger Lancaster explains in his contribution to this volume, "the redistributive welfare state, which once governed through ideals of health, well-being, and discipline, has given way to a punitive neoliberal regime, which takes the crime scene as the basic paradigm of governance and conditions assistance on varied forms of *victimization* (or otherwise subjects benefits to means-testing as opposed to universal entitlement).... Mass incarceration is only one of the punitive state's techniques, and what goes unexamined is the role of sexual fear and loathing in promoting expansive new extra-carceral modes of securitization."

The carceral state itself has been the object of growing critical attention. Activists, scholars, and the media have highlighted the expansion of the prison population in the United States. And as the economic fallout from the 2008 financial crisis has continued to devastate state budgets, even some conservative state governments have been forced to reconsider their tough-on-crime policies, which swell the prison population and drain scarce resources needed for other urgent purposes. In this context, activists and progressive organizations have had some success in rallying broad-based support for campaigns against punitive drug policies and minimum sentencing requirements.

As a result, opposition to the prison-industrial complex, once limited to academic and activist critics of structural racism, has gone mainstream. Speaking at Columbia University on April 29, 2015, Hillary Clinton declared, in one of her first presidential campaign appearances, "It's time to end the era of mass incarceration." President Barack Obama chimed in on July 14, 2015, calling for an end to mandatory minimum sentencing and for congressional action to fix "a broken system." Strong bipartisan support for that objective has in fact emerged in the U.S. Congress as well as across the entire political spectrum; Koch Industries and the MacArthur Foundation, FreedomWorks and the Center for American Progress, along with a number of right-wing and left-wing political leaders and groups, have all come together to form the Coalition for Public Safety in order to lobby for criminal justice reform.[12] Of course, it remains to be seen how substantial or significant any actual reforms prove to be, and in any case the effects of overhauling the federal criminal justice system alone will be felt by only about 10 percent of the entire U.S. prison population. Whatever the outcome, the anti-incarceration movement has made undeniable progress, but it has been less unified, less vigorous, less interested, and less successful in countering the war on sex.

Nonetheless, the war on sex has not gone entirely unchallenged by activists, critics, scholars, lawyers, political commentators, and journalists.[13] Anyone who reads the writings assembled in this volume, who takes the trouble to look into the political mobilizations of resistance and critique that they describe, or who pursues the scholarly leads provided by their citations will recognize how many individuals, organizations, and political coalitions have identified, and contested, the various ways that sex is currently being targeted for regulation and control. A long list of activist groups fighting against the war on sex can be found in the afterword to this volume. Efforts to oppose the war on sex have often been strikingly courageous, astute, and forward-looking, and they have achieved some important victories. But they have had to struggle for broad acceptance. And, in terms of actual progress, this movement is still at its very beginning.

It is perhaps symptomatic of the current state of sexual politics that the war on sex has yet to receive, even from feminists and queer theorists, the urgent attention it deserves. Those who have been defending sexual freedom all along would benefit from a wider political, critical, and scholarly consensus in their favor as well as from more vigorous and principled support. One purpose of this volume, accordingly, is to underwrite their efforts — if only by highlighting the existence of the war on sex and by bringing it to the attention of those who might well challenge it if they actually recognized its extent or the magnitude of the threat it poses to sexual freedom and civil liberties. The writings assembled here should provide renewed inspiration for a broad and powerful response to the war on sex from progressive forces both inside and outside the academy.

Another purpose of this volume is to call for renewed critical analysis of the politics of sex itself.

The politics of sex cannot be reduced to a politics of identity. On the contrary, as the evidence collected here shows, it is a politics that cuts across identity — across differences of race, class, gender, sexuality, and other social categories. That is both a *challenge* and an *opportunity*. It is a challenge because it calls into question some of the dominant, recent, identity-based ways of organizing both knowledge and political movements around sex and sexuality. It is an opportunity because it offers to bring together, across differences of identity, many distinct constituencies affected by the politics of sex.

As a number of essays in this volume make clear, racial and sexual minorities, as well as women, transgender people, and the poor, are sometimes exposed to the harshest kinds of sexual policing. Young transgender people of color are at particular risk of discrimination and mistreatment. Black communities are disproportionately affected: sex offender registration rates for Black men in the United States are roughly twice those for Whites.[14] In other words, the inequalities produced by sexual politics are often stratified according to the same axes of social difference as many other kinds of social inequality.

Often — but not always.

As the contributors to this volume demonstrate, sex as a target of state power is more than just a vehicle for the consolidation of existing social hierarchies. Rather, sex — understood as a continuum of practices ranging from the acceptable and approved to the disreputable and disapproved, along with the regulatory categories of persons those practices generate — has its own politics. It should be seen as an axis of social difference in its own right. Sex gives rise to specific kinds of regulation and control, and it is subject to its own forms of oppression and demonization.[15]

More than thirty years ago, Gayle Rubin argued in her foundational essay, "Thinking Sex," that the politics of sex was not entirely reducible to the politics of gender; it constituted its own axis of inequality and required analysis in its own right.[16] The work collected in this volume dramatizes that point, extends it further, and demands a new engagement with it. As the evidence gathered here argues with particular force and eloquence, sexual politics cuts across the identity politics of gender, race, class, and sexuality.

Take, for example, Louisiana's 200-year-old Crime Against Nature law, which was expanded in 1982 to include "Solicitation" (offering to engage in oral or anal sex for money). The Louisiana state legislature massively reaffirmed its commitment to the law as recently as 2014, when it voted 66–27 against its repeal. Alexis Agathocleous, in his contribution to this volume, highlights the real-world consequences of this law: he shows "how a statute, passed in the context of virulent homophobia in the early 1980s, came to be predominantly wielded against African American women. . . . [The law] was adopted and then enforced in ways that involve sometimes overlapping and sometimes distinct discriminatory purposes." Sexual politics, in other words, is often a solvent of identity. It can override the divisions among different social groups that define themselves by reference to specific identity markers. Sexual politics requires its own analysis.

Why sex? What is it about sex itself that makes it such a ready site for social control? And how do we mobilize politically around it? If the essays in this volume do not offer a single answer to that question, they provide a number of salient clues, and they increase the pressure on all of us to find both theoretical and practical solutions.

II

As of December 7, 2015, there were 843,680 persons registered in the United States as sex offenders.[17] (That is more people than the entire population of states like North Dakota, Wyoming, or Alaska.) The names, photographs, addresses, workplaces, criminal histories, and personal information of these sex offenders are recorded in public, searchable databases, accessible via government websites to anyone with an Internet connection or a smartphone (the specific details posted online vary somewhat by state). Sex offenders must register with the local police in all the jurisdictions where they live, work, and attend school; in many jurisdictions, they must comply with strict residency restrictions as well as restrictions on places where they may be present, and they must regularly update their information (including whenever they move to a new address), on pain of incurring additional penalties, such as prison time. In Louisiana, they must personally notify their neighbors of their presence, for example by distributing handbills with their photos or by taking out advertisements in local newspapers at their own expense. In Texas, the Department of Public Safety must provide written notice to the immediate neighbors of certain sex offenders. In Oklahoma and Louisiana, the words "sex offender" appear in large orange-red letters on their drivers' licenses. In 2003, the U.S. Supreme Court upheld the constitutionality of Alaska's Sex Offender Registration Act, finding that it could be applied to convicted criminals retroactively *because its complex provisions were merely regulatory and not punitive* — a precedent-setting decision.[18]

Very few registered sex offenders — a mere 1 percent in some states — fall into the category of violent sexual predators.[19] Many of those on the sex offender registries were found guilty of crimes that did not involve any contact with another person. Others were convicted of misdemeanors (rather than felonies) of a sexual nature or of crimes involving consensual sexual activity that elicited no complaint from the alleged victims or from bystanders. Among the offenses subject to registration in a number of states in 2007, according to Human Rights Watch, were paying for sex, urinating in public, flashing or streaking, and sexual relations between underage teenagers.[20] In Britain, a man was placed on a sex offender registry in 2007 because he was caught having sex with a bicycle in the privacy of his home.[21] The vast majority (72.4 percent) of the 2,317 sex offenders convicted under *federal* statutes in the United States in 2010 (the most recent year for which the statistics have been analyzed) were charged with "the possession, receipt, transportation, or distribution of sexually oriented images of children": that is, they were found guilty of noncontact crimes — specifically, child pornography offenses that involved no actual physical relations with or direct abuse of a minor on their part.[22]

Judith Levine notes in her chapter that "a quarter of convicted sex offenders are [themselves] minors, eleven to seventeen years old; 16 percent are under twelve." Of all sex offenses against minors "known to the police," according to a comprehensive U.S. Department of Justice report from December 2009, more than a third (35.6 percent) are committed by other minors, many of them quite young: "The number of youth coming to the attention of police for sex offenses increases sharply at age 12 and plateaus after age 14." Even more troubling is the fact that the juvenile sex offenders identified by the police, and recorded in the DOJ's National Incident-Based Reporting System, include "a small number of children younger than 6 years of age." The authors of the 2009 DOJ report decided to exclude that group from its statistics.[23]

Children can of course cause serious sexual harm to other children. Some of them may simply be engaging in routine sexual exploration and experimentation and may therefore require relatively little in the way of intervention. Some of them, however, commit forcible sexual assault, rape, or other acts of sexual violence: such conduct calls for more elaborate intervention and thoughtful, humane punishment. Since children often have unimpeded access to younger children, they can inflict sexual harm unobserved. So it is important to be aware of the risk of sexual abuse among minors and to prevent it as well as to punish it appropriately. If efforts to identify and to discipline juvenile perpetrators of sexual abuse have multiplied of late, that is in part because communities and law enforcement are trying quite properly to make up for a long history of ignoring and of underreporting the sexual abuse of minors by other minors. But the sheer numbers of very young children currently being accused of sex offenses, and the draconian ways in which they are being punished, also raise the possibility that sex offenses are being defined far too broadly and treated out of all proportion to the real danger they present — the possibility, in other words, that sex, not harm, is the actual target of regulation. The DOJ report just cited estimates that in 2004 alone the police in the United States would have identified about 89,000 juveniles as sex offenders.[24]

Those figures may surprise, but what is really surprising is that they aren't higher. As Owen Daniel McCarter, Erica R. Meiners, and R. Noll point out in their contribution to this volume, transgender youth, especially transgender women of color, are often treated as sexual deviants by their schools and accused of sexual offenses. And starting in 2009, when the news media fastened on an epidemic of "sexting" among students at Tunkhannock Area High School in rural Pennsylvania, there has been an avalanche of reports about teenagers taking, and often sending one other via their smartphones, sexually explicit photographs of themselves. Such photos qualify under federal law as child pornography if the subject is under the age of eighteen. Child pornography is illegal to possess (to say nothing of distributing) *even when it consists of images of yourself*. No wonder, then, that high school students all around the United

States have fallen into the clutches of the law and have been subject to a wide variety of disciplinary and punitive measures.[25]

In November 2014, the parents of all children enrolled in the School District of Rhinelander, Wisconsin, received a prerecorded telephone message from the school administration in coordination with the Oneida County Sheriff's Department. The robocall announced the conclusion of an investigation into "numerous students who were sharing inappropriate photos via personal cell phones." The message, as quoted in the Rhinelander *Star Journal*, pointed out that, although no criminal charges had been filed against any of the students involved, "Wisconsin law does consider incidents such as this as *felony offenses*, and it does not have disciplinary alternatives for such offense."[26] Law enforcement officials in many school districts across the country have been obliged in recent years to explain to astonished assemblies of high school students that taking (and, worse, exchanging) explicit photos of themselves makes them felons, who if convicted risk lifelong registration on public, searchable databases as sex offenders, with potentially devastating consequences for their subsequent abilities to find housing, employment, and schooling. As Hanna Rosin summed up the situation in the November 2014 issue of the *Atlantic*, "in most states it is perfectly legal for two 16-year-olds to have sex. But if they take pictures, it's a matter for the police."[27]

Rosin's point is illustrated by the case of Brianna Denson and Cormega Zyon Copening, two African American sixteen-year-olds in Fayetteville, North Carolina. State law permits them to have sex but not to sext: that is a felony, which in North Carolina means that they can be charged as adults — and that journalists can publish their names. Accordingly, on September 2, 2015, a reporter for the *Fayetteville Observer* mentioned the case and described Denson's situation as follows:

> After a 16-year-old Fayetteville girl made a sexually explicit nude photo of herself for her boyfriend last fall, the Cumberland County Sheriff's Office concluded that she committed two felony sex crimes against herself and arrested her in February. The girl was listed on a warrant as both the adult perpetrator and the minor victim of two counts of sexual exploitation of [a] minor — second-degree exploitation for making her photo and third-degree exploitation for having her photo in her possession. A conviction could have put the girl in prison and would have required her to register as a sex offender for the rest of her life. A plea

bargain arranged for her in July [2015] should clear her record next summer.[28]

Of what did that plea bargain consist?

> This is how Denson is settling her case. In court on July 21, Denson told District Court Judge Stephen Stokes that she was responsible for the crime of disseminating harmful material to minors. This is a misdemeanor and does not have the life-ruining requirement that she register as a sex offender. One of [the Cumberland County district attorney's] assistants dropped the felony sexual exploitation charges. Stokes put Denson on probation for a year. He ordered her to pay $200 in court costs, stay in school, take a class on how to make good decisions, refrain from using illegal drugs or alcohol, not possess a cellular phone for the duration of her probation and to do 30 hours of community service. If Denson stays out of trouble, [the district attorney] next July will drop the misdemeanor charge. She will be able to move on with her life with a clean criminal record.[29]

Her boyfriend was not so fortunate, even though he did not disseminate the photos. In fact, neither teen was accused of sharing their photos with anyone besides each other. The sheriff's office still "hit Copening with five sexual exploitation of a minor charges — four for making and possessing two sexually explicit pictures of himself and the last for possessing a copy of the picture that Denson made for him. Copening, who was 16 at the time and is now 17, also faces possible prison time and the requirement to register as a sex offender if convicted. The charges have already forced him off the football team at Jack Britt High School. He had been the quarterback."[30] Copening eventually avoided prison time with a plea bargain similar to Denson's, including a year of probation, during which he will be subject to warrantless searches.[31]

Denson and Copening narrowly escaped lifelong restrictions on their movements. On February 1, 2016, the U.S. Congress unanimously passed H.R. 515: International Megan's Law to Prevent Child Exploitation and Other Sexual Crimes through Advanced Notification of Traveling Sex Offenders. The law forbids the secretary of state to issue passports to any individuals who have ever been convicted of a sex offense with someone below the age of eighteen unless those passports display a "unique identifier," defined as "any visual designation affixed to a conspicuous location on the passport indicating that the individual is a covered sex offender" (by "covered," the text means "covered by that description": i.e., guilty of a sex offense with a minor). Travel documents issued to covered sex offenders before the passage of the law are subject to revocation. No other category of criminal — indeed, no other category of *person* — has until now been identified as such on a U.S. passport, let alone by a visibly conspicuous scarlet letter. Unlike some other countries, the United States has never demanded that its citizens carry papers indicating their religious affiliation or ethnicity, or anything having to do with their medical, criminal, or sexual histories. Never, that is, before now.[32]

The new federal statute also establishes a special center within the ICE "to send and receive notifications to or from foreign countries regarding international travel by registered sex offenders" and to monitor foreign travel by American "child-sex offenders," who must now provide "information relating to [their] intended travel . . . outside the United States, including any anticipated dates and places of departure, arrival, or return, carrier and flight numbers for air travel, destination country and address or . . . any other itinerary or other travel-related information required by the Attorney General." Sponsored by Republican Representative Chris Smith of New Jersey, citing a 2010 Government Accountability Office (GAO) report that found 4,500 passports were being issued annually to sex offenders, the legislation was intended, in Smith's words, to hinder U.S. citizens from abusing "little children" overseas; the State Department, however, had rebutted the implications of the GAO's finding in an appendix to the report, indicating that it "already has the authority to deny passports to people convicted of sex tourism involving minors and those whose probation or parole terms forbid them from traveling." The new law, then, will impose an additional burden on the lives of former sex offenders, long after they have completed their sentences and been released from supervision, and will put them at the mercy of foreign governments whenever they are abroad. And it will do all this without producing any real gains in terms of effective crime prevention. President Barack Obama signed the new legislation into law on February 8, 2016.[33]

At least six other countries in the world (Australia, Canada, France, Ireland, South Africa, and the United Kingdom) require the registration of sex offenders, according to Human Rights Watch. But the United States "is alone in the scope of the registries, in particular the public and easily accessible nature of the information on the registries, the onerous conditions imposed on registrants, the imposition of residency restrictions, and the broad application of many of these aspects to youth sex offenders."[34]

The practice of listing the names and whereabouts of convicted criminals on public registries for many years after they have completed serving their sentences has been largely restricted, so far, to those who have committed crimes that are specifically sex-related. Most other criminals — even those who have been convicted of violent crimes, such as murder, robbery, or assault with a deadly weapon — do not have to register publicly once they have done their time and been released from correctional supervision. (Nor should they: one of the oldest tenets of formal, reasoned law is the idea that every punishment is specific and finite, with fixed limits, including a set period of time, clear sanctions, explicitly stated deprivations, and nothing more.) The treatment of sex offenders, then, cannot be explained by their sheer dangerousness. Rather, the danger that they represent qualifies as extreme *because* it involves sex.

A few states are starting to institute public registries to incorporate other classes of criminals besides sex offenders. In this way, the treatment of sex offenders risks becoming generalized and providing a model for the management of all ex-convicts. As Judith Levine points out in her contribution to this volume, "What happens to sex offenders can eventually happen to all offenders. For instance, states have instituted registries for offenses from drunk driving to methamphetamine manufacture. Florida lists all prisoners released from custody." Roger Lancaster agrees: "If we want to see what social control could look like over the course of the twenty-first century, we should look to the sex offender."

Lancaster goes on to expand on this point. The treatment of sex offenders, he argues,

> should worry us more than it apparently does, in part because the techniques used for marking, shaming, and controlling sex offenders have come to serve as models for laws and practices in other domains. Electronic ankle bracelets and techniques of house arrest are being applied to an expanding list of offenders and defendants — including undocumented immigrants who have been released from custody to await processing (on civil, not criminal, charges). It is estimated that a quarter of a million people are currently manacled to some form of electronic monitoring. Public registries, which make visible any stain on a person's record, have proved especially popular with government agencies, civic

organizations, and private vigilante groups. A victims' rights clearing-house in New Mexico posts an online database of everyone convicted in the state of driving while intoxicated. Several states publish online listings of methamphetamine offenders, while lawmakers in Texas, Nevada, and California have introduced initiatives to create public registries of those convicted of domestic violence.

Gregory Tomso, another contributor to this volume, sees a troubling convergence between the increased governmental regulation of sex and popular movements to contain sexual danger. Noting how "the state's new, aggressive interest in HIV dovetails with an extremist and increasingly popular view of HIV-infected persons as dangerous disease carriers who pose a threat to local communities," Tomso remarks how easy it is for HIV-positive people to be assimilated by the public to the category of sex offenders: "In some cases, people with HIV and violent sex offenders appear to be completely fungible in popular discourse, one standing in for the other amid calls to deprive those with HIV of their civil rights, including their right to privacy. Extremists are using the Internet to promote a form of crowdsourced, vigilante justice targeting sex offenders and so-called HIV predators. The website STDcarriers.com, for example, publishes the names and photographs of thousands of people worldwide who have tested positive for sexually transmitted infections or who have been prosecuted for criminal HIV transmission."

Despite these incipient moves to institute public registries for other types of criminals, only those who have been found guilty of certain sex-related offenses by a court of law are required at this time to register in all fifty of the United States. In that sense, sex remains exceptional in U.S. jurisprudence.

The age at which one may be liable to disciplinary punishment as a sex offender is rapidly decreasing. The age at which it is permissible to exercise sexual agency and freedom is on the rise.

In April 2014, five-year-old Eric Lopez was spotted by a teacher on the playground of the Ashton Ranch Elementary School in Surprise, Arizona. According to Eric's mother, who recounted the story to a local radio station, a somewhat older student had told Eric to pull down his pants or else he would do it for him. Eric complied, pulling down his pants and underwear in front of other students. The teacher took Eric to the office of the principal, who discussed the incident with Eric and got him to sign a form (Eric signed only his first name, that being as much as he knew how to do at his young age), acknowledging that he had been disciplined for "sexual misconduct." To be sure, school officials did not present Eric's behavior to him in that light, since they did not consider such a term "age appropriate," and Eric, for his part, didn't know how to read. The form was placed in his file as part of his permanent scholastic record. Eric's mother was not informed at the time; she discovered the incident a couple of months later and tried to have the incriminating document removed from her son's file. The school refused her request on the grounds that, according to the policy of the Dysart Unified School District, indecent exposure qualifies as a form of sexual misconduct and the school is not obliged to summon a parent to a disciplinary hearing unless the student explicitly invokes his right to have her there. The Las Vegas affiliate of cbs News reported that the assistant superintendent defended the school's actions in a written statement to the local radio station; he said, "Our school district uses consistent language for disciplinary infractions in order to provide clarity and track discipline data accurately," explaining that the district must follow state and federal guidelines and definitions set to define a sexual offense.[35]

Less than a year later, on January 13, 2015, the Faculty of Arts and Sciences (fas) at Harvard University promulgated a new policy banning all sexual or romantic relations between professors and undergraduate students. It states, "No fas Faculty member shall request or accept sexual favors from, or initiate or engage in a romantic or sexual relationship with, any undergraduate student at Harvard College."[36] This prohibition is not limited to professors and students who have some professional association: it does not take into account, for example, whether the professor is the instructor or supervisor of the student. Rather, it forbids relationships between all professors and all undergraduates, even if they have no institutional affiliation with each other and know each other only from a chance meeting off campus or online. The purpose of the categorical prohibition, as Harvard freely acknowledged, was not only to prevent abuse but also to "reflect the faculty's expectations of what constituted an appropriate relationship between undergraduate students and faculty members."[37] The faculty simply happened to disapprove of sex between undergraduates and professors, whether or not it involved any misconduct. Here, once again, the target of regulation is not confined to actual harm; it extends to sex itself. The new policy also does not take into account the age of either the student or the professor, only their official status at Harvard. No matter how old you may be, if you are an undergraduate at Harvard, you remain a statutory minor for sexual purposes insofar as you cannot freely consent to have sexual relations with another adult, of any age, if the latter happens to be a member of the Harvard faculty.

In short, while you are never too young to be guilty of sexual misconduct, you may never be old enough to make certain kinds of sexual decisions for yourself.

III

Let us turn now to the disproportionate sentences often handed out for sexual crimes. Take the case of Daniel Enrique Guevara-Vilca. A stockroom worker in East Naples, Florida, with no previous criminal record, Guevara-Vilca was twenty-four years old when police raided the home he shared with his mother and brother and found a laptop computer that contained 300 sexually explicit pictures of children and 38 hours of taped child pornography. Guevara-Vilca claimed he did not know the images were there: he often downloaded a quantity of pornography from various sites late at night without watching it first. He was found guilty by a six-person jury in 2011 and sentenced by a Collier County Circuit Court judge to serve 454 concurrent life terms, one for each count of possessing an illicit image, amounting to life in prison without the possibility of parole. "Had Mr. Vilca actually molested a child," the *New York Times* pointed out, "he might well have received a lighter sentence." Life without the possibility of parole is a sentence typically given for crimes like first-degree murder, but not for crimes of lesser violence.

In Florida, however, as the *Times* explained, "possession of child pornography is a third-degree felony, punishable by up to five years in prison."[38] In fact, under Guevara-Vilca's sentencing scoresheet, "the minimum permissible sentence was 152.88 years in prison." So remarked Appellate Judge Stevan T. Northcutt of Florida's Second District Court of Appeal on April 10, 2015, when he reversed Guevara-Vilca's conviction on a technicality and remanded the case for a new trial. Judge Northcutt also observed that "if Guevara-Vilca had been charged with possession of child pornography with intent to promote [illegal sex acts involving a minor], he could have been convicted and sentenced for only one second-degree felony count rather than 454 third-degree felony counts."[39]

In this respect, the case of Guevara-Vilca resembles that of Morton R. Berger, an Arizona man who received a 200-year prison sentence, which the U.S. Supreme Court let stand in 2007, for possessing twenty pornographic images of children. This sentence amounted to twenty consecutive sentences of ten years each, since "Arizona law imposes a mandatory minimum sentence of 10 years for 'sexual exploitation of a minor,' and it requires that sentences for multiple convictions [for a range of "dangerous crimes against children"] be served consecutively," as Linda Greenhouse of the *New York Times* explained.[40]

It is reasonable to argue that purchasers of photographic images of the sexual abuse of children drive the market for them and contribute financially to the production of them, thereby indirectly causing real and grievous harm to minors. It is legitimate to criminalize commercial forms of child pornography on that basis and to prosecute and punish those who produce them as well as those who purchase them. When the same images are downloaded repeatedly for free from online sites, however, it is not clear (despite occasional assertions to this effect) that actual, additional harm is being inflicted on minors by Internet users — let alone harm comparable to first-degree murder.

Let us consider the harsh punishments meted out for another category of sexual crime. Twenty-four U.S. states currently make it illegal for HIV-positive people to have sex without first disclosing their infection to their sexual partners. Less than 5 percent of those prosecuted for breaking such laws are accused of infecting their partners; the others, evidently, are accused of failing to inform their sexual partners of their HIV infection before engaging in sexual activity that did not result in the transmission of HIV. Sean Strub, in his contribution to our volume, mentions the well-known case of Nick Rhoades in Iowa, who in 2009 was sentenced to twenty-five years in prison for having failed to disclose his HIV-positive status to another man, whom he did not infect with HIV during sexual intercourse, no doubt because the sexual contact in question actually carried little or no risk of transmitting HIV (Rhoades was under antiretroviral treatment at the time and used a condom for anal sex; the only unprotected sexual contact he had was oral and did not involve ejaculation).[41] He was later released on probation and placed on a sex offender registry; then, in 2014, the Iowa Supreme Court overturned Rhoades's conviction.

Even more remarkable is the case of Willy Campbell, an HIV-positive man currently serving a thirty-five-year prison term in Texas for spitting at a police officer — who, of course, was not infected, since spitting is not a means of HIV transmission: according to the U.S. Centers for Disease Control and

Prevention (CDC), "HIV cannot be spread through saliva, and there is no documented case of transmission from an HIV-infected person spitting on another person."[42] Nonetheless, in 2008, a Dallas jury found that Campbell's saliva was "a deadly weapon," which means that Campbell has to serve half of his sentence before being eligible for parole.[43] These lengthy prison terms for behavior that occasioned no harm to others, but that is associated with socially stigmatized sex, far exceed criminal sentences normally handed out for manslaughter.

Thirty years of research into the sexual dimensions of the HIV/AIDS epidemic have quantified the risky sexual practices of seemingly every conceivable population, at an annual cost of many millions of dollars. But only a small handful of studies have examined the impact of criminalizing HIV on the epidemic itself and on human rights more broadly. The fact that it is still not possible to determine with any degree of exactitude the number of HIV-positive people who have been incarcerated under HIV disclosure laws (a thousand? several thousand?) is a telling indication of how little is known about the expanding regulation of sex.

Excessively harsh or lengthy punishments for sex crimes — even, in some cases, for behavior that caused no injury — are not the most terrifying consequences of the war on sex. Indefinite detention without trial by jury is even more disturbing. In her contribution to this volume, Laura Mansnerus describes how civil commitment policies enacted as part of wide-ranging sex offender legislation have allowed twenty states, the District of Columbia, and the U.S. federal government to keep certain sex offenders locked up for life in high-security treatment facilities, sometimes without a second jury trial, even though those detained did not receive life sentences when they were originally tried in a court of law. In *Kansas v. Hendricks* (1997), the Supreme Court ruled that such detention extending far beyond actual court-ordered sentences is permissible: it does not qualify for inclusion among the "cruel and unusual punishments" prohibited by the Eighth Amendment to the U.S. Constitution because it is not a punishment at all. It is, in theory at least, treatment.[44] Never mind that the treatment facilities where such sex offenders are held bear a striking resemblance to prisons. Or that in some states almost no one ever completes the so-called treatment and ends up getting released.

Regina Kunzel reminds us in her contribution to this volume that civil commitment has a long history, stretching back to the late 1930s and the

1940s, when a widespread panic over sexual deviance resulted in many new innovative and draconian state laws. Those laws provided for the indefinite psychiatric confinement, without any criminal charges, of individuals identified as "sexual psychopaths." In the majority of cases, this term really meant homosexuals, since the legislation "was used most extensively" in order to suppress and to punish "consensual sex between adults of the same sex."

When the chapters by Mansnerus and Kunzel are placed side by side, they make an important political point. As Kunzel argues, the midcentury historical developments that she chronicles provide "a preview and genealogy of the seemingly ever-expanding regime of sex offender surveillance and punishment that we live with today." In particular, by showing how "the discourse of medicine — the language of illness, treatment, and cure — masked a midcentury expansion of the carceral state," Kunzel "offers some clues to understanding the ambivalent and often muted response of early gay rights activists to sexual psychopath legislation, and perhaps even the silence on the part of contemporary LGBT politics in response to the more recent and sweeping national wave of laws criminalizing sexual offenders since 1990." Kunzel suggests that the determination of some LGBT groups to distance themselves and their constituents from the imputations of pathology and criminality with which they had long been stigmatized, and thereby to "dislodge homosexuality from its classification as a mental illness," led them to approve of "sexual psychopath legislation [in general] while seeking to remove homosexuals from its criminalizing purview."

As Kunzel shows, LGBT political organizations have not always known what position to take in the war on sex, especially since they have had to worry that by defending the wrong people they would discredit themselves and their constituencies. That political point about gay activists' fears of reinforcing negative stereotypes in the minds of the heterosexual majority is confirmed by Scott De Orio, in another historical study included in this volume. De Orio describes an almost identical political scenario in California in the 1970s, when "gay activists, liberal state officials, and law-and-order conservatives redefined what it meant to be a 'sex offender' by transforming California's sex offender registry to focus less on gay sex and more on rape and sex with minors." In this case, the issue was not sexual psychopath laws but a vaguely worded section of the state penal code criminalizing "lewd or dissolute conduct," which was used primarily against "gay men who sought intimacy in bars, parks, and other public places." Those convicted under that statute were required to register with the local police as sex offenders.

"Gay activists challenged that regime," De Orio continues, "by forming an alliance with liberals who supported the reform of laws punishing victimless crimes." As a result, "the gay-liberal coalition" was able to end "the police enforcement of the lewd conduct law in semiprivate spaces like gay bars and to remove those convicted under the law from the sex offender registry." But that victory entailed a certain cost. For conservatives — with the endorsement of "liberals and some gay activists," De Orio observes — successfully "spearheaded a campaign to make the registry entail much harsher punishments than it did before." Furthermore, "the broad consensus that registration was appropriate for the 'real' sex offenders completely overshadowed the minority of gay activists, feminists, and civil libertarians who argued that the registry should be abolished entirely. Through these battles, gay activists, liberals, and conservatives produced a new raison d'être for sex offender registration that the federal government would later adopt when it started requiring all states to maintain a registry in the 1990s."[45]

All this historical background is highly significant because it helps to explain our current situation. In particular, it allows us to understand how a sinister legal mechanism like civil commitment, invented in the late 1930s and the 1940s before temporarily falling into disuse in the late 1960s and the 1970s, could be successfully revived in the 1990s and maintain its legitimacy today. As a result, it has become acceptable to treat sex offenders, like sexual psychopaths and homosexuals before them, as dangerous predators who may be held in high-security treatment facilities without limit and without trial, unable to appeal their detention by the usual legal methods.

In some cases, those treatment facilities provide very little effective treatment. For example, the Associated Press reports that only three of the offenders involuntarily confined by the State of Kansas in Larned State Hospital have been released since the program began operating in 1994. Meanwhile, the number of sex offenders being held without any term limit has grown to 258, according to the state's own Department for Aging and Disability Services, which administers the program.[46] In Missouri, 206 offenders have been designated sexually violent predators and have been civilly committed against their will to the maximum-security Sex Offender Rehabilitation and Treatment Services at facilities in Farmington and at Fulton State Hospital, supposedly for the purpose of mental health care, following the end of their criminal sentences. Not a single one of them "has successfully completed treatment and been released into the community" since the program was created by statute in 1999.[47]

The record holder among the states is Minnesota. As of June 2015, it held 715 sex offenders without term limits in maximum-security treatment centers in Moose Lake and St. Peter (including 67 whose only crimes were committed while they were juveniles). At the current rate of civil commitment, the number of such detainees will rise by the year 2022 — according to the state's own projections — to a total of 1,215. The Minnesota Sex Offender Program was once used to detain dangerous sex offenders, but it was extended in 2003 to include any sex offender who met expanded legal qualifications for civil commitment. No offender has ever been fully discharged since the program's inception in 1994. As U.S. District Court Judge Donovan Frank concluded on June 17, 2015, "no one has any realistic hope of ever getting out of this 'civil' detention."[48]

As Mansnerus reports, there are "about 5,000 sex offenders, [confined] involuntarily and indefinitely, who [because they are not serving prison sentences] are not in the criminal justice system at all." Since they are considered to present a threat to society if released, their incarceration can be challenged only by a motion from the public defender's office claiming that the detainee "is not as dangerous as the state says he is." Mansnerus adds, "The argument rarely succeeds."

This is preventive detention, a human rights issue, which should raise obvious constitutional questions, as it is starting to do both in Missouri (where U.S. District Judge Audrey G. Fleissig ruled on September 11, 2015, that the application of the state's civil commitment program was unconstitutional) and in Minnesota. While neither Judge Frank nor Judge Fleissig challenged civil commitment itself — they could not very well do so, since the Supreme Court signed off on it in *Kansas v. Hendricks* — Judge Frank did appeal for authority to Justice Anthony Kennedy's concurring opinion in that case, which cautioned against using civil commitment as an alternate form of punishment. Accordingly, he found that "*the Minnesota statutes governing civil commitment and treatment of sex offenders are unconstitutional as written and as applied.* . . . The overwhelming evidence at trial established that Minnesota's civil commitment scheme is a punitive system that segregates and indefinitely detains a class of potentially dangerous individuals without the safeguards of the criminal justice system."[49] Judge Fleissig reached a similar conclusion about civil commitment in Missouri, finding that "the Constitution does not allow [Missouri officials] to impose lifetime detention on individuals who have completed their prison sentences and who no longer pose a danger to the public, no matter how heinous their past conduct."[50]

These recent cases confirm that certain sex offenders now have "their own place in constitutional jurisprudence," as Mansnerus says: they are "different not just from other citizens but also from other criminals." Nothing accounts for this difference but sex itself — that is, the sexual nature of the offense. Sex changes the nature of crime and of criminal jurisprudence alike. As Mansnerus succinctly puts it, "All kinds of criminals have personality disorders and failures of self-control," which could in theory justify detaining them indefinitely after the end of their criminal sentences, but such indefinite detention is normally considered unconstitutional. "As to why sex offenders are different from the others," Mansnerus remarks, "the best apparent answer is that their crimes involved sex."

Mansnerus adds, "Indeed, some men in indefinite confinement would be better off if they had simply killed their victims. It is not the magnitude but the nature of the threat that has brought on fear and revulsion — and punishment beyond what the courts sanction for other criminal behavior. Sex *is* different, even if the Constitution does not say so."

IV

We have few analytic tools for understanding the urgent political and theoretical questions raised by the continued expansion of punitive policies aimed at regulating and controlling sex. The war on sex calls for new ways of thinking about sexual politics. The frameworks available to those of us in the academy — psychology, criminology, public health, jurisprudence, and scholarship on sexual orientation, class, gender, race, and mass incarceration — may help to reveal particular facets of the socio-legal regulation of sex, but they do not account for all the limitations currently being placed on sexual expression across a wide range of regulatory contexts. They do not explain how it is that sexual prohibitions, once consolidated into law, invariably outrun the purposes for which they were devised and get extended to encompass others; how sex crime laws constantly morph and branch out and trickle down, infiltrating and shaping all sorts of administrative procedures; why such laws tend to expand, including new categories of acts, both sexual and nonsexual, and new categories of persons; why the ages of those targeted by such laws keep falling while the ages of those accountable under them keep rising — in short, why sex constitutes such an important, independent vector of social control.

Nor can the available analytic tools bring out the links between, say, the prosecution of sex work and HIV criminalization, or similar combinations of issues, because different aspects of the criminalization and social control of sex are often treated independently. This silo effect, as Amber Hollibaugh and Mary Anne Case both point out in their contributions to this volume, extends beyond the academy and into social movements. As a result, the criminalization of sex is glaringly absent from the agendas of a number of existing progressive political projects, which often cannot resist the temptation, as Hollibaugh puts it, "[to move] as far away from sex as possible." Mary Anne Case similarly laments the fact that the various constituencies affected by the war on sex "too rarely make common cause or even seem to see the connections between the issues to which they are committed." Accordingly, Case warns students of sexual politics about the perils of "silo-ization": that is, the tendency to enclose "a set of issues and constituencies far from fruitful interaction with others." Let's review some unfortunate effects of these political and theoretical tendencies to silo-ization.

Although the burden of criminal law falls most severely on the poor, and in particular on poor Black men, civil rights organizations no longer take much of a specific interest in the war on sex or in the forms of sexual politics that contribute to the mass incarceration of Black men — such as the wrongful conviction rate of Black men for sexual misconduct with White women. Earlier generations of Black civil rights activists did protest the disproportionate use of rape charges against Black men as well as the high conviction rate for them; as far back as the end of the nineteenth century, Black clubwomen and suffragists refused to join the campaign by White purity reformers to raise the age of sexual consent or to impose criminal penalties on male sex offenders, fearing that such measures would simply compound the mistreatment of Black men by the criminal justice system.[51] But with the decline of lynching, the political impetus behind this resistance faded, disappearing by the late 1960s.

The LGBT political movement took shape in the late 1940s and early 1950s as a coordinated resistance to the police harassment of gay men and other minorities, but it has not consistently opposed the rise of the carceral state. In recent years, most large LGBT organizations have actually supported the carceral state, insofar as they have lobbied for state and federal hate crime statutes that impose harsher penalties for certain offenses and have advocated for the rights of LGBT crime victims while paying relatively little attention to the plight of LGBT persons caught in the net of the criminal justice system.[52] Meanwhile, the movement has tended to abandon the struggle for sexual freedom in favor of fighting for same-sex marriage and an end to discrimination against lesbians, gay men, and (sometimes) transgender people in housing, employment, and public accommodation.[53] When Rentboy.com was dismantled and its staffers arrested by the U.S. federal government and the NYPD, criticisms of the prosecutors and the police appeared on the websites of such organizations as the ACLU, Human Rights Watch, Lambda Legal, the National LGBTQ Task Force, the National Center for Lesbian Rights, and the Transgender Law Center, but the Human Rights Campaign — the most important, Washington-based gay lobby group — remained silent.

And yet, as Laura Mansnerus shows, there is good reason to believe that "gay men are overrepresented among those chosen for lifetime detention" and incarcerated by means of civil commitment. In fact, if you are a male between the ages of eighteen and twenty-five, and if you have sex with another male under eighteen who was not related to you or whom you just met, and if you have never "lived with [a] lover for at least two years," *you belong in the moderate- to high-risk category* according to the tabulation devised by Static-99, "an instrument designed to assist in the prediction of sexual and violent recidivism for sexual offenders," which is widely used in North Atlantic countries in sentencing scoresheets: in other words, you qualify as a "sexually violent predator" for the purposes of civil commitment.[54]

Hans Tao-Ming Huang, in his contribution to this volume, wonders about the relation between the cause of gay marriage and the abandonment of other struggles against sexual oppression: "It is curious that efforts to control and punish deviant HIV-positive subjects [in Taiwan] coincide with efforts to mobilize the AIDS surveillance industry to support the cause of gay marriage. Campaigns to secure same-sex marriage rights have reached new heights in the past two years. Is the current advocacy of HIV rights and LGBT rights in Taiwan premised upon the foreclosure of the deviant HIV subject? Must the 'community' be cleaned up before it can seek legal recognition?"

Some feminists have an ambivalent relationship to laws relating to sex crimes, while others firmly take positions for or against. Many find themselves torn between the need to protect women from sexual violence and the goal of underwriting female sexual self-determination. A number of our contributors single out for critique what one of them, Elizabeth Bernstein, calls "the rise of carceral feminism." Bernstein explores "the significance of feminism's own widening embrace of the neoliberal carceral state," along with "the rise of a carceral feminist framework." She correlates these developments with "a neoliberal *gender* strategy that securitizes the family and lends moral primacy to marriage" rather than to sexual autonomy and sexual freedom for women.

"Criminal justice," Bernstein concludes, "has often been the most effective vehicle for binding feminists and evangelicals together around historically and socially specific ideals of sex, gender, and the family."

Judith Levine and Roger N. Lancaster agree with Bernstein when she writes that "cross-ideological alignments . . . have occurred around both sex and crime. . . . In the present historical moment, sex is often the vehicle that joins 'left' and 'right' together around an agenda of criminal justice." In short, the war on sex cannot be blamed on right-wing extremists or religious radicals alone but also needs to be understood as the result of a long-standing collaboration between the Left and the Right. As Lancaster insists, "we misunderstand the stark future that has already crept up on us if we see in it only a reflection of conservative agendas, defunct authoritarianisms, and intolerant puritanisms of times past. Not a single element of the punitive turn is exempt from the democratic longings of liberal subjects, in some permutation or other, for liberation, freedom, and empowerment. The constituencies for continuous control lie as much on the liberal Left as on the conservative Right."

V

The contributors to this collection cannot confront all the dimensions of the war on sex in all their specificity. The subject is too vast to be encompassed by a single volume. The work assembled here tends to cluster around three main themes: the criminalization of HIV, both in the United States and overseas; the criminalization of commercial sex and sex work; and the history and operation of sex offender registries, along with the punishment of sex offenders in general. I have already touched on sex offender registries and the criminalization of HIV, and I will say more about the criminalization of sex work in a moment, so let me glance now at some relevant topics that this collection does not take up in sufficient detail. Since its omissions do not result from any specific preferences or intentions on the part of the editors, but simply from an inability to deal with all the urgent issues, it may be useful to list some of those issues here. For if they cannot all be covered in a single volume, a number of them can at least be mentioned. The purpose of this section, then, is to highlight and to indicate the importance of some topics of major concern that this collection as a whole does not adequately address.

First, it will already be evident that the contents of this volume bear mostly on criminal law. Further analysis of the war on sex will need to deal in detail with three additional areas: administrative regulation, civil law, and federal policy. Recent developments in all three of those areas are responsible for the production and multiplication of new and highly repressive mechanisms for controlling sex.

I have already noted some disquieting examples of administrative regulation. There is the increasing surveillance of student behavior in primary and secondary schools, along with the introduction of new, stringent, and overly broad sexual misconduct codes in higher education and the workplace. In these administrative contexts, enforcement procedures usually do not replicate judicial procedures in use by the state that conform to established requirements of the criminal justice system; rather, employers and educational institutions tend to apply their own, less systematic and less stringent definitional and evidentiary criteria for what is and is not punishable. Although they do so in an effort to respond to the changing legal and political environment, their administrative regulations often represent an alternative, for better or for worse, to legal prohibitions against sexual misconduct.[55]

Antioch College's notorious Sexual Offense Prevention Policy, which required students to request and to receive explicit affirmative verbal consent before initiating each step in sexual relations,[56] was widely ridiculed when it was introduced in 1991. But in retrospect it would seem to have been prophetic, for versions of it have recently become law in California (2014) and in New York (2015).[57] (Whoopi Goldberg and Lady Gaga actively lobbied for the New York statute.) State legislators elsewhere have proposed similar measures, and many colleges and universities are already implementing them by adding them to their administrative regulations.

Under these regulations, college disciplinary boards must use an "affirmative consent standard" in adjudicating complaints of sexual assault. The California law defines that standard as imposing on individuals the obligation to make an "affirmative, conscious, and voluntary agreement to engage in sexual activity" before proceeding to engage in it (the standard is informally dubbed "yes means yes"), with the further proviso that "affirmative consent must be ongoing throughout a sexual activity." As a result, sexual partners have to be able to document both initial and continuing consent, at least in cases where they are accused of sexual assault, if they ever hope to clear themselves of sexual misconduct charges.

"How might a student demonstrate that he repeatedly obtained consent?" asks attorney Wendy Kaminer; she cites the response of Bonnie Lowenthal, the California assemblywoman "who coauthored that state's law": "Your guess is as good as mine."[58] Under these circumstances, it should come as no surprise that software companies have started to market apps that enable sexual partners to register their consent at each stage of their relations, in case one of them happens to accuse the other of sexual assault at some point in the future.[59]

This may have the welcome result of reducing sexual assault on campus, which is perceived to be widespread, but it could also result in a trivialization of the meaning of sexual assault and in a sexually repressive blurring of its very definition. As Matt Kaiser, an attorney quoted by *Time*, puts it, "Assault can [now] mean touching somebody's butt when making out and they didn't want you too [*sic*] and didn't say you could."[60] Feminist legal scholar Janet Halley makes a more ambitious argument:

> Affirmative consent requirements — in part because of their origin in a carceral project that is overcommitted to social control through punishment in a way that seems to me to be social-conservative, not emancipatory — will do a lot more than distribute bargaining power to women operating in contexts of male domination and male privilege. They will foster a new, randomly applied moral order that will often be intensely repressive and sex-negative. They will enable people who enthusiastically participated in sex to deny it later and punish their partners. They will function as protective legislation that encourages weakness among those they protect. They will install traditional social norms of male responsibility and female helplessness. All of these will be the costs we pay for the benefits affirmative consent requirements deliver.

In some circumstances, Halley argues, "even 'yes' is not enough" to mean yes or to eliminate the possibility of coercion: according to some feminist understandings of affirmative consent and some rules of evidence, ultimate epistemic authority over the question of whether the accuser truly gave her consent rests with her, residing in her own subjective knowledge of her feelings and her intent, irrespective of any outward affirmation she might have provided at the time she engaged in sexual activity.[61]

There are further, potentially troubling consequences. Like Halley, Judith Shulevitz points out that the affirmative consent standard "shifts the burden of proof from the accuser to the accused" — something that "represents a real departure from the traditions of criminal law in the United States" (in fact, the war on sex has been shifting that burden from accusers to accused for some time now, effectively requiring defendants to prove their innocence).[62]

Worse, affirmative consent is now migrating from college handbooks to state penal codes, where it is starting to define the boundary between consensual sex and criminal assault. "Most people think of 'yes means yes' as strictly for college students," Shulevitz remarks, but "it is actually poised to become the law of the land. About a quarter of all states, and the District of Columbia, now say sex isn't legal without positive agreement, although some states undercut that standard by requiring proof of force or resistance as well." A model statute, intended to redefine the legal meaning of "sexual assault and related offenses," and designed for consideration and eventual adoption by the federal government and the states, is in the process of being formulated and discussed by the American Law Institute: an early draft not only featured the affirmative consent standard but also extended "contact" to include any touching of any body part (clothed or unclothed) with the aim of sexual gratification (reaching out on a date to take another person's hand without that person's express prior permission would qualify). That provision was not retained, but the point remains: campus policy risks becoming U.S. law.[63]

Meanwhile, more and more students are in effect coming under protective custody, with Title IX of the Education Amendments Act of 1972 being used to justify disciplinary action against students or teachers who have the kinds of sex that decision-makers don't like. As Laura Kipnis writes, "with the extension of Title IX from gender discrimination into sexual misconduct has come a broadening of not just its mandate but even what constitutes sexual assault and rape." In fact, Kipnis herself was the target of a Title IX complaint merely for *publishing an article* in the *Chronicle of Higher Education* that criticized how current sexual harassment codes had shaped "the narratives and emotional climate of professor-student interactions" at U.S. universities, including on her own campus: a graduate student at her school, who was otherwise unknown to Kipnis, complained that the article "had a 'chilling effect' on students' ability to report sexual misconduct."[64] No wonder that college professors are hastily removing sexual content from the courses they teach, in order to avoid being accused by students of making their classrooms "hostile environments" or "unsafe spaces" for those who may be easily susceptible to feelings of sexual discomfort.[65]

Turning now from administrative regulation to civil law, I should indicate that further research is needed to examine the sexually repressive effects of current developments, including the use of domestic violence restraining orders, the rise of sexual fault grounds in divorce hearings, and the expansion of emotional harm torts. In family courts in the United States today, it is becoming easy to turn divorce into an endless and insoluble conflict by making an unprovable accusation of sexual abuse or domestic violence against a former spouse, and courts are beginning to institutionalize their practices to deal with this move.

Fathers now face social expectations to participate in child care, but they are prosecuted and punished under child molestation laws for engaging in the kinds of physical contact with their children (such as bathing naked with them) that, when performed by mothers, do not provoke concern from prosecutors. As one feminist legal scholar comments, "We want men to share responsibility for children and are critical of them when they do not do so. At the same time, we do not seem to trust men with children in the same way we do mothers."[66] Recent prosecutions dramatize that point.

Many of these regulatory or punitive measures arise from laudable impulses to identify and eliminate sexual abuse and to protect victims or potential victims from harm. But a certain number of them miss their mark and end up hurting the very individuals they are intended to help. They also end up having the effect of constraining intimacy and punishing sex itself.

Federal policy offers the following instructive example of such unintended consequences. In 2003, George W. Bush asked Congress to approve a measure he called the President's Emergency Plan for AIDS Relief (PEPFAR). This initiative would go on to become the largest global development program funding HIV treatment and prevention in Africa. But as the legislation was making its way through the various congressional committees, Republican Representative Chris Smith from New Jersey (sponsor of the recent International Megan's Law discussed earlier) added an amendment to it that requires any group or organization receiving U.S. government funds not "to promote or advocate the . . . practice of prostitution" and to have "a policy explicitly opposing prostitution or sex trafficking." The U.S. Supreme Court struck down the second of those two provisions ten years later, in 2013, but only as it applies to organizations based in the United States: the restriction continues to govern all foreign governments and all NGOs outside the United States that receive funds from PEPFAR. Meanwhile, the first provision remains in force.[67]

The two clauses, collectively known as the Anti-Prostitution Loyalty Oath (APLO) or Pledge, were ostensibly designed to prevent taxpayer dollars allocated to the global fight against HIV/AIDS from contributing in any way to human trafficking or the sexual enslavement of women. Accordingly, the APLO mandates that NGOs receiving U.S. government funds adopt an organization-wide policy opposing prostitution and declare their opposition to it in their materials. The evidence, however, suggests that victims of sex trafficking have been hurt, rather than helped, by this measure. The APLO has been widely criticized by members of the public health community, not only because it compounds the stigma associated with sex work, but also because it prohibits U.S.-funded NGOs from partnering with sex workers to devise practices that reduce the transmission of HIV; furthermore, it impedes those NGOs from determining the most effective HIV/AIDS prevention strategies to adopt in specific social contexts. For example, the APLO makes it difficult for public health organizations to establish trust with sex workers, brothel owners, and other commercial sex businesses; to set up drop-in centers for sex workers and victims of sex trafficking; and to offer sex workers various kinds of practical advice about how to deal with clients while protecting themselves from HIV infection. Such advice is now financially risky because it could be construed as promoting prostitution.

"In the field," according to the Center for Health and Gender Equity, "the policy has not resulted in a single documented positive result. To the contrary, advocates have documented numerous examples of the harmful effects of the pledge, which can endanger the lives of sex workers, their clients, and their families." In 2005, accordingly, Brazil refused $40 million in U.S. global HIV/AIDS funding so that it could retain the possibility of continuing to sponsor programs that had been found to be successful in reducing the spread of HIV.[68]

Recent research has shown that "HIV prevention has been less successful since the inclusion of the pledge," which can be correlated with a corresponding rise in infections "particularly among sex workers and people presumed to be sex workers, including some gay men and transgender people." As funding restrictions have kicked in, drop-in centers have had to close: "in some instances sex workers no longer have access to places to bathe and use a toilet. Sex workers have been denied clinic services. Sex workers have less access to condoms and personal lubricant," necessary for preventing HIV transmission. Another effect has been to stifle information sharing among NGOs about what programs are effective in stopping the spread of HIV among sex workers and their clients.[69] In January 2015, The Lancet published a series of articles showing that "sex workers face substantial barriers in accessing prevention, treatment, and care services," not all of them legal, "and remain underserved by the global HIV response"; until the specific needs of sex workers are met, not only by decriminalization but also by the elimination of social and economic factors interfering with their ability to protect their health, it will be difficult to combat the worldwide HIV/AIDS epidemic.[70]

In short, any study of the regulation of sex in the world today will need to look beyond the sphere of criminal law. The dimensions and consequences of the war on sex far exceed the sorts of activities that are subject to criminalization and the sorts of disciplinary measures that are designed to prohibit and punish sexual offenses.

While civil law, administrative regulation, and public policy are not the primary focus of this volume, the work contained in it does afford a few perspectives on sexual regulation that look beyond issues of criminalization. A vivid glimpse into the intensifying bureaucratic and administrative management of sex is offered, for example, by Hans Tao-Ming Huang's study of the blending of social welfare with policing in Taiwan's HIV services. Like South Korea and China, Taiwan uses household registration techniques for the purposes of HIV surveillance. In that context, Huang reveals a particularly sinister development whereby HIV case managers — including nurses, buddies, and other hospital-based personnel — monitor patients' compliance with treatment regimes and report disapproved but not necessarily harmful behavior to state agencies. In some cases, the result may be criminal prosecution, but in many instances greater bureaucratic surveillance and practices of self-care are prescribed: punishment is reserved for those who do not cooperate. "As HIV testing and treatment have been scaled up," Huang remarks, "militarized social control comes to be reactivated under the current regime of HIV surveillance." The administrative regulation of sex, then, can have repressive effects without resorting to criminal prosecution.

Public employment can be denied for purely moral reasons related to sex. Melissa Petro was never prosecuted for a crime. She did lose her job as a teacher for reasons entirely unrelated to her job performance, which was apparently stellar. As Petro recounts in her contribution to this volume, what got her into trouble was not sex but writing about it. She published an op-ed on the website of the *Huffington Post*, in which she "criticized the recent censoring of the adult services section of Craigslist." In the course of that column, she mentioned that she had once worked as a stripper and a prostitute. "Because

I was arguing that sex workers shouldn't be ashamed to speak for themselves, I signed my name to it." Her column caught the attention of the *New York Post*, which put the story on the cover of its September 27, 2010, issue. Petro was removed from her job as a teaching fellow in a New York City public school, reassigned to the Department of Education administrative offices, and charged with conduct unbecoming a professional. No one questioned her competence as a teacher. A year later, she still could not find a job, despite "two master's degrees, five years' experience in the nonprofit sector, and three years' experience teaching."

Petro's case recalls that of Julie Gagnon, an administrative assistant at Etchemins Secondary School (a public high school in Lévis, on the south shore of Quebec City in Canada), who was fired in 2011 when a fourteen-year-old student recognized her from a pornographic film he had seen online and then created a Facebook profile for her under her stage name. The school board chair, Leopold Castonguay, unblinkingly justified her dismissal to reporters as follows: "We considered the facts and actions that led to this incident were inappropriate, unacceptable and incompatible not only with our mission but also with our values that we wish to teach our young students."[71] The students appear to have had other ideas.

A few weeks later, the *San Francisco Chronicle* reported that a state appeals court had "upheld the dismissal of a San Diego schoolteacher who was fired [in November 2008] for posting a sexually explicit ad and photos in the 'men seeking men' section of Craigslist." Frank Lampedusa did not identify himself by name in the ad, but he was apparently recognized by a user of the website (restricted to persons eighteen years of age and older), who made an anonymous tip to a police dispatcher, describing himself as the father of a student at Farb Middle School, where Lampedusa had taught since 2004 and served as dean of students. According to the *Chronicle*, "Lampedusa's firing had [earlier] been overruled by a state commission that said the ad was unrelated to his ability to teach middle-school students. But the appeals court disagreed, saying Lampedusa's conduct showed he was unfit to teach and 'serve as a role model' for his students. A teacher's private life can constitute grounds for dismissal if it demonstrates 'indecency and moral indifference,' said the Fourth District Court of Appeal in San Diego," which intended its 3–0 ruling to serve "as a statewide precedent for future cases." In the words of Justice Gilbert Nares, "Lampedusa's public posting of his pornographic ad is inconsistent with teaching middle-school students and serving as an administrator." Jose Gonzales, a lawyer for the district, explained the decision as follows: "Like judges and police officers," teachers "are held to a higher standard of off-duty conduct . . . because of their critical function in our government."[72]

In all three of the cases just mentioned, it seems likely that the stigmatized character of the sex at issue — commercial, pornographic, homosexual — played some role in the decision to dismiss the employee from the school. The inference to be drawn from these cases, then, is that what is often at stake in sexual regulation cannot be captured by the politics of identity (the female or gay identity of the employee). It has to do, rather, with *the kinds of sex* that are subject to social disapproval. Because they are already disliked, those kinds of sex turn out to be easy or plausible targets of both state and civil regulation. Sex has its own politics.

VI

Even when it comes to criminal law, we have not been able to take stock of all the new forms of intensified interdiction or the full range of legal measures with sexually repressive effects. In the context of the war on sex, even progressive reforms in criminal law can have unintended repressive consequences. Take, for example, the federal Prison Rape Elimination Act. Passed by the unanimous consent of Congress in 2003, the Prison Rape Elimination Act (PREA) was designed to address the epidemic of sexual violence in U.S. prisons. It required the U.S. Attorney General to devise national standards for detecting, preventing, reducing, and punishing rape and other forms of sexual abuse, whether by prisoners or by prison staff. Those standards came into effect on August 20, 2012; they apply to all federal, state, and local confinement facilities (the Department of Homeland Security belatedly issued its own regulations for immigration detention facilities in March 2014). Whereas the PREA standards came into force immediately in the Federal Bureau of Prisons, few states fully comply with them as yet. Most states, however, have assured the Department of Justice of their intention to do so — since they risk losing 5 percent of certain federal funds if they don't.

Despite the slow pace of its implementation, PREA has already had a significant impact. It offers numerous protections against sexual assault and provides important measures of safety for lesbian, gay, bisexual, and — crucially — transgender detainees. But it remains unclear how much practical benefit PREA has actually provided prisoners. Some of its consequences have turned out to be undeniably harmful, insofar as they have licensed prison officials to punish not only sexual violence, assault, and abuse but also many nonviolent forms of sex and gender expression that those officials consider inappropriate.[73] As Dean Spade has written, "It is unclear whether the new rules have reduced sexual violence, but it is clear they have increased punishment."[74]

According to a May 2014 report by Columbia Law School's Center for Gender and Sexuality Law, "LGBT prisoners have ... experienced unanticipated negative impacts from the Prison Rape Elimination Act (PREA), including being punished through new policies purportedly created to comply with PREA that forbid gender non-conforming behavior and punish consensual physical contact."[75] The act provides prison officials with a new pretext, in other words, to punish gay prisoners for having consensual sex with each other and to discipline transgender prisoners.

For example, Idaho has invoked PREA and the need to prevent sexual assault in order to clamp down on gender expression among prisoners, forbidding inmates in women's prisons from having masculine haircuts and inmates in men's prisons from having feminine haircuts; its regulation states, "To foster an environment safe from sexual misconduct, offenders are prohibited from dressing or displaying the appearance of the opposite gender."[76] Prison officials in Massachusetts cited PREA to justify denying a transgender woman medically necessary hormone treatment on the grounds that it would make her vulnerable to sexual assault, though the U.S. Court of Appeals for the First Circuit rejected their claim as a patent expression of bad faith.[77]

Meanwhile, in Arkansas, a prisoner was placed in administrative segregation because he was found guilty of engaging in consensual sex. "Administrative segregation" is the technical term for solitary confinement, which is sometimes considered torture by human rights groups and was the target of a vehement critique by U.S. Supreme Court Justice Anthony Kennedy in 2015.[78] As of late 2014, between 80,000 and 100,000 prisoners in the United States were held in solitary confinement, though on January 25, 2016, President Obama imposed a ban on the solitary confinement of juveniles in federal prisons and eliminated its use for minor infractions, which may have the effect of reducing the number of federal prisoners in solitary confinement by 10,000.[79] Under PREA, administrative segregation (typically used to isolate prisoners who are judged to be threats to others) has been extended to isolate prisoners deemed likely to commit a sexual assault. But one consequence has been that solitary confinement is now used quite often to punish anyone who expresses same-sex desire. In Kansas, a prisoner who had written a note inviting a fellow inmate to engage in a consensual sexual relationship was put in PREA segregation. "Because segregation and solitary confinement, as well as labeling someone as a sexual predator, can actually create greater vulnerability to sexual abuse," legal scholar Gabriel Arkles points out, "these actions may undercut the purported goal of preventing sexual abuse."[80]

In his contribution to this volume, Jay Borchert documents the extent to which prison officials continue to prohibit and punish consensual sex among prisoners: he uncovers a number of cases from Michigan in which prisoners who were accused not of sexual assault but merely of "consensual touching of each other," were sentenced to lengthy terms of administrative segregation, as if they represented a threat to the general prison population. The Supreme Court's decriminalization of gay sex in private and sanctification of it in marriage, Borchert shows, have yet to extend to the two million Americans who are incarcerated. Chase Strangio, an attorney with the ACLU, agrees: "All corrections agencies continue to prohibit consensual sexual contact or touching of any kind. Consensual contact is often punished as harshly as rape. . . . The West Virginia Supreme Court upheld a disciplinary infraction against a prisoner for kissing another prisoner on the cheek. He served 60 days in solitary. Unfortunately, PREA is becoming another mechanism of punishment used by corrections officials, often especially targeting LGBT prisoners."[81]

Accordingly, the authors of the May 2014 report from Columbia Law School's Center for Gender and Sexuality Law called on the Department of Justice to "amend the PREA regulations to require prisons to eliminate bans on consensual sex among incarcerated people . . . with the purpose of creating a policy that allows for appropriate, consensual sexual contact among prisoners but does not undermine the purposes of PREA or authorize relationships between a prisoner and a prison staff member." The DOJ, they argue, "should convene a working group of relevant agency personnel and outside experts, including people who have been incarcerated and survivors of sexual assault," in order to "investigate and address instances of prison staff using PREA as a pretext for punishing non-sexual displays of affection, [instances] which tend to be based on homophobia and transphobia."[82]

Similar kinds of criticisms have been leveled against New York's new statewide Human Trafficking Intervention Initiative, which has the unfortunate potential to perpetuate the criminalization of sex workers under the guise of eliminating sex trafficking and, especially, the sexual exploitation and victimization of minors. Many anti-trafficking measures, in fact, either conflate trafficking with mere sex work or ignore the differences between them. As Carole Vance points out, both the understandable outrage and the sometimes elaborately marshaled panic over sex trafficking (based on wildly inflated estimates of the numbers of victims, which no amount of debunking ever succeeds in discrediting) can lead to this category confusion: "the distinction between the 'exploitation of prostitution' and 'prostitution' is often lost, along with the distinction between prostitution and trafficking."[83] And while the language of the law is often clear enough, its implementation on the ground can produce, as Vance says, "another reality altogether."[84]

Let us then consider in this light New York's Human Trafficking Intervention Initiative. This measure created a statewide system of eleven Human Trafficking Intervention Courts (HTICs), the first such system in the nation, "designed to intervene in the lives of trafficked human beings and to help them to break the cycle of exploitation and arrest," according to New York State Chief Judge Jonathan Lippman (now retired), who announced the launch of this reform by the New York judiciary on September 25, 2013. The new courts, Lippman continued, are expected to cover "close to 95 percent of those charged with prostitution and trafficking related offenses" in the state of New York.[85] Similar programs have emerged in cities across the country, from Baltimore to Columbus, Ohio, from Phoenix to West Palm Beach, Florida; in addition, Texas and Connecticut have special courts and programs to deal with prostitution.[86]

These initiatives reflect a laudable determination, modeled on the reform of the treatment of drug offenders, to replace interdiction with harm reduction and to avoid compounding the abuse of victims of sex trafficking, especially minors, who are all too often prosecuted and punished as criminals, instead of simply being freed from their captors and restored to their communities. If one wishes to oppose sex trafficking in the name of human rights, and if one wishes to protect the human rights of those who are victims of trafficking, it makes no sense to use the criminal law to prosecute victims as if they were offenders. Adopting this enlightened and progressive logic, New York's HTICs are supposed to make it possible to refer the majority of those arrested for prostitution-related misdemeanors to treatment programs and social services instead of to the criminal justice system. "Defendants who [cooperate and] complete a mandated program obtain an adjournment [in] contemplation of dismissal (ACD), and if they are not rearrested for any offense for six months, the charge is dismissed and sealed."[87]

While New York's Human Trafficking Intervention Initiative was at first hailed by sex worker groups and by progressives for providing an alternative to harsh and unfair punishments, its implementation has since been criticized. Here, for example, is the finding of Truthout, a progressive Internet news website, published on October 26, 2014: "A Truthout review of state and other data shows that, despite the increased focus on trafficking, the vast majority of prostitution-related arrests in New York City are for low-level charges like loitering and simple prostitution, not human trafficking. Sex workers and even trafficking victims are far more likely to end up in handcuffs than the sex traffickers allegedly lurking in the shadows." Truthout found that 917 defendants had participated in the Brooklyn HTIC since the court was established, with 211 more cases pending, but that no major sex trafficking cases or convictions had been listed on the Brooklyn district attorney's website in 2014. "The Queens HTIC has heard more than 2,400 cases since its pilot program began keeping track in February 2010 . . . but a review of the office's press releases shows seven people have been charged with sex trafficking in four major cases since the HTIC program expanded in September 2013." Instead of sex traffickers, the HTICs seem to be processing hundreds of people engaged in ordinary prostitution, whether buying or selling.[88]

It is perhaps no surprise that the unintended consequences of New York's policies are not evenly felt across the community. The Red Umbrella Project (RUP), a largely queer Brooklyn-based organization of sex workers and their advocates, found that "in Brooklyn, Black people are present in the HTIC and face prostitution-related charges at a disproportionately high rate. Black defendants in the Brooklyn HTIC faced 69% of all charges, 94% of loitering for the purpose of engaging in a prostitution offense charges, and were 88% of the defendants who faced three or more charges." The RUP also pointed out that police are not informed of which defendants have been granted ACDs or had their charges dismissed and sealed. "Therefore, receiving an ACD does not protect someone who is no longer doing sex work from being rearrested for a loitering for the purposes of prostitution charge if they spend time in public space in a neighborhood where they have previously been arrested, or near an area that the police have identified as a stroll where people trade sex."[89]

Although being sent to therapy or yoga classes is more humane than being sent to prison, it is not an entirely appropriate way of treating adults who have simply decided to sell sex in order to earn money, as various commentators have noted. Nor does it address the social and economic factors that motivate some people to engage in prostitution. At the same time, the redefinition of *all* sex work as human trafficking does serve to justify the continuing criminalization of sex work and to perpetuate police sweeps of sex workers, without apparently providing effective means for fighting human trafficking and punishing traffickers, who still seem to slip through the net of the law.

As for sex workers themselves, it is not clear that being arrested by the police is the best way to gain access to social services. Nor can law enforcement address the conditions that impel disadvantaged youth to resort to sex work. Lisa Duggan reports in *The Nation* that the Urban Institute, in partnership with Streetwise and Safe, has published a series of studies

> outlining the reasons young LGBTQ New Yorkers engage in what they call "survival sex" or sex in exchange for housing, food, or cash. As Audacia Ray, director of RUP, explained to me, the language of "trafficking" covers over the intertwined conditions of migration, domestic violence, and poverty — which only sometimes come together with the kind of organized force and coercion conjured by the term. When used as an umbrella term for nearly all sex work, as it is in the HTICs, "trafficking" effectively erases the systemic conditions that shape the experience of sex work, substituting individual criminal "traffickers" for the traps of poverty and homelessness. The trafficking framework also erases the agency of women. Sex work becomes a kind of statutory crime, with women as legal children, with issues of coercion assumed and questions of consent rendered irrelevant for the court.[90]

Legal definitions of trafficking also sometimes fail to make a rigorous distinction between the family and friends of sex workers and their "pimps," criminalizing the former as if they were necessarily the latter. That is not to deny that the two categories often coincide, but they do not do so in every case.

The fact that the burden of the punishments meted out under anti-trafficking programs, such as New York's Human Trafficking Intervention Initiative, seems to fall squarely on sex workers and not, as it turns out, on sex traffickers, should raise red flags. So should the tendency of interdiction efforts to focus on sex work instead of on other kinds of human trafficking involving coerced labor. Once again, everything here points less to a program to eradicate abuse than to a determination to regulate and constrain sex itself. In her contribution to this volume, Elizabeth Bernstein notes that " 'trafficking' as defined in international protocols and in current federal law could conceivably encompass sweatshop labor, agricultural work, or unscrupulous labor practices on [U.S.] military bases in Iraq," but that is not how those regulations are usually applied. Instead, they are often used to constrain and to punish sex work in particular, along with sex workers and their families.[91]

Bernstein goes on to discuss the international versions of these anti-trafficking initiatives: "With 'women's human rights' understood as pertaining exclusively to questions of sexual violence and to bodily integrity (but not to the gendered dimensions of broader social, economic, and cultural issues), the human rights model in its global manifestation has become a highly effective means of disseminating feminist carceral politics on a global scale." She continues, "Within the context of campaigns to combat the global 'traffic in women,' this efficacy has been manifest in the United States' tier ranking and economic sanctioning of countries that fail to pass sufficiently punitive anti-prostitution laws, in the transnational activist push to criminalize male clients' demand for sexual services, in the tightening of international borders as a means to 'protect' potential trafficking victims, and in the implementation of new restrictions upon female migrants' capacity to travel." Such restrictions sometimes have the further effect of forcing female migrants to rely on smugglers to transport them across borders, which makes these women less autonomous and therefore *more* vulnerable to sex trafficking.[92]

Bernstein's critique converges with the analysis of California's Proposition 35 that Carol Queen and Penelope Saunders contribute to this volume. Overwhelmingly approved by popular referendum in November 2012, with 81 percent of voters casting ballots in its favor, Prop 35, known as the CASE Act (Californians Against Sexual Exploitation), claimed to criminalize human trafficking. Queen and Saunders argue, however, that the new law will actually do the following instead:

"expand the definition of trafficking well beyond that currently recognized by global experts;

expand prison sentences and sex offender registration, including in some cases for the people the law claimed to protect;

further criminalize sex workers' associates, including their partners and families;

erode affected persons' online privacy through requirements to register their Internet accounts with law enforcement;

channel fines to police agencies, sex work abolition agencies, and non-profits associated with Homeland Security—limiting or eradicating entirely funds that would, under earlier anti-trafficking strategies, be available to support victims directly."

One effect of the Prop 35, in other words, is further to elide "the differences between sex trafficking and sex *work* (e.g., prostitution, exotic dancing, and other forms of eroticized labor)," thereby blocking efforts to protect sex workers from harm and make sexual labor safer for those who freely choose to engage in it. In response to developments such as Prop 35, which punish rather than protect sex workers, Amnesty International adopted on August 11, 2015, a new policy defending the rights of sex workers and calling for "the full decriminalization of all aspects of consensual sex work." Other human rights organizations, such as Human Rights Watch, UNAIDS, the World Health Organization, the Global Commission on HIV and the Law, and the Open Society Foundations, now also support the decriminalization of sex work.[93]

VII

Although the transnational dimensions of the war on sex largely escape our purview, this volume does include articles on Taiwan by Hans Tao-Ming Huang, on the Netherlands by Gregory Tomso, and on the Caribbean by Maurice Tomlinson. Analysis of transnational issues is hampered by a paucity of adequate tools to address the delicate political issues raised by the war on sex outside the context of the established industrialized democracies. Recent critiques of "homonationalism" within queer theory, for example, whatever their other uses, are singularly ill-equipped to respond to the challenges posed by new state persecutions of homosexuals in Russia and Uganda. Particularly in countries that used to belong to the Soviet bloc, or that fall within the current sphere of Russian influence, there has been an uncanny echoing of queer theory's critique of LGBT rights as an alien, inapt, Westernizing imposition of a liberal model on local sexual cultures and norms (similar arguments for the inapplicability of LGBT rights to Asian countries were once advanced by the autocratic government of Singapore).[94] Liberals have had a loud and forceful response to the neo-orthodox reaction in these post-Soviet countries, and the prospect of EU admission was enough to force Moldova to retreat from its Putinesque laws, but queer theorists seem to be paralyzed in the face of these developments, apparently worried that academics who advocate for gay rights will be seen as homonationalist or merely liberal. The current geopolitical climate for sexual justice therefore gives rise to a number of extremely thorny questions.

In conclusion, to say that the developments described in this essay and in this volume constitute a war on sex is not to imply that all those developments are the same. Is the war on sex to be understood as a redirected expression of social hostility, an oblique attack on already stigmatized but otherwise innocent groups, such as racial minorities and sexual dissidents? Or do current sexual regulations actually target the right people but end up going too far? Do they err in being overly inclusive and in criminalizing the innocent along with the guilty? Or is it that the expanding restrictions on sex, which bypass *persons* and identify harmful, injurious *activities* (e.g., the production of sexually explicit images of children), define those targets too broadly (so as to include teenagers taking nude selfies)? Or is the problem that the right practices (rape, sex trafficking) are being correctly opposed but in ways that produce bad and unintended consequences along with counterproductive effects? Or is it simply the case that the guilty, who deserve to be punished, are being punished out of all proportion to the seriousness of their crimes?

It should be clear at this point that *all of these factors* are involved in the war on sex. But it should also be clear that *all of these factors are different from one another* and bring different dynamics or logics of practice into play. They should not be conflated; rather, they should each be described in all their specificity, then analyzed and confronted on an issue-by-issue basis — even if they are all driven, to varying degrees, by a single underlying animus against sex itself.

To denounce the war on sex is not to call for the decriminalization or liberation of all sexual practices. It is certainly not to condone sexual violence; the sexual exploitation and victimization of women, children, the poor, and the vulnerable; or to express indifference to the reality and gravity of various kinds of sexual harm. It is not even to indicate approval of prostitution, pornography, or risky sexual practices in an age of epidemic disease. It is to suggest, rather, that moral disapproval should not be translated automatically into prohibition or repression, much less criminalization. Personal feelings about good and bad sex, even considered views about right and wrong sex, should acquire the force of law or social policy only after much careful, critical, collective reflection.

There are many aspects of contemporary sexual life and contemporary sexual culture that are deeply troubling. It should be possible, accordingly, to critique on feminist grounds the increasing sexualization of images of women in the mass media or the routine pornographization of women's and men's bodies in mainstream advertising without engaging in puritanical overkill — without, for example, demonizing recreational or nonreproductive sex and without promoting familialism or imposing conjugal domesticity on the unwilling or the recalcitrant. It is certainly not appropriate or desirable to suppress the free expression of opinions about the differences between good and bad sex. People have a right to object to sex that they regard as wrong or immoral. But in passing laws, framing regulations, and formulating policy, they should place the emphasis on reducing harm rather than inculcating virtue — or someone's idea of it. It ought to be possible to detect, deter, prevent, and punish sexual misconduct while maximizing sexual freedom and the sexual agency of individuals.

Many of the contributors to this volume focus on the damage done to sexual civil liberties by the recent convergence between certain elements in the women's movement and certain elements in the conservative movement, which agree on using the power of the state and other institutions to police sex, to restrict sexual choices, and to punish sexual infractions. The resulting consensus among some feminists and some conservatives has persuaded many people today that rape, abuse, domestic violence, and sexual exploitation should be combated by increased penalties — by stricter, harsher, and continually more expansive forms of repression, restriction, surveillance, prohibition, criminalization, and punishment. Nonetheless, feminism is not the enemy: the authors whose work is collected here see no fundamental, substantive, irreconcilable opposition between feminism and sexual freedom. It is women, after all, who often have suffered the most from the carceral turn in sexual politics. As Judith Levine argues in her own contribution, "if we are to end sexual violence by cracking down on sexual freedom, we are trading one oppression for another."

Here, as so often in the context of political struggles, it is a question of identifying the principal enemy. For example, readers of this volume will have to ask themselves which is worse: rare, horrific crimes committed by deranged individuals or a systematic, increasing, massive, generalized encroachment on civil liberties by the state? At the moment, the balance between sexual freedom and the need for protection from sexual danger has shifted to the advantage of the latter. Can we redress the balance in a responsible way? Is it possible to confront structural violence, systematic injustice, and the persistent forms of social inequality (between men and women, adults and children) without bearing down unfairly on already disempowered individuals and groups or depriving them of agency? And is it possible to re-equilibrate the criminal justice system by devising appropriate penalties for crimes of sexual harm that do not over-criminalize and over-punish those who are guilty of them?

These are not easy questions to answer. But we must try. How well we succeed in answering them is likely to determine the positions we take in the war on sex.

NOTES

I wish to acknowledge and to thank a number of friends and colleagues who have read the text of this essay, sometimes more than once, who have provided me with timely and up-to-date information, and who have given me expert, extensive, detailed, rigorous, subtle, painstaking, thoughtful, challenging, and invaluable advice, though I hasten to add that none of them should be held responsible for the opinions I have expressed, which are entirely my own. I am immensely indebted to Bill Dobbs, Janet Halley, Trevor Hoppe, and Roger Lancaster; also to Scott De Orio, Roger Mathew Grant, Myra Jehlen, Rostom Mesli, Stephen Molldrem, Gayle Rubin, Timothy Stewart-Winter, Marie Ymonet, and the anonymous referees for Duke University Press. I could never have completed this essay as it stands without their help. Nor could I have completed it without the support of a fellowship from the Wissenschaftskolleg zu Berlin and a paid leave from the University of Michigan, which gave me the leisure and the resources needed to undertake the research presented here. My gratitude to all!

1. Richard Nixon, "Annual Message to the Congress on the State of the Union," January 22, 1970. Available online by Gerhard Peters and John T. Woolley, *The American Presidency Project*, http://www.presidency.ucsb.edu/ws/?pid=2921 (accessed April 25, 2015).

2. Richard Nixon, "Special Message to the Congress on Drug Abuse Prevention and Control," June 17, 1971. Available online by Peters and Woolley, *The American Presidency Project*, http://www.presidency.ucsb.edu/ws/?pid=3048 (accessed April 25, 2015).

3. Press Release, Department of Justice, U.S. Attorney's Office, Eastern District of New York, "Largest Online Male Escort Service Raided: Rentboy.com CEO and Six Current and Former Employees Arrested," August 25, 2015, http://www.justice.gov/usao-edny/pr/largest-online-male-escort-service-raided; E.D.N.Y. Docket

No. 15-MJ-780; Lisa Duggan, "What the Pathetic Case against Rentboy.com Says about Sex Work," *The Nation*, January 7, 2016, http://www.thenation.com/article /what-the-pathetic-case-against-rentboy-com-says-about-sex-work/. The federal indictment of Jeffrey Hurant, founder and CEO of Rentboy.com, which was filed on January 27, 2016, in the U.S. District Court for the Eastern District of New York, does actually attempt to associate the website with sex trafficking and underage sex, but it tellingly omits to include such charges in the three counts on which Hurant is indicted: they comprise one count of promoting prostitution and two counts of money laundering. See Scott Shackford, "The Official Indictment of Rentboy.com's Founder Will Infuriate You: Human Trafficking Issues Are Raised to Make Site Operators Look Bad, but the Charges Don't Match," Reason.com, January 28, 2016, http:// reason.com/blog/2016/01/28/the-official-indictment-of-rentboycoms-f.

4. See, for example, Dan Herbeck, "Child Porn Raid Wrong, But No Apology by Feds; W. Side Businessman Traumatized at Home Because of 'Wi-Fi Theft,'" *Buffalo News*, March 17, 2011, http://www.buffalonews.com/Child_porn_raid_wrong_but _no_apology_by_feds__W._Side_businessman_traumatized_at_home_because _of_aposWi-Fi_theftapos.html.

5. Griswold v. Connecticut, 381 U.S. 479 (1965); Eisenstadt v. Baird, 405 U.S. 438 (1972); Carey v. Population Services International, 431 U.S. 678 (1977).

6. Roe v. Wade, 410 U.S. 113 (1973); Stanley v. Georgia, 394 U.S. 557 (1969); Lawrence v. Texas, 539 U.S. 558 (2003).

7. Melissa Chan, "Utah Governor Declares Pornography a Public Health Crisis," *Time*, April 19, 2016, http://time.com/4299919/utah-porn-public-health-crisis; Brady McCombs, "Utah Leaders Call Pornography a Plague Damaging Young Minds," *Washington Post*, April 19, 2016, http://bigstory.ap.org/article/7568aaf511b948639ddf4 7cd50ac6530/utah-leaders-call-pornography-plague-damaging-young-minds. Cf. Joe Kort, "If Porn Was ACTUALLY Killing Boners, Wouldn't Men Be FREAKING Out?" YourTango, April 14, 2016, http://www.yourtango.com/2016287733/porn-addiction -public-health-crisis-slut-shaming; Mark Simpson, "Today's Porn Panic Is No Different to the Anti-Masturbation Movements of the 19th Century," *The Telegraph*, April 29, 2016, http://www.telegraph.co.uk/men/thinking-man/todays-porn-panic -is-no-different-to-the-anti-masturbation-movem.

8. U.S. Sentencing Commission, *Report to the Congress: Mandatory Minimum Penalties in the Federal Criminal Justice System* (October 2011), p. 300.

9. See Trevor Hoppe, "Punishing Sex: Sex Offenders and the Missing Punitive Turn in Sexuality Studies," *Law & Social Inquiry* 41, no. 3 (2016): 573–594.

10. Hoppe, "Punishing Sex."

11. Bernard E. Harcourt, "Neoliberal Penality: A Brief Genealogy," *Theoretical Criminology* 14, no. 1 (2010): 1–19 (quotation on p. 4; italics in original). See, further,

Bernard E. Harcourt, *The Illusion of Free Markets: Punishment and the Myth of Natural Order* (Cambridge, MA: Harvard University Press, 2012).

12. See Bill Keller, "Where Right Meets Left: The Odd-Couple Alliance on Justice Reform Is Not as Odd as It Seems," Marshall Project, February 20, 2015, https://www.themarshallproject.org/2015/02/20/where-right-meets-left, who comments, "Nobody wants to grapple with the draconian treatment of sex offenders."

13. For some journalistic challenges, see Editorial Board, "Banishing Sex Offenders Doesn't Help," *New York Times*, September 8, 2015, A26 (criticizing residency restrictions for former sex offenders); Editorial Board, "Male Escorts a Homeland Security Threat?" *New York Times*, August 29, 2015, A18 (criticizing the federal raid on Rentboy.com); Editorial Board, "Indefinite Imprisonment, on a Hunch," *New York Times*, August 16, 2015, SR8 (criticizing the practice of civil commitment for sex offenders); Julie Bosman, "Teenager's Jailing Brings a Call to Fix Sex Offender Registries," *New York Times*, July 5, 2015, A1 (the front page of the Sunday *Times*); and Ian Lovett, "Restricted Group Speaks Up, Saying Sex Crime Measures Go Too Far," *New York Times*, October 2, 2013, A11.

14. See Hoppe, "Punishing Sex."

15. For a particularly eloquent statement to this effect, see Andrew Extain, "Beyond the Headlines: How We See Sex Offenders," Center for Sexual Justice, July 27, 2015, http://www.centerforsexualjustice.org/2015/07/27/beyond-the-headlines-how-we-see-sex-offenders/.

16. Gayle S. Rubin, "Thinking Sex: Notes for a Radical Theory of the Politics of Sexuality," in *Pleasure and Danger: Exploring Female Sexuality*, ed. Carole S. Vance (Boston: Routledge and Kegan Paul, 1984), 267–319; repr., with additional material, in Gayle S. Rubin, *Deviations: A Gayle Rubin Reader* (Durham, NC: Duke University Press, 2011), 137–193.

17. According to statistics compiled from state registries by the National Center for Missing and Exploited Children, http://www.missingkids.org/en_US/documents/Sex_Offenders_Map2015.pdf (accessed February 8, 2016).

18. Smith v. Doe, 538 U.S. 84 (2003). The Supreme Court decision invoked an unfounded and, it now seems, false statistic about the high recidivism rate among sex offenders to justify the practice of putting the names of convicted sex offenders on public registries, a statistic that thereby gained undeserved authority in subsequent jurisprudence: see Ira Mark Ellman and Tara Ellman, "'Frightening and High': The Supreme Court's Crucial Mistake about Sex Crime Statistics," *Constitutional Commentary* 30, no. 3 (fall 2015): 495–508.

19. "More than 20,000 sex offenders are registered in Georgia. . . . Of that 20,000, only 244 offenders are considered violent sexual predators required to wear a monitor for life, GBI [Georgia Bureau of Investigation] statistics show": Joy Lukachick

Smith, "Georgia Drops Hundreds from Sex Offender Registry," *Chattanooga Times Free Press*, November 13, 2011, http://www.timesfreepress.com/news/news/story/2011/nov/13/georgia-drops-hundreds-from-sex-registry/63812/. Similar figures have been quoted for Vermont, which as of 2007 had 24,000 registered sex offenders, of whom 282 were classified by the state as "sexual predators" or were convicted of sexually violent crimes, according to Human Rights Watch, *No Easy Answers: Sex Offender Laws in the US* 19, no. 4(G) (September 2007): 62.

20. Human Rights Watch, *No Easy Answers*, 39–40; Human Rights Watch, *Raised on the Registry: The Irreparable Harm of Placing Children on Sex Offender Registries in the US* (2013), 21n.

21. BBC News, "Bike Sex Man Placed on Probation," November 14, 2007, http://news.bbc.co.uk/2/hi/uk_news/scotland/glasgow_and_west/7095134.stm; BBC News, "Bike Sex Case Sparks Legal Debate," November 16, 2007, http://news.bbc.co.uk/2/hi/uk_news/scotland/glasgow_and_west/7098116.stm.

22. U.S. Sentencing Commission, *Report to the Congress: Mandatory Minimum Penalties in the Federal Criminal Justice System*, 295, 300. Sex offenders convicted under federal statutes represent a small fraction of the total number of convicted sex offenders in the United States, but the detailed statistical information about them that is available makes it possible to characterize them with some precision.

23. David Finkelhor, Richard Ormrod, and Mark Chaffin, "Juveniles Who Commit Sex Offenses against Minors," Office of Juvenile Justice and Delinquency Prevention, Office of Justice Programs, U.S. Department of Justice, *Juvenile Justice Bulletin* (December 2009), 1–4, http://www.ojp.usdoj.gov. The statistics provided by the report are based on very spotty and incomplete data from the National Incident-Based Reporting System, which (though more informative than any previous collection of crime data in the United States) "is not yet nationally representative, nor do its data represent national trends or national statistics" (2). The authors also caution that "very few of the youth described [as sex offenders in this report] are convicted as adults would be. Many were only alleged to have engaged in illegal behavior, and, if subject to justice system action, were adjudicated delinquent rather than convicted of a crime" (1n). An additional clarification: "It is also important to note that the offender ages recorded in NIBRS reflect the ages of the youth at the time the incidents are reported, not the ages at the time the incidents occurred, which are different in 19 percent of cases" (3).

24. Finkelhor, Ormrod, and Chaffin, "Juveniles Who Commit Sex Offenses against Minors," 4.

25. In one 2004 Pennsylvania case, "a 15-year-old girl was charged with manufacturing and disseminating child pornography for having taken nude photos of herself and posted them on the Internet. She was charged as an adult, and as of 2012 was

facing registration for life" as a sex offender (Human Rights Watch, *Raised on the Registry*, 35). In another instance, police in Manassas City, Virginia, not only charged a seventeen-year-old boy with two counts of child pornography for sending his fifteen-year-old girlfriend a photo of his own penis, but they attempted to pin the rap on him by inducing him to have an erection so they could photograph it themselves in order to complete a positive identification of the culprit. The teenager received a year's probation, and the detective in the case later killed himself when he was about to be arrested on charges of making sexual advances to two thirteen-year-old boys whom he had been coaching in hockey. See Julie Carey, David Culver, and the NEWS4 [NBC Washington] Team, "Va. Teen Could Be Jailed for 'Sexting' Girlfriend," July 3, 2014, http://www.nbcwashington.com/news/local/Va-Teen-Could-be-Jailed-for -Sexting-Girlfriend-265770831.html; Tom Jackman, "In 'Sexting' Case Manassas City Police Want to Photograph Teen in Sexually Explicit Manner, Lawyers Say," *Washington Post*, July 9, 2014, http://www.washingtonpost.com/blogs/local/wp/2014 /07/09/in-sexting-case-manassas-city-police-want-to-photograph-teen-in-sexually -explicit-manner-lawyers-say/?tid=sm_fb; Michael McLaughlin, "Police Abandon Plans to Photograph Teen's Penis in Virginia Sexting Case," *Huffington Post*, July 10, 2014, http://www.huffingtonpost.com/2014/07/10/manassas-city-teen-sexting_n _5572316.html; Tom Jackman, "Manassas City Teen Placed on Probation in 'Sexting' Case Where Police Sought Photos," *Washington Post*, August 1, 2014, https://www .washingtonpost.com/local/manassas-city-teen-placed-on-probation-in-sexting-case -where-police-sought-photos/2014/08/01/c4d6ff62-19ad-11e4-85b6-c1451e622637 _story.html; Tom Jackman, "Manassas City Police Detective in Teen 'Sexting' Case Commits Suicide," *Washington Post*, December 15, 2015, https://www.washingtonpost .com/local/public-safety/manassas-city-police-detective-in-teen-sexting-case -commits-suicide/2015/12/15/de88f7c4-a356-11e5-9c4e-be37f66848bb_story.html.

26. http://starjournalnow.com/Content/News/Local-News/Article/School -District-of-Rhinelander-concludes-sexting-investigation/7/46/8906 (accessed April 26, 2015). Emphasis added.

27. Hanna Rosin, "Why Kids Sext," *The Atlantic*, November 2014, http://www .theatlantic.com/magazine/archive/2014/11/why-kids-sext/380798/#sthash .lC73Bowv.dpuf. Cf. Samantha Allen, "Colorado's Sexting Nightmare," *The Daily Beast*, November 9, 2015, http://www.thedailybeast.com/articles/2015/11/09/colorado-s -sexting-nightmare.html: "a 16-year-old in Colorado can legally consent to sex with a 26-year-old but a 17-year-old cannot send a nude photo to another 17-year old." For a general survey of this issue, see Amy Adele Hasinoff, *Sexting Panic: Rethinking Criminalization, Privacy, and Consent* (Urbana: University of Illinois Press, 2015).

28. Paul Woolverton, "NC Law: Teens Who Take Nude Selfie Photos Face Adult Sex Charges," fayobserver.com, September 2, 2015, http://www.fayobserver.com/news

/local/nc-law-teens-who-take-nude-selfie-photos-face-adult/article_ce750e51-d9ae
-54ac-8141-8bc29571697a.html.

29. Woolverton, "NC Law."

30. Woolverton, "NC Law."

31. Danielle Wiener-Bronner, "Teen's Probation for Nude Selfies Includes Accept-
ing Warrantless Searches," Fusion.net, September 16, 2016, http://fusion.net/story
/198000/north-carolina-teens-nude-selfies-plea-deal/.

32. For the text of the law, see Congress.gov, "H.R.515 — International Megan's
Law to Prevent Child Exploitation and Other Sexual Crimes through Advanced Notification of Traveling Sex Offenders," https://www.congress.gov/bill/114th-congress
/house-bill/515 (accessed February 2, 2016). See also David Post, "The Yellow Star,
the Scarlet Letter, and 'International Megan's Law,'" *Washington Post*, January 6,
2016, https://www.washingtonpost.com/news/volokh-conspiracy/wp/2016/01/06
/the-yellow-star-the-scarlet-letter-and-international-megans-law/; Beth Schwartz-
apfel, "Congress Acts to Mark Passports of Sex Offenders: Target of Legislation Is
Sex-Traffickers; Critics Call It a 'Scarlet Letter,'" *Marshall Project*, February 2, 2016,
https://www.themarshallproject.org/2016/02/02/congress-acts-to-mark-passports
-of-sex-offenders#.wS2garTkv; Christopher Moraff, "The Long Arm of Sex Offender
Laws: America's Broken Sex Offender Policy Goes Global," *Al Jazeera America*, February 8, 2016, http://america.aljazeera.com/opinions/2016/2/the-long-arm-of-sex
-offender-laws.html.

33. See White House Office of the Press Secretary, "Statement by the Press Secretary on H.R. 515, H.R. 4188, S. 2152," February 8, 2016, https://www.whitehouse
.gov/the-press-office/2016/02/08/statement-press-secretary-hr-515-hr-4188-s
-2152-0.

34. Human Rights Watch, *Raised on the Registry*, 98. On the lifelong consequences
of registration for children convicted of sex offenses, see the detailed account by
Sarah Stillman, "The List," *New Yorker*, March 14, 2016, http://www.newyorker.com
/magazine/2016/03/14/when-kids-are-accused-of-sex-crimes.

35. CBS Las Vegas, "School: 5-Year-Old Committed 'Sexual Misconduct' By Pulling Pants Down On Playground," http://lasvegas.cbslocal.com/2014/07/01/school
-5-year-old-committed-sexual-misconduct-by-pulling-pants-down-on-playground/
(accessed April 25, 2015); "'My Son Is Not Sexualized': Mother's Fury as her Kin-
dergartner Son, 5, Is Accused of Sexual Misconduct for Pulling his Pants Down in
the Playground after Another Student Threatened Him," *Daily Mail*, June 26, 2014,
http://www.dailymail.co.uk/news/article-2671699/Arizona-kindergartner-accused
-sexual-misconduct-pulling-pants-playground-pupils-threatened-him.html; Crystal
Shepeard, "5-Year-Old Cited for Sexual Misconduct for Taking Off Pants on Playground," Care2, July 4, 2014, http://www.care2.com/causes/5-year-old-cited-for

-sexual-misconduct-for-taking-off-pants-on-playground.html. See, generally, the detailed report by Human Rights Watch, *Raised on the Registry*.

36. "Sexual and Gender-Based Harassment Policy and Procedures for the Faculty of Arts and Sciences, Harvard University," January 13, 2015, available at http://www.fas.harvard.edu/sexual-gender-based-harassment-policyresources (accessed April 28, 2015).

37. Quoted in Ashley Southall and Tamar Lewin, "New Harvard Policy Bans Teacher-Student Relations," *New York Times*, February 6, 2015, A15.

38. Erica Goode, "Life Sentence for Possession of Child Pornography Spurs Debate over Severity," *New York Times*, November 4, 2011, A9.

39. Daniel Enrique Guevara-Vilca v. Florida, Florida Second District Court of Appeal, Case No. 2D11–5805 (April 10, 2015), 5, 8. The two other judges on the Court of Appeal for Florida's Second District concurred in the decision.

40. Linda Greenhouse, "Justices Decline Case on 200-Year Sentence for Man Who Possessed Child Pornography," *New York Times*, February 27, 2007, http://www.nytimes.com/2007/02/27/washington/27scotus.html?_r=1&; the case is Berger v. Arizona, No. 06-349.

41. For more details, see Sergio Hernandez, "Sex, Lies and HIV: When What You Don't Tell Your Partner Is a Crime," *ProPublica: Journalism in the Public Interest*, December 1, 2013, http://www.propublica.org/article/hiv-criminal-transmission.

42. CDC, "HIV Transmission," January 16, 2015, http://www.cdc.gov/hiv/basics/transmission.html.

43. Campbell, in addition to being homeless and intoxicated at the time of his clash with the police officer, was convicted of harassment of a public servant. He had an alleged history of spitting at police officers and biting fellow jail inmates, and was indicted under a habitual-offender statute that mandated a minimum penalty of twenty-five years. The police officer testified that Campbell's saliva hit him in the eye and mouth. See Tiara M. Ellis, "HIV-Positive Man Gets 35 Years for Spitting on Dallas Police Officer," *Dallas Morning News*, May 15, 2008, http://www.hivjustice.net/case/us-texas-man-gets-35-years-for-spitting-saliva-was-deadly-weapon/; Gretel C. Kovach, "Prison for Man with H.I.V. Who Spit on a Police Officer," *New York Times*, May 16, 2008, http://www.nytimes.com/2008/05/16/us/16spit.html.

44. Kansas v. Hendricks, 521 U.S. 346 (1997).

45. De Orio doesn't mention it, but that later development produced a bizarre sequel. Timothy Stewart-Winter recounts that "the passage of California's version of Megan's Law resulted in thousands of elderly gay men, convicted under lewd conduct or sodomy statutes decades [earlier], being forced to register [as sex offenders] with the state and notify their neighbors in the late 1990s. The response of gay rights groups was to lobby the California assembly to alter the classification so as to

exclude them — a successful effort. They mounted no other objection to the law."
See Timothy Stewart-Winter, "Queer Law and Order: Sex, Criminality, and Policing
in the Late Twentieth-Century United States," *Journal of American History* 102, no. 1
(June 2015): 61–72 (quotation on p. 72).

46. Nicholas Clayton, "Kansas Faces Criticism for Cost of Sex Offender Program,"
Washington Times, April 27, 2015, http://www.washingtontimes.com/news/2015/apr
/27/kansas-faces-criticism-for-cost-of-sex-offender-pr/.

47. "Editorial: Missouri's SORTS Program Looks a Lot like Prison," *St. Louis
Post-Dispatch*, April 27, 2015, http://www.stltoday.com/news/opinion/editorial
-missouri-s-sorts-program-looks-a-lot-like-prison/article_466a148c-d3bd-50a0-8152
-98e8beab68d1.html?print=true&cid=print; see also Jesse Bogan, "Class Action Lawsuit
Begins over Missouri's Treatment of Sexually Violent Predators," *St. Louis Post-Dispatch*,
April 22, 2015, http://www.stltoday.com/news/local/crime-and-courts/class-action
-lawsuit-begins-over-missouri-s-treatment-of-sexually/article_2dcbc31d-bee9-53b0
-ba1b-68a101cf2a82.html?print=true&cid=print.

48. Peter Cox and Matt Sepic, "Federal Judge: Minnesota Sex Offender Program
Unconstitutional," MPR News, June 17, 2015, http://www.mprnews.org/story/2015
/06/17/sex-offender-program-unconstitutional; U.S. District Court, District of Minnesota, Civil No. 11-3659 (DWF/JJK), Document 966 (June 17, 2015), 4, 12, 14; also 11–
12: "the MSOP [Minnesota Sex Offender Program] has developed into indefinite and
lifetime detention. Since the program's inception in 1994, no committed individual
has ever been fully discharged from the MSOP, and only three committed individuals have ever been provisionally discharged from the MSOP. By contrast, Wisconsin
has fully discharged 118 individuals and placed approximately 135 individuals on supervised release since 1994. New York has fully discharged 30 individuals — without
any recidivism incidents, placed 125 individuals on strict and intensive supervision
and treatment ('SIST') upon their initial commitment, and transferred 64 individuals
from secure facilities to SIST."

49. See U.S. District Court, District of Minnesota, Civil No. 11-3659 (DWF/JJK),
Document 966 (June 17, 2015), 2 and 4. Italics added.

50. As quoted by Jesse Bogan, "U.S. Judge Rules Handling of State's Sexual Predator
Program Is Unconstitutional," *St. Louis Post-Dispatch*, September 12, 2015, http://www
.stltoday.com/news/local/crime-and-courts/federal-judge-rules-that-missouri-s
-sexually-violent-predator-program/article_8ea46baa-5e3f-5773-a1d1-9465c9d08fe9
.html.

51. Mary E. Odem, *Delinquent Daughters: Protecting and Policing Adolescent Female
Sexuality in the United States, 1885–1920* (Chapel Hill: University of North Carolina
Press, 1995), 26–30. Cf. Estelle B. Freedman, *Redefining Rape: Sexual Violence in the
Era of Suffrage and Segregation* (Cambridge, MA: Harvard University Press, 2013), 119.

52. Note also a ballot initiative in California sponsored by Michael Weinstein and his AIDS Healthcare Foundation that could have the effect of criminalizing the local pornography industry: "FSC: Adult Industry Facing Gravest Threat Since Nixon Administration," AVN, January 21, 2016, http://business.avn.com/articles/legal/FSC -Adult-Industry-Facing-Gravest-Threat-Since-Nixon-Administration-619867.html.

53. See Stewart-Winter, "Queer Law and Order."

54. Andrew Harris, Amy Phenix, R. Karl Hanson, and David Thornton, "STATIC-99 Coding Rules: Revised — 2003," http://www.static99.org/pdfdocs/static-99-coding -rules_e.pdf, p. 71 and coding forms on pp. 79–80. See, for example, the case of Galen Baughman, who successfully challenged his civil commitment in court: James Ridgeway, "How 'Civil Commitment' Enables Indefinite Detention of Sex Offenders," Guardian, September 26, 2013, http://www.theguardian.com/commentisfree/2013/sep/26 /civil-commitment-sex-offenders. A new version of the Static-99 tabulation, Static-99R, was released in 2009, but it would not change the risk assessment for the hypothetical gay male teenager or young adult mentioned. On Static-99, see Peter Aldhous, "These 10 Questions Can Mean Life Behind Bars," BuzzFeed News, April 22, 2015, http://www .buzzfeed.com/peteraldhous/these-10-questions-can-mean-life-behind-bars.

55. For example, Harvard states that its Sexual Harassment Policy "is designed to ensure a safe and non-discriminatory educational and work environment and to meet legal requirements, including: Title IX of the Education Amendments of 1972, which prohibits discrimination on the basis of sex in the University's programs or activities; relevant sections of the Violence Against Women Reauthorization Act; Title VII of the Civil Rights Act of 1964, which prohibits discrimination on the basis of sex in employment; and Massachusetts laws that prohibit discrimination on the basis of sex, sexual orientation, and gender identity. It does not preclude application or enforcement of other University or School policies." See Harvard University, "Sexual and Gender-Based Harassment Policy: Policy Statement," http://diversity.harvard .edu/pages/hu-sexual-harassment-policy (accessed April 28, 2015).

56. Antioch College, "Sexual Offense Prevention Policy (SOPP) & Title IX," http:// www.antiochcollege.org/campus-life/residence-life/health-safety/sexual-offense -prevention-policy-title-ix (accessed June 6, 2015).

57. New York State, "Governor Cuomo Signs 'Enough Is Enough' Legislation to Combat Sexual Assault on College and University Campuses," July 7, 2015, http://www .governor.ny.gov/news/governor-cuomo-signs-enough-enough-legislation-combat -sexual-assault-college-and-university.

58. Wendy Kaminer, "Don't Expect Students to Follow New Sexual Consent Rules," Boston Globe, July 27, 2015, https://www.bostonglobe.com/opinion/2015/07/26/don -expect-students-follow-new-sexual-consent-rules/D2ui6BG7WxUszVpgpvABmM /story.html.

59. Nosheen Iqbal, "How Can You Be Sure Someone Wants to Have Sex with You?" *Guardian*, July 27, 2015, http://www.theguardian.com/lifeandstyle/2015/jul/27/sure-sex-affirmative-consent-apps-yes-mean-yes.

60. Eliza Gray, "This Is the New Frontier in the Fight against Campus Rape," *Time*, June 5, 2015, http://time.com/3910602/campus-rape-sexual-assault-california-law/. The New York statute stipulates that " 'sexual activity' shall have the same meaning as 'sexual act' and 'sexual contact' as provided in 18 U.S.C. 2246(2) and 18 U.S.C. 2246(3)," where the term "sexual contact" is defined to mean "the intentional touching, either directly or through the clothing, of the genitalia, anus, groin, breast, inner thigh, or buttocks of any person with an intent to abuse, humiliate, harass, degrade, or arouse or gratify the sexual desire of any person."

61. Janet Halley, "The Move to Affirmative Consent," *Signs: Journal of Women in Culture and Society* 42, no. 1 (2016): 257–279, 259, 270.

62. Judith Shulevitz, "Regulating Sex," *New York Times*, June 28, 2015, SR1. See also Teresa Watanabe, "UC San Diego Didn't Give Male Student Fair Trial in Sex Case, Judge Rules," *Los Angeles Times*, July 14, 2015, http://www.latimes.com/local/lanow/la-me-ln-ucsd-sexual-misconduct-20150713-story.html.

63. Shulevitz, "Regulating Sex."

64. Laura Kipnis, "Sexual Paranoia Strikes Academe," *Chronicle of Higher Education*, February 27, 2015, http://chronicle.com/article/Sexual-Paranoia/190351/; "My Title IX Inquisition," *Chronicle of Higher Education*, May 29, 2015, http://chronicle.com/article/My-Title-IX-Inquisition/230489/?cid=at&utm_source=at&utm_medium=en. For an expansion of Kipnis's argument about the misuse of Title IX, see Jeannie Suk, "Shutting Down Conversations about Rape at Harvard Law," *New Yorker*, December 11, 2015, http://www.newyorker.com/news/news-desk/argument-sexual-assault-race-harvard-law-school.

65. For a survey of problematic issues connected with emerging campus sexual assault policies, see Janet Halley, "Trading the Megaphone for the Gavel in Title IX Enforcement," *Harvard Law Review Forum* 128 (2015): 103–117.

66. Katharine Bartlett, "Suspicious Eyes: The Uneasy Relationship between Feminism, Male Parenting, and Child Molestation Laws," JOTWELL, November 2, 2012, http://family.jotwell.com/suspicious-eyes-the-uneasy-relationship-between-feminism-male-parenting-and-child-molestation-laws/, reviewing Camille Gear Rich, "Innocence Interrupted: Reconstructing Fatherhood in the Shadow of Child Molestation Law," *California Law Review* 101, no. 3 (June 2013): 609–698.

67. United States Leadership against HIV/AIDS, Tuberculosis, and Malaria Act of 2003, 22 U.S.C. §§ 7601–7682 (2003); Agency for International Development v. Alliance for Open Society International, Inc., 570 U.S. ___ (2013), 133 S. Ct. 2321.

68. "Anti-Prostitution Pledge," Center for Health and Gender Equity, http://www.genderhealth.org/the_issues/us_foreign_policy/antiprostitution_pledge/ (accessed May 20, 2015); for more details, see the comprehensive report prepared by the Center for Health and Gender Equity, *Implications of U.S. Policy Restrictions for Programs Aimed at Commercial Sex Workers* (Takoma Park, MD: Center for Health and Gender Equity, August 2008), esp. 5.

69. Melissa Hope Ditmore and Dan Allman, "An Analysis of the Implementation of PEPFAR's Anti-Prostitution Pledge and Its Implications for Successful HIV Prevention among Organizations Working with Sex Workers," *Journal of the International AIDS Society* 16, no. 1 (2013): 17354 (p. 11).

70. *The Lancet* 385, nos. 9962–9964 (January 3, 10, 17, 2015).

71. Shannon McKarney, "High School Secretary Fired for Appearing in Porn," Care2, April 8, 2011, http://www.care2.com/causes/high-school-secretary-fired-for-appearing-in-porn.html.

72. Bob Egelko, "Teacher's Sex Ad on Craigslist Grounds for Firing," SF Gate, May 5, 2011, http://www.sfgate.com/news/article/Teacher-s-sex-ad-on-Craigslist-grounds-for-firing-2372856.php.

73. See Gabriel Arkles, "Prison Rape Elimination Act Litigation and the Perpetuation of Sexual Harm," *New York University Journal of Legislation & Public Policy* 17, no. 4 (fall 2014): 801–834.

74. Dean Spade, *Normal Life: Administrative Violence, Critical Trans Politics, and the Limits of Law* (Brooklyn, NY: South End Press, 2011), 91, cited and quoted in Arkles, "Prison Rape Elimination Act Litigation," 830n.

75. Catherine Hanssens, Aisha C. Moodie-Mills, Andrea J. Ritchie, Dean Spade, and Urvashi Vaid, *A Roadmap for Change: Federal Policy Recommendations for Addressing the Criminalization of LGBT People and People Living with HIV* (New York: Center for Gender and Sexuality Law at Columbia Law School, 2014), 22.

76. Idaho Department of Corrections, Procedure Control No. 325.02.01.001, Prison Rape Elimination 5 (2009), quoted in Hanssens et al., *A Roadmap for Change*, 21.

77. Battista v. Clarke, 645 F.3d 449–454 (1st Cir. 2011), cited and discussed in Arkles, "Prison Rape Elimination Act Litigation," 815.

78. Davis v. Ayala, 576 U.S. ___ (2015) (Kennedy, J., concurring). Solitary confinement has come under increasing critique: see Erica Goode, "Solitary Confinement: Punished for Life," *New York Times*, August 4, 2015, D1.

79. Timothy Williams, "Locked in Solitary at Age 14: The Risks of Juvenile Isolation," *New York Times*, August 16, 2015, A1; The Liman Program, Yale Law School Association of State Correctional Administrators, "Time-In-Cell: The ASCA-Liman 2014 National Survey of Administrative Segregation in Prison" (August 2015), 3,

cited in Barack Obama, "Why We Must Rethink Solitary Confinement," *Washington Post,* January 25, 2016, https://www.washingtonpost.com/opinions/barack-obama -why-we-must-rethink-solitary-confinement/2016/01/25/29a361f2-c384-11e5-8965 -0607e0e265ce_story.html?tid=a_inl; Juliet Eilperin, "Obama Bans Solitary Confinement for Juveniles in Federal Prisons," *Washington Post,* January 25, 2016, https:// www.washingtonpost.com/politics/obama-bans-solitary-confinement-for-juveniles -in-federal-prisons/2016/01/25/056e14b2-c3a2-11e5-9693-933a4d31bcc8_story.html.

80. Arkles, "Prison Rape Elimination Act Litigation," 818, citing McKnight v. Hobbs, 2:10CV00168 DPM HDY, 2010 WL 5056024 (E.D. Ark. Nov. 18, 2010), *report and recommendation adopted,* 2:10CV168 DPM HDY, 2010 WL 5056013 (E.D. Ark. Dec. 6, 2010); Everson v. Cline, No. 101,914, 2009 WL 3172859 (Kan. App. Oct. 2, 2009), both also cited in Hanssens et al., *A Roadmap for Change,* 68n58.

81. See Hanssens et al., *A Roadmap for Change,* 21.

82. Hanssens et al., *A Roadmap for Change,* 22–23.

83. Carole S. Vance, "States of Contradiction: Twelve Ways to Do Nothing about Trafficking While Pretending To," *Social Research* 78, no. 3 (fall 2011): 933–948 (quotation on p. 934), citing Kate Butcher, "Confusion between Prostitution and Sex Trafficking," *The Lancet* 361 (June 7, 2003): 1983, who draws the basic distinctions very clearly, in direct response to the U.S. government's adoption of the APLO provision in the 2003 legislation authorizing PEPFAR. Butcher adds, "By merging trafficking and prostitution, the agency of sex workers is overlooked. Rather than promoting opposition to prostitution we would do better to promote human rights. The right to resist being drawn into prostitution by trafficking certainly, but so too the right to work [i.e., to sell sex] with the law's protection from harm, be it rape, violence, robbery, or other violations." See also Carole S. Vance, "Innocence and Experience: Melodramatic Narratives of Sex Trafficking and Their Consequences for Law and Policy," *History of the Present: A Journal of Critical History* 2, no. 2 (fall 2012): 200–218, esp. 202.

84. Vance, "States of Contradiction," 934.

85. Chief Judge Jonathan Lippman, "Announcement of New York's Human Trafficking Intervention Initiative," Center for Court Innovation, http://www.courtinnovation .org/research/announcement-new-yorks-human-trafficking-intervention-initiative (accessed June 1, 2015).

86. William K. Rashbaum, "With Special Courts, State Aims to Steer Women Away from Sex Trade," *New York Times,* September 26, 2013, A22.

87. Red Umbrella Project, *Criminal, Victim, or Worker? The Effects of New York's Human Trafficking Intervention Courts on Adults Charged with Prostitution-Related Offenses* (October 2014), Executive Summary, 1.

88. Mike Ludwig, "Want the Truth about New York's Human Trafficking Courts? Ask a Sex Worker," *Truthout,* October 26, 2014, http://www.truth-out.org/news

/item/27036-want-the-truth-about-new-york-s-human-trafficking-courts-ask-a-sex-worker.

89. Red Umbrella Project, *Criminal, Victim, or Worker?* Executive Summary, 2.

90. Duggan, "What the Pathetic Case against Rentboy.com Says about Sex Work."

91. On this point, see also Vance, "States of Contradiction," 933–934; Vance, "Innocence and Experience," 201–202.

92. Vance, "States of Contradiction," 935.

93. See Emily Bazelon, "Should Prostitution Be a Crime? A Growing Movement of Sex Workers and Activists is Making the Decriminalization of Sex Work a Feminist Issue," *New York Times Magazine,* May 5, 2016, http://www.nytimes.com/2016/05/08/magazine/should-prostitution-be-a-crime.html?emc=edit_th_20160508&nl=todaysheadlines&nlid=27430306.

94. See the analysis, and brilliant rejoinder, by Chris Berry, *A Bit on the Side: East-West Topographies of Desire* (Rose Bay [Sydney], NSW: EM Press, 1994), 73–104. Cf. Joseph A. Massad, *Desiring Arabs* (Chicago: University of Chicago Press, 2007), 160–190.

PART I

The
Politics
of Sex

ROGER N. LANCASTER

|1|

The New Pariahs

Sex, Crime, and Punishment in America

Beware of those in whom the will to punish is strong.
FRIEDRICH NIETZSCHE | *Thus Spake Zarathustra*

Along the way to the third millennium, something changed in the ebb and flow of what we call progress in American culture. This change would involve new social movements of various sorts, novel arrangements among the institutions of civil society, revamped rationales for the role of the state, not to say a restructuring of important elements of everyday life — and, ultimately, peculiar economic effects. Now it is a curious fact that not even the most engaged and creative soothsayers — experts at reading the entrails of legal documents and deciphering the hidden mysteries of political-economic trends — foresaw this sea change. Humanist diviners of power, stigma, shame, feeling, and other such enigmas of the human condition were largely silent as well. Even the queerest of theorists took little notice of the shifting tide; perhaps this was selective amnesia on our part.

More curious still, our theoretical models remain halting and incomplete in the wake of events. We say that the United States has become a more fearful and, by that measure, a more punitive society. We begin to see that panic and rage have been institutionalized and that this has had corrosive effects on the public sphere and thus on the democratic process. We can discern the broad outlines of those effects: the redistributive welfare state, which once governed through ideals of health, well-being, and discipline, has given way to a punitive neoliberal regime, which takes the crime scene as the basic paradigm of governance and conditions assistance on varied forms of *victimization* (or otherwise subjects benefits to means-testing as opposed to universal entitlement). But what still goes unmarked is the role of liberalism in fostering these illiberal developments. What remains poorly understood is the glaring fact that mass incarceration is only one of the punitive state's techniques, and what goes unexamined is the role of sexual fear and loathing in promoting expansive new extra-carceral modes of securitization.

Before giving this changeover a name and trying to work out its implications, let me tell, in broad outlines, the story of what actually happened. In the first section, I will lay out a picture of general trends in crime and punishment over the last half century. In the next section, I will chart the social and political currents in play in these developments. Then, I will track the evolution and dissemination of modern sex laws against that wider backdrop. Only then, in the final section, will I take stock of the resulting picture and hazard a few guesses about where the currents of social change seem to be taking us.

TRENDS IN CRIME AND PUNISHMENT

Start in the 1960s: a time when new social movements and youthful rebellions threw durable hierarchies based on age, race, gender, and sexuality into question; a decade when antidraft, antiwar, and anti-imperialist movements laid siege to the militarized masculinity that had undergirded U.S. power for decades. These were the best of times, as an optimistic, upbeat counterculture strove to develop forms of life outside the confines of the nuclear family, the nine-to-five workaday world, and sober, stultifying suburbia. But all was not copacetic in the Age of Aquarius, and from another perspective these were also the worst of times: an epoch of urban disorders, violent crime, and white flight from the cities. Crime rates rose dramatically during the 1960s and through the early 1970s; then they remained elevated, with periodic alarming peaks, until about 1992.[1]

The Great American Crime Spree in Perspective

These disruptions seemed to burst upon the scene like a sudden summer thunderstorm. But America had seen its crime scares before. During the 1930s, J. Edgar Hoover stoked reportage on spectacular gangland violence and lurid sex crimes to kite the authority of the newly formed FBI. Closer to the cusp of the Great American Crime Spree, at the end of the socially tranquil 1950s, the incidence of certain forms of lawbreaking actually began to climb, with juvenile delinquency scares first airing as journalism and "social problem" movies. What is often forgotten, however, is that the United States was born in rampant lawlessness. Consider the long historical trajectory: Violent crime rates were high in the nineteenth century (and, all evidence suggests, higher still during the colonial period) — much higher than during the 1960s, 1970s, or 1980s. These rates had registered a gradual, almost continuous decline (with exceptions in the wake of major wars) until bottoming out in the early 1950s. What happened to crime rates after the 1960s, then, graphically tracks less like a backward *L* (commencing low then suddenly taking off) or even a standard *U* (high, then low, then high again) than like a reverse *J* (a long decline followed by a smaller uptick).[2]

Explanations for such historical trends abound, and it is useful to keep this larger picture in mind, as it provides an antidote to just-so stories about crime's causes and effects. Some historians say crime rates fell over a century and a half because Americans became more religious; others say the rates fell because new industrial modes of life encouraged social conformity. Some attribute the decline to the benefits of public education and new bureaucratic modes of socialization. Others see in the crime figures a general, long-term "civilizing process." As Michael Tonry and Joan Petersilia point out, virtually no one who studies these matters attributes this historic, much-researched decline to innovative policing strategies, stiffer sentencing provisions, or the institutionalization of a modern criminal justice system. These latter are of course the prevailing, official explanations for the second, less dramatic and shorter-term decline from 1992 until the present, but, as Franklin Zimring meticulously shows, they do not hold much water.[3]

Tolerance and Lockdown

American society metabolized the changes of the 1960s in uneven and complicated ways. Much of its response was reactive, even reactionary. America got religion — again — and the resulting evangelical counter-counterculture proved every bit as resilient as "the great disruption" it resisted (to steal a useful term from a conservative political theorist).[4] Often insinuated but seldom called out, race continued to color American politics; Republicans won seven out of ten presidential elections between 1968 and 2004 by adopting Richard Nixon's "Southern Strategy," with its coded appeals to white solidarity. Meanwhile, culture warriors waged a grim twilight struggle over how to organize what Antonio Gramsci had once dubbed "the institutions connected with sexual life": that is to say, marriage, the family, and kinship. If it remained unclear for a long time exactly how these various struggles would play out, we might today describe the resulting social formation in terms of a dialectical tension between progress and regress, liberation and repression. The civilizational clock — if we could believe in such a thing — appears to be running forward and backward at the same time.

On the one hand, something that was set in motion during the 1960s remains in motion today. Forms of prejudice based on gender, race, and sexuality were stripped of their standing as "natural" hierarchies and have been progressively delegitimized in the respectable political sphere. Radicals once had aspired to more, of course. Some wanted a far-reaching overhaul of the everyday institutions; others aspired to an upending of the class system; and virtually no one would have welcomed the prevailing new rationale for military adventures, "humanitarian intervention." But this is not to say that radical critique is dead. The spirit of headier times lives on in chastened form today: a lively queer Left militates against gay marriage as the be-all and end-all of the modern gay movement, while Walter Benn Michaels has contrasted *discrimination* to *exploitation* in order to suggest that anti-discrimination has become the official ethos — the reigning ideology of neoliberalism — at a time of intensifying class exploitation and widening social inequalities.[5] It will be clear that I am in sympathy with such negative views of the new status quo (many of which were prefigured in Herbert Marcuse's 1969 essay, "Repressive Tolerance").[6] Still, it is useful to mark the advances signified by the abolition of Jim Crow, the gradual accretion of women's rights, the repeal of sodomy laws, and the end of an official, public white monoculture. These were no mean feats; they have altered the institutional nexus in profound ways; and they represent genuine triumphs of the social movements that began their ascent at a time when large sections of the white working class were drifting into alignment with a conservative "middle-class" outlook.

On the other hand, accompanying developments on the American scene represent radical subtractions from the regime of formal human rights, the expansion of the democratic franchise, and civic inclusion. Beginning in 1973, incarceration rates in the United States began an unprecedented thirty-five-year continuous climb. The incarcerated population swelled from around 360,000 in 1973 to more than 2,300,000 in 2008, and the incarceration rate soared from about 170 per 100,000 (which was already high for a democracy) to more than 750.[7] At the peak of this mania for locking people up, one in every ninety-nine adults was behind bars. Even after these numbers have leveled off and posted modest declines, the basic contours of this picture remain intact. When it comes to incarceration, the United States ranks first in the world, and this is true whether measured in terms of the incarceration rate (which remains five to ten times that of other developed democracies) or in terms of the absolute number of people in prison.[8]

No doubt the United States does suffer from a higher incidence of violent crime than do other developed democracies. But higher crime rates account for only a fraction of the country's elevated prison statistics, and mass incarceration appears to be a "logical" response to high crime rates only when other options — poverty alleviation, jobs programs, and rehabilitation for first-time offenders — are taken off the table. The rapid expansion of the U.S. penal system was fueled less by a crime surge than by draconian laws passed in the name of assorted wars on crime, drugs, and gangs. That is, in the 1970s the U.S. criminal justice system began implementing stiffer sentences, longer incarcerations, and more onerous terms of release and surveillance to far, far more people than any of the nations Americans like to think of as their peers. As a result, a large percentage of people in U.S. prisons today — even many inmates serving extremely long sentences — were not convicted of a violent crime. Many were convicted for offenses against public order or morality: they are drug offenders of one sort or another. Others serve long sentences for property crimes that once would have drawn a short term, a fine, or a suspended sentence. The image of the "repeat offender" looms large in the public imagination, but data from the Bureau of Justice Statistics show that the great run-up in the prison population results from an increase in first-time incarcerations. So strong was the tug of incarceration that even policies originally designed to reduce the prison population came to feed the carceral system: in 1999 alone the United States sent about as many people to prison for parole violations as it sent to prison for any reason in 1980.[9]

Harsh laws were combined with harsher enforcement. A staggering fourteen million Americans were being arrested each year by the mid-2000s, excluding traffic violations — up from a little more than three million in 1960. (That is, the annual arrest rate as a percentage of the population nearly tripled: from 1.6 percent in 1960 to 4.5 percent in 2009.) Thirty percent of the adult population is said to have a rap sheet — an arrest record.[10]

Numbers pile up. At prevailing rates of incarceration, one in every fifteen Americans will serve time in a prison during his or her lifetime. For men the rate is more than one in nine. For African American men the expected lifetime rate is roughly one in three.[11] Such figures have no precedent in the United States: not under Puritanism, nor even under Jim Crow. Some point to the crime rate decline after 1992 as evidence of these policies' success. But by reasonable, informed estimates, locking up millions of people for long periods contributed to as much as 27 percent or as little as 10 percent of the overall reduction in crime.[12]

These inflated numbers could not help but have large economic effects, and the distinctively harsh version of neoliberalism that developed on U.S. soil appropriated such facts on the ground as an enabling and productive condition. For mass incarceration solves two of capitalism's socioeconomic problems at the same time. First, as sociologist Loïc Wacquant has explained, it contains and controls what Marx called a "reserve army of labor": the deproletarianized sections of the working class whose chronic unemployment might otherwise lead to social unrest.[13] Second, it produces stable employment in law enforcement at a time when secure unionized jobs in the industrial sector have become virtually nonexistent. These twin functions — which I have called penal Keynesianism — appear to have buttressed and stabilized the post-1970s American experiment in deregulation, privatization, and outsourcing. It has been estimated that during the 1990s, America's zeal for incarceration shaved two percentage points off the unemployment figures.[14] Roughly 4 percent of the civilian labor force is employed by the penal system or works to put people in prison. If one adds to these numbers those employed in private security positions, plus those whose work responsibilities include the monitoring and guarding of other laborers, the results are striking: in an increasingly "garrisonized" economy, one out of every four or five American laborers is employed in what Samuel Bowles and Arjun Jayadev call "guard labor."[15]

American Gulag

That this remarkable social transition, so inimical to the spirit of a free society, occurred under formally democratic conditions — indeed, was prodded by electoral pressures to "get tough on crime" — mocks any grand conception of democracy in America. Angela Davis registers something of the shock of these numbers:

> When I first became involved in antiprison activism during the late 1960s, I was astounded to learn that there were then close to two hundred thousand people in prison [this figure does not include jail inmates — RNL]. Had anyone told me that in three decades ten times as many people would be locked away in cages, I would have been absolutely incredulous. I imagine that I would have responded something

like this: "As racist and undemocratic as this country may be [remember, during that period, the demands of the Civil Rights movement had not yet been consolidated], I do not believe that the U.S. government will be able to lock up so many people without producing powerful public resistance. No, this will never happen, not unless this country plunges into fascism."[16]

Certainly, policies of mass incarceration, disproportionately directed against racial minorities, begin to resemble fascist techniques of coercion. In the past, we would have referred to the resulting form of government as "authoritarian" or called it a "police state." I have used the term "punitive state" to describe a shift in the dominant rationale for governance: from the postwar era's welfare perspective to the present era's culture of crime control. Strictly speaking, it involves no exaggeration whatever to say that the United States has become a *carceral society*, in which a bloated prison system provides the normative model for governance in general and in which organizations of civil society collude with elements of the state to intensify punitive norms and to feed ever more prisoners into the penal system.

The criminologist David Garland describes this system of control in the bleakest of terms. The present prison system "serves as a kind of reservation system, a quarantine zone," where "purportedly dangerous individuals are segregated in the name of public safety." In form, number, and arbitrariness it "resembles nothing so much as the Soviet gulag — a string of work camps and prisons strung across a vast country, housing [more than] two million people most of whom are drawn from classes and racial groups that have become politically and economically problematic. . . . Like the pre-modern sanctions of transportation or banishment, the prison now functions as a form of exile."[17]

Many of the procedures associated with the justice system wed a primal rage to punish with a modern mania for the privatization of government functions. At the front end of the system, assorted application fees and charges for people who seek court-appointed attorneys undermine the defendant's Sixth Amendment right to counsel. At the back end of the system, more fees, charges, and procedures pile on. Indeed, "almost every encounter with the criminal justice system these days can give rise to a fee," reports Adam Liptak of the *New York Times*, among them court costs, restitution fees, recovery costs for such services as incarceration or electronic monitoring, and mandatory contributions to various high-minded funds.[18]

And once the system gets its hooks into a person, it is loath to let him go. Nearly 5 million Americans are on probation or parole. Added to the 2.2 million behind bars, this means that one in every thirty-five adults — roughly 3 percent of the adult population — is actively caught up in the long reach of the penal system.[19] What happens to convicts upon their release from prison is instructive. Some 45,000 laws and rules nationwide serve to strip ex-convicts of basic rights, according to a study by the National Association of Criminal Defense Lawyers. These elaborate encumbrances, known as "collateral consequences," restrict access to voting, housing, education, professional licensing, and interstate travel; they affect a person's immigrant status, parental rights, and access to public benefits. That is to say, they relegate a large population to a permanent second-class status — or worse.[20]

VICTIMS' RIGHTS IN THE PUNITIVE TURN

This "punitive turn" in penal policy did not happen all at once, but it did happen very quickly.[21] All the more remarkably, it represents a sharp reversal of long-standing trends. In countries of the North Atlantic, including the United States, penal models stressing rehabilitation, reform, and welfare had gained ground steadily from the late nineteenth century on, and by the mid-twentieth century these were the prevailing approaches almost everywhere. Indeed, in the wake of liberal legal reforms of the 1960s, the prison population was slowly shrinking and alternatives to incarceration were being developed. Michel Foucault brilliantly traces this long shift from punitive to welfare models of social control in *Discipline and Punish* — although nothing in Foucault's analysis (or anyone else's) could have predicted what soon followed in the United States: the return of a punitive orientation, specifically designed to subtract from life or enjoyment ("incapacitation") rather than to produce well-being.[22] The question, then, is how rehabilitation came to be discredited and how a "lock 'em up" approach — which diverts funds from health, education, and social services, uproots social support networks, devastates poor minority communities, and imposes other enormous social costs — came to be acceptable.

The short explanation has to do with the victims' rights movement, which amplified the howl on the lips of the crime victim into a comprehensive political program for the transfer of his or her blameless suffering to its proximate blameworthy cause. This movement provided the moral underpinnings for a punitive approach to crime; it persuaded voters to identify with crime victims, to deemphasize the rights of the accused, and to countenance excessive policing. It aggressively lobbied for the harsher laws, enhanced penalties, zealous prosecution, and court procedures that put the prison system on steroids. The longer explanation has to do with the unique conjunctures that made the last third of the twentieth century propitious for the rise of such a victims' rights movement, and this explanation will take all manner of twists and turns as it wanders through diverse political precincts. Let me sketch here something of the interplay of multiple causes and effects in bringing about this distinctively American outcome.

Genealogies of the Punitive Turn

The United States was becoming a palpably more fearful place in the 1970s, a time when serial killers, slasher movies, religious cults, drug scares, and sex crimes came to occupy an outsized portion of the mediascape. As Philip Jenkins sums it up, the liberal and libertarian optimism of the 1960s gave way to "a more pessimistic, more threatening interpretation of human behavior" and to "sinister visions of the enemies facing Americans and their nation."[23] The perception that crime was raging out of control (and that liberal or welfare methods of crime control were not working) was key to this mood swing — which laid the groundwork for a political swing to the right. The old joke is apposite: "What's a conservative?" "A liberal who's been mugged."

Conservatives — who have always had a simple approach to crime: put the bad man in jail and keep him there — stoked anxieties about crime to reap political benefits. They began to get the upper hand on crime policy long before they were able to implement any of the economic theories that had been hatched in neoliberal think tanks, sometimes many decades before.[24] I give away no secrets when I say that racial antagonisms were involved in these developments. Racially skewed crime statistics made law-and-order politics a natural venue for the expression of white backlash, hardhat conservatism, and Southern revanchism. And racially skewed law enforcement made mass incarceration a blunt instrument of racial domination. So much is well known. With and since Nixon, a tough approach to crime came to be expressly associated with the patriotism, loyalty, and work ethic of a steely silent (white) majority.[25]

What might be less obvious is the role played by liberals and progressives in bringing about the present state of affairs. Let me put it this way: whereas the Right played up expressive punishment (harsh penalties and long sentences), the liberal Left, too, undermined penal welfarism in its own way: by shifting the focus of public concern away from the rehabilitation of the lawbreaker to the suffering of his victim, by promoting new "technologies of the self"[26] — new ways of knowing ourselves and deciphering our experiences based on an acute sense of victimization — and by fostering a consensus that government exists, essentially, to protect the innocent.

Elements of this approach were present on the American scene all along, of course. Liberalism (as opposed to any variant of socialism) construes the rationale for government action narrowly, as intervention on behalf of the weakest and most vulnerable; it aims to correct or curb "worst abuses" rather than to address the logic of the system as a whole.[27] In other words, the liberal view of government action is already conditioned and its approach to public good is already hemmed in. In this sense, modern or progressive liberalism, with its activist bent, retains a family resemblance to classical liberalism (modern conservatism), which begins from the premise that there might be such thing as *too much* government and thus construes freedom as the *absence* of state intrusion into "private" affairs (notably, economic activities). By contrast, socialism begins from the premise that inequalities, vulnerabilities, and other invidious outcomes are neither "excesses" nor anomalies but rather *expressions* of the intrinsic logic of the capitalist system; socialists thus view an enlarged, democratically controlled state sector as desirable — and hope that its gradual expansion will culminate in social control over the means of production. Because it lacks a viable socialist tradition, American politics is essentially a contest between two forms of liberalism: one party sees discrimination, abuses of power, or systemic perturbations as the main sources of victimization; the other party sees victimization as consisting in government attempts to correct or eliminate these dysfunctions.

But that is not all. Limitations on the American political imagination are further exacerbated by institutional constraints imposed at the time of the country's founding. To be sure, New Deal and Great Society programs pushed modern liberalism in a moderately social-democratic direction. But under the U.S. constitutional structure, with its separation of powers and sharp delineation of federal and state governments, it proved impossible to develop a full-fledged welfare state comparable to those that exist in "even the most conservative European societies," as Jonathan Simon has noted.[28] In any case, because well-being on the American model is construed as a private matter ("the pursuit of happiness"), political elites are effectively barred from making it the permanent focus of statecraft; instead, they have often constructed their authority as a response to crises, perils, emergencies, and wars. The sounding of alarms, often over statistically anomalous happenings, has been a recurring part of this political package; similarly, the *innocence* of the victim is a perennial trope of reform efforts under the logic of American liberalism: for if a citizen's own private actions played any role in her unhappy predicament, then she would be ineligible for public empathy or government remedy, and state intervention would be unjustifiable. Welfare programs or reforms positively require both emergencies and innocent victims.

For deep structural reasons, then, moral panic is as American as apple pie. Victimized innocents have served as poster children for missions of rescue, social uplift schemes, and assorted variants of activist liberalism over many decades of American history. This durable mode of political mobilization staged a comeback in the 1970s, at a time of narrowing political options.

The cultural reaction of the 1970s typically tilted against the "excesses" of the 1960s. But interdiscursive dynamics incubated in the countercultural movements themselves also contributed to the changing political climate. These developments bear closer inspection.

Feminist cultural critic Elayne Rapping has shown in detail how modern self-help and recovery movements devolved from the countercultural mobilizations of the 1960s: the derivative movements borrowed heavily from feminist consciousness-raising groups, with their discovery of victimization in everyday life experiences and their emphasis on organization, support, and immediacy — but without an earlier feminist vision of expansive freedoms and radical social change.[29] Rapping celebrates these latter-day popularizations of a feminist sensibility while lamenting the loss of a political focus. But the kernel of the problem is more vexing than her analysis admits, and the speed with which this devolution occurred lends credence to Russell Jacoby's early observation that "the personal" was depleting "the political" from the very start in what he dubbed the New Left's "cult of subjectivity." Declarations like "I feel oppressed by your statement" or "I feel excluded by this discussion" mark the spot where political concepts have been shrunk down to personal size and hauled into the service of petty envy and *ressentiment*.[30] Such staples of New Left discussion groups were discursive incubators for the development of new technologies of the self, which were then exported to assorted recovery, survivor, and therapeutic movements.

Above all, the new techniques of self-inspection and confession were designed to assign blame. Fanned by TV melodramas, yellow journalism, and legal and medical professions, these techniques proliferated rapidly. By the 1980s, expansive victim industries were in place — replete with self-help books, tracts on recovery, therapeutic techniques, academic advocates, and political lobbies — and victimization emerged as a durable new source of identity.[31] The pump was primed for the production of victimization on a hitherto unimagined scale: on the one side, new cadres of specialists staked their professions on a constantly expanding field of victimization; on the other side, the victim role afforded those who claimed it some relief from the rising neoliberal demand for individual responsibility. Victims — and *only* victims — might be entitled to support, services, and assistance, at a time when "welfare" was being made a dirty word. All that was required was the naming of a victimizer.

And so over the course of the 1970s and 1980s, the quintessential American hero of yore — the risk-taking individual who takes responsibility for his or her own fate and triumphs over adversity — gave way to the aggrieved victim who perpetually recounts unhappy experiences and recriminates against others. This redefinition of core values did not go unnoticed or uncontested. The essential case against it was laid out early on in sex-positive feminist critiques of the anti-pornography campaigns. Carole Vance and others showed how feminist assertions that sexual images intrinsically harm women redound to the benefit of social conservatives and serve to curb freedoms, which will always involve risks and dangers.[32] By the early 1990s, others took up similar threads and criticism was coming in from all segments of the political spectrum.[33]

Wendy Brown develops stark claims in her influential book of the period, *States of Injury*, a theoretical broadside against the politics of victimology she sees as inherent in modern liberalism, especially its feminist and LGBT variants. Attempts to "outlaw" injury, she reasons, build a certain kind of state and foster certain kinds of identities: they legitimize law and the state as "protectors against injury" while casting "injured individuals as needing such protection by such protectors." Freedom, now defined as protection, comes to mean subjection: it cultivates "wounded attachments," identities whose relation to the state is defined by grievance. Caught up in the resulting "economy of perpetrator and victim," the injured party seeks neither emancipation nor power but only aspires to punish and preempt: to make the perpetrator suffer as she or he has suffered.[34] (In like vein, Kristin Bumiller has argued that civil rights and sex discrimination laws effectively trap people in victim identities, reinforcing a sense of victimization and dependency — to the detriment of more robust approaches that might foster power, freedom, or social equality.[35])

Constructing Victimization

Whereas the rhetoric of individual liberation, freedom, and autonomy had prevailed during the upsurge of 1960s radicalism, the rhetoric of personalized grievance, injury, and victimization increasingly came to the fore with the decay of the New Left social movements. Talk about victimization on the Left joined powerfully with nascent trends on the Right. Positioned at the intersection of street crime and sexual violence, the victims' rights movement proved a logical vehicle for blending liberal rhetorics with conservative goals.

Ironically, it did not start out that way. The victims' rights movement was gestated in the welfare state of the 1960s, which addressed the socioeconomic causes of crime (poverty, institutional racism, alienation) while taking a holistic approach to crime's effects on communities. Aid for victims of violent crime was understood as the flip side of attempts to rehabilitate convicts through counseling, education, and job training. But by the early 1970s, political tides were turning and victims' support groups had become a pointed instrument of the "war on crime," with its decidedly non-holistic approach to crime's causes and effects. Attributing low conviction rates to a lack of cooperation by victims and witnesses, the federal Law Enforcement Assistance Administration (LEAA) launched demonstration projects designed to get victims and witnesses involved in the war on crime; it funded conferences for victims' organizations and encouraged the formation of victims' assistance programs nationwide. The state thus sponsored or seeded a host of private organizations, including the umbrella group for victims of violent crime, the National Organization for Victims' Assistance (NOVA) (1975). Other prominent victims' organizations founded during this period of ferment include Families and Friends of Missing Persons (1974), Parents of Murdered Children (1978), and Mothers Against Drunk Driving (1980). By the beginning of the 1980s, the nascent movement was directly pitting victims' rights *against* the rights of the accused in widespread campaigns for the passage of a "Basic Bill of Rights for Crime Victims and Witnesses." The Reagan administration would eventually draw the movement "securely within the compass of the right," according to a logic that Bruce Shapiro has described.[36]

To date, all fifty states and the District of Columbia have passed some version of a victims' bill of rights, thirty-four as amendments to their state constitutions.[37] The main elements of these bills tilt law enforcement practices away from a constitutional emphasis on the rights of the accused; they also institutionalize emotional, personal recrimination, to various degrees, in the workings of the justice system. For example, one provision in victims' rights bills asserts the victim's right to be protected from the accused. The concern that accusers might be stalked or harassed is a valid one, but once codified as a legal norm this "right" reverses the traditional presumption of innocence and favors pretrial detention, giving prosecutors a powerful weapon against the accused. (Defendants are far more likely to enter a guilty plea when jailed and cut off from family and friends.)

Other provisions in victims' rights bills assert the right of victims to confer with prosecutors in cases to which they are a party and to be heard at any public hearings regarding sentencing, parole, or release. Advocates of this approach stress the supposed therapeutic benefits of involvement for the victims. It remains unclear whether such participation accelerates healing or reinforces a sense of perpetual victimization and bereavement; nonetheless, emotional presentencing testimony by victims and their families is now as much a regular part of criminal trials as it is a standard practice at congressional hearings. The mandatory admission of such testimony strains against one of the most ancient principles of Western law: the idea that law ought to be dispassionate, free of emotion. As legal scholar Paul Robinson has put it, victim influence on sentencing is "inconsistent with our reasons for being so careful to have impartial judges, jurors, and prosecutors . . . who will look only to the facts of the case." Justice, moreover, ought not be influenced by whether a crime victim has family members who make impact statements, nor should it be affected by whether victims and their loved ones are reputable or disreputable, forgiving or vengeful.[38] Prima facie, presentencing testimony would seem to be a recipe for unequal justice.

Meanwhile, a distinctly *privatized* notion of justice is enshrined in victims' rights amendments in various states, which typically include mandates for financial restitution — as though punishment were "payment" and justice a cash transaction. The periodic assertion that vengeance is a basic right reiterates the idea that justice is punishment and that punishment is a settling of accounts between individuals.[39] Such notions turn back the clock on key principles of rational law, which have for millennia sought to restrain vengeance and to cultivate a corrective and preventive logic. "Not that he is punished because he did wrong, for that which is done can never be undone," Plato reasoned 2,400 years ago, "but in order that in future times, he, and those who see him corrected, may utterly hate injustice, or at any rate abate much of their evil-doing."[40]

The politicization of crime issues in victims' support groups followed a path that had already been blazed by consciousness-raising groups, a path leading from the personal experience of victimization to political campaigns for redress. In this way, the Left provided the organizational template for victims' rights. But it was also party to the development of punitive laws in more direct ways.

If I had to identify one crucial turn in the ramshackle sequence of events that led to the present state of affairs, it would be neither the emergence of white backlash nor the rise of the Christian New Right (both of which were important factors), but rather the development of "carceral feminism," as Elizabeth Bernstein calls it in her contribution to this volume: that is, the gradual process whereby mainstream white feminists came to view rape, sexual abuse, and domestic violence through a law-and-order lens and came to make harsh criminal penalties their central demand. White middle-class women were receptive early on to this approach, in no small part because they could afford to ignore the very different experiences black and brown women had with the police, not to mention the role historically played by rape accusations in structuring racial violence, as the political scientist Marie Gottschalk has pointed out.[41] Carceral feminism achieved two simultaneous results: it undermined the educated middle class's historic commitment to enlightened humanitarianism, social tolerance, and progressive reform, especially as these related to issues of crime and punishment; and it gave free rein to the worst rhetorical excesses of the victims' rights movement, whose activists, now shielded by their progressive feminist credentials as well as by their perceived unimpeachable innocence, could lash out at various species of criminal predators without fear of reproof.

A political reverb effect was thus orchestrated. The victims' rights movement of the 1980s and 1990s adopted early feminist rhetoric around rape and domestic violence — for example, the assertion that crime victims are victimized a "second time" by their experiences with the police and court system.[42] Meanwhile, rape shield laws — which protect rape victims from having to be cross-examined about their past sexual behavior but which have been criticized by some feminists and civil libertarians — set a precedent for later laws protecting accusers while diminishing the rights of the accused.[43] Not only did language and concepts pass back and forth between crime control advocates and mainstream feminists; political collusions between them multiplied: in many states, white feminist groups worked with law-and-order conservatives to insert their favored provisions into local anti-crime bills. Alternative welfare-based approaches supported by socialist feminists — broad policies that would have enhanced the economic independence of women, and thus would have reduced their (and their children's) vulnerability to domestic and sexual violence — were increasingly given short shrift.[44]

Before long, local police departments and victims' rights groups began sponsoring "Take Back the Night" rallies, giving the sheen of progressivity to what in fact were punitive anti-crime campaigns. By the time Congress passed the Violence Against Women Act (VAWA) as part of the 1994 Violent Crime Control and Law Enforcement Act, the incorporation of law-and-order feminism into the punitive state seemed inevitable, natural. VAWA expanded federal jurisdiction over domestic violence, pumped federal money into the prosecution of violent crimes against women, imposed restitution requirements, created a federal rape shield law, and provided a federal "civil rights remedy" (subsequently struck down by the courts). It also increased penalties for some sex offenders while the wider Crime Control Act named sixty new death penalty offenses and eliminated support for inmate higher education. Mainstream feminist groups actively lobbied for passage of the omnibus act; they were comparatively quiet in the debates two years later, when Congress passed and Clinton signed the Personal Responsibility and Work Opportunity Act — a bill to "end welfare as we know it" — despite that bill's profoundly antifeminist content.[45]

The dangers of viewing rape and domestic violence through a law-and-order lens should have been obvious from the start. U.S. history, Gottschalk notes, is "littered with punitive efforts to address violence against women and children that ended up idealizing the nuclear family and motherhood and emboldening political conservatives." Feminism did not take this sharply punitive turn in other countries, and with few exceptions women's movements internationally have tended to maintain a critical distance from the repressive power of the state.[46] The reasons for the political collusion between crime control advocates and mainstream feminists in the United States ultimately have to do with our truncated political spectrum and the limitations of liberalism. In the context of a liberal emphasis on formal equality, and in the absence of viable radical, socialist, or social-democratic alternatives, feminist demands naturally gravitated to the grievance-redress model, reinforced victim narratives, and tended to promote a criminal justice approach to violence against women and children.

The placement of the victim center stage in the national drama; the elaboration of his or her precarious innocence, as justification for state action, over against the utter depravity of the predator; the erasure of the latter's backstory, so that he becomes nothing more than an example of mute, inglorious evil; the institutionalization of constitutionally suspect procedures favoring detention, conviction, and incarceration; a conceptual shift in the focus of welfare, from universal entitlement to the special needs of the harmed or wounded; the redefinition of justice *as* punishment — and above all the lifting of the bar against excessive punishment (a linchpin of the disciplinary approach associated with penal welfarism): these were the results of long-term collaborative projects that emanated from many quarters spanning the political spectrum. There was no one single cause for these developments. Rather, elements old and new came into play. No doubt owing to its diverse sources, the punitive turn proved capable of putting down deep institutional roots while reproducing itself long after the original conditions that had initiated it (rising crime rates, urban riots, racial backlash) abated. No doubt the economic effects derived from mass incarceration also reinforced these trends. They became bolder under the Clinton administration than during the Reagan-Bush era.

It should scarcely come as a surprise that in the land of puritan revolutionaries and prurient liberal social reformers, some of the most exacting punishments would involve sex.

MODERN SEX CRIME LAWS

Today, we seem poised on the cusp of another era of transformation. Some have declared an end to the age of mass incarceration — a tad hastily, in my view. Still, something no doubt is happening, and it would be good to know just what.

Limits of the Carceral Society

There are many good omens. The long tide of punitive lawmaking shows signs of receding. Upbeat journalists occasionally produce pieces on the advent of a more rational approach to crime; this advent is perhaps especially evident where drug laws are concerned. Notably, racial sentencing disparities have become a point of national embarrassment, and in 2007 the U.S. Sentencing Commission intervened to reduce retroactively the sentences of some (not all) federal inmates convicted on crack-related drug charges, effectively bringing their sentences into closer alignment with those for cocaine-related charges. The Obama administration has continued these modest efforts. Meanwhile, even in some conservative states there has been renewed interest in rehabilitation, especially in the juvenile justice system. These are important developments, as the expansion of the prison system was driven by state laws more than by federal policies. A notable milestone: in 2009 the State of New York rescinded much of what remained of its 1973 Rockefeller drug laws, whose mandatory minimum sentencing provisions for low-level drug offenders had been a harbinger of nationwide policies of mass incarceration. Mundane budget pressures have played no small part here. In the wake of the 2008 financial crisis, cash-strapped states found themselves hard-pressed to maintain prison populations at prerecession levels, while California — a major contributor to overall prison numbers — was under federal orders to ease prison overcrowding.

As a result of these and other developments, increases in the rate of incarceration slowed over the course of the last decade; rates peaked in 2008 or 2009 (depending on one's measure) and have posted small — sometimes very small — decreases every year since.[47] These developments give cause for cautious celebration. However, the numbers remain elevated, and a closer inspection of the data reveals contradictory trends. For example, the number of African Americans sent to prison declined from the beginning of the twenty-first century, but the number of whites and Latinos sent to prison increased rapidly enough to keep the system growing for several more years.[48] After 2008, the federal system — especially the immigration detention system — has sometimes grown while state prison systems have shrunk. Some elements of the carceral system appear to have become self-sustaining. Recent studies document high recidivism (and reincarceration) rates, and a "life of crime" may be virtually all that remains now for millions of people who were churned through penitentiaries at a time when legislatures were shrinking or eliminating prison rehabilitation, job training, and educational programs, while piling on collateral consequences that make legitimate employment all but impossible.[49] Everything seems to work out as though a great beast were struggling to maintain equilibrium. And while penalties for some drug crimes have become less severe, penalties for other offenses are being ramped up. Penalties for violent crimes, second offenses, and crimes committed with a handgun continue to increase.

This is where sex crimes come in. Harsher sex crime laws contributed to the rise of the mass incarceration more than is usually acknowledged. Today, escalating penalties and long mandatory minimum sentences for first-time sex offenders continue to feed the prison pipeline and to keep incarceration rates elevated. Marie Gottschalk surveys some of the numbers. Nationwide, convictions for sex offenses of various kinds — mostly non-rape — ballooned between 1993 and 2000, increasing by 400 percent. This rate of increase vastly exceeded the overall rate of expansion of the prison system and occurred during a period when sex offense rates (like other crime rates) were falling rapidly. After 2000, incarceration rates for sex offenses continued to rise, while incarceration rates for other crimes stabilized or fell. Some subsets of sex offenses have registered extraordinary growth. For example, the number of federal prisoners serving time for possession (not production) of sexually explicit materials, usually child pornography, increased sixtyfold between 1996 and 2010. "Thanks to tougher sanctions, sex offenders have become the fastest growing segment of state and federal prison populations. Between 10 and 20 percent of state prisoners are now serving time for sex offenses; in some states, however, the rate is nearly 30 percent."[50]

Role of the Sexual Predator

At a time when the system seems ripe for reform, most criminal justice advocates have been reluctant to talk about sex offender laws, much less to lobby for their reform. The reluctance has deep roots.

Narratives of sexual danger are older than the republic itself. Indeed, the drama of protection — what Susan Faludi calls "the guardian myth" — serves as something of a foundational national storyline about the wresting of white civilization from sexual savagery.[51] During the colonial, antebellum, Jim Crow, and Progressive eras, white Americans were variously preoccupied with tales of sexual danger to white women and children. The retrograde racial and gender politics involved in guardianship could not be clearer. Historically, the guardian myth cast white men as protectors of white women and children; the villains of the piece were depraved red, black, brown, or yellow men. But Depression and McCarthy-era paranoias put a new spin on this old storyline. With the decline of lynch law in the 1930s, the focus of white middle-class sexual anxieties shifted from external threats to internal deviations, and a new species of sexual monster — the "sexual psychopath," who was raced as white and sexed as homosexual — lurched onto the historical stage.[52] After a brief hiatus during the 1960s, he resumed his stalking of children in the wake of gay liberation — at about the same time that Americans started to repeal sodomy laws while getting tough on crime. (See Regina Kunzel's and Scott De Orio's essays in this volume.) The sexual psychopath eventually would morph into the modern "pedophile," just in time for new plot twists, such as stories about satanic ritual abuse, stranger danger, and a host of subsequent perils to children.[53] Meanwhile, the role of the protector, too, would undergo various rewrites, in alignment with the shifting focus of white sexual anxieties and changing gender politics. Over time, the guardians were recast: today, they are not an ensemble of white men but rather an assemblage of victims' rights advocates, mainstream feminists, and social workers.

Keeping in view the wide sweep of these trends and motifs, I shall try to take a step beyond existing analyses of what is now well established: mass incarceration's roots in racial domination. For mass incarceration is only one element (albeit a very substantial one) of the present system of social control, and racial domination is only one function (again, a very prominent one) of that system. In wider terms, the present system is an expansive new reticulum that includes such components as lockdown schools, gated communities, video surveillance technologies in public and private places, secure key-card entry systems, antitheft devices, elaborate performance monitoring procedures, and corps of security specialists — supported by platoons of private guards — everywhere.[54] Repression, too, is only one of the mechanisms in play. Increasingly, subject citizens are primed to *crave* the new techniques of supervision — for their own "good," even for their own sense of *freedom* — which are silently disseminated across a rebuilt landscape.

The (implicitly white) sexual predator has played an important role in the production of this wider system. His crimes are understood as being both uniquely horrific and uniquely widespread; they are thus to be constantly anticipated and guarded against. Because his predations occur in secret, and because they often invade otherwise safe spaces, they must be constantly flushed out and exposed. The merest suspicion of the predator's presence justifies, even demands, the laying of traps, the deployment of decoys, the staging of "stings," the application of surveillance technologies at new sites. And if, in Foucauldian terms, the sexual predator's stealth and guile have proved to be less "enemy" than target and support for an array of preventive procedures,[55] the fear and loathing he evokes have proved to be important *political* resources. The emotions he stirs have played a crucial part in stoking public outrage, in mobilizing an inflamed citizenry, and in cementing the prevailing tabloid storyline around innocence, vulnerability, and victimization.

"Innocence," of course, is an especially precarious concept, never more so than when it is imagined as "sexlessness," and it would appear that the sexual predator is an absolutely indispensable element in underwriting this concept: it is ultimately *he* who secures the existence of innocence, diacritically, by threatening to snatch it away. In the mutually constitutive interplay between innocent sexlessness and sexual evil, innocence serves as a stand-in for *health*, not only for the child but for the species as well: its preservation, up to a certain unclear age, points to a happy, well-adjusted future. Correlatively, the predator's pernicious sexuality constitutes a kind of *disease*: the perils he poses circumscribe the normal, desired state, and their intrusion into the closed world of childhood — more so than poverty, neglect, or violence — is deemed uniquely capable of diverting the child from the proper developmental path. This dialectic between innocence and its despoliation has given rise to a biopolitical system every bit as expansive as any variant of nineteenth-century sexual hygienics, replete with corps of specialists, advocates, and disciplinarians. The most successful new social movement of the late twentieth century, the victims' rights movement, could scarcely have staged so many notable triumphs in the fields of law, policing, and court procedures without the help of that massive new hygienic infrastructure and without invoking, as its foil, the ignominious figure of the sexual predator. Expansive new cadres of professional child protectors could scarcely have occupied an increasingly crowded field except in the shadow of his outsized existence.

A dark suspicion begins to form: Might we think that in a society committed both to a war on crime (with its mass incarceration of black men) and to ridding itself of racism (through formal adherence to a regime of civil rights), the feared figure of the white pedophile is *necessary*? Might we wonder whether part of the psychosocial work he performs is to absolve the guilty conscience of racism at a time when so many fears are focused on the black gangbanger or the brown border menace? Perhaps. Facts in evidence: Penalties for a variety of sex crimes have continued to intensify, even as drug crime laws have been relaxed. The population administered by sex laws continues to grow, even as the prison population has stabilized.

I therefore venture a working hypothesis. Sexual fears and strategies for the containment of sexual dangers are key threads of the new reticulum. They figure prominently in ongoing redefinitions of norms of governance. They provide a reusable template, suitable for application in other domains. If we want to see what social control could look like over the course of the twenty-first century, we should look to the sex offender.

Sex Offender Laws

America's current sex offender laws have smaller-scale precedents in mid-twentieth-century sex panics, when, in the name of child protection, thirty states devised civil commitment procedures for sexual psychopaths and a trickle of states imposed sex offender registries. With the sexual and due process revolutions of the 1960s, some of these statutes were modified or retired. But then a new series of sex panics began in the 1970s, and by the 1980s some states were passing sex offender laws that resembled those of the McCarthy era. Still, as late as 1993, only twelve states had sex offender registries.

This picture changed dramatically in 1994, when Congress passed and President Bill Clinton signed into law a federal statute named for Jacob Wetterling, an eleven-year-old Minnesota boy who was abducted by a masked gunman in 1989. (Although nothing was known of Wetterling's fate or his abductor's identity for the better part of 27 years, activists and reporters generally — and, it turns out, correctly — interpreted the tragedy as an instance of abduction, rape, and murder.) The Wetterling Act required convicted sex offenders to register with authorities upon release, parole, or probation. It mandated annual registration for a ten-year period for some offenses (any sexually violent offense and certain criminal offenses against a victim who was a minor) and lifetime registration on a quarterly basis for persons determined to be "sexually violent predators." It also required local authorities to transmit registry information to state law enforcement and the FBI.

Then, under a 1996 amendment to the Wetterling Act, all states were required to adopt statutes collectively known as Megan's Law, named for Megan Kanka, a seven-year-old girl who was raped and murdered in New Jersey in 1994. This amendment required local law enforcement authorities to notify neighbors about a sex offender's presence in their community. Although registration and notification requirements varied, all states came to post searchable online lists of at least some categories of registered sex offenders.

More recently, the 2006 Adam Walsh Act enhanced and systematized registry and notification requirements. Named for the abducted and murdered son of John Walsh, who went on to become the host of Fox Broadcasting Company's *America's Most Wanted*, the legislation was expressly drafted "in response to the vicious attacks by violent predators" against seventeen other named victims who died over a sixteen-year period. The act's preamble cites these anomalous child murders as evidence of "deadly loopholes" in the antecedent Wetterling Act and Megan's Law. (There is no evidence that sex was involved in Walsh's kidnapping and murder, but as in the Wetterling case, this was the motive assumed by family members, advocates, and reporters.) And so the Walsh Act tightened sex offender registration requirements and established a three-tier system based on the type of offense committed (a break with earlier classifications that purported to be based on the risk of recidivism): Tier 1 offenders are subject to annual registration for a period of fifteen years; Tier 2 offenders must update their registration every six months for twenty-five years; and Tier 3 registrants are required to register their whereabouts every three months for life. In addition to enhancing penalties for an array of sex crimes, the legislation established a national public sex offender database (over and above existing state registries) and made failure to register or update one's registration a felony. Other sections of the act, each named for a different child victim, contain provisions for DNA collection and, in a striking display of petty punitiveness, make it more difficult for the relatives of anyone ever convicted of a sex offense to obtain green cards. Ex post facto law is usually viewed as inimical to democratic norms, but the Walsh Act also gives the U.S. attorney general the authority to apply its provisions retroactively.

The marking and tracking of sex offenders leapt beyond national borders with the enactment of International Megan's Law. Passed by the House in a unanimous voice vote after only forty minutes of floor debate, the bill was signed into law by President Obama in 2016. The new law purports to allow authorities to preempt sex tourism and child exploitation: it requires registered sex offenders convicted of crimes involving minors to pre-report all international travel, and it provides for a newly created Angel Watch Center to share these travelers' itineraries with foreign governments. The law also requires a "visual designation affixed to a conspicuous location on the passport indicating that the individual is a covered sex offender."

One might well hope for a legal classification system that distinguishes menace from nuisance, with nuanced criteria for sorting violent repeat offenders, who belong in prison or require supervision, from nonviolent or one-time offenders. But as Gayle Rubin observed in her indispensable essay on sex panics, American thinking admits little nuance or proportion when it comes to sex.[56] This lack of nuance is not merely a cultural legacy of Puritanism; it is constantly stoked in raw, emotional campaigns by victims' rights and child advocacy groups, crusading journalists, and opportunistic politicians. Every victim-named law tells the story of an elaborate institutional collaboration to exaggerate risk and to conflate categories of harm: its naming commemorates the true story of a helpless child who suffered a terrible death at the hands of a hardened criminal; its legislative content applies stringent measures against a host of minor, first-time, and nonviolent offenders.[57]

The most intense form of public dread is directed at the lurking stranger, the anonymous repeat offender. In fact, the crimes that most spur public outrage — the abduction, rape, and murder of children — are exceedingly rare. In a nation whose population includes roughly 74 million minors, about one hundred high-risk abductions of children by strangers occur every year, and about half end in murder. Statistically, then, a child's risk of being killed by a sexual predator who is a stranger (1 in 1,480,000) is lower than the chance of being killed by lightning (1 in 1,200,000). Most perpetrators of sexual abuse are family members, close relatives, or friends or acquaintances of the victim's family. And in 70 to 80 percent of child deaths resulting from abuse or neglect, a parent is held responsible.[58]

Advocates for laws to register, publicize, and monitor sex offenders after their release from custody typically assert that those convicted of sex crimes pose a high risk of sex crime recidivism. But studies by the Justice Department and other organizations show that recidivism rates are significantly lower for convicted sex offenders than for burglars, robbers, thieves, drug offenders, and other convicts. And only a tiny portion of sex crimes are committed by repeat offenders, which suggests that current laws are misdirected and ineffective. A federally financed study of New Jersey's registration and notification procedures found that sex offense rates were already falling before the implementation of Megan's Law; the study also found no discernible impact on recidivism and concluded that the growing costs of the program might not be justifiable. Other studies have suggested that public registries actually promote recidivism by relegating registrants to a status of permanent social exclusion, thus depriving them of any interest in their own rehabilitation.[59]

The "typical" sex offender is a less exceptional figure than official narratives suggest. Contrary to the common belief that burgeoning registries provide lists of child molesters, the victim need not have been a child and the perpetrator need not have been an adult. Child abusers may be minors themselves.

(Up to 41 percent of child sex abuse perpetrators are said to be juveniles.)[60] First-degree rape is always a registry offense. Statutory rapists — who are not rapists at all, insofar as their crimes involved neither coercion nor violence — are variously covered in many states. Some states require exhibitionists and "peeping Toms" to register. Louisiana once compelled some prostitutes to do so. "Forcible touching" is a registry offense, and this designation may apply even to adolescent boys who "copped a feel," as it was called on my junior high playground. (In New Jersey a neurologically impaired twelve-year-old boy who groped his eight-year-old brother in the bathtub was required to register as a sex offender.)[61] Fully two-thirds of the North Carolina registrants sampled in a 2007 study by Human Rights Watch had been convicted of the nonviolent offense of "indecent liberties with a minor," which does not necessarily even involve physical contact. (Virtually all of the five hundred registrants randomly sampled — 98.6 percent — were one-time offenders; that is, the offense for which they were registered was their first and only conviction for a sex offense.)[62] Culpability and harm vary greatly in these offenses. Some are serious. Some would not be classified as "criminal" under European laws, which set lower ages of consent than do American laws. Some defy common sense. And because sex crimes are broadly defined and closely monitored, the number of people listed in sex offender registries has grown rapidly: 843,680 at latest count, more than the population of San Francisco (currently the thirteenth largest city in the country).[63]

Talk about "risk" was ubiquitous in deliberations around registry requirements. Risk assessment models usually purport to provide calibrated calculations and bias-free assessments of probability. But applied to sex offenders, actuarial logic has deteriorated into something else: panicky risk-aversion, arbitrary judgments, and a rapid expansion of sanctions targeting broad populations for registration and other forms of "waste management."[64] Registry procedures involve not one but two leaps of actuarial logic. First, the recidivism of some becomes tantamount to the recidivism of all, with the result that "there can be no such thing as an 'ex-offender' — only offenders who have been caught before and will strike again," as David Garland succinctly puts it. Under this distorted logic, "criminals" will "have few privacy rights that could ever trump the public's uninterrupted right to know."[65] Second, since the commission of lower-level sex offenses with willing participants is understood to be preliminary to the commission of horrendous, brutal crimes, this anticipated escalation must be deterred by escalating penalties. Thus, gradations that were first haltingly elaborated to *distinguish* degrees of risk or harm subsequently have become the basis for *blurring* those very distinctions, and in many locales mid- and lower-level nonviolent offenders have become subject to invasive, onerous notification procedures: web listings, the distribution of electronic notices or paper flyers, to say nothing of increasingly punitive federal rules.

This is associative logic — or magical thinking, as the anthropologists would have it: the logic of panic.[66] It aligns not with "science" in any meaningful sense of the word, much less with rational risk assessment, but with much older ideas about danger, taboo, and ritual pollution. It has the force of an irrefutable argument; it takes the form of extortion; and it gathers like an unstoppable wave: Who but a moral monster would oppose a law, no matter how draconian, named for a murdered child?

Registration and notification rules violate basic legal principles and amount to an excessive and enduring form of punishment. They render registrants all but unemployable and unhousable. But these are only the beginning of added-on penalties and collateral measures. Other laws go much further. At last count, forty-one states and the District of Columbia have passed laws that require some sex offenders to be monitored — sometimes for life — with electronic ankle bracelets that use radio frequency or global positioning systems (GPS). The Walsh Act includes a federal pilot program to use global positioning to keep an eye on sex offenders. Nine states either allow or require chemical castration for some categories of sex offenders.

In addition, new civil commitment laws in twenty states and the District of Columbia resurrect that odd institution from the 1950s, allowing for the indefinite detention of sex offenders after the completion of their sentences. (See the essay by Laura Mansnerus in this volume.) The Walsh Act created a federal civil commitment program. Civil libertarians oppose civil confinement on principle: it violates due process, it represents a form of double jeopardy, and it is tantamount to indefinite preventive detention. The Supreme Court has repeatedly swatted aside these objections: civil confinement is not deemed punitive if psychological treatment is provided. Such a rationale for civil commitment would seem to display an inherent illogic: the accused is deemed mentally fit for trial and sentencing but mentally unfit for release.[67] Moreover, psychological treatment for civilly confined sex offenders is largely unscientific, based more on therapeutic fad and conjecture than on any body of informed evidence or double-blind studies. Still, inmates are presented with a legal catch-22: One condition of release from civil commitment is the successful completion of psychological therapy. But since therapy typically requires a complete recounting of past crimes — including those unknown to authorities — and since the number of crimes committed is a factor in determining whether the detainee is subject to civil commitment, many logically refuse therapy and do so on the advice of counsel.[68]

In theory, these procedures are applied against the worst of the worst: violent repeat offenders. In practice, civil commitment is applied to a mixed group that sometimes includes minors and nonviolent offenders such as exhibitionists but not violent, garden-variety rapists. One detainee shared his story with me in a letter: When he was eighteen, he was charged with sending pornographic material via email to a respondent he believed to be his fourteen-year-old male cousin. The recipient was actually a decoy, planted by an aggressive prosecutor. And because this was the young man's *second* offense — his first offense had involved voluntary relations with a same-sex partner when he was fifteen and the younger partner was thirteen — he was classified as a "violent sexual predator" and sent directly to civil commitment. Such are the judgments that can go into designating a violent sexual predator. The most recent survey of sex offender civil commitment programs, dating to 2013, found 5,640 detainees.[69]

Meanwhile, laws in more than twenty states and hundreds of municipalities restrict where a sex offender can live, work, or walk. Where a sex offender lives has no known bearing on whether he will commit new crimes. But residency restrictions have proved popular, promoted by citizens' groups, victims' rights advocates, crusading journalists, and politicians in a wide variety of settings. California's Proposition 83 prohibits all registered sex offenders (felony and misdemeanor alike) from living within two thousand feet of a school or park, effectively evicting them from the state's cities, rendering them homeless, or scattering them into isolated rural areas. The law also mandates lifelong electronic tracking of all felony sex offenders, whether deemed dangerous or not, through GPS.

A lawyer describes his client's shattered life in 2008: the uprooted offender perpetually circulates through the streets of the Bay Area, where there are no places he can live. He and his wife must move their trailer constantly to avoid violating a rule tacked on by the Department of Corrections and Rehabilitation, which prohibits sex offenders from being in the same noncompliant place for two hours. His original registry offense was indecent exposure: mooning his sister-in-law during a family argument.[70]

There are signs of corrective movement on some of the most excessive "child safety zone" laws. California courts have scaled back the statewide law in a succession of rulings, a U.S. District Court judge has thrown out Michigan's one-thousand-foot buffer zone, and the Massachusetts Supreme Judiciary Court has broadly ruled residency restrictions an unconstitutional form of "banishment." A few states and municipalities have modified their laws in the wake of chaotic displacements. Still, lawmakers are loath to appear "soft" on sex crime, so these modifications usually give something with one hand and take away something with the other. Legislation in Iowa is instructive. In 2009 Iowa retained its ban on sex offenders' living within two thousand feet of a school or daycare center but scaled back its application to a smaller subset of sex offenders: those convicted of more serious crimes. At the same time, however, the state imposed stringent new daytime rules on where any offenders might set foot and raised the fees it charges sex offenders to register with authorities.

The scene under the Julia Tuttle Causeway proved iconic of the overreach of U.S. laws. In 2007, a small camp of sex offenders took up residency under the Miami bridge. The authorities charged with monitoring sex offenders allowed this because they could find no other place for the men to live. Javier Diaz, thirty, was among those rendered homeless; he had been sentenced in 2005 to three years' probation for lewd and lascivious conduct involving a girl younger than sixteen. Because he lived under the causeway, Diaz had "trouble charging the tracking device he is required to wear; there are no power outlets nearby." Diaz elaborated on his plight: "You just pray to God every night, so if you fall asleep for a minute or two, you know, nothing happens to you."

That was 2007. By 2009, the camp had swelled to as many as 140 squatters. The scene raised health and safety concerns; it also gave rise to bad publicity. So in 2010 Miami-Dade County commissioners passed a new sex offender ordinance that created a single countywide standard. The new ordinance had the effect of repealing twenty-four competing sex offender statutes passed by Miami and various other municipalities within the county. Authorities then began relocating homeless sex offenders to new motels, apartments, and campgrounds. Civil libertarians hailed the new comprehensive law as a step in the right direction but noted that it did not go far enough. Florida state law still prohibits all sex offenders from living within a thousand feet of a school, daycare center, park, playground, bus stop, or other places where children gather. And the new Miami-Dade law still prohibits sex offenders from living within 2,500 feet of a school; it simply eliminated the profusion of other competing laws that kept sex offenders from living within 2,500 feet of various other places that children might frequent.

"It's the end of the Julia Tuttle, but it's not the end of this kind of place," commented Patrick, described as "a registered sex offender who has lived under the rat-infested bridge for three years." "There will be another Julia Tuttle, another place where people will put us so that we are out of sight and out of mind."[71]

CONTINUOUS CONTROL

The most modern aspect of the spectacle is thus also the most archaic.

GUY DEBORD | *The Society of the Spectacle*

Digital scarlet letters, electronic tethering, and practices of banishment have relegated a growing number of people to the logic of "social death," a term introduced by the sociologist Orlando Patterson, in the context of slavery, to describe a condition of permanent dishonor and exclusion from the wider moral community. The creation of a pariah class of unemployable, uprooted criminal outcasts largely escaped the notice of academic queer theorists, who in their heyday supposedly earned their keep by accounting for such phenomena. But it has drawn the attention of human rights activists, and even a journal as staid as the *Economist* has decried U.S. sex offender laws as harsh and ineffective.[72]

This business should worry us more than it apparently does, in part because the techniques used for marking, shaming, and controlling sex offenders have come to serve as models for laws and practices in other domains. Electronic ankle bracelets and techniques of house arrest are being applied to an expanding list of offenders and defendants — including undocumented immigrants who have been released from custody to await processing (on civil, not criminal, charges). It is estimated that a quarter of a million people are currently manacled to some form of electronic monitoring.[73] Public registries, which make visible any stain on a person's record, have proved especially popular with government agencies, civic organizations, and private vigilante groups. A victims' rights clearinghouse in New Mexico posts an online database of everyone convicted in the state of driving while intoxicated. Several states publish online listings of methamphetamine offenders, while lawmakers in Texas, Nevada, and California have introduced initiatives to create public registries of those convicted of domestic violence. Gregory Tomso's contribution to this volume discusses "the website STDcarriers.com, for example, [which] publishes the names and photographs of thousands of people worldwide who have tested positive for STIs or who have been prosecuted for criminal HIV transmission." Mimicking Megan's Law, Florida maintains a website that gives the personal details (including photo, name, age, address, offenses, and periods of incarceration) of all prisoners released from custody. Some other states post similar public listings of paroled or recently released ex-convicts. It goes without saying that such procedures work against rehabilitation and reintegration.

Other things merit saying, however. Costly and inefficient as they are, such techniques of supervision are cheaper than incarceration. They invite adoption in a time of budget shortfalls and ever-less-expensive digital technologies. They resonate well with public opinion, which would like to see fewer people in prison but also favors putting all ex-convicts under some form of supervision, if recent survey results are any guide.[74] And they satisfy liberal urges to look for supposedly more humane alternatives to mass incarceration.

It thus seems reasonable to venture a guess or two about future trends, in the absence of countervailing political pressures or oppositional social movements. On the one hand, the prison population will continue to register modest declines over the coming years. (Already, intakes have declined and prisons are rapidly graying, foretokening a smaller prison population of old men in the future.) On the other hand, decentralized techniques of supervision and surveillance — enhanced parole requirements, public notices, ankle bracelets and varied forms of house arrest, perhaps even residency restrictions — will continue to spread and expand. The way has already been marked.

Call the forty-year era just behind us "the carceral society." I stress the uniqueness of this social formation. This regime of power renounced the "gentle punishments" of penal welfarism, and it deployed supplementary techniques of supervision beyond the walls of the carceral less to rehabilitate offenders or to regulate conduct than to catch lawbreakers and thereby feed ever more people into the maw of the prison system. In these regards the American carceral society represents a radical break with the logic and aims of the disciplinary regime theorized by Michel Foucault, although it retained many of the previous regime's signature traits: the tendency of modern forms of power to keep branching out, penetrating "even the smallest details of everyday life" through the "capillary actions" of the disciplines; the production of a "carceral archipelago," which exports nonstop surveillance "from the penal institution to the entire social body."[75] The carceral will not disappear anytime soon, of course, and its modified U.S. version will remain bloated both by historical standards and by comparison with other democracies. But its methods seem too coarse and too expensive for modern goals. So superimposed upon it — or, better yet, networked around it and reciprocally working with it — will be what we provisionally might call a "system of continuous control," to borrow a phrase from Gilles Deleuze.

In his prescient essay, "Postscript on the Societies of Control," Deleuze contrasts walled-in "spaces of enclosure" (prisons, schools, hospitals) with the "ultrarapid forms of free-floating control" made possible by electronic collars or electronic cards, which might "raise a given barrier" but "could just as easily be rejected on a given day or between certain hours; what counts is not the barrier but the computer that tracks each person's position — licit or illicit — and effects a universal modulation."[76] This emergent decentered system, as I have been describing it, relies on depersonalized technologies to activate highly personal monitory techniques that Thomas Mathiesen has dubbed the Synopticon: not the surveillance of the many by the few — a model of social control that Foucault derived from the Panopticon, the ideal prison designed by Jeremy Bentham — but rather the surveillance of the few by the many.[77]

And what happens when ultra-rapid technologies foster the proliferation of unbounded laws and hypervigilant techniques? What happens when "the few" — miscreants, lawbreakers, potential recidivists — become more and more numerous? The synoptic technique flattens out: already the many are observing *the many*, a crisscrossing web of harsh glares and discerning gazes. These, I suggest, are substantively new conditions and relations.

Synopticism and Securitization

Synopticism — decentralized or dispersed techniques of surveillance and supervision — flourishes on what seems most "futuristic" about the present: advanced technologies, digitized systems of accounting, and new communications media. But it also revives the most ancient techniques of punishment:

spectacle, shaming, shunning — practices that would have been deemed "primitive" or "backward" only forty years ago. Accordingly, the emerging system of continuous control destabilizes long-standing cultural oppositions between "the modern" and "the archaic," as well as theoretical models that rely on them directly or indirectly.[78] We might mark the resulting ironies, antinomies, and relapses in a variety of theoretical idioms.

For example, we could invoke Max Horkheimer and Theodor Adorno's *Dialectic of Enlightenment* to try to understand how, in these techniques, rational law has permutated into its opposite: how reason itself has become irrational. Social regress is tied to technological progress in the present case because rational techniques (advanced technologies) have been applied to instrumental tasks (controlling and managing certain classes of lawbreakers) in uncritical ways (that is, via procedures that ignore classical injunctions against disproportionality, termless punishments, and ex post facto law). Or we might see in present trends a curious wrinkle on Norbert Elias's conception of the "civilizing process." As standards associated with self-restraint and shame become higher, cruel punishments should decline. Yet the banishment of unpleasant topics from polite society — which is part of the civilizing process — opens up spaces where civilization "runs in reverse." Fear of crime, stoked by social entrepreneurs and modulated by assorted institutions, produces something of this boomerang effect: the savagery of "primitive" violence solicits "civilized" brutality. Sex panic would seem paradigmatic of this paradoxical process: a more "civilized" sensitivity to child maltreatment unleashes the "barbarism" of current sex offender laws.[79]

An improvised reading of Foucault underscores different ironies. Foucault had discerned two broad, overlapping dispensations of power. *Sovereign power* was the archaic right of the king to punish: it aimed to harm, maim, or "subtract" from life. By contrast, modern *bio-power* aims not to subtract from life but to regularize or normalize it. Bio-power developed in a historically staggered sequence. Disciplinary techniques emerged first, in the seventeenth and eighteenth centuries: the "gentle punishments" associated with Enlightenment prisons strove to "correct" miscreants, to straighten out crooked ways. Then, in the eighteenth and nineteenth centuries, biopolitics further refined the techniques of normalization. The effect of demographic and biomedical sciences, it works less to correct than to modulate, invest in, or "produce" life.[80]

Continuous control could be depicted as the unanticipated mutant offspring of sovereign power and biopolitics. In the new amalgam, the middle term of the suite, disciplinary power, all but disappears from the scene. Deleuze signals just this possibility in his terse essay on the subject. Contrasting modern electronic tracking devices with the forms of confinement located in the prison, he writes, "It may be that older methods, borrowed from the former societies of sovereignty, will return to the fore, but with the necessary modifications."[81]

Giorgio Agamben's key works model a variant of this approach. Recasting Foucault's argument about the emergence of biopolitics, Agamben argues that since Aristotle, Western juridico-political thought has distinguished between "bare" (biological) life and forms of life bound by laws and imbued with rights (citizenship). Sovereign power, in his account, is basically the power to decide the exception — that is, to suspend laws and strip away the rights associated with citizenship. (Usually exercised by the executive branch of modern governments, this power also might be wielded by legislatures or judiciaries.) Agamben's writings provided the framework for a powerful critique of U.S. actions in the wake of 9/11. The designation of "enemy combatants" in the war on terror, the construction of a detention camp at Guantánamo, and elements of the Patriot Act all suggest that, by degrees, "exception" is becoming the norm — or, to be more precise, "the declaration of the state of exception has gradually been replaced by an unprecedented generalization of the paradigm of security as the normal technique of government." Agamben foregrounds a crucial point here: the current strategy of power is called "securitization," a strategy that continuously attempts to preempt and prevent, to absolutely forestall shadowy figures from committing any evil deeds, and to batten down the hatches and dig in against even remote threats. Sex offenders might seem a paradigmatic case of Agamben's arguments: their rights have been peeled away and permanently suspended in response to various panics or emergencies. But what Agamben's approach has gained in grandeur it has given up in specificity. Parables that stretch from Aristotle to Guantánamo will not afford much analytic traction on the kinds of institutional practices and conflicts that Foucault's historicism was designed to uncover, and it seems to me that the philosopher overshoots his mark by making Auschwitz paradigmatic of the modern exercise of sovereign power over bare life. These moves are too broad to serve purposes other than rhetorical ones.[82]

Perhaps closer inspection of the sex offender's place in the system of continuous control, along with some reflection on the peculiar variant of governmentality that this system spawns, might bring us back to a rather more obvious reading of Foucault, applied to the decades following the 1960s. Mapping a broad epistemic shift from clerical to scientific forms of authority, Foucault famously describes the appearance of new sub-races of sexual degenerates from the end of the late eighteenth century onward: their elaboration in whimsical medical nosologies, their subjection to moral campaigns of various sorts, and the multiplication of legal sanctions against them.[83] Congenital criminals, evolutionary throwbacks, and sexual degenerates thus were among the earliest inventions of the life-investing disciplines, and the hunt for the biopolitical monster is a recurring feature of bio-power.

Present-day conditions reproduce something of the logic of this earlier period. As moral hierarchies based on race or ethnicity have become politically inadmissible, and as old variants of homophobia have become less acceptable in polite society, the pivot has turned to new moral hierarchies based on sex — and this unsettling of established patterns of authority has set the stage for new institutional collaborations, for the production and containment of new species of monsters. Consequently, certain types of sexual dread and deterrence are intensifying at a time when other sexual taboos are relaxing. The intensified prohibitions invariably target intergenerational sex, and they have expanded in three ways: Ages of consent have been pushed upward — even though young people are having sex at earlier ages, creating more crime by definition. Penalties and collateral consequences for a wide variety of sexual transgressions involving minors have become harsher — even though such expressive punishments are known to be counterproductive. And medico-political authorities have waged continuous campaigns to variously flush out, taxonomize, diagnose, treat, and persecute the resulting new species of sexual degenerate.

These institutional moves reinforce ongoing redefinitions of key concepts in the culture at large: "child" (redefined to include minors up to the age of eighteen, or twenty-one in the case of alcohol consumption — and sometimes beyond, in the case of new sex codes at many universities), "sex" (redefined to include a wide range of acts, such as touching clothed body parts for the purpose of erotic gratification), "abuse" (redefined to include events that were not experienced as traumatic). Meanwhile, notions of sexual violence have become increasingly hyperbolic: unwanted touching becomes synonymous with sexual assault, which becomes synonymous with rape, and protection against sexual assault becomes a high priority.[84]

Consider, in this context, the statement attributed to a police spokeswoman in a news story about a molestation case against a twenty-eight-year-old substitute teacher: "We're not going into details, but the contact was so subtle that some of the victims may not realize they were victims."[85] See, too, the recent furor over locker-room hazing by football players at a New Jersey high school. What the *New York Times* called "the sexual penetration of one of the juvenile victims" and a parent described as "a violent ritual involving anal sexual attacks by seniors who routinely preyed on freshmen" actually was no more than "the pressing of a digit or digits against the shallow dent between [the victim's] clothed buttocks," as Judith Levine makes clear. Other "sexual assaults" in the case, she adds, "amount to grabbing of butts and genitals." If the hazing case offers a gauge of the hyperbolization of sexual violence in public culture, it also suggests a measure of disproportionality in the criminal justice system. The county prosecutor charged seven boys, ages fifteen to seventeen, with a variety of sex crimes, including aggravated sexual assault, aggravated criminal sexual contact, conspiracy to commit aggravated criminal sexual contact, and criminal restraint. Conviction on the most serious of these counts could carry a prison sentence of twenty-five years to life. Conviction on any one of them could involve a minimum of fifteen years on the public sex offender registry.[86]

Sexual Peril and the New Governmentality

The redoubling of taboos around *age* at a time when other taboos have been reexamined, deemphasized, or modified serves wider social functions. It revives the idea that sex is *the* basis for morality, and it disallows on principle what Gayle Rubin calls a "concept of benign sexual variation."[87] It secures childhood as the last repository of purity — and can only allow one response to the inevitable crisis of defilement: expand and fortify childhood. It tethers law, ever more securely, to functions associated with spectacles of punishment. These are no small matters; they circumscribe crucial features of our social dispensation, which in so many ways stage the Innocent over against the Monster.

It almost seems beside the point to say that the resulting webs of institutional authority have spawned expansive subfields of pseudoscience: fanciful psychological profiles of super-predators, imaginative therapeutic programs, inventive diagnostic tools said to predict future recidivism, not to say unsupported metrics for the calculation of power inequalities by age difference, along with implausible notions of innocence, trauma, and risk. It might be more to the point to note that these protocols often betray a volatile and unstable relationship to the old-style homophobias whose logics they replace. For example, Static-99, the actuarial assessment instrument widely used in sex offender programs, recycles findings from homophobic medicine by citing Nazi orchidectomies to assess the benefits of castration. (The Nazis castrated thousands of sex offenders, a flexible category that included child molesters, homosexuals, and others deemed "undesirable." Castration continued to be practiced on vague and shifting categories of sex offenders in parts of Europe afterward; cumulatively these provide the basis for the cited "recidivism" studies.)[88] Other administrative procedures are no less problematic. A simple scorecard used by parole officers in the California Department of Corrections and Rehabilitation automatically classifies "same-sex pedophilia" as "high risk," and this checkbox can be ticked irrespective of the age of the minor or whether force (or even sex) was alleged in the case. Often-repeated claims about the incurability of the sex offender whose preference is for males clearly mark the genealogy of the pedophile, while freehand theories about "the cycle of abuse" (abused children become adult abusers) echo yesteryear's notions of homosexual contagion (the "vicious circle of proselytism"). And even in the wake of the Supreme Court's 2003 ruling against sodomy laws in *Lawrence v. Texas,* some courts and statutes still adhere to homophobic precedent. The California Supreme Court just reinstated a distinction between oral sex and intercourse: adults convicted for having noncoercive oral sex with sixteen- and seventeen-year-olds must register as sex offenders, whereas in cases of intercourse judges are left free to determine whether registration is appropriate. (The two dissenting justices called attention to the role of homophobia in the decision and noted that the five-member majority would treat gays and lesbians more harshly than heterosexuals.)

Tabloid culture amplifies these muddled themes and transmits them to the wider public. For example, the liberal *Daily Show with Jon Stewart* heaped derision on U.S. House representative Mark Foley when word got out of the Republican congressman's flirtations with a sixteen-year-old congressional page. There were ironies to be mined, of course: Foley potentially faced prosecution under harsh federal laws that he himself had written regulating Internet communications with minors under the age of eighteen. But the imbalance of such laws was not the satirists' point, and the writers exculpated themselves from charges of homophobia by pointedly insisting that Foley was a *pedophile* (despite the fact that sixteen is the age of consent in Washington, D.C.), not a gay man. Writing about the disproportionate attention given to gay pedophiles in child abuse scandals in the United States and Canada, Kevin Ohi summarizes such narratives this way: "The discourse around child abuse has given stalwart homophobes . . . a seemingly unassailable venue for homophobic ecstasy in the guise of inflamed righteousness."[89]

Perhaps, then, what has happened is that U.S. culture, under contending pressures since the 1960s, has "retrogressed" to an earlier mode of bio-power — or, better put, has reproduced the conditions under which elementary forms of bio-power emerge. Nascent forms of disciplinary authority over deviant sexualities do seem decidedly old-fashioned: they reflect naive preoccupations perpetually at odds with modern scientific understandings of risk or reflexive models of harm; their leitmotifs are neo-Victorian notions of peril and contagion. The resulting varieties of social action recycle old tropes and update the themes of nineteenth-century social hygiene campaigns: the imperiled child is cast in the lead role of the national melodrama;[90] Victorian and Progressive Era crusades against "white slavery" have morphed into North Atlantic campaigns to end "sexual trafficking" (see Elizabeth Bernstein, as well as Carol Queen and Penelope Saunders, in this volume); missions of rescue have become the steady state, the dominant justification for political action; and the hunt for the monster has become a perpetual condition. We thus seem caught in a time warp, crystallized by new communications technologies in a quaint, daguerreotype version of modernity. This is moral panic 2.0.

The notion of a "retrogression" might seem implausible at first blush. But I do not claim that modern institutional forms recapitulate exactly those of bygone eras, only that there has been a return to methods, aims, and tactics previously thought to be obsolete. Under the progressivist historical narratives that define American civilization and gauge it in its own terms, these moves can only be understood as "primitive," "atavistic," "premodern," and so on.[91] On this reckoning, we count not one but two leaps backward. The first retrogression was a return to the brute methods of colonial subjugation to deal with exploding crime rates and inner-city turmoil; punishment replaced rehabilitation as the goal of justice, and a militarized police force was deployed with the blunt aim of containing and controlling the black "underclass." The second retrogression took up the techniques of nineteenth- and early twentieth-century social reformers, when the birth of bio-power was tied to miscellaneous sex panics and moral fortification movements, to manage the varied and contradictory aftereffects of the sexual revolution. Today, the dispersed and multifarious techniques of the latter approach seem to be superseding the blunt instruments of the former. History moves forward after all.

Metaphors aside, what has undeniably happened is this: in the wake of a succession of crime scares, moral panics, and spectacles of predation, the terms of democracy's functioning and the citizenry's place in it have been reconfigured — radically, one might say. The daily occurrence of marginal outrages, amplified by old and new media, positions the public as victim or potential victim; tales of wanton abuse, orchestrated by social movements right and left, narrowly channel politics into the demand for protection; the same movements and their institutional allies agitate and lobby to intensify punitive laws, to widen their prohibitive scope, and to deploy new surveillance techniques everywhere. As public opinion thus gives way to what Paul Virilio calls "public emotion,"[92] the citizen's role is increasingly reduced to a judicial function: the constant staging of emotionally-manipulative morality plays, passed off as news or analysis, casts the citizen as chorus and jury, her vote as verdict. Sped and intensified by the second machine age, the forms of civic responsibility associated with such citizenship mean, basically, that we all are to assume responsibility for policing each other — an idea that Americans used to associate with totalitarian states.[93]

In the resulting dispensation, then, it is neither the defense of liberty nor the redistribution of wealth that defines the legitimacy of government and the moral fitness of officeholders. Rather, the modern state traffics in *fear* as the justification for its existence, as ballast and support for its rule, and as the very definition of its democracy. It can only brace itself as against ominous threats, some real, some imagined, and it can only realize the general will in these terms. It governs less through rational self-interest, scientific risk-management, or conventional notions of well-being than through anxiety, neurosis, and crime. (I borrow freehand from Engin Isin's notion of "governing through neurosis" and Jonathan Simon's concept of "governing through crime."[94])

In this nascent form of governmentality, sex offenders appear to be not so much the last pariahs — the outcasts who are left over after the destigmatization of homosexuality, fetishism, and so on — as the first ones: models for the production of perpetual criminalization and unremitting punishment, harbingers of a brave new world of social regulation, prototypes for an emergent system of continuous control after the topping-out of the carceral system.

Intensification and Escalation: Current Trends

An abundance of recent scholarship attempts to make sense of these punitive trends, starting with mass incarceration, by interpreting them as an extension of the logic of neoliberalism. But this school of thought assumes what it claims to show, effectively reversing cause and effect. To be sure, neoliberal forms of accountability and profit-taking have indeed inflected the punitive state's various institutions and practices after the fact. But it cannot be assumed that whatever intensifies capitalism will also necessarily intensify forms of coercion. In point of fact, punitive states have emerged under socialist projects; they did not have to await capitalist intensifications.[95] In point of fact, neoliberalism is a global phenomenon; the punitive state, with its policies of mass incarceration, burgeoning public sex offender registries, and so on, is — at least so far — a distinctly American phenomenon.[96] The true sequence of events suggests just the opposite of the prevailing academic storyline: it was actually the punitive turn, with its pitiless approach to losers, lawbreakers, and racial subalterns, that paved the way for the subsequent imposition of a deregulated and nakedly predatory variant of capitalism, not vice versa.

Nor is it even clear that the aim of the punitive state is to produce docile, disciplined bodies, ready for work under new productive conditions at the high noon of neoliberalism. Perhaps what is most challenging about the present conjuncture is that it portends the production of ever-larger surplus populations, unassimilable persons who are subject to coercion but not to discipline. This becomes all the plainer as the carceral society gives way to continuous control. What remains unclear is whether, within the deepest logic of the system, there is any natural limit to the production of pariahs.

Michalis Lianos attempted to theorize power after Foucault around a familiar *dispositif*, the antitheft device, which distributes suspicion equally but at least has the advantage of operating free of prejudice or animus.[97] By contrast, Alice Goffman describes the wreckage of the carceral society from the vantage of a black inner-city community, many of whose residents live "on the run," perpetual fugitives from the law. They are tracked and hounded by a variety of monitory techniques (checkpoints, home visits, and reviews of various databases) whose operational goal is to entrap or ensnare them. No one could conclude that the system is designed to inculcate in these fugitives any semblance of self-control, lawful conduct, or market discipline.[98] Like the picture of huddled masses living under the Julia Tuttle Bridge, these scenes of inner-city blight provide real-world models for the operation of continuous control. It is to be suspected that no one could really regulate his conduct under the emergent regime's increasingly exacting demands, as neoliberalism would seem to require; it is to be suspected that this is exactly the system's aim. Nothing could be less liberal, neo- or otherwise.

What I have dubbed "the magical power of the accusation" means essentially that accusation is already condemnation and that we are all always under suspicion, if not actually on trial — at least as far as sex is concerned.[99] New technologies embed this suspicion in the productive infrastructure and implant it in the pores of social life. As surveillance takes increasingly decentered and involute forms, electronic monitoring, sting operations, and digital vigilantism are escalating, while standards of evidence — to say nothing of distinctions between investigation and entrapment, science and magic — show signs of great lability.

Experimenting with virtual reality headsets, criminologists can now track the eye movements of sex offenders — the better to understand and predict their behavior, supposedly.[100] "Sweetie," a computer-generated avatar launched by a children's charity–cum–vigilante group, poses as a chatty ten-year-old Filipina girl to catch online voyeurs and give their names to the police. Sweetie doesn't actually look like a real girl, at least not on the BBC feed that reported the story, so it's not clear whether the people she entraps are real pedophiles.[101] In this regard the civic organization's amateur sleuthing resembles that of government agents: Internet sex stings often involve neither children nor victims nor even offenders strictly speaking. In Florida, police detectives in some jurisdictions go further: They troll adult online dating sites, where they meet men who are looking for other adults. After baiting and grooming the men, sometimes over the course of days, and after steering the conversation to sex, the decoys then switch the age they claim to be, indicating that their "real" age is fourteen or fifteen — and try to convince the sting targets to continue the conversation anyway. Alternatively, the undercover detective introduces the idea that the man on the hook might have sex with the decoy's underage "child" or "sister." Men who say no to this latter proposition are arrested anyway just for talking to the detective. Even men who cut off such conversations and report them to authorities are kept nonetheless under "active investigation."[102]

New social media accelerate the democratization of social control and provide a ready bullhorn for mob-like orchestrations of vox populi. When

John Grisham opined in an interview that U.S. penalties for child porn were unnecessarily harsh, social media virtually exploded with condemnations, including innuendo about Grisham's motives and predilections. The lawyer and author of legal thrillers quickly issued a retraction and an apology. Hot on the heels of their victory, bloggers and tweeters conducted a similar campaign against pop culture icon Lena Dunham, labeling her a "child molester" after she wrote about engaging in the ordinary explorations of childhood — basically, "playing doctor" — as a young girl with her younger sister. To her credit, Dunham stood her ground.

Anxiety (Dis)Order

The predispositions and structures of feeling that prepare the way for this brave new world are deeply rooted in American concepts of liberal democracy and free choice, and they are already widely distributed in the biometrics of everyday life. The informed suburban consumer ventures out from behind the poliorcetic walls of a gated community. He drives a new car that is equipped with a built-in global positioning navigation system. He thinks he needs this device to help him find his way when he is lost and to report his whereabouts in case of trouble — but it can also be used to track his movements, should police, prosecutors, or corporations wish to do so. (A great many of his favorite creature comforts have such dual function, by design or not.) He chooses this shopping mall over that one because the former's parking lot is watched over by closed-circuit cameras. He believes that this degree of security is beneficial. An up-to-date parent, he downloads any one of several sex offender locator apps, available for iPhones or Android devices, which compile information from sex offender databases to provide the names, addresses, and photographs of registered sex offenders living or working in the vicinity. He believes he has a genuine need to have this sort of information — and he believes that this technology will empower parents to "turn the tables" on predators.

Crime-conscious routines and surveillance technologies purport to make us feel safer, but there is good reason to think that they have the opposite effect: they produce subject citizens who are always thinking about crime. They induce, not relieve, anxiety. I pause to ponder some of the possible psychological consequences of expansive lawmaking and obsessive thinking about crime, sex crime in particular. Judith Levine, Janice Irvine, and other sex-positive feminists have argued that the established culture of child protection — with its fetishization of virginity and its constant battery of alarmist messages that equate sex with risk and danger — actually harms children and impedes their social development.[103] A lifeworld dominated by sexual fear certainly discourages experimentation, pleasure, and autonomy. More than that, it tacitly redefines sex, like smoking, as a form of *harm*, permitted only to adults (who are allowed to accept responsibility for their own decisions). James Kincaid goes further to suggest that in the prevailing storyline about harm, "innocence" itself has been eroticized: the purer the child is imagined to be, the greater the danger of his or her defilement — and the greater the thrill some adults will experience in performing rites of protection.[104] Speculations along these lines purport to delve into the nether regions of the psyche.

But what if what lurks in the closet and stirs anxieties there is more literal than figurative? The kinds of laws that I have been enumerating are themselves logical sources of anxiety. Harvey Silverglate has suggested that the average American unwittingly commits three felonies per day. Or, more accurately put, expansive, vaguely written laws give prosecutors great leeway in pinning raps, and America's sex laws supply prosecutors with a veritable trove of actionable material. What sort of leeway? Silverglate gives the example of a respected lawyer who was charged with obstruction of justice when he destroyed a hard drive containing images of naked boys that were discovered on his client's — an Episcopal church's — computer. The attorney acted in good faith: he recommended immediately firing the church's organist (who had stored the images) and he destroyed the hard drive without any knowledge that the feds had begun an investigation of the organist. Many attorneys would have done the same. Child pornography "is illegal to possess ('contraband') and therefore holding, rather than destroying it, arguably would be criminal."[105] The lawyer's dangerous predicament illustrates a recurring dilemma in modern sex laws: the difference between licit and illicit behavior becomes so slight as to be a matter of point of view.

Anxiogenic catches and snares abound in American sex laws, as do laws criminalizing noncoercive practices that are probably widespread. It seems plausible to think that a substantial chunk of the population has had amorous, physical, or moral contact with someone somewhere in some manner at some point in their lives that a prosecutor might construe as unlawful. Arrests for "public" sex, for example, typically target men who "[believe] they are alone or out of view," but who are observed by police using peepholes or hidden cameras, or who are responding to overtures from police decoys.[106] Lawyers and researchers tell me that a large percentage of defendants in statutory rape cases credibly believed that they were involved with a partner who was above the age of consent. (Many states do not allow defendants to argue that the minor impersonated an adult.) Of course, mature adults have no monopoly on misjudgments, momentary lapses, indiscretions, or reckless passions. Many young people do not realize that they are violating their states' consent or abuse laws when they engage in standard routines of courtship and seduction. Cell phones put the tools for serious lawbreaking — "sexting" among underage teens, which violates child pornography laws — in everyone's hands. (A recent survey finds that nearly 20 percent of teens under the age of eighteen have sent a sexually explicit picture of themselves via cell phone; nearly 40 percent had received such images, with a substantial number of those forwarding them on to others.)[107]

In view of rampant legal hazards, it is unclear just where the search for "monster" might lead us. Tabloid scandals give hints. A headline, typical of its genre, announces a citizenry's shock and consternation: "Town Is Shaken after Prosecutor's Arrest in a Child-Sex Sting." The first line of a story in *USA Today* reads, "A Bible camp counselor and a Boy Scout leader were among 125 people arrested nationwide in an Internet child pornography case." An article on a lawsuit against Richard Roberts, then president of Oral Roberts University, obliquely refers to cell phone text messages sent to "under-age males — often between 1 A.M. and 3 A.M." An all-too predictable headline announces "Foes of Sex Trade Are Stung by the Fall of an Ally."[108] The monster, we are told, is hiding in plain sight!

Such narratives ricochet and whiplash in the culture at large. The dynamics they set in motion are not mysterious, nor do they require elaborate psychological models to explain them; they require only that we understand first that panic is a discursive form, a communicative strategy, a means of suasion.[109] Sad stories about fallen figures or exposed pretenders trade in schadenfreude: they allow tellers and listeners to revel in exposing the hypocrisy of others; and in this telling, they reveal the capacity for recursive regression in sex panics. That is, whenever those who have been most zealous about protecting innocence find themselves caught up in scandal, the result is not a reconsideration of the ground from which this business started — inflated notions of harm, the politics of protection — but instead, remorse on the part of the fallen and panicked calls for greater zeal, tighter laws, tougher enforcement, more continuous control. In so denouncing hypocrisy, we exculpate ourselves. In exculpating ourselves, we also absolve the law. The structure of the scandal thus conduces to the stabilization of a wider field of anomic (normless, lawless) law. When the law gapes after what it aims to devour, when the distinction between lawful and unlawful becomes intolerably tenuous, when the difference between protection and abuse gets whittled down to almost nothing and we all become implicitly blackmailable as real or potential malefactors, *then* we are pushed, inexorably and violently, to reassert the barrier between opposed concepts: law and crime, fair and foul, protection and abuse.

Jean Baudrillard once notoriously argued that Watergate was not a scandal at all but a trap laid by the system to catch its adversaries in a diversionary moral panic. Diversion, in all its senses, is part of what moral panics do, and I am developing a similar line of argument here, one that sees both law and crime as part of a system. This institutional system, by the nature of its functioning, not only necessarily generates excess, lapse, or scandal; it also possesses the uncanny ability to recapture and reinvest that excess in the operational logic of the system itself. The friction between the one thing and the other — the nobility of the protector, the iniquity of his fall from grace — serves as an inexhaustible resource, a constant point of intensification. Nothing exceeds, nothing escapes the perpetual feedback loop. Of course, the ruse of liberalism, on either socialist or Foucauldian readings, is just this: to draw attention to scandal, individual pathology, and worst abuses — to the spectacle of transgression — thereby diverting attention from the workaday functioning of the larger disciplinary social system, which demands not remedial or corrective action but global discreditation and radical overhaul. The curiously self-reinforcing dynamic I am describing here reproduces this diversionary tactic, causes it to mutate into illiberal, punitive form, and perpetually ratifies the apprehension that gave rise to the system of reactive laws, which thereby continues to expand and thus to produce panics and scandals anew.

"This is every parent's worst nightmare," goes the recurring phrase, a staple of news reports helpfully proffered to *USA Today* by the federal prosecutor involved in a nationwide sweep. "It is just deeply disturbing to know that there are people like this out there in our neighborhoods," he added.[110] Deeply disturbing, yes, but deeply reassuring as well, according to the feedback dynamic I have just described — and *that* is indeed our worst nightmare, one from which we have yet to awaken.

Postscript on Sex and Suspicion in the Society of Continuous Control

I have taken a wide-angle view of recent American history, surveying the punitive turn not only in terms of the usual categories (fear of crime, structures of racial domination, and assorted wars on drugs, gangs, and violence) but also with regard to an ongoing series of sex panics, resultant laws for the regulation of sexuality, and especially techniques for monitoring and managing sex offenders. This view suggests a two-part periodization of the social formation that emerged in the post-1960s. The first phase, starting in 1973, I call the carceral society. No name could be more apposite for the unmodulated practices of mass incarceration that have prevailed for the better part of four decades. All signs suggest that mass incarceration is poised to recede as a strategy of social control; it is now being succeeded by plural techniques whose onset cannot be so clearly marked and whose end date is nowhere in sight. This is what I tentatively have called the society of continuous control. It remains unclear whether the incipient regime amounts to a transmutation of the internal logic of the carceral society or whether it ought to be understood as the latter's second phase; it remains unclear at what point quantitative changes might amount to qualitative transformations.

In any case, the structural features of these developments bear scrutiny: How does the system of power embedded in the criminal justice system operate today? How are its operations different from those of past dispensations, especially in terms of sexual regulation, and what might extant trends bode for the future? I draw out a dozen points here, tracking various aspects of the transitions from discipline to mass incarceration to continuous control.

1. The Enlightenment prison transformed punishment into a *penitent* practice, and a complex of specialized disciplines translated its associated techniques (observation, normalization, reform) into a network of far-flung institutions (schools, hospitals, charities).[111] So much is well established about the regime of power that Foucault theorized as *disciplinary*. The carceral society that emerged on American soil in the wake of the 1960s represents a departure from this regime: Its technicians renounced the goal of rehabilitation, which had served as goal and justification of the disciplinary regime, in favor of punishment, and they vastly expanded the penal system — at the expense of the other institutions that were part of the disciplinary network (e.g., public education, social medicine). This, the turn away from a model of social control based on the cultivation of well-being and its replacement with one based on the administration of punishment, was only the first of a series of steps.

2. Excessive punishment, formerly barred under penal welfarism and even under much older formulas dating to classical antiquity, was intrinsically linked to the new regime's signature practice, incapacitation. It is not only

at the more serious levels of infraction that lawbreakers are to be pursued and punished. "Broken windows" theories, "quality of life" and "order maintenance" policing, zero-tolerance policies, tiered sex offender registries, and myriad other widespread practices all express the simple premise that minor infractions ought to be closely policed and scrupulously punished so as to deter more serious offending. Remarkably little evidence supports this premise, which conflates nuisance with menace and diverts law enforcement from devising penalties and procedures that attend to actual harm.

3. More than mere disproportionality is at stake here. Bernard Harcourt describes how "quality of life" policing really amounts to *aesthetic* policing: it expresses *distaste* for certain kinds of expression and certain kinds of people, who are linked to the remarkably subjective concept "disorder."[112] We prohibit the squeegee man from cleaning car windows at traffic stops because we don't want his kind of person in our neighborhood. We impose harsh sanctions on graffiti artists because we don't like the way subway trains or urban wallscapes look covered with glyphs and symbols. An abundance of sex offender laws similarly express distaste, a moral judgment about the nature of certain acts with certain persons. If sex offender rolls were peeled down to persons who committed violent assaults, they would be considerably smaller than they are. By degrees, such criteria for judgment push law into an increasingly arbitrary and anomic state.

4. Both the society of the carceral and the society of continuous control entail monitory and enforcement techniques hitherto associated with total institutions or military operations (e.g., SWAT teams, used in the routine service of warrants; closed-circuit TVs, used to secure streets and other public spaces).[113] These moves intensify the penal system's ancillary powers and push techniques first utilized in disciplinary societies to a new level of development.

5. Even so, more than intensification, acceleration, and development have occurred in the new stratagems of social control, for their center of gravity has shifted with the redefinition of punishment *as* justice: they ensnare without any hope, however fragile, of redemption. Under the new dispensation, the miscreant can never serve his time, can never pay his debt to society, can never make good his trespass, can never complete his penance. He can never prefix an "ex" to his "con," can never be anything except an offender. *Precisely* what the new regime does, within its closely written laws, is to produce the lawbreaker as unassimilable, so as to cast him into hell, and this hell extirpates even that age-old romance that once attached to the breaking of the law. This becomes especially clear with sex offender laws. There can be no "lyricism of

marginality" in the image of the sexual outlaw, that homeless and debased social nomad "who prowls on the confines of a docile, frightened order."[114] This is not your father's Subject of Discipline, heir to the project of Enlightenment.

6. Of course, sex is not the only conceivable object of continuous control. It is notable that techniques developed to manage sex offenders were deployed in the "war on terror" (e.g., registries and the elaboration of implausible legalisms to permit indefinite detention), and it is significant that the application of other such techniques (e.g., electronic tethering) continues to widen. So let us say instead that sex was a privileged entry point, a useful laboratory for the development of new methods, a key nexus in the passageway from the carceral society to the society of continuous control. Likely, too, it will remain a focal node in the ongoing evolution of the system, as illustrated in the next point.

7. However intrusive its vast mechanisms had been, the disciplinary regime retained within its function certain implicit and explicit zones of privacy. It is true that these zones were never absolute: social services could invade and inspect homes with less warrant than policemen. It is true, too, that privacy implied responsibility for self-inspection and hygiene maintenance. Still, time-honored laws protected these no-go zones against arbitrary intrusion. Those limits receded under the carceral state, and newer geographies of power threaten to erase the distinction between public and private altogether. Perpetual recourse to the construction and containment of sexual peril has been key to this development. Because sexual perils take shape within that stronghold of privacy rights, the home, what goes on behind closed doors — or at private computer terminals, or on personal cell phones, etc. — is now of special interest to law enforcement. Whereas the crime-conscious routines of the carceral society had secured the borders between safe and unsafe *neighborhoods*, or strove to protect the domestic interior from threats that originated *from without*, the sex-crime-conscious routines of continuous control secure the relations between safe and unsafe *persons*; that is, they securitize the institutions of everyday life *from within*. The result is a double-pincer movement. On the one side, the new sexual economy sorts not curable perverts from normal people but rather incurably bad men from the rest. On the other side, the verdict always remains out on those who have not yet been accused, convicted, and isolated, so the capillary actions of laws and technologies transport a concern for detection into every domain. The new procedures batter down old walls. Not even zones of trust and privacy between parents and their children are sacrosanct, as prosecutions of parents for taking nude

photos of their children have dramatized. Some states require parents to report to the police if they discover that their teenage kids are having sex — and make it a crime not to do so. Taking into account some of the myriad routes through which crime control enters into family matters, a clever wag quipped that the child-centered family had become the crime-centered family: one more apparatus for surveillance and detection.[115]

8. The regulation of sex has produced similarly exigent demands for the unbounding of laws on both temporal and spatial fronts. Historically, statutes of limitations set maximum time limits for filing charges in noncapital criminal cases — and with good reason: memories fade or change. But not even time poses a barrier to continuous control, and successive revisions to federal law have extended the statute of limitations for many sex offenses involving young victims, including nonviolent crimes, to the life of the minor. Historically, too, the scope of laws was coterminous with the borders of the states that passed them. States seldom claimed jurisdiction over events beyond their boundaries. However, a strange thing happened to long-standing concepts of sovereignty and citizenship in the aftermath of wave after wave of sex panic: new sex crime laws attach to the body, the person, in unprecedented ways. Evolving sex trafficking statutes now extend the long arm of earlier laws that primarily regulated interstate travel and U.S. maritime jurisdiction. These federal laws make it a crime to travel abroad for purposes of having sex with a minor or, even less purposefully, to have sex while abroad with a person who is younger than eighteen years old. These statutes apply without regard for the age of consent in the traveler's home state or the traveler's destination. Continuous control is potentially infinite in its scope and span.

9. Past forms of enforcement largely relied on the monitory practices of professionals to augment those of the police: teachers, doctors, social workers. . . . By contrast, forms of synoptic responsibilization today increasingly tend toward vigilantism. The looming oculus of Neighborhood Watch organizations enjoins the public to act as eyes of the police. Television shows like Fox Broadcasting Company's *America's Most Wanted* and NBC's *To Catch a Predator* (once a sweeps-week staple) turned crime and punishment into commercial spectacles while urging the public to keep a constant state of vigilance. (During its long and successful run, *America's Most Wanted* reenacted crime scenes and exhorted the audience to call in with tips on the whereabouts of fugitives.) For a time Oprah got in on the act, launching a national manhunt for fugitive sex offenders. Post-9/11 slogans — "If you see something, say

something" — adjure members of the public to be diligent in monitoring each other for signs of transgression and to call out whatever strikes them as unusual. Parents and citizens' groups exchange information on sex offenders in their neighborhoods via email, flyers, and neighborhood postings. By such turns, citizenship becomes tantamount to surveillance, the introjection of a fear-based ethics into everyone. By such hooks, synopticism gets its hold on the "soul" of the subject citizen more thoroughly than panopticism ever could.

10. To put this another way, the geometrical form of the carceral society was still a pyramid: the few panoptically observed the many. The transitional form of continuous control was an inverted pyramid: the many synoptically observed the few. The emergent shape, pioneered by expansive public sex offender registries, is perhaps that of a spiral: the many are observing the many in a continuous circuit of nonreciprocal surveillance. Not just teachers, doctors, or social workers, but we, all of us, are to act as "judges of normality."[116] This is a great "democratization" of social control.

11. The return of the spectacle is no secondary feature of continuous control. It is essential to both its monitory and its punitive techniques. Public registries allow citizens simultaneously to supervise registrants *and* to view their most exacting punishment: perpetual exposure, perpetual shaming, perpetual enclosure in an electronic public pillory. And the prohibition against spectacularization was only the first of a series of fragile barriers against barbarism to be struck down. Indefinite detention, ex post facto law, and practices of banishment — to say nothing of torture for those suspected of terrorist activities — followed in rapid succession. Such practices display the law not in its majesty but in its banality, we might say.

12. Perhaps what comes most clearly to the fore with continuous control is that it works off a distorted actuarial logic, which admits no level of acceptable risk and demands a variety of *cheap* forms of incapacitation. New systems of accountability and algorithms of deterrence intensify this logic and blur the distinction between lawful and unlawful activity. For example, the sorting of multiple databases means that suspicion is broadly distributed. Not, "he is suspect because he broke a law"; rather, "he is suspect because he checked certain books out of the library or visited certain web sites or ran Google searches on certain subjects."[117] Today's stratagems of power thus seek to anticipate, detect, manage, and segregate broader categories of miscreants than were thinkable under previous regimes: the potential offender, the

future recidivist, the risky individual, the minor offender whose crimes can be forecast to escalate. . . . In effect, the new methods purport to provide so many forms of mind reading.

Just how long this state of affairs might last, whether such trends will be turned back by political reform or systemic breakdown, or whether the social impulses that gave rise to the incipient regime will simply burn out: these remain to be seen. What ought to be clear is that we misunderstand the stark future that has already crept up on us if we see in it only a reflection of conservative agendas, defunct authoritarianisms, and intolerant puritanisms of times past. Not a single element of the punitive turn is exempt from the democratic longings of liberal subjects, in some permutation or other, for liberation, freedom, and empowerment. The constituencies for continuous control lie as much on the liberal Left as on the conservative Right. The sooner we wrap our heads around this contradictory business the better.

I hope that oppositional social movements — already present in the antiprison movement and in the movement to reform sex offender laws — will continue working to roll back the wheel that every day advances farther along its indicated path. I harbor no illusions that this will be easy. Meaningful headway will involve the reversal of not one or two but many intertwined trends. Our efforts will run headlong into well-established precepts: the public's right to know, the dangerousness of the world, the subject citizen's apparent desire for ever-greater levels of personal safety. . . . Writing nuance and proportionality into law will require considering the humanity and human rights of the most vilified and demonized classes of queer criminals since the McCarthy-era homosexual. And it will mean, among other things, letting our guard down — when everything over the last forty years has contributed to the building of a garrisonized society.

If this piece gives any insights of any value, perhaps it also lays out a general path for the struggles ahead. The effort to turn back the tide of punitive policies has to involve an expansion of the concept of justice. It must involve long, difficult thoughts about the place of sexuality in personal development. It must make a case for child welfare and public safety in the round. And it should take a broader view of women's liberation and queer rights than what now obtains in the historically triumphant versions.

The stakes are high. Little will have been gained if we trade a bloated prison system for sprawling forms of electronic surveillance that offload the costs of imprisonment onto offenders, their families, and their communities. Little will have been gained if we trade one form of the punitive state for another.

NOTES

Thanks to Andy Bickford, Bob Chatelle, James D'Entremont, Liza Featherstone, Doug Henwood, Jeff Maskovsky, Yasmin Nair, Debbie Nathan, and Judith Levine for careful readings and instructive feedback. I have benefited enormously over the years from my conversations with James Faubion, Setha Lowe, Michael Sherry, Jonathan Simon, and Loïc Wacquant on this subject matter. Special thanks to David Halperin for close readings, indispensable suggestions, generosity — and helpful lessons on Foucault.

1. See, for example, Alexia Cooper and Erica L. Smith, "Homicide Trends in the United States, 1980–2008," Bureau of Justice Statistics, Patterns and Trends, November 2011, NCJ 236018: 2.

2. Michael Tonry and Joan Petersilia, "American Prisons at the Beginning of the Twenty-first Century," in *Crime and Justice 26: Prisons* (Chicago: University of Chicago Press, 1999), 3. Manuel Eisner, "Long-Term Historical Trends in Violent Crime," *Crime and Justice* 30 (2003): 83–142. See also Claude Fischer, "A Crime Puzzle: Violent Crime Declines in America," *Berkeley Blog*, June 16, 2010, http://blogs.berkeley.edu/2010/06/16/a-crime-puzzle-violent-crime-declines-in-america/.

3. Tonry and Petersilia, "American Prisons," 3; Franklin E. Zimring, *The Great American Crime Decline* (Oxford: Oxford University Press, 2007).

4. Francis Fukuyama, *The Great Disruption: Human Nature and the Reconstitution of Social Order* (New York: Free Press, 2000).

5. Ryan Conrad, ed., *Against Equality: Queer Revolution, Not Mere Inclusion* (Oakland, CA: AK Press, 2014); Walter Benn Michaels, *The Trouble with Diversity: How We Learned to Love Identity and Ignore Inequality* (New York: Metropolitan, 2006).

6. Herbert Marcuse, "Repressive Tolerance," in *A Critique of Pure Tolerance*, ed. Robert Paul Wolff, Barrington Moore, Jr., and Herbert Marcuse (Boston: Beacon, 1969), 95–137.

7. Exact numbers and dates will vary, depending on which jurisdictions are included in the tallies. By some measures, 2009 was the peak year. Thanks to Roy Walmsley, director, World Prison Brief, International Centre for Prison Studies, for these numbers, which include jails and prisons. Walmsley elaborates: "The numbers in state and federal prisons started to rise in 1973. There were 196,000 at the end of 1972 and 204,000 at the end of 1973. There were probably around 160,000 jail inmates in 1973, based on there being 161,000 in 1970 (Department of Justice LEAA) and

158,000 in 1978 (BJS). The totals in 2007–09 were: 2,298,000 in 2007 (780,000 jails, 1,518,000 prisons), 2,307,500 in 2008 (785,500 jails, 1,522,000 prisons) and 2,292,000 in 2009 (767,400 jails, 1,524,600 prisons)" (personal communication).

8. The Pew Center on the States, "One in 100: Behind Bars in America, 2008" (Washington, D.C.: Pew Charitable Trusts, 2008). The Centre for Prison Studies keeps up-to-date figures on incarceration worldwide at http://www.prisonstudies.org.

9. Michael H. Tonry, *The Handbook of Crime and Punishment* (New York: Oxford University Press, 1998); Henry Ruth and Kevin Reitz, *The Challenge of Crime: Rethinking Our Response* (Cambridge, MA: Harvard University Press, 2003), 95–96. Ruth and Reitz discern specific periods in the long-term hike in incarcerations: During the 1970s and early 1980s courts began sending more "marginal" felons (burglars, auto thieves) to prison. From the mid-1980s through the early 1990s, the war on drugs was the main engine of prison growth. During the 1990s longer sentences for a variety of crimes continued to fuel the growth of the prison state. Thomas P. Bonczar, "Prevalence of Imprisonment in the U.S. Population, 1974–2001," *Bureau of Justice Statistics Special Report*, August 2003, NCJ 197976: 3.

10. "The Attorney General's Report on Criminal History Background Checks," U.S. Department of Justice, June 2006: 51. Howard N. Snyder, "Arrest in the United States, 1980–2009," *Patterns and Trends*, Bureau of Justice Statistics, September 2011, NCJ 234319.

11. Bonczar, "Prevalence," NCJ 197976: 8.

12. Bruce Western, *Punishment and Inequality in America* (New York: Russell Sage, 2006), 168–188; Franklin E. Zimring, *The Great American Crime Decline* (Oxford: Oxford University Press, 2007), 55; William Spelman, "The Limited Importance of Prison Expansion," in *Crime, Inequality, and the State*, ed. Mary E. Vogel (New York: Routledge, 2007), 150–164.

13. Loïc Wacquant, "From Slavery to Mass Incarceration: Rethinking the 'Race Question' in the U.S.," *New Left Review* 13 (January–February 2002): 53.

14. Bruce Western and Katherine Beckett, "How Unregulated Is the U.S. Labor Market? The Penal System as a Labor Market Institution," *American Journal of Sociology* 104, no. 4 (1999): 1040–1041.

15. See Peter Wagner, *The Prison Index: Taking the Pulse of the Crime Control Industry* (Northampton, MA: Prison Policy Initiative, 2003), http://www.prisonpolicy.org/prisonindex/; Samuel Bowles and Arjun Jayadev, "Garrison America," *Economists' Voice*, March 2007, 1–7; Samuel Bowles and Arjun Jayadev, "One Nation Under Guard," The Great Divide (Opinion Pages), *New York Times*, February 15, 2014. http://opinionator.blogs.nytimes.com/2014/02/15/one-nation-under-guard/.

16. Angela Y. Davis, *Are Prisons Obsolete?* (New York: Seven Stories, 2003), 11. Unattributed brackets in the original.

17. David Garland, *The Culture of Control: Crime and Social Order in Contemporary Society* (Chicago: University of Chicago Press, 2001), 178.

18. Adam Liptak, "Debt to Society is Least of Costs for Ex-Convicts," *New York Times*, February 23, 2006, http://www.nytimes.com/2006/02/23/us/debt-to-society-is-least-of-costs-for-exconvicts.html.

19. Lauren E. Glaze and Erinn J. Herberman, "Correctional Populations in the United States, 2012," *U.S. Bureau of Justice Statistics Bulletin*, December 2013, NCJ 243936: 2.

20. National Association of Criminal Defense Lawyers, *Collateral Damage: America's Failure to Forgive or Forget in the War on Crime — A Roadmap to Restore Rights and Status After Arrest or Conviction*, May 2014.

21. I draw the term "punitive turn" from Michael Sherry, "Dead or Alive: American Vengeance Goes Global," in "Special Issue on Force and Diplomacy," *Review of International Studies* 31 (December 2005): 246–263.

22. "Not even the most inventive reading of Foucault, Marx, Durkheim, and Elias on punishment could have predicted these recent developments — and certainly no such predictions ever appeared." David Garland, *Culture of Control*, 3.

23. Philip Jenkins, *Decade of Nightmares: The End of the Sixties and the Making of Eighties America* (Oxford: Oxford University Press, 2006), 11.

24. See Jamie Peck, *Constructions of Neoliberal Reason* (Oxford: Oxford University Press, 2010), for a history of neoliberal ideas, especially between the 1930s and the 1960s.

25. See Rick Perlstein, *Nixonland: The Rise of a President and the Fracturing of America* (New York: Scribner's, 2008).

26. Foucault describes technologies of the self as one of the sorts of "truth games" that human beings engage in to understand themselves. These techniques of self-examination are designed to decipher the self's experiences, with the aim of producing happiness or rectification or some other goal. Michel Foucault, "Technologies of the Self," in *Technologies of the Self: A Seminar with Michel Foucault*, ed. Luther H. Martin, Huck Gutman, and Patrick H. Hutton (Amherst: University of Massachusetts Press, 1988), 16–49.

27. See Barbara Nelson, *Making an Issue of Child Abuse: Political Agenda Setting for Social Problems* (Chicago: University of Chicago Press, 1984).

28. Jonathan Simon, *Governing through Crime: How the War on Crime Transformed American Democracy and Created a Culture of Fear* (Princeton, NJ: Princeton University Press, 2007), 26.

29. Elayne Rapping, *The Culture of Recovery: Making Sense of the Self-Help Movement in Women's Lives* (Boston: Beacon, 1996).

30. Russell Jacoby, "The Politics of Subjectivity," *New Left Review* 79 (May–June 1973): 37–49.

31. Joel Best, "Victimization and the Victim Industry," *Society* 34, no. 4 (May–June 1997): 9–17. See also *Random Violence: How We Talk about New Crimes and New Victims* (Berkeley: University of California Press, 1999), 119–141.

32. See various essays in Carole S. Vance, ed., *Pleasure and Danger: Exploring Female Sexuality*, 2nd ed. (London: Pandora, 1992).

33. See Wendy Kaminer, *I'm Dysfunctional, You're Dysfunctional: The Recovery Movement and Other Self-Help Fashions* (New York: Addison-Wesley, 1992); Robert Hughes, *The Culture of Complaint: The Fraying of America* (New York: Oxford University Press, 1993); Alan Dershowitz, *The Abuse Excuse: And Other Cop-Outs, Sob Stories, and Evasions of Responsibility* (New York: Little, Brown, 1994); Charles J. Sykes, *A Nation of Victims: The Decay of the American Character* (New York: St. Martin's, 1992).

34. Wendy Brown, *States of Injury: Power and Freedom in Late Modernity* (Princeton, NJ: Princeton University Press, 1995), 5–6, 27; see also 8 and 21.

35. Kristin Bumiller, *The Civil Rights Society: The Social Construction of Victims* (Baltimore: Johns Hopkins University Press, 1992). A similar argument has been made recently by Janet Halley, "The Move to Affirmative Consent," *Signs: Journal of Women in Culture and Society* 42, no. 1 (forthcoming).

36. Bruce Shapiro, "Victims and Vengeance: Why the Victims' Rights Amendment Is a Bad Idea," *Nation*, February 10, 1997, 13.

37. National Victims' Amendment Constitutional Passage, http://www.nvcap .org/ (accessed June 29, 2014).

38. Paul H. Robinson, "Should the Victims' Rights Movement Have Influence over Criminal Law Formulation and Adjudication?" *McGeorge Law Review* 33, no. 4 (summer 2002): 756–757.

39. For a wider review of the development of the victims' rights movement, see Roger N. Lancaster, *Sex Panic and the Punitive State* (Berkeley: University of California Press, 2011), 194–203.

40. Plato, *Laws*, trans. Benjamin Jowett (Amherst, MA: Prometheus, 2000), 274.

41. Marie Gottschalk, *The Prison and the Gallows: The Politics of Mass Incarceration in America* (Cambridge: Cambridge University Press, 2006), 129.

42. Marlene Young and John Stein, "The History of the Crime Victims' Movement in the United States: A Component of the Office for Victims of Crime Oral History Project," Office for Victims of Crime, Office of Justice Programs, and U.S. Department of Justice, December 2004, https://www.ncjrs.gov/ovc_archives/ncvrw/2005 /pdf/historyofcrime.pdf; Political Research Associates, "Conservative Agendas and Campaigns," in *Defending Justice: Activist Resource Kit*, ed. Palak Shah (Somerville, MA: Political Research Associates, 2005), 199; Patricia Yancey Martin and R. Marlene Powell, "Accounting for the 'Second Assault': Legal Organizations' Framing of Rape Victims," *Law and Social Inquiry* 19, no. 4 (autumn 1994): 853–890.

43. Early on, feminist legal theorist Vivian Berger sketched additional and substitute practices in rape trials and urged an approach that would "dignify the complainant's role without imperiling the person accused." See "Man's Trial, Woman's Tribulation: Rape Cases in the Courtroom," *Columbia Law Review* 77, no. 1 (January 1977): 1–103. For a review of feminist arguments for and against rape shield laws, see Aya Grueber, "Rape, Feminism, and the War on Crime," *Washington Law Review* 84 (2009): 581–658.

44. Debbie Nathan and Michael Snedeker convincingly unfold this argument in the final chapter of their classic, *Satan's Silence: Ritual Abuse and the Making of a Modern American Witch Hunt* (New York: Basic, 1995).

45. Gottschalk, *Prison and the Gallows*, 150–151, 153.

46. Gottschalk, *Prison and the Gallows*, 163, 2, 64, 133–138.

47. Glaze and Herberman, "Correctional Populations, 2012," NCJ 243936.

48. William J. Sabol, Heather C. West, and Matthew Cooper, "Prisoners in 2008," *U.S. Bureau of Justice Statistics Bulletin*, December 8, 2009 (revised April 1, 2010), NCJ 228417: 5–6.

49. Matthew R. Durose, Alexia D. Cooper, and Howard N. Snyder, "Recidivism of Prisoners Released in 30 States in 2005: Patterns from 2005 to 2010," Special Report, April 2014, NCJ 244205.

50. Marie Gottschalk, *Caught: The Prison State and the Lockdown of American Politics* (Princeton, NJ: Princeton University Press, 2015), 199–200.

51. Susan Faludi, *The Terror Dream: Fear and Fantasy in Post-9/11 America* (New York: Metropolitan, 2007), 215–216, 262, 289. See also Faludi, "America's Guardian Myths," *New York Times* (Op-Ed), September 7, 2007. Susan Jeffords developed an earlier version of this argument in an essay about what she calls "scenarios of protection"; see Jeffords, "Rape and the New World Order," *Cultural Critique* 19 (autumn 1991): 201–215.

52. Estelle B. Freedman, "'Uncontrolled Desires': The Response to the Sexual Psychopath, 1920–1960," *Journal of American History* 74, no. 1 (1987): 83–106. Neil Miller, *Sex-Crime Panic: A Journey to the Paranoid Heart of the 1950s* (Los Angeles: Alyson Books, 2002). George Chauncey, "The Post-War Sex Crime Panic," in *True Stories from the American Past*, ed. William Graebner (New York: McGraw-Hill, 1993), 160–178. David K. Johnson, *The Lavender Scare: The Cold War Persecution of Gays and Lesbians in the Federal Government* (Chicago: University of Chicago Press, 2003).

53. Nathan and Snedeker, *Satan's Silence*; Richard Ofshe and Ethan Watters, *Making Monsters: False Memories, Psychotherapy, and Sexual Hysteria* (Berkeley: University of California Press, 1996); Philip Jenkins, *Moral Panic: Changing Concepts of the Child Molester in Modern America* (New Haven, CT: Yale University Press, 1998).

54. See, for instance, Simon, *Governing through Crime*, 257.

55. Michel Foucault, *The History of Sexuality*, Volume 1, *An Introduction* (New York: Vintage, 1980), 41–42.

56. Gayle Rubin, "Thinking Sex: Notes for a Radical Theory of the Politics of Sexuality," in *Pleasure and Danger: Exploring Female Sexuality*, 2nd ed., ed. Carole S. Vance (London: Pandora, 1992), 267–319.

57. See my longer discussion of victim-named laws in Lancaster, *Sex Panic and the Punitive State* (Berkeley: University of California Press, 2011), 98–100.

58. I derive these numbers from various studies produced by the Office of Juvenile Justice and Delinquency Prevention and published in *National Incidence Studies of Missing, Abducted, Runaway, and Thrownaway Children (NISMART)*, U.S. Department of Justice, Washington, D.C., as well as from the U.S. Department of Health and Human Services Child Maltreatment Annual Reports.

59. Patrick A. Langan, Erica L. Schmitt, and Matthew R. Durose, "Recidivism of Sex Offenders Released from Prison in 1994," U.S. Department of Justice, Washington, D.C., November 2003, NCJ 198281. Compare with Patrick A. Langan and David Levin, "Recidivism of Prisoners Released in 1994," U.S. Department of Justice, Washington, D.C., June 2002, NCJ 193427. See also Lawrence A. Greenfeld, "Sex Offenses and Sex Offenders: An Analysis of Data on Rape and Sexual Assault," U.S. Department of Justice, Washington, D.C., February 1997, NCJ 163392; Kristen M. Zgoba and Karen Bachar, "Sex Offender Registration and Notification: Limited Effects in New Jersey," U.S. Department of Justice, April 2009, NCJ 225402. See also Jeffrey C. Sandler, Naomi J. Freeman, and Kelly M. Socia, "Does a Watched Pot Boil? A Time-Series Analysis of New York State's Sex Offender Registration and Notification Law," *Psychology, Public Policy, and Law* 14, no. 4 (2008): 284–302; Amanda Y. Agan, "Sex Offender Registries: Fear without Function?" *Journal of Law and Economics* 54 (February 2011): 207–239; J. J. Prescott and Jonah E. Rockoff, "Do Sex Offender Registration and Notification Laws Affect Criminal Behavior?" *Journal of Law and Economics* 54 (February 2011): 161–206.

60. Emily M. Douglas and David M. Finkelhor, "Childhood Sexual Abuse Fact Sheet," Crimes Against Children Research Center, May 2005, http://www.unh.edu/ccrc/factsheet/pdf/childhoodSexualAbuseFactSheet.pdf, 10.

61. Judith Levine, *Harmful to Minors: The Perils of Protecting Children from Sex* (New York: Thunder's Mouth, 2003), 47.

62. "No Easy Answers: Sex Offender Laws in the U.S.," *Human Rights Watch* 19, no. 4G (September 2007): 31–32.

63. According to statistics compiled from state registries by the National Center for Missing and Exploited Children, http://www.missingkids.com/en_US/documents/Sex_Offenders_Map2015.pdf (accessed February 8, 2016).

64. See Malcolm M. Feeley and Jonathan Simon's prescient essay on actuarial logic in crime control, "The New Penology: Notes on the Emerging Strategy of Corrections and Its Implications," *Criminology* 30, no. 4 (1992): 449–474. See also Jonathan Simon, "Managing the Monstrous: Sex Offenders and the New Penology," *Psychology, Public Policy, and Law* 4, nos. 1/2 (1998): 452–467; Wayne Logan, "A Study in 'Actuarial Justice': Sex Offender Classification Practice and Procedure," *Buffalo Criminal Law Review* 3 (2000): 592–637. Bernard E. Harcourt composes a comprehensive case against actuarial law in *Against Prediction: Profiling, Policing, and Punishment in an Actuarial Age* (Chicago: University of Chicago Press, 2007).

65. Garland, *Culture of Control*, 180–181.

66. See my discussions in Lancaster, *Sex Panic and the Punitive State*, 7, 41, 81, 237–238.

67. Kansas v. Hendricks, 521 U.S. 346 (1997); Allison Morgan, "Civil Confinement of Sex Offenders: New York's Attempt to Push the Envelope in the Name of Public Safety," *Boston University Law Review* 86 (2007): 1034.

68. Monica Davey and Abby Goodnough, "For Sex Offenders, Dispute on Therapy's Benefits," *New York Times*, March 6, 2007, A1.

69. Deirdre D'Orazio, Rebecca Jackson, Jennifer Schneider, and Alan Stillman, "Annual Survey of Sex Offender Civil Commitment Programs 2013," Sex Offender Civil Commitment Programs Network, October 28, 2013, http://www.soccpn.org/images/SOCCPN_survey_presentation_2013_in_pdf.pdf.

70. Marc Gardner, a defense attorney living in the Bay Area, has written about this case: "When Mooning Is a Sex Crime," *Counterpunch*, November 18, 2008, http://www.counterpunch.org/2008/11/18/when-mooning-is-a-sex-crime/.

71. Greg Allen, "Bridge Still Home for Miami Sex Offenders," NPR, July 21, 2009, http://www.npr.org/templates/story/story.php?storyId=106689642; Julie K. Brown, "Iowa Statute May Provide Answer to Bridge Sex-Offender Saga," *Miami Herald*, July 24, 2009, A1; Julie K. Brown, "Sex Offender Camp beneath Julia Tuttle Causeway Finally Being Dismantled," *Miami Herald*, February 27, 2010, B1; Julie K. Brown, "'There Will Be Another Julia Tuttle,' Sex Offender Says," *Miami Herald*, March 6, 2010, B3.

72. Orlando Patterson, *Slavery and Social Death: A Comparative Study* (Cambridge, MA: Harvard University Press, 1982); Georgia Harlem, "America's Unjust Sex Laws," *Economist*, August 6, 2009, 9. For a notable exception to queer theory's inattentiveness, see James R. Kincaid's daring study, *Erotic Innocence: The Culture of Child Molesting* (Durham, NC: Duke University Press, 1998). Under the editorship of Carolyn Dinshaw and David Halperin, GLQ published a number of notable pieces on sex panics and the demonization of intergenerational sex: see Kevin Ohi, "Molestation 101: Child Abuse, Homophobia, and the Boys of Saint Vincent," GLQ 6, no. 2 (2000):

195–248; Ellis Hanson, "Screwing with Children in Henry James," GLQ 9, no. 3 (2003): 367–391; Steven Angelides, "Feminism, Child Sexual Abuse, and the Erasure of Child Sexuality," GLQ 10, no. 2 (2004): 141–177. See also Jon Davies, "Imagining Intergenerationality: Representation and Rhetoric in the Pedophile Movie," GLQ 13, nos. 2–3 (2007): 369–385.

73. This estimate was given by Robert Gable, a student of B. F. Skinner who code-signed the first electronic monitoring system with the aim of providing positive social support for the rehabilitation of offenders and parolees. Instead, laments Gable, the tool is being (mis)used "almost exclusively as an information system to document rule violations." See Mario Koran, "Lost Signals, Disconnected Lives: Concerns Raised over Reliability of State's GPS Monitoring of Offenders," *WisconsinWatch.org*, March 24, 2013, http://wisconsinwatch.org/2013/03/lost-signals-disconnected-lives/.

74. Public Opinion Strategies and the Mellman Group, "Public Opinion on Sentencing and Corrections Policy in America," March 2012.

75. Michel Foucault, *Discipline and Punish: The Birth of the Prison*, trans. Alan Sheridan (New York: Vintage, 1977), 198, 298.

76. Gilles Deleuze, "Postscript on the Societies of Control," *October* 59 (winter 1992): 3–7, esp. 4, 7.

77. Thomas Mathiesen, "The Viewer Society: Michel Foucault's 'Panopticon' Revisited," *Theoretical Criminology* 1, no. 2 (1997): 215–232. See also Michalis Lianos, "Social Control after Foucault," *Surveillance and Society* 1, no. 3 (2003): 412–430.

78. For the record, I do not argue that "primitive law" in small-scale or rural societies invariably tends toward punitive as opposed to restorative or harmonizing practices. The opposition I trace here is internal to Western and American cultures: we fling the label "primitive" at practices we do not like in order to convince ourselves that we, and practices we do like, are modern; see Lancaster, *Sex Panic and the Punitive State*, 236. This opposition has a long history in legal theory. Elsewhere, I trace the opposition between deontological and consequentialist approaches to punishment, from classical antiquity to Enlightenment ideas and in modern social theories. See Roger N. Lancaster, "Punishment," in *A Companion to Moral Anthropology*, ed. Didier Fassin (Oxford: Wiley Blackwell, 2012), 519–539.

79. Max Horkheimer and Theodor W. Adorno, *Dialectic of Enlightenment* (1947; repr., New York: Continuum, 1990), 30, 36, 41–42; Norbert Elias, *The Civilizing Process: Sociogenetic and Psychogenetic Investigations*, rev. ed. (1939; repr., Oxford: Basil Blackwell, 1994).

80. Foucault, *History of Sexuality*, 135–145.

81. Deleuze, "Postscript," 7.

82. Giorgio Agamben, *State of Exception* (Chicago: University of Chicago Press, 2004), 14 (see also 6–7). Lancaster, *Sex Panic*, 95–96.

83. Nineteenth-century entomologies produced not only homosexuals but also zoo-philes and zooerasts, auto-monosexualists, presbyophiles, and other now-forgotten terms for specifying aberrant sexualities. Foucault, *History of Sexuality*, 40, 44.

84. See Lancaster, *Sex Panic*, 48–49, 57–58.

85. Reagan Morris, "Teacher Admits Molesting Pupils," *New York Times*, August 5, 2006, A9.

86. Judith Levine, "The 'Sex Offender' Regime Is Cruel and Unusual Punishment," *Counterpunch*, October 24, 2014, http://www.counterpunch.org/2014/10/24/the-sex-offender-regime-is-cruel-and-unusual-punishment/; NJ.com, "7 Sayreville foot-ball players charged in hazing, sexual assault of teammates," October 10, 2014, http://www.nj.com/middlesex/index.ssf/2014/10/sayreville_football_players_charged_in_hazing.html.

87. Rubin, "Thinking Sex," 283.

88. Thanks to Andrew Extein for calling this to my attention. See also Geoffrey J. Giles, " 'The Most Unkindest Cut of All': Castration, Homosexuality and Nazi Jus-tice," *Journal of Contemporary History* 27, no. 1 (January 1992): 41–61.

89. Ohi, "Molestation 101," 195, 197.

90. See the prescient Lauren Berlant, *The Queen of America Goes to Washing-ton City* (Durham, NC: Duke University Press, 1997). See also Lee Edelman, *No Future: Queer Theory and the Death Drive* (Durham, NC: Duke University Press, 2004).

91. See Paul Smith, *Primitive America: The Ideology of Capitalist Democracy* (Min-neapolis: University of Minnesota, 2007).

92. Paul Virilio, *The Original Accident*, trans. Julie Rose (Cambridge: Polity, 2007), 26, 62.

93. Mark Andrejevic, "The Work of Watching One Another: Lateral Surveillance, Risk, and Governance," in "People Watching People," ed. David Wood, special issue of *Surveillance & Society*, 2, no. 4 (2005): 479–497.

94. Engin F. Isin, "The Neurotic Citizen," *Citizenship Studies* 8, no. 3 (2004): 217–235. Simon, *Governing through Crime*.

95. In any case, early neoliberal theories of crime and punishment gave no hint of the carceral state to come, and as late as 1979 Foucault showed that these theo-ries augured a more tolerant penal practice. Neoliberal penal policy "does not aim at the extinction of crime, but at a balance between the curves of the supply of crime and negative demand. . . . This amounts to posing as the essential question of penal policy, not, how should crimes be punished, nor even, what actions should be seen as crimes, but, what crimes should we tolerate?" Michel Foucault, *The Birth of Biopoli-tics: Lectures at the College de France, 1978–1979*, ed. Michel Senellart, trans. Graham Burchell (New York: Palgrave Macmillan, 2008), 258–259, 256.

96. Loïc Wacquant detects signs that the punitive approach is spreading across the Atlantic. See "The Prison Is an Outlaw Institution," *Howard Journal of Criminal Justice* 51, no. 1 (2012): 1–15.

97. Lianos, "Social Control after Foucault," 419–422.

98. Alice Goffman, "On the Run: Wanted Men in a Philadelphia Ghetto," *American Sociological Review* 74 (2009): 343. See also Goffman, *On the Run: Fugitive Life in an American City* (Chicago: University of Chicago Press, 2014).

99. Lancaster, *Sex Panic*, 21, 52, 104–136.

100. Alistair Charlton, "Virtual Reality Headsets to Help Predict Sex Offender Behaviour," *International Business Times*, November 3, 2014, http://www.ibtimes.co.uk/virtual-reality-headsets-help-predict-sex-offender-behaviour-1472840.

101. Angus Crawford, "Computer-Generated 'Sweetie' Catches Online Predators," BBC News, November 3, 2013, http://www.bbc.com/news/uk-24818769.

102. Noah Pransky, "Officers Accused of Bending Rules on Sex Sting Arrests," *USA Today*, August 8, 2014, http://www.usatoday.com/story/news/nation/2014/08/08/sexual-predator-stings/13770553/.

103. Levine, *Harmful to Minors*; Janice M. Irvine, *Talk about Sex: The Battles over Sex Education in the U.S.* (Berkeley: University of California Press, 2004).

104. James R. Kincaid, *Erotic Innocence: The Culture of Child Molesting* (Durham, NC: Duke University Press, 1998), esp. 14–16, 54–55, 102–106.

105. Harvey Silverglate, *Three Felonies a Day: How the Feds Target the Innocent*, foreword by Alan M. Dershowitz (2009; repr. New York: Encounter, 2011). See esp. 159–166.

106. Robert L. Jacobson, " 'Megan's Laws' Reinforcing Old Patterns of Anti-Gay Police Harassment," *Georgetown Law Journal* 81 (1998–1999): 2456.

107. Donald S. Strassberg, Ryan K. McKinnon, Michael A. Sustaíta, and Jordan Rullo, "Sexting by High School Students: An Exploratory and Descriptive Study," *Archives of Sexual Behavior* 42, no. 1 (January 2013): 15–21.

108. Abby Goodnough, "Town Is Shaken after Prosecutor's Arrest in a Child-Sex Sting," *New York Times*, September 29, 2007, A8; "Feds Arrest 125 People Nationwide in Child-Porn Investigation," *USA Today*, October 19, 2006, http://usatoday30.usatoday.com/news/nation/2006-10-19-child-porn-arrests_x.htm; Ralph Blumenthal, "Professors Sue Oral Roberts President," *New York Times*, October 11, 2007, A22; Nina Bernstein, "Foes of Sex Trade Are Stung by the Fall of an Ally," *New York Times*, March 12, 2008, A1.

109. See Janice M. Irvine, "Emotional Scripts of Sex Panics," *Sexual Research and Social Policy* 3, no. 3 (September 2006): 82–94.

110. "Feds Arrest 125 People."

111. Foucault, *Discipline and Punish*, 298.

112. Bernard Harcourt, "Policing Disorder," *Boston Review*, April–May 2002, http://new.bostonreview.net/BR27.2/harcourt.html.

113. For an explanation of the term "total institution," see Erving Goffman, *Asylums: Essays on the Social Situation of Mental Patients and Other Inmates* (New York: Anchor Books, 1961).

114. Foucault, *Discipline and Punish*, 301.

115. Simon, *Governing through Crime*, 204–206.

116. Foucault, *Discipline and Punish*, 304.

117. Jeremy W. Crampton, "Surveillance, Security and Personal Dangerousness" (paper presented at the American Association for the Advancement of Science Annual Conference, St. Louis, MO, February 16–20, 2006).

|2|

Sympathy for the Devil

*Why Progressives Haven't Helped the Sex Offender,
Why They Should, and How They Can*

UNTOUCHABLE

On November 18, 2013, Kristie Mayhugh, Elizabeth Ramirez, and Cassandra Rivera walked out of the Bexar County Jail in San Antonio, Texas, into the arms of their families. Their friend Anna Vasquez had been released a year earlier.

The quartet of working-class Chicana lesbians — the San Antonio Four — had been convicted in 1997 and 1998 of the sexual molestation of Ramirez's nieces, then seven and nine. Ramirez, tried separately as the "ringleader," was sentenced to thirty-seven and a half years; the others got fifteen. All were under twenty-one years old. Ramirez and Vasquez both had children. All were innocent.

Poverty, racism, sexism, and homophobia — plus junk science and satanic panic — played powerfully in the trials of the San Antonio Four. The girls' accusations were made under pressure by their father, Javier Limón, who was divorced from their mother, Ramirez's sister; he'd sent love letters to Ramirez, who rebuffed him. Then his mother told him she was alarmed when she noticed her granddaughters playing with Barbie dolls in a way she considered sexualized. The accusations were improbable and inconsistent: putting objects and "white powder" into the girls' vaginas, threatening them with guns and knives. The prosecution's case rested on discredited forensic "science" about how little girls' untouched hymens are supposed to look. No gun or any other material evidence was found. But far crazier accusations of child abuse had been made — and believed — all over the country, including in Texas, and the "satanic ritual abuse" panic was still alive in San Antonio.

Self-avowed homophobes were allowed to serve on the jury. The sister of one of the defendants counted seventy-five references to their lesbianism in court.

In prison, the San Antonio Four wrote to anyone who might help them. No one did. Finally, a guy named Darrell Otto, who was living in the Yukon with his dogs, discovered them online. He got in touch with the National Center for Reason and Justice (NCRJ), an organization that helps people falsely accused of crimes against children. The NCRJ (on whose board I serve) pulled together a support committee, worked with local reporters and a documentarian to produce exposés of the case, and in 2010 persuaded the Innocence Project of Texas to appeal the conviction. The lawyers took advantage of a new Texas law allowing defendants to appeal if they'd been convicted on subsequently discredited "junk science." Expressing deep sorrow and asking forgiveness, the younger niece, Stephanie Limón Martinez, recanted her accusations. "I was only 7," she wrote, "and I was scared."[1]

The women have still not been exonerated. In fact, for the first year after her release, Anna Vasquez was subject to sex offender registry restrictions, as are all sex offenders released from custody. Among the things she was forbidden to do: talk on the phone with anyone who has children, which includes almost all of her family and friends.

These women are as compelling as any victim of injustice you are likely to find. They are beautiful, dignified, articulate, pious — and innocent as Jesus in the cradle. Their tribulations reflect every form of disadvantage and bigotry America has to offer.

When no one responded to their many letters for help, the four started praying. Their families and friends prayed. When they were released, they thanked God.

But other than a mysterious Canadian, the NCRJ, and (possibly) God, the world ignored the San Antonio Four for two decades.

None of the organizations that might have been expected to take on their plight did so — not LGBT, people of color, women's, or criminal justice reform groups. When the women got out of jail, the mainstream media, from the local papers to *Time* to the *Guardian*, reported the story. But Bill Dobbs, a lawyer and press secretary for queer and left movements who helped NCRJ with the San Antonio Four press work, got no traction with the progressive media. "LGBT organizations and news outlets zoom in on LGBT crime victims and very rarely take notice if one of us is accused or convicted," he wrote in an email. "Left news media miss or mangle so much sex and LGBT-related news they may as well be legally blind to those topics."

The women's innocence made no difference. They were labeled sex offenders; worse, they had allegedly harmed children. And for that reason, they were untouchable. People who have actually committed crimes might as well be radioactive.

A PRISON NATION WITHOUT THE PRISON

The most bizarre charges of satanic ritual abuse may be a thing of the past. Journalist Debbie Nathan, who is coauthor, with attorney Mike Snedeker, of *Satan's Silence: Ritual Abuse and the Making of a Modern American Witch Hunt*, called the San Antonio case "the last gasp of the satanic ritual abuse panic."[2] But false accusations and wrongful convictions of child sexual abuse continue apace.[3]

At the same time, as the carceral state metastasizes, the body of criminal law known collectively as Megan's Laws and the policies that fall under the rubric of sex offender registration and notification, or SORN, have thickened and hardened even more rapidly, with far less opposition.

Every former felon is disenfranchised and virtually condemned to poverty by the myriad collateral consequences of conviction. The 38,000 state and federal sanctions inventoried by the American Bar Association include everything from the prohibition of working as a radiologist's assistant to bans from public housing and food stamps to permanent disenfranchisement.[4] But thanks to a coincidence of state insolvency due to endless tax rebellion, growing activism against the prison-industrial complex, and the election of a black president, that is starting to change. The war on drugs — the main contributor to mass incarceration — shows signs of de-escalation, such as the grant of early release to some nonviolent federal drug offenders. Some states have passed laws requiring states to apprise defendants of the collateral consequences of conviction before a plea bargain and to devise mechanisms for the restoration of rights. But there is no equivalent cease-fire in the war on sex. In fact, the model legislation for those laws, written by the national Uniform Law Commission, categorically excludes registered sex offenders from relief.[5]

As of June 2014, there were more than 795,000 people on the sex offender registries (SORs) of the states and U.S. protectorates — a number equal to more than 15 percent of the 5.1 million people on probation or parole in America.[6] Not every registered sex offender is listed on the public Internet registries. But federal law mandates the registration and publication of the names, faces, and criminal and personal information of an ever-growing swath of people convicted of an ever-wider breadth of offenses, including transgressors as young as fourteen.[7] Beth E. Richie, anti-violence feminist, prison abolitionist, and director of the Institute for Research on Race and Public Policy at University of Illinois at Chicago, called the registry "a prison nation without the prison."[8]

In the two decades of their existence SORN laws and their concomitant sanctions — from prohibitions on giving out candy on Halloween to mandatory chemical castration[9] — have yielded little or no positive impact on public safety.[10] Meanwhile, they act as a quiet invitation to vigilante violence. Recently in South Carolina, skinheads Jeremy and Christine Moody were sentenced to life for the murder of registered sex offender Charles Parker and his wife, Gretchen. Being led to the police car, Christine shouted, "Killing that pedophile was the best day of my life" — she'd gladly do it again. She almost got the chance. When apprehended, Jeremy had the name and address of his next target written on an envelope — information he'd gotten from the registry.[11] It wasn't the first time a registered sex offender was assaulted or killed, his family harassed, or his house vandalized, and it will not be the last.

Although the U.S. Supreme Court has ruled SORN measures to be "administrative," not punitive — therefore not subject to the Eighth Amendment's prohibition of cruel and unusual punishment[12] — human rights advocates condemn U.S. sex crimes laws as violations of international standards and covenants.[13]

The sex offender regime does not affect only sex offenders. Coupled with the stigma it produces, the regime stands as a symbol and model of what Yale University queer legal scholar Joseph Fischel calls "debility," personal vulnerability and dysfunction imposed by the state.[14] What happens to sex offenders can eventually happen to all offenders. For instance, states have instituted registries for offenses from drunk driving to methamphetamine manufacture. Florida lists all prisoners released from custody.

Still, social justice activists have stayed as far as they can from sex offenders and the laws that govern their lives. What Northeastern University gender studies professor and queer prison abolitionist Erica R. Meiners wrote in 2008 is still true today:

My research suggests that no anti-prison movement has developed a campaign to draw attention to escalating [sex offender registries] as public policy failures or to name how they participate in expanding the [prison-industrial complex]. National, visible feminist organizations that work on issues related to violence against women and children have not publicly challenged the expansion of SORS, or, more broadly, directly addressed the way that strategies that turn to the state to protect women and children do not make our communities, or children and women, any safer. . . . [D]espite the criminalization of queers, a population historically defined as sex offenders, national . . . LGBT organizations have not documented how current SORS potentially impact those who identify as LGBT or non-heteronormative.[15]

When Meiners talked about sex offenders on a panel on "prison abolition as a feminist issue" in Chicago in 2012, the moderator nervously introduced her subject as "complicated and hard." Unlike the other talks, Meiners's presentation lasted less than two minutes; her tone was almost apologetic.[16]

The only organizations actively pressing for reform or repeal of sex offender laws consist almost entirely of incarcerated or registered sex offenders and their loved ones. The local chapters of this somewhat fractious network, called Reform Sex Offender Laws (RSOL), function largely as self-help circles and ministries. Some lobby to waylay anti-sex-offender bills; sadly, these efforts sometimes soften the worst proposals, making slightly less draconian plans palatable enough to gain wider support among lawmakers. But besides this focused legislative action, the RSOLs are politically unsophisticated. Beyond a few individuals, progressives have not approached the RSOLs either to offer a broader analysis or to invite them into a larger political movement.[17]

Why? What can be done to change this neglect of a population constantly subject to clear and grave injustice?

The answers lie in the tangled histories of the movements that should recognize these issues as akin to their own. From the mid-1970s through the early 1980s, incipient conservatism inside these movements began to emerge — in particular, the strain of gender essentialism coupled with a punitive impulse that became what Elizabeth Bernstein and others call "carceral feminism."[18] Many anti-violence and sexual liberationist feminists of color and queer activists rejected such essentialism early on and began to understand it as a vital enzyme in producing that punitive feminist impulse. They also began to recognize the negative consequences for women of color and poor communities when criminalization became the predominant response to sexual violence; many eventually joined the movement against mass incarceration. These resisters have brought a richer understanding — a "racing" and "queering" — of the function and fallout of the prison state.

That movement has also acquired powerful theoretical and strategic coherence with Michelle Alexander's *The New Jim Crow*, an analysis of mass incarceration as the perpetuation — indeed, the worsening — of historic systematic racism.[19] Unfortunately, the sex offender, who is perceived to be white and middle class, does not fit easily into this analysis.

In tracing the significant role that the essentialist strain of feminism has had in preventing progressives from making common cause with sex offenders, I do not wish to suggest that this strain of feminism — or even it plus the various formations among women of color who opposed it — represents all the feminism that emerged in the 1970s or since. From the start, feminism was divided. Ann Snitow conceptualized that divide as the "equality feminists," who want every opportunity men have (including lousy ones), versus the "difference feminists," looking for a better deal in an implacably gendered world, even extolling the natural superiority of women.[20] The two aren't wholly separate or mutually exclusive. Nevertheless, the former, "equality" strain has reproduced and mutated into numerous collections of women and genderqueers who, like their progenitors, seek sexual liberation rather than sexual protection, freedom as much as safety.

Yet even many people who consider themselves sex radicals have a hard time confronting sex offender issues. This reluctance is not just a matter of theory or tactics. Meiners calls the sex offender regime the "affective" carceral state, built upon and reproduced by politically manipulated emotion — revulsion, fear, and vengeance — compounded by disinformation. Any movement that declares solidarity with sex offenders, who are by now imaginatively synonymous with "pedophiles," must face those explosive public emotions. But progressives must also interrogate their own, often unfair and unsubstantiated, feelings in order to rout them from their hearts.

GAY LIBERATION: THE SEX PANIC BEGINS

In December 1977, in the outer-Boston precincts of Revere, Massachusetts, twenty-four men were indicted on over one hundred counts of statutory rape of boys ages eight to fifteen. Suffolk County District Attorney Garrett Byrne — known for his attempts to censor *Naked Lunch* and *Hair* — called the men a "sex ring" that conspired to lure the boys with drugs, money, and games into a house, where they were raped and photographed.

The press leapt on the story. But as the police investigation proceeded, it turned out that much of what they were reporting was not true. Most of the men didn't know each other; there was no "ring." None of the boys was under thirteen. The vast majority of the sex involved two fifteen-year-old hustlers who had found a discreet place to conduct business in the home of one Richard Peluso. Six months earlier, when Peluso was arrested for child molestation, the police found pictures of sixty-four youths in his home; they rounded up the boys and pressured them to name names. Thirteen cooperated, yielding the twenty-four indictments.[21]

The Suffolk DA's office proposed a hotline for anonymous tips about men having sex with underage boys. A witch hunt was in the offing. In response, the radical collective that produced the publication *Fag Rag* formed a committee to oppose the hotline and support the rights of the defendants. Addressing itself to the "vulnerable" members of the gay community — "children, prostitutes, promiscuous, working class, transvestites" — the *Fag Rag* group believed that if anyone in the gay community was threatened, everyone was in danger.

Events elsewhere certainly bespoke peril. The same month in Toronto, vice cops raided the offices of the radical gay paper *Body Politic*, seizing twelve crates of materials including the subscription lists. For the crime of publishing "Men Loving Boys Loving Men," a defense of intergenerational sex by Gerald Hannon, the magazine and its publisher were charged with criminal obscenity.[22]

In Washington, D.C., social worker Judianne Densen-Gerber testified before a congressional committee that there were an estimated 1.2 million children victimized by child prostitution and pornography, including snuff films in which they were murdered for the viewer's delectation. Her partner, Los Angeles vice cop Lloyd Martin, told the panel that sexual exploitation of children was "worse than homicide."

Although Densen-Gerber's claims turned out to be massively exaggerated,[23] the scare inspired Congress only months later to pass the first of a body of new laws criminalizing a broadening category of images as child pornography.[24] In the public imagination the child molester was not yet the polymorphously perverse "pedophile," lusting after any young body of any sex. He was, as he'd been in the 1920s, a gay man. At that hearing, the head of the National Coalition for Children's Justice averred that "most agree that child sex and pornography is basically a boy-man thing."[25]

Meanwhile, in Florida, under the banner "Save Our Children," orange-juice spokesmodel Anita Bryant was organizing a campaign to repeal a new Dade County ordinance forbidding discrimination based on sexual orientation.

The repeal won overwhelmingly. Other cities and states followed suit. In California, queers organizing aggressively managed to defeat the Briggs Initiative, which would have barred homosexuals from teaching in public schools. But celebration was short-lived. Twenty days after the polls closed in 1978, the out gay San Francisco city supervisor Harvey Milk, a leader in the anti-Briggs campaign, was assassinated.

A few weeks later, Illinois police arrested John Wayne Gacy for the rape and murder of thirty-three teenage boys and young men. There could not have been a less auspicious time for the founding, in Boston, of the North American Man/Boy Love Association, or NAMBLA.

In the late 1970s, progressive psychologists and educators were advocating a more liberal attitude toward children's and teen sexuality. Still, few professionals defended gay and lesbian teenage sex. A queer kid had to be crazy to come out in high school. Families rejected their gay and lesbian children, as they still do. Many kids ran away to gay urban communities like Boston's. Some found each other, others found loving older partners. Some ended up working the streets alongside working-class boys like those involved in the Revere arrests; some turned to survival sex, using and used by adults.[26]

Still, the sixties and early seventies counterculture, including the gay liberation movement, was a youth culture, where sharp lines between young and older were blurred. All over the country, activists, including teens, undertook drives to relax or repeal age-of-consent statutes. Among the "basic rights" New York's Gay Activists Alliance (GAA) enumerated in its 1969 constitution was "the right to make love with anyone, anyway, anytime, provided only that such action be freely chosen by individuals involved." In the early 1970s, GAA vowed to fight for an end to all legal restrictions "related to homosexual acts between consenting persons."[27]

But if Boston's gay community generally agreed that sex between consenting adults should be legal, sex between any-aged "persons" was another matter. What Leigh Goodmark, a family law practitioner and professor specializing in intimate violence, calls dominance feminism — the idea "that in a male-dominated society, women exist as sexual objects to be exploited by men at their pleasure" — was gaining sway.[28] Dominance feminism was a close cousin of gender essentialism — the notion that men are biologically built and programmed to be one way (aggressive, predatory) and women the opposite (peaceful, submissive). In 1975, Susan Brownmiller's *Against Our Will: Men, Women and Rape* married the two. She argued that since the start of human history rape had been "nothing more or less than a conscious process of intimidation by which all men keep all women in a state of fear." Men were made to rape, she suggested: "By anatomical fiat — the inescapable construction of their genitals — the human male was a predator and the human female served as his natural prey."[29] The following year, Andrea Dworkin went further, indicting all heterosexual intercourse as rape. "Fucking," she wrote, "is the means by which the male colonizes the female."[30]

As feminists exposed the family secrets of incest and child sexual abuse, as well as domestic violence against women, a similar theory took shape around men and children. In *Father-Daughter Incest* (1981), the feminist psychologist Judith Lewis Herman read incest as a structural inevitability of the patriarchal family.[31] From heterosexual rape and family abuse, the view that gendered power was the crux of all sexual politics expanded. Soon, according to these "dominance feminists," any structural imbalance of power, whether of gender, wealth, or age, implied coercion by the one who yielded more social clout.

Among some of Boston's politicized lesbians, this galvanizing idea lent intellectual coherence and emotional and moral power to a vague distaste for an urban gay bar-and-baths culture that tolerated consensual cross-generational sex as one expression of desire among many. So when *Gay Community News* (GCN), the major forum for queer political debate in Boston, published NAMBLA's manifesto in 1978, declaring the "rights" of children of any age to engage in sex with adults, condemnation poured in, mostly from women.

The fire spread nationally. The 1979 Philadelphia planning conference for the first gay march on Washington adopted a demand from the Gay Youth Caucus for "Full Rights for Gay Youth, including revision of the age of consent laws." Lesbian members of the newly elected coordinating committee offered a substitute: "Protect Lesbian and Gay Youth from any laws which are used to discriminate against, oppress, and/or harass them in their homes, schools, jobs and social environments" — deleting both sex and age of consent. The lesbians threatened to walk out if their amendment wasn't adopted. In a mail vote, it was.

Around the country, other women withdrew from mixed-sex actions when organizers refused to pull NAMBLA representatives from the speakers' rosters.[32] In New York, Lesbian Feminist Liberation (LFL) issued a news release accusing "so-called Man/Boy Lovers" of trying to "make palatable" the sexual exploitation of children, a ploy that "feminists easily recognize." The group also threatened, "We will not passively march alongside pederast banners or signs, nor quietly stand and listen to pederast speeches at any march or rally. Lesbian Feminist Liberation will not support pederasts within the Lesbian and Gay movements nor anywhere else."[33]

The battle lines were drawn almost entirely by sex. "For the gay movement to refuse to support the demands of gay youth and boy-lovers is like refusing to support [the Equal Rights Amendment]," declared one man at a New York forum on intergenerational sex. A woman countered, "What NAMBLA is doing is tearing apart the movement. If you attach [the man/boy love issue] to gay rights, gay rights will never happen."[34] In other words, it was the perverts, not those who refused solidarity with them, who were destroying the movement.

The issue appeared strategic: What would advance the movement? But smuggled in under cover of strategy was a more personal question: What was good for gay and lesbian people themselves, especially teenagers? Some radical sexual liberationists argued that as long as no one was forced, how and with whom anyone had sex was not "the movement's" affair. Young gays weighed in. "Children do have the power adults are denying them to protect themselves," a representative of Gay Youth told the New York gathering. He said that better sex education and stronger rape law would allay exploitation better than enforcement of age-of-consent statutes.[35]

But it didn't matter what young people said. Age difference was a power imbalance, NAMBLA's opponents argued. Power imbalances equaled coercion. Ergo, sex between lovers of different ages made the younger partner a victim. The Victorian notion behind age-of-consent law — that "children," capaciously defined, are sexually ignorant, thus categorically unable to say yes to sex — had received the imprimatur of feminist theory.

Gender essentialism reinforced these fixed ideas about age. In the pages of GCN several women announced that intergenerational sex was a men's thing; women "don't do that," declared Amy Hoffman, an editor. This claim moved Beth Kelly to contribute an article confessing the lovingly sexual relationship she had had between the ages of eight and eleven with a great-aunt fifty years her senior. "Taboos on childhood sexuality when it blossoms at all, or on adolescent sexuality that crosses age boundaries, are so deeply entrenched in our culture that for years I was ashamed and afraid to admit [this], even to myself," Kelly wrote. The vilification of NAMBLA was a case of gay people oppressing each other, their youth, and themselves, she said: "It's time to stop selling out young people, and to begin being honest, with ourselves and with each other."[36]

Kelly's testimony, like the Gay Youth member's, evaporated in the heat. What also may have been lost — as it always is when the Child becomes an abstraction — was a nuanced discussion of the real experiences of gay kids, especially those living on the margins. In 1978, for instance, members of the

Boston gay youth organization Project Lambda were interviewed for a piece in the Michigan publication *Growing Up Gay*. Ironically, the kids lamented that gay adults in their community were more focused on Anita Bryant's "Save Our Children" campaign than they were on the youth panhandling in their own streets.[37]

It may have been a sign of how dominant were gender essentialist voices that as experienced and clear-sighted an activist as Eric Rofes echoed it in a GCN piece urging "sisters and brothers" to work together "on the issues that we can unite behind." Among these unifying issues he did not include man-boy love, sadomasochism, pornography, and public sex, which he cordoned off as male tastes. Then he spoke of the lesbian dissidents, who "as women"

> have seen how pornography has been used to fuel violence against women, including lesbians. They see sado-masochism used as a weapon by men to keep women submissive, in a society which already works to make women powerless. In a culture that seems to support the coercion and rape of young women by heterosexual men, the issue of intergenerational sex is understandably volatile to lesbians.[38]

Moral outrage gave way to political expediency: a measure of legitimacy could be gained by exiling boy-lovers beyond the walls of anthropologist Gayle Rubin's fortress of sexual acceptability.[39] Soon NAMBLA had virtually no defenders left in the LGBT (even Q) community.

Nor was it long before the brand of feminism that saw masculine coercion everywhere discovered it even where there was no man involved: within lesbians who had purportedly internalized patriarchal oppression. In 1982, Women Against Pornography (WAP) attacked the Barnard Scholar & Feminist Conference on Sexuality and some of its participants personally, charging that they were promoting "anti-feminist sexuality" — pornography, lesbian sadomasochism, and butch-femme relations.[40]

QUEEREST OF THE QUEERS: THE SEX OFFENDER

Then in 1984 an eighteen-year-old working-class gay Massachusetts daycare worker was arrested for the mass molestation of preschoolers, and the mainstream gay and lesbian movement was silent. The defendant, Bernard Baran, declared his innocence from the start and never wavered. Baran was the first person to be convicted in what would become a nationwide daycare abuse panic. The accusations against him — which began when a couple of parents objected to a homosexual teaching their son — were vague, contradictory, and in some cases outlandish. The videotapes of the children's accusations that the grand jury saw had been extensively edited to delete the parts in which the toddlers were bribed, hectored, and threatened to give the "right" answers. In the full interviews, in fact, the kids denied everything, which they continued to do sporadically throughout the trial.

In the courtroom Berkshire County District Attorney Daniel Ford adopted what journalist Jim D'Entremont called a "diseased-pariah strategy." A four-year-old alleged victim tested positive for gonorrhea of the throat. Baran's gonorrhea tests were negative. There was evidence suggesting the child had been abused by a family member. Nevertheless, Ford brought in an expert witness to testify to the prevalence of gonorrhea among homosexuals. In his closing argument he described the defendant's "primitive urge to satisfy his sexual appetite" — echoes of the "uncontrollable desires" of the gay molester of the last sex panic, thirty years earlier.

Baran received three concurrent life sentences. He was tortured by inmates and guards throughout the decades. He was in prison, innocent, for twenty-one years before being released on bail.

Yet throughout his ordeal, "no gay organization of any kind acknowledged the existence of Bernard Baran," wrote D'Entremont, who, with his partner, Bob Chatelle, started the Free Baran defense committee. That committee became the National Center for Reason and Justice, which helped to secure Baran's release and exoneration more than two decades later. After only eight years of freedom Baran died, not yet fifty years old.

The gay organizations that ignored Baran also ignored Margaret Kelly Michaels, whose prosecutors in 1988 spent two days detailing a same-sex relationship she'd had, "implying that lesbianism had impelled her to force toddlers of both sexes to lick peanut butter off her cervix at the Wee Care Nursery School in Maplewood, New Jersey," wrote D'Entremont.[41] They ignored the San Antonio Four.

Police registries of "known homosexuals" and those arrested for engaging in acts such as "outraging public decency" were inaugurated in the 1940s — Bayard Rustin, the gay civil rights organizer and close associate of Martin Luther King, was on one — but had fallen into disuse by 1980s. They didn't languish long. In 1986, Illinois set up the first public registry of people convicted of sex offenses against children, and other states followed. In 1990, Washington state passed the first community notification act. In 1994, the federal Jacob Wetterling Crimes Against Children Sex Offender Registry Act mandated that every state set up a registry. The 2006 Adam Walsh Child Protection and Safety Act mandated that all the registries be put on the Internet. It also significantly increased the number of offenses requiring notification and directed states to list offenders as young as fourteen.

Because some states require registration of people convicted long before the new laws went into effect, and because sex and vice statutes have for decades been disproportionately enforced against same-sex actors and gender nonconformers as well as racial minorities, the registries perpetuate these inequities.[42] But, by the 1990s, mainstream LGBT groups were busy trying to get married and join the military. They said nothing about the registries.

Many feel the mainstream LGBT movement bought the wedding band and the army fatigues by selling out queerer queers — not just boy-lovers but also young closeted men of color with HIV/AIDS, street kids, incarcerated transsexuals. To this list of queer untouchables, Yale's Fischel adds sex offenders.[43]

A new sex panic had begun, and people within the LGBT movement pushed it along by magnifying the personal and political damage that might be inflicted by a small group of sexual outliers. Today, writes Meiners, LGBT organizations have not "initiated any public campaigns or research about how [sex offender registries] could potentially augment 'fear of the queer' by recirculating public discourses on 'sex offenders.' "[44] But the problem is more than a failure to act. By refusing to defend — and actively ostracizing — the queerest among them, mainstream lesbian and gay organizations perpetuated their own "fear of the queer."

ANTI-VIOLENCE FEMINISTS:
PARTNERS IN PUNISHMENT

Most histories of the early feminist anti-violence movement are similar: In the early 1970s consciousness-raising and speak-outs brought the stark facts of rape and domestic abuse to light. While law enforcement stood back and let the violence reign, women set up a homegrown shelter system, at the same time demanding that the state give female citizens equal protection under the law by providing prompt and respectful police and court responses, as well as medical care and social services for victims. Buttressing all this was a feminist analysis of the root causes of masculine violence: a gendered system of economic and social inequality.

It's the next chapter — the late 1970s and later — where the stories diverge. Here is one typical version, from *Up Against a Wall: Rape Reform and the*

Failure of Success, by Rose Corrigan, Drexel University law and social policy scholar and longtime volunteer in rape care centers:

> During the initial wave of rape law reform conservative writers, thinkers, and legislators jumped on the sexual abuse awareness bandwagon as a way to demonstrate their "get tough on crime" credentials, and to call for ever more punitive and repressive sentences for sex offenders. Many of these conservatives, however, rejected feminist arguments about the origins of sexual violence in gender inequality and male supremacy.... In the end, conservatives supported the feminist rape reform agenda when it suited their own interests ... even as they sought to maintain the very systems of inequality feminists argued created and sustained gender-based violence.

In this telling, feisty feminist institutions struggled for years, sticking to their ideals in a hostile culture. But they were poor; around them, politics were moving rightward. The feminists did their best to hold onto their ideals against pressure from conservatives. But just as in the gay and lesbian movement, realism pointed to compromise. Feminists began to work with law-and-order proponents "in strategic ways," says Corrigan, "co-opting ... rather than being co-opted."[45]

Eventually, the state started to come around. Some of those legal reforms passed in some places — rape shield laws, the criminalization of marital rape. Police were compelled to arrest perpetrators of domestic violence, hospitals to train staffs on how to attend to rape victims. Some funding flowed to victims' services. Feminists — or so this narrative goes — were suspicious of their macho and paternalistic suitors in the police departments and prosecutors' offices. But as the movement matured — by now the crisis center workers had earned their social work degrees and bought some new typewriters — its rightward drift continued. Both professionalism and the bureaucratic demands of accessing state support carried it in a conservative direction.

Having gingerly climbed into bed with the forces of law and order, feminists found themselves married, financially dependent, and knocked up with a baby they didn't really want. Worst of all, as Corrigan's "rape care center" informants tell it, the system that had perverted their values still was not enforcing the law.

This is a melodrama of stolen innocence, of seduction and betrayal. And like all melodramas, it is part fiction.

The fact is, feminists did not learn to love the law and its enforcers by hanging around, reluctantly, with Republicans. An essentialist belief in the incorrigibility of men and a concomitant resort to coercive and punitive measures had infected feminism at least as far back as nineteenth-century "social purity" crusades. In the earliest days of the second-wave women's movement, rage at sexism was balanced by the late-sixties utopianism, a virago on one shoulder, a love child on the other. But by the mid-1970s, as women continued to limp into battered-women's shelters and rape crisis centers, anger turned hopes for social transformation into a desire for retribution. Even before the laws changed, moral conservatives were there beside feminists to attack sexual violence.[46]

Social worker Densen-Gerber and vice cop Martin were a paradigmatic child-saving team; Women Against Pornography and the 1985–1986 Attorney General's Commission on Pornography (the Meese Commission) was a later one. But an early example of such a feminist-conservative marriage was Parents United, a network of federally funded Alcoholics Anonymous–like support groups founded in the early 1970s to deal with child battery and, later, with incest. Parents United satisfied grassroots feminist values by assisting battered women and abused children in finding housing, welfare, and other social services. But rather than challenge the supremacy of the nuclear family, as feminists like Herman were doing, the network's goal was to save marriages, by any means necessary.

Actually, *support* group is too benign a description of what went on in Parents United. According to Nathan and Snedeker, the groups re-educated incestuous fathers "amid a totalistic climate of ascetic discipline, intense religiosity, zealous group cohesion, twelve-step rituals, confessions, and expiations of sin" — the men's, that is. In response, the group "might praise [the father] warmly for his efforts [or] viciously denounce him . . . and urge him to do the same to himself."

Praising Parents United for its success in rendering men "more submissive and nurturant" toward their wives and children, Herman enthusiastically compared the methodology to re-education in revolutionary societies — "little concerned that the students in such classes are political prisoners under threat of death if they do not learn their lessons."[47] This denouncer of masculine authoritarian power created by social inequality was willing to turn the tables and anoint women men's inquisitors and disciplinarians.

Nor was collaboration with law enforcement and the abridgment of defendants' rights foisted on feminists in a Faustian bargain, the quid pro quo for victims' services. The two traveled hand in hand from the first. In the early 1980s, Seattle's Harborview Sexual Assault Center director Lucy Berliner undertook to ease child testimony and thus make convictions more attainable in abuse trials. Firmly holding to the orthodoxy that "children never lie" (a contention anyone who's ever been or known a child can easily contest), she promoted the relaxation of such bedrock Sixth Amendment protections of criminal defendants as the exclusion of hearsay testimony, the right to face one's accuser (children would be allowed to testify in another room before a video camera), and the right to ascertain a child witness's capacity to understand and speak rationally and truthfully.[48] These were the first "victims' rights" policies, and they were also dear to conservatives, who had long viewed the Sixth as a get-out-of-jail-free pass for the guilty. In 1982, President Ronald Reagan impaneled a Task Force on Victims of Crime, which concluded that "the victims of crime have been transformed into a group oppressively burdened by a system designed to protect them." The committee recommended that the Sixth Amendment be "augmented" to guarantee protections of victims commensurate to those of the accused.[49]

Thirty years later, the draft amendment has grown longer, trespassing more deeply into defendants' protected territory. Congress keeps proposing it, and feminists keep complaining that victims don't get enough ("Why do rape victims have so few rights — either on the books or in practice?" asks Corrigan).[50] But, as the civil libertarian feminist Wendy Kaminer pointed out when the amendment came up in 2001, the victims' rights strategy is not only anti-constitutional; it's ineffective. "It's hard to argue with the desire to reform trials [and institute other prosecution-friendly policies] in order to help victims heal," Kaminer wrote. But curtailing defendants' rights does not cede those rights to victims; it grants them to the state. "Victims need and deserve services, but with [more than] 2 million people already behind bars, the state needs no more power to imprison us."[51]

FEMINISTS VERSUS SATAN

"What began as a 'gender war' led to more generalized fears about the epidemic of sexual abuse and the pandemic threat of sex criminals," wrote Elizabeth Bumiller in 2013.

These apocalyptic fears, to some degree, can be attributed to feminist warnings about the pervasive risk of stranger violence and depictions of horrible attacks. Feminists also produced narratives about sadistic violence that took place in the home, often fixated on a primal scene of incest, ripe for appropriation within a larger cultural setting.[52]

Bumiller doesn't blame feminists alone for the production of those hysterical narratives. Neither do I. But if you're looking for the door through which Satan and his minions entered the scene, it is as likely to open into a feminist therapy clinic as into a snake-handling fundamentalist church.

Densen-Gerber considered herself a feminist. The child pornography panic she launched now makes felons of teens who "sext" their friends or lovers and imposes decades-long federal sentences for downloading images of naked sixteen-year-olds even in states where it is legal to have sex with those sixteen-year-olds. Feminist psychologist Ann Burgess, originator of "rape trauma syndrome," was the first to propose the fantastical notion that gay men were organizing themselves into "sex rings" to abuse children. The FBI and police routinely announce that they have broken up child prostitution or pornography "rings," offering little or no evidence of coordination.[53] As director of Children's Institute International in Los Angeles, social worker Kee MacFarlane pioneered the suggestive and coercive questioning of children that elicited the hundreds of accusations of satanic abuse in the McMartin Preschool trials; those methods and almost identical accusations fed a decades-long witch hunt. MacFarlane was also a feminist.

And even while the nation woke up from the shared hallucination of satanic ritual abuse, feminists like Gloria Steinem refused to open their eyes. "Ritual Abuse Exists," shouted the cover of *Ms.* magazine in 1993. "Believe It!" A former fact-checker at the magazine recently told me she was instructed not to check the facts in that story.

How could feminists, cultural critics by inclination and training, swallow charges of nursery school teachers inviting pedophilic clowns into the classroom, mutilating animals, flying children to Mexico to be sexually tortured, or forcing them to lick peanut butter off genitals — all within wide-open classrooms during the eight hours of a school day? How could they square the large number of women among the accused with the fact that upward of 98 percent of rapists are men — not just a fact but the basis of their own worldview? And why did feminists — for whom childcare was a founding demand — not see the backlash in attacking the very people enabling women to take steps toward social and economic equality while giving their children a secure place to be?

Fear trumps reason; feminists had helped create and stoke the fear. Ideology also trumps reason, especially when the ideology is based in fear of an overblown danger. Sexual essentialism, moreover, is a Manichaean worldview. That is why it settles comfortably in the criminal justice system, with its good guys and bad guys, its perpetrators and victims, its guilty and its innocent — a system in which justice for the victim means only one thing: punishment of the criminal.

And although it is secular, feminist Manichaeism can sit in a pew with fire-and-brimstone Christianity, where life on earth is a battle between the Prince of Darkness and the forces of light. To contemplate the innocence of the accused in a daycare abuse case in the 1980s or the injustice of the sex offender regime today is to ask people who believe they are defending the innocent to take the part of the guilty, to urge people on the side of the angels to sympathize with the Devil.

WOMEN OF COLOR OBJECT

From the start, women of color bridled at the separatism of the white lesbian feminist movement and the gender essentialism of the mainstream white women's anti-violence movement. In 1977, as Boston's gay and lesbian community was splintering along gender and ideological lines, the black feminist lesbians of the Combahee River Collective published a statement expressing their misgivings, as well as a different vision of liberation:

> We have a great deal of criticism and loathing for what men have been socialized to be in this society: what they support, how they act, and how they oppress. But we do not have the misguided notion that it is their maleness, per se — i.e., their biological maleness — that makes them what they are. As Black women we find any type of biological determinism a particularly dangerous and reactionary basis upon which to build a politic. We must also question whether Lesbian separatism is an adequate and progressive political analysis and strategy, even for those who practice it, since it so completely denies any but the sexual sources of women's oppression, negating the facts of class and race.

Along with anger at men, the statement evinced solidarity: "We struggle together with Black men against racism, while we also struggle with Black men about sexism."[54]

In spite of some progress, major fissures between the mainstream women's anti-violence movement and communities of color did not heal. Legal reforms championed by the former did not account for the violence disadvantaged women suffer not only in their homes and neighborhoods but also at the hands of the state. So new law enforcement policies, epitomized in the 1994 Violence Against Women Act, ended up delivering more safety to some women — white, educated, straight — and more scrutiny and penalty to those already in economically or personally compromised situations. Legal strategies that positioned abused women as the antagonists of their partners, without allowing them to decide what to do, took power from the already disempowered. Meanwhile, violence marched on.[55]

Increasingly, the priorities and tactics of mainstream anti-violence feminists were antipathetic to those, such as queers and communities of color, who were trying to get out from under the hand of the carceral state. It was a logical progression for anti-violence feminists of color and anti-prison activists to join forces.

Since the 1980s, most feminists have moved past those old narrow categories of masculine and feminine and embraced the lability of gender and sexuality, bodies and desires. Criminal justice reform activism is also being "queered."[56] A campaign in New Orleans in 2012, for instance, brought together LGBTQ activists and sex workers, mostly women and transwomen of color at the lower rungs of their occupation, to defeat a new state law classifying oral and anal sex as "crimes against nature" (CAN) subject to registry. Since it came after *Lawrence v. Texas*, the Supreme Court ruling that protects private consensual homosexual acts, the CAN law singled out prostitutes and men having sex in public as sex offenders. The New Orleans campaign was the rare political organizing effort outside the Reform Sex Offender Laws (RSOL) network that challenged any aspect of the sex offender registry. But solidarity goes only so far. The campaign did not call out the essential injustice of the registry itself, for all registrants.

ENEMIES OF THE CARCERAL STATE: VEXED BY WHITENESS?

A visit to NationInside.org, an online clearinghouse of activism against the prison-industrial complex, finds a plethora of efforts both broad (Decarcerate Michigan) and specific (Campaign for Prison Phone Justice, which targets the high cost of calls from prison). The names signal inclusiveness (All of Us or None). Apart from individual posts, however, there is nothing on the site about sex crime laws and policies.

Why isn't a ten-year sentence for possessing one image of a naked child seen as an injustice deserving equal attention to expensive phone calls? If it is right to "ban the box" on job applications asking if the jobseeker has a criminal record, should we not also ban the words "sex offender" on drivers' licenses?

It's not hard to sympathize with anti-prison people who might want to shy away from sex offenders. Already representing a host of designated ogres — the "gangbanger," the drug "kingpin" — they have little to gain by taking on another. That's the cynical reason not to adopt these issues. The principled reason is that if your goal is to resist the state's authority to assign permanent identities based on the laws people have broken, you are not going to divide people up by criminal category.

But my guess is the main impediment to integrating this glaring example of criminal injustice is theoretical. The movement's foundational text, Michelle Alexander's *The New Jim Crow*, shows mass incarceration to be the principal instrument by which the state perpetuates the impoverishment and disenfranchisement of black and brown people. It provides the movement an intellectually powerful and a morally persuasive theory, along with extensive documentation — not to mention a phrase that succinctly knits together 250 years of American history with the current scourge on people of color.

The book does not mention sex, let alone sex offenders (it hardly mentions gender either, but there's lots of other good scholarship to fill that gap). Is this because the sex offender is — or is believed to be — white and, compared with the rest of the criminal population, relatively well off? A recent article on the correctional facility for sex offenders in Avenel, New Jersey, noted that more than half the inmates were white and "include[d] former attorneys and doctors, psychologists and community leaders, and once-successful businessmen."[57]

Movements are not birthed by theories, but theory can help limn the boundaries of a movement. *The New Jim Crow* — the book and the political discourse that flows from it — is essentially about the African American experience. Whiteness fits awkwardly inside it. Yet impoverished, uneducated white people suffer similar maltreatment within the criminal justice system. In the war on drugs, while crack and powder cocaine now carry equivalent — thus racially unbiased — penalties, tougher sentences for methamphetamine production and sale, primarily a white rural phenomenon, are feeding an increase in white incarceration, under increasingly long sentences.[58]

But whiteness plays an important role in the historic construction of blackness; the purportedly white sex offender is a critical player in the late twentieth-century dissemination of fear into every lane and hamlet of America. And, as new research shows, the sex offender is not as white as has been thought (see later discussion). Understanding all this can enrich progressive approaches to the intersections between race and the enforcement of sexual morality. Attention to the sex offender, whose lot is analogous to that of the drug offender, also opens opportunities for solidarity and collaboration.

PREDATORS AND PEDOPHILES

In the 1980s, the daycare abuse panic spread and the statute books filled with sex crimes laws — Megan's Law, Jessica's Law, the Jacob Wetterling Act, the Adam Walsh Act — each passed after the spectacular violation and/or killing of its child namesake. The geography of terror shifted from poor black urban communities to the white middle-class suburbs (after September 11, it spread again, everywhere). The term "predator," originally denoting an amoral, probably crack-maddened black teenage killer, came to stand for a psychologically sick sex fiend.

The black beast haunting white America's nightmares did not go into hibernation, of course. One of the highest-profile cases of the 1980s was the 1989 near-fatal rape of a white investment banker jogging in Central Park. The police forced confessions from four teenage boys of color; all were convicted, along with a fifth who had not confessed. It was thirteen years before they were exonerated. From the arrest to the verdict and beyond, the press and prosecutors seized the time-honored figure of the black sex-crazed beast: the boys were "savage," "feral," a "wolf pack," traveling from Harlem to the park (read: from the jungle to civilization) to go "wilding" — a word that may have been coined by some creative headline writer.[59]

But in the newspaper police blotter a new character was appearing: the "pedophile." And the mugshot at the top of the column was white. As George Mason University anthropology and cultural studies professor Roger Lancaster shows in *Sex Panic and the Punitive State*, the symbolic "predator" — the larger-than-life monster — did not become white in isolation. Lancaster traces this racial transmogrification alongside the rise of "white victimist politics" and of the neoliberal state. While 1970s recession bled into Reaganist austerity and privatization, a racialized politics of crime and resentment of redistributive policies ("taxes" allegedly flowing from white to black) carried the white working class from liberalism to conservatism.

The mainstream feminist anti-violence movement had a hand in these neoliberal trends.[60] As the penal system grew and the welfare system shrank, "the figure of the victim preside[d] over a weird transformation," writes Lancaster. Victim advocacy "install[ed] a distorted little welfare state in the middle of savage capitalism." Crime victims got free counseling, medical care, job training, housing assistance, and sympathy. "The citizen" got none of these.[61] Indeed, thanks to the social and civic disenfranchisement of criminal offenders, millions of people, especially men and boys of color, are effectively no longer citizens at all.

The whiteness of the "pedophile" both obscures and serves racism, says Lancaster. "Shall we say, then, that in a society committed both to a war on crime (with its mass incarceration of black men) and to ridding itself of racism (through formal adherence to a regime of civil rights) the feared figure of the white pedophile is necessary?" he writes. "Perhaps part of the psychic work he performs is to absolve the guilty conscience of racism at a time when so many other fears are focused on the black gangbanger and brown border menace."[62]

The sex offender, figured white, reassures Americans that they live in a "post-racial" society. I can almost hear Chief Justice John Roberts making the case that race-based applications of the equal protection clause of the Fourteenth Amendment are obsolete because more white people are going to prison for running meth labs and the sex offender registries are filling up with white faces.

HOW WHITE IS THE SEX OFFENDER?

But are the registries in fact full of white faces? For the last thirty years, we — and in that pronoun I include progressives — have had little more than anecdote, media, and political rhetoric to inform us about who the sex offender is. It's been hard to find out the truth. Researchers of the SORN laws are frustrated by the same problems that trouble study of U.S. criminal data generally, especially if the goal is to compile or compare information from more than one state. Records are inconsistent and spottily available; similarly named statutes define crimes differently; most criminal records, including the registries, do not indicate the relationship of the offender to the victim (for instance, only some registries include a category on the list called "Incest").

Federal data bunches crimes in categories, not according to specific offenses. Thanks to plea bargaining, conviction records don't reveal the original charges, much less what actually happened.

Still, new quantitative analyses of data accrued over more than twenty years of the registries' existence are adding to our understanding of the ways the criminal justice system views and deals with the people who transgress the state's version of licit sexual behavior. The information that emerges confirms some popular beliefs and upends others. One aspect of the narrative that these new findings complicate is the role of race in the sex offender regime.

This much is true: Within the racially skewed penal state, the convicted sex offender is uniquely white. Thanks mostly to gross disparities in arrests and sentencing for drug-related offenses, six in ten prison inmates are people of color.[63] But two-thirds of sex offenders are white.[64] Among offenders who are publicly listed on the registries,[65] more than two-thirds are also white, according to an ongoing analysis by Alissa Ackerman and colleagues of over 445,000 publicly registered sex offenders in 2010 in all fifty states, the federal government, and the U.S. protectorates. Crime victims are almost always the same race as the perpetrators.

In other words, sex offenders compose the only criminal population in which whites are represented roughly in proportion to their numbers in the general population — a striking exception to the rule of the New Jim Crow.

DARKNESS VISIBLE

How much of an exception is it, though? In fact, even while whites represent two-thirds of registered offenders, among those whose names and faces appear on the Internet for all to see, "blacks appear to be over-represented . . . and especially so in the states of Delaware, Minnesota, New Jersey, New York, and North Carolina," concluded Ackerman and her colleagues in their first rounds of parsing the data in the public sex offender registries. Beyond that white majority, "the remainder included minorities who were primarily black." Although some states' black-to-white ratios were more consonant with their overall demographics, nationally African Americans composed 22 percent of the Ackerman sample, compared with only 13 percent of the U.S. population.

Other racial and ethnic inequities showed up in state registries — or not. In Alaska, for instance, American Indian and Alaskan Natives represented about 15 percent of the state population, and Native Hawaiian and Pacific Islanders another 1 percent, according to the 2010 U.S. Census. Yet more than half (57 percent) of Alaska's publicly registered sex offenders were Native American. On the other hand, in California Hispanics (the census category is "Hispanic or Latino") were slightly underrepresented: 31 percent of publicly listed registered sex offenders, compared with 37 percent of Californians.[66]

Ten years ago, Drexel University Law School professor Daniel M. Filler came to similar conclusions about the races of offenders subject to community notification — that is, those deemed threatening enough to public safety to warrant informing the neighbors that they're coming out of prison and moving into the community. The results of his meticulous 2004 investigation were unambiguous:

> African-Americans are grossly overrepresented on notification rolls. In some states an African-American person is over 16 times more likely to appear on a notification website than a white person. The inequities extend well beyond statistical disparities, however. By including offenders convicted well before several landmark anti-discrimination cases, and during periods of documented informal discrimination, registries perpetuate historical racism.[67]

Unexpectedly, racial disparities were the least cockeyed in Southern states. But a black person in Nebraska was three times more likely to be subject to notification than a white person; in Montana, six times more likely; and in North Dakota, more than fourteen times. The imbalance in the North, while not as acute, nevertheless found the percentage of African Americans on the rolls "well out of line" with those in the states' populations. No jurisdiction Filler studied escaped this bias. Overall, a black person's odds of being subject to notification requirements ranged from 1.35 to 14.4 times those of a white person's, with a median of 1.91 times.[68]

Roger Lancaster, using numerous sources including Filler, created a valuable set of race-sensitive comparisons of general incarceration, sex offender registration, community notification, and civil commitment rates. His tables reconcile the comparative whiteness of the sex offender, both in reality and in the public imagination, with the ubiquity of black faces on the rolls: African Americans are overrepresented on sex offender registries and in community notification, he finds. "But they are far more overrepresented in prisons and jails."[69]

In 2004, Filler could not supply reliable explanations for the disparities he found, and therefore he did not judge them. They would be "unproblematic if, for instance, African-Americans offended at higher rates and Megan's Laws are a narrowly tailored and effective prevention policy," he ventured. They'd be troubling if the decisions reflected intentional or unintentional racial bias.[70]

Especially since the Adam Walsh Act of 2006, Megan's Laws are anything but narrowly tailored. Research is piling up to show that their effectiveness is minuscule to nonexistent. But one thing the racial discrepancies probably do not reflect is intentional, or even individual, bias on the part of decision-makers. Rather, the racial biases are historical, cultural, and political, and they are written into the assessment tools most commonly used to determine the "tiers" of risk of reoffense that trigger community notification.

For instance, the assessment instruments, such as the Static-99, assign risk points to a prior record of nonsexual violent crimes. They rate the assault of a stranger as an indicator of more dangerousness than the sexual molestation of a family or household member or close family friend, the most common unwanted sexual intrusion on children. They associate the use of physical force in the commission of the crime with higher risk of reoffense. By contrast, perpetrators of acquaintance or family aggressions, which the assessment systems read as "nonviolent," are assigned lower tiers.[71]

A 2010 analysis by researchers at Roger Williams University of about 320 convicted sex offenders of different races and ethnicities indicates that these assessed factors have racial dimensions. In their sample, about three-quarters of the African Americans and more than half of the Latinos had been convicted of at least one nonsexual violent crime in addition to their sex crime; three-quarters of the whites had not. Whites were also far more likely than African Americans to be convicted of noncontact crimes — offenses involving no use of force — such as exhibitionism and child pornography possession, according to this analysis. Blacks and Latinos were more likely to assault strangers than were whites.[72]

In other words, the description of crimes indicating high risk on the most used assessment instruments would seem to belong to those committed by men of color: stranger attacks using physical force by men who have prior records of nonsexual violent crimes. It makes sense, then, that African Americans are disproportionately assigned high-tier status, subject to community notification.

Of course, the other factor that rings up the highest risk points is having a child victim. Whites in the Roger Williams sample were twice as likely to have offended against a child as African Americans were.[73] This may contribute to boosting the white count on the registries and in community notification. More than half of white sex offenders in the sample committed *incest* with a child, as compared with just over a third of the African Americans. Many states exempt incest perpetrators from public websites to protect the privacy of their victims, who may share their assailants' names or addresses. The black or brown rapist is rendered visible. The white family abuser disappears.

But hidden behind the faces on the police blotter, the Internet registry, and the community notification fliers are many uninvestigated questions and possibly confounding influences. Is there actually more incest in white families? Anti-violence feminists of color have pointed out that people of color are reluctant to call the authorities if they're suffering family abuse, since they rightly do not trust the authorities to help them more than they harm them. Are white children and their mothers simply more willing to report child sexual abuse than black ones? Decades of research confirm that poverty and its attendant troubles — drug and alcohol addiction, disorganized and over-crowded households, parental stress — are strong predictors of child mal-treatment and neglect.[74] A recent study finds that child abuse increases with income inequality.[75] If social service agencies did more to assist and less to punish parents and guardians, would impoverished families of color report incest more and the statistics change?

Similarly, longer rap sheets of nonsexual violent crimes for men of color must be, at least in part, an artifact of race-based disparities in policing and conviction rates. The most notorious inequalities show up around drug-related offenses, but African Americans are also arrested for forcible rape at three times the rate whites are, and for other sex offenses at twice the rate.[76] There is no reason to assume that police practices regarding rape are any less racially biased than around drugs.[77] In fact, an analysis in 2011 of the first 250 DNA ex-onerations in the United States found that 62 percent of the defendants falsely convicted of rape were African American; adding Latinos, the percentage rose to 70.[78] Meanwhile, the overwhelming prevalence of whites convicted for downloading child pornography over the past two decades might reflect no more than a historic race gap in Internet use, which is now narrowing to insignificance.

The biases that invisibly guide systemic practices in the carceral state are also inscribed in the sex offender assessment tools, as well as scholarly interpretations of the data. The Roger Williams researchers discerned in their sample of convicted offenders "a pattern in which whites exhibit more sexual deviance," whereas "African-Americans were found to have higher rates of involvement in aggression," including nonsexual violence. This distinction between "deviance" and "aggression" reproduces racialized notions of antisocial sexual behavior: that the "normal" black man perpetrates harm willfully, because he is bad (masculine aggression being wrong but not pathological), whereas the white man who commits a similar act cannot help himself, because he is psychologically ill. In fact, a majority of people in civil commitment are white, diagnosed with a "mental abnormality or personality disorder" that "predisposes" them to committing sexually violent acts.[79]

Critics have noted that because contemporary sex crimes law grew out of hysteria around sensationalized crimes by white strangers against white middle-class children, the system exaggerates peril to white children in low-crime neighborhoods while understating the dangers facing disadvantaged children in high-crime neighborhoods. Filler suggests the "white narrative" of sex crimes accounts for the silence on racial disparities in the registries.[80] In fact, the same story may account for the silence his own findings have met among criminologists and other analysts of the sex offender regime.

In some ways the white narrative is accurate when it comes to the sex offender regime. In other ways, SORN policies and practices fit the New Jim Crow analysis. There is a great deal more we need to know. But one thing is certain: the closer we look, the more complex the racial chiaroscuro of the sex offender regime becomes.

THE INNOCENT — OR GUILTY — CHILD

As the 1990s progressed and sex crimes against children, real or spectral, filled the news, adult rapes seemed to be fading from view. In fact, they were. While 400,000 rape kits were sitting around unopened, "a thorough analysis of federal data published [in early 2014] concluded that between 1995 and 2012, police departments across the country systematically undercounted and underreported sexual assaults" — to the tune, "conservatively," of a million or more, The Nation reported. "Conservatively" because the researcher limited her purview to cases within the FBI's pre-2012 definition of rape: "carnal knowledge of a female forcibly and against her will." This definition did not include anal or oral rape, cases involving drugging or alcohol, or the rape of boys and men. The real numbers, in other words, could be higher.[81]

Feminists have long noted that few women are "innocent" enough — sober, dressed modestly, not out late alone — to make "good" victims in a rape or abuse indictment or trial. If a woman is poor, a single or teen mother, a prostitute, a former prisoner, or a drug user, she is not innocent at all. She asked for it. Historically, no black woman is innocent. "The mythical [black] rapist implies the mythical whore," wrote Angela Davis in 1978, "and a race of rapists and whores deserves punishment and nothing more."[82]

The rigorous criteria for victimhood have left only one incontrovertible innocent: the child.[83] Make that the white child. In *Racial Innocence*, Robin Bernstein shows how "the concept of 'childhood innocence' has been central to U.S. racial formation since the mid-nineteenth century." White children have been "imbued with innocence, black ones excluded from it, and others of color erased by it . . . until the Civil Rights Movement succeeded not only in legally desegregating public spaces, but in culturally desegregating the concept of childhood itself."[84]

But childhood innocence requires not just whiteness; it requires sexual ignorance and chastity. And just as the black child is not innocent by virtue of being black, the sexual child is not innocent by virtue of being sexual. The child or teen of color — figured as a teen mother or "baby daddy" — is not innocent by virtue (or vice) of being both black and sexual. In the minds of most white New Yorkers in 1989, the boys accused of raping the Central Park jogger were not children any more than a wolf pup is a child. In fact, the case inspired legislation nationwide to prosecute juveniles as adults, policies that have largely affected youth of color.

Those prosecutions, coupled with the broadening and hardening of sex crimes law, are capturing more and more children of all races. A quarter of convicted sex offenders are minors, eleven to seventeen years old; 16 percent are under twelve. "The single age with the greatest number of offenders from the perspective of law enforcement was age 14" — the same age at which the Adam Walsh Act mandates certain offenders be registered.[85]

What did these young criminals do? My own research suggests that the answer is not much. Some engaged in consensual sex — mutual masturbation and blowjobs mostly — with teens or pubescent kids a little younger than themselves. Some viewed online images of other naked kids.[86] Like their adult counterparts, many end up on the registry for "indecent liberties with a minor" — a crime that in most states includes such noncontact offenses as speaking "lewdly" to a child or (more commonly) to an agent masquerading as a thirteen- or fourteen-year-old online. In 1999, the papers reported a "child sex ring" in York Haven, Pennsylvania, in which "children as young as 7 . . . taught each other to have sex" (children can be "ring" members too). One of the defendants, an eleven-year-old girl, was convicted of rape.[87] The two most common transgressions of minor-age sex offenders, according to the Bureau of Justice Statistics, are "forcible sodomy" — anal or oral sex — and "forcible fondling." Under BJS definitions, a "forcible" offense is one committed by physical force or psychological coercion, "or *not forcibly or against the person's will where the victim is incapable of giving consent because of his/her youth* or because of his/her temporary or permanent mental or physical incapacity" (italics mine). That is, a child engaged in sex play with a minor child may be "forcing" him or her statutorily, but not actually.[88]

Also adding to the criminalization of child sexuality is a diagnosis introduced in the 1980s of "sexual behavior problems," manifested by "children who molest," who may be as young as three. Sometimes kids do coerce, bribe, or threaten others. But mostly their questionable — or prosecutable — acts include such normative behaviors as putting things inside orifices and masturbating a lot. The treatment, which if the child is old enough happens in juvenile detention, involves keeping daily diaries of "deviant fantasies" and detailing every masturbatory episode; interdictions on swearing, touching, or being touched; and, once the child is broken, apologizing on his knees before the "victim." Some of it resembles the dolorously destructive 1950s and '60s "cures" for homosexuality. It is interesting to note that the diagnosis and early treatment were developed at Children's Institute International, by the feminist social worker Kee MacFarlane — pioneer of extracting accusations of satanic ritual abuse from toddlers in the McMartin trials — and her colleague Toni Cavanaugh Johnson.[89]

TWO PANICS, POINTS OF CONVERGENCE

The war on drugs and the war on sex are both legal campaigns born in moral panic. Both target stigmatized behaviors — from using drugs to queer sex, including sex for money and sex with or between minors — as vices to be eradicated. Both exaggerate the harms of these behaviors to society and conflate victimless transgressions with crimes of violence. The first has overwhelmingly targeted poor men of color. The second has created a new class of outcasts, many of them white. Both enlist citizens as informants, guards, and enforcers of a police state that divides communities, devastates families and individuals, including children, and fills our prisons to bursting.

This chapter has identified some of the divisions and limitations —ideological, strategic, and theoretical— within and among the feminist anti-violence, gay liberation, anti-racist, and anti-carceral movements that have prevented progressives from working to eradicate one of the sex panic's most egregious legacies, Megan's Laws and the SORN regime. But there are also many points where the grievances and visions of these movements and of sex offenders themselves converge. Mapping some of these may suggest routes toward ending sexual violence without sacrificing social or legal justice.

Stigma: An Equal-Opportunity Destroyer

There might be some ways to equal the racial scores in the SORN regime. For instance, some anti-violence feminists (like those Rose Corrigan interviews) seem to favor eliminating the incest exemption for public registration and community notification. The desired end is public awareness: alerting people to the prevalence of family abuse and the magnitude of the harm it inflicts.[90]

Doing this might have the side effect of sprinkling more white faces around the Internet registries. But it makes no sense as policy. Community notification is meant to enhance public safety. But the *only thing* public registry accomplishes is social and economic isolation of the registrant, which may contribute to recidivism rather than reduce it.[91] Successful reintegration into the community is the best approach to crime prevention. As for preventing incest, broadcasting the personal information of an uncle who has sexually abused his niece does not improve her private safety either.

At this point, any reason the state cooks up for preserving the offender's privacy is a good one — *even if it results in furthering misconceptions* about the prevalence and harm of various sex acts. Activists and public intellectuals should educate the public about the causes and harms of sexual violence. But the sex offender registry is not a teaching tool.

Similarly, racial stereotypes have shaped our ideas about what constitutes a sex crime and who commits it. Daniel Filler argues that the pain of sex offender registration and notification is especially acute for African American men. Within communities "already devastated by the social consequences of mass incarceration," he says, "the side effects of Megan's Laws — shame, social disconnection, and exclusion — take a uniquely high toll."[92]

Perhaps this is true. But sex offender laws disperse pain beyond its usual sufferers, creating a new population of the vilified, impoverished, and disenfranchised that crosses race, class, and age. Interviews and surveys of registered sex offenders universally elicit feelings of extreme anger, fear, frustration, and despair.[93]

There is no justice in trying to make SORN more racially balanced or "fair." Registration and notification policies are another weapon in the war on men of color and also on sexual nonconformers of all races. In fact, the registry may be more pernicious than incarceration, in that it enlists the community in enforcing the offender's punishment. Justice demands that progressives work together to shut the sex offender registry down altogether.

Sex Panic Victimizes Women . . .

Just as women and girls are overwhelmingly the victims of sex crimes, just as legal reforms to combat sexual violence against women have inflicted state violence on some women, the child sex abuse panic disproportionately hurts women, too.

Women may be more likely than men to be falsely accused and convicted of harm to children. Among the 1,281 reported exonerations in the University of Michigan and Northwestern Law Schools' National Registry of Exonerations at the end of 2013,[94] fewer than 8 percent were women. The crimes for which these women were convicted were similar to those of the men. But there was one "conspicuous exception. Nearly a third of both genders were convicted of sexual assaults, but the men were overwhelmingly convicted of raping adult victims, and the women were all convicted of child sex abuse."

Women were also "heavily concentrated" among exonerations for what the registry calls "fabricated crimes" — cases in which no crime occurred (as opposed to those in which the wrong person was convicted). Almost two-thirds of the female exonerees were convicted of such nonexistent crimes (compared with 19 percent of men); most of the charges involved child sex abuse. In fact, more than half (55 percent) of all the exonerations for fabricated crimes involved child sex abuse convictions. Of these, two-thirds "were generated in a wave of child sex abuse hysteria that swept the country 30 years ago."[95] When they are exonerated, the San Antonio Four will be entered on the registry in this category.

By understanding the multifarious, sometimes contradictory workings of sexism, women's advocates of all stripes can find common cause in challenging it.

Most responsible for the alarming rise in criminal sex convictions of both minors and young adults is the gradual rise of the age of consent from as young as ten to as old as eighteen, depending on the state. The age below which a person's picture may be called child pornography is eighteen, which covers a lot of pictures, including mainstream advertising.

Much grief, not only for the convicted party but also for the "victim" inveigled into testifying against him, would be avoided by lowering the age of consent.[96] If we are concerned about adult exploitation of young people, as we should be, we could adopt a law like the one on the Netherlands' books from 1990 to 2002: people from twelve to sixteen could have sex with whomever they pleased, but they could also bring a claim of adult exploitation to the state, to be adjudicated in the family welfare system, not the criminal courts. The law recognized both the sexual autonomy of young people and also their vulnerability to harm from adults.[97]

Working toward such change makes sense for queer activists. So outré has child sexual activity become in the United States that we might as well call it queer. It makes sense for incarceration's opponents of color, too, who have seen sexuality used to stigmatize their girls and push both boys and girls into the juvenile justice system. But reducing the age of consent can also be a feminist position, as a little-known chapter of women's history reminds us.

In 1978, the year Boston's lesbian feminists took up arms against NAMBLA in the name of exploited gay boys, a group of New Jersey feminists led by the National Organization for Women (NOW) successfully lobbied lawmakers to lower the age of consent from sixteen to thirteen. The initiative was part of a revision of the state's penal code that also abolished anti-sodomy statutes, a change lesbian and gay activists pushed for. The feminists — no pack of radicals, these — argued that the higher age of consent "watered down" enforcement of rape laws. By prosecuting consensual teen sex, they said, it diverted attention from forcible rape. They wanted protection for unwanted sex without punishing girls for being sexual.[98]

The statute New Jersey ended up with was not perfect. Bowing to protests by a coalition of parents, priests, and police, the women accepted a compromise that kept the age of consent at sixteen, with a "Romeo and Juliet" exception for partners less than four years apart in age (gay activists defended the removal of sodomy provisions). But just like the insight of women of color that rape law reform without attention to race or poverty could harm marginalized women, the New Jersey feminists understood that without thinking about age, such laws could backfire against the intended objects of protection.

The women's liberation movement began with a utopian vision of sexual liberation. It also revealed the pervasiveness of sexual violence. But if we are to end sexual violence by cracking down on sexual freedom, we are trading one oppression for another. The Left has a bad record where freedom is concerned, especially sexual freedom and even more especially the sexual freedom of women, queers, and the nonconformers of desire. In the past, the first priority was economic justice, from which freedom was supposed to follow naturally (it didn't). Criminal justice and personal safety must not be bought at the price of sexual justice and freedom. We can be safe and free too.

Sexual McCarthyism Divides and Conquers

People labeled perverts are tempted to win credibility by promoting the punishment of someone more perverted than they. Yes, it is regrettable, they aver, but the "worst of the worst" must be in solitary confinement, sentenced to life without parole, on the registry, chemically castrated, and so on. Even convicted pedophiles demonize the offenders they believe are worse than themselves. A sample letter to the U.S. Sentencing Commission posted on the RSOL-affiliated CautionClick.com asked visitors to the website to press for lighter penalties for viewing child pornography. But, it stressed, producers and distributors "should be sentenced to the maximum under the law."[99] Reading this, I was reminded of the thick book of ACLU policies I examined in the mid-1990s. The statement on child pornography — the organization could not settle on a policy — was the only one including a recommendation for what *should* be censored.[100]

The "worst of the worst" have included communists, terrorists, gang members, and pedophiles, to name a few. The boundaries around citizenship keep shifting and shrinking, as more people are exiled to Constitution-free zones. "First, they came for the sex offenders," I titled a book review. Anyone could be next. Let's not turn each other in.

The Enemies of Our Friends

On the neo-Nazi white supremacist online forum Stormfront.org, the word "pedophile" multiplies the loathsomeness of the racial or religious Other, and vice versa (*sic* all, pun intended):

"Jew Rabbi pedophile arrested in California from charges in NY"
"See what islam promotes, all of these pedophile worshipers should be made to stay in their own country. Deport this muslim w(B)itch."
"Minor Sexually Assaulted By Black Pedophile Turcuois Gay"
"Samantha Runnion, age 5. Kidnapped, raped, and murdered by a mestizo."

Sometimes it takes being lumped together by those who hate us to recognize how much we have in common.

WHAT ABOUT THE REFORM SEX OFFENDER LAWS (RSOL) NETWORK?

Where is the sex offender in all this? How does he understand his predicament? What does he want? With varying degrees of eloquence, the RSOLs articulate the troubles with the laws: they don't protect children but inflict suffering on registrants' families; they make no distinctions between the dangerous and the harmless; they exact punishment beyond the sentence and are therefore unconstitutional. In fact, they do nothing less than banish people from civilization. "The label of sex offender is so widely and indiscriminately used that it has dehumanized thousands of people who pose no threat to public safety, hampering their ability to become productive members of society," reads the website of Texas Voices for Reason and Justice.

Texas Voices is a good example of the challenge of politicizing the RSOLs. It is the largest of the groups — more than 700 members, out of the state's 80,500-plus registered offenders — and probably the most effective, thanks to its executive director, an indefatigable organizer, savvy lobbyist, and compassionate and patient person, whose son is a sex offender.

Like RSOLs around the country, Texas Voices has given some of its members the courage and support to speak publicly as registered offenders about the sex offender regime. Some Texas Voices members participated in a letter-writing campaign to the *San Antonio Express-News* to urge the editor to let an investigative reporter finish and publish a piece about the San Antonio Four, who live in the organization's home city; some went to screenings of the documentary-in-progress, where supporters gathered. But most of the offenders and their families who sign up with Texas Voices are so consumed and demoralized by the registry, so desperate and poor, that any activity beyond survival is a superhuman task. Formal disenfranchisement is not the only way mass incarceration and its collateral consequences prevent felons from participating as citizens.

But sex offenders are also crippled by the effects of sex offender treatment, which figures the person who commits a sex "crime" in much the same way that Alcoholics Anonymous regards the alcoholic — as incurable and in need of close self-management. Coupled with the treatment, the effort of compliance with the myriad rules of registration constantly reminds the registered sex offender, as the 613 daily obligations of *halachah* remind the Jew of her Jewishness, of his identity as a guilty man.

Lots of people convicted in the war on drugs know the laws are crazy: smoking weed should not be a crime. But it is the rare sex offender who will venture that the law he broke shouldn't be a law in the first place. Just as the law makes few distinctions between serious crimes and obnoxious or simply unconventional sexual behavior, even the sex offender who has harmed no one rues his "mistake" or "stupidity" — implying that he deserved punishment, just not forever. The sample letter to the Sentencing Commission posted on CautionClick.com does not argue for decriminalization of viewing child pornography, after all, only for lighter penalties.

The sex offender regime promotes solipsism, docility, guilty conscience, and self-disgust in its subjects — not exactly a recipe for militancy. How can such a demoralized and humiliated population be politically mobilized?

RESTORATIVE JUSTICE

The first step in politicizing and mobilizing the sex offender is to rehumanize him, both in his own eyes and in the eyes of others, including progressives, enabling those who have been queasy about making alliances with "child molesters" to understand them as brothers under the thumb of the carceral state.

A personal, quasi-clinical way this happens for sex offenders coming out of prison are Circles of Support and Accountability, or COSAs. A COSA is a small group of trained community volunteers who support the "core member" — he's not called an ex-prisoner or offender — in dealing with the practical, social, and emotional problems of reentering life on the outside. The volunteers also attempt to help him learn new thoughts and behaviors to prevent committing another crime, doing everything from driving him to the doctor's office to receiving his midnight phone calls. COSAs have shown significant success in reducing reoffense in the clients, who are not uncommonly compulsive repeat violent offenders.[101]

The COSA is a form of restorative justice (RJ), a set of practices based on the idea that if it's the state's job to enforce the law, it's up to the community to restore peace (COSAS are actually a hybrid, financed by the Department of Corrections and run by nonprofits or churches, which work in collaboration with parole officers). As state-administered retribution for lawbreaking continues to make no dent in interpersonal violence, and to inflict its own violence on millions, restorative justice is gaining the commitment of a growing number of clinicians, lawyers, educators, child protection and even corrections professionals, as well as feminist anti-violence activists, criminal justice reformers, and prison abolitionists.

The applications of RJ range from "peace circles" for families torn by abuse or high school students threatening other students to truth and reconciliation commissions in countries riven by civil war and massive neighbor-on-neighbor atrocities.

Restorative justice does not talk about offenders and victims; it speaks in terms of harm: the person responsible for it and the person subjected to it. It recognizes that harm to an individual is harm to a community as well. On the principle that hurt people hurt others, it cares about both the harm-doer and the person he harms. Violence is not just an act; it also implies a relationship, even if it's a bad one.

At every step, RJ is the antithesis of the criminal justice system. In court, the prosecutor represents the "people" but the victim may never be heard. In RJ, the victim speaks, gives testimony to her pain, and expresses her needs and desires. In the criminal justice system, the defense attorney endeavors to minimize or disprove her client's accountability, even if the person did the crime; the harm-doer may come to believe that story, or even feel like a victim himself. Community participants in RJ hold the harm-doer accountable, with reparations realized in words and deeds.

The state-administered partner to restorative justice is "responsive regulation," which uses the least coercive and intrusive measures possible to move people into accord with prosocial norms. These tactics are built on the proven principle that people treated with fairness and respect by government are more likely to obey the law.[102]

In recognizing that everyone has harmed and been harmed — that we are all offenders and victims, guilty and innocent — restorative justice resists essentialism. Mimi Kim, a longtime anti-violence worker in communities of color in the San Francisco Bay Area, remembers that she and her comrades "feared that if we slipped away from the binaries, we risked colluding with the people doing harm [and] endangering people." On the us-against-them, criminal/victim, innocent woman/guilty man matrix, there was no room for a batterer who was sometimes a good father or a woman subjected to abuse who considered her relationship worth keeping — minus the violence.[103] It was not until the twenty-first century, in an experimental program called Creative Interventions, that Kim and her coworkers began "to address power inequalities without getting trapped in binaries" and to "reclaim community spaces of authority," where violence is condemned and restitution pursued without police or legal intervention.[104]

I met Kim in the summer of 2014 at a restorative justice conference in Vermont, whose keynote speaker was University of Pennsylvania sociologist and legal scholar Dorothy Roberts, author of the seminal *Killing the Black Body: Race, Reproduction, and the Meaning of Liberty*. Roberts called for moving "beyond reforming dominant forms of punishment to fundamentally transform the meaning of justice."

From restoration to transformation to liberation: that's the cry of generationFIVE and allies like INCITE! Women of Color Against Violence and the prison abolitionist group Critical Resistance. Gen5's mission bespeaks both realism and vision: to eliminate sexual abuse in five generations — a hundred years at least, but still an almost giddily ambitious timeline. Many activists, even the most radical, are resigned to living with the sex offender registry for the long foreseeable future. They'd rather focus on campaigns that have a better chance of success. But is abolishing the registry any less daunting than, say, putting the private prison industry out of business or ending sexual abuse in a century?

Restorative justice may offer a space within which mainstream anti-violence feminists and anti-essentialist anti-violence workers, queers, people of color, and prison abolitionists can talk to one another, in spite of unhappy histories and even enduring hostilities.

It may also be a safe place to hear the isolated sex offender. The RSOLS do not generally speak the same language as left and progressive movements. In large part, where their members have any identifiable political analysis at all, right-wing libertarianism would be the closest description: get the state out of my life, period. It's not hard to see why. But rejecting the state's punitive intrusion does not have to mean resigning oneself to the state's neglect. Ex-felons have their citizenship rights seized. They don't forfeit their human rights at the same time.

Similarly, if women and children subjected to intimate abuse encounter only additional abuse if they call the police, they learn not to ask for the state's assistance.[105] Restorative justice offers avenues to confronting interpersonal violence without involving the criminal justice system. Still, victims' services are now so entwined with the courts that it is difficult to get public services, especially in an emergency, without knocking on the prosecutor's door. Movements that seek to untangle personal conflict resolution from the penal system need at the same time to hold the state accountable for bettering citizens' lives in other ways.

This is one of neoliberalism's most brilliant sleights of hand: whittle government down to its most noxious functions, generate such hostility to the state that people cannot conceive of a benign, much less helpful or just, state; sit back and wait until people cease to demand assistance and then grow suspicious of and even hostile toward it — namely, popular opposition to Obamacare. Communities of color experience every day the replacement of public services with hyper-policing. Members of RSOLs come to need public services because the state is hyper-policing them and taking away their ability to find housing, make a living, or look after their children. Understanding these shared predicaments and strategizing to overcome them may be a point of convergence between progressive movements and the grassroots movement of sex offenders.

HUMAN RIGHTS FOR ALL

The sex offender's voice is important because the regime that oppresses him does not oppress only him. The state uses his treatment to habituate the public to the dehumanization of all offenders. His position as scum of the earth stands for all who were left behind when the factories closed and the prisons went up: hazardous waste to be inventoried, warehoused, and destroyed.

This is the function of the supermax prison as well, which selects the human detritus supposedly so toxic that it must be quarantined in lead boxes for years. A campaign to shut down Illinois's torturous Tamms supermax prison offers an example that progressives could follow to end the sex offender regime.

Tamms Year Ten, a coalition of artists, community activists, civil libertarians, and former inmates and their families organized by "legislative artist" Lauri Jo Reynolds and others, was launched in 2009. The campaign employed techniques ranging from conventional lobbying and petitions to the collective creation of enormous outdoor art pieces, slowly winning over skeptical lawyers, hostile union members, timid legislators, and quiescent human rights advocates. After four years, Illinois governor Pat Quinn signed the order to close Tamms.

What the organizers understood was that in order to generate the public sympathy to mobilize sufficient political will to get the government to close Tamms, they had first to humanize the men inside. That effort began by sending the prisoners poems and photographs. Letters came back expressing astonishment: "Hi Committee, is this for real? I can't believe someone cares enough to send a pick-me-up to the worst-of-the-worst." After a while, the inmates were speaking up for themselves. The crowning moment may have come when Quinn put pen to paper. But the campaign's supreme achievement — one that other progressives can look to as model and inspiration — was persuading both people on the outside and those inside the box that the "worst of the worst" are people.

One of the most beautiful actions of Tamms Year Ten was a march of mothers and former inmates, who carried placards modeled on those of the striking Memphis sanitation workers, an all-black force whom Martin Luther King Jr. addressed the night of his assassination in 1968. "I *Am* a Mom," the women's signs declared. The men's: "I *Am* a Man." The sex offender is a man, possessor of inalienable human rights and worth.

NOTES

I'd like to thank Ann Snitow, Debbie Nathan, Roger Lancaster, Trevor Hoppe, David Halperin, and Erica Meiners, whose generous and incisive readings improved this manuscript greatly.

1. Michelle Mondo, "Woman Recants Accusation of Sex Assault," *San Antonio Express-News*, September 15, 2012; Linda Rodriguez McRobbie, "How Junk Science and Anti-Lesbian Prejudice Got Four Women Sent to Prison for More Than a Decade," Slate.com, December 4, 2013.

2. Deborah Esquenazi, dir., *Southwest of Salem: The Story of the San Antonio Four* (Motto Pictures and Naked Edge Films, 2016).

3. Two recent cases: Millionaire Gigi Jordan murdered her autistic son to protect him from further abuse by his father, one of more than twenty people he allegedly

told her sexually tormented him and performed satanic abuse such as forcing him to drink blood and kill animals. James C. McKinley Jr., "At Murder Trial, Mother Tells of Abuse She Believes Son Suffered," *New York Times*, October 16, 2014, A29. Another is Malthe Thomsen, a Danish teaching intern accused, against all evidence to the contrary, of sexually abusing children at a New York preschool. Javier C. Hernandez, "At Manhattan Preschool Accounts of Sex Abuse Case Differ," *New York Times*, July 24, 2014, A22.

4. American Bar Association, National Inventory of the Collateral Consequences of Conviction, http://www.abacollateralconsequences.org/.

5. Uniform Law Commission, Uniform Collateral Consequences of Conviction Act, http://www.uniformlaws.org/Act.aspx?title=Collateral%20Consequences%20Of%20Conviction%20Act.

6. These data, compiled from the state governments and the National Center for Missing and Exploited Children, do not include Native American reservations, which also maintain registries. Also, numbers of people on the registries are kept separately from others on parole and probation. Parents for Megan's Law and the Crime Victims Center, "Number of Registrants Reported by State/Territory," March 31, 2016, https://www.parentsformeganslaw.org/public/meganReportCard .html.

7. Jacob Wetterling Crimes Against Children Act 1994; Megan's Law 1996; Adam Walsh Child Protection and Safety Act 2006.

8. Yasmin Nair, "Beth Richie on Race, Gender and the 'Prison Nation,'" *Windy City Times*, May 22, 2013.

9. This is the policy, on second offense, in California, where the state auditor also recently reported that as late as 2013, prison medical practitioners were sterilizing female inmates without their informed consent. California State Auditor, "Sterilization of Female Inmates: Some Inmates Were Sterilized Unlawfully, and Safeguards Designed to Limit Occurrences of the Procedure Failed," Report 2013-120 (2013).

10. Most convincing to me are data showing they've had no effect on crime one way or the other. See, e.g., A. Y. Agan, "Sex Offender Registries: Fear without Function?" *Journal of Law and Economics* 54 (February 2011): 207–239.

11. Jonathan McFadden, "SC Couple Sentenced to Life for Killing Convicted Sex Offender," *Charlotte Observer*, May 6, 2014.

12. Smith v. Doe (01-729) 538 U.S. 84 (2003), Connecticut Dept. of Public Safety v. Doe, 538 U.S. 1 (2003). In Kansas v. Hendricks, 521 U.S. 346 (1997), the Supreme Court majority upheld the state's civil commitment law, deciding tautologically that because the law did not establish criminal proceedings, the involuntary confinement it effected was not double jeopardy.

13. See, e.g., Human Rights Watch, *Raised on the Registry: The Irreparable Harm of Placing Children on Sex Offender Registries in the US* (2013); Human Rights Watch, *No Easy Answers: Sex Offender Laws in the US* 19, no. 4(G) (September 2007).

14. Joseph Fischel, "Against Nature, against Consent: A Sexual Politics of Debility," *differences* 24 (2013): 55–103.

15. Erica R. Meiners, "Never Innocent: Feminist Troubles with Sex Offender Registries and Protection in a Prison Nation," *Meridians: feminism, race, transnationalism* 9 (2009): 34.

16. She subsequently told me not to make too much of the brevity of her presentation — she was sick that day. Still, the tension around the topic is palpable, even in the video.

17. One interesting attempt at synthesis was a University of Chicago symposium called "Are Sex Offenders the New Queers?" It was held off campus to make it available to the community, but sex offenders in the audience reportedly met insensitive responses from some panelists. Thoughtful preparation for such encounters is needed.

18. Elizabeth Bernstein, "Carceral Politics as Gender Justice? The 'Traffic in Women' and Neoliberal Circuits of Crime, Sex, and Rights," *Theory and Society* 41, no. 3 (2012): 33–259.

19. Michelle Alexander, *The New Jim Crow: Mass Incarceration in the Age of Colorblindness* (New York: The New Press, 2010)

20. Ann Snitow, *The Feminism of Uncertainty: A Gender Diary* (Durham, NC: Duke University Press, 2015).

21. Only one case went to trial. The defendant was convicted of two counts of fellating a fifteen-year-old male hustler and sentenced to five years' probation. Art Cohen, "The Boston/Boise Affair, 1977–78," *Gay & Lesbian Review Worldwide*, March 1, 2003, http://www.thefreelibrary.com/The+Boston%2fBoise+Affair%2c+1977–78.+(Essay). -a098247486.

22. "History of the Body Politic: A Timeline," University of Western Ontario Hudler Archives, http://www.uwo.ca/pridelib/bodypolitic/bphistory/timeline.htm (accessed August 3, 2016).

23. Densen-Gerber later confessed she'd gotten to 1.2 million by quadrupling a figure a journalist said he had "thrown out" to get a rise from law enforcement. She subsequently doubled that quadrupled estimate. No snuff films have ever been found. Densen-Gerber later left Odyssey House under suspicion of embezzlement and humiliating and coercive methods. Martin was removed from his post for harassing witnesses and falsifying evidence. See Judith Levine, *Harmful to Minors: The Perils of Protecting Children from Sex* (Minneapolis: University of Minnesota Press, 2002), 239nn62–69.

24. Protection of Children Against Sexual Exploitation Act of 1977, Pub. L. No. 95-225, 92 Stat. 7 (codified as amended at 18 U.S.C. §§ 2251–2252, 2256, 2423 (2006)) (originally enacted Feb. 6, 1978).

25. U.S. House of Representatives, *Sexual Exploitation of Children: Hearings Before the Subcommittee on Crime of the Committee on the Judiciary* (Washington, D.C.: Government Printing Office, 1977).

26. See, e.g., JoAnn Wypijewski, "The Passion of Father Paul Shanley," *Legal Affairs*, September/October 2004, http://www.legalaffairs.org/issues/September-October -2004/feature_wypijewski_sepoct04.msp.

27. NB: persons, not adults. Gay Activists Alliance, "Repeal the New York Consensual Sodomy Statute!" New York (n.d.).

28. Leigh Goodmark, "Reframing Domestic Violence Law and Policy: An Anti-Essentialist Proposal," *Journal of Law & Policy* 31 (2009): 40.

29. Susan Brownmiller, *Against Our Will: Men, Women and Rape* (New York: Simon & Schuster, 1975), 15–16.

30. Andrea Dworkin, "Sexual Economics: The Terrible Truth," reprinted in *Letters from a War Zone: Writings 1976–1989* (New York: Dutton, 1989), 119.

31. Judith Lewis Herman, *Father-Daughter Incest* (Cambridge, MA: Harvard University Press, 1981).

32. E.g., Philip Schehadi, "Conflict Over Speaker Splits March on Albany, *Gay Community News*, April 26, 1980, 3; James Jackson, "Boy Love Controversy Erupts at Gay Conference," *Gay Community News*, November 13, 1982, 3.

33. David Thorstad, "Man/Boy Love and the American Gay Movement," in *Male Intergenerational Intimacy*, ed. Theo Sandfort and JD Edward Brongersma (New York: Harrington Park Press, 1991), 258–259.

34. Philip Schehadi, "Adult/Youth Relationships Discuss[ed?] at NYC Forum," *Gay Community News*, July 5, 1980, 7.

35. Ibid.

36. Beth Kelly, "On Woman/Girl Love — Or, Lesbians Do 'Do It,'" *Gay Community News*, March 3, 1979, 5.

37. "Lack of Support from Adult Gays Makes Life Difficult in Boston," in *Growing Up Gay* [pamphlet] (Ann Arbor, MI: Youth Liberation Press, 1978).

38. Eric E. Rofes, "On the Viability of Coalitions of Lesbians and Gay Men: New York and Beyond," *Gay Community News*, June 28, 1980, 5.

39. Gayle Rubin, "Thinking Sex: Notes for a Radical Theory of the Politics of Sexuality," in *Pleasure and Danger: Exploring Female Sexuality*, ed. Carole S. Vance (Boston: Routledge and Kegan Paul, 1984), 267–319.

40. In response to the protest, Barnard College confiscated the seventy-two-page conference "diary" the organizers had prepared, and the Rubinstein Foundation

canceled funding of the next year's conference. Carole S. Vance, *Pleasure and Danger*, 431–439. Members of WAP would later apply the same reasoning to sex work: no matter what a worker said, nobody could conceivably volunteer to strip or give blow jobs for a living. Therefore, they must be victims of coercion. Still later, they began conflating all sex work with trafficking.

41. Jim D'Entremont, "The Devil in Gay, Inc.: How the Gay Establishment Ignored a Sex Panic Fueled by Homophobia," Friends of Justice, http://bobchatelle.net/the-devil-in-gay-inc-2 (accessed July 15, 2016). See also http://freebaran.org.

42. Daniel M. Filler, "Silence and the Racial Dimension of Megan's Law," *Iowa Law Review* 89 (2004): 1547–1548, http://works.bepress.com/daniel_filler/2.

43. "What's Queer about Sex Offenders? Or Are Sex Offenders the New Queers?" University of Chicago public symposium, 2010.

44. Meiners, "Never Innocent," 34–38.

45. Rose Corrigan, *Up Against a Wall: Rape Reform and the Failure of Success* (New York: NYU Press, 2013), 9.

46. For a discussion of the role of rage in feminism, see Judith Levine, *My Enemy, My Love: Man-Hating and Ambivalence in Women's Lives* (New York: Doubleday, 1992).

47. Debbie Nathan and Michael Snedeker, *Satan's Silence: Ritual Abuse and the Making of a Modern American Witch Hunt* (New York: Basic, 1995), 22–23. Judith Lewis Herman, *Father-Daughter Incest* (Cambridge, MA: Harvard University Press, 1981), 160.

48. Lucy Berliner and Mary Kay Barbieri, "The Testimony of the Child Victim of Sexual Assault," *Journal of Social Issues* 40 (summer 1984): 125–137; Lucy Berliner, "The Child and the Criminal Justice System," in *Rape and Sexual Assault*, ed. Ann W. Burgess (New York: Garland Publishing, 1985), 199–208; Stephen J. Ceci and Maggie Bruck, "Suggestibility of the Child Witness: A Historical Review and Synthesis," *Psychological Bulletin* 113 (May 1993): 403–439.

49. President's Task Force on Victims of Crime Final Report, December 1982.

50. Corrigan, *Up Against a Wall*, 17.

51. Wendy Kaminer, "Victims vs. Suspects," *American Prospect*, December 19, 2001.

52. Elizabeth Bumiller, "Feminist Collaboration with the State in Response to Sexual Violence: Lessons from the American Experience," in *Gender, Violence, and Human Security*, ed. A. M. Tripp, M. M. Ferree, and C. Ewig (New York: NYU Press, 2013), 191–213.

53. For example, Nolan Feeney, "FBI Recovers 168 Children from Sex-Trafficking Rings across the U.S.," *Time*, June 23, 2014.

54. Combahee River Collective Statement 1977. In 1986, Gloria Hull, Patricia Bell Scott, and Barbara Smith would elegantly sum up the conundrum of black lesbians

in their anthology *All the Women Are White, All the Blacks Are Men, But Some of Us Are Brave.*

55. Kate Pickert, "What's Wrong with the Violence Against Women Act?" *Time*, February 27, 2013.

56. Elias Walker Vitulli, "Queering the Carceral: Intersecting Queer/Trans Studies and Critical Prison Studies," GLQ 19 (2012): 111–123; Queers for Economic Justice, http://q4ej.org (now closed).

57. Arielle Levin Becker, "Preparing Prisoners for Return to Society," *Gannett New Jersey*, January 12, 2007.

58. Karen van Gundy, "Substance Abuse in Rural and Small Town America," Carsey Institute Reports on Rural America (Durham, NH: University of New Hampshire, 2006); Eugene Jarecki, *The House I Live In* (Charlotte Street Films, 2012).

59. Natalie Byfield, "The Legacy of the Central Park 'Wilding' Case," *Huffington Post*, May 27, 2014, http://www.huffingtonpost.com/natalie-byfield/the-legacy-of-the-central_b_5398013.html.

60. See Bernstein, "Carceral Politics as Gender Justice?"; Bumiller, "Gender, Justice, and Neoliberal Transformations," *Scholar & Feminist Online* 11 (fall 2012/spring 2013), ed. Elizabeth Bernstein and Janet Jakobsen, http://sfonline.barnard.edu/gender-justice-and-neoliberal-transformations/.

61. Roger Lancaster, *Sex Panic and the Punitive State* (Berkeley: University of California Press, 2011), 221–223.

62. Lancaster, *Sex Panic and the Punitive State*, 94.

63. Sentencing Project, "Racial Disparity" (chart and blog), http://www.sentencingproject.org/template/page.cfm?id=122.

64. Alissa R. Ackerman, Andrew J. Harris, Jill S. Levenson, and Kristen Zgoba, "Who Are the People in Your Neighborhood? A Descriptive Analysis of Individuals on Public Sex Offender Registries," *International Journal of Law and Psychiatry* 34 (2011): 153.

65. Another several hundred thousand are registered and not publicly listed.

66. Ackerman et al., "Who Are the People in Your Neighborhood? 153; U.S. Census 2010, http://www.census.gov/2010census/.

67. Filler, "Silence and the Racial Dimension of Megan's Law," 1539.

68. Filler, "Silence and the Racial Dimension of Megan's Law," 1550.

69. Lancaster, *Sex Panic and the Punitive State*, 247–251.

70. Filler, "Silence and the Racial Dimension of Megan's Law," 1557.

71. Douglas L. Epperson, Static-99 Coding Rules (Revised 2003), http://www.static99.org/; Minnesota Department of Corrections, Minnesota Sex Offender Screening Tool Revised (MN-SOST-R). Various analyses show that having a victim who is not a family member does correlate with higher rates of offending again, but

the level of force used has little predictive effect. Mario J. Scalora and Calvin Garvin, "A Multivariate Analysis of Sex Offender Recidivism," *International Journal of Offender Therapy and Comparative Criminology* 47 (2003): 310. But such predictions should be viewed cautiously. Tamara Rice Lave has shown that the Static-99 produces a massive number of false positives. In one calculation, the test "would recommend releasing 15 people who would re-offend and would recommend [civil commitment for] 275 people who would not re-offend." T. R. Lave, "Controlling the Offender: Sex, Mental Illness and the Static 99," Social Science Research Network, May 16, 2007, http://ssrn .com/abstract=987586 or http://dx.doi.org/10.2139/ssrn.987586.

72. Alejandro Leguizamo, Brooke Peltzman, Nicolas Carrasco, Michelle Nosal, and Leslie Woods, "Ethnic Differences among Incarcerated Sex Offenders" (Feinstein College of Arts & Sciences Faculty Papers, 2010), http://docs.rwu.edu/fcas_fp/37/.

73. Leguizamo et al., "Ethnic Differences."

74. See, e.g., Maria Cancian, Kristen Shook Slack, and Mi Youn Yang, "The Effect of Family Income on Risk of Child Maltreatment," Institute for Research on Poverty Discussion Paper no. 1385-10, http://www.irp.wisc.edu/publications/dps/pdfs /dp138510.pdf.

75. J. Eckenrode, E. G. Smith, M. E. McCarthy, and M. Dineen, "Income Inequality and Child Maltreatment in the United States," *Pediatrics* (2014), DOI: 10.1542/ peds.2013-1707.

76. Christopher Hartney and Linh Vuong, "Created Equal: Racial and Ethnic Disparities in the US Criminal Justice System," National Council on Crime & Delinquency (March 2009), 11.

77. On the other hand, racial disparities in sentencing and parole — in which African Americans are disproportionately sentenced to prison while whites get probation — may have less effect on the sex offender registries, since virtually no defendant whose plea bargain results in parole escapes registration and its collateral restrictions.

78. Brandon L. Garrett, *Convicting the Innocent: Where Criminal Prosecutions Go Wrong* (Cambridge, MA: Harvard University Press, 2012); Matthew Johnson, "Sex, Race, and Wrongful Conviction," *The Crime Report*, October 4, 2013, http://www .thecrimereport.org/news/articles/2013-10-sex-race-and-wrongful-conviction.

79. Lancaster, *Sex Panic and the Punitive State*, 247. The population at the Adult Diagnostic and Treatment Center in Avenel, New Jersey, a civil commitment facility for sex offenders, supposedly was about 56 percent white in 2005, compared with the state's general prison population, which is 63 percent black. Becker, "Preparing Prisoners for Return to Society." The racialized badness/illness distinction produces an ironic twist in a twisted system — the one instance in which being black or brown is an advantage: Nabbed, convicted, or locked up for an act presumably guided by

cold, conscious sanity, the man of color at least retains constitutional habeas corpus protections and Sixth Amendment due process rights. His white counterpart completes his prison term and, diagnosed as mad by a few state-appointed psychiatrists, ends up in the sex offender gulag with no constitutional rights and no definite date of release.

80. Filler, "Silence and the Racial Dimension of Megan's Law," 1539.

81. Soraya Chemaly, "How Did the FBI Miss Over 1 Million Rapes?" *The Nation*, June 30, 2014. It's also possible they are not higher, if rapes have in fact declined. Widely varying definitions of rape confound statistics almost fatally.

82. Angela Davis, "Rape, Racism and the Capitalist Setting," *Black Scholar* 9 (1978): 28.

83. The recent focus on college campus rape doesn't contradict this contention. American college students, especially girls, are regarded as children.

84. Robin Bernstein, *Racial Innocence: Performing American Childhood from Slavery to Civil Rights* (New York: NYU Press, 2011); see a synopsis at http://racialinnocence.blogspot.com/.

85. Howard N. Snyder, "Sexual Assault of Young Children as Reported to Law Enforcement: Victim, Incident, and Offender Characteristics" (U.S. Bureau of Justice Statistics, 2000), 8. So catastrophic are the lifelong effects on children of the sex offender registry that Human Rights Watch recently released a 114-page report called *Raised on the Registry: The Irreparable Harms of Placing Children on Sex Offender Registries in the US*.

86. Because it is illegal for any civilian, including journalists and scholars, to look at the images the state calls child pornography, it is impossible to know what images people are being convicted of viewing or possessing.

87. Levine, *Harmful to Minors*, 47.

88. Snyder, "Sexual Assault of Young Children as Reported to Law Enforcement," 8, 13.

89. Levine, *Harmful to Minors*, 45–67.

90. See, e.g., Corrigan, *Up Against a Wall*, 205–248.

91. A careful analysis of several data sets by Amanda Y. Agan at the University of Chicago finds that sex offender registration neither increases nor decreases the likelihood of reoffense. A. Y. Agan, "Sex Offender Registries: Fear without Function?" *Journal of Law and Economics* 54 (2011): 207–239.

92. Filler, "Silence and the Racial Dimension of Megan's Law," 1539.

93. Alissa R. Ackerman, Meghan Sacks, and Lindsay N. Osier, "The Experiences of Registered Sex Offenders with Internet Offender Registries in Three States," *Journal of Offender Rehabilitation* 52 (2013): 29–45. For some heartbreaking examples of life on the registry, go to http://PrisonTalk.com.

94. As of July 2014 there were 1,403 known exonerations. University of Michigan and Northwestern University National Registry of Exonerations (2014).

95. Samuel R. Gross, "Exonerations in the United States, 1989–2012: Report by the National Registry of Exonerations" (2012), 80, http://www.law.umich.edu/special /exoneration/Documents/exonerations_us_1989_2012_full_report.pdf.

96. Joseph Fischel advances an intriguing argument for getting rid of the concept of consent altogether. Fischel, "Against Nature."

97. Evidence of changing values about child sexuality: in 2001 the Dutch Parliament raised the age of consent from twelve to sixteen, with a rare unanimous vote. Gert Hekma, "How Libertine Is the Netherlands," in *Regulating Sex: The Politics of Intimacy and Identity*, ed. Elizabeth Bernstein and Laurie Shaffner (New York: Routledge, 2004), 211.

98. "A Look at New Jersey's Controversial New Sex Law for Minors," *Children's Legal Rights Journal* 31 (1979–1980), http://heinonline.org/HOL/LandingPage?handle =hein.journals/clrj1&div=28&id=&page=; Thorstad, "Man/Boy Love and the American Gay Movement," 257.

99. CautionClick: National Campaign for Reform, Sample letter to U.S. Sentencing Commission, July 2014, http://www.cautionclick.com/docs/ccncr-action-alert -senetencing-commission-20140624.pdf.

100. Civil libertarians were slow in general to catch on to the sex panic. For a long time, only the small National Coalition Against Censorship had the courage to challenge censorship of the newly expanding category called child pornography. In the early 1990s, when retired attorney Morton Stavis proposed to the Center for Constitutional Rights (CCR) that it support his appeal for Kelly Michaels, the board of the organization he founded wanted her first to be examined by a psychiatrist, presumably to assess whether she might actually have raped babies with forks and spoons and forced them to eat her feces. Ultimately, CCR's board refused to join Stavis. From a conversation with Debbie Nathan, who was at the board meeting.

101. Robin J. Wilson, Janice E. Picheca, and Michelle Prinzo, "Evaluating the Effectiveness of Professionally-Facilitated Volunteerism in the Community-Based Management of High-Risk Sexual Offenders: Part Two — A Comparison of Recidivism Rates," *Howard Journal* 46 (September 2007): 327–337.

102. Ian Ayres and John Braithwaite, *Responsive Regulation: Transcending the Deregulation Debate* (Oxford: Oxford University Press, 1995).

103. The other side of this coin: Lenore Walker, who developed the "battered woman's syndrome," testified for the defense in O. J. Simpson's trial, arguing that because the murder victim, Nicole Brown Simpson, had resisted, for instance, by calling the police numerous times, she was not suffering battered women's syndrome and therefore it was plausible that Simpson had not battered (or killed) her.

104. "Creative Interventions: Bridging the Gap between Restorative Justice and Grassroots Community Interventions Addressing Domestic Violence," breakout session, Restorative Justice, Responsive Regulation, and Complex Problems Conference, Burlington, VT, July 16, 2014.

105. See, e.g., Catherine Kaukinen, "The Help-Seeking Strategies of Female Violent-Crime Victims: The Direct and Conditional Effects of Race and the Victim-Offender Relationship," *Journal of Interpersonal Violence* 19 (2004): 967–990.

OWEN DANIEL-MCCARTER,

ERICA R. MEINERS, AND R. NOLL

|3|

Queer Disavowal

"Controversial" Crimes and Building Abolition

While unlikely actors such as Newt Gingrich, member of the conservative prison reform organization Right on Crime, lobby for sentencing reform and prison closure and herald the "end of mass incarceration," facets of our carceral regime remain untouched.[1] People convicted of sex crimes are, according to political scientist Marie Gottschalk, "the fastest growing segment of state and federal prison populations" due to "tougher sanctions."[2] Punishment continues after exiting prison. With over 800,000 individuals on sex offender registries, many convicted as minors, surveillance persists after release from prison.[3] In 2014 in New York, as the state pushed to close prisons, the *Washington Post* reported that dozens of people with convictions for sexual offenses were held after their release date because of their inability to secure housing thanks to laws that restricted their residences to more than 1,000 feet away from a school (including state- or non-state-sponsored shelters).[4] The hyper-vilification and increased criminalization of "sex offenders" stands in stark contrast to the growing bipartisan consensus that the "war on crime" and "war on drugs," in the words of President Bill Clinton, "sent everybody to jail for too long."[5] As criminal justice reform gains a tenacious foothold, interrogating the function of sex offender registries and community notification laws grows more imperative.

State and federal definitions of what qualifies as a sex offense vary and continue to expand. Gottschalk suggests that "pedophilia came to be viewed as interchangeable and synonymous with all sex offenders" in the 1980s, thereby fueling the escalating, unique, and exceptionally punitive state responses.[6] In

Illinois, sex offenses include criminal sexual assault, sexual abuse, child pornography, sexual exploitation of a child, and soliciting a child.[7] Juveniles are particularly vulnerable. A minor texting a nude selfie, an act done by one in five teenagers, is creating and circulating child pornography.[8] An adult engaging in this behavior (with other adults) would not be committing a crime. Once convicted, individuals are restricted in where they can live and are required to "register" their location through posted public notices, in online databases, and in some states, such as Louisiana, on state identification cards. Depending on the conviction and jurisdiction, this registration requirement can last for years or for a lifetime.

Notably, research consistently concurs that registries and community notification laws do *not* reduce child sexual violence, and "stranger danger" sexual violence against children is the *least* significant risk.[9] Available data clearly establish that for all children under eighteen, strangers are consistently the least likely to be the perpetrators of sexual assaults, generally less than 10 percent.[10] Gottschalk summarizes available research: "friends, acquaintances, and family members are responsible for more than 90 percent of all sexual abuse of children."[11] Yet the figure of the "stranger danger" child molester fuels harsher sentencing structures and longer registration requirements, and persistently presents a political roadblock to imagining a world without prisons. Registries and community notification requirements have also failed to prevent child sexual violence — which is still frequently unreported to law enforcement — or to produce accountable channels for public safety.

As many scholars have documented, pre-Stonewall-era gay (and lesbian) organizing featured anti-prison organizing: "publishing newsletters, investigating and publicizing prison conditions, offering legal counseling, organizing prison ministries, sponsoring pen-pal and outreach projects, and assisting parolees."[12] As policing and punishment shaped queer lives, liberation movements required prison justice analysis and organizing.[13] This roundtable suggests that not only do linkages between queers and "sex offenders" persist and necessitate closer interrogation, but dismantling our investments in a racialized carceral regime requires challenging our queer feelings, disavowals, and indifference to the supposedly "worst of the worst." Solidarities and shared analysis are critical in these moments of rethinking "mass incarceration." Yet mainstream gay and lesbian movements — with an emphasis on legislative and other "rights-based" agendas — are glaringly absent from critical criminal justice dialogues.

Located in Chicago, the three of us — Owen, Erica, and R. — continue to research, educate, advocate, and organize around and against the U.S. prison nation with a particular emphasis on naming how race, gender, and sexuality intersect with criminalization. Owen is a transgender activist who cofounded the Transformative Justice Law Project of Illinois (TJLP), which provides legal services, activist support, and educational materials for criminalized trans and gender-nonconforming people inside and outside of detention throughout the state of Illinois. The TJLP operates under a commitment to three core values: the right to gender self-determination, vision toward a long-term goal of prison abolition, and dedication to resisting state-sponsored systems of control through transformative justice and community empowerment models. Owen has also taught gender studies, U.S. civil rights law, and critical criminology at DePaul University and works with an organization that, among other things, provides advocacy in public K–12 school systems in Illinois to promote transformative justice practices as a response to bias-based violence. Erica has been working for the last sixteen years alongside people exiting prisons and jails through a "re-entry" program that assists people in accessing housing, employment, and education. Erica is member of the national organization Critical Resistance and is also involved with a number of local restorative and transformative justice initiatives, particularly alongside young people. As an academic, Erica struggles to support productive interventions in our prison nation. R. is currently a graduate student in political theory and anthropology at University of Chicago, trying to think and doubt and work around prison abolition, surveillance, and the politics of refusal. For the past six years, R. has been involved in informal support for queer folks incarcerated in a Midwest "women's" detention facility.[14]

The three of us have crossed paths in many ways. We are colleagues, comrades, and friends, and we continue to share resources, students, communities, support networks, and activism. This roundtable on overlapping sex offender, queer, and criminalization/incarceration organizing tensions provided an opportunity to reflect on the wider implications of our very local work, to build shared analysis, to consider accountability across our labors, and to think through our shared experiences of having to respond to questions about "the worst of the worst" in any discussion of prison abolition. Our conversation offers a snapshot — not any definitive state of queer anti-prison work. This dialogue unfolded, largely online, over several months, with editing assistance by Lark Mulligan, another collaborator from TJLP.

How does the category of "sex offender" emerge within your queer work?

ERICA: Queer is not typically how I define any of the work I do around the "criminal justice" landscape, in part because few of the people I work with within these spheres use this term. Yet in a sense all people coming out of prison and in prison could be understood as queer — marginal, marked, disqualified.

For most trying to rebuild life after prison, being on the registry complicates an already precarious pathway. Having any criminal record ensures that finding housing and employment will be difficult. For those convicted of sexual offenses the requirement to register is an added hurdle and stigma, and it ensures that finding a job and a place to live will be almost impossible.

I also work with young LGBTQ people, particularly those in public schools. Queer, in these spheres, is just one among many terms and tools for gender and sexual self-identification that are always tethered to race. Of course, just like the variance across our vocabularies in this roundtable, the language people use to describe their identity — specifically forms of racialized gender and sexuality — exceeds the institutional or standard terms made available (gay or lesbian or possibly transgender or trans) and is rarely static. Despite a significant increase in rights for select white, privileged lesbian and gay people, and a shift in access to formal state recognition for select non-heterosexuals and non-gender-conforming people, the lives of marginal, particularly non-white, LGBTQ young people are heavily regulated, often through institutions and structures less popularly associated with surveillance or policing: schools, healthcare, nonprofits, and/or child or social services. Queer self-advocacy, or young people's self-determination, is often marked by these institutions as disruptive and predatory.

R: Like Erica, few of the people I talk with who are confined in a "treatment unit" for those classified as women by the state in the large Midwest jail where I work use the term "queer," yet many identify as lesbian, gay, bisexual, transgender, and so on. This gender-responsive treatment unit provides supportive services and individualized treatment plans for what is assumed to be issues specific to women, such as trauma and substance abuse. In this jail the category of "sex offender" emerges most often in people's discussions of being violated, or written up or charged with a violation, for *any* alleged sexual contact within the unit. Jail staff and officers often regard any form of intimacy between those who are incarcerated as "sexual offenses," as the state assumes that forms of intimacy in custody are nonconsensual and therefore predatory.

Those most frequently designated as "predators," and thus vulnerable to accusations of a "sex offense," are often masculine-presenting folks of color on this unit.

OWEN: The majority — and I'd even wager the *vast* majority — of my abolitionist legal advocacy has been centered around transgender women. It is rare for me to hear one of my clients identify as "queer" and yet I think many would fall into the definition you suggest, Erica: marginal, marked, disqualified. Like R., I often hear painful accounts of people's experiences of sexual violence and, also quite commonly, how this sexual violence went unnoticed by the criminal legal system. Often the "offender" is a family member, a partner, or all too frequently a police officer or prison guard who is held completely unaccountable by our hyper-criminalization system. Sometimes I wonder who these "sex offenders" are who are actually prosecuted, because in my seven years of working with hundreds of transgender people, I know of only *one* person who was able to find a prosecutor to charge the man who raped her (a guard at a juvenile detention facility) in a criminal court.

The most common criminal charges I see are misdemeanor crimes of survival: prostitution, retail theft, loitering, trespass, drug possession, robbery, fraud, and resisting arrest. I've only worked with a few women who pled guilty to sex offenses. I've also worked with several folks who haven't been charged with a sex offense per se but have certainly had the stigma of their gender expressions used to inflate charges or to charge them with other sexualized crimes, such as the criminal transmission of HIV.[15] As many of the folks I've worked with are detained in the Illinois Department of Corrections (IDOC), I most commonly see how "violations" — the tickets prisoners get for violating the inmate code of conduct — are disproportionately issued against transgender and gay detainees.[16] These violations can have devastating consequences, including sending someone to "the hole" (solitary confinement), taking away their work "privileges" (which may be a source of necessary income), and even adding time to their detention period. Like the plea bargaining system, these violations have the (dis)advantage of an even less impartial adjudication than in a criminal court, a lower burden of proof, and absurd evidentiary standards. Many I've talked to were not even present for the administrative hearing that decided whether the violation had occurred. The charges are often profoundly vague and open to wide discretionary interpretation on the part of a prison guard. A prisoner can be punished for *gesturing* in a way that is intended to sexually arouse. I've known visibly gender-expansive clients who have been faced with a violation for the way they walked near a guard, how they used their hands, the way they smiled, or how they blinked their eyes. They are punished not because of what they are accused of but rather because of how they present.

What are some specific ways that queers are most vulnerable in terms of being charged with sexual offenses?

ERICA: In a project focused on systems-involved LGBTQ youth, an unsurprising and important finding has emerged: gender-nonconforming people (often black transgender women) report institutional harassment and climate policies being used to police their self-advocacy. In one example a young transgender woman of color — a fierce advocate for her rights in a school where she experienced repeated (and often violent) and unchecked aggression from predominantly white peers and staff — was formally sanctioned for verbally insulting a peer who harassed her. The perpetrator was not sanctioned as his harm was made invisible — no one noticed the repeated name-calling, how he and his friends threw forks at her, mimed sexual acts, and on and on. She was suspended, punished, and labeled a sexual harasser. The school informed her that if she received one more sexual harassment "report" she could be labeled a sex offender and suspended for up to one hundred days. Yet her reports of the harm she experienced would require corroborating witnesses. Staff and her peers at the school continued to create an unsafe environment for her, which neither counts as harassment nor merits any formal sanction.

When young queer people try to survive or resist gender-coercive and heterosexist institutions, disciplinary sanctions are ready and waiting. Sexual activities considered non-heterosexual or between non-white and/or non-gender-conforming youth are flagged as deviant, not natural, and are under surveillance. This is visible in many of the cases about youth "sex offenders" that have made it to mainstream media. For example, Kaitlyn Hunt, a white high school honor student and cheerleader, was charged with two counts of lewd and lascivious battery of a child twelve to sixteen years of age. Hunt acknowledges having a consensual same-sex sexual relationship with a fourteen-year-old female when she was seventeen years old.[17]

A 2009 research brief from the U.S. Department of Justice indicates that across the United States, young people between twelve and fourteen are overrepresented on the sex offender registry: "juveniles account for more than one third (35.6 percent) of those known to police to have committed sex offenses."[18] This can be attributed to the expansion of categories that require registration and to the requirement to include those convicted in juvenile courts, but it is also due to the visibility of non-adults and their specific vulnerability. Their bodies, behavior, and mobility are constrained by laws; their sexuality, in particular, is highly regulated. For many young people, engaging in sexual practices with another minor requires breaking the law. A non-adult's inability to legally consent triggers the carceral state to produce crime and harm. Forms of surveillance are uneven: whiter, wealthier, and/or *less queer* young people are not only less likely to be under surveillance (and therefore to get caught breaking the law) but, if "caught," possess access to varied forms of capital that enable differential routes through punitive systems (less likely to be charged, more likely to be released to parents, less likely to be tried as an adult, shorter sentences, etc.).

R: The logic of determining a "sexual offense" in the space of the jail is predicated on some form of authenticity. What I mean by this is that those who are assumed to have continuity of "queerness" outside of the jail are most at risk of being designated as predatory inside the jail; authentically performing an "outside" queer life rather than "gay for the stay" results in specific forms of recognition — the potential for rapacious intimacies. Perhaps the choice term of the jail staff is "bulldagging," a term with a long association with queer women of color, especially those in prison, being accused of "turning out" heterosexual women. The jail then becomes the location of "stranger danger," as it is presumed to not hold one's heterosexual life as a point of direct accountability. The spatial and temporal mismatch of life outside and life inside becomes blurred with the persistence (or continuity) of queer women. Because of this, I believe those who are perceived as "authentically" queer are believed to be more of a threat, and therefore more often threatened with charges that might result in being required to register.

I have yet to hear of an official case from this unit where accusations of a sexual offense led to a charge or conviction (even when such threats by officers and treatment staff are common). Most often, when someone receives a violation (usually a write-up by an officer or staff as a mark of "bad behavior") for a sexual offense, it is common for this person to be moved from this unit to general population. Since access to this specialized housing unit is often mandated by a judge, such a violation can lead to changes in the terms of sentencing, as such violations are detailed and provided to the judge to determine if one is to be released from the program. These violations often result from accusations by just *one* officer and as Owen noted are frequently not investigated. Therefore, my observations suggest that it is common for queer folks, specifically those who are gender-nonconforming, to be targeted for these accusations and then to receive a violation. These violations can often determine the trajectory and time of one's release or the length of monitoring or probation requirements. Beyond the targeting of queer folks of color in policing, these forms of violations based on "sexual offenses" ensure that queer folks in jails receive more interaction, policing, and monitoring in carceral systems.

OWEN: The collateral consequences of sex offense convictions are devastating across the United States. I often find it difficult to assess how these laws weave into the lives of transpeople because of the significant lack of reliable data about the number of transpeople incarcerated. There are no functional methods for "tracking" queer and trans identities in the criminal legal system. Courts, detention sites, and police departments rarely document when someone in their custody is queer or transgender. In a few jurisdictions in the United States there is a clear policy that mandates that someone's gender identity be documented (such as the Chicago Police Department), but in practice I've found that the culture of the institution (prison or police) so deeply rejects the very *existence* of transpeople that even when arrestees clearly self-express that they are transgender upon arrest, they are unlikely to be institutionally classified as transgender.[19] In addition to lack of data collection or outright refusal to collect data, I've found many transpeople choose not to disclose their trans identity on intake into detention or try to "pass" as non-trans to reduce harm. Thus, unless we are in community, family, support systems, or legal relationships with transpeople in the criminal legal system, it is very hard to know how sentencing enhancements like the registry exacerbate vulnerabilities. That said, the few stats we do have of involvement in the criminal legal system are staggering. For example, in a 2011 study where trans and gender-nonconforming participants were asked about their experiences with police and detention, 47 percent of black transgender respondents *who were not currently incarcerated* reported having been incarcerated at some point in their lives.[20] We can only imagine how high those numbers would be if they included the transgender people currently detained across the country.

The cause of such disproportionate numbers of transpeople in detention — especially black, indigenous, and Latino/a transpeople — is linked to a legacy of the criminal sexualization of trans bodies of color. Even from the time of first conquest on what is now known as North America, people who today might identify as transwomen, gender expansive, or Two Spirit were labeled "berdache," a term which derives from the French and Arabic word for "prostitute." Transpeople have been profiled on this land as sexual deviants since, and this legacy leads to what I would consider a "trans panic" toward sexual encounters with transpeople. Similar to the youth you mention, Erica, the few transpeople I have worked with who have been charged with sex offenses were engaging in consensual sex only to later be accused of committing a sex crime. Amplified by the trans, racial, and gender bias woven into the very fabric of our criminal legal system, these transwomen were painted as barbaric and deceitful. With the knowledge that juries also possess these deep biases, these women took plea deals instead of risking fighting their cases. A guilty plea to a sex offense crime ensures they will never be able to change their names in Illinois and seal their criminal records; they are almost completely excluded from many types of employment, housing, and licensure. Had they been immigrants, their convictions would have made them deportable and permanently *inadmissible* in the United States. What's worse is that all of these institutions are *already* less accessible to transpeople — particularly transpeople of color. Transgender people are overwhelmingly at risk of homelessness, unemployment, and deportation.

What are some ways that people are pushing against/responding to these policies or practices?

R: Over the past few years, people on the unit discuss how each may or may not be targeted differently based on race and gender presentation along the lines of sexuality. I have learned a lot from those who have tried to push back and resist accusations by officers regarding "predatory" sex practices by refusing much of the language of being "turned-out" and "turning out" that addresses the dispersion of risk for those who are intimate: one might call these strategies of refusal *dispersed intimacies*. These are small efforts to make forms of intimacies — feet overlapping on chairs and hands through the same hole in a jacket — more *regular* of an occurrence to undermine claims that even an exhausted, slumped head on the shoulder of another is a mark of an assumed "gay" relationship. These strategies seek to overwhelm risk instead of anticipating and calculating the ongoing persistence of risk. Dispersion meets the risk head-on; it stops it in its tracks — it *refuses*, it is not paranoid, and it does not run alongside risk. It does not desire the accumulation of sexual practices for the sake of shaking the statistical norm; rather, these strategies want a grounded account of intimacy beyond the sexual. Put more crudely, these strategies do not desire everyone to be "gay" on the unit with the assumption that *more bodies* would mean something against surveillance. Instead, the act of overwhelming is in the increasing of touching and the boldness of contact that disorientate the marker of the sexual in its regularity. These strategies push back against the tactics of normalization so familiar to many in mainstream gay and lesbian movements, suggesting that the stakes of surveillance on queer bodies necessitate a way of accounting for these more slight bodily contestations.

OWEN: The clients I have worked with who have been officially charged with sex offenses (or with sex violations while in detention such as "sexual misconduct") are resilient. Perhaps it's my own (white, lawyer, formally educated) lens, but I would expect more shame and internalization of the label "sex offender"—a classification that will follow them for the rest of their lives. Instead, the folks I know are *angry*. Often the charge of "sexual misconduct" stems, as we've all named, from consensual sexual relationships with targeted disproportionate criminalization. In one instance someone was actually criminally prosecuted inside the prison where she was already serving a sentence. In my legal practice and related advocacy work, folks on the inside are entirely aware that the systems of sex offenses and sexual violations are about *masking* the causes of sexual violence which are glaringly obvious in the criminal legal system—power and control, submission and domination, feminization as "weakness," and lasting overt racism.

ERICA: I did think visibility, or just telling the facts, was key to dismantling the false narrative that registries equal child (sexual) safety. But in my forays into doing public work around this, a thicket of issues have emerged. Facts don't sway people.

The few current groups that critically engage registries and community notification laws, including Reform Sex Offender Laws (RSOL), often focus on how these systems harm the people on the registry, but they also appear to fail to acknowledge that sexual violence, overwhelmingly perpetrated by cisgendered men, is, if not pervasive, persistent. Yes, the state's purported response to this harm is not only inadequate but unjust, but cisgendered men still harm people, particularly women and children. A small number of other advocacy groups working against registries, including Human Rights Watch, frequently lift up examples of juveniles' acts that resulted in a conviction and aim to engender sympathy for juveniles or the "wrongfully convicted." In line with many criminal justice reform initiatives that seek to highlight the "innocent," these strategies identify sympathetic individuals to exonerate or that merit preferential treatment, but they don't interrogate deeper issues of the failure of criminalization to address sexual violence or our unparalleled affective investments in expanding registries.

Some days it feels like the figure of the "sex offender" is too weighted and monstrous a specter and there is no organizing from this identity, this standpoint. Yet to claim innocence — that this figure is not monstrous — is a too dangerous path. This was painfully evident in 2014 when Laverne Cox, star of the Netflix series *Orange Is the New Black* and longtime advocate for transgender folks in prison, backed away from a campaign that sought to raise the visibility of the treatment of transpeople in prison. Cox distanced herself from the campaign that included the experiences of Synthia China Blast when news sources revealed that Blast was in prison for convictions including child sexual violence.[21] Despite being a transwoman in prison, Blast was, in the words of a mainstream LGBTQ paper, too "controversial" to defend.[22]

As this figure "sex offender" is such an impossible site to organize from or even to deconstruct — a category so saturated, layered with the monstrous and not fully human — I have shifted to a parallel track of organizing and research. Perhaps chipping away at the racialized and heterogendered artifact of childhood might open up avenues to rethink normal. Deconstructing or even just blurring the fictions of childhood and the associated racialized illusions of innocence, consent, and reason seems easier than humanizing the hideously impossible figure of the "sex offender" and holds the potential to raise critical questions.

How do you respond to the "alternatives" question? How do we hold the reality of (child) sexual violence next to the (failed) state responses to this harm? What is the relationship between struggles to dismantle/critique registries and abolition movements that respond to harm and violence without building up police and prisons?

OWEN: Prison abolition is about truly ending violence. When I teach about prison abolition, I am always taken aback when met with the "but what about the child molester?" question. First, it seems odd to center a system of mass incarceration on approximately 3 percent of the entire prison population. I believe this question is really about perceived personal safety presented by cages, and I try to gently engage in a deeper conversation.

In these moments, I first make sure that those in the room know some fairly basic but largely masked statistics, such as that the United States incarcerates more people than any country in the world; the majority of detainees are black and brown; Cook County Jail — the largest jail system in the country — is also our state's largest mental health treatment center; nearly all of those convicted of a crime used a state-appointed attorney, which meant they were living in poverty at the time they were convicted; women are the fastest-growing prison population. I ask students what the *purpose* of the criminal legal system is and they often say, "To deter crime by punishing people who commit crime." I respond by asking whether anyone in the room has experienced sexual violence or knows someone closely who has. Without fail, nearly all respond "yes." At this point, generally the group begins to acknowledge that the criminal legal system did nothing to deter or punish these instances of sexual violence that have touched their lives. They begin to acknowledge that the criminal legal system has not reduced the rates of sexual violence. Thus, at its very core, if you believe that the criminal legal system is about stopping violence and (in particular) is about stopping sexual violence, and most importantly stopping *child* sexual violence, it is a failed system: it does not stop this violence.

At this point, I often let the room just sit with this realization: the criminal legal system does not prevent sexual violence. I ask the group to reconsider the question "but what about the child molester?" I ask them to think about what causes someone to sexually abuse children. Some say that the person has a mental illness, that they are "sick." Some say they are "immoral." And a few say "they are survivors of child sexual violence themselves." I ask the group whether there are any ways to prevent sexual violence without courts, cages, registries, or electronic monitoring. Responses vary: mental health treatment and social support at a young age; increased involvement in spiritual or faith communities; comprehensive sexual health education and a more sex-positive culture; less sexual violence in media, television, and pornography. While these ideas may not be precisely *my* vision of a world without prisons, these "alternatives" are better than a world with prisons. Of course, some answer this question with a resounding "no" — there are no preventive measures outside of prisons. But I try to leave the group with an understanding that human beings are not "born" as "child molesters" or "sexual predators," and in fact the notion that someone could be born inherently sexually aggressive is racist. It is an ideology that fuels oppression, that gets politicians elected, and if you examined it closely, it is an ideology that clarifies that the criminal legal system is not about preventing sexual violence.

Acknowledging that the criminal legal system's remedy for acts of sexual violence does not deter sexual violence is a critical first step. Further conversations need to think about systemic sexual violence, the way we teach violence in classrooms, media outlets, families, and communities, and the ways that the criminal legal system itself actually fuels sexual violence.

ERICA: As Owen stated, I argue that registries, like other forms of state violence including prisons, often mask origins or forms of violence. The carceral state increases vulnerability and forms of violence. *What will be built to replace prisons?* obscures the harm and ineffectiveness of our carceral regime. This question also demands from those who engage in critique a response or a "solution." *If not registries, then what?* I can't count the times I have been asked this question. Even engaging with this "alternatives" question (I am beginning to hate that word) can strengthen the dismissal of critique, subsequently erase the harm done by the police and prisons, and mask the ineptitude of, for example, the registry to meaningfully address child sexual violence.

I generally offer the *both/and* response, perhaps contradictory to some. It seems vital to name how our current prison nation exacerbates and reproduces forms of state or structural violence and makes many, even those who count as children, profoundly unsafe. I also highlight that critique does not require knowing "the response." I try, in a range of ways, to think through and practice this form of engagement with a wide range of audiences. It is tricky because people want to feel and to be safe. The affective dimensions of our anti-prison movements are under-specified. *If not registries, then what?* is often tied to bodily engagements, feelings.

And yet. Despite my desire to *not* respond to this question, I do feel strongly about naming how everyday people continue to imagine and build — sometimes unimaginable, temporal — *alternatives*. People are addressing harm without involving the state. For many communities, calling the cops has never been an option. Ad hoc and formal groups are building and practicing responses to (child) sexual violence "outside" law enforcement. One of the most visible organization in the United States is generationFIVE, but other initiatives and organizations are in motion across the globe.[23]

As *child protection* and child sexual violence are so intimately tethered to feelings about the "the worst of the worst" — the monstrous figures who exemplify the reason why we must have prisons — unpacking child sexual violence is central not only to dismantling the architecture of our prison nation but also to building forms of safety for all, including children.

R: I worry about this question, both it being asked and responding to it. I do think it is necessary to be critical of the shifts we are witnessing at this moment: the expansion of treatment programs such as those discussed, the implementation of "LGBTQ programs" as an ascendency of something quite insidious in carceral expansion. But I will not respond directly to these shifts, and not because I do not regard such lines of thought as critical, but rather because much of this work has been carefully done.[24] It is clear that the presence of queer programming at a large jail does little to undermine sex offender registries. Increasingly I consider abolition movements as a form of politics of refusal, and of course the narratives of any work predicated on a "sympathetic" turn toward LGBTQ movements as worthy projects of self-governance makes me weary. If we take seriously that queers are tethered to the identity of the sex offender, then of course this logic carries through in terms of propping up such programs to battle a specific kind of (undesirable) queer.

Because of this, I want to be careful to differentiate between what I might consider as "alternatives" and "attentiveness." I think alternatives, as Erica has said, are about describing a new world, which I believe we are not necessarily obligated to imagine. Alternatives are often equated with reforms in the name of urgency, yet it always stinks of compromise — the baggage of what we allow as potential. What I like about the term "attentiveness" is that it provides a promise of what is not yet here while still calling claims to the present discussion — the non-congratulatory acknowledgment that one *has arrived*. It allows abolitionists to sidestep the expectation that the present and the future are our only breaks. Perhaps being attentive in the unit at the jail is about arriving at forms of intimacies that many of us might not want to replicate (as we would not want to replicate the conditions of such intimacy, that is, the prison), yet we make adequate room for the possibility of strategies of standstill that come with such conditions. This demand (or just attentiveness) is not about valorizing the potential of politics under lockdown, nor about abandoning such places as spaces of quasi-becoming: taking them seriously means being attentive toward arrangements that are always precariously in the present and does not underscore the reformist narrative. Those thinking through registries and abolitionist politics must carve out a language for partial spaces that are not swiped out by either abolition as non-presence or alternatives as "better-than" logics. Attentiveness is not a middle ground, nor a compromise. As evidenced in the practices of many negotiating survival under state violence, and the lives of people inside and on the registry are no exception, forms of refusal are an important politics of arriving that demands to be taken seriously. Of course, forming this collective disposition of attentiveness is a whole other matter, but perhaps this is precisely where the place and urgency of critique as a partnership become the most meaningful.

NOTES

1. Right on Crime, http://www.rightoncrime.com; "End Mass Incarceration Now," Editorial, *New York Times*, May 25, 2014, http://www.nytimes.com/2014/05/25/opinion/sunday/end-mass-incarceration-now.html?_r=0.

2. Marie Gottschalk, *Caught: The Prison State and the Lockdown of American Politics* (Princeton, NJ: Princeton University Press, 2015), 199.

3. Emily Horowitz, *Protecting Our Kids: How Sex Offender Laws are Failing Us* (Santa Barbara, CA: Praeger, 2015); Roger N. Lancaster, *Sex Panic and the Punitive State* (Berkeley: University of California Press, 2011).

4. Associated Press, "Housing Rules Keep NY Sex Offenders behind Bars," *Washington Post*, August 22, 2014, http://www.washingtontimes.com/news/2014/aug/22/housing-rules-keep-ny-sex-offenders-behind-bars/#ixzz3QK6DIbFY.

5. Kasie Hunt, "Bill Clinton: Prison Sentences to Take Center Stage in 2016," *MSNBC News*, October 8, 2014, http://www.msnbc.com/msnbc/bill-clinton-prison-sentences-take-center-stage-2016.

6. Gottschalk, *Caught*, 198.

7. Sex Offender Registration Act (730 ILCS 150).

8. Joshua Herman, "Sexting: It's No Joke, It's a Crime," *Illinois Bar Journal* 98 (2010): 192.

9. Richard Wright, "Sex Offender Registration and Notification: Public Attention, Political Emphasis, and Fear," *Criminology and Public Policy* 3 (2003): 97–104; Howard N. Snyder, "Sexual Assault of Young Children as Reported to Law Enforcement: Victim, Incident, and Offender Characteristics in 2000," Bureau of Justice Statistics, July 2000, http://www.bjs.gov/content/pub/pdf/saycrle.pdf.

10. Horowitz, *Protecting Our Kids*; Gottschalk, *Caught*.

11. Gottschalk, *Caught*, 124.

12. Regina Kunzel, "Lessons in Being Gay: Queer Encounters in Gay and Lesbian Prison Activism," *Radical History Review* 100 (2008): 11–37, 12.

13. With one exception: historian Regina Kunzel notes that the issue of intergenerational sex, or men charged with or convicted of sex with minors, even if legally recognized as consensual, continually posed challenges for aspects of gay and lesbian organizing (Kunzel, "Lessons in Being Gay," 24).

14. For more on TJLP, see www.tjlp.org; on Critical Resistance, see www.criticalresistance.org.

15. In Illinois the criminal transmission of HIV is a Class 2 felony and the statute is written to encompass a wide range of practices, placing those who are HIV positive and who engage in any sexual practices at risk of being charged. See 720 ILCS 5/12-5.01 (2012).

16. Technically these violations are defined as offenses under Illinois Department of Corrections law, and tickets are what are given to the prisoner after the violation/offense.

17. Charged just days after her eighteenth birthday, Hunt eventually pled no contest to charges including battery and interference with child custody and agreed to a deal, which included four months in jail, house arrest for two years, and three years of probation and gave the state power to monitor her electronic communications. Carlos Harrison, "Florida Student, 18, Arrested for Sex with Teammate, 14," *New York Times*, May 21, 2013, http://www.nytimes.com/2013/05/22/us/florida-18-year-old-arrested-for-encounters-with-friend-14-gets-online-support.html?_r=0.

18. David Finkelhor, Richard Ormrod, and Mark Chaffin, *Juveniles Who Commit Sex Offenses against Minors* (Washington, D.C.: U.S. Department of Justice, Office of Justice Programs, Office of Juvenile Justice and Delinquency Prevention, 2009), https://www.ncjrs.gov/pdffiles1/ojjdp/227763.pdf.

19. See, for example, Chicago Police Department General Order G02-01-03, http://directives.chicagopolice.org/directives/data/a7a57b38-1394a4ae-75313-94a4-b606a68cfab99615.pdf?hl=true.

20. Jaime M. Grant, Lisa A. Mottet, Justin Tanis, Jack Harrison, Jody L. Herman, and Mara Keisling, *Injustice at Every Turn: A Report of the National Transgender Discrimination Survey* (Washington, D.C.: National Center for Transgender Equality and National Gay and Lesbian Task Force, 2011).

21. Parker Molloy, "Laverne Cox Distances Herself from Controversial Trans Inmate," *The Advocate*, August 26, 2014, http://www.advocate.com/politics/transgender/2014/08/26/laverne-cox-distances-herself-controversial-trans-inmate.

22. Molloy, "Laverne Cox Distances Herself."

23. On generationFIVE, see http://www.generationfive.org.

24. I find Morgan Bassichis, Alexander Lee, and Dean Spade's "Building an Abolitionist Trans and Queer Movement with Everything We've Got" in *Captive Genders: Trans Embodiment and the Prison Industrial Complex*, ed. Eric A. Stanley and

Nat Smith (Chico, CA: AK Press, 2015) helpful for those who don't realize that "saving" LGBTQ folks actually undermines the broader stakes of carceral logics. Lynne Haney's *Offending Women: Power, Punishment, and the Regulation of Desire* (Berkeley: University of California Press, 2010) addresses how to understand governance through "alternative" programming of incarceration. Lisa Duggan's *The Twilight of Equality?* (Boston: Beacon, 2004) outlines the co-optation of queer politics in the ascendancy of neoliberal identity movements.

J. WALLACE BORCHERT

| 4 |

A New Iron Closet

Failing to Extend the Spirit of Lawrence v. Texas
to Prisons and Prisoners

INTRODUCTION

During the seven years I spent as a prisoner in California, Minnesota, and Illinois, one of the most troubling conditions of my confinement was the recriminalization of my identity as a gay man. At any given moment, my sexuality could bring about swift and durable punishment from the state. Segregated into Los Angeles County Jail's gay and transgender K6G unit (well documented by Sharon Dolovich and by Russell Robinson), I witnessed the systematic mistreatment of LGBT prisoners.[1] In all, I was classified, housed, and watched over in eight additional county jails and fourteen prisons. In each, I experienced mistreatment and fear, and I watched as other LGBT prisoners — particularly transgender prisoners — were degraded and punished on a daily basis.

Of course, prisons are intended to punish. But what I witnessed was not the ordinary state-sanctioned punishment doled out every day in prisons across America (which has its own set of problems). The mistreatment of LGBT prisoners goes above and beyond the normal degradation meted out by the state, enacting a disparate set of punishments for LGBT people markedly different from the punishment of prisoners perceived as heterosexual or gender-conforming. Through my personal experience and the experience of others like me, I came to believe that America's prisons are iron closets for LGBT citizens — backward spaces void of the legal, cultural, and social recognition and protections that, outside prison walls, have emerged since Stonewall.

As I show in this chapter, America's prisons and jails regularly police and punish consensual, same-sex sex. These punitive policies have continued unabated in the wake of the Supreme Court's 2003 groundbreaking ruling in *Lawrence v. Texas*, which struck down sodomy statutes nationwide and thus forbade the state from criminalizing private, same-sex sex. But the Supreme Court's reach did not penetrate prison walls. Beyond sexuality, I also show how prisons regulate gender by policing and punishing prisoners who do not conform to traditional gender roles and presentations.

This essay will explore the current state of what can ostensibly be categorized as LGBT criminalization in state and federal prisons in the United States.[2] First, I introduce the reader to the characteristics of contemporary prison rules that construct an iron closet for LGBT prisoners, criminalizing both sexual and gender identity as well as same-sex sex. These administrative rules, known as "sexual misconduct rules," are institutionalized in every prison and jail nationwide. Second, I will present cases obtained through Freedom of Information Act (FOIA) requests that can be viewed as typical violations of sexual misconduct rules, both for engaging in consensual same-sex sex between prisoners and for nonconforming gender presentation among prisoners. Third, I discuss the legal and institutional logics that construct these rules as legitimate for prisons and explain how such rules persist despite LGBT progress in broader society. Last, I will argue that prison officials must reconsider prisons as situated within (rather than outside of) the expanding landscape of cultural and social acceptance for LGBT citizens. Until officials ameliorate the conditions that make prisons a new iron closet, LGBT prisoners will continue to be forced to time-travel to a place that existed prior to our social movements, to a place that criminalizes our very identities and behaviors.

CRIMINALIZING LGBT PRISONERS

Today LGBT citizens have more legal rights, protections, and social acceptance than could have been imagined before Stonewall. Yet this expansion of legal recognition has been slow to reach American prisons and jails and the millions of prisoners incarcerated behind their fences and walls. Outside prison gates, same-sex sex is legal and LGBT couples and transgender citizens enjoy access to an ever-greater number of legal protections. Within our prisons from coast to coast, the picture is starkly different, as LGBT identity and same-sex sex remain criminalized. Administrative rules barring consensual, same-sex sex between prisoners are a part of each and every prison system across the United States. Plainly speaking, it is against prison rules for prisoners to have any type of intimate physical contact with one another. If prisoners are caught kissing, hugging, or hand-holding or found engaging in oral or anal sex, they can be written up for violating sexual misconduct rules.

A sexual misconduct ticket is a serious matter. The *Federal Inmate Handbook* — the guide for the more than 200,000 prisoners residing in our Federal Bureau of Prisons facilities — ranks "engaging in sexual acts" and the "proposal of sexual acts" in the "high category of code prohibited acts," which also includes aggravated assault.[3] Only murder, rape, and sexual assault rank as higher-category physical offenses within the federal prison system's 116 facilities nationwide. Violations of "high-category" acts are punishable by lengthening time to parole, forfeiture of good time, disciplinary transfer, segregation, loss of privileges, removal from program and group activities, loss of job, and restriction to quarters.[4]

State prisons nationwide, housing over 1,500,000 prisoners, similarly structure sexual misconduct rules. The Iowa Department of Corrections defines sexual misconduct as follows:

> An offender commits sexual misconduct when the offender proposes a sexual contact or relationship with another person through gestures, such as, kissing, petting, etc., or by written or oral communications, or engages in a consensual sexual contact or relationship. Gestures of a sexual nature designed to cause, or capable of causing, embarrassment or offense to another person shall also be punishable as sexual misconduct.[5]

What we see is that the meaning and the context of the rule are remarkably subjective. What exactly is a "sexual proposal"? What is a "gesture of a sexual nature"? Who determines when that line in the sand has been crossed? Today, after decades of ever-greater acceptance for LGBT citizens, an out and proud individual can be pushed back into an iron closet by a prison system that criminalizes his or her desire.

Contrary to what some of us may logically assume "sexual misconduct" means, this rule category is not applied to violent sexual assault or rape between prisoners; there are separate administrative rules dedicated to prohibiting and punishing violent sexual behaviors.[6] It applies to consensual sex. The Iowa Department of Corrections rules are explicit on this point: "an offender commits sexual misconduct when the offender . . . engages in a consensual sexual contact or relationship." The sexual misconduct rule pertains in fact to two things: consensual sex between prisoners, who are usually of the same gender (as prisons are segregated by objective gender assignment at birth), and the active presentation of transgender identity as normatively understood by prison officials.

For instance, a female transgender prisoner housed in a male prison facility may be written a sexual misconduct ticket for wearing makeup or having her hair in a style normatively understood as appropriate for cisgender female prisoners. The Michigan Department of Corrections (MDOC), in its "Prisoner Discipline Policy Directive," details examples of sexual misconduct such as "wearing clothing of the opposite sex; wearing of makeup by male prisoners," as well as "consensual touching of the sexual or other parts of the body of another person for the purpose of gratifying the sexual desire of either party."[7]

Punishments for infractions can be severe.[8] They include relegating the prisoner to non-resourced areas of the prison, where education, substance abuse treatment, recreation, religious services, employment, and library and visiting privileges are unavailable or drastically reduced. The Indiana Department of Corrections notes that violating the sexual misconduct rule carries up to 180 days in "administrative segregation." More commonly known as solitary confinement, this prison within a prison is a punishment with widely known, highly deleterious consequences for the physical, mental, and emotional health of prisoners; many view it as a form of torture that violates basic human rights.[9]

Prison authorities may also decide to change the security level of a prisoner who violates sexual misconduct rules, which can trigger her relocation to a higher-security facility such as a supermax prison with isolative housing arrangements mimicking solitary confinement and its associated damages. Rules violations in general, and sexual misconducts specifically, can lengthen time to parole, can contaminate parole hearings, and may affect the crucial relationships that released prisoners have with their parole agents by defining these prisoners as rule-breakers as well as sexual and gender deviants.

Beyond these direct consequences, sexual misconduct rule violations can have simultaneous, collateral consequences for prisoners during incarceration and beyond. The MDOC notes, "a prisoner cannot earn good time or disciplinary credits during any month in which s/he engaged in [rules violations]"; the prisoner "shall accumulate disciplinary time" (which is time added that lengthens the original sentence); "each prisoner . . . shall be reviewed by the Security Classification Committee" (which often results in transfer to disciplinary facilities with fewer resources and opportunities for rehabilitation); and "a prisoner may be reclassified to administrative segregation based solely on a guilty finding without a separate hearing being conducted" — thus prefiguring an array of harsh penalties for violating Michigan's sexual misconduct rule.[10] In short, violating the sexual misconduct rule can result in grave consequences for incarcerated citizens.

Readers may be wondering, "But didn't the Supreme Court in *Lawrence v. Texas* strike down sodomy laws that criminalized same-sex sex?" Technically, this is true. But the high court's 2003 decision has had a rather delimited effect. *Lawrence* stops at the prison gate; prisons and prisoners do not fall under its purview. Legal scholars have criticized *Lawrence* for its vagueness, which has necessarily limited its application to other forms of injustice faced by LGBT people. One of these injustices is the failure to establish liberty interests for prisoners in the *spirit* of the landmark decision, which could allow prison officials to reconsider the validity of these rules in an era of expanding LGBT rights and legal protections.

The retrograde nature of these rules and punishments in prisons is remarkably similar to the violent legal landscape that existed for LGBT citizens (including those individuals who do not identify as LGBT but engage in same-sex sex) prior to *Lawrence*. Dale Carpenter, an expert in constitutional law, describes the Texas Homosexual Conduct Law that initiated the arrest of the plaintiffs in *Lawrence* as follows:

> What was nominally a law criminalizing homosexual conduct in fact was a law criminalizing the status of being homosexual. In Texas, being gay became a crime. As John Lawrence responded when his partner, Jose Garcia, asked why they had been charged, "We were arrested for being gay." In a technical sense that was untrue, but in the real world, simply being gay was a crime in Texas. The Homosexual Conduct law was, in practice, a Homosexual Status law.[11]

If we read this quotation, substituting "prison" for "Texas," we instantly see an analogy: the "homosexual conduct law" is remarkably similar to the "sexual misconduct" rule in our nation's prisons as each activates a set of instrumental and symbolic punishments for LGBT citizens and those who engage in same-sex sex. In prison, just as in Texas before 2003, "if persons engaged in that prohibited conduct, they violated the law — no matter whether they were actually gay or were straight and experimenting or settling for second-best sex."[12]

Sexual misconduct rules have both instrumental and symbolic effects on prisons as state institutions, as well as on the prisoners within their walls. In my work with state prison officials, I interviewed a director of a state prison system in the South who noted,

> I think that throughout the U.S. you'll find that consensual sexual be-
> havior between prisoners is prohibited. It doesn't mean that the rules
> do not get violated. Yes, they do get violated, but when they're violated
> the sanctions, in most jurisdictions, the sanctions are swift and certain.
> So, we do not accept or acknowledge consensual sexual relationships
> between offenders.

And this sanctioning of homosexuality resounded throughout my incarceration. Symbolically, these rules and punishments targeted a central feature of
my identity. They weighed heavy on my mind and on the minds of other similarly situated prisoners during our incarceration. Answering W. E. B. DuBois
in this context, it simply did not feel good at all to be a social problem who
could expect "swift and certain" retribution from the state for our consensual
same-sex desires.

PUNISHING SAME-SEX SEX

As I noted in the beginning of this chapter, same-sex sex is criminalized and
punished in prisons nationwide. The following incident reports have been
retrieved through FOIA requests to the Michigan Department of Corrections
in order to detail the types of sexual misconduct rules that same-sex sex commonly violates in Michigan prisons.[13]

The first case involves two prisoners and is a "Notice of Intent to Classify to Segregation" — an administrative order that justifies a defendant being
placed in administrative segregation, or what is commonly known as solitary
confinement:

> Prisoner Jackson was found guilty of sexual misconduct. Prisoner
> Jackson was found by unit staff to be in an embrace and kissing Pris-
> oner Munson. Prisoner Jackson was also found guilty of sexual mis-
> conduct in 2008 where he was caught with another prisoner in a sexual
> act. Both of these incidents indicate that prisoner Jackson is sexually
> active and should not be housed in a general population housing unit.
> A hearing needs to be held to determine if prisoner Jackson should be

classified to administrative segregation because of his sexually active nature.

Following this notice, a hearing was held for Prisoner Jackson with the following severe result:

> Prisoner Jackson was classified to Administrative Segregation for two major sexual misconducts. The first incidence [sic] took place where Jackson and another prisoner were directly observed in a cell together with erect penises. The second incident took place in 2009 where Jackson and the same prisoner were directly observed standing face-to-face in an embrace, kissing each other on the lips. Prisoner Jackson has been classified to Administrative Segregation for a period of 1 year.

Despite *Lawrence*, consensual same-sex sex is criminalized in Michigan prisons to the extent that kissing and embracing are regarded as violating the sexual misconduct rule. And this rule violation clearly brings about severe consequences, as Prisoner Jackson is subsequently sent to administrative segregation — solitary confinement — for a period of one year.

In addition to preventing prisoners from having access to important prison resources, solitary confinement produces potential psychiatric damage: according to expert testimony, "The Courts have recognized that solitary confinement can cause a very specific kind of psychiatric syndrome, which in its worst stages can lead to an agitated, hallucinatory, confusional psychotic state often involving random violence and self-mutilation, suicidal behavior, agitated, fearful and confusional kinds of symptoms."[14]

A "MDOC Class 1 Misconduct Hearing Report" from 2011 presents an additional case of criminalizing same-sex contact. The offense involved may be difficult for some to view as same-sex sex or misconduct of any sort. Here is what we read in the reporting officer's report: "Prisoner Franzen was kissing Prisoner Johnson's neck as Johnson rubbed Franzen's feet. I find that this was consensual touching of each other that was done for the purposes of sexual gratification. The charge is upheld. Prisoner Johnson is being placed in Administrative Segregation."

To make matters more complicated, in a third case we see that the MDOC uses prisoners as confidential informants, revealing dubious, impossible to verify instances of same-sex sex between prisoners. Prisoners with bias against LGBT prisoners can thus make confidential reports of same-sex sex between prisoners who can be punished, as they would be as a result of reports that originated with prison staff. Here, Prisoner Davidson, who has been accused of having sex, claims that he "had conflicts with [the informants] and now they're getting back at him by saying they saw him having oral sex with another prisoner [Peterson]." The report goes on to note, "Based on confidential statements, Prisoner Peterson was seen with Prisoner Davidson's penis in Prisoner Peterson's mouth. This sexual act is a violation; prisoners are prohibited from having any sexual contact with another prisoner." As in the previous cases, the prisoners were found guilty of violating the sexual misconduct rule — "as confirmed by witnesses, it is found that Davidson had mutual physical contact for sexual gratification." Peterson and Davidson were then sent to administrative segregation, with the possibility of irreparable physical and mental harm, for the *crime* of "mutual physical contact for sexual gratification" in a Michigan prison as reported, but not verified, by prisoner informants who may have been motivated by LGBT bias.

MISUNDERSTANDING TRANSGENDER PRISONERS
TROUBLES THE EQUATION

We now know that consensual same-sex sex is a crime in our prisons. To complicate the case, we can again look to Michigan as one of numerous states with correctional departments that conflate non-normative gender presentation with heightened sexuality. The following cases demonstrate how transgender prisoners in Michigan can be issued sexual misconduct rule violation tickets for wearing clothing of the "opposite" gender in facilities that are gender segregated and how prison officials target transgender prisoners disproportionately for additional surveillance and security procedures. These cases are illustrative of common trends in the treatment of transgender prisoners in prisons nationwide.

I became aware of the case at hand during my time collaborating with the American Friends Service Committee Michigan Criminal Justice Office (AFSC), a leader in the broad-based, collaborative effort to reform policy and practice within the Michigan Department of Corrections and nationwide. Through FOIA requests beginning in 2011 and continuing through 2014, AFSC sought to obtain evidence documenting the treatment of transgender prisoners in Michigan's prisons to verify prisoner narratives, claims, and anecdotal evidence that indicated widespread mistreatment of transgender prisoners. The records obtained reveal a normative conflation of sexuality with gender identity on the part of prison officials, from line staff to the executive leadership, which drives disproportionate surveillance and punishment of the bodies of transgender prisoners.

This systemic mistreatment of transgender prisoners makes an already difficult situation (prison) worse. The records obtained by AFSC reveal extraordinary levels of sexual and identity harassment on the part of prisoners and prison officials alike. One transgender female, Candace (a pseudonym), notes how her fellow male prisoners treat her: "It's all kids and they are tormenting me daily. I am the only one like myself here and feel very lost." Within this hostile environment, staff also bully and ridicule Candace, reportedly telling her, "You have a wide load. How do you expect to be the prison whore if you can't bend over and grab your ankles?" She goes on to state, "I was so embarrassed I had to leave the chow hall." In addition to the verbal abuse, Candace has been written up multiple times for violating the sexual misconduct rule, with officers' claims of "impersonating a female" to justify the ticketing and subsequent punishment:

> [Corrections Officer] Tom asked me if I had make-up on. I told him no, that I fill in my eyebrows because they do not grow from tweezing them so long. He inferred that I was impersonating a female. I explained that I am a female — that I lived my entire life as a female. He stated, "Do you want to go in your cell and take care of it or let Major Court decide if you have a gender disorder?" He seemed very upset with the explanation and I did not want to get in a debate with him so I said, I'll let the court decide.

In Candace's case, she was found guilty of sexual misconduct numerous times for her nonconforming gender identity in prison. These violations contaminated the remainder of her prison sentence, including her possibility for parole. In total, Candace has spent nearly four years in the iron closet of administrative segregation or solitary confinement for the crime of being transgender.

The following email from the MDOC headquarters in Lansing, Michigan, to all MDOC wardens, captains, and lieutenants details the way sexual misconduct rules are understood and operationalized by prison officials, revealing an environment of abuse, characterized by heightened surveillance and punishment directed toward transgender prisoners:

> They [prisoners] know that we, I will not tolerate the behavior and that it is a policy violation to wear effeminate appearing clothing, et cetera. I am good with sexual misconducts if they are upheld. Just the other day I told Candace to lose the eye liner, Kool-Aid, and scrunchy in his hair.

Let's have staff search their cells and confiscate anything that violated policy and we can go from there. If they want attention, we will oblige.[15]

Following up on the executive-level directive, a subsequent email from MDOC headquarters indicates the approach that the MDOC takes toward its transgender prisoners.

We have been having problems with prisoners wearing homemade make up and wearing their hair like a women [sic]. I have reviewed the policy directive and was unable to find any information that allows them to wear makeup or wear their hair like a women [sic]. They have been warned numerous times by Officer Tom. Today Officer Tom took photographs and wrote Class I Sexual Misconduct tickets.[16]

We know that sexual misconduct violations can spell trouble for prisoners. In a review of Candace's file and the files of other transgender female prisoners in Michigan prisons, a pattern of systematic abuse emerges in which transgender prisoners spend a high proportion of their incarceration spells in administrative segregation or solitary confinement. In fact, prisoners like Candace are criminalized for their identity without engaging in behavior that remotely resembles a normative understanding of "sexual" misconduct.

This treatment makes conditions of confinement particularly harsh for transgender prisoners and is not unusual. In my own experience as a prisoner in over twenty facilities in California, Minnesota, and Illinois, I witnessed countless cases of prison staff treating transgender prisoners with extra administrative hurdles, surveillance, punishment, abuse, and isolation. In a forthcoming paper, Lori Sexton and Valerie Jenness provide additional detail on the environment of abuse that transgender prisoners experience in California prisons. One male prisoner reports, "Most transgenders [sic] on this yard, well, they get called cum buckets. These guys here have no respect for them and they have no respect for themselves."[17] This lack of respect and understanding is clearly part of the logics of sexual misconduct rules as applied to transgender prisoners such as Candace.

PRISON LOGICS AND PRISON JURISPRUDENCE

Why do sexual misconduct rules go unquestioned? For the better part of American prison history, prison officials have been allowed broad latitude and professional expertise to operate prisons as they see fit. In this sense, correctional officials can be seen as sovereign in their ability to conceptualize and actualize the ways their prisons operate.[18] From roughly 1871 until the early 1970s, judicial and legislative relationships with corrections were informed by the "Hands-off Doctrine" as delineated in *Ruffin v. Commonwealth* (1871). That doctrine claimed that a prisoner forfeits his liberty and all his personal rights, except what the law in its humanity accords him, as "he is for the time being a slave of the state."[19]

Since then, there has only been one brief period in which the rights of prisoners were expanded. This short-lived change developed as an outgrowth of the civil rights movement and, in the field of penology, is referred to as the "rehabilitative turn" in corrections. During the 1960s and 1970s, a set of federal and Supreme Court cases[20] forced prison officials to adopt a new orthodoxy and praxis to conform to new rehabilitative frameworks for managing prisoners. These policy directives redefined constitutional protections under the law for prisoners and facilitated their ability to have their voices heard at court.[21]

At the height of the prison reform era and in line with broader social movements, the Supreme Court maintained that "prisoners are still persons entitled to all constitutional rights unless their liberty has been constitutionally curtailed by procedures that satisfy all of the requirements of due process."[22] In line with general social trends promising greater equality among and between citizens that led to the Civil Rights Act of 1964, the Voting Rights Act of 1965, the Fair Housing Act of 1968, President Johnson's War on Poverty, and the introduction of the Equal Rights Amendment in 1972, prisons began generating programming designed to rehabilitate prisoners and help them reenter society.

However, the Supreme Court began to take a dimmer view of prisoners' rights in the late 1970s, adopting a deferential stance toward the expertise of prison officials. For the court, prisons have become special places with special orderings and necessities — so exceptional, in fact, that the court must defer to the specialized knowledge of correctional authorities. By 1987, Justice O'Connor effectively ended prisoner rights expansion by writing,

> Running a prison is an inordinately difficult undertaking that requires expertise, planning, and the commitment of resources, all of which are peculiarly within the province of the legislative and executive branches of government. Prison administration is, moreover, a task that has been committed to the responsibility of those branches, and separation of powers

concerns counsel a policy of judicial restraint. Where a state penal system is involved, federal courts have, as we indicated in Martinez, additional reason to accord deference to the appropriate prison authorities.[23]

O'Connor goes on to write that "when a prison regulation impinges on inmates' constitutional rights, the regulation is valid if it is reasonably related to legitimate penalogical [sic] interests." This reasoning contradicts reform-era precedent, which held that a prisoner's constitutional rights did *not* stop at the prison gate.[24] Steering corrections toward wider autonomy, the Court's opinion in *Turner v. Safley* is a decisive move away from reform-era standards and assists in the operation of the punitive turn that ultimately brought about today's system of mass incarceration.

Shortly after the early deference decisions, legal scholars began to detect a retreat by the Supreme Court toward a "new hands-off" doctrine and a deliberate evasion of judicial responsibility in prison law cases.[25] The opinion in *Turner* thus provides wide latitude to correctional officials as experts, capable of answering myriad questions regarding good corrections or the proper shape of confinement, who need not be concerned with strict constitutional review of their orthodoxy and praxis.[26] Deference thus provides state prison officials a legitimate, jurisprudential framework for ignoring or dismissing rights expansion for LGBT citizen prisoners.

Building on the instrumental and symbolic barrier to successful prisoner litigation constructed in *Turner*, the Prison Litigation Reform Act of 1996 (PLRA) further incapacitates incarcerated individuals by limiting prisoner access to courts. The PLRA codifies a widespread belief that prisoners too frequently engage in frivolous litigation over issues that could perhaps be resolved by prison administration. The PLRA requires prisoners to exhaust internal prison due process and grievance procedures before accessing the court. Yet accessing the court is difficult for prisoners. Previous research has noted that "prisoners who miss a filing deadline or otherwise fail to comply with a procedural requirement in the prison grievance process might be forever barred from bringing their claim to court," thus allowing the court to evade through various technicalities having to answer the tough questions that may be present in prisoners' claims.[27]

In response, some state Departments of Corrections have erected additional barriers to filing grievances (usually time-based), thus making it increasingly difficult for prisoners to reach the court for relief. The primary method of constructing these barriers is to narrow the window of time to file internal grievances. Prisoner petitions for relief can thus be thrown out at court on procedural, time-based grounds as opposed to being rejected on the merits of their claims. Since the advent of the PLRA, prison litigation has dropped by nearly 50 percent.[28]

With these legal developments, scholars note that prisons are once again structured as highly autonomous, lacking transparency or accountability in their day-to-day operations.[29] Deference and the PLRA operationalize the logics of mass incarceration, including sexual misconduct rules that target same-sex sex and gender-nonconforming prisoners. For today's prisoners and their advocates, access to the courts is blocked; it is nearly impossible for them to challenge the logics of sexual misconduct rules as violating norms that are within, at a minimum, the *spirit* of *Lawrence* in order to escape the iron closet. Shay goes on to note,

> Despite its importance, the area of corrections regulation is a kind of "no-man's land." In many jurisdictions, and in many subject areas, prison and jail regulations are formulated outside of public view. Because of deference afforded prison officials under prevailing constitutional standards, such regulations are not given extensive judicial attention. Nor do they receive much focus in the scholarly literature.[30]

In this light, the prison is purposefully constructed to hide the damages it inflicts upon vulnerable populations behind prison walls and fences, at great social and geographical distance from those who are not incarcerated.[31]

Of course, many prisoners engage in consensual, same-sex sexual activity, regardless of their self-reported sexual identity, during their incarceration spells. Recent research has found that over 40 percent of prisoners engaged in consensual sex while incarcerated, and the Bureau of Justice Statistics found that only 7 percent of prisoners sampled classified themselves as homosexual or bisexual.[32] A recent report from the U.S. Department of Justice notes that many prisoners (40 percent) are punished for being victims of rape and sexual assault.[33] Sexual assault victims are often treated as culpable participants. Of the 10,200 respondents to the 2008 National Former Prisoner Survey who reported being victims of sexual assault, 34 percent reported being placed in segregation or protective custody; 24 percent reported being confined to their cell; 14 percent reported being classified to a higher level of custody; and 28.5 percent reported being given a disciplinary write-up for being the *victim* of sexual assault.[34] As such, rules barring consensual same-sex sex in prisons extend even to victims of rape and assault, punishing them for being victims of violence perpetrated against them.

CONCLUSION

Deference as well as the PLRA reinforce the independence and autonomy of prison officials by allowing them to construct and maintain rules and punishment frameworks targeting LGBT prisoners and prisoners who engage in consensual same-sex sex. Correctional orthodoxy and practice, regardless of their motivations, are thus prevented from interacting with *Lawrence* to extend the expanded landscape of LGBT rights since Stonewall to prisons and prisoners.

Aside from these legal barriers limiting prisoner access to the courts, there are myriad reasons officials choose to define sexual misconduct rules in prisons as rules rather than crimes. By defining these violations as "rule breaking," prison officials are able to draw attention away from the hostile climate faced by LGBT prisoners (as well as non-LGBT-identifying prisoners who practice same-sex sex). Thus, the state can claim that same-sex behavior is not *criminalized* — it is merely managed administratively.

In practice, the distinction between a "rule violation" and a "crime" is largely academic. Viewing the prison as its own society — with its own set of rules, regulations, and codes of conduct — helps to explain why this is so. Like the removal of individuals who commit crimes from everyday society, prisoners who violate prison regulations are segregated from the general prison population. They are removed from where they live and taken to an alternate space where heightened restrictions are placed on them, limiting their freedom and access to resources; in essence, they are taken to a virtual *jail within the prison.* Indeed, during these instances, prisoners often claim that they are being "taken to jail" as they are hauled in for violating formal behavioral codes. Thus, while authorities maintain that rule infractions do not constitute "crimes" in the conventional sense, the prisoner — whose rights and freedoms are infringed upon in either circumstance — would not be blamed for viewing this distinction as entirely meaningless.

By categorizing the arbitrary processes the state employs to punish same-sex sex and gender nonconformity among prisoners as "rule breaking," the state is able to reframe the unjust treatment of LGBT prisoners in largely bureaucratic terms. Simple "rule breaking" does not connote the harsh punishments and significant damages that prisoners may incur through long-lasting periods in isolation and segregation. As I have shown, by framing these practices as "rules," prison officials have helped to seal prisons walls against the expansion of LGBT rights occurring in broader society. I argue that the term "crime" more accurately describes the way sexual and gender infractions in prison are treated, which raises serious social questions of inequality, marginalization, and citizenship.

Despite this bleak scenario, there may be an opening for reconsideration. I have interviewed a number of pragmatic correctional directors who have indicated that consensual, same-sex sex is a frequent characteristic of prison life. As such, they believe it requires less attention and less punishment. One long-term state correctional department director from the Southwest asks,

> Are we going to not recognize that there's sex in prisons between inmates? Or are we going to say if we don't recognize it, it's not happening? It's going to happen. It's the nature of the most complex creature, the human being. That drive is there. Inmates will tell you that they're not gay, but the best sex they ever had was in prison and once they get out they go back to being totally heterosexual.

Zygmunt Bauman advises us of the danger of bureaucracy "to disguise, or even subsume, profound questions of morality that should detain us all."[35] Bauman thus provides leverage to examine why prisons have viewed themselves as special places, as places outside the contemporary understanding of human rights, where a disjoint legality, morality, or landscape of rights between prison and society makes sense. However, as my interviews with correctional directors suggest (and as the prison reform era proves), shifting cultural attitudes are able to support new ways of managing prisoners. In this light, emerging correctional logics informed by LGBT rights movements could lead to a wider belief that alternative identities and behaviors are unsuitable for punishment.

None of this should be read as diminishing the significance *Lawrence* has had in the landscape of legal and societal changes for LGBT citizens in American society. These structural, cultural, and epistemological changes have fostered greater acceptance and inclusion of LGBT Americans in social institutions and popular culture, including the church, television, politics, and the media. Yet the ability of *Lawrence* to impact social institutions such as the military, marriage, and prisons has varied. The inability to extend the spirit of *Lawrence* to the military was remedied in 2012 with the repeal of "Don't Ask, Don't Tell," which brought to light a clear and persistent social fact: LGBT citizens are part of our military and have defended our country for decades. In particular, changes in military policy have reshaped concepts of citizenship that have historically reinforced the policing of identity and same-sex sex. Thus, an expansion of the spirit of *Lawrence* to prisons and prisoners could potentially be delivered through a critical interrogation of correctional logics to determine if sexual behavior between prisoners or alternative sexual and gender identity necessarily violates prison rules and norms. If it is determined that behaviors and identities do violate rules and norms, are the current severe responses appropriate to the case at hand? Is the iron closet constructed for these prisoners commensurable with broader societal, legal, and cultural acceptance?

These broader cultural changes are signaled by Justice Thomas in his dissent to *Lawrence*. Although he did not agree with the Court's finding that sodomy laws violated basic constitutional protections, he did nonetheless argue that "punishing someone for expressing his sexual preference through noncommercial consensual conduct with another adult does not appear to be a worthy way to expend valuable law enforcement resources."[36] Justice Thomas goes on to acknowledge that broad-based cultural change can generate institutional change. Given that both Justice Kennedy and Justice Thomas agree that laws criminalizing consensual sexual behavior are at the very least (in the words of Thomas) "uncommonly silly," why do prisons remain outside this realm of logic? Why do our prisons continue to punish, criminalize, and damage prisoners like Candace, Jackson, Davidson, and countless others? Why are our prisons iron closets for LGBT prisoners? The presence of LGBT prisoners and the reality of consensual same-sex sex in prisons are social facts. By viewing prisons as within the contemporary landscape of expanding rights and acceptance for LGBT citizens, we can begin to believe that prisons and the prisoners within them are a part of the LGBT community and its social movements; in so doing we might remove the rules barring consensual same-sex sex and gender nonconformity from prison rulebooks or, at a minimum, lessen their harsh punishments.

NOTES

1. See Sharon Dolovich, "Strategic Segregation in the Modern Prison," *American Criminal Law Review* 48, no. 1 (2010): 1–110; and Russell K. Robinson, "Masculinity as Prison: Sexual Identity, Race, and Incarceration," *California Law Review* 99, no. 5 (2011): 1309–1408.

2. Catherine Hanssens et al. note that "LGBT people and PLWH are overrepresented in U.S. prisons and jails, and face widespread and pervasive violence, inadequate healthcare, nutritional deprivation, and exclusion from much needed services and programs. LGBT prisoners and prisoners with HIV are more likely to be placed in administrative segregation or solitary confinement . . . and to be denied access to mail, jobs, and programs while in custody. LGBT prisoners have also experienced unanticipated negative impacts from the Prison Rape Elimination Act (PREA), including being punished through new policies purportedly created to comply with PREA that forbid gender non-conforming behavior and punish consensual physical contact." *A Roadmap for Change: Federal Policy Recommendations for Addressing the Criminalization of LGBT People and People Living with HIV* (New York: Center for Gender & Sexuality Law at Columbia Law School, 2014).

3. Federal Bureau of Prisons, "Statistics," *U.S. Department of Justice*, 2014, http://www.bop.gov/about/statistics/population_statistics.jsp, accessed July 2014.

4. Federal Bureau of Prisons, "Statistics."

5. Iowa Department of Corrections, *Policies and Procedures* (Des Moines: Iowa Department of Corrections, 2006).

6. However, even in cases of violent sexual assault and rape, victims who are LGBT identified are often charged with sexual misconduct as well, indicating that prison officials view LGBT prisoners as sexual instigators who are somehow deserving of the assaultive behavior perpetrated upon them.

7. Michigan Department of Corrections (MDOC), *Prisoner Discipline Policy Directive* (Lansing, MI, 2012).

8. There is a hearing process for prisoners who are charged with violating prison rules, including sexual misconduct rules. However, the prison rules hearings adjudication process is fraught with procedural hurdles and barriers to the effective representation of facts, including the use of anonymous prison informants, in order to mount an accurate defense against biased claims made by guards in same-sex sex and LGBT identity cases. See Giovanna Shay, "Ad Law Incarcerated," *Berkeley Journal of Criminal Law* 14, no. 2 (2010): 329–392.

9. Rachael Kamel and Bonnie Kerness, *The Prison Inside the Prison: Control Units, Supermax Prisons, and Devices of Torture* (Philadelphia: American Friends Service Committee, 2003); Juan E. Mendez, "Torture and Other Cruel, Inhuman or Degrading Treatment or Punishment: In 66th Session of Promotion and Protection of Human Rights: Human Rights Questions, Including Alternative Approaches for Improving the Effective Enjoyment of Human Rights and Fundamental Freedoms," United Nations General Assembly, 2011. The American Friends Service Committee as well as Juan E. Mendez — the United Nations' Special Rapporteur of the Human Rights Council on torture and other cruel, inhuman, or degrading treatment or

punishment — view solitary confinement, otherwise known as administrative segregation or protective custody, as a violation of human rights and an extreme form of torture that leads in many cases to extremely deleterious physical, mental, and emotional health outcomes for prisoners unfortunate enough to spend even short stays in these conditions of confinement.

10. MDOC, *Prisoner Discipline Policy Directive.*

11. Dale Carpenter, *Flagrant Conduct: The Story of Lawrence v. Texas* (New York: W. W. Norton, 2012), 109.

12. Carpenter, *Flagrant Conduct*, 106–107.

13. In the following cases describing the criminalization and punishment of same-sex sex as well as gender nonconformity, pseudonyms are used to protect the identity and confidentiality of prison staff and prisoners alike.

14. Kamel and Kerness, *Prison Inside the Prison*, 3

15. Email from Michigan Department of Corrections to Richard Handlon Correctional Facility Officials, "Gender Identity Disorder in Prisoners," August 29, 2012.

16. Michigan Department of Corrections, "Gender Identity Disorder in Prisoners."

17. Lori Sexton and Valerie Jenness, "The Social Allocation of Allegiance: Collective Identity and Collective Efficacy among Transgender Prisoners" (unpublished manuscript).

18. Carl Schmitt, *Political Theology* (1922; repr., Chicago: University of Chicago Press, 1985).

19. Ruffin v. Commonwealth, 62 Va. 790 (1871).

20. Prominent prisoner rights cases during the reform era include Cooper v. Pate, 378 U.S. 546 (1964); Hutto v. Finney, 437 U.S. 678 (1978); Pugh v. Locke, 406 F.2d 318 (M.D. Ala. 1976); Procunier v. Martinez, 416 U.S. 396 (1974); Ruiz v. Estelle 503 F. Supp. 1265 (S.D. Tex. 1980); Wolff v. McDonnell, 418 U.S. 539 (1974).

21. Malcolm Feeley and Edward Rubin, *Judicial Policy Making and the Modern State: How the Courts Reformed America's Prisons* (New York: Cambridge University Press, 1999).

22. *Procunier*, 416 U.S. 428.

23. Turner v. Safley, 482 U.S. 78 (1987).

24. *Procunier*, 416 U.S. 396.

25. Sharon Dolovich, "Exclusion and Control in the Carceral State," *Berkeley Journal of Criminal Law* 16, no. 2 (2011): 259–339; Sharon Dolovich, "Forms of Deference in Prison Law," *Federal Sentencing Reporter* 24, no. 4 (2012): 245–259; Sharon Dolovich, "Incarceration American Style," *Harvard Law & Policy Review* 3 (2009): 237–262; Dolovich, "Strategic Segregation in the Modern Prison"; Cheryl Dunn Giles, "Turner v. Safley and Its Progeny: A Gradual Retreat to the 'Hands-Off' Doctrine," *Arizona*

Law Review 35 (1993): 219–236; Paul Horwitz, "Three Faces of Deference," *Notre Dame Law Review* 83, no. 3 (2008): 1061–1165.

26. The 1987 *Turner* decision provided a highly subjective *rational basis test* to be used by the judiciary to affirm or deny claims made by prisoners. Known as the *Turner Test*, the decision-making method operates with less scrutiny than the *strict scrutiny* standards spelled out in *Procunier*. With the *Turner Test* a prison practice, rule, or regulation may be ruled as legitimate if it meets four discrete, yet highly subjective, criteria: (1) if there is a "valid, rational connection between the prison regulation and the legitimate government interest put forward to justify it"; (2) "whether alternative means of exercising the right(s) that remain open to prison inmates" are available; (3) "the impact accommodation of the asserted constitutional right will have on guards and other inmates"; and (4) if there are "ready alternatives" to choose from such that prison officials can achieve their intended goal(s) (*Turner*, 482 U.S. 78).

27. Shay, "Ad Law Incarcerated," 342.

28. Todd Clear and Natasha A. Frost, *The Punishment Imperative: The Rise and Failure of Mass Incarceration in America* (New York: NYU Press, 2013).

29. Dolovich, "Exclusion and Control in the Carceral State"; Dolovich, "Forms of Deference in Prison Law"; Dolovich, "Incarceration American Style"; Dolovich, "Strategic Segregation in the Modern Prison"; Horwitz, "Three Faces of Deference"; Shay, "Ad Law Incarcerated."

30. Shay, "Ad Law Incarcerated," 331.

31. Michel Foucault, *The Archaeology of Knowledge and the Discourse on Language* (New York: Vintage, 1972); Michel Foucault, *Discipline and Punish: The Birth of the Prison* (New York: Vintage, 1979); David Garland, *The Culture of Control: Crimes and Social Order in Contemporary Society* (Chicago: University of Chicago Press, 2001); Jonathan Simon, *Governing through Crime: How the War on Crime Transformed American Democracy and Created a Culture of Fear* (New York: Oxford University Press, 2007); Jonathan Simon, "The Ideological Effects of Actuarial Practices," *Law & Society Review* 22, no. 4 (1988): 771–800; Jonathan Simon, "Punishment and the Political Technologies of the Body," in *The Sage Handbook of Punishment and Society*, ed. Jonathan Simon and Richard Sparks, 60–90 (New York: Sage, 2013); Jonathan Simon, "The 'Society of Captives' in the Era of Hyper-Incarceration," *Theoretical Criminology* 4, no. 3 (2000): 285–308.

32. Christopher Hensley, Richard Tewksbury, and Jeremy Wright, "Exploring the Dynamics of Masturbation and Consensual Same-Sex Activity within a Male Maximum Security Prison," *Journal of Men's Studies* 10, no. 1 (2001): 59–71; Bureau of Justice Statistics, *Sexual Victimization in State and Federal Prisons Reported by Inmates* (Washington, D.C.: Department of Justice, 2009).

33. U.S. Department of Justice, *Sexual Victimization Reported by Former State Prisoners: National Former Prisoner Survey* (Washington, D.C.: Bureau of Justice Statistics, 2008), 31.

34. U.S. Department of Justice, *Sexual Victimization*, 31.

35. Zygmunt Bauman, "Modernity and Ambivalence," *Theory, Culture & Society* 7, no. 2 (1990): 143–169.

36. Lawrence v. Texas, 539 U.S. 558 (2003) (Thomas, J., dissenting).

MARY ANNE CASE

|5|

Seeing the Sex and Justice Landscape through the Vatican's Eyes

The War on Gender and the Seamless Garment of Sexual Rights

Over the course of the last half century, just as the United States was in the throes of the war on sex described by David Halperin in his introduction to this volume, the Vatican and those operating under its influence have been waging a global war on gender, with multiple fronts on every continent and armies on its side ranging from clerics and academics to naked male protestors on the streets of Paris.[1] The Vatican's declared aim in this war is to put a stop not only to the English word "gender" as it is used in legal and policy-making documents by such bodies as the United Nations and the European Union, but also to those many reforms in secular law governing the sexes, sexuality, reproduction, and the family that the Vatican associates with what it calls "the gender theory" or "the ideology of gender."[2] These include laws leading to the dismantling of sex roles, to the acceptance of homosexuality, to the recognition of a diversity of family forms and of sexual and gender expression, and to access to the new reproductive technologies, condoms, other contraceptives, and abortion — in short, most of what goes under such diverse headings as women's sexual and reproductive rights, protections for sexual orientation and gender identity (SOGI), family law reform, and the elimination of sex stereotyping. Especially inasmuch as it fights against the legal and social acceptance of non-marital, non-procreative, non-heterosexual sex, and more generally against sexual freedom, the Vatican's war on gender is a major front in the war on sex.

To a much greater extent than other fronts in the war on sex Halperin describes, the Vatican's war on gender is "a single, integrated phenomenon" or "a deliberate strategic plan coordinated at some high level of centralized author-ity."[3] One can trace the development of the Vatican's strategic plan at every level. In the highest echelons of the hierarchy, the fears first expressed in *The Ratzinger Report* of the 1980s were cathected in the word "gender" and pro-mulgated by the so-called Panzer Cardinal Joseph Ratzinger as Prefect of the Congregation for the Doctrine of the Faith (CDF) in his *Letter to the Bishops of the Catholic Church on the Collaboration of M[a]n and Wom[a]n in the Church and in the World* in May 2004 and, after his ascension to the papacy as Benedict XVI, in an address to the Roman Curia in 2008.[4] The scouting report *Gen-der: The Deconstruction of Women, Analysis of the Gender Perspective in Prep-aration for the Fourth World Conference on Women*, which Catholic blogger Dale O'Leary provided from the trenches of the 1995 Beijing Conference to Ratzinger and John Paul II, had by 2003 led to the Pontifical Council for the Family's thousand-page *Lexicon: Ambiguous and Debatable Terms Regarding Family Life and Ethical Questions* and to a myriad of related works.[5] Interna-tional networks of training sessions put on by authors represented in the lexi-con, such as the French Lacanian psychoanalyst priest Tony Anatrella, and by other activists operating in Vatican orbits now help warn of dangers and implement counter-strategies.[6] In part motivated by such training sessions, activists have flooded not only the corridors of power but the streets, as, for example, hundreds of thousands of French citizens came out to demonstrate against the inclusion of same-sex couples in a law extending "Marriage Pour Tous" (Marriage for Everyone) in the spring of 2013, marching under slogans such as "Don't touch our gender stereotypes."[7]

From the beginning of this war on "gender," the Vatican made strategic alli-ances with other political actors and faith traditions, for example, cooperating with the Organization of the Islamic Conference at Beijing and thereafter in the United Nations. In late 2014, Pope Francis personally welcomed an inter-national who's who of self-described proponents of traditional marriage and opponents of same-sex marriage from diverse faith traditions and continents to the Vatican for an International Colloquium on the Complementarity be-tween Man and Woman ("Humanum Conference") sponsored by the CDF.[8] These strategic alliances have coincided with an almost centripetal increase in conservatism with respect to gender issues among participating religious denominations, as, for example, American evangelical Protestants over time moved closer to the Catholic position in opposition to abortion and birth control while the Vatican gave center stage at the Humanum Conference to Southern Baptists, Orthodox Jews, and Mormons, whose views on male headship in marriage would be a step backward for the Catholic Church.

The stakes in the war on the ideology of gender, as the Vatican sees it, could not be greater — human nature itself risks being destroyed if advocates for feminism and gay rights, seen as the enemy in this war, have their way with the law. I am one of those advocates, yet, paradoxically, the way I see the landscape of sex and justice has much more in common with the Vatican's vision than with the approach of so many on my side of the battle for sexual rights. In this chapter, I will briefly sketch the Vatican's view of the landscape and set forth some of my reasons for finding it compelling and recommending it to my side, even as I completely reject the normative imperatives the Vatican applies to what it sees.

Since at least 1984, Ratzinger thought it "necessary to get to the bottom of the demand that radical feminism draws from the widespread modern culture, namely the 'trivialization' of sexual specificity that makes every role interchangeable between man and woman. . . . Detached from the bond with fecundity, sex no longer appears to be a determined characteristic, as a radical and pristine orientation of the person. Male? Female? They are questions that for some are now viewed as obsolete, senseless, if not racist. The answer of current conformism is foreseeable: 'whether one is male or female has little interest for us, we are all simply humans.' This in reality has grave consequences even if at first it appears very beautiful and generous."[9] It is no wonder that, to Ratzinger, the view that "we are all simply humans . . . at first appears very beautiful and generous": this had long been a view central to Christianity, as manifest in such proof texts as Galatians 3:28.[10] But it is also little wonder that Ratzinger was inclined to reject it, because it was precisely in his lifetime, in the second half of the twentieth century, that the Catholic Church first adopted a theological anthropology of complementarity, to wit that "man and woman" have "equal dignity as persons" but that this equal dignity is premised on and manifest in essential and complementary differences, "physical, psychological and ontological."[11] The move to complementarity coincided with Vatican pronouncements against artificial birth control and abortion (e.g., *Humanae Vitae* in 1968), against homosexuality (e.g., *Persona Humana* in 1975), and against the ordination of women to the ministerial priesthood (e.g., *Inter Insigniores* in 1976).[12] Among the grave consequences Ratzinger identified as resulting from a move away from essential sex differences were those made possible through technological intervention, such as "the right to be made male or female at one's will or pleasure . . . through surgery" and "separating fecundity from sexuality with the purpose of making it possible to procreate at will."[13]

Ratzinger was inclined to see radical feminism at the root of the various dangers associated with gender:

> In order to avoid the domination of one sex or the other, their differences tend to be denied, viewed as mere effects of historical and cultural conditioning. In this perspective, physical difference, termed sex, is minimized, while the purely cultural element, termed gender, is emphasized to the maximum and held to be primary. The obscuring of the difference or duality of the sexes has enormous consequences on a variety of levels. This theory of the human person, intended to promote prospects for equality of women through liberation from biological determinism, has in reality inspired ideologies which, for example, call into question the family, in its natural two-parent structure of mother and father, and make homosexuality and heterosexuality virtually equivalent, in a new model of polymorphous sexuality.
>
> While the immediate roots of this second tendency are found in the context of reflection on women's roles, its deeper motivation must be sought in the human attempt to be freed from one's biological conditioning. According to this perspective, human nature in itself does not possess characteristics in an absolute manner: all persons can and ought to constitute themselves as they like, since they are free from every predetermination linked to their essential constitution.[14]

Of particular concern to Ratzinger and others in the Vatican orbit were any moves toward "liberation from biological determinism" in matters of sexuality, whether in the form of "sexuality . . . separated from procreation" or "procreation without sexuality." Once these separations are effected, "[n]o longer having an objective reason to justify it, sex seeks the subjective reason in the gratifying of the desire," and "it naturally follows that all forms of sexual gratification are turned into 'rights' of the individual," with "homosexuality becom[ing] an inalienable right" and "abortion . . . another form of 'liberation.' "[15] Thus, from the start, at the core of what became the Vatican's war on what it calls the ideology of gender was a war on sex.

As Ratzinger's analysis indicates, the Vatican sees, and assumes its opponents also see, a tight connection between and among all the components it incorporates under the "gender agenda."[16] Perhaps one reason for this is that, at the time of the Beijing conference, when the Vatican's attention was first drawn to "gender," advocates did indeed focus on "Creating a Broad Sexual Rights Agenda," as Rachel Rosenbloom wrote in a 1996 International Gay and Lesbian Human Rights Commission (IGLHRC) report:

> All over the world, women face violence, harassment, and discrimination because they reject socially imposed gender roles. . . . For instance, compulsory marriage, while it is sometimes used by parents specifically to put an end to lesbian relationships, is also imposed on many girls and women regardless of sexual orientation, and the policing of same-sex relationships cannot be seen in isolation from the policing of relationships which cross lines of race, class, or religion.[17]

Unfortunately, so far in the twenty-first century, the feminists and sexual rights advocates on the other side of the "gender agenda" from the Vatican too rarely make common cause or even seem to see the connections between the issues to which they are committed.[18] Their dominant tendency in recent decades has been silo-ization. Whether these metaphorical silos are hoarding grain in the form of funding or protecting missiles to be launched at the opposition, the result is that each silo (the SOGI silo, the reproductive rights silo, etc.) tightly encloses a set of issues and constituencies far from fruitful interaction with others, and some constituencies are left without a well-filled and fortified silo of their own.

This leaves someone like me in a paradoxical position with respect to the Vatican's articulation of the "gender agenda." As a descriptive matter, the Vatican and I draw very similar connections between the various components of feminist, LGBT, sexual and reproductive rights, and family law reform — when we connect the dots we see a similar figure. The principal difference is the normative spin we each put on it, in that the Vatican's nightmares concerning gender are my dreams and vice versa. (I have noticed similar points of descriptive commonality and diametrically opposed normative spin when I have in the past compared my own vision of sex, gender, and sexuality with that of Justice Scalia.[19]) Unfortunately, those who share more of my normative preferences when it comes to the laws and policies governing sex, gender, sexuality, and the family are all too rarely inclined to make the connections the Vatican and I both see as inescapable. Perhaps part of the reason is that, unlike many other scholars and activists on my side of the "gender agenda," I am strongly inclined to resist the identitarian turn: I find much that is appealing in what for the Vatican is a nightmare vision of "liberation from biological determinism" and from essentialized identity categories.[20] The war over gender is indeed a war of liberation, reminiscent of the late-twentieth-century liberation movements I wish were more central to today's sexual rights advocacy. I would like to see rights extended not on the basis of sex, gender, or orientation identity categories, but to all regardless of the identity categories they may identify with or be categorized into. My dream vision is of people being free and equal no matter who or what they are, not because of who or what they are.[21] Instead of reinforcing the SOGI silo, I would like to see greater recognition by advocates for freedom of sexual and gender expression that not only gays and lesbians have a sexual orientation and not only those who identify as trans have a gender identity in need of protection. I would also like to see my side of debates on the meaning of gender in law — the side of the feminists, the gay rights advocates, the queer theorists — be clear about the relationship our most vehement and thoroughgoing opponents so clearly see between a commitment to traditional sex roles rooted in the subordination of women and an opposition to equal rites and rights for gay and lesbian couples.[22]

Not only do many other advocates for components of the gender agenda today tend to draw too few of the connections the Vatican does between and among their causes, but they also tend to misinterpret the Vatican itself as being almost exclusively obsessed with homosexuality and transsexuality even when a careful reading of the Vatican's pronouncements makes clear much broader concerns about sex and gender are at issue. For example, headlines reporting on the 2008 Christmas speech Benedict XVI made to the members of the Roman Curia tended to read along the lines of "Pope says saving heterosexuality like saving the rainforest."[23] Speaking far more broadly, however, Benedict XVI said the Church "has a responsibility towards creation, and must also publicly assert this responsibility. In so doing, she must not only defend earth, water and air as gifts of creation belonging to all. She must also protect man from self-destruction. What is needed is something like a human ecology, correctly understood. . . . Rain forests deserve indeed to be protected, but no less so does man, as a creature having an innate 'message' which does not contradict our freedom, but is instead its very premise."[24]

Taking seriously the notion of a "human ecology" put at risk by the "gender agenda" has a number of fascinating implications. First, it indicates that Benedict XVI thinks of feminists and advocates for sexual rights in much the same way as environmentalists think of logging companies: they are on the verge, if they are not stopped, of clear-cutting human nature the way loggers are the rainforest. This imagines a level of power and influence, not only on law but on lived human experience, that even the most hopeful supporters and severest critics of what Janet Halley calls "governance feminism" have not hitherto ascribed to feminists or to SOGI activists.[25] It also helps make sense of the Vatican's emphasis on shaping secular law: the Vatican is seeking the equivalent of an endangered species act for the traditional family.

Even more intriguing, it suggests that, in Benedict XVI's view, just as it would be possible to destroy the rainforest, it would also be possible, though similarly inadvisable and contrary to the will of the Creator, for human beings to effect the "self-destruction of man himself" by destroying what he sees as "the nature of the human being as man and woman."[26] In his dire warnings against the imminent risk of human self-destruction, Benedict XVI sounds to me a bit like the Charlton Heston character in *Planet of the Apes*, crying, "You Maniacs! You blew it up! Ah, damn you! God damn you all to hell!"[27]

For all his vaunted more pastoral approach to repentant sexual sinners and his broader environmental consciousness, Pope Francis also sees what he calls "the gender theory" in apocalyptic terms: "Let's think of the nuclear arms, of the possibility to annihilate in a few instants a very high number of human beings. Let's think also of genetic manipulation, of the manipulation of life, or of the gender theory, that does not recognize the order of creation," he said in listing examples of how "every period of history has its own 'Herods' who destroy, plot schemes of death, and disfigure the face of man and woman, destroying creation."[28] Francis's Argentinian background leads him to invoke personal experience when he adds charges of "ideological colonialization" and imperialism to the litany of evils associated with gender. Comparing the indoctrination he associates with programs of gender mainstreaming to those imposed "by dictators of the last century" through "Fascist Youth under Mussolini [and] the Hitler youth," he inveighs against those who tie grants for the education of the poor to the condition that "gender theory [be] taught," something he said happened to an Argentinian woman of his acquaintance in 1995 and of which the African bishops complained at the 2014 Synod.[29] Because both gender mainstreaming and women's and LGBT equality are commitments of the European Union, even Polish bishops complain of imperialism and colonization when describing pressure to implement sex equality in the newer EU member states.[30] Francis and his Church share this rhetoric of colonization in the face of indigenous traditions with notorious fellow warriors in the war on sex and gender, from Putin's Russia to the African nations, which, influenced by American evangelicals, have declared homosexuality to be an un-African imperialist import from colonizing nations.[31]

Proponents of sexual rights have, I think, much to learn from their opponents' fight against gender. We should not just become aware of our opponents' strategies and tactics, but in some cases we should take them as a model. And we should strive more closely to resemble our opponents' vision of who we are and what we stand for. Let me conclude by briefly suggesting a few examples of how this might be done. The first is that we should actively embrace the radical possibility for change the Vatican ascribes to us — just as the notion that all men are born free and equal was a transformative innovation in the face of millennia of subordination by race, class, and ethnicity, so too the notion that sex and gender roles should no longer imprison and subordinate individuals could indeed transform — but would not destroy — humanity.[32]

Second, we should recognize that sexual rights are what the Vatican would call a seamless garment.[33] In recent years, silos have rent this garment in ways foresighted activists long warned against.[34] Thus, for example, the same-sex marriage movement in the United States may have offered what the Supreme Court describes as new "dignity" and protection from "humiliation" to same-sex couples willing to marry and to their children,[35] but it has left those individuals of all sexes and orientations who are unwilling or unable to conform their sexual relationships or their family lives to such a marital model with fewer possibilities for recognition and acceptance. In the world of the UN and of international NGOs, gender and sexual rights have been divided into the territories of women's rights, reproductive rights, and SOGI, which compete for funds and attention rather than weaving a seamless vision fostering cooperation.[36] While the Vatican sees the fight against abortion, contraception, the new reproductive technologies, and gay rights as part of a single war, its opponents by and large do not, forgoing what may be opportunities not only for fruitful alliances, but also for a less narrowly focused vision of their struggles.

The field of education has been a central battleground in the war on gender as well as the war on sex, nationally and internationally. As noted earlier, Pope Francis focused on conditions placed on education funding in inveighing against ideological colonization in Africa and Latin America. In France, the first skirmish in the most recent outbreak in the war on gender came in September 2011, when eighty deputies from Nicolas Sarkozy's ruling UMP party seconded a call previously made by officials of the French Catholic Church for the immediate withdrawal of new French public high school textbooks in life sciences because the textbooks included discussion of "gender theory, or the idea that masculinity and femininity are socially constructed."[37] Anti-gender activists in countries across Europe have delayed or hindered adoption of educational programs designed to promote sex equality, whether it be France's ABCDs of Equality, replaced in 2014 after protests from Catholics and other activists, or the European Union's Estrela Report on sexual and reproductive health and rights, which dealt with age-appropriate sexual education as well as with contraception and abortion, and which was rejected in 2013 as a result of lobbying by those under Vatican influence.[38] In the United States anti-gay culture warriors from Anita Bryant in the last millennium to the proponents of Proposition 8 in California have made a central part of their campaign their fears about what would be taught to children concerning sex and gender. Government-funded abstinence-only sex education programs have failed in their aim of preventing teen pregnancy and disease but have succeeded in inculcating constitutionally problematic sexual stereotypes.[39]

Perhaps more clearly than any battles since those at the Beijing conference in 1995, these national and international battles over sex education in the schools illustrate the inextricable connections Ratzinger highlighted decades ago between the war the Vatican has declared on gender and the war on sex analyzed in this volume, or, to put it more affirmatively, between the achievement of a broad sexual rights agenda and the repudiation of "fixed notions concerning the roles and abilities of males and females."[40] It is therefore particularly unfortunate that, while unity of purpose still strengthens conservative opponents of comprehensive sex education in U.S. schools, who set themselves against favorable discussion of contraception, abortion, homosexuality, sex outside of marriage, and gender fluidity, a tendency to silo-ization still limits those who favor sexual freedom and empowerment. Instead of continuing down a path of silo-ization, the ubiquitous Gay Straight Alliances of students should routinely go beyond supporting queer kids to also provide much needed support for straight girls' rights to sexual self-determination and pleasure. Instead of enforcing sex-specific dress codes with exceptions only for those willing to identify as trans, U.S. schools should make dress codes sex neutral; indeed, they might follow the French ABCDs of Equality's example of "skirt day," when boys are encouraged to wear traditionally female clothing. Nearly a quarter century after Surgeon General Jocelynn Elders lost her job for acknowledging at a UN conference on AIDS that "masturbation is something that is a part of human sexuality and perhaps should be taught," we should at long last take up her suggestion. We should do these things because not until we weave a seamless garment of sexual rights for the next generation will there be hope for a just peace in the war on sex.[41]

NOTES

This chapter forms part of a much larger project on the Vatican and gender, and incorporates portions of my earlier work from *After Gender the Destruction of Man? The Vatican's Nightmare Vision of the Gender Agenda for Law*, 31 PACE L. REV. 802 (2012) and "The Role of the Popes in the Invention of Sexual Complementarity and the Anathematization of Gender," *Religion and Gender*, March 29, 2016, https://www .religionandgender.org/articles/abstract/10.18352/rg.10124/.

1. In imitation of the tactics of the topless feminist protest group Femen, a group of anti–gay marriage activists calling themselves Hommen covered their faces and bared their bodies in street protests in the spring of 2013, after the passage of a bill opening marriage to same-sex couples.

2. For the objections raised by the Vatican to the use of the word "gender" in Beijing, see *U.N. Report on the Fourth World Conference on Women, Beijing, China*, U.N. Doc. A/Conf.177/20 (Sept. 4–15, 1995), 162. For its more recent objections to "a radical definition of 'gender,' which asserts that sexual identity can somehow be adapted indefinitely to suit new and different purposes" in the 55th session of the Commission on the Status of Women of the United Nations Economic and Social Council, see The Permanent Observer Mission of the Holy See to the United Nations, *Statement of the Holy See in Explanation of Position on the Agreed Conclusions*, http://www .holyseemission.org/statements/statement.aspx?id=73. As critics repeatedly point out, there is, of course, no single "theory of gender." Two different usages of the word "gender" are at the root of the Vatican's distress, however. First, academics use the word to distinguish cultural or attitudinal characteristics associated with the sexes from biological characteristics (i.e., to distinguish masculine and feminine from male and female). Second, policymakers and lawyers, following the example of Ruth Bader Ginsburg, use the terms "gender" and "sex" interchangeably in legal documents. These two uses of the term "gender" may seem antithetical, with the first stressing the distinction between sex and gender, the second using the terms interchangeably and synonymously. But, from the Vatican's perspective, there is the same reason to be concerned about both usages: each is associated with what Pope Benedict XVI condemned as "the obscuring of the difference or duality of the sexes," discussed below.

3. Halperin, "Introduction: The War on Sex," this volume.

4. Joseph Cardinal Ratzinger and Vittorio Messori, *The Ratzinger Report: An Exclusive Interview on the State of the Church* (San Francisco: Ignatius, 1985), 95; Ratzinger, *Letter to the Bishops of the Catholic Church on the Collaboration of M[a]n and Wom[a]n in the Church and in the World,* May 31, 2004, http://www.vatican.va/roman_curia/congregations/cfaith/documents/rc_con_cfaith_doc_20040731_collaboration_en.html; Pope Benedict XVI, *Address of His Holiness Benedict XVI to the Members of the Roman Curia for the Traditional Exchange of Christmas Greetings,* December 22, 2008, http://www.vatican.va/holy_father/benedict_xvi/speeches/2008/december/documents/hf_ben-xvi_spe_20081222_curia-romana_en.html. I have made the alteration in the title of *Letter to the Bishops* because, although the official English translation speaks of the "Collaboration of Men and Women," the Italian and every other official language I can read speaks of the sexes in the singular — for example, "Uomo e . . . Donna" or "Mann und Frau." The use in particular of "woman" in the singular, as an essential or ideal type, is one of the most problematic aspects of the theological anthropology of complementarity, on which the Vatican bases its repudiation of what it calls the gender agenda.

5. Pontifical Council on the Family. *Lexicon. Termini ambigui e discussi su famiglia, vita e questioni etiche* (Bologna: Edizioni Dehoniane, 2003). English translation: *Lexicon: Ambiguous and Debatable Terms Regarding Family Life and Ethical Questions* (Front Royal, VA: Human Life International, 2006).

6. See, for example, John L. Allen Jr., "Secularism, Africa and Characters in Rome," *National Catholic Reporter,* August 20, 2010, http://ncronline.org/blogs/all-things-catholic/secularism-africa-and-characters-rome.

7. For a collection of such slogans from the follow-up demonstration in 2014, see Marie Piquemal and Catherine Lemoël, "Récit de la journée: Manif pour tous, l'heure de la dispersion," *Libération,* February 2, 2014, http://www.liberation.fr/societe/2014/02/02/manif-pour-tous-le-retour_977189.

8. See Humanum, http://humanum.it/ (accessed February 1, 2016). Those in attendance included, from the United States, Rick Warren, Russell Moore, officials of Focus on the Family, Robert George, and other marquee names in the fight against same-sex marriage.

9. Ratzinger and Messori, *The Ratzinger Report,* 95.

10. In the Douay-Rheims translation, "There is neither Jew nor Greek: there is neither slave nor free: there is neither male nor female. For you are all one in Christ Jesus."

11. Ratzinger, *Letter to the Bishops.* For a discussion of how complementarity came to be Catholic orthodoxy, see Case, "The Role of the Popes."

12. Paul VI, *Humanae Vitae,* July 25, 1968, http://w2.vatican.va/content/paul-vi/en/encyclicals/documents/hf_p-vi_enc_25071968_humanae-vitae.html; Sacred

Congregation on the Doctrine of the Faith, *Persona Humana: Declaration Concerning Certain Questions on Sexual Ethics*, December 29, 1975, http://www.vatican.va/roman _curia/congregations/cfaith/documents/rc_con_cfaith_doc_19751229_persona -humana_en.html; Sacred Congregation on the Doctrine of the Faith, *Inter Insigniores: Declaration on the Admission of Women to the Ministerial Priesthood*, October 15, 1976, http://www.vatican.va/roman_curia/congregations/cfaith/documents/rc_con _cfaith_doc_19761015_inter-insigniores_en.html.

13. Sacred Congregation, *Inter Insigniores*.

14. Ratzinger, *Letter to the Bishops*.

15. Ratzinger and Messori, *The Ratzinger Report*, 84–86.

16. While the term "gender agenda" has been embraced by the United Nations, I am using the term here as imagined, defined, and rejected by the Vatican and by religiously motivated conservatives under its influence. Compare, for example, United Nations, *Global Gender Agenda and the United Nations*, http://www.un.org/ecosocdev /geninfo/women/gender.htm (accessed December 14, 2011) with, for example, Dale O'Leary, *The Gender Agenda Redefining Equality* (Lafayette, LA: Vital Issues Press, 1997), which describes from a Catholic perspective the process by which the Vatican and other religious participants opposed the feminist use of the term "gender" at the 1994 International Conference on Population and Development in Cairo and the 1995 Fourth World Conference on Women in Beijing.

17. Rachel Rosenbloom, "Introduction," in *Unspoken Rules: Sexual Orientation and Women's Human Rights*, edited by Rachel Rosenbloom (London: Cassell, 1996), ix.

18. See, for example, Ali Miller, *Fighting Over the Figure of Gender*, 31 PACE L. REV. 837, at 847, 840–1 (2011), describing "two superficially distinct guises of gender territorialization in the U.N.": an "overt . . . turf fight" and "a tension . . . discernible in a deafening silence" between "advocacy groups representing 'gender as identity/ woman'" and "groups representing 'gender as gay or trans identity/male.'"

19. See, for example, Mary Anne Case, "*The Very Stereotype the Law Condemns*": *Constitutional Sex Discrimination Law as a Quest for Perfect Proxies*, 85 CORNELL L. REV. 1447, 1448 (2000), discussing Scalia's dissent in the VMI case.

20. Sacred Congregation, *Persona Humana*; and Case, "*The Very Stereotype the Law Condemns.*"

21. Among the many works in which I have previously defended such a vision of liberation from rigid identity categories are *Disaggregating Gender from Sex and Sexual Orientation: The Effeminate Man in the Law and Feminist Jurisprudence*, 105 YALE L.J. 1 (1995); *Unpacking Package Deals: Separate Spheres Are Not the Answer*, 75 DENV. U. L. REV. 1305 (1998); and *What Feminists Have to Lose in Same-Sex Marriage Litigation*, 57 UCLA L. REV. 1199, 1203–09 (2010).

22. See Case, *What Feminists Have to Lose*, at 1209. In this earlier essay, I argued that "recognition of same-sex marriage and elimination of enforced sex roles are as inextricably intertwined as the duck is with the rabbit in the famous optical illusion." *Id.* at 1233.

23. See, for example, "Pope Says Saving Heterosexuality Like Saving the Rainforest," *Reuters*, December 22, 2008, http://blogs.reuters.com/faithworld/2008/12/22/pope-says-saving-heterosexuality-like-saving-the-rainforest/.

24. Pope Benedict XVI, *Address of His Holiness*.

25. See Janet Halley et al., *From the International to the Local in Feminist Legal Responses to Rape, Prostitution/Sex Work and Sex Trafficking: Four Studies in Contemporary Governance Feminism*, 29 HARV. J.L. & GENDER 335, 340 (2006).

26. Benedict XVI, *Address of His Holiness*. His argument here echoes similar arguments made in twentieth-century French family law reform debates by public intellectuals with Catholic connections, who invoked Lacanian psychoanalytic theories and philosophical anthropology to argue that any move to eliminate traditional sex distinctions in French family law (for example, through recognition of same-sex couples, new reproductive technologies, gay and single-parent adoptions) could, by disrupting the symbolic order, "bring about a generalized state of social chaos and psychic distress, in a worst case scenario turning society and all within it psychotic." See Camille Robcis, *French Sexual Politics from Human Rights to the Anthropological Function of the Law*, 33.1 FRENCH HIST. STUD. 129, 132 (2010).

27. *Planet of the Apes* (APJAC Productions, 1968). Perhaps one reason why this image springs to mind is that Charlton Heston's character, George Taylor, also laments, in tones reminiscent of the Vatican's concerns about sexual freedom's threat to a marriage culture, that on Earth there was "Lots of love-making but no love. You see, that was the kind of world we'd made."

28. Andrea Tornielli and Giacomo Galeazzi, *This Economy Kills: Pope Francis on Capitalism and Social Justice* (Collegeville, MN: Liturgical Press, 2015), 149–150.

29. "Apostolic Journey of His Holiness Pope Francis to Sri Lanka and the Philippines (12–19 January 2015)," In-Flight Press Conference of His Holiness Pope Francis from the Philippines to Rome, January 19, 2015, http://w2.vatican.va/content/francesco/en/speeches/2015/january/documents/papa-francesco_20150119_srilanka-filippine-conferenza-stampa.html. ("This is ideological colonization. They enter with an idea that has nothing to do with the people; but with groups of people yes, but not with the people. It colonizes the people with an idea that wants to change a mentality or a structure.")

30. See, for example, Slawomir Sierakowski, "The Polish Church's Gender Problem," *New York Times*, January 26, 2014, http://www.nytimes.com/2014/01/27/opinion

/sierakowski-the-polish-churchs-gender-problem.html, describing how "gender" became the 2013 word of the year in Poland, largely because of protests by Polish clergy that the "ideology of gender presents a threat worse than Nazism and Communism combined."

31. For Francis to use the charge of "ideological colonization" as a slur against feminists and sexual rights activists is particularly ironic as he prepared to canonize Father Junipero Serra, despite Serra's lack of the ordinarily requisite number of miracles and in the face of active protests by Native American groups who claim the missionary enslaved and tortured their ancestors. Similarly, many have noted the irony in African nations still enforcing sodomy laws imported in the colonial era from Britain claiming that homosexuality, rather than its condemnation, is a colonial import.

32. As I and others have previously argued, this is a vision with deep roots in Christianity, a vision which, in earlier times, the Catholic Church itself embraced more than it seems to do today.

33. The term, stemming from the garment Jesus is said to have worn before the crucifixion, has been applied by spokespersons for the Catholic Church in a variety of contexts to issues that should not be artificially isolated from one another. Most relevant to the present discussion, Joseph Cardinal Bernardin, following the lead of Catholic peace activist Eileen Egan, who coined the term, wrote about "The Seamless Garment" in the context of "A Consistent Ethic of Life," which would unite Catholic teaching and activism against abortion, birth control, and euthanasia with that against the death penalty, war, and hunger. See, for example, Joseph Cardinal Bernardin, "A Consistent Ethic of Life: Continuing the Dialogue," The William Wade Lecture Series, St. Louis University, March 11, 1984, http://www.priestsforlife.org/magisterium/bernardinwade.html.

34. See, for example, Nancy D. Polikoff, We Will Get What We Ask For: Why Legalizing Gay and Lesbian Marriage Will Not "Dismantle the Legal Structure of Gender in Every Marriage," 79 VA. L. REV. 1535 (1993).

35. Language about the "dignity" of marriage was central to Justice Kennedy's majority opinions in both of the recent Supreme Court opinions concerning same-sex marriage — Obergefell v. Hodges, 135 S. Ct. 2584 (2015) and Windsor v. U.S., 133 S. Ct. 2675 (2013) — each of which expressed concern about the "humiliation" of children raised by same-sex couples were same-sex marriage not to be fully recognized.

36. See, for example, Miller, Fighting Over the Figure of Gender.

37. Ruadhán Mac Cormaic, "French Schoolbook Ignites Gender Debate," Irish Times, September 7, 2011, http://www.irishtimes.com/newspaper/world/2011/0907/1224303639424.html.

38. See for example, Martine Storti, "L'abandon des ABCD de l'Egalité, symbole de l'abdication idéologique de la gauche," Le Monde, July 2, 2015, http://www.lemonde

.fr/idees/article/2014/07/02/l-abandon-des-abcd-de-l-egalite-symbole-de-l
-abdication-ideologique-de-la-gauche_4448865_3232.html; European Parliament
Committee on Women's Rights and Gender Equality, *Estrela Report on Sexual and
Reproductive Health and Rights*, December 3, 2013, http://www.europarl.europa.eu
/sides/getDoc.do?pubRef=-//EP//TEXT+REPORT+A7-2013-0426+0+DOC
+XML+Vo//EN.

39. For discussion, see Cornelia T. L. Pillard, *Our Other Reproductive Choices: Equality in Sex Education, Contraceptive Access, and Work-Family Policy*, 56 EMORY L.J. 941, 956–57 (2007).

40. Miss. Univ. for Women v. Hogan, 458 U.S. 718, 724–25 (1982).

41. See Mary Anne Case, *Feminist Fundamentalism on the Frontier Between Government and Family Responsibility for Children*, 2009 UTAH L. REV. 381, 391-5, discussing conservative efforts to limit education about sexual freedom and sexual equality; Mary Anne Case, *Legal Protections for the Personal Best of Each Employee: Title VII's Prohibition on Sex Discrimination, the Legacy of Price Waterhouse v. Hopkins, and the Prospect of ENDA*, 66 STANFORD L. REV 1333 (2014), discussing sex specific school dress codes; Jack Schonfeld, "Remember That Time Bill Clinton Fired His Surgeon General for Encouraging Masturbation Education," *Newsweek*, February 5, 2016, http://www.newsweek.com/remember-time-bill-clinton-fired-his-surgeon-general
-encouraging-masturbation-423302.

PART II

The
Invention
of the
Sex Offender

|6|

Sex Panic, Psychiatry, and the Expansion of the Carceral State

In 1949, George Raymond was brutally beaten by two men he and a friend picked up for sex. After the assault, he ran toward the road, hailed a car, and asked to be taken to the police. "I don't recall why I did this," he stated, "for later I had every reason not to call the police."[1] Rather than chasing down Raymond's assailants, the police took Raymond to jail. He was later examined by two psychiatrists, who, when they learned of his sexual history with other men and with adolescent boys, determined him to be a sexual psychopath. So diagnosed, and without a criminal charge or conviction, he was committed indefinitely to Saint Elizabeths Hospital, the federal institution for the mentally ill in Washington, D.C.

Raymond was institutionalized under what became known as Public Law 615 or the Miller Law, passed in the District of Columbia a year before his arrest in 1948 and named for its sponsor, Nebraska Representative Arthur Lewis Miller. The new law increased the punishment for sexual offenses with minors as well as for sodomy, defined in the law as penetration "however slight" of the mouth or anus of one person with the sexual organs of another. The Miller Law amended that anatomically precise definition to cast its net more widely by including under sodomy's scope "any other unnatural or perverted sexual act with any other person or animal."[2] That strategic vagueness dramatically expanded the law's purview.

With the exception of sodomy, the Miller Law did not name the specific sexual acts it deemed immoral or criminal, nor did it differentiate between felonies and misdemeanors, violent and nonviolent crimes, or consensual and nonconsensual sexual acts. The aspect of the law that most radically enlarged its scope was its criminalization of behavior characterized sweepingly as "inviting for the purpose of immorality."[3] Under the Miller Law, a person identified as a "recidivist" in any of these categories of sexual offense was examined by two psychiatrists to determine whether they were a sexual psychopath — in the law's definition, "a person, not insane, who by a course of repeated misconduct in sexual matters has evidenced such lack of power to control his sexual impulses as to be dangerous to other persons" — and if found to be so, they would be committed indefinitely to Saint Elizabeths Hospital.[4] No criminal charge was required. Once institutionalized, people diagnosed as sexual psychopaths were treated according to the therapeutic trends of the day: individual and group psychotherapy, insulin and electro-shock therapy, chemotherapy, and in rare instances, lobotomy.[5]

While propaganda about the Miller Law evoked the dangers posed by sexual psychopaths to children, the law was used most extensively to criminalize consensual sex between adults of the same sex (as were sexual psychopath laws passed in twenty-nine states by the late 1950s).[6] Although not a pioneering law (by the time it was introduced in 1948, seven states already had similar laws on the books), the Miller Law was distinguished by the fact that it was initiated and passed at the federal level by the U.S. Congress.[7] And so while it governed the relatively small geographical territory of the District of Columbia, it bore the imprimatur of the federal state. Passed in the period known to historians for witnessing the height of hostility toward sexual and gender nonconformity, the Miller Law was part of a national wave of sexual psychopath laws that vastly expanded the criminalization of non-normative sex, especially homosexual sex between men, and part of a larger state project of regulating and policing homosexuality.

The midcentury sexual psychopath scare has been analyzed by historians George Chauncey, Estelle Freedman, and others who have tracked the way in which panics were sparked by sensationalizing media reporting on sex crimes, usually involving the spectacularly brutal murder of a child. Bills criminalizing a range of sexual offenses were promoted by grassroots citizens groups and then sponsored by state legislators and enacted into law. Historians have exposed those scares' exaggerated imaginings of risk and the ways in which panic about sexual psychopaths functioned as proxies for other postwar social anxieties: about the hypermasculinization and potential violence of returning veterans, the wartime dislocation of sexual and gender norms, Cold War threats to national security, and the heightened visibility of postwar gay and lesbian urban subcultures.[8]

This essay joins those critical examinations of how non-normative sex became the focus of state regulation and social control in the postwar United

States, with an interest in understanding the criminalization of sexual differ-ence in that formative historical period as well as the sexual politics of the decades that followed. The evolution of Washington, D.C.'s Miller Law offers a study in the codification of a sex panic into law, and also a preview and ge-nealogy of the seemingly ever-expanding regime of sex offender surveillance and punishment that we live with today. Looking closely at the extensive con-gressional debate over the Miller Law, this essay locates psychiatric authority at the center of its justifying logics and proposes that the discourse of medi-cine — the language of illness, treatment, and cure — masked a midcentury expansion of the carceral state that anticipated the more widely examined carceral explosion of the 1970s, 1980s, and 1990s.

Medical discourse helped usher in sexual psychopath legislation; it also mystified the laws' criminalization of sexual difference in ways that made them difficult to challenge, both at their moment of origin in the 1940s and 1950s and in their later incarnations as sex offender legislation after 1990. Attend-ing to the importance of the psychiatric authority and medical discourse that underwrote midcentury sexual psychopath laws, as well as the efforts to chal-lenge and overthrow psychiatric authority on the part of gay activists in the 1960s and early 1970s, offers some clues to understanding the ambivalent and often muted response of early gay rights activists to sexual psychopath legisla-tion, and perhaps even the silence on the part of contemporary LGBT politics in response to the more recent and sweeping national wave of laws criminal-izing sexual offenders since 1990.

THE MILLER LAW, MEDICALIZATION, AND CRIMINALIZATION

When the Miller Law was proposed in Washington, D.C., in 1948, the con-text of sexual panic that made laws like it seem so necessary and made the rationales for the expansion of criminal categories and the policing of deviant sexuality so persuasive were already part of the national common sense, set in legal precedent and declared constitutional in higher courts. The Minne-sota sexual psychopath statute upon which the Miller Law was modeled had survived constitutional challenge in the state's highest court in 1939, and the U.S. Supreme Court approved the Minnesota law in 1940. When the Miller Law was proposed in 1948, seven states already had sexual psychopath laws on the books. While it was perhaps inevitable, then, that the bill would move quickly through Congress, some lawmakers expressed concerns about the law's dramatic expansion of state power despite a solidifying consensus around the virtue and legitimacy of sexual psychopath laws. In the congressional subcommittee hearings on the bill, Iowa Congressman Joseph O'Hara poked fun at the potentially awesome reach of the proposed law and its structuring paranoia, remarking that its broad and vague definition of sexual psychopaths as persons who lacked the power to control their sexual impulses reminded him "of a little quip. 'All the world is queer but thee and me, and even thou art a little queer.' "[9] Saint Elizabeths psychiatrist Benjamin Karpman, invited to testify before Congress as an expert in the psychiatric treatment of criminals, raised a hypothetical question about the husband and wife who, "to prevent having more children, . . . indulge in what [the Miller Law termed] sodomy." What if the wife were to sue for divorce and charge her husband with violation of the law? he asked. "Are you going to send him to St. Elizabeths?" Karpman also raised questions about the law's more likely targets. Anticipating claims about privacy that would come to be so important more than half a century later in arguments for the decriminalization of homosexuality, Karpman asked about the man "who is a pervert in the strictest sense of the word, but makes it a business of his own?"[10]

These voices of skepticism were quickly stifled in congressional hearings on the bill. Representative George MacKinnon, sponsor of that 1939 Minnesota sexual psychopath law, shot down Karpman's suggestion that a man's perversion might be his own business. Although the imperiled child was the privileged subject of community outrage and media reporting on sex crimes and has been characterized by historians as the instigating motor of these laws, MacKinnon responded to Karpman's criticisms by referencing not the murderer of children but rather, and revealingly, the person who "is a constant menace to society, particularly to younger boys and young men." That person, not identified explicitly as homosexual, presumably because the equation of homosexuality and predation was so familiar, was particularly dangerous, MacKinnon insisted, in contexts of hierarchical relations among men such as the military and the labor force: "They go around and they may not force them, but the fact that they may have a superior rank, they may be a chief petty officer where the boy is in a subordinate capacity; and the same thing exists out in the ordinary, everyday life where somebody may be an employer. . . . And while it is true there is no act of force, such a person is a substantial menace to society."[11] While historians have characterized gay men as the collateral victims of midcentury sexual psychopath laws that targeted violent sexual crimes and children, the congressional debate on the Miller Law reveals male homosexuality to have been a central target. The virtue of the Miller Law, in the eyes of its proponents, was in criminalizing such acts of "social menace" that would not have been captured by existing criminal law but were newly understood as indicative of dangerous sexual psychopathy.

Advocates of the Miller Law succeeded both in expanding the criminalization of non-normative sex and effectively mystifying that expansion by medicalizing sexual deviance. When the bill was first introduced, sexual deviance was described in criminal terms, emphasizing the law's punitive aims. In calling to order the hearing of the congressional subcommittee on February 20, 1948, Representative Miller described the bill as one "to provide for the *commitment, detention, and treatment of criminal sexual psychopaths.*"[12] But as the bill was discussed and revised, references to criminality, detention, and punishment were whittled away. In the law's final form just three months later, passed on May 20, 1948, it was described as providing for "the treatment of sexual psychopaths in the District of Columbia, and for other purposes."[13]

The question of the law's intent with respect to issues of punishment and treatment came up repeatedly in subcommittee hearings. When Kentucky Representative Frank Chelf asked for clarification about the "penalty" or "final punishment" for a person charged under the Miller Law in order to be certain that the proposed law would not weaken punishment for sexual crimes, Congressman MacKinnon explained that it "does not provide for any criminal penalty. It provides that such persons shall be considered as sick persons, and they are to be handled in that way rather than as criminals."[14] Saint Elizabeths superintendent Winfred Overholser, called upon to testify in the hearings, offered his professional authority to support this position, stating, "As a physician I would rather see them dealt with outside the criminal law."[15]

In line with the Miller Law's medicalized conception of sexual psychopathy, the person charged under its statutes was not referred to as "the defendant" or "the accused." The language of the act explained that "a person against whom a statement is filed . . . is referred to throughout as a 'patient.' This is in accordance with the theory that the title essentially provides treatment rather than punishment."[16] The virtue of the law, in Overholser's understanding, was in recognizing "a very large group of offenders as essentially sick people rather than vicious ones."[17]

The Miller Law's insistence on the conceptualization of the sexual psychopath as a "patient" rather than a "defendant" and its use of the medical language of treatment instead of incarceration and punishment had several important effects. Since it mandated the hospitalization and ideally the rehabilitation of the sexual psychopath rather than punitive incarceration, it allowed supporters to characterize the law as progressive and humane. The description of the bill that went before Congress touted it as being "in conformity with the most up-to-date thinking in the fields of psychiatry and criminal law."[18] MacKinnon described the Miller Law as "dealing in what you might call a more modern way with these psychopathic personalities."[19] Overholser praised the proposed legislation "as progressive, as practical, as indicating a closer union of the law with medicine, and as indicating that the law is ready to take advantage of the scientific knowledge concerning behavior."[20] Medical language aligned sexual psychopath laws rhetorically with modernity and progress.

The medicalization of the sexual psychopath had important juridical effects as well. In taking the determination of sexual psychopathy out of the courtroom and into the psychiatric clinic, the Miller Law effectively evaded due process. While people formally defined as "defendants" required a trial by jury, privilege against self-incrimination, and protection against double jeopardy, people defined as "patients" did not. "Since the proceedings here in question are not of a criminal character," MacKinnon stated, "the constitutional right to a jury trial does not apply to proceedings of this type."[21] This was the case even for what members of Congress and Overholser acknowledged would potentially result in lifelong carceral institutionalization.

A generous reading of the Miller Law might take the law at its progressive word, viewing its investment in treatment and cure as part of a more general swing of the pendulum of U.S. penal history away from retribution and toward rehabilitation. In fact, the postwar period is characterized by historians of the prison as a time when the "rehabilitative ideal" held sway, and sexual psychopath laws were heralded by some at the time as the pinnacle of progressive thinking about crime as psychologically motivated and the criminal as rehabilitatable. But the psychiatric language of treatment and cure did not evade what Michel Foucault called "the sordid business of punishing."[22] On the contrary, removing the language and apparatus of criminalization at once erased and facilitated the enlargement of the scope of the law and the expanded powers of the state. The Miller Law's advocates understood and valued that expansion. Saint Elizabeths superintendent Overholser recognized the intent and aim of the law as the "widening ... of the scope as to the group of persons who are recognized by the law as needing treatment for their benefit and for the benefit of society."[23] In proposing changing the law's subject from "criminal sexual psychopath" to "sexual psychopath," MacKinnon rejected the language of "criminal" not simply as unmodern in its punitive stance but also as "too restrictive." He continued by explaining that "a lot of these acts of a sexual nature are not what might be classed as criminal. . . . I think if you are going to make it necessary to show that there is a criminal propensity, that is too strict a burden."[24]

When the bill came to a vote, MacKinnon referred to a tacit common understanding of the purpose of this expansion of the law, stating, "I am sure we are all familiar with a great many of the circumstances surrounding many of these offenses, or breaches of good conduct, and I don't think . . . that it is desirable to make it necessary to first file a criminal charge before you can subject the individual to treatment."[25] MacKinnon made clear that while the bill included "some provisions dealing with what may be classed as sex crimes," and that the law "provides for increased penalties" for those crimes, the proposed law "adds additional offenses and penalties therefore for breaches of public decorum that have not previously been covered by District statutes."[26] The virtue of this kind of legislation, two psychiatrists noted shrewdly several years after its passage, was that it "satisfied the diverse strivings and tendencies of both the treatment-minded and the punishment-minded."[27] When the Miller Law was presented in Congress, the main line of questioning had to do with whether it would weaken or strengthen the sex laws in the District. With the reassurance from its sponsors that it would strengthen them "very much," it passed.[28]

The medicalized underwriting of criminalization in the Miller Law and other sexual psychopath laws is especially striking given the ambivalence on the part of psychiatrists regarding the laws and the psychiatric concepts that underwrote them. The term "sexual psychopath" connoted medical authority. It was a more purportedly scientific term than the terms "sex pervert," "sex deviate," or "sexual degenerate" that circulated around the same time in the press and popular culture (although vernacular references to the "sexual pervert" did appear in congressional discussion of the bill).[29] As MacKinnon pointed out, "It is true that the term 'psychopathic' is not a part of the working vocabulary of most people. Yet the reasonably well informed recognize it as having reference to mental disorders."[30] In fact, that was the term's great advantage: it sounded more like a diagnosis than an expression of disgust.

It seemed to matter little to legislators that many psychiatrists had long dismissed the diagnostic category of the "psychopath" as a "wastebasket diagnosis."[31] As early as 1924, the distinguished psychiatrist William Alanson White proclaimed that the category of the psychopath had become "a sort of middle ground for the dumping of odds and ends" and was not a meaningful medical category.[32] Psychoanalyst Benjamin Karpman, holding that mental disorder was at the root of all crime and envisioning a future when mental hospitals would replace prisons, stated provocatively in congressional subcommittee hearings, "I object to the use of the word 'criminal,' and I object to the use of the word 'psychopath.'"[33] Although Karpman was recognized as an expert in the study of the psychopathic criminal and authored some of earliest work in the 1930s linking criminality to sexual deviance, by 1951 he had come to the conclusion that "the terms 'sexual psychopath' and 'sexual psychopathy' have no legitimate place in psychiatric nosology or dynamic classification."[34] The first edition of the *Diagnostic and Statistical Manual of Mental Disorders* (*DSM*) in 1953 did not include sexual psychopathy as a diagnostic category. Many psychiatrists in this period were reluctant to subsume homosexuality in particular under the diagnostic label of psychopathy, even though there was broad consensus among psychiatrists that it was a neurosis or personality disorder worthy of its own *DSM* classification.

Psychiatrists were especially critical of the portion of the Miller Law and other sexual psychopath laws that compelled defendants under penalty of law to answer questions asked by psychiatrists who were charged by the court with determining whether they met the statutory standard for sexual psychopathy. As Overholser observed, "you cannot expect to get the truth from him when you are holding a club over his head."[35] Psychiatrists were also less optimistic than legislators about a "cure" for sex offenders. While Karpman boasted about his success in curing "sex perverts," Overholser expressed his reservations about the Miller Law's imperative that sexual psychopaths be institutionalized until they were deemed "'fully and permanently recovered.'"[36] Nearly a decade later, in 1956, psychiatric experts reported in a public forum on sex offenders that "neither a prison term nor surgery may make him change his ways."[37] Such a determination of cure was especially difficult "if not impossible to render," psychiatrist Karl Bowman later claimed, in the case of homosexuals.[38]

The expanded criminalization of non-normative sex, then, was promoted, justified, and effectively erased as such through the discourse of medicine. The carceral and criminal expansion sanctioned by new sexual psychopath laws was accomplished through the language of illness, treatment, and cure. Medicalized language and the support, however ambivalent, of psychiatrists, emboldened by their new prestige after the war and eager to expand their professional purview into the criminal justice system, licensed this carceral

expansion. As Overholser told members of Congress about sexual psychopaths, "[i]t is an interesting group from a therapeutic point of view and we
should welcome the opportunity to deal with them."[39]

NONPATIENT HOMOSEXUALS

In 1948, the year the Miller Law was passed, and as the postwar policing of homosexuality intensified, Harry Hay first conceived of an activist group committed to reconceptualizing homosexuality as something comprising a minority
group worthy of protection from persecution and discrimination rather than
as an individual problem or pathology. With a group of friends in Los Angeles
in 1950, Hay founded the Mattachine Society, and local branches were formed
across the country in the years that followed.

Mattachine organizations often courted allies among professionals and experts and invited them to speak at their meetings, and in 1964, D.C. attorney
Sidney Sachs met with members of the Mattachine Society of New York to
discuss the Miller Law, then sixteen years in operation. Sachs noted that in the
ten years between 1954 and 1964 there had been ninety-three Miller Law admissions to Saint Elizabeths Hospital, averaging between nine and ten people
per year. At the time of his talk, he reported, there were forty-nine people on
the hospital's rolls listed as sexual psychopath admissions.[40] Of course, this
number was very small in relation to the number of people arrested in the
District for same-sex sex. "So you can see," Sachs told Mattachine members,
"that the statute is very seldom used." Sachs encouraged his audience to take
comfort in the fact that "everything on the books that is oppressive to homosexuals is not carried out to the letter."[41]

The responses of Mattachine members to Sachs's presentation captured the
complex and critical relationship that gay men and lesbians were forging in
the 1960s to psychiatric authority and to the pathologization and criminalization of homosexuality that it sanctioned. Mattachine members in attendance
at Sachs's talk seemed to understand that the terrorizing effect of the Miller
Law and other sexual psychopath laws — naming homosexuality a form of
sexual psychopathy and identifying it as a social menace, erasing distinctions
between consensual same-sex sex and violent sexual assault, conflating the
male homosexual and the pedophile, and licensing a massive upsurge in the
policing of gay cruising areas — had a much longer reach than the law itself.
Some reasonably imagined themselves to be the potential targets of such

laws. One Mattachine member countered Sachs's efforts to de-dramatize and minimize the effects of the Miller Law, observing that "the weight of these laws is such that homosexuals per se can be hospitalized by some arbitrary decision, that somehow this status falls within the purview of the law."[42] That comment was an astute one, capturing the way that sexual psychopath laws targeted a "status" — a kind of personality or type defined by a lack of control over sexual impulses — rather than a particular crime. Another noted that, in the terms of the law, he was clearly a "recidivist": "I am a homosexual," he stated boldly, and "I commit the act habitually."[43] Other homophile activists, however, were eager to put some distance between themselves and the public targets of sexual psychopath laws: people who were sexually sick, those who were sexually uncontrolled, and especially people who had sex with children. One man declared to Sachs that he was "in sympathy with the general concept of the sexual psychopath laws." His only concern, he stated, was "in the possibility of their misuse."[44]

That distancing move — approving of sexual psychopath legislation while seeking to remove homosexuals from its criminalizing purview — aligned with the broader effort on the part of gay activists to dissociate themselves from attributions of sexual pathology and dislodge homosexuality from its classification as a mental illness. To Mattachine leader Frank Kameny, the argument against conceiving of homosexuality as a form of mental illness was a grounding political move, essential to the political intelligibility of gay people. "The entire homophile movement is going to stand or fall upon the question of whether homosexuality is a sickness," Kameny wrote, "and upon our taking a firm stand on it."[45] That position was stated boldly in the Washington, D.C., Mattachine's "anti-sickness" resolution, approved in 1965, that "in the absence of valid evidence to the contrary, homosexuality is not a sickness, disturbance, or other pathology in any sense, but is merely a preference, orientation, or propensity, on par with, and not different in kind from, heterosexuality."[46] The effort to distance homosexuality from the stigma of mental illness would become a defining project of the emerging gay rights movement.

Recognizing the importance of medicalized discourse to sexual psychopath laws allows us to see the broader stakes and political edge of gay activists' anti-sickness stance, aimed not only at the stigma created by psychiatry's position on homosexuality or the damage done to individuals who were led to understand themselves as mentally ill, but also at the codification of psychiatric stigma in law. Kameny and others were aware of the ways in which psychiatric authority over homosexuality enabled the expansion of the criminalization of non-normative sexuality under the guise of progressive, humane, and medical treatment. They understood as well that the insidious reach of the medical model went beyond the power of psychoanalysts to undermine the "self-respect, self-esteem, self-confidence, and self-image" of individual homosexuals, and beyond the promotion of a cultural climate of homophobia by portraying homosexuality as a curable mental disorder.[47] The labeling of homosexuality as pathological also supported a range of laws and restrictions against homosexuals, including sexual psychopath laws. The fight against sickness, then, was also a fight against criminalization.

It is clear what was gained by such claims. Kameny did not underestimate the extent to which the understanding of homosexuals as sick undergirded a larger structure of stigma, exclusion, discrimination, and criminalization. The American Psychiatric Association's declassification of homosexuality as a mental illness in 1973 was celebrated by gay activists at the time and has been trumpeted by historians as a milestone in the history of social justice. I conclude, though, by pondering the possible narrowing of political vision produced by the move to distance homosexuality from a larger group of "sex psychopaths" and more generally from "sickness." That question runs so counter to familiar and triumphalist stories of the victory of gay activists over psychiatric stigma, counter even to common sense, that it is difficult to frame. But it was a question anticipated by the person perhaps most associated with the anti-sickness position, Frank Kameny. Kameny was clear-eyed in his appraisal of the costs of psychiatric stigma: "Whatever definitions of sickness one may use," he wrote, "sick people are NOT EQUAL to well people in any practical, meaningful sense."[48] Kameny seemed to comprehend (and to excuse) the exclusionary effects of his own anti-sickness position when he wrote, "Properly or improperly, people ARE prejudiced against the mentally ill. Rightly or wrongly, employers will NOT hire them. Morally or immorally, the mentally ill are NOT judged as individuals, but are made pariahs. If we allow the label of sickness to stand, we will then have *two* battles to fight — that to combat prejudice against homosexuals per se, and that to combat prejudice against the mentally ill — and we will be pariahs and outcasts twice over. One such battle is quite enough."[49]

In his defense of the Washington, D.C., Mattachine's anti-sickness resolution, Kameny articulated the pragmatic strategy of organizing around a single axis of oppression. His words also suggest an awareness of the stigmatizing dynamics that Erving Goffman described in moments of "mixed encounter," when, as Jonathan Metzl states, an "affirmation of one's own health depends on the constant recognition, and indeed the creation, of the spoiled health of others."[50] As disability scholars Paul K. Longmore and Lauri Umansky write plainly, "To be associated with disabled people . . . is stigmatizing."[51] Gay men had been cast as mentally disordered sexual psychopaths. The success of the gay liberation movement depended, in considerable measure, on cutting those stigmatizing ties. The strategy of attempting to attain rights and respect by distancing one's own group from associations of stigma was far from unique to the gay rights movement. Both disability and queer studies scholars have detailed the ways in which stigmatized people have struggled to be included under the umbrella of the normal by distancing themselves from the even more stigmatized. As Michael Warner has observed, the most common strategy for displacing sexual shame is to "pin it on someone else."[52]

The popular story of the gay triumph over psychiatric assessments of homosexuality as a form of mental illness assumes "health" to be a transparent, self-evident good. It is difficult to be "against health," as Jonathan Metzl and others have recently observed.[53] But health is not simply a category of worth; it can function as well as an ideology that produces norms and exclusions and creates hierarchies of worthiness. The anti-sickness agenda required gay activists to shear off the rights-deserving homosexual from other forms of stigmatized and criminalized sexual difference. Given the discursive and political centrality of the endangered child to sexual psychopath laws, many of these efforts involved distinguishing the homosexual from the pedophile.[54]

The expansion of the criminalization of sexual offenses was just beginning its long history in the mid-twentieth century. Although sexual psychopath laws fell by the wayside in the 1960s and 1970s, the category of disordered "sex offender" that they created was resurrected in the wave of legislation that began in Washington state in 1990. In 1996, Congress passed "Megan's Law," a package of laws that mandated community notification, civil commitment of some sex offenders after completion of their criminal sentences, and mandatory registration of all released sex offenders. Community notification and civil commitment statutes swept across the United States in the 1990s and the following decade. Current sex offender laws, in their positioning of the sexual criminal as fundamentally different in kind from other criminals, their certainty in assessing the "risk" posed by various forms of non-normative sex, their strong populist support, and their often perpetual punishment and permanent criminalization, have in their genealogy the sexual psychopath laws of the mid-twentieth century. Although midcentury goals of rehabilitation and cure have been largely replaced by explicitly punitive interests, and although many of the major psychiatric professional organizations have opposed the new statutes, current-day sex offender legislation relies upon a judgment of mental disorder and the promise of "treatment" to justify the civil commitment statutes of every state and the federal government.[55]

Mainstream LGBT politics have been primarily silent in response to the new wave of state and federal sex offender legislation. Instead, contemporary LGBT rights organizations have prioritized access to the civil institutions of marriage and the military and successfully fought the criminalization of homosexual sex in sodomy laws through arguments about the primacy of privacy and love. Is it possible that in the process of insisting on the mental health of gay men and lesbians, LGBT politics lost a critical purchase on the sweeping criminalization of non-normative sex under sex offender legislation?[56] In disaggregating gays and lesbians from the sick and the criminal, did we lose the possibility of recognizing the expansion of the criminalization of sexual offenders, and criminalization more broadly, as a queer issue? What political traction might we have lost in our insistence on distinguishing between the private, consensual, legal sex between same-sex partners and the forms of non-normative consensual sex that remain criminalized?

NOTES

My thanks to Stephen Dillon for research assistance and to Stephen Dillon, David Halperin, Trevor Hoppe, Siobhan Somerville, and Dara Strolovitch for their helpful responses to earlier drafts of this essay.

1. George Raymond (pseudonym), "My Life History," 29–30, Benjamin Karpman papers, University of Minnesota.

2. "A Bill to Provide for the Treatment of Sexual Psychopaths, Public Law 615, H.R. 6071," in *United States Statutes at Large, 80th Congress, 2nd Session, 1948*, vol. 62, part 1, *Public Laws* (Washington, D.C.: Government Printing Office, 1949), 4–5.

3. It went on to prohibit such invitations "upon any avenue, street, road, highway, open space, alley, public square, enclosure, public building or other public place, store, shop, or reservation at any public gathering or assembly in the District of Columbia, to accompany, go with, or follow him or her to his or her residence, or to any other home or building, enclosure, or other place," for prostitution "or any other immoral or lewd purpose" (H.R. 6071, 2).

4. H.R. 6071, 5–6.

5. See George N. Thompson, "Electroshock and Other Therapeutic Considerations in Sexual Psychopathy," *Journal of Nervous and Mental Diseases* 109 (June 1949): 531–539. Thompson wrote that "neurosurgery is probably the form of treatment offering the greatest hope in this so far hopeless field" (531).

6. See Morris Ploscowe, *Sex and the Law* (New York: Prentice-Hall, 1951), 216; Estelle B. Freedman, " 'Uncontrolled Desires': The Responses to the Sexual Psychopath, 1920–1960," *Journal of American History* 74, no. 1 (June 1987): 83–106.

7. Prior to World War II, California, Illinois, Michigan, and Minnesota had enacted laws for the civil commitment and psychiatric treatment of sexual psychopaths. By the end of 1947, Massachusetts, Vermont, and Wisconsin had also enacted similar provisions.

8. See George Chauncey, "The Postwar Sex Crime Panic," in *True Stories from the American Past*, ed. William Graebner (New York: McGraw-Hill, 1993), 160–178; Freedman, " 'Uncontrolled Desires' "; Simon Cole, "From the Sexual Psychopath Statute to 'Megan's Law': Psychiatric Knowledge in the Diagnosis, Treatment, and Adjudication of Sex Criminals in New Jersey, 1949–1999," *History of Medicine and Allied Sciences* 55, no. 3 (2000): 292–314; Elise Chenier, *Strangers in Our Midst: Sexual Deviancy in Postwar Ontario* (Toronto: University of Toronto Press, 2008); Fred Fejes, "Murder, Perversion, and Moral Panic: The 1954 Media Campaign against Miami's Homosexuals and the Discourse of Civic Betterment," *Journal of the History of Sexuality* 9, no. 3 (June 2000): 305–347; Philip Jenkins, *Moral Panic: Changing Concepts of the Child Molester in Modern America* (New Haven, CT: Yale University Press, 1998). A critique of the sexual psychopath laws was articulated at the time by Edwin H. Sutherland, "The Diffusion of Sex Psychopath Laws," *American Journal of Sociology* 56 (1950): 142–148.

9. H.R. 2937–H.R. 5264, Criminal Sexual Psychopaths, Committee on the District of Columbia, February 20, 1948, 99.

10. H.R. 2937–H.R. 5264, 112.

11. H.R. 2937–H.R. 5264, 114. When Representative Miller introduced the bill to Congress, on the other hand, he observed, "The present laws of the District of Columbia do not seem adequate to handle sex crimes against children" (H.R. 6061, Treatment of Sexual Psychopaths in the District of Columbia, Congressional Record, April 26, 1948, 4886).

12. Congressional Record — House, February 3, 1948, 1038.

13. H.R. 6071, May 21, 1948, 1.

14. Congressional Record — House, April 26, 1948, 4887.

15. H.R. 2937–H.R. 5264, 101.

16. "Providing for the Treatment of Sexual Psychopaths in the District of Columbia," 80th Congress, 2nd Session, Report No. 1377, 6.

17. H.R. 2937–H.R. 5264, 103.

18. "Providing for the Treatment of Sexual Psychopaths in the District of Columbia," 8. Elise Chenier makes a similar argument, tracing the genealogy of sexual psychopath laws in Canada to Progressive Era laws that named the "defective delinquent," in her analysis, a "medicalized version of the habitual criminal" (Chenier, *Strangers in Our Midst*, 21). Chenier writes, "It is . . . useful to see criminal sexual psychopath legislation as one point on a century-long trajectory of psycho-medical thinking about criminality, sexual, and legal responsibility, and as part of a long tradition of social reform that took a dim view of punishment and repression" (40).

19. H.R. 2937–H.R. 5264, 7.

20. Hearings on "Criminal Sexual Psychopaths," 97.

21. H.R. 2937–H.R. 5264, 39–40. In the discussion of the bill in the Committee on the District of Columbia, O'Hara noted that the committee "endeavored in considering this subject, realizing the danger which might exist in a wave of hysteria of social workers or anything of that nature, that the right of the accused or the rights of an individual are safeguarded to the greatest extent that we could do so, even to the right of counsel, to insist upon counsel to appear before him in any and all of these cases" (H.R. 6071, March 31, 1948, 16–17).

22. Michel Foucault, *Abnormal: Lectures at the Collège de France, 1974–1975*, trans. Graham Burchell (New York: Picador, 2003), 23.

23. H.R. 2937–H.R. 5264, 103.

24. H.R. 2937–H.R. 5264, 83.

25. H.R. 2937–H.R. 5264, 64.

26. Congressional Record — House, April 26, 1948, 4887.

27. Frederick J. Hacker and Marcel Frym, "The Sexual Psychopath Act in Practice: A Critical Discussion," *California Law Review* 43, no. 5 (December 1955): 767.

28. H.R. 6061, 4887; Sutherland, "The Diffusion of Sexual Psychopath Laws," 146.

29. In response to Chelf's question about the law's penalty for the "sexual pervert," MacKinnon responded, "Title II of the bill is not aimed at the ordinary sexual pervert, nor is it limited to perverts" (H.R. 6061, 4885–4887).

30. H.R. 2937–H.R. 5264, 34.

31. "The Psychopathic Individual: A Symposium," *Mental Hygiene* 8 (1924): 175. See also Hacker and Frym, "The Sexual Psychopath Act in Practice," 770.

32. "The Psychopathic Individual: A Symposium," 175.

33. H.R. 2937–H.R. 5264, 117.

34. Benjamin Karpman wrote, "Psychopaths exhibit a combination of hypersexuality with a strong homosexual component. Despite their intellectual capacity, they are unable to foresee the consequences of their acts since their primitive emotional

organization presses for immediate release." *The Individual Criminal: Studies in the Psychogenetics of Crime* (Washington, D.C.: Nervous and Mental Disease Publishing, 1935).

35. H.R. 2937–H.R. 5264, 107.

36. U.S. House of Representatives, Committee on the District of Columbia, discussion of H.R. 2937–H.R. 5264, Criminal Sexual Psychopaths, February 20, 1948, 115; H.R. 2937–H.R. 5264, 105.

37. "2,000 Hear Experts on Sex Deviates and Star Forum Meeting," ONE 4, no. 3 (1956), 13.

38. Karl M. Bowman and Bernice Engle, "A Psychiatric Evaluation of the Laws of Homosexuality," *American Journal of Psychiatry* 112, no. 6 (February 1956): 577–583.

39. H.R. 2937–H.R. 5264, 104.

40. The law was used even less frequently in the years immediately after its passage. The Saint Elizabeths Hospital Annual Report in 1951 noted that "very few sexual offenders are being committed under this act; it is doubtful, in fact, just how great an added sense of security the community should feel on the basis of the operation of this law" (4). The hospital's annual report of 1952 stated, "For the moment the act seems to have lapsed into a state of desuetude," noting that only three sexual offenders had been committed under the act during the fiscal year (4).

41. David Johnson points out that despite the passage of the Miller Sexual Psychopath Law in 1948, most men arrested for same-sex sex in the District of Columbia were charged with disorderly conduct, allowed to post a $25 fine, and released. Johnson, *The Lavender Scare: The Cold War Persecution of Gays and Lesbians in the Federal Government* (Chicago: University of Chicago Press, 2006), 117. The Miller Law was not unusual in this regard. Sutherland wrote in 1950 that "the states which have enacted such laws make little or no use of them" (Sutherland, "The Diffusion of Sexual Psychopath Laws," 142). As such, Matthew Gambino points out, the Miller Law "became the basis for an expanded campaign of harassment and intimidation aimed at gay men in the District." Gambino, "Mental Health and Ideals of Citizenship: Patient Care at St. Elizabeths Hospital in Washington, D.C., 1903–1962" (PhD diss., University of Illinois at Urbana-Champaign, 2010), 237. See also Johnson, *Lavender Scare*, 55–63; Genny Beemyn, *A Queer Capital: A History of Gay Life in Washington, D.C.* (New York: Routledge, 2014).

42. Sidney S. Sachs, "A Short Discussion of the Miller Act," 1964, Mattachine Society of New York papers, IGIC, New York Public Library, Box 4, Fol. 1 ("Legal Matters"), Reel 11.

43. Sachs, "A Short Discussion of the Miller Act."

44. Sachs, "A Short Discussion of the Miller Act."

45. Frank Kameny, "Speech," quoted in John D'Emilio, *Sexual Politics, Sexual Communities: The Making of a Homosexual Minority in the United States, 1940–1970* (Chicago: University of Chicago Press, 1983), 163.

46. "Policy of the Mattachine Society of Washington," adopted March 4, 1965, reprinted in *Eastern Mattachine Magazine* 10, no. 4 (May 1965): 22–23.

47. Kameny, "Gay Liberation and Psychiatry," in *The Homosexual Dialectic*, ed. Joseph A. McCaffrey (Englewood Cliffs, NJ: Prentice-Hall, 1972), 189.

48. Kameny, "Emphasis on Research Has Had Its Day," *Ladder* 10, no. 1 (1965): 13.

49. Kameny, "Does Research into Homosexuality Matter?" *Ladder* 9, no. 8 (1965): 16–17.

50. Jonathan Metzl, "Why Against Health?" in *Against Health: How Health Became the New Morality*, ed. Jonathan Metzl and Anna Kirkland (New York: NYU Press, 2010), 5. See Erving Goffman, *Stigma: Notes on the Management of Spoiled Identity* (New York: Prentice-Hall, 1973).

51. Paul K. Longmore and Lauri Umansky, "Introduction," in *The New Disability History: American Perspectives*, ed. Paul K. Longmore and Lauri Umansky (New York: NYU Press, 2001), 51.

52. Michael Warner, *The Trouble with Normal: Sex, Politics, and the Ethics of Queer Life* (Cambridge, MA: Harvard University Press, 2000), 3.

53. Metzl and Kirkland, *Against Health*.

54. Gay claims to health also required the separation of same-sex sexual attraction and gender non-normativity. The removal of homosexuality from the DSM in 1973 depended in part on its disaggregation from gender variance and on the rhetorical appeal on the part of gay activists and supportive psychiatrists to the distinction between transsexuality and homosexuality. The third edition of the DSM, published in 1980, the first that did not include an entry for "homosexuality," was also the first that named a new diagnosis: "Gender Identity Disorder." As Eve Kosofsky Sedgwick observes, "This is how it happens that the *de*pathologization of an atypical sexual object-choice can be yoked to the *new* pathologization of an atypical gender identification." Sedgwick, "How to Bring Your Kids Up Gay," *Social Text*, no. 29 (1991), 21.

55. See Jeslyn Miller, "Sex Offender Commitment: The Treatment Paradox," *California Law Review* 98 (2010): 2093–2128.

56. Roger Lancaster suggests as much in his study of the cultural phenomenon of sex panic and its manifestations in criminal law, when he proposes that because of "current political strategies for evading stigma and managing unspoken accusations," especially circulating around the figure of the pedophile, mainstream LGBT rights cannot speak to the "absent presence" or spectral figure of the homosexual in the current sex panic. Lancaster writes, "When, as the price of entry into the 'properly

political sphere,' mainstream gay rights organizations promote a hypernormal image of homosexuality, maintain silence about sex offender registries and 'child safety zones,' and . . . avoid discussions of age-of-consent laws, they reinforce a dynamic that Lee Edelman has described: everyone wants to offload the burden of queerness onto someone else; no one wants to be holding the stigma." Roger N. Lancaster, *Sex Panic and the Punitive State* (Berkeley: University of California Press, 2011), 233. See also the essay by Judith Levine in this volume, chapter 2.

SCOTT DE ORIO

| 7 |

The Creation of the
Modern Sex Offender

In 1968, a former policeman and liberal candidate for Los Angeles district attorney named Michael Hannon published an article in the gay magazine *Tangents* criticizing laws that punished what he called "victimless crimes." Hannon inveighed in particular against California's sex offender registry — the first of its kind in the nation — which allowed the police to identify and track the whereabouts of individuals convicted of certain sex crimes. The problem with the sex offender registry, he argued, was that it criminalized a hodge-podge of harmless as well as harmful offenses without any apparent rhyme or reason. While registration might be an appropriate legal response to violent sex crimes, it was a waste of public resources for lesser offenses that did not involve a victim. For example, the registry's inclusion of "lewd or dissolute conduct" — a law that the police used primarily to crack down on gay cruising — was a particularly frivolous use of police power. "I take no offense," he explained, "at the idea of the police informing themselves of the whereabouts of rapists in a community, but expenditure of time and money to keep track of persons whose only crime is to offend against quaint Victorian ideas of the proper way to perform a sex act strikes me as absurd." Drawing on the idea of the victimless crime, Hannon proposed to modify the sex offender registry by removing crimes that did not involve harm in order to home in on ones that did.[1]

In the 1970s, gay activists, liberal state officials, and law-and-order conservatives redefined what it meant to be a "sex offender" by transforming California's sex offender registry to focus less on gay sex and more on rape and sex with minors. The 1950s and '60s was a period of intense police repression of gay men who sought intimacy in bars, parks, and other public places. Gay activists challenged that regime by forming an alliance with liberals who supported the reform of laws punishing victimless crimes. By the early 1980s, the gay-liberal coalition had persuaded the California Supreme Court to prohibit the police enforcement of the lewd conduct law in semiprivate spaces like gay bars and to remove those convicted under the law from the sex offender registry. At the same time, liberals and some gay activists supported registration for rape and sex involving minors. With their endorsement, conservatives spearheaded a campaign to make the registry entail much harsher punishments than it did before. The broad consensus that registration was appropriate for the "real" sex offenders completely overshadowed the minority of gay activists, feminists, and civil libertarians who argued that the registry should be abolished entirely. Through these battles, gay activists, liberals, and conservatives produced a new raison d'être for sex offender registration that the federal government would later adopt when it started requiring all states to maintain a registry in the 1990s.[2]

Recent work in queer theory has promoted an increasingly accepted notion that the gay movement has become more and more conservative since the 1970s. The gay movement, or so this story goes, has gradually deemphasized the pursuit of sexual freedom and focused more on the right to marriage. It has supported gentrification and the war on terror. It has become characterized increasingly by a "homonormative" sexual politics, to use Lisa Duggan's term, that "does not contest dominant heteronormative assumptions and institutions but upholds and sustains them."[3] While it is true that the gay movement has become more conservative in a variety of ways in the last four decades or so, this scholarship runs the risk of making the gay movement bear a disproportionate responsibility for larger social and political developments that stem from other causes.[4]

The goal of this essay is to show why it is important to contextualize this much-discussed turn to the right in gay politics and to resituate it in the larger political landscape — specifically, to see how it developed within the limitations of the larger political culture in which gay activists were operating. To place preponderate blame on gay activists for helping to make sex offender registration more punitive since the 1970s would be simply to misunderstand who caused that shift. Mainstream conservatives and liberals were the main groups responsible for radically expanding the carceral state's sphere of control over sex offenders. Some gay activists, too, endorsed the idea that registration was an appropriate legal response to rapists and child molesters. However, they did not invent this argument, and they were not its most vigorous promoters. Furthermore, conservatives put a great deal of indirect pressure on the gay movement to endorse that position through the use of stigmatizing rhetoric that portrayed gays as child molesters. It is probable that the reason more gay activists did not argue for abolishing the registry altogether is that they were afraid of confirming that stereotype in the minds of the straight majority and jeopardizing their goal of getting gay cruising off the registry. Of all the groups that supported amplifying sex offender registration for crimes involving victims, gay activists were the least influential, and they had the most to lose.

This historical account yields two lessons, one theoretical and one political. First, queer theory needs to distinguish the relative contributions of mainstream conservatives, mainstream liberals, and various gay activists to the war on sex — their different responsibilities for the spread and intensification of sex offender registration in recent decades. Second, LGBTQ politics should take a more vigorous role in conceptualizing and promoting constructive ways for the state to respond to sexual violence. Those two goals are interdependent, because truly progressive political activism requires a different style of engagement with the history of the gay movement. This style of engagement would focus less on blaming some gay activists for having bad politics and more on recuperating the insights of other gay activists who argued in the 1970s that the sex offender registry should be abolished altogether. This group pointed out that sex offender registration illogically singles out *sex* crimes as deserving of exceptionally stigmatizing punishment. They also produced an analysis of rape and child sexual abuse as social problems whose root cause was not deviant individuals but women's and children's systemic dependence on men in the institution of the family. However, the registration abolitionists of the 1970s did not manage to elaborate their analysis with enough power and sophistication to persuade lawmakers to deal with sexual violence in more effective and constructive ways. Now more than ever, it is imperative for queer theorists to pick up where these critics left off and develop their intellectual tradition further so that we might be in a position to proffer concrete policy alternatives to sex offender registration.[5]

THE LEWD CONDUCT LAW BEFORE 1968

When the California legislature enacted the first state-level sex offender registry in the country in 1947, legislators included gay sex among the deviant sexual practices that they identified as dangerous. They created the registry in the context of a national wave of concern about deviant sex. Between 1937 and 1967, twenty-six states passed "sexual psychopath" laws that authorized the indefinite detention of sex offenders, many of them gay men, in state hospitals. Unlike the ubiquitous sexual psychopath laws, though, only four other states besides California — Arizona, Nevada, Ohio, and Alabama — had enacted a sex offender registry by 1976. The architects of the California registry framed it as a surveillance system that would provide "local police authorities with the knowledge of the whereabouts of habitual sex offenders and sex deviates" — including the perpetrators of gay-related offenses like sodomy, indecent exposure, and, as it was called before 1961, "being a lewd or dissolute person." Some law enforcement officials believed the registry was "effective as a deterrent to homosexual activity," while others argued it was necessary because "homosexuals are prone to commit violent crimes and crimes against children." For the lawmakers who created it, the sex offender registry was a means through which to suppress the harmful behavior of gay men.[6]

Of all the gay offenses to which the registry applied, the lewd or dissolute person law was the statute that police enforced most frequently. In the earliest case litigated by a gay rights organization in 1952, activists attacked the law for facilitating police entrapment — the practice in which a police officer would dress as a civilian and make sexual overtures at unsuspecting gay men to trick them into committing the crime of being a lewd or dissolute person. The defendant in the case was a gay rights activist named Dale Jennings who was entrapped by a plainclothes police officer in Los Angeles. According to Jennings, the officer had followed him home uninvited after the two met in the bathroom of a public park. The officer forced his way into Jennings's home and "sprawled on the divan making sexual gestures and proposals. . . . At last he grabbed my hand and tried to force it down the front of his trousers. I jumped up and away. Then there was the badge and he was snapping the handcuffs on with the remark, 'Maybe you'll talk better with my partner outside.'"[7] After contacting his associates at the homophile organization the Mattachine Society, Jennings made the rare and brave decision to defend his innocence in court; most men in his position would have pled guilty in the hope of getting the opportunity to plea-bargain for a lighter sentence. Mattachine formed the Citizens Committee to Outlaw Entrapment (CCOE) to publicize the case and raise money for legal fees. "THE ISSUE HERE," one of the CCOE's flyers emphasized, "IS NOT WHETHER THE MAN IS A HOMOSEXUAL OR NOT, BUT WHETHER THE POLICE DEPARTMENT IS JUSTIFIED IN USING SUCH METHODS."[8] At the trial, Jennings's attorney, too, defended the legitimacy of his client's homosexual identity and called the practice of police entrapment into question instead; though Jennings was openly homosexual, his conduct had been neither "lewd" nor "dissolute." The jury voted eleven to one for an acquittal, and a new trial was scheduled. Before the trial took place, though, the city requested the case be dismissed. The CCOE heralded the outcome as "the first time in California history an admitted homosexual was freed on a vag-lewd [lewd vagrancy] charge" and a "GREAT VICTORY for the homosexual minority."[9]

That great victory was, however, an isolated one. In the main, the California legislature and court system tacitly or explicitly endorsed the police's discretionary use of the lewd or dissolute person law to repress gay men and their sexual culture throughout the 1950s and 1960s. In order to rectify the fact that the law unconstitutionally criminalized a type of person as opposed to a type of behavior, the legislature reformed it in 1961 by removing the word "person" from "lewd or dissolute person" and replacing it with "conduct." However, the reform had little practical effect on the enforcement of the law, since the new statute still left it up to the police to define what behaviors fell under "lewd or dissolute conduct." Indeed, the statute did not even require the presence of an offended person besides a police officer for a lewd conduct conviction to be valid. The courts' claim that gay men offended the "public," then, was usually made in bad faith, since the only so-called victim involved in most cases was the police officer, who went out of his way to catch gay men who were seeking a sexual assignation. Even worse, the reformed statute intensified the police repression of gay men by specifically proscribing solicitation — the mere act of inviting someone to have sex — for the first time.[10]

The courts, too, afforded the police complete discretion to use the lewd conduct law to criminalize just about any gay behavior. Judges relied on a very broad understanding of what constituted a "public" place, such as when a Los Angeles Municipal Court convicted a man in 1963 for "kissing another man on his lips for three seconds" in a bar.[11] In 1967, the Los Angeles Superior Court held it was legitimate for the police to use the statute to criminalize the mere act of asking another person in public to go have gay sex in private. "We cannot believe," the court argued, "the Legislature intended to subject innocent bystanders, be they men, women or children, to the public blandishments of deviates so long as the offender was smart enough to say that the requested act was to be done in private."[12] A California Court of Appeal affirmed in 1968 that it was "manifest that the legislature believed that the subjection in public to homosexual advances or observation in public of a homosexual proposition would engender outrage in the vast majority of people."[13] Along with the legislature and the police, judges sustained the idea that gay men were a deviant social element against which the heterosexual public required protection and whose social world needed to be suppressed.[14]

Otherwise gay-friendly liberal law reformers still supported the state repression of gay cruising during this period. In 1962, the American Law Institute, an organization dedicated to the scholarly study of the law, published its Model Penal Code to provide state legislatures with a prototype to refer to when revising their criminal codes, many of which were about a century old. The Model Penal Code proposed to reform how the state regulated sexuality to decriminalize behaviors that did not harm others while retaining criminal sanctions on ones that did. It removed laws punishing sex practiced by consenting adults in private, including gay sex, while prohibiting rape, prostitution, sex involving minors, "open lewdness," and gay cruising (which it described as loitering "in or near any public place for the purpose of soliciting or being solicited to engage in deviate sexual intercourse"). In order to dispute the lewd or dissolute conduct law, gay activists in California would have to find a way to convince liberals that gay men's public sexual culture was, in fact, victimless.[15]

THE BATTLE TO REFORM THE LEWD CONDUCT LAW

In the late 1960s, a surge of gay activism produced the first-ever large-scale attempt to reform California's lewd conduct law. While the Mattachine Society had been the lone resister to the law in the 1950s, a critical mass of gay organizations, including the Homophile Effort for Legal Protection, the National Committee for Sexual Civil Liberties (NCSCL), and the Gay Rights Chapter of the American Civil Liberties Union (ACLU), now existed to exert a stronger influence on public policy about gay cruising. Building on the pioneering efforts of the homophile movement, the new cohort of gay activists and lawyers invented direct-action protest strategies, crafted legal arguments, and formed political alliances with liberal city and state officials to curtail the state repression of gay men.

In Los Angeles, gay activists had to contend with the virulent homophobia of Police Chief Edward "Ed" Davis, who defended the LAPD's frequent crackdowns on gay cruising by portraying gay men as dangerous psychopaths who preyed on children. The "open and ostentatious merchandising of the concept of homosexuality is a clear and present danger to the youth of our community," Davis claimed when justifying his refusal to establish a police liaison to the gay community in 1972. Later that year, he argued in a lecture before the Beverly Hills Bar Association that there was "no such thing as a victimless crime." "The homosexual who hangs out in the park, and we get a complaint because kids playing ball are molested by this guy who wants to hang out in the men's toilet, he certainly has victims." Davis justified making it a police priority to suppress gay male sexual culture by associating gay men with child molestation.[16]

One way in which gay activists countered the stigmatizing rhetoric of law-and-order conservatives like Ed Davis was by arguing that it was unjustifiable to criminalize homosexual activity when it took place in private places like bars and bedrooms. Such was the argument of the Homophile Effort for Legal Protection (HELP). Founded in 1968, HELP was a legal aid society for gay men that maintained a twenty-four-hour answering service for members who needed legal assistance, representation, or money for bail. Its newsletter helped gay men avoid being arrested for cruising by publishing a segment that identified "local trouble spots" that were currently being targeted by the LAPD. However, HELP did not argue for the complete decriminalization of gay cruising. As a contributor to the newsletter put it, the organization did not believe that gay men "should be permitted to engage in activities which, when committed in public view, are offensive to the average person. What goes on behind closed doors is another matter — be these the doors to a bar which is known to have nude entertainment or the door to your bedroom." HELP disputed the idea that gay men were a menace to the public by drawing attention to the fact that the police were targeting even those portions of their sexual culture that played out in arguably private settings.[17]

The police, gay activists also pointed out, used the lewd conduct law to suppress not just sex acts but any expression of intimacy at all, no matter how minor. On New Year's Eve in 1966, eight police officers launched a brutal assault on a bar called the Black Cat in Silver Lake and arrested fifteen men, thirteen of whom they charged with lewd conduct for kissing when the clock struck midnight.[18] The mere possibility of police harassment cast a pall over gay social life in the bars, even when the police were not actually present. In September 1970, the Gay Liberation Front (GLF) organized a protest they described as a "touch-in" at the Farm, a popular gay bar in West Hollywood, in order to contest the bar's policy prohibiting kissing, holding hands, and other physical contact. The Farm's owner defended the policy as a necessary precaution to prevent the police from "bust[ing] the bar for encouraging 'lewd conduct.'" A flyer for the protest queried angrily, "DO YOU BELIEVE THAT

TWO MEN OR TWO WOMEN WITH THEIR ARMS AROUND EACH OTHER
CONSTITUTES 'LEWD CONDUCT'?" At the protest, about eighty men and
women marched in mock shackles and chains while loudspeakers played
music like the Beatles' "I Want to Hold Your Hand."[19] Later that month, GLF
and the Farm arrived at an agreement securing "touch privileges" for bar patrons. (The bar endured still more grief the following year, though, when a
county official urged the Public Welfare Commission not to renew its dancing and entertainment license because of a recent series of arrests for lewd
conduct on or near the premises.) In these ways, activists challenged the notion that gay men were dangerous sex predators by highlighting the utterly
quotidian nature of the behaviors for which they were being arrested.[20]

When gay men contested a lewd conduct charge in court, they greatly increased the risk that they would actually be put on the sex offender registry. While many prosecutors and judges thought that the "lewd or dissolute"
behaviors for which the police arrested gay men were indeed criminal, they
did not believe those behaviors were serious enough to warrant registration.
Often, prosecutors would add another charge after the arrest and offer to
waive the charge for lewd conduct as long as the accused pled guilty to the
non-registrable offense. On the whole, then, the most punitive aspect of sex
offender registration during this period was not the requirement that the offender contact the local police once a month. Rather, prosecutors wielded
the threat of registration to coerce defendants into pleading guilty to a lesser
criminal charge. In this context, men accused of lewd conduct displayed considerable bravery when they refused a plea bargain. In 1970, for example, after
plainclothes vice officers arrested GLF activist John Platania in Griffith Park
in Los Angeles, Platania chose to represent himself at a jury trial instead of
hiring a lawyer to get the charge reduced and avoid public exposure. "With
the full support of the GLF," a journalist for the gay magazine the *Advocate*
commented approvingly, "[Platania] is turning his arrest by vice squad officers into a full-scale, public challenge of police entrapment procedures."[21]
Likewise, when the Metropolitan Community Church reverend Ronald
Thaxton Pannel took his lewd conduct case to court in 1973, he refused to plea
bargain for the lesser charge of "disturbing the peace" because he wanted to
see through his dispute of the lewd conduct law's constitutionality. "As long
as the 647(a) [lewd conduct issue] has not been resolved," he told the *Advocate*, "then I don't have to enter a plea of my 415 [charge for disturbing the
peace]. I'm hoping that by the time I'm forced to plead one way or the other,
I will have enough money to plead innocent and demand a jury trial."[22] Es-

sential to activists' challenge to the lewd conduct law was the courage of individual gay men who risked their livelihoods in order to challenge the statute's constitutional basis.

Scholars, too, contributed to the movement to reform the lewd conduct law by furnishing empirical evidence backing up activists' claim that the LAPD did, in fact, practice discrimination by enforcing the statute disproportionately against harmless gay male behaviors. A study from 1966 published in the UCLA *Law Review*, titled "The Consenting Adult Homosexual and the Law," found that only 10 of the 434 arrests that LAPD officers had made for lewd conduct violations during the previous year involved private citizens as complaining witnesses. It noted, moreover, that most of the men who had been arrested pursued sexual contact only with other consenting adults and approached them through the use of circumspect body language. "The majority of homosexual solicitations," the 185-page report noted, "are made only if the other individual appears responsive and are ordinarily accomplished by quiet conversation and the use of gestures and signals having significance only to other homosexuals."[23] The sociologist Laud Humphreys reported similar findings in his 1970 ethnography *Tearoom Trade: Impersonal Sex in Public Places*. A report from 1973 written by law students Thomas Coleman and Barry Copilow argued that the LAPD enforced the lewd conduct law against gay men "as a class of persons" in a purposefully discriminatory way. Together, these studies undermined the stereotype that portrayed gay men as dangerous sex offenders, and they made it possible for lawyers to argue instead that the lewd conduct law was a mode of state-sanctioned homophobia.[24]

Gay activists formed alliances with liberal public officials who shared their perspective about the need to restrain the police from suppressing gay men's harmless behavior. When a lawyer named Burt Pines ran for Los Angeles city attorney in 1973, he pledged to "take a strong, tough look at any prosecutions under 647 [the lewd conduct law] dealing with homosexual activity, and it's certainly going to be an area that I would seek to de-emphasize." Pines's promise contrasted sharply with the proposal of his rival candidate Roger Arnebergh, who suggested gay bars incorporate as private clubs to help gay men "avoid unintentionally or unknowingly offending" a bystander.[25] After Pines prevailed in the race for city attorney, he made good on his vow through a new policy that reduced the number of cases his office prosecuted involving arrests for lewd conduct in gay bars. Between June and August 1974, the *Advocate* conjectured, Pines's policy had singlehandedly prompted a 48 percent reduction in arrests in Hollywood. Los Angeles mayor Tom Bradley also took the view that the police should deprioritize relatively minor crimes. In a key-note address to a police association in 1975, Bradley called for police depart-ments to reexamine the enforcement of "the whole range of activities which are generally described as victimless crimes," from "penny ante-poker [sic] to surveillance of gay bars." These key city officials lent unprecedented main-stream support to gay activists' goal of reforming the lewd conduct law.[26]

The statutory basis of the solicitation portion of the lewd conduct law eroded in 1975 when California decriminalized anal and oral sex between consenting adults in private. In 1963, the California legislature had formed the Joint Legislative Committee for Revision of the Penal Code to overhaul the state's nearly century-old code.[27] In a 1971 report detailing its revision proposals, the committee recommended that sodomy be legalized between consenting adults in private, though, as a consulting attorney to the Society for Individual Rights noted, it "in no way corrects the present harmful result of [the lewd conduct law]."[28] Around the same time, Willie Brown, a Demo-cratic assemblyman (and future mayor) from San Francisco, began introduc-ing a separate consenting adults bill in the legislature. A number of profes-sional associations, responding to pressure from the NCSCL and other gay rights organizations, passed resolutions in support of the idea, including the American Bar Association in 1973. When an iteration of the "Brown bill" fi-nally passed in 1975, gay activists had new cause to question the validity of the lewd conduct law's prohibition of solicitation.[29] As Peter Thomas Judge, the president of the Gay Rights Chapter of the ACLU of Southern California, underscored in a letter to Willie Brown, "Since [the Brown bill] became law the courts and legal enforcement agencies continue to maintain the posture that it is illegal to ask someone to engage in an act that is now legal."[30] Though neither the penal code revision nor the Brown bill altered the lewd conduct law directly, the decriminalization of sodomy between consenting adults in private provided gay activists with a fresh round of ammunition with which to attack it.[31]

After the passage of the Brown bill, several disputes in the Los Angeles City Council signaled that gay activists were gaining ground in the argument over the lewd conduct law. In 1975, the Democratic Senator George Moscone of San Francisco (another future mayor of the city) sponsored a bill proposing to remove the word "solicit" from the statute. The bill did not pass the Cali-fornia Senate, but, at the same time, conservative city council members in Los Angeles who tried to gather enough votes to pass a resolution opposing the bill were unsuccessful.[32] The next year, the city council made major cuts to the LAPD vice squad in the wake of a police raid on a gay charitable fundraiser. Citing Penal Code Section 181's prohibition of involuntary servitude, the police had deployed sixty officers, thousands of dollars, and a helicopter to disrupt a mock "slave auction" at the Mark IV bathhouse, the proceeds of which were to go to the Los Angeles Gay Community Services Center. Outraged by the raid and faced with an $18 million deficit, the city council voted to remove forty-seven vice officers from the department. The former consensus that gay men were a threat to public decency was coming undone.[33]

In the 1979 case *Pryor v. Municipal Court*, the California Supreme Court affirmed gay organizations' view that the lewd conduct law permitted the police to be too repressive of gay social life. In that case, the defendant Don Pryor had been arrested in Los Angeles in 1976 for soliciting an undercover vice officer for oral sex. In its friend-of-the-court brief in support of Pryor, the NCSCL argued that, since the Brown bill had decriminalized anal and oral sex between consenting adults in private, the state was now obligated to "afford a reasonable opportunity to all persons to communicate their desire to engage in the now-licit conduct." Moreover, the statute's vague wording was a "standing invitation to police corruption" and "capricious enforcement" against gay men.[34] In its majority opinion, the *Pryor* court reviewed over seventy years of statutory interpretations of the law in search of a coherent legal definition of "lewd or dissolute conduct." "The answer," the court determined, "of the prior cases — such acts as are lustful, lascivious, unchaste, wanton, or loose in morals and conduct — is no answer at all," and it constrained the police's discretionary prerogative by requiring the presence of an offended private citizen for a conviction to be valid. The one disadvantage of the opinion, as the NCSCL saw it, was that, since Pryor had not actually been convicted of lewd conduct, the court deemed him ineligible to challenge the statute's registration requirement. Still, the new restrictions *Pryor* placed on the legal definition and police regulation of lewd or dissolute conduct signaled that the law's conceptualization of gay men as dangerous sex offenders was softening.[35]

THE BATTLE TO REMOVE SEX OFFENDER
REGISTRATION FOR LEWD OR DISSOLUTE CONDUCT

After the *Pryor* decision, gay rights attorneys had reason to believe that they could also persuade the courts to remove lewd conduct from the category of crimes requiring those convicted under them to be listed on the sex offender registry. In two key cases from the 1970s, judges had indicated that they would be amenable to such a change. In 1973, the California Supreme Court set aside the sentence of a man who had been convicted of lewd conduct for urinating outside a Taco Bell in downtown Los Angeles around 1:30 AM. The court argued his conviction must be overturned because the judge who sentenced him had not properly advised the defendant that pleading guilty to lewd conduct would mean he would have to register as a sex offender. "Although the stigma of a short jail sentence should eventually fade," the court reasoned, "the ignominious badge carried by the convicted sex offender can remain for a lifetime."[36] In the 1978 case of *People v. Mills*, a California Court of Appeals upheld the validity of sex offender registration in the case of a man who was convicted of fondling and attempting to rape a seven-year-old girl. However, the court went out of its way to make clear it was not ruling on the validity of registration for those guilty of lewd conduct violations. Referring to the aforementioned case, the judges pointed out that they were "not concerned with a private urination at 1:30 in the morning in a semi-private area, but with a compelled sexual molestation of a seven-year-old female. If there be an ignominious badge imposed it would appear deserved."[37] These cases established a legal precedent supporting the idea that the registry was appropriate for violent sex offenses but not for victimless crimes like lewd conduct.

The state legislature supported that idea, too. A 1979 bill introduced by the Republican state senator H. L. Richardson proposed to establish a mandatory jail term of ninety days for failure to register as a sex offender and make certain categories of offenders ineligible for community release programs — including individuals convicted of lewd conduct.[38] Responding to complaints from the ACLU and the NCSCL, the legislature amended the bill before passing it to omit lewd conduct from its scope. "This is the first time," Thomas Coleman of the NCSCL noted, "the Legislature has acknowledged that registration requirements for rapists and child molesters are different issues from registration of lewd conduct defendants."[39] Gay activists and their liberal allies were securing for gay men immunity from the heightened criminal sanctions that a bipartisan majority of lawmakers was otherwise bringing to bear on sex offenders.

Some gay activists, liberals, and civil libertarians believed sex offender registration was bad policy, but they did not propose some superior alternative to address crimes involving victims like rape and child molestation. In 1972, the San Francisco Mental Health Advisory Board formed its Subcommittee on Homosexual Activity and the Law in response to complaints from gay activists about police entrapment. In addition to opposing entrapment, the committee's report recommended the sex offender registry be repealed entirely, since it entailed "a gross *lifetime* condemnation of a person."[40] In a report to the California legislature, the Joint Legislative Committee for Revision of the Penal Code argued that it seemed "illogical to register sex offenders but not robbers, burglars, and others who pose a greater statistical threat to the safety and well-being of the population."[41] E. H. Duncan Donovan of the Gay Rights Chapter of the ACLU of Southern California described sex offender registration as "a modern version of the Scarlet A for adultery. This dehumanizing practice . . . is not inflicted on ax murderers who have paid their debt to society."[42] These activists pointed out that sex offender registration focused illogically on sex as a specific attribute of a crime that, supposedly, made it particularly harmful. The registry created a situation in which the state punished sex crimes in an exceptionally harsh way compared with violent crimes not related to sex. However, critics of sex offender registration did not advance — or, perhaps, were unable to imagine — some better legal response to sexual violence.

It is noteworthy that some gay activists and feminists generated a critique of child sexual abuse during this period as a problem of the heterosexual family, though that critique did not enter into discussions in the legal arena about whether sex offender registration was good policy. In 1977, the ACLU's Gay Rights Chapter and the National Organization for Women (NOW) jointly published a pamphlet titled "Sexual Child Abuse: A Contemporary Family Problem" that framed child sexual abuse as a form of exploitation endemic to the "family and friends of the family."[43] A pamphlet from Parents and Friends of Gays called "About Our Children" asserted that "Gay persons RESPECT CHILDREN"; most commonly, it was "fathers, stepfathers, grandfathers, uncles, and mothers' boy friends" who perpetrated child sexual abuse. As they challenged the stereotype that gays and lesbians were child molesters, these activists also transcended the facile notion that child sexual abuse was caused by a few sick or evil individuals; rather, it was a social problem that was woven into the fabric of the heteronormative family. As such, the family itself was amenable to a political critique.[44]

The argument gay activists made that succeeded in court called for the deregistration of gay men's harmless behaviors but endorsed sex offender registration for crimes involving victims. Jerry Blair contended in the *San Diego Law Review* in 1976 that the "compulsory registration of obscene misdemeanants severely dilutes the effectiveness that registration might otherwise provide in the prevention of child molestation, forcible rape, and other violent sex crimes."[45] In a friend-of-the-court brief in a lewd conduct case from 1979, the ACLU affiliates of Northern and Southern California and the Pride Foundation argued that individuals who committed sex crimes against women or children were especially likely to be repeat offenders. "The great majority of sex offenses," the brief contended, "with the exception of rape and child molesting, are one-time events."[46] In the context of a political culture in which conservatives were vigorously promoting sex offender registration and ambivalent liberals either agreed with them or lacked an alternative policy to put forward, gay activists, too, capitulated to conservatives in order to shift the registry's focus away from gay men's behavior.

The 1983 California Supreme Court case *In re Reed* codified this shift. In that case, the court determined that the lewd conduct law's registration requirement was a form of punishment that was out of proportion to the crime. The petitioner, Allen Eugene Reed, had been arrested by an undercover vice officer in a public restroom and, upon conviction, was required to register as a sex offender. The language the court used to describe Reed's behavior could not have been more different from the way courts had talked about deviant gay men in the 1950s and 1960s: Reed was "not the prototype of one who poses a grave threat to society." At the same time, the court made clear that its decision to remove the lewd conduct law's registration requirement was contingent on the fact that Reed had challenged registration as it applied to that particular statute but not registration overall. His "relatively simple sexual indiscretion" did not "place him in the ranks of those who commit more heinous registrable sex offenses."[47] The culmination of three decades of political conflict, the *Reed* case reconstructed the legal definition of the sex offender, deemphasizing homosexuality and concentrating instead on sex crimes against women and children.

CONCLUSION: SEX OFFENDER REGISTRATION AFTER THE GAY RIGHTS REVOLUTION

Although a conviction under the lewd conduct law no longer entailed registration as a sex offender, the statute still threatened the livelihoods of many gay men. After the *Reed* decision, lewd conduct remained a crime of "moral turpitude" that required the automatic suspension of teaching and other professional licenses — a consequence that did not follow from other misdemeanors, such as battery, that did not involve sex. Moreover, after *Reed*, individuals convicted of lewd conduct were no longer allowed to enter a plea bargain to a lesser offense, meaning a teacher, for example, was now forced to contest the testimony of a vice officer in court if he wanted keep his job. Though gay activists achieved major reforms of the lewd conduct law, they were not able to overturn the legal framework that supported it. The basic idea that there existed something called "lewd or dissolute conduct" persisted, leaving gay men who cruised for sex vulnerable to criminalization.[48]

If gay cruising was still exposed to state repression, it was now, at least, exempt from sex offender registration, which became a ubiquitous legal response to rape and child sexual abuse in the 1990s. In 1994, Congress passed the Jacob Wetterling Crimes Against Children and Sexually Violent Offender Registration Act, requiring all states to create and maintain a sex offender registry.[49] In 1996, the U.S. Congress passed Megan's Law, which amended the Wetterling Act to require that states create a public database allowing citizens to track the whereabouts of registered sex offenders, making the registry much more punitive than it was before.[50] Though the cast of characters to which sex offender registration applies has changed, the policy's narrowminded reliance on stigmatizing individuals as a way of controlling sexual violence persists. Alongside other tough-on-crime campaigns like the War on Drugs, the War on Sex Offenders has contributed to the massive expansion of the carceral state in the United States.[51]

The political exigencies of our contemporary situation call for queer theorists to start using the history of gay politics in a different way. It is not enough to criticize gay activists for being complicit in the rise of sex offender registration in the late twentieth century, even though it is true that some of them were. Gay activists were not the most influential group driving that shift; mainstream liberals and conservatives were. When the historical context is recovered and taken into consideration, it becomes clear why many gay activists steered clear of challenging the widespread demand for harsher punishments for sex involving minors. They did not want to risk corroborating the accusation made by conservatives that gays were themselves child molesters. Understanding the pressures that gay activists were facing at the time makes it possible for queer theorists nowadays to focus less on blaming the gay movement for helping sustain the registry and more on trying to reform the sexual politics of the majority.

In order to contest the regime of sex offender registration, queer theorists must recuperate and extend the ideas of those who once called for the abolition of the registry altogether. Laws that stigmatize individuals as "sex offenders" oversimplify the complex structural origins of sexual harm. Drawing on the intellectual tradition of the registration abolitionists, we should conceptualize alternative ways for the state to address sexual violence. These will include policies geared toward closing the wage gap to make women and children as a group less dependent on men within the family — the site, as gay activists, feminists, and civil libertarians argued in the 1970s, where most sexual violence occurs.

There are other good reasons to oppose sex offender registration besides the fact that it is a shallow response to sexual violence. It should be opposed also because it contributes to the stigmatization and demonization of sex itself as well as to the repression of benign sexual variation. The sex-specific nature of the registry enshrines in the law the assumption that sex is something that is uniquely harmful, rather than a key aspect of human flourishing. "Sex" is not a synonym for "harm," and the law should not treat it as such.[52]

NOTES

1. Michael Hannon, "Victimless Crimes: A Legal Dilemma," *Tangents* 2, no. 7 (June 5, 1968): 4–8. The movement to reform laws punishing victimless crimes opposed the criminalization of a range of activities, including the private consumption of illegal drugs, gambling, pornography and obscenity, prostitution, and public drunkenness. See Wendy Serbin Smith, *Victimless Crime: A Selected Bibliography* (Washington, D.C.: National Institute of Law Enforcement and Criminal Justice, Law Enforcement Assistance Administration, U.S. Department of Justice, 1977).

2. Feminist activists played a key role advocating for tough-on-crime sex offender policies in other contexts, but they did not do so in the specific battle over California's sex offender registry that I examine here. See Marie Gottschalk, "The Battered-Women's Movement and the Development of Penal Policy," in *The Prison and the Gallows: The Politics of Mass Incarceration in America* (Cambridge: Cambridge University Press, 2006), 139–164.

3. Lisa Duggan, "The New Homonormativity: The Sexual Politics of Neoliberalism," in *Materializing Democracy: Toward a Revitalized Cultural Politics*, ed. Russ Castronovo and Dana D. Nelson (Durham, NC: Duke University Press, 2002), 179.

4. Michael Warner, *The Trouble with Normal: Sex, Politics, and the Ethics of Queer Life* (Cambridge, MA: Harvard University Press, 1999); Jasbir K. Puar, *Terrorist Assemblages: Homonationalism in Queer Times* (Durham, NC: Duke University Press, 2007); Dean Spade and Craig Willse, "Sex, Gender, and War in an Age of Multicul-

tural Imperialism," QED: A Journal in GLBTQ Worldmaking 1, no. 1 (2014): 5–29; Christina B. Hanhardt, *Safe Space: Gay Neighborhood History and the Politics of Violence* (Durham, NC: Duke University Press, 2013).

5. Some critics have already begun this work. See Rose Corrigan, "Making Meaning of Megan's Law," *Law & Social Inquiry* 31, no. 2 (April 2006): 267. Corrigan argues that Megan's Law, the federal statute requiring states to create publicly accessible databases of registered sex offenders, "excludes many of the most common offenders from reach of the law, thus deflecting attention away from assaults committed by family and friends in favor of reviving stereotypes about deviant strangers." See also Roger N. Lancaster's discussion about "pointers for a sounder public discourse" in *Sex Panic and the Punitive State* (Berkeley: University of California Press, 2011), 243–245, and Eric S. Janus, "Feminism, the Culture Wars, and Sexual Violence," in *Failure to Protect: America's Sexual Predator Laws and the Rise of the Preventive State* (Ithaca, NY: Cornell University Press, 2006), 75–92.

6. E. A. Riddle, "Compulsory Registration: A Vehicle of Mercy Discarded," *California Western Law Review* 3, no. 195 (1967): 199; Tamara Rice Lave, "Only Yesterday: The Rise and Fall of Twentieth Century Sexual Psychopath Laws," *Louisiana Law Review* 69, no. 3 (spring 2009): 549; Robert L. Jacobson, "'Megan's Laws' Reinforcing Old Patterns of Anti-Gay Police Harassment," *Georgetown Law Journal* 87, no. 7 (July 1999): 2443; George Chauncey, "The Postwar Sex Crime Panic," in *True Stories from the American Past*, ed. William Graebner (New York: McGraw-Hill, 1993), 160–178; Estelle B. Freedman, "'Uncontrolled Desires': The Response to the Sexual Psychopath, 1920–1960," *Journal of American History* 74, no. 1 (June 1987): 83–106.

7. Dale Jennings, "To Be Accused, Is To Be Guilty," ONE 1, no. 1 (January 1953): 12.

8. "NOW is the time to fight," [1952], box 1, folder 14, Mattachine Society Project Collection, Co112008-016, ONE National Gay and Lesbian Archives, USC Libraries, University of Southern California.

9. "Victory!," [1952], box 1, folder 14, Mattachine Society Project Collection, Co112008–016, ONE National Gay and Lesbian Archives, USC Libraries, University of Southern California; An Open Letter to Friends of the Citizens' Committee to Outlaw Entrapment, [c. 1952], box 1, folder 14, Mattachine Society Project Collection, Co112008-016, ONE National Gay and Lesbian Archives, USC Libraries, University of Southern California. For more on the Jennings case, see John D'Emilio, *Sexual Politics, Sexual Communities: The Making of a Homosexual Minority in the United States, 1940–1970* (Chicago: University of Chicago Press, 1983), 70–74. The police practice of using plainclothes officers to entrap gay men was an invention of the postwar period. See Nan Alamilla Boyd, "Policing Queers in the 1940s and 1950s: Harassment, Prosecution, and the Legal Defense of Gay Bars," in *Wide-Open Town: A History of Queer San Francisco to 1965* (Berkeley: University of California Press, 2003), 108–147.

10. Two events in particular precipitated the 1961 legislative revision of California's vagrancy law of which the lewd or dissolute person statute was a part. The first was the 1960 California Supreme Court decision *In re Newbern*, which deemed unconstitutional the "common drunk" provision of the statute. The second was Arthur H. Sherry's influential law review article "Vagrants, Rogues and Vagabonds — Old Concepts in Need of Revision," *California Law Review* 48, no. 4 (1960): 557–573. For a useful discussion about the legislative history of California Penal Code Section 647(a), see the majority opinion in Pryor v. Municipal Court, 25 Cal. 3d 238 (1979).

11. "Male Kisses in Public Ruled 'Lewd,'" *Los Angeles Herald-Examiner*, August 27, 1963.

12. People v. Dudley, 250 Cal. App. 2d Supp. 955 (1967).

13. People v. Mesa, 265 Cal. App. 2d 746 (1968).

14. A California District Court of Appeals decision from 1955 involved a man named Perfecto Martinez, who was convicted of "being an idle, lewd and dissolute person" for wearing female apparel in public. Martinez was committed to the State Medical Facility at Terminal Island for treatment as a sexual psychopath. *In re Martinez*, 130 Cal. App. 2d 239 (1955). In the 1956 case *People v. Woodworth*, a Los Angeles Municipal Court convicted William Woodworth of lewd conduct for supposedly soliciting sex from a police officer. People v. Woodworth, 147 Cal. App. 2d Supp. 831 (1956).

15. Louis B. Schwartz, "Morals Offenses and the Model Penal Code," *Columbia Law Review* 63, no. 4 (1963): 681; Walter Barnett, "Court Left Solons with Key to Reform," *The Advocate*, May 12–25, 1971.

16. "Ed Davis New L.A. Top Cop," *Los Angeles Advocate*, October 1969; "LAPD Chief Compares Gays, Lepers," *The Advocate*, January 5, 1972; "Victimless Crime? No Such Thing, Says Chief Davis," *The Advocate*, February 2, 1972.

17. "HELP Is Here," [1968], box 1, folder 1, Homophile Effort for Legal Protection, Incorporated (HELP, Inc.), Records, Co112008-052, ONE National Gay and Lesbian Archives, USC Libraries, University of Southern California; HELP, Inc. Newsletter, March 15, 1972, box 4, folder 2, Homophile Effort for Legal Protection, Incorporated (HELP, Inc.), Records, Co112008-052, ONE National Gay and Lesbian Archives, USC Libraries, University of Southern California.

18. Jim Highland, "RAID!" *Tangents* 2, no. 4 (January 1967): 4–7.

19. "Touch-In" at the Farm, [1970], box 1, folder 15, Gay Liberation Front (GLF), Los Angeles Records, Co112012.031, ONE National Gay and Lesbian Archives, USC Libraries, University of Southern California; Protest at the Farm, 1970, box 1, folder 22, Gay Liberation Front (GLF), Los Angeles Records, Co112012.031, ONE National Gay and Lesbian Archives, USC Libraries, University of Southern California.

20. "GLF Wins Touch Privileges at Bar," *The Advocate*, October 28–November 10, 1970; "Gay Leaders Defend License of L.A. Bar," *The Advocate*, January 6, 1971.

21. "LAPD Entrapment Victim Fighting Back," *The Advocate*, December 23, 1970.

22. Rob Cole, "Crack in California Lewd Law," *The Advocate*, January 3, 1973.

23. Project, "The Consenting Adult Homosexual and the Law: An Empirical Study of Enforcement and Administration in Los Angeles County," UCLA *Law Review* 13, no. 3 (March 1966): 686, 796.

24. Laud Humphreys, *Tearoom Trade: Impersonal Sex in Public Places* (Chicago: Aldine, 1970); Barry Copilow and Thomas F. Coleman, "Enforcement of Section 647(a) of the California Penal Code by the Los Angeles Police Department," 1973, Unmarried America, http://www.unmarriedamerica.org/Archives/1973-1974-coleman-Copilow -Toy-Reports/1973-Coleman-Copilow-Report.pdf. For an example of lawyers drawing on this scholarship to challenge the constitutionality of the lewd conduct law, see Brief for the Pride Foundation, the American Civil Liberties Union of Northern California, and the American Civil Liberties Union of Southern California as amicus curiae, *In re Anders*, 25 Cal. 3d 414 (1979).

25. Martin St. John, "Pines Pledges Ear for Gays If He's Elected L.A. City Attorney," *The Advocate*, February 14, 1973; Martin St. John, "L.A. City Attorney Would Turn Gay Bars into Private Clubs," *The Advocate*, March 14, 1973.

26. Joel Tlumak, "Pines Eases Gay Prosecutions," *The Advocate*, May 22, 1974; "Hollywood Lewd Busts Off 48%," *The Advocate*, October 9, 1974; Jim Kepner, "Bradley Tells Police: Shift Priorities," *Entertainment West*, 1975 (full date unavailable).

27. "Revised Penal Code on Coast to Be Proposed to Legislature," *New York Times*, September 23, 1971.

28. The quote comes from Earl G. Stokes to James M. Foster, [1972], box 1, folder 4, Society for Individual Rights (SIR) Records, Co112011-075, ONE National Gay and Lesbian Archives, USC Libraries, University of Southern California; Arthur C. Warner to American Bar Association, June 3, 1972, Thomas F. Coleman and Jay Kohorn Papers, Acc103-3, ONE National Gay and Lesbian Archives, USC Libraries, University of Southern California.

29. "Law Students Narrowly Back Consent Laws," *The Advocate*, June 7, 1972; "Psychiatrists in California Support Gays," *The Advocate*, June 7, 1972; Thomas Coleman, "Nation's Lawyers Call for Consent Laws," *The Advocate*, August 29, 1973; George Mendenhall, "Gov. Brown Signs Sex Bill — Referendum Possible," *The Advocate*, June 4, 1975.

30. Peter Thomas Judge to Willie Brown, July 18, 1978, box 7, folder 4, American Civil Liberties Union of Southern California Lesbian and Gay Rights Chapter records, Co112007-013, ONE National Gay and Lesbian Archives, USC Libraries, University of Southern California.

31. For more on the role Willie Brown played in the effort to decriminalize sodomy between consenting adults in private in California, see Jonathan Bell, *California Crucible: The Forging of Modern American Liberalism* (Philadelphia: University of Pennsylvania Press, 2012), 261–262.

32. Judy Willmore, "Victory Claimed in L.A. Council," *The Advocate*, August 27, 1975.

33. "The Great Slave-Market Bust: A Story Only Los Angeles Could Produce," *The Advocate*, May 5, 1976; "47 Vice Cops Axed in Budget Crunch," *The Advocate*, June 16, 1976.

34. Arthur C. Warner, "Non-Commercial Sexual Solicitation: The Case for Judicial Invalidation," *SexuaLaw Reporter* 4, no. 1 (January–March 1978): 1, 10–20, 17.

35. Pryor v. Municipal Court.

36. *In re Birch*, 10 Cal. 3d 314 (1973).

37. People v. Mills, 81 Cal. App. 3d 171 (1978).

38. S.B. 13 Press Release, [1979], box 5, folder 5, American Civil Liberties Union of Southern California Lesbian and Gay Rights Chapter records, Co112007-013, ONE National Gay and Lesbian Archives, USC Libraries, University of Southern California.

39. Memorandum of Points and Authorities in Support of Objection, Motion and Request re: Registration under P.C. §290, p. 21, *In re Reed*, 33 Cal. 3d 914 (1983).

40. Press release re: San Francisco Mental Health Advisory Board, [1972], box 1, folder 4, Society for Individual Rights (SIR) Records, Co112011-075, ONE National Gay and Lesbian Archives, USC Libraries, University of Southern California.

41. Exhibits for the Petition for Writ of Habeas Corpus and Application for Stay, Law Offices of Jay M. Kohorn, p. E-64, *In re Reed*, 33 Cal. 3d 914 (1983)

42. Draft of Transcript of Public Hearings, November 1981, box 14, Arthur C. Warner Papers, Public Policy Papers, Department of Rare Books and Special Collections, Princeton University Library.

43. Sexual Child Abuse, [1977], box 24, folder 11, American Civil Liberties Union of Southern California Lesbian and Gay Rights Chapter records, Co112007-013, ONE National Gay and Lesbian Archives, USC Libraries, University of Southern California.

44. "About Our Children," 1978, box 4, folder 1, Adele Starr collection on Parents and Friends of Lesbians and Gays, Co112009-012, ONE National Gay and Lesbian Archives, USC Libraries, University of Southern California.

45. Jerry D. Blair, "Sex Offender Registration for Section 647 Disorderly Conduct Convictions Is Cruel and Unusual Punishment," *San Diego Law Review* 13, no. 2 (1976): 402. "The Consenting Adult Homosexual and the Law" made the same argument. See Project, "The Consenting Adult Homosexual and the Law," 737.

46. Brief for the Pride Foundation as amicus curiae, *In re Anders*, 25 Cal. 3d 414, 33.

47. *In re Reed*, 33 Cal. 3d 914.

48. National Committee for Sexual Civil Liberties, "Implications of Reed," [1983], Unmarried America, http://www.unmarriedamerica.org/Archives/1980-1983-sex -registration-law-challenge/reed-implications.pdf.

49. Jacob Wetterling Crimes Against Children and Sexually Violent Offender Registration Act, Pub. L. No. 103-322, Title XVII, Subtitle A, § 170101, 108 Stat. 2038 (September 13, 1994).

50. Megan's Law, Pub. L. No. 104-145, 110 Stat 1345 (May 17, 1996).

51. On the repressive turn in American sex crime law since the 1960s, see Corey Rayburn Yung, "The Emerging Criminal War on Sex Offenders," *Harvard Civil Rights–Civil Liberties Law Review* 45 (2010): 435–481. On the expansion of the carceral state in the United States since the 1960s, see Gottschalk, *The Prison and the Gallows*, and Heather Ann Thompson, "Why Mass Incarceration Matters: Rethinking Crisis, Decline, and Transformation in Postwar American History," *Journal of American History* 97, no. 3 (December 2010): 703–734.

52. As Alfred Kinsey once wrote, "It is ordinarily said that criminal law is designed to protect property and to protect persons, and if society's only interest in controlling sex behavior were to protect persons, then the criminal codes concerned with assault and battery should provide adequate protection. The fact that there is a body of sex laws which are apart from the laws protecting persons is evidence of their distinct function, namely that of protecting custom." Alfred C. Kinsey, Wardell B. Pomeroy, and Clyde E. Martin, *Sexual Behavior in the Human Male* (Philadelphia: W.B. Saunders, 1948), 4. On the concept of benign sexual variation, see Gayle Rubin, "Thinking Sex: Notes for a Radical Theory of the Politics of Sexuality," in *The Lesbian and Gay Studies Reader*, ed. Henry Abelove, Michèle Aina Barale, and David M. Halperin (New York: Routledge, 1993), 3–44; and Rostom Mesli, "Gayle Rubin's Concept of 'Benign Sexual Variation': A Critical Concept for a Radical Theory of the Politics of Sexuality," *South Atlantic Quarterly* 114, no. 4 (October 2015): 803–826.

LAURA MANSNERUS

| 8 |

For What They Might Do

A Sex Offender Exception to the Constitution

Crime inflicts harm, and the state inflicts harm in return, in a form of retribution that is visible in prisons everywhere. But it is also evident in institutions that confine about 5,000 sex offenders, involuntarily and indefinitely, who are not in the criminal justice system at all. They have completed prison terms and are now housed as mental patients, though most are not mentally ill. They live in cells and dormitories, herded by uniformed guards to meals and work details, often denied unsupervised communication with the outside world. Visitors are fiercely discouraged. These men — and all but a handful are men — are confined because of what they might do someday, exactly the kind of preventive detention that seems like an obvious constitutional problem. But the constitutional objections that once looked equally obvious were exhausted years ago. Now, for each offender entering this system, or trying to leave, the only challenge available is a motion from the public defender's office arguing that he is not as dangerous as the state says he is. The argument rarely succeeds.

So thousands of former convicts remain locked away, held under the ominously named "predator laws." In almost all of the twenty states that have them, they are called Sexually Violent Predator Acts.[1] They are the ultimate measures in a vast scheme of social controls — longer sentences, public registries, residency restrictions, tighter parole supervision — that have walled off sex offenders from the rest of us. These measures have assigned sex offenders their own place in constitutional jurisprudence, different not just from other citizens but also from other criminals.

In the early 1990s, as a string of sexually motivated child murders lit up the media and sent bands of citizen-advocates to statehouses across the country, legislators faced a problem: While trying to answer demands to dispel the menace in any way possible, they could not employ the criminal justice system very efficiently to do it. Sentences for sex crimes could be (and were) increased, but even the most vengeful legislature would probably not adopt mandatory life sentences for crimes short of murder. And offenders already in prison could not be re-sentenced. The criminal justice system confines people, but it cannot confine them prospectively or indefinitely.

A state could do both under general civil commitment laws, but that system also had limits. To involuntarily commit someone to a mental institution, the state had to prove that they were both mentally ill *and* dangerous; the U.S. Supreme Court had made clear that that rule applied to people who had committed criminal acts as much as it did to anyone else.[2] The challenge, then, was to design a workaround just for sex offenders about to be released from prison, a workaround that would loosen the requirements for commitment, extend offenders' confinement, and still satisfy the courts. A few states adopted the medical model to turn prisoners into patients, promising to try to rehabilitate them even if they could not be rehabilitated. But requiring a diagnosis of mental illness limited the kind of offender that could be controlled under the law to only those suffering from conditions identified by a fairly strict set of medical criteria. In an effort to broaden the scope of civil commitment laws, states devised a new scheme that applied not just to those who suffered from diagnosable mental illnesses but also to those identified as having a "mental abnormality" or "personality disorder." These measures were called the Sexually Violent Predator (svp) Acts. The new laws were premised on a confounding logic: The same person who exercised the volition legally required to commit a crime and stand trial for that violation is suddenly found to be lacking in volition, so much so that he must be confined *indefinitely*. That determination comes years after the offense, sometimes decades — decades in which he may well have aged out of the highest-risk group and is, actuarially speaking, more likely than ever to exercise self-control. In those years, he probably received no treatment; but now, the state says, treatment must start immediately.

Some lower courts resisted, but the Supreme Court took the authors of the new legislative regime at their word. In 1997, in its first ruling on the issue, *Kansas v. Hendricks*, the Court upheld the Kansas Sexually Violent Predator Act.[3] The Court's overall rationale was that the law was intended to treat rather than punish the offenders and therefore was not just extended punishment by another name. Then, the Court said, instead of a strict requirement of mental illness, the Kansas statute's "mental abnormality or personality disorder" standards would be enough, so long as they were disorders that caused "volitional impairment," rendering the person likely to commit future sex crimes. Refinements would come later, but with that decision the SVP laws were approved, the new standards set, and the commitment machinery allowed to keep running.

"Sexually violent predator" is a term that tells a story about how a legal fiction can work in practice. Legislators imported a horror-story metaphor into law and then into the news media. And if "predator" is a metaphor, "violent" is a recasting of an ordinary dictionary definition, or a term of art. As defined in these laws, "violent" crimes can include consensual sex with a minor, public indecency, and downloading child pornography. A sexually violent predator statute, then, can apply to an exhibitionist or a twenty-three-year-old who had sex with a willing fifteen-year-old — people who are, in the common understanding of the words, neither violent nor predators. And it often does. The laws, enacted with pronouncements about trapping the worst of the worst, have ended up trapping the somewhat worse. They have committed thousands of men bearing little resemblance to the toddler-kidnappers and torture-murderers who prompted the laws. They have confined thousands who are not mentally ill. They have confined people never even found to have touched their victims.

The courts have not endorsed that result, but they have enabled it. As the literature on moral panics has documented, legislatures react quickly to spectacular, horrifying crimes and growing public fear.[4] That response is part of the job. But the courts are supposed to moderate these responses. They are supposed to disregard the overheated language that has slipped into common usage — the term "predator," for example — and at least appear to apply a morally neutral lens to their reading of the Constitution. If sex offenders warrant a constitutional doctrine of their own, the courts are supposed to explain why. But they have only fleetingly acknowledged a central problem in the new scheme: all kinds of criminals have personality disorders and failures of self-control. As to why sex offenders are different from the others, the best answer apparently is that their crimes involved sex. The Supreme Court in particular did not squarely address this problem, and may never be required to address it, unless it is presented with a statute that involuntarily commits arsonists or animal abusers. Some legal scholars argue persuasively that the Supreme Court might very well approve of detaining other groups on the basis of risk, and certainly the Court has acquiesced before to public panics.[5] Still, there's no panic like a sex panic.

The wave of public alarm that prompted the SVP laws was not the nation's first and not the first to prompt specialized civil commitment laws. An earlier twentieth-century panic, actually more hyperbolized than the most recent one, began when some gruesome but scattered sex crimes against children in the 1930s and 1940s brought on a tabloid rampage. As it worked its way into the expanding national media, the fear was stoked by, among many others, the outsize figure of J. Edgar Hoover. In one of many articles inveighing against "sex fiends," Hoover wrote, "Should wild beasts break out of circus cages, the whole city would be mobilized instantly. But depraved human beings, more savage than beasts, are permitted to rove America almost at will."[6] Another growing industry, psychiatry, was consulted for guidance as almost thirty states enacted civil commitment laws to contain the perceived menace of the "sexual psychopath." In Roger Lancaster's account of the era, the arc looks eerily familiar:

> Child rape and murder figured prominently in public discussions of sex offenses. These extreme events triggered mob attacks and the organization of citizens' groups or children's protective societies in a number of cities and towns. They also stimulated wider preemptive measures. The rationale offered for the sexual psychopath laws often stressed liberal aims: treatment, not punishment. But because every sex offender was viewed as posing the threat of violence, nonviolent offenders charged with sodomy and exhibitionism could also be incarcerated under sexual psychopath laws.[7]

The era had its dissenters, including the psychiatric experts whose authority had been enlisted for cover and even some state legislatures and governors. And while few of the sexual psychopath laws were struck down, the Supreme Court balked at their vague criteria of deviance and dangerousness. The Court upheld Minnesota's statute in 1940 by interpreting it as limited to those persons showing "an utter lack of control of sexual impulses."[8] Any broader reading of the statute, the Court said, would be unconstitutional. Still, more and more states enacted sexual psychopath laws, and by the time they were finished they had locked up thousands of men (the women were generally left alone), many of them exhibitionists, Peeping Toms, and ordinary gay men who had done nothing that would be illegal today.

By the early 1970s, America was at the sputtering end of the panic. The country was seeing a flowering of previously unthinkable ideas about sexual liberty, including the recognition of adolescent and even childhood sexuality. One workmanlike guide published in 1974, *The Sex Handbook: Information and Help for Minors*, assured, "If you're old enough to want to have sex, you're old enough to have it."[9] In the vast bulge of baby boomers entering adulthood, "sex fiend" and "pervert" had become terms of irony.

Legislatures accommodated the growing skepticism about victimless offenses, the demonization of homosexuality, and the criminalization of teenage sex. (For a brief time in 1978, New Jersey's age of consent was lowered to thirteen.) Criminal codes everywhere were rewritten. Their treatment of actual violent sex crimes did not change, of course; lawmakers were finally recognizing the difference between brutality and deviance.[10]

At the same time, judicial attention to individual liberties, and especially the Supreme Court's attention, was waxing. In a string of decisions in the late 1960s and early 1970s, the Court flagged the "defective delinquent" and sexual psychopath laws, acknowledging what Justice Marshall called "a massive curtailment of liberty" inherent in civil commitment.[11] (The specific crime was technically not relevant to the legal conclusion, but Justice Marshall began his opinion in that case, *Humphrey v. Cady*, by noting that the offender had been convicted of contributing to the delinquency of a minor, a misdemeanor. For that, he had been sent to a "sex deviate facility" in a Wisconsin prison.) The rule that the Court reinforced, for sex offenders as for anyone else, was that civil commitment was permissible only for someone who had a recognized mental illness and posed an imminent danger to himself or others. Some of the sexual psychopath laws were repealed in the wake of the Supreme Court's admonitions; others fell into disuse as lawmakers turned away from civil commitment altogether during a national wave of deinstitutionalization.

The Court's warnings crystallized in a 1992 decision that seemed to leave little room for the preventive detention model. The case involved a Louisiana man named Terry Foucha who was arrested on burglary and weapons charges, acquitted by reason of insanity, and committed to a mental institution.[12] While he suffered from what was described as a drug-induced psychosis when he committed the crime, he recovered his grip on reality after being hospitalized. Everyone agreed that Foucha was no longer mentally ill. However, during his hospitalization, he was diagnosed as having an antisocial personality disorder. Finding a number of constitutional problems with Foucha's detention, the Supreme Court was emphatic in asserting that the diagnosis would not be enough:

> The state asserts that because Foucha once committed a criminal act and now has an antisocial personality disorder, a disorder for which there is no effective treatment, he may be held indefinitely. This rationale would permit the state to hold indefinitely any other insanity acquittee not mentally ill who could be shown to have a personality disorder that may lead to criminal conduct. The same would be true of any convicted criminal, even though he has completed his prison term. It would also be only a step away from substituting dangerousness for our present system.[13]

If Terry Foucha had come before the Court five years later, in 1997, he probably would have gotten the same result. But that's because Terry Foucha was a burglar. Foucha was impulsive and aggressive, but so are many burglars, and Louisiana had no law aimed at locking them up indefinitely. As a criminal, he was unexceptional, inhabiting a universe of criminals generally regarded as bad but not mad, troubling but not incomprehensible.

What the Court did face in 1997 was a sex offender confined through civil commitment, caught in a net of new laws designed just for sex offenders. In fact, in Leroy Hendricks the justices had a walking advertisement for those laws. His criminal record showed ten child victims, and he described himself as an incorrigible pedophile. He told one physician that treatment was "bullshit" and that the only way he could stop abusing children was "to die." When his last term in a Kansas prison expired, he became the first man committed under the state's Sexually Violent Predator Act.

At the same time that the court was hearing Hendricks's appeal, a new panic had flared. Although national crime statistics showed no spike in sex crimes or child molestation in the early 1990s, newspapers and cable TV and politicians reported an epidemic of monsters.[14] Their names were widely broadcast: Westley Alan Dodd in Washington state, Jesse Timmendequas in New Jersey, Richard Allen Davis in California. All had sexually attacked and murdered children, and all had long, atrocious records. Even President Clinton joined the pageant of the outraged; he mourned Richard Davis's victim, twelve-year-old Polly Klaas, in his 1994 State of the Union address, opening his campaign for a national registry of sex offenders.[15] Reflecting broader trends, the prison population of sex offenders had risen sharply in the 1980s, the result of stricter sentencing laws and shifting prosecutorial priorities.[16] The growing number of sex offenders in prison seemed all the more reason to dread — and track — their eventual release. The states responded by enacting registration laws and, in some, the new regimes for civil commitment.

Meanwhile, the "predator," a stylized image from crime fiction, entered reporting about real crimes, almost always sex crimes. In 1991, an episode of NBC's 48 Hours, titled "Predators," examined child sex murders.[17] A search in the online news archive NewsLibrary, a compilation of newspaper articles from around the country, evidences this trend: In 1985, in almost every article where the word "predator" appeared, it was used in reference to the animal kingdom. A handful of stories used the word in general references to badly behaving humans; two referred to specific criminals (with the word "predator" appearing in quoted statements by judges or prosecutors); and a single story referred to a rapist as a "predator." By 1990, about 10 percent of the "predators" lurking in news articles were sex offenders. Most of these references appeared in articles about Washington state's new SVP law, the first in the nation and the subject of intense news coverage. (The law was, after all, called the Sexually Violent Predator Act, or, for short, "the predator law.") The remainder of the "predator" sex offender references described identified individuals, often in quoted statements — or, in just a few instances, sex offenders in general. By 1995, "predator" had become a common term for sex offenders, individually and collectively, accounting for 24 percent of all uses of the word. Many of these were un-ironic uses of the word, not in quotation marks, as a term for sex offenders in general. The new concept had entered America's vernacular.

After legislators enacted Washington state's SVP law, other state legislatures followed suit. Lawmakers in Wisconsin, Minnesota, and, most important, Kansas all quickly passed similar SVP laws. Although the SVP law in Washington state law had been struck down by a lower federal court and was in jeopardy, Kansas legislators were undeterred and used it as a model for their own law, enacted in 1994. In legislative testimony, a member of the Kansas Parole Board, who later became the state's attorney general, said that the bill was aimed at keeping certain offenders "locked up for life." "We cannot open up our prison doors and let these animals back into our communities," she said.[18] One legislator said, "Because there is no effective treatment for sex offenders, this bill may mean a life sentence for a felon who is considered a risk to women and children. So be it."[19] Another said, "That's why it's called a sex predator law. They'll be out prowling the streets. I want to err on the side of public safety." A colleague in the Kansas House, a former judge, protested:

"Believe me, you don't have to be a constitutional scholar and you don't even have to be a retired judge to see this bill for what it is," he said. "This is pure preventative detention, which is constitutionally impermissible."[20] But his side lost in the 102–23 House vote. The Senate vote was unanimous: 40–0.

Like Washington's law, Kansas's new statute allowed the commitment of a sex offender with a "mental abnormality or personality disorder." When the Kansas Supreme Court ruled on Leroy Hendricks's case, it struck down the state's svp law, holding under the *Foucha* decision that a "personality disorder" was not sufficient cause for civil commitment. But in a 5–4 decision, the U.S. Supreme Court reversed the Kansas court and resuscitated the law. The opinion was written by Justice Thomas, who had dissented vehemently in *Foucha*. "The term 'mental illness' is devoid of any talismanic significance," he wrote. "Indeed, we have never required state legislatures to adopt any particular nomenclature in drafting civil commitment statutes." At the same time, the Court said that whatever definition the state chose, the disorder would have to be one that made it "difficult, if not impossible, for the person to control his dangerous behavior." The minority, in an opinion written by Justice Breyer, dissented on another ground: that the Kansas law was punitive in intent. Noting the overheated language used by the law's proponents in the legislature, the dissenters argued that the law violated the constitutional prohibition of ex post facto laws.

The *Hendricks* decision might have looked like a historical happenstance, turning on a single vote among what had recently become the most conservative Supreme Court bench in decades. Without that one vote, the svp laws might have been choked off in 1997. But all nine justices approved the new "mental abnormality" standard.

Five years after *Hendricks*, it was Justice Breyer's turn to write for the majority in a 7–2 decision that again upheld the Kansas law. At issue was the commitment of Michael T. Crane, whose conviction stemmed from an odd, one-day spree in which he exposed himself to a tanning salon attendant and then went to a video store, exposing himself again, grabbing a clerk, and threatening to rape her before giving up on the whole enterprise and running out of the store. Crane had a history of other "inappropriate behavior," but he was no Leroy Hendricks; he was diagnosed with antisocial personality disorder and exhibitionism. The Kansas Supreme Court again struck down the law, and the U.S. Supreme Court again brought it back to life. "It is enough to say that there must be serious difficulty in controlling behavior," Justice Breyer wrote, difficulty "sufficient to distinguish the dangerous sexual offender" who is being considered for commitment "from the dangerous but typical recidivist convicted in an ordinary criminal case."[21]

In pages of verbal contortions over degrees of self-control, the justices in *Kansas v. Crane* struggled to resolve what the American Psychiatric Association had declined to resolve when it said, in the context of the insanity defense, that "the line between an irresistible impulse and an impulse not resisted is probably no sharper than that between twilight and dusk."[22] But, having to define what is constitutional and what is not, the Court had to settle on some words. The words applied only in the context of the SVP laws; the old, stricter standard still applied to most criminals, including assailants who brutalize their victims — as long as no genitalia are involved. But when the Court was asked whether sex offenders could be indefinitely detained on *some other* basis, the answer was yes.

While psychiatrists and psychologists agree with the courts that legal and medical definitions of mental illness are not necessarily congruent, they are generally dismayed that legislators and prosecutors use their diagnoses to circumvent the criminal process. A task force of the American Psychiatric Association said in a 1999 report that "confinement without a reasonable prospect of beneficial treatment of the underlying disorder is nothing more than preventative detention."[23] The *Hendricks* and *Crane* decisions brought a flurry of objections from mental health professionals. One forensic psychiatrist wrote scathingly about the "inchoate jurisprudence of the United States Supreme Court" and the elusive medical distinction that the Court said would limit eligibility for commitment: "Because this distinction is not one of principle but rather of diagnostic labeling, the protections guaranteed by our constitution become matters of sovereign grace rather than clear entitlement."[24] The Court's next major statement came in 2010, in a ruling on a new federal sex crimes law, the Adam Walsh Child Protection and Safety Act. The law authorized civil commitment of "sexually dangerous persons" held in federal prisons, where the once-negligible number of sex offenders was burgeoning because of recently expanded child pornography laws. The only question before the Court was whether Congress had the constitutional authority to enact a civil commitment program, normally a species of legislation left to the states; the Court held that it did. The justices did not address the issue of whether the due process clause permitted civil commitment for the predicate crime of downloading pictures. That was not exactly the situation of the named plaintiff, Graydon Earl Comstock, who had also molested four boys, though others held by the federal Bureau of Prisons in Butner, North Carolina, had been convicted of nothing more than consuming child pornography.[25]

After *United States v. Comstock*, the legal landscape was more hospitable than ever to the SVP laws.[26] Nothing was going to dislodge the practice, and even civil liberties advocates settled into dull acceptance. This is how social change — in this case, change that demonizes and punishes — comes about: the losers retreat, and the winners frame a new orthodoxy that bends our views about justice. The courts abet the change, and then they sustain it. When their cautions are ignored, retributive practices and procedural shortcuts seep into the new (or, by now, old) scheme. But the Supreme Court said it was all right, so who's going to do anything?

WHAT THE COURT HAS WROUGHT

Justice Thomas's opinion in *Hendricks* assumed that the element of "volitional impairment" would ensure that the Kansas law targeted "only a narrow class of particularly dangerous individuals." While assuming as they must that prosecutors and lower courts would take their direction, at least some of the justices seemed uneasy. In a separate concurring opinion, Justice Kennedy wrote, "If, however, civil confinement were to become a mechanism for retribution or general deterrence, or if it were shown that mental abnormality is too imprecise a category to offer a solid basis for concluding that civil detention is justified, our precedents would not suffice to validate it."[27]

Justice Kennedy's caution aside, commitments have proceeded apace. No states have enacted SVP laws since 2007, mostly because they are hugely expensive, but the twenty in place are now embedded in the vast web of government controls over sex offenders. The courts struggle with unwieldy "conditions of confinement" complaints, which often can be expected to live longer than the people who filed them, but very few have released anyone on due process grounds. Only a handful of lower courts have questioned the constitutionality of the statutes as written. Meanwhile, most states have settled into a processing routine, stamping psychiatrists' certifications, filing boilerplate petitions, hiring more staff, and buying more beds. By 2006, about 4,500 people were being held under the SVP laws.[28] According to a 2014 survey, about 5,300 were in custody. In the states that reported further information on that survey (not all did), about 1,500 had been released since the programs' inception and 260 had died in custody.[29]

Courts settled into routines, too. A court authorizes temporary detention and then — sometimes years later — decides at a hearing whether to grant the state's commitment petition. Some states provide for periodic review hearings after that, but in practice the reviews are often delayed for years. Some states' laws, including the Kansas statute blessed by the Supreme Court, require jury trials and proof beyond a reasonable doubt to support a commitment, but other states require neither.

It is hard to tell who, exactly, gets fed into the machinery. An even administration of justice would see roughly proportional numbers of civil commitments across the country, but the numbers are wildly disparate. The number of commitments per one million people is 54 in Wisconsin, for example, and 129 in Minnesota, though both states started their SVP programs the same year. Over the first seven years of their programs, New Hampshire had 0.8 commitments per one million residents, whereas New York had 15.[30] In thirty states, of course, the rate is zero. While law-enforcement officials still assure the public that they are capturing the worst of the worst, exactly what constitutes "the worst" might mean something else in the state next door. In every state, meanwhile, the worst of the worst remain in prison, serving ever-longer terms, or in forensic hospitals for those with severe mental illness. It turns out that the Supreme Court's limiting language has had little apparent effect, as the "distinction" that was supposed to separate the bad-plus from the merely bad never materialized. In practice, the distinction simply served to underscore the line between sex offenders and everybody else.

THE PROCESSING OF JUSTICE

In the criminal justice system, the courts are monitors of accuracy: if the state is going to lock up someone, the courts are supposed to make sure that it's the right person and that there is ample evidence for doing so. Sometimes due process protections end up excluding information that might be useful — hearsay, for example, or self-incriminating statements — but the rules are generally intended to sift out information that is unreliable. In the civil commitment system, the sifting mechanism all but vanishes. The candidate for commitment does have certain constitutional protections, like the right to counsel and cross-examination, but the court will hear piles of evidence against him that would not be admissible in a criminal case. That's the whole point.

Criminal courts also exclude some evidence that *is* potentially quite useful but would grossly prejudice a jury. Information about a defendant's prior convictions and "prior bad acts," as well as more general evidence about his character, is subject to a rough balancing test weighing its probative value against its prejudicial effect. Such evidence is almost always ruled inadmissible. A civil commitment proceeding is not constrained by constitutional concerns about fair treatment, and so evidence of the subject's general turpitude — or, in the state's view, his likelihood of reoffending — is almost always admissible. Again, that's the whole point. As explained by Eric Janus, probably the leading critic of the SVP laws among legal scholars, "the relevant 'facts' are psychological constructs, whose only reality is in the expert judgment of mental health professionals."[31]

In most cases, mental health professionals are the *only* witnesses. They are enlisted to gather evidence for the government and then, when judges defer to their expertise, effectively become decision-makers.[32] They not only make diagnoses but also administer the "actuarials," the tests designed to measure risk of recidivism, and act as expert witnesses to testify to the importance of those tests. The tests are the subject of widespread debate among researchers, who have established only that they are somewhat more reliable than a coin toss. But the actuarials, like the psychiatric diagnoses, are essential to the court's ultimate decision. They satisfy a need for facts.

Common diagnoses include both obvious sexual disorders, like pedophilia, and a basket of "paraphilias," denoting deviant sexual interests. Sometimes those diagnoses are tagged with the term "not otherwise specified," or "NOS," meaning that the disorder doesn't fall within a clear diagnostic category in the profession's *Diagnostic and Statistical Manual*. Some people are simply diagnosed with "antisocial personality disorder," though even the *Crane* court pointed out that 40 percent to 60 percent of the general male prison population could be diagnosed with antisocial personality disorder,[33] and other sources use a higher estimate. "Narcissistic personality disorder," mood disorders, and substance abuse are common diagnoses as well.

The psychiatrist or psychologist testifying as an expert witness has usually interviewed the inmate but relies more heavily on their "official record," which often reaches back to juvenile offenses and even infractions in school. The inmate's record in treatment is also heavily mined in the proceedings against him. This cache of evidence, incorporating notes and impressions from therapists and attendants, is naturally rife with hearsay. But staff members' observations are typically folded into the testimony or report of the state's expert witness. And the courts have carved out exceptions to the hearsay rule for expert witnesses, who may discuss anything they relied upon in forming their conclusions. So if a social worker notes, for example, that Patient X has been hostile in group therapy, that observation can be cited by the psychiatrist who testifies later at Patient X's review hearing that he has an antisocial personality disorder.

Finally, treatment is itself a massive exercise in self-incrimination. During treatment, an inmate is supposed to recall every victim he ever had, whether or not the incident was reported. If he complies, he is obviously incriminating himself. If he doesn't, he is demonstrating evasion and denial, which count as risk factors. If he describes struggling with self-control, he is making the state's case. If he asserts a measure of self-control, he is lacking insight, if not lying. If he disagrees with the staff's assessments, he is resistant to treatment or, worse, defying reality. Some men refuse treatment altogether but by doing so lose all chance of release.

The deep fear that generated the SVP laws is, of course, that the demons in the headlines would strike again. They are, we have been told, helpless recidivists — who have already shown that they can't control themselves — and are, in this way, different from other criminals. Sex offender recidivism is a morass for researchers, especially since so many sex crimes go unreported. And among those who are committed, so few are released that it's impossible to measure recidivism at all. But most research shows that sex offenders are *less* likely than other criminals to reoffend and are often generalists in crime, a rape or other sexual assault just one entry on a long rap sheet. For example, the Bureau of Justice Statistics, in a study following 10,000 sex offenders for three years after their release from prison, found that 5.3 percent had been re-arrested for sex crimes, although some meta-analyses have found higher rates over longer periods.[34] Among non-sex offenders in the study, the re-arrest rate was 68 percent.[35] A New Jersey study found that, among a group of 102 sex offenders considered for civil commitment but released, 10.5 percent were convicted of a new sex offense during the next six years. That same group of 102 offenders had an overall reconviction rate for all offenses (sexual or otherwise) of 67 percent, indicating that sex offenders are a lot like people in prison for other crimes.[36]

Many judges apparently still subscribe to the conventional wisdom about recidivist sex offenders, however. One 2007 decision by the U.S. Court of Appeals for the Fifth Circuit cited as authority a probation officer's testimony that in his "professional experience," sex offenders have "a recidivism rate of approximately 70 percent."[37] Another federal appeals court relied on the unsubstantiated finding that sex offender recidivism rates are 20 percent to 25 percent.[38] Their assertions only reflect widely held assumptions about the people before them. They are the same assumptions that led Chief Justice William Rehnquist to ask, in oral argument in the *Hendricks* case, "So what's the state supposed to do? Just wait till he goes out and does it again?"[39]

NOT SO SPECIAL: CIVIL COMMITMENT IN NEW JERSEY

New Jersey is the home not just of Megan's Law, which established the public registry of sex offenders, but also of a robust civil commitment program. The state has a higher commitment rate for its total population than most SVP states do, but it is probably a fair illustration of how law-enforcement officials and courts make their decisions.[40] Since 1999, New Jersey has incarcerated almost seven hundred men. As of December 2013, thirty-seven had died, five had been deported, and an undisclosed but small number sent to prisons or to the Ann Klein Forensic Center for the seriously mentally ill.[41] The state reported that 171 had been released, but of those many were elderly and debilitated, some sent to nursing homes where they died not long afterward.[42]

Public information on the SVP program is sparse. Because the inmates are classified as mental patients, their names are never released. Hearings are closed to the public and all records impounded. It's hard for an outsider even to know that this program exists. The Special Treatment Unit is run by the Department of Corrections, in a previously abandoned prison's solitary confinement wing, but the department's website does not list the facility. The Department of Human Services, which provides the treatment staff, also does not release information on the program.

The state did release some data, however, to researchers from the John Jay College of Criminal Justice of the City University of New York, who submitted their report to the National Institute of Justice in 2011.[43] The study aimed, in part, to compare the committed offenders with a randomly chosen group of sex offenders who were released after their prison terms. Of all the sex offenders leaving prison, 12 percent were referred for commitment by corrections officials to the state attorney general's office, which filed SVP commitment petitions in 79 percent of those cases.[44]

The study addressed a question that should be unnecessary: *Are* there differences between SVPs and other sex offenders? Unsurprisingly, the answer is yes. The SVPs had more prior convictions and significantly higher risk-assessment scores — which is largely how they came to be candidates for commitment. But if the law aims to confine the worst of the worst, the differences should be enormous. And they are not.

First, the researchers tried to quantify violent tendencies. They found that in committing the index crime, 40 percent of SVPs threatened their victims, versus 16 percent of non-SVPs, and 25 percent used a weapon (versus 7 percent of non-SVPs). These numbers affirm that SVPs are more violent as a group than other sex offenders, but since well over half did *not* use threats and three-quarters did not use weapons, they are a decidedly less menacing group than the robbery and assault convicts in New Jersey's prisons. In fact, the study discloses that 5 percent of SVPs (and 7 percent of non-SVPs) were in prison for a "non-contact sex crime."

The SVPs were more likely to have victimized strangers (30 percent) than were the other sex offenders (12 percent), but that means, of course, that 70 percent knew the people they victimized. Twenty-three percent victimized family members (versus 35 percent of non-SVPs) — hardly a validation of the stranger-danger fears that generated the law. Finally, SVP victims were twice as likely to be male, 23 percent among SVPs compared to 12 percent among non-SVPs; it is likely, then, that gay men are overrepresented among those chosen for lifetime detention.

As for the courts' handling of the SVP laws, New Jersey would be a likely place to look for thoughtful decisions. Judges are appointed, not elected, and governors of both parties have put accomplished practitioners and academics on the bench. But they are no more likely than popularly elected judges in other states to question the commitment machinery.

The commitment petitions from the attorney general's office go to a judge, who almost always issues a temporary commitment order, and then go before one of two or three judges designated to conduct full hearings in SVP cases. The same judge may see the same inmate in repeated review hearings over the years. In only a few cases has one of these judges ordered an inmate's release over the state's objections. (In Massachusetts, by contrast, which requires jury trials, the state loses so many cases that it has had to release more than seven hundred people from temporary commitment.[45] Massachusetts seems to be an extreme outlier, however.) The trial judges' rulings may be appealed, of course. But the appellate courts, which hear all kinds of cases, almost always defer to the experience of the SVP judges and stress that their scope of review is narrow in any event.

Still, the appellate court opinions — which, unlike the SVP judges' opinions, are accessible in judicial archives — provide a catalog of stories about the inmates' days in court. The appellate judges, assessing the evidence heard below, delve into the smallest of complaints from therapists. One fairly typical appellate opinion, for example, noted a psychiatrist's observation that the inmate, M.C., "evinced 'traits of narcissism,' as he enjoys being the center of attention." The court continued, "She also noted M.C. had difficulty with social cues." Another recounted a psychiatrist's testimony: "At the hearing, Dr. McAllister acknowledged that discussion of sexual offenses is an integral part of the treatment process, and R.B.B. was 'quite open' about his sexual offenses. On the other hand, it seemed to him that R.B.B. took 'some pleasure' in these accounts." In case after case, the courts invoke evidence like this, signs that the inmate is making no progress — and is therefore a sexually violent predator.

Unless the system's mistakes emerge somehow in an appellate review, they are locked away along with the inmates. But occasionally news of mistakes escapes by another route. That's what happened in the case of Rodney Roberts.

Roberts was committed to the Special Treatment Unit in 2006, after two convictions involving rape charges. The first stemmed from his role in a gang rape — though in Roberts's case it was an attempted rape — in 1986. While on parole, in 1996, he was identified by a seventeen-year-old who said a stranger had grabbed her on a street in Newark and raped her. Roberts was arrested and quickly pled guilty to a reduced charge of kidnapping. Seven years later, at the end of his prison term, he was determined to be a sexually violent predator.

Through the years at the Special Treatment Unit, his story shifted somewhat, but he told psychiatrists and psychologists that he did not commit the 1996 rape. He had taken the plea bargain, he said, because he was afraid of spending the rest of his life in prison. For this, Roberts paid a price in his civil commitment hearings. At the first, a psychiatrist who diagnosed him with "paraphilia, non-consent" testified that by committing a rape while still on parole for the first assault Roberts showed he was unable to control himself. Another psychiatrist said that Roberts "denies he committed the offense. I do not believe him." Roberts's own expert witnesses both testified that he did not suffer from any sexual disorder and voiced doubts about his guilt. But in her ruling, the trial judge said she was disregarding their testimony because "both misjudged the reliability of the evidence of the rape, giving credence to the incredible fiction" that Roberts was maintaining.[46] In other words, anyone who thought Roberts might be telling the truth could not be a reliable expert witness. Months later, the appeals court embellished the record a bit. The panel described the 1996 rape victim's distress, noting that when the victim was shown pictures of possible suspects, she "began sobbing and crying when she saw R.R.R.'s black and white photograph."[47] The appeals court confirmed, as it almost always does, that the man before them was a sexually violent predator.

Meanwhile, in a tortuous journey through the criminal courts in Newark, Roberts was challenging the 1996 conviction, pursuing the only conceivable means out of lifetime confinement. Because he had pled guilty so soon after his arrest, the police investigation had been closed and, he was told years later, the rape kit lost. Roberts persisted, and in 2013, a police detective found it. The prosecutor's office ordered DNA tests, which cleared Roberts.[48] After he had spent years in the civil commitment system, based on predictions that he would strike again, the criminal justice system unearthed an annoying fact: *Rodney Roberts didn't do it.*

Roberts was released from the Special Treatment Unit in 2014. The staff members and expert witnesses who kept him there for eight years will not be held accountable for their judgments. Nor will the judges have to explain themselves, including the judge who was so incensed by Roberts's "incredible fiction." They were only doing what the Supreme Court said they could do to protect the public.

SEX IS DIFFERENT

The *Hendricks* decision in theory opened the door to detaining other groups deemed dangerous, and some legal scholars see ominous results. Eric Janus, discussing the "outsider jurisprudence" that had supposedly been discarded in the last half century, argues, "The predator laws — adopted and embraced in what seems like the limited context of the universally despised sex offender — now stand ready to provide a constitutional template for the expansion of government control on a much more massive scale."[49] Corey Yung invokes the wartime metaphor in explaining the causes and effects of the SVP laws: "America has begun what can only be described as a criminal war on sex offenders akin to the war on drugs that has continued for nearly 40 years. And as in any war, domestic or foreign, the normal rules of liberty are suspended and significant exceptions are made to allow for wartime action."[50]

The Supreme Court has acquiesced before to demands to warehouse threatening groups. The obvious example, now renounced, is *Korematsu v.*

United States, the 1944 decision upholding President Roosevelt's executive order confining Japanese Americans to internment camps.[51] More recently, the federal courts have countenanced the long-term detention of noncitizens charged with, but not yet convicted of, immigration violations. And the best-known use of preventive detention now is Guantánamo Bay.

These examples are distinguishable from the sex offender detentions, however, in several ways. No American citizens were ever sent to Guantánamo. The Supreme Court determined in 2004 that noncitizens held there can challenge their status as "enemy combatants" in federal civilian courts, where the normal constitutional protections would apply.[52] The few Americans designated "enemy combatants" awaited trial like other criminal suspects in the United States. While some foreign-born U.S. residents were jailed after the September 11, 2001, terrorist attacks and held on immigration charges, the goal was to deport them, not to detain them indefinitely.

Most regimes of preventive detention have arisen during wartime panics, whereas moral panics driven by internal threats are handled, however terribly, by the criminal justice system.[53] The more apposite question raised by the Supreme Court's SVP decisions is how they might affect the large universe of American criminals who are not sex offenders. A state might, by the logic of *Hendricks*, enact a law using the same, lower standard to commit arsonists or drunk drivers. But there is no panic over arson or drunk driving. There is no such panic even over child abuse — a far more common threat to children than strangers with sexual compulsions and a crime commonly committed by recidivists. The panic sets in when a child's sexual innocence is threatened.

Indeed, some men in indefinite confinement would be better off if they had simply killed their victims. It is not the magnitude but the nature of the threat that has brought on fear and revulsion — and punishment beyond what the courts sanction for other criminal behavior. Sex *is* different, even if the Constitution does not say so.

As both Janus and Yung observe, while terrorism suspects have few sympathizers, they at least have public attention. Lawyers and academics, television anchors, newspaper columnists, and politicians are discussing them. The discussion itself encourages scrutiny and, in an optimistic view, political and legal limits to the urge to punish. The sex offenders locked away from view have no public attention at all. They are different, so different that no one wants to hear about them. The public's mission has been accomplished.

1. Arizona, California, District of Columbia, Florida, Illinois, Iowa, Kansas, Massachusetts, Minnesota, Missouri, Nebraska, New Hampshire, New Jersey, New York, North Dakota, Pennsylvania, South Carolina, Virginia, Washington, and Wisconsin, in addition to the federal government.

2. See Foucha v. Louisiana, 504 U.S. 71 (1992) for an extensive discussion of precedents.

3. Kansas v. Hendricks, 521 U.S. 346 (1997).

4. See, for example, Estelle B. Freedman, " 'Uncontrolled Desires': The Responses to the Sexual Psychopath, 1920–1960," *Journal of American History* 74, no. 1 (June 1987): 83–106; Philip Jenkins, *Moral Panic: Changing Concepts of the Child Molester in Modern America* (New Haven, CT: Yale University Press, 1998); Eric S. Janus, *Failure to Protect: America's Sexual Predator Laws and the Rise of the Preventive State* (Ithaca, NY: Cornell University Press, 2006); John Douard and Pamela D. Schultz, *Monstrous Crimes and the Failure of Forensic Psychiatry* (Dordrecht: Springer Netherlands, 2013); Chrysanthi S. Leon, *Sex Fiends, Perverts and Pedophiles: Understanding Sex Crime Policy in America* (New York: NYU Press, 2011); Roger N. Lancaster, *Sex Panic and the Punitive State* (Berkeley: University of California Press, 2011).

5. See, for example, Janus, *Failure to Protect*, 93–1091; Corey Rayburn Yung, "Sex Offender Exceptionalism and Preventive Detention," *Journal of Criminal Law and Criminology* 101 (2011): 994–1003.

6. J. Edgar Hoover, "How Safe Is Your Daughter?" *American Magazine*, July 1947, p. 33.

7. Lancaster, *Sex Panic and the Punitive State*, 34. See also Kunzel, chapter 6 this volume.

8. Minnesota *ex rel.* Pearson v. Probate Court of Ramsey County, 309 U.S. 270, 274 (1940). See also Kunzel, chapter 6 this volume.

9. Heidi Handman, *The Sex Handbook: Information and Help for Minors* (New York: Putnam, 1974), 2.

10. See, for example, Jenkins, *Moral Panic*, 106–117; Lawrence M. Friedman, *Crime and Punishment in American History* (New York: Basic, 1993), 241–257.

11. Humphrey v. Cady, 405 U.S. 504 (1972). Regarding "defective delinquent," see for example, McNeil v. Director, Patuxent Institution, 407 U.S. 245 (1972). For sexual psychopath laws, see for example Specht v. Patterson, 386 U.S. 605 (1967).

12. Foucha v. Louisiana, 504 U.S. 71 (1992).

13. *Id.* at 82–83.

14. Leon, *Sex Fiends, Perverts and Pedophiles*, 163–164.

15. Jenkins, *Moral Panic*, 199.

16. For an analysis of the "spectacular growth of sex offender incarceration," see Leon, *Sex Fiends, Perverts and Pedophiles,* pp. 161–167.

17. Jenkins, *Moral Panic,* 194.

18. Quoted in ACLU amicus curiae brief in Kansas v. Hendricks, No. 95-1649 (Oct. 1, 1996) at 10.

19. *Hendricks,* 521 U.S. at 385 (Breyer, J., dissenting [quoting statement of Jim Blaufuss]).

20. Julie Wright, "Predator Bill Sent to Finney; Objections Can't Overcome Fear of Violent Sex Crimes," *Wichita Eagle,* April 28, 1994.

21. Kansas v. Crane, 534 U.S. 407, 413 (2002).

22. American Psychiatric Association, Statement on the Insanity Defense II, 1982.

23. See American Psychiatric Association, *Dangerous Sex Offenders: A Task Force Report of the American Psychiatric Association* (Washington, D.C.: American Psychiatric Association), 175.

24. Sameer P. Sarkar, "From Hendricks to Crane: The Sexually Violent Predator Trilogy and the Inchoate Jurisprudence of the United States Supreme Court," *Journal of the American Academy of Psychiatry and the Law* 31 (2003): 242–248.

25. See, for example, Rachel Aviv, "The Science of Sex Abuse," *New Yorker,* January 14, 2013.

26. United States v. Comstock, 560 U.S. 126 (2010).

27. 521 U.S. at 373.

28. Washington State Institute for Public Policy, "Comparison of State Laws Authorizing Involuntary Commitment of Sexually Violent Predators: 2006 Update."

29. Sex Offender Civil Commitment Programs Network [SOCCPN], "Annual Survey of Sex Offender Civil Commitment Programs 2014," http://soccpn.org/images /SOCCPN_Annual_Survey_2014_revised.pdf (link no longer active). The 2014 survey did not incorporate figures from Iowa, Kansas, and Washington State, which did not report. Counts for those states come from the organization's 2013 survey, http://soccpn.org/images/SOCCPN_survey_presentation_2013_in_pdf, and from Washington State sources. The latest reports on deaths are from the 2013 survey.

30. SOCCPN Annual Survey 2014.

31. Janus, *Failure to Protect,* 33.

32. See Fred S. Berlin, Report to Schiff Hardin & Waite and the American Civil Liberties Union in Hargett v. Adams (N.D. Ill., 2003), at 10–11. See Adam J. Falk, "Sex Offenders, Mental Illness and Criminal Responsibility: The Constitutional Boundaries of Civil Commitment After *Kansas v. Hendricks,*" *American Journal of Law and Medicine* 25 (1999): 117–147.

33. 534 U.S. at 412.

34. Lawrence A. Greenfield, *Recidivism of Sex Offenders Released from Prison in 1994* (Bureau of Justice Statistics, 2003), 24. http://www.bjs.gov/content/pub/pdf/rsorp94.pdf.

35. Greenfield, *Recidivism of Sex Offenders*, 14.

36. Cynthia Calkins Mercado et al., *Sex Offender Management, Treatment, and Civil Commitment: An Evidence-based Analysis Aimed at Reducing Sexual Violence* (Washington, D.C.: National Institute of Justice, 2001), 61.

37. United States v. Emerson, 231 F. App'x 349, 352 (2007).

38. Doe v. Miller, 405 F.3d 700, 707 (8th Cir. 2005).

39. Transcript of oral argument, 1996 U.S. Trans. LEXIS 80 at 41.

40. SOCCPN 2014 annual survey.

41. New Jersey Department of Corrections rosters obtained by researcher from the Special Treatment Unit.

42. SOCCPN 2014 annual survey.

43. Mercado et al., *Sex Offender Management*.

44. Mercado et al., *Sex Offender Management*, 55, 57–58.

45. SOCCPN 2013 annual survey.

46. *In the Matter of the Commitment of R.R.R.*, Superior Court of New Jersey, Appellate Division, Docket No. A-2663-05T2, Oct. 2, 2007.

47. *In the Matter of the Commitment of R.R.R.*

48. Thomas Zambito, "Newark Man Set Free After Serving 17 Years for a Rape He Says He Did Not Commit," *Star-Ledger*, April 8, 2014.

49. Janus, *Failure to Protect*, 97.

50. Yung, "Sex Offender Exceptionalism and Preventive Detention," 997.

51. Korematsu v. United States, 323 U.S. 214 (1944).

52. Hamdi v. Rumsfeld, 124 S. Ct. 2633 (2004).

53. See, for example, Douard and Schultz, *Monstrous Crimes and the Failure of Forensic Psychiatry*; Stanley Cohen, *Folk Devils and Moral Panics: The Creation of the Mods and Rockers* (Berkeley: University of California Press, 1972).

PART III

Sex Work *and the* Trouble *with* Trafficking

|9|

The "Hooker Teacher"
Tells All

I have two master's degrees, five years' experience in the nonprofit sector, and three years' experience teaching — and I cannot get a job. Why? Just google me. I'm the "Hooker Teacher" — at least that's what I've come to be called ever since September 27, 2010, when I found myself on the cover of the *New York Post*.

"Meet Melissa Petro," the story began," the teacher who gives a new twist to sex ed." The piece describes me as a "tattooed former hooker and stripper" who was "shockingly upfront about her past." Indeed, earlier that month, I'd written an op-ed on the *Huffington Post* that criticized the recent censoring of the adult services section of Craigslist and came clean about my own sex-worker past. Because I was arguing that sex workers shouldn't be ashamed to speak for themselves, I signed my name to it. The *New York Post* wasn't interested in my politics, however; its interest seemed only in cooking up shock that an elementary school teacher would dare admit such a shady history.

The Internet shaming was fast, intense, and seemingly unending, summed up in February by columnist Andrea Peyser, who wrote, "Hooker turned teacher Melissa Petro is a disgrace."

Eight months after the story broke, I am jobless. I cannot get hired. And even my biggest supporters ask me privately, "But seriously, what were you thinking?" The answer is complicated. I was being idealistic. I was being provocative. I was naive. I picked a fight that I thought I could win — and I was wrong.

One reason I was so casual about the disclosure was that I had been writing about my past long before becoming a teacher. As a student at the New School, where I earned a degree in creative nonfiction, I began work on a memoir that details, in part, how I began stripping while living in Mexico as a student abroad. As an undergraduate at Antioch, I conducted ethnographic research across Europe and in the United States, interviewing women from all aspects of the industry about their lives and their professions (published in the collection *Sex Work Matters: Power and Intimacy in the Sex Industry*). The subject of sex work and workers' rights became a passion about which I've written in print and online, everywhere from academic and literary journals to political blogs.

Another reason I didn't think my story would be shocking is because, well, my story isn't shocking. Whereas some women's road to sex work entails coercion and last-ditch survival, for me, this wasn't the case. I was the product of a working-class home — the first in her family to go to college, let alone study abroad — and my working as a stripper began as a means to an end. Prior to stripping, I'd worked in fast food. I'd worked in retail. I even spent one summer delivering singing telegrams. I was used to long hours, unreasonable bosses, and very little pay; stripping — at least at first — was the ideal job.

But sex work, I would learn, was a far from perfect occupation. Prostitution, in particular, was not the job for me. I was simply not suited for a profession that relied on dishonesty. I got caught up in the industry's pull toward materialism and greed. The industry's criminalized and stigmatized nature only exacerbated the rigors of the work. I kept my job a secret, even from my family and friends. Living a lie, I lied to myself. My own denial and self-justification made it near impossible to extricate myself from the business. It was only by writing about my experiences that I was able to see my truth.

Around my twenty-seventh birthday, I gave up sex work for good. It was some months later when — unemployed and working on a book — teaching presented itself as an option. I was attracted to the flexibility and creativity of the profession. I liked the idea of working with children and of making a difference in my community, not to mention the summer vacation. After graduating from the New School, I landed a spot as a New York City teaching fellow, which bills itself as a highly competitive program that recruits "high quality, dedicated individuals from different backgrounds" to become teachers in New York City's struggling public schools. My first year as a teacher, I earned my master's in childhood education in the evenings while working full-time at an elementary school in the South Bronx. I taught art and creative writing to students in grades K–5, nearly 700 students each week. In the three years I spent there, I grew to love my job.

My past had no bearing on my competence as a teacher, and so I refused to operate as if it did. The idea that an elementary school teacher wasn't entitled to a life in her off-hours I found equally absurd. Sure, I'd seen other teachers get in trouble for stupid things like pictures or comments posted on Facebook. Even so, I did not think it would happen to me. I was well appreciated at my school. When it came to my administration and my colleagues, my personal life was just that: personal. Many of them knew I was a writer, and those who had bothered to google me knew I wrote about my past. It had never been an issue — until the day it became front-page news.

There it was, my name and likeness — a most unflattering shot, by the way — under varying versions of the "hooker teacher" headline (which always made it sound like I was still involved in sex work, as though I were heading from the reading circle straight to working the streets): "Bronx art teacher blabs about exploits as stripper and hooker," "Prostitute teacher a reason to end tenure." I was called an "idiot prosti-teacher" in one *New York Post* headline. One photo caption by the same publication read, "Attention whore." More offensive than my past, it seemed, was the fact I'd had the gall to talk about it. The women's blog the Frisky supposed it was "all part of Petro's media-savvy plan to get publicity for her upcoming memoir," which the writer called "disgusting." The *Daily News*, *Inside Edition*, and *Us Weekly* all sent their female reporters, women ironically similar to me — young professionals, well-dressed, writers themselves — to get in my face, demanding to know how I could refer to myself as a feminist.

As an advocate, I had long ago realized the media generally treats current and former sex workers in one of two ways: we are portrayed as victims, looked down upon and felt sorry for, too stupid to realize our own victimization; or else we are made out to be villains — dirty, cheap, and willing to do anything to satisfy our greed. For years, I'd fought these gross stereotypes. Now I found myself on the receiving end of it.

To some, it was unfathomable to think that a woman could have once been a prostitute and, at another time, served her community competently as a teacher. Even New York's Mayor Bloomberg made a statement personally requesting my permanent removal from the classroom. It was as though I were a monster needing to be stopped.

I'm not a monster or a moron. I'm a human being, and — like everyone else — I've made mistakes. In the community where I grew up, girls didn't become writers and teachers; they became strippers. I worked hard to earn my degrees. Of my sex work past, I have no regrets. Why, hadn't I done exactly what critics of prostitution would have wanted? I had exited the sex industry to become a "productive" member of society. And yet no one seemed to accept that I might not be ashamed of my past. That I might, on the contrary, be proud of it.

I thought my perspective deserved to be heard. I thought that my speech was protected. I did not believe a government employee could lose her job for publishing an op-ed. Like I said, I was naive.

The night before the *Post* article came out I received a phone call from the superintendent of schools in my district informing me that I'd been put in reassignment. Instead of teaching I would report to the Department of Education administrative offices and sit awaiting instruction, where I sat for months until this past Friday, my last day. After months of investigation, I was formally charged. The charges — conduct unbecoming a professional — were a direct result of my published writing, the evidence cited against me consisting entirely of my quoted work. The fact that I was competent in my role as a teacher was never called into question. Even the *Post* could find no way of describing me other than "well liked." But my job performance was never a consideration. The only fact that seemed to matter, apparently, was that I'd been a whore.

In the days and weeks following my reassignment, I learned a number of hard lessons about constitutional law. The constitutionality of a government employee's speech is contingent on whether or not that speech creates a distraction in the workplace and, if it does, it is not protected so long as the distraction outweighs its political worth. This is the same reason that a soldier, according to people like John McCain, shouldn't announce that he or she is gay. Doing so, the argument goes, would create a "mortal distraction." In the case of the hooker teacher, in order to fire me the DOE needed only to prove that my writing created a disruption in my school community and that such a disruption had little societal value. Whether it was my speech or the speech of the *New York Post* that created the disruption was, of course, an argument to be made.

Meanwhile, the actual political import of my work was impossible to gauge, my own words buried in Google searches underneath inflammatory news pieces, sensational headlines, and cherry-picked excerpts from my creative work that, printed out of context, suggested I wrote at length about marijuana-fueled shenanigans and lesbian love affairs. Contrary to how I was being painted in the headlines, I was not a teacher blogging recklessly in her off-hours on WordPress about her sexual escapades. I was a writer and, as a writer, I was establishing a platform as a social commentator on an issue of cultural importance.

In the wake of hooker teacher headlines no one was debating the censoring of Craigslist, the legality of prostitution, or even the constitutionality of my reassignment. The heated debate in the commentary section of the *Daily News*, for example, was whether I was hot enough to be paid for sex. The papers printed my personal Facebook statuses as if they were news. The CBS news published a slide show of my personal pictures, implicating my family and friends. The home where I lived was revealed on the nightly news so that anyone who wanted to could easily come find me. I was personally insulted and put at risk, then made to feel that by publishing a work of serious nonfiction, I had been "asking for it."

Sure, I knew I was taking a risk. I stated that in the original *Huffington Post* piece. But knowing there is a risk doesn't mean you realize how great a risk it is or what the consequences will be. And the consequences, in a word, have been devastating.

While I was paid by my employer through April, I had been relying on two after-school jobs to make ends meet. The day the *Post* story hit I was unceremoniously fired from both, including a position working in the childcare section of my gym. Other than an offer to be in a porn mag and another paid opportunity to be interviewed on *Inside Edition* — an agreement that felt a little like Red Riding Hood signing on to have dinner with the wolves — there were no silver linings in my dark cloud of publicity. Like the teenager I had once been, this past winter I would've done almost anything for cash. No one willing to hire the hooker teacher meant that I skipped meals. I walked instead of taking the train and didn't launder my clothes as often as necessary. This, I understand, is the predicament of the unemployed and working poor, and it reminded me a lot of how I grew up. I worked hard to escape those circumstances, and the fact that I was back there — with student loans to boot — felt unfair.

I suppose I could've just gone back to hooking. Instead, I made the arguably antifeminist decision to give up my apartment and move in with my boyfriend. If this situation has taught me anything, it is that sometimes we must put ideals aside and think practically — much like I did at nineteen years old, when I became a stripper. So, in the end, I resigned from my job, rather than pursuing a trial. I quit rather than be fired because, had I not signed their agreement, the DOE threatened to contest my unemployment. As much as I believed in the merits of my case, it was a risk I couldn't take.

Now, I send out rafts of résumés, and I can't find work. Whether that's partly the economy, I can't say, but these days it seems my most important former occupation is the one not on my résumé. Despite all I've lost, though, I refuse to let this defeat me. I know there would be something worse than living with the consequences of speaking my truth: living in silence. Let's hope potential employers take note: I didn't lose my job for being a hooker. I lost my job for being a writer.

ELIZABETH BERNSTEIN

| 10 |

Carceral Politics as Gender Justice?

The "Traffic in Women" and
Neoliberal Circuits of Crime, Sex, and Rights

On a cold and windy February afternoon, I approach the fifth in a series of lunchtime rallies on behalf of a new N.Y. State law which would
stiffen the potential criminal penalties against men who are convicted
of patronizing a prostitute, from 90 days to a year in prison.[1] When I
arrive at Foley Square, I encounter a group of fifty or so women (mostly
white or Asian, and all conspicuously middle class as indicated by their
stylish attire and educated patterns of speech) as well as a gathering pool
of journalists and onlookers. Present too are several influential City and
State-level political figures who have been invited by the organizers to
speak.

Women from the rally's two sponsoring feminist organizations (NOW-
NYC and Equality Now) as well as a smattering of other groups are
gathered on the steps behind the speakers, holding up signs from their
respective organizations and handing out press packets. Periodically,
they coax the rest of the crowd to join together in a chant: "What do we
want? A strong trafficking law! When do we want it? Now!" Or, "Elliot
Spitzer, take the lead! A strong trafficking bill is what we need!"[2]

In their depictions of the sex industry, all of the speakers at the rally
deploy the new anti-trafficking buzzwords ("victim," "predator," "perpetrator," "exploiter"), along with stock anecdotes of innocent women
having their papers confiscated, being forced to sell their bodies, and
being trapped and tricked. The narratives of women's victimization are
coupled with an insistence upon the need to "focus on demand" and to
aggressively pursue the perpetrators of sexual violence. Criminal law is

rendered as a surprisingly powerful and effective deterrent to men's bad behavior: "We need to have laws that will make men think twice about entering the commercial sexual exploitation business," one passionate City Council member explains.

The final speaker at the event is Angela Lee from the New York Asian Women's Center. Fashionable and fortyish, dressed in a black leather jacket and fitted slacks, she makes no mention of the role played by global poverty in the dynamics of trafficking or prostitution, instead framing the issue in terms of the sexual integrity of families. "This is a family issue," she declares outright, "especially as Chinese New Year approaches and there are so many victims' families who won't be able to celebrate."[3] Lee goes on to link the dangers faced by trafficking victims to New York State's lack of success thus far in imposing a law that would provide severe enough criminal penalties for traffickers and pimps. She concludes her speech with the emotional declaration that "We need to punish the traffickers and set the victims free!"

AUTHOR'S FIELD NOTES | February 2007, New York City

Although a decade of feminist research and activism has addressed the role of the neoliberal state in criminalizing the survival strategies of poor women, and of poor women of color in particular, the significance of feminism's own widening embrace of the neoliberal carceral state has only begun to come into focus.[4] "The contemporary women's movement in the United States helped facilitate the carceral state," explains Marie Gottschalk, noting that some of the very same historical and institutional factors that made the U.S. women's movement relatively successful in gaining public acceptance (including its firm foothold in elite politics, the absence of competing Marxist currents, and a strong national tradition of political liberalism) were important building blocks for the carceral state that emerged simultaneously in the 1970s.[5] In a similar vein, Kristin Bumiller has argued that once feminism became fatally inflected by neoliberal strategies of social control, it could serve as an effective inspiration for broader campaigns for criminalization (such as the war on drugs).[6]

While Gottschalk and Bumiller single out U.S. feminism as an exceptional case, scholars have pointed to similar trends within an array of different national contexts.[7] Writing about the confluence of French feminism and anti-immigrant sentiment, for example, Miriam Ticktin notes that contemporary feminist concern with issues of sexual violence "is often recognized only through the framework of racial, cultural, and religious difference."[8] As Ticktin demonstrates, by "fighting sexism with racism," feminist campaigns around sexual violence have become increasingly powerful accessories to French state interests in border control and policing.[9]

Another recent domain of feminist activism in which the carceral turn has become apparent is in gathering political and cultural attention to the "traffic in women." Until the mid-1990s, an incipient sex workers' rights movement had sought to decriminalize and to destigmatize women's sexual labor and to gain rights and protections for sex workers from within a labor frame, but in more recent years these efforts have been undercut by a bevy of new federal, state, and international laws that equate all prostitution with the crime of "human trafficking" and that impose harsh criminal penalties against traffickers and prostitutes' customers. This pivot first occurred within the context of transnational feminist organizing at the United Nations, an attention that brought with it "a focus on crime control methods and rescue, to the detriment of the promotion of the full range of rights needed by trafficked persons."[10] Within the United States, although some anti-trafficking activists continue to pay lip service to the goal of decriminalizing and securing economic rights for sex workers, the overwhelming thrust of current feminist attention has been similarly oriented toward widening — rather than eliminating — the sphere of criminal justice intervention in the sex industry.

Although "trafficking" as defined in international protocols and in current federal law could conceivably encompass sweatshop labor, agricultural work, or unscrupulous labor practices on military bases in Iraq, it has been the far less common instances of sexually trafficked women and girls that have stimulated the most concern by feminist activists, the state, and the press. In the 2000 UN Protocol Against Trafficking in Persons, for example, "trafficking" is understood to include "the exploitation of the prostitution of others or other forms of sexual exploitation, forced labour or services, slavery or practices similar to slavery, servitude or the removal of organs."[11] Yet, in the Protocol definition, "prostitution occupies an asymmetrical place in the list" as distinct from the specific criteria for force or coercion that qualify other forms of labor. In this context, two intertwined themes emerge: "the site of sexual exchange as a priority for state intervention and a criminal response as the main response to exploitation."[12]

Feminist anti-trafficking activists have themselves acknowledged that a focus on sexual violation, rather than the structural conditions of exploited labor more generally — in addition to their strategic partnership on this issue with evangelical Christians — has been crucial to transforming it into a legal framework with powerful material and symbolic effects.[13] At events such as the February 2007 anti-trafficking rally that I attended at Foley Square in New York City, the political efficacy of conjoining the threat of sexual violence with calls for an expanded carceral state apparatus was apparent, with political leaders and feminist activists in strong agreement that human trafficking was primarily an issue of family values, sexual predation, and victimized women and children.

Commentators who have critically assessed the rise of the anti-trafficking movement in the United States have often attributed its ascendance to what they perceive to be the moralistic sexual politics of its two principal groups, "radical feminists" and conservative Christians.[14] They have argued that both groups harbor "archaic and violated visions of femininity and sexuality," that they embrace a sexual ideology that is "pro-marriage" and "pro-family," and that they share an antipathy toward nonprocreative sex.[15] By the late 1990s, feminists and evangelicals were well poised to forge transnational alliances around this issue, as a greater reliance upon NGOs by the United Nations encouraged many newly formed evangelical NGOs to enter the international political fray.[16]

Other critics have pointed to the strong parallels between feminist uprisings around sex trafficking in the current moment and those that surrounded the white slavery scare in the postbellum years of the last century, which similarly derived their impact from tropes of violated femininity, shattered innocence, and the victimization of "women and children."[17] Commentators have situated contemporary mobilizations against trafficking in terms of successive waves of "sex panics" that have occurred at periodic intervals in the United States through the twentieth and twenty-first centuries.[18] The marked historical resonance between the current U.S. anti-trafficking campaign and the Meese Commission anti-pornography hearings that took place during the 1980s (in which conservative Christians and a segment of the feminist movement once again joined forces for the sake of sexual reform) has also been explored.[19]

Although ample critical attention has been devoted to the conservative legacy of feminist sexual politics that underpins contemporary anti-trafficking campaigns, most accounts have stopped short of looking at another sociologically significant linkage between the feminist and evangelical Christian activist constituencies that has catapulted the "traffic in women" to its current position of political and cultural prominence — specifically, a carceral and far from historically inevitable paradigm of state engagement, both domestically and internationally. Left unaddressed by most commentators are the questions of *why* a vision of sexual politics that is premised upon a version of (feminist) family values should reign ascendant at this particular historical moment, or how these values might couple with broader sets of political and economic interests. Whereas theorists such as Garland, Wacquant, and Simon astutely describe the rise of the carceral state but provide only a partial sketch of the dynamics of sex and gender that have facilitated its emergence, an equally significant deficit resides in analyses of sexual politics that fail to adequately consider feminist activists' newfound and nearly ubiquitous insistence upon carceral versions of gender justice.[20] In contemporary anti-trafficking campaigns as in neoliberal governance more generally, the left and right ends of the political spectrum are joined together in a particular, dense knot of sexual and carceral values. A consideration of the rise of carceral feminism alongside other dimensions of neoliberal governance will allow us to unravel this tangle of factors.

NEOLIBERALISM'S (FEMINIST) FAMILY VALUES

In the 1970s our feminist goal was "liberation": liberation from discrimination at work, liberation from sexual constraints, liberation from forced sex, forced pregnancy and forced domestic service.... Our focus was less violence per se, than the function of violence in keeping us down. Feminist marches ... were not about punishing men or protecting women; if anything, we denounced punishing women and protecting men. We were determined to occupy our cities, our jobs, our homes, our lives in courageous defiance of punitive — or protective — curfews and controls. We knew our movement was transgressive and, thus, dangerous, but we had no illusion about the sanctity or security of home.

GAIL PHETERSON | "Tracing a Radical Feminist Vision from the 1970s to the Present"

As the feminist theorist Gail Pheterson has recently observed, a previously hegemonic feminist critique of family and home has receded at precisely the same time that the movement's embrace of carceral politics has escalated, with a drift toward punitive or "protective" curfews and controls.[21] Although this latter shift might be explained simply in terms of the "new middle class punitiveness," the mainstream feminist embrace of family values and its primary focus upon extrafamilial forms of sexual violence is sociologically significant in and of itself.[22] Such a trend stands in marked contrast to the analyses offered by classic sociological works such as Kristin Luker's *Abortion and the Politics of Motherhood* (1984) and Arlene Stein's *The Stranger Next Door* (2001), as well as to Thomas Frank's celebrated journalistic account, *What's the Matter with Kansas?* (2004), which posited diverse ways in which the right-wing adhesion to family values could be read as a class-based reaction to the hegemonic sexual cultures of elites.[23] In these volumes, activists' ideological commitments are underpinned by their material circumstances, with conservative investments in sexual politics attributed to the gendered class strategies of those whom the global economy has left behind.

Yet neoliberal carceral politics and the "conservative" sexual politics that are their accompaniment are also increasingly situated within the liberal-leaning, professional middle classes. In contemporary anti-trafficking campaigns, it is ironically secular feminists who are advocating for family values, together with a new middle-class contingent of evangelical Christians who are engaged in a sexually modernizing project that literally transports them to the farthest corners of the global sex industry.[24] Two recent shifts in feminist and conservative Christian sexual politics have made their current alliance against sex trafficking possible: a secular feminist shift in focus from bad men inside the home (sexually abusive husbands and fathers) to sexual predators outside of it (traffickers, pimps, and clients), and the feminist-friendly shift of a new generation of evangelical Christians away from sexually improper women (as prior concerns with issues like abortion suggest) and toward sexually improper men. For both constituencies, the masculinist institutions of big business, the state, and the police are reconfigured as allies and saviors, rather than the enemies of migrant sex workers, and the responsibility for trafficking is shifted from structural factors and dominant institutions onto individual (often racially coded) criminal men. To slightly rework Gayatri Spivak's famous formulation regarding the gendered logics of postcolonial politics, in contemporary anti-trafficking campaigns, it is white women who have joined forces with key sites of institutional power in order to save brown women from brown men.[25]

While secular feminists have no doubt also been drawn toward anti-trafficking advocacy by the opportunities that this work presents for professional advancement and travel, important, too, is the potential that contemporary feminists perceive in this issue to symbolically enhance their own power in domestic-sphere heterosexual relationships — a power which the global sex industry is understood to erode.[26] "Seeing prostitutes shapes men's view of what sex is, who women are, and how they should be treated," remarked one white, middle-class activist at a recent anti-trafficking event that was sponsored by the feminist anti-trafficking NGO the Coalition Against Trafficking in Women (CATW). "The idea that you can contain the value system of prostitution, and it will only affect *those* women, or those women in that country, and that it won't spill over into society as a whole . . . is an illusion," suggested another. As the British cultural theorist Jo Doezema has written, in regard to Western feminists' " 'wounded attachment' to the third world prostitute," "the 'injured body' of the 'third world trafficking victim' in international feminist debates around trafficking in women serves as a powerful metaphor for advancing certain feminist interests, which cannot be assumed to be those of third world sex workers themselves."[27]

The link between global sex trafficking and the gendered power relations of heterosexual domesticity is also made explicit in a recent collection of essays published by a feminist anti-trafficking NGO entitled *Pornography: Driving the Demand in International Sex Trafficking.* In one essay, the activist Chyng Sun emphasizes the damage that commercialized sex does to private-sphere, heterosexual relationships when it serves as the new standard for how all women "should look, sound, and behave."[28] In another recent feminist collection, *Not for Sale,* the author Kristen Anderberg issues a condemnation of the global sex industry after describing how watching pornographic videos with her male lover led to debilitating body issues and to plummeting self-esteem.[29] In the same way that a set of material and symbolic interests in heterosexual marriage undergirded the sexually "puritanical" nineteenth-century feminist battles against white slavery, abortion rights, and even birth control, so too do contemporary feminist activists harbor a set of investments in "family values" and home that are decipherable in terms of the global interconnections of late-capitalist consumer culture.[30] While contemporary discussions of the impact of the sex industry on normative heterosexual relations have ample historical precedent, the expanding scope and reach of sexual commerce under conditions of globalization, or what one influential anti-trafficking activist has termed "the prostitution of sexuality," have served to rapidly accelerate feminist concerns.[31]

For contemporary anti-trafficking activists, one key ambition is to make the institution of heterosexual marriage more egalitarian and more secure by restoring an amative sexual ethic to sexual relations. Although anti-trafficking activists come from both heteronormative, liberal-feminist lineages and more "radical" lesbian-feminist traditions (as illustrated, for example, by the alliance between NOW-NYC and Equality Now at the 2007 rally), what binds the two groups to one another, as well as to their evangelical Christian counterparts, is their shared commitment to a relational, as opposed to a recreational, sexual ethic.[32] More pivotal than the heterosexual/lesbian-feminist divide of generations past, the conviction that sexuality should be kept within the confines of the romantic couple serves to cement a political alliance between ideologically disparate constituencies.[33] As one feminist activist explained to me in recounting the initial forging of the alliance between the divergent groups that constitute the anti-trafficking coalition, "A whole consortium from the farthest left to the farthest right was in favor of making all prostitution trafficking. . . . What was really interesting is the coalition of people . . . a coalition that included the Salvation Army and the lesbian-feminist Equality Now, and CATW up in New York and Michael Horowitz who's very conservative. . . . That's new politics. I had never before seen a group like that."[34]

From the perspective of anti-trafficking feminists, it is thus not the "changing gender roles" wrought by feminist social transformations that have created new social insecurities (*contra* Garland, Wacquant, and Simon), but rather the sexual revolutions of the 1960s and 1970s that have served to alter the balance of gendered power by creating extrafamilial sexual temptations for men. The renowned anti-trafficking activist Donna Hughes thus attributes the existence of human trafficking not only to prostitution but also to the advent of a culturally liberal and permissive attitude toward sex that generates men's demand for sexual services.[35] Another anti-trafficking activist that I interviewed about her engagement in the issue similarly sketched her perception of feminists' sexual dilemma in broad strokes, explaining that "through TV commercials, through billboards, through marketing, the sexuality continuously keeps increasing where there is no . . . protection anymore over our physical bodies, there are no more parameters, everything is acceptable." A third feminist commentator who is active in contemporary anti-trafficking debates has expressly attributed the "traffic in women" to the mainstreaming of prostitution, pornography, and sexually explicit mass media.[36] These activists are not mistaken in their identification of a new consumer-driven paradigm of sexuality that has co-emerged with other late-capitalist cultural transformations and which might best be defined as recreational, rather than relational, in its underlying ethic. What is ironic and surprising is the extent to which feminist anti-trafficking activists have embraced a pro-familial strategy for battling this trend, one which is itself intricately interwoven with neoliberal commitments to capitalism and criminalization.

Rather than regarding the heterosexual nuclear family as another institution of male domination to be abolished (and itself a key incarnation of the "traffic in women"), contemporary anti-trafficking discourse situates the family as a privatized sphere of safety for women and children that the criminal justice system should be harnessed to protect.[37] It was thus that one invited speaker at another CATW anti-trafficking event, a young woman who had previously worked in the sex industry and who therefore described herself as a "survivor" of sex trafficking, attributed this experience to a combination of "no father figure" and an abundance of sexualized mass media. Conversely, she signaled that she had successfully overcome her ordeal by pointing out that she was now married and working full time at "a good paying, real job." In contrast to an earlier moment in radical-feminist sexual politics, one which sought to link the sexual exploitation of prostitution to questions of violence against women more generally, including within the home, in contemporary anti-trafficking campaigns it is specifically nonfamilial forms of heterosexuality that have become the exclusive political targets.[38]

This commitment to the home as safe haven undergirds what the feminist theorist Inderpal Grewal has described as the "gender of security" in the early twenty-first century United States.[39] As a gender-specific emblem of the sequestered middle-class lives that theorists such as Jonathan Simon have also evoked, Grewal identifies the figure of the "security mom" as one who seeks to harness the power of a securitized state apparatus to protect herself and her children. Akin to Grewal's analysis, my ethnographic observations with feminist anti-trafficking activists reveal a specifically gendered set of investments in the neoliberal carceral state, one which is intricately interwoven with activists' own social locations as racially and class-privileged women. At the meetings with the anti-trafficking activists that I attended, the interlocking of multiple structures of privilege with a prosecutorial bent was manifest in various ways — from the professional settings of the conferences (at the American Bar Association, at the headquarters of the New York County Lawyers' Association, at assorted white-shoe law firms) to the sets of interpersonal connections that activists drew upon in their strategizing sessions. "Are there any women judges that are there for us?" asked one activist at the Lawyers' Association meeting. "Are we on talking relations with the wife of the governor?" queried another. The professional upper-middle-class orientation of anti-trafficking activism that I observed in my research is also consistent with research on the class profiles of anti-prostitution activists in other national contexts and of contemporary transnational feminist activism more generally.[40]

As members of the class fraction that is most likely to reap strong material and symbolic rewards from marriage, anti-trafficking activists are heavily invested in the maintenance and reproduction of this status and are ready to enlist the state apparatus on behalf of the gendered and sexual interests that are most pertinent to themselves: a version of "feminist" family values that is premised upon liberal understandings of formal equality between women and men, and the safe containment of sexuality within the pair-bonded couple.[41] As with Grewal's analysis of the "security mom," these women utilize and promote the carceral state in order to securitize the sexual boundaries of home.

The feminist embrace of carceral politics and the articulation of these politics through a pro-familialist ideal of gender and sexuality were evident at the meetings of the anti-trafficking caucuses of NOW-NYC and the American Association of University Women (AAUW) that I attended between 2006 and 2008. At a November 2006 conference on Violence Against Women that was cosponsored by the AAUW and other feminist organizations, several hundred professional women, predominantly white, spent the day discussing the necessity of abolishing prostitution for women's equality, while dozens of black and Latina women dressed in catering uniforms circulated among them arranging tables and chairs and serving drinks. The keynote speaker was a lawyer from the feminist NGO Equality Now, who took the podium after being very graciously introduced as "a former prosecutor of sex crimes and a mother." Visibly pregnant with a prominent diamond ring on her left finger, this well-coiffed and well-dressed lawyer reminded her audience of the important deterrent effects of the criminal law and conveyed the horrors of human trafficking as follows:

> I'd like to tell you the story of Christina, who . . . was a victim of human trafficking. She came here as a 19 or 20 year old woman in response to an ad for what she thought was a babysitting job. And when she arrived at JFK airport . . . she was then informed that the babysitting job wasn't available anymore. . . . Of course . . . she was forced to work in a brothel. And she describes that experience with the same words that any of us would use to describe it. She describes the sex of prostitution as disgusting, as degradation, and profoundly traumatic to her. And what I want to talk to you about is [what] some of the lasting effects are for her, after she escaped the experience. She is infertile. She can never have children.[42]

Nearly identical narratives were presented at the multiple anti-trafficking conferences that I attended throughout the course of my fieldwork, the only significant alteration being the victim's name.[43] Yet there is much to unpack in this exposition of the harms of trafficking though the presentation of "Christina's story," which in its sheer generality suggests that it is at least partially fictionalized and at best a strategically constructed composite case. Particularly notable is the moral and political legitimacy afforded to domestic care work as late-capitalist informal-sector employment,[44] the invocation of a single gendered (and uniformly negative) experience of "the sex of prostitution,"[45] and the construal of reproductive failure as the worst possible harm that could result for female victims. While elements of this narrative undoubtedly can and do happen to real individuals, as a representation of human trafficking the scenario described was far from the most empirically prevalent case.[46] Even more curiously, according to case files compiled from the U.S. Department of Justice, no trafficking case matching this description has ever been prosecuted.[47] The lawyer's simultaneous commitments to the carceral state, the capitalist service sector, and the ideology of feminist family values perfectly paralleled the underlying neoliberal logic which united these realms, in which the social inequalities that globalization has wrought are legitimate so long as the sexual boundaries of middle-class family life can be maintained.

At a discussion focused upon "ending demand" for sex trafficking at the Commission on the Status of Women meetings that I attended at the United Nations in March 2007, the link between sexual and carceral politics was once again revealed. At this meeting dedicated to problematizing men's "demand" for the services of sex workers, the panelists used the occasion to directly showcase how the carceral state could be effectively harnessed to achieve amatively coupled and sexually egalitarian nuclear families. The opening speaker from the CATW explicitly hailed the five white, middle-class men in the room as exemplars of a new model of enlightened masculinity and urged the audience members to "to bring their husbands, sons, and brothers" to future meetings. The model of prostitution and trafficking that the CATW panelists invoked bore little if any connection to structural or economic factors, rendering prostitution wholly attributable to the actions of bad men: husbands within the family who might appeal to the sexual services of women outside of it or bad men outside the family (coded as non-white and foreign) who might entice women and girls within it to leave.[48] Although the CATW regards itself as a progressive feminist organization, members displayed no hesitation in appealing to a punitive state apparatus. As the panel chair repeatedly emphasized during her sharply condemnatory presentation about heterosexual men's purchase of sex, "The only thing that prevents recurrence is fear of arrest."

Though numerous studies have shown that the arrest of clients serves primarily to drive prostitution indoors rather than to eradicate it, what was at stake for the CATW activists were the broader symbolic effects that a politics of criminalization could offer — not simply in turning the figure of the "sex predator" into a grotesque parody, as Wacquant has argued, but also for delegitimizing markets in female sexual labor and the commercialization of sexuality more generally.[49] The state is thus able to assume a feminist rationale for arresting those who stand in the way of neoliberal agendas of urban restructuring and the removal of race and class Others from public space.[50]

In my fieldwork with feminist activists, the utility of the carceral state for securitizing the middle-class family — and more specifically, for domesticating heterosexual men — was also manifest in frequent appeals to the case of Sweden as an exemplar of enlightened anti-trafficking policy. The criminalization of male sex purchasers, a policy model first implemented in Sweden in 1998, is often referred to by transnational feminist activists as the "Swedish Plan" in order to convey its feminist origins and impact, since Sweden is considered by many to be the most gender-egalitarian country in the world. It was thus that at a subsequent CATW panel that I attended, "Abolishing Sex Slavery: From Stockholm to Hunts Point," the Swedish policy of criminalizing the clients of sex workers was endorsed by speakers who not only applauded Sweden's reputation for gender equality, but who explicitly referenced the Swedish welfare state's commitment to "promoting men to be home with their children at a young age." Left unremarked upon in the transnational dissemination of this carceral strategy is that Sweden itself embraced it only after its hallmark welfare state (which earned it its feminist reputation in the first place) had been seriously weakened in the 1990s.[51]

In a related vein, feminist theorists of neoliberalism such as Lisa Duggan and Kate Bedford have pointed out the ways in which the ideology of "family values" becomes particularly critical when other possibilities for social relations are eclipsed.[52] Marriage as an institution is "grounded in the privatization of social reproduction, along with the care of human dependency needs, through personal responsibility exercised in the family and in civil society — thus shifting costs from state agencies to individuals and households."[53] The demise of the welfare state and the ascendance of law-and-order politics, both premised upon the promotion of "personal responsibility" and the condemnation of public disorder, are thus directly correlated not just as institutional alternatives to managing the racialized poor (as Wacquant has suggested) but also via "the dense interrelations" among neoliberalism's economic and (gendered) cultural projects.[54] Whereas Wacquant identifies but does not explain the shift to the "masculine" penal state or the familialist sexual politics that are its accompaniment, Duggan and Bedford demonstrate that the rise of "family values" politics is necessary to fill in the caring gaps that the obliterated welfare state has left vacant. They demonstrate that the neoliberal state can be harnessed to notions of "domesticating men" that operate simultaneously at two different levels: men, particularly poor and working-class men, are encouraged to do more care work within the home and to take on the burdens of social reproduction that arise when women themselves move into the sphere of paid work. At the same time, professional middle-class men are encouraged to constrain their commercial consumption in ways that are compatible with heterosexual domesticity and amative love.

A NEOLIBERAL CIRCUITRY OF CRIME, SEX, AND RIGHTS

The prior examples serve to illustrate how the rise of a carceral feminist framework is connected to the collapse of a social welfare state in more ways than one — both as a new social strategy for regulating race and class Others and as part of a neoliberal *gender* strategy that securitizes the family and lends moral primacy to marriage. Viewed as such, it becomes clear that as neoliberal economic policies extend their reach around the globe, they will serve to diffuse a new criminal justice–focused social agenda (as Wacquant has aptly demonstrated) *in tandem with* a new political paradigm of gender and sexuality that is premised upon the (feminist) family value of amative, sexually egalitarian couples. This new paradigm has been disseminated through such disparate means as stepped-up laws and controls against sex offenders (including proposals for a new pan-European sex offender registry), the insertion of men into private-sphere caring labor via official World Bank development policy, and burgeoning international campaigns against the "traffic in women."[55] Indeed, one of the reasons that anti-trafficking campaigns have become such a galvanizing issue for feminists, evangelicals, and other activists is because the interlinked sexual, carceral, and economic commitments that comprise them can be harnessed to the now hegemonic internationalist discourse of "women's human rights." As the political theorist Kristin Bumiller has observed, "human rights conventions attempt to improve conditions for women by putting pressure on states to promote serious and effective enforcement of criminal laws against interpersonal violence."[56] With "women's human rights" understood as pertaining exclusively to questions of sexual violence and to bodily integrity (but not to the gendered dimensions of broader social, economic, and cultural issues), the human rights model in its global manifestation has become a highly effective means of disseminating feminist carceral politics on a global scale.[57]

Within the context of campaigns to combat the global "traffic in women," this efficacy has been manifest in the United States' tier ranking and economic sanctioning of countries that fail to pass sufficiently punitive anti-prostitution laws, in the transnational activist push to criminalize male clients' demand for sexual services, in the tightening of international borders as a means to "protect" potential trafficking victims, and in the implementation of new restrictions upon female migrants' capacity to travel.[58] Feminist anti-trafficking activists have lobbied hard for all of these measures in addition to strongly endorsing the U.S. government's "anti-prostitution pledge," which stipulates that NGOs that do not explicitly take a stand in condemnation of prostitution will lose their capacity to receive U.S. funding.[59] Feminists have also offered their support for the vigilante brothel raids that evangelical Christian groups such as the International Justice Mission have conducted in India, Cambodia and other countries in partnership with the local police.[60] Although Wacquant, Garland, and Simon neglect to identify the political efficacy of human rights discourse for extending the nationally rooted carceral agendas that they describe, as Bumiller, Halley, Grewal, and other critical feminist scholars have observed, it has become an indispensable tool for the international spread of the increasingly mainstream paradigm of feminism-as-crime-control.[61]

From the perspective of U.S.-based anti-trafficking advocates, the shift to the international human rights field has also been crucial in relocating a prior set of internecine political debates among feminists about the meaning of prostitution and pornography (one which had divided the U.S. feminist movement throughout the 1980s and early 1990s and in which liberationist factions were emerging triumphant) to a humanitarian terrain in which the anti-prostitution constituency was more likely to prevail.[62] As one of the founding members of a prominent feminist anti-trafficking NGO explained to me during an interview, framing the harms of prostitution and trafficking as politically neutral questions of humanitarian concern about third-world women, rather than as issues that directly impacted the lives of Western feminists, was pivotal to waging the fight against commercial sexuality successfully:

There was an earlier wave of consciousness about exploitation that took both pornography and prostitution almost together as a kind of commercial sexual exploitation of women. And they got battered down by ACLU types . . . who were the same people who were also against prosecution of rape because it was discriminatory prosecution against people of color. . . . It wasn't even just priorities. It was really just a basic understanding of human rights. After that [we] went underground . . . and then trafficking brought these issues right back.[63]

Another human rights activist that I interviewed further observed that by the time of the 1995 Beijing World Conference on Women, the frameworks around both trafficking and prostitution had irrevocably shifted: "Beijing is where trafficking as a labor issue was first transformed into a sexual violence and slavery issue." According to these activists, feminists who had participated in earlier waves of domestic struggle for the state curtailment of prostitution and pornography had initially been hampered by other liberal constituencies (including divergent feminist factions and the ACLU) who were opposed to the potentially discriminatory effects of a criminal justice frame. But by resituating their issues in terms of the "traffic in women" overseas and as a violation of international commitments to women's human rights, they were able to wage the same sexual battles unopposed.

The most recent twist in the transnational feminist campaign against human trafficking has occurred with gathering attention to so-called "domestic" forms of sex trafficking. The 2005 reauthorization of the U.S. Trafficking Victims Protection Act (TVPRA) established the crime of "domestic trafficking" on a moral and legal par with previous cross-border understandings of the crime.[64] With the aim of shifting enforcement priorities toward street prostitution in urban areas, the TVPRA established $5,000,000 in federal grants to local law enforcement agencies to investigate and prosecute sex trafficking within the United States.[65] Some commentators have speculated that the shift from an international to a domestic focus in U.S. anti-trafficking policy has occurred because the U.S. government has consistently failed to identify the overwhelming numbers of transborder victims that it previously claimed existed.[66]

According to a U.S. Department of Justice summation of 2,515 human trafficking investigations conducted between 2008 and 2010, of 389 confirmed incidents of trafficking, 85 percent were sex trafficking cases, 83 percent of victims were U.S. citizens, and 62 percent of confirmed sex trafficking suspects were African American (while 25 percent of all suspects were Hispanic/ Latino).[67] The racial impact of anti-trafficking laws is also heightened by the fact that men who are convicted of pimping can now be given ninety-nine-year prison sentences as "domestic sex traffickers" (versus the prison sentences of several months that were previously typical), while migrant sex workers are themselves increasingly arrested and deported for the sake of their "protection."[68] Both domestically and globally, U.S. anti-trafficking policies have thus contributed to unprecedented police crackdowns on people of color who are involved in the street-based sexual economy (pimps, clients, and sex workers alike), and they have facilitated a sharp reversal of the trend toward the increasing legitimacy of sexual labor which prevailed up until the late 1990s.[69] In this way, contemporary anti-trafficking campaigns can be viewed as an effective, feminist embodiment of neoliberalism's joint carceral and sexual projects, ushering in agendas of family values and crime control while asserting new understandings of gender justice and "women's human rights."

CONCLUSION

If the postmaterialist politics tends towards good and evil,
crime is a natural metaphor for evil.
THEODORE CAPLOW AND JONATHAN SIMON | Crime and Justice

This article has sought to synthesize and push forward arguments made by recent social theorists concerning the emergence of the carceral state and its relationship to more general patterns of cultural and political transformation.[70] Drawing upon diverse accounts of the relationship between neoliberalism and the turn toward punitive modes of justice in contemporary social policy, I have highlighted the implicit gendered dimensions of this shift as well as its disparately raced and classed impact, melding theories of carcerality and punishment with insights drawn from my own empirical research on campaigns against sex trafficking. I have sought to show how an understanding of recent transformations within feminism, and within the politics of sex and gender more generally, is critical to the broad, sweeping analyses of the neoliberal carceral state that theorists such as Garland, Wacquant, and Simon have formulated. Via successive encodings of issues such as rape, sexual harassment, pornography, sexual violence, prostitution, and trafficking into federal and now international criminal law, mainstream feminists have provided crucial ideological support for ushering in contemporary carceral transitions.[71] Most recently, the burgeoning discourse of "women's human rights" has served to re-circuit feminist attention from the domestic spheres of home and nation to an expanding international stage, asserting carceral versions of feminism on a global scale.

It is important to understand the underlying gendered and sexual dynamics that have inspired this shift in feminist emphasis and strategy. Assumptions such as Garland's, Simon's, and Wacquant's that late-modern conditions of "gender flux" have led to a reactive embrace of carceral politics on the part of the once-liberal middle classes fail to consider the gendered interests that underpin feminist advocacy on behalf of the neoliberal carceral state. Whereas Garland correctly asserts that late-capitalist social transformations have destabilized certain aspects of middle-class life and fomented middle-class punitiveness, he misidentifies not only the reality of criminal threat but also the gendered and sexual instabilities that are the source of this trend. In contemporary anti-trafficking campaigns it is not "changing gender roles" in the abstract but rather reconfigured norms of *male sexuality* that are perceived as the greatest threat to middle-class feminist and evangelical Christian activists, for which both criminal justice and family values are perceived to be the remedies. Though Wacquant astutely demonstrates the correlation between the eclipse of the welfare state and the advent of the penal state (as well as the pivotal symbolic role played by the sex offender in ushering in these transitions), he fails to account for feminists' own investment in facilitating this shift. My own ethnographic research in combination with other feminist critiques of sexuality and neoliberalism helps to clarify this allegiance, demonstrating how the intersecting race, class, and gender locations of a prominent contingent of Western feminists have created deep political investments in the contemporary security state and in the middle-class family form.

Finally, Simon usefully reveals the ways in which the contemporary security state serves not only to police the poor but also to create middle-class understandings of securitized "freedom," pointing to the important role played by feminism in advancing this project.[72] My research on the contemporary anti-trafficking movement helps to illuminate precisely how and why feminists have reoriented their political aims toward carceral ends, situating ideological transitions in terms of the new political-economic horizons that feminists are confronting: contemporary feminist commitments to both "family values" and to a law-and-order agenda are facilitated by a neoliberal state apparatus in which poor as well as middle-class lives are increasingly governed through crime, and in which the privatized family is designated as the optimal institution for social support. Under such circumstances, the impetus to find non-economic means to equalize the dynamics of sexual power within the family — such as governing through crime — becomes compelling to many feminist (and evangelical Christian) social justice advocates. Rather than pursuing materially redistributive strategies, the versions of feminism that have survived and thrived are those which deploy the mutually reinforcing sexual and carceral strategies that a reconfigured neoliberal state is likely to support.[73]

Most generally, this essay has shown how attention to social actors' carceral commitments is pivotal to understanding the politics that have joined together "left" and "right," and feminists and evangelicals, on sexual issues — and vice versa. I have used the case study of human trafficking to illuminate how neoliberal sexual politics and carceral politics work together, highlighting the cross-ideological alignments that have occurred around both sex and crime. As theorists such as Garland, Wacquant, and Simon have persuasively argued, in the present historical moment, sex is often the vehicle that joins "left" and "right" together around an agenda of criminal justice. My own analysis of contemporary anti-trafficking campaigns has demonstrated how the reciprocal is also true: criminal justice has often been the most effective vehicle for binding feminists and evangelicals together around historically and socially specific ideals of sex, gender, and the family. To fully understand the rise of the carceral state and its relationship to late-capitalist social transformations, we need a feminist analytics of neoliberalism that is cognizant of how mutually reinforcing sexual and carceral strategies have come to circulate together.

NOTES

1. The bill, New York SB 5902, passed with broad support from New York feminist organizations on June 6, 2007.

2. Spitzer was ironically a strong ally of the New York feminist movement before resigning from office on March 13, 2008, for patronizing a prostitute. Michael Powell and Nicholas Confessore, "4 Arrests, Then 6 Days to a Resignation," New York Times, March 13, 2008, http://www.nytimes.com/2008/03/13/nyregion/13recon.html.

3. Such claims disregard a body of social scientific evidence which has found that women and girls often enter into prostitution at their families' behest, so as to better provide for their parents and children; see, for example, Heather Montgomery, Modern Babylon? Prostituting Children in Thailand (Oxford: Berghahn, 2001); Laura María Agustín, Sex at the Margins: Migration, Labour Markets and the Rescue Industry

(London: Zed Books, 2007); Elizabeth Bernstein, *Temporarily Yours: Intimacy, Authenticity, and the Commerce of Sex* (Chicago: University of Chicago Press, 2007).

4. See, for example, Angela Y. Davis and Cassandra Shaylor, "Race, Gender, and the Prison Industrial Complex: California and Beyond," *Meridians: Feminism, Race, Transnationalism* 2, no. 1 (2001): 1–25; Angela Y. Davis, *Are Prisons Obsolete?* (New York: Seven Stories Press, 2003); Laurie Schaffner, *Girls in Trouble with the Law* (New Brunswick, NJ: Rutgers University Press, 2005); Julia Sudbury, ed., *Global Lockdown: Race, Gender and the Prison-Industrial Complex* (London: Routledge, 2005); Lynne Haney, *Offending Women: Power, Punishment and the Regulation of Desire* (Berkeley: University of California Press, 2010).

5. Marie Gottschalk, *The Prison and the Gallows: The Politics of Mass Incarceration in America* (Cambridge: Cambridge University Press, 2006), 115.

6. Kristin Bumiller, *In an Abusive State: How Neoliberalism Appropriated the Feminist Movement against Sexual Violence* (Durham, NC: Duke University Press, 2008).

7. Miriam Ticktin, "Sexual Violence as the Language of Border Control: Where French Feminist and Anti-Immigrant Rhetoric Meet," *Signs: Journal of Women in Culture and Society* 33, no. 4 (2008): 863–889; Kamala Kempadoo, "Victims and Agents of Crime: The New Crusade against Trafficking," in *Global Lockdown: Race, Gender and the Prison-Industrial Complex*, ed. Julia Sudbury (London: Routledge, 2005), 35–55; Don Kulick, "Sex in the New Europe: The Criminalization of Clients and the Swedish Fear of Penetration," *Anthropological Theory* 3, no. 2 (2003): 199–218.

8. Ticktin, "Sexual Violence as the Language of Border Control," 865.

9. Sherene Razack, "Domestic Violence as Gender Persecution: Policing the Borders of Nation, Race, and Gender," *Canadian Journal of Women and the Law* 8, no. 1 (1995): 72, quoted in Ticktin, "Sexual Violence as the Language of Border Control," 865.

10. Alice Miller, "Sexuality, Violence against Women, and Human Rights: Women Make Demands and Ladies Get Protection," *Health and Human Rights* 7, no. 2 (2004): 32.

11. United Nations Office on Drugs and Crime, "Protocol to Prevent, Suppress and Punish Trafficking in Persons, Especially Women and Children, Supplementing the United Nations Convention against Transnational Organized Crime," 2000, https:// treaties.un.org/Pages/ViewDetails.aspx?src=IND&mtdsg_no=XVIII-12-a&chapter =18&lang=en.

12. Miller, "Sexuality, Violence against Women, and Human Rights," 32.

13. Elizabeth Bernstein, "The Sexual Politics of 'New Abolitionism,'" *Differences: A Journal of Feminist Cultural Studies* 18, no. 3 (2007): 128–151; Elizabeth Bernstein, "Militarized Humanitarianism Meets Carceral Feminism: The Politics of Sex, Rights, and Freedom in Contemporary Anti-Trafficking Campaigns," in "Feminists Theorize

International Political Economy," ed. Kate Bedford and Shirin Rai, special issue, *Signs: Journal of Women in Culture and Society*, 36, no. 1 (autumn 2010): 45–71; Janie A. Chuang, "Rescuing Trafficking from Ideological Capture: Anti-Prostitution Reform and Anti-Trafficking Law and Policy," *University of Pennsylvania Law Review* 158 (2010): 1655–1728.

14. The term "radical feminist" may be largely a misnomer given a political trajectory that has carried many of the original activists associated with this point of view to prominent positions in national and international governance, including within the Bush White House (see Bernstein, "Militarized Humanitarianism Meets Carceral Feminism").

15. Penelope Saunders, "Traffic Violations: Determining the Meaning of Violence in Sexual Trafficking Versus Sex Work," *Journal of Interpersonal Violence* 20, no. 3 (2005): 343–360; Ron Weitzer, "The Social Construction of Sex Trafficking: Ideology and Institutionalization of a Moral Crusade," *Politics and Society* 35, no. 3 (2007): 447–475; Gretchen Soderlund, "Running from the Rescuers: New U.S. Crusades against Sex Trafficking and the Rhetoric of Abolition," NWSA *Journal* 17, no. 3 (2005): 64–87.

16. Doris Buss and Didi Herman, *Globilizing Family Values: The Christian Right in International Politics* (Minneapolis: University of Minnesota Press, 2003).

17. See, for example, Kempadoo, "Victims and Agents of Crime"; Amy Foerster, "Contested Bodies: Sex Trafficking NGOs and Transnational Politics," *International Journal of Feminist Politics* 11, no. 2 (2009): 151–173; Agustín, *Sex at the Margins*; Jo Doezema, "Ouch! Western Feminists' 'Wounded Attachment' to the 'Third World Prostitute,'" *Feminist Review* 67 (2001): 16–38.

18. Roger N. Lancaster, *Sex Panic and the Punitive State* (Berkeley: University of California Press, 2011); Carole Vance, "Thinking Trafficking, Thinking Sex," GLQ: A *Journal of Lesbian and Gay Studies* 17, no. 1 (2010): 135–143.

19. Weitzer, "The Social Construction of Sex Trafficking"; see also Carole Vance, "Negotiating Sex and Gender in the Attorney General's Commission on Pornography," in *The Gender/Sexuality Reader: Culture, History, Political Economy*, ed. Roger N. Lancaster and Micaela di Leonardo (New York: Routledge, 1997), 434–440; Lisa Duggan and Nan D. Hunter, *Sex Wars: Sexual Dissent and Political Culture* (London: Routledge, 1995).

20. In this regard, Lancaster, *Sex Panic*, constitutes an important exception. David Garland, *The Culture of Control: Crimes and Social Order in Contemporary Society* (Chicago: University of Chicago Press, 2001); David Garland, ed., *Mass Imprisonment: Social Causes and Consequences* (London: Sage, 2001); Loïc Wacquant, *Prisons of Poverty* (Minnesota: University of Minnesota Press, 2009); Loïc Wacquant, *Punishing the Poor: The Neoliberal Government of Social Insecurity* (Durham, NC: Duke University Press, 2009); Jonathan Simon, *Governing through Crime: How the War on*

Crime Transformed American Democracy and Created a Culture of Fear (New York: Oxford University Press, 2007).

21. Gail Pheterson, "Tracing a Radical Feminist Vision from the 1970's to the Present: Left-Right, North-South," talk presented at Graduate Gender Program (GGeP) of the University of Utrecht, Netherlands, September 25, 2008.

22. On the "new middle class punitiveness," see Garland, *The Culture of Control*.

23. Kristin Luker, *Abortion and the Politics of Motherhood* (Berkeley: University of California Press, 1984); Arlene Stein, *The Stranger Next Door: The Story of a Small Community's Battle over Sex, Faith, and Civil Rights* (Boston: Beacon, 2001); Thomas Frank, *What's the Matter with Kansas? How Conservatives Won the Heart of America* (New York: Holt, 2004).

24. Bernstein, "Militarized Humanitarianism Meets Carceral Feminism."

25. Gayatri Spivak, "Can the Subaltern Speak?" in *Marxism and the Interpretation of Culture*, ed. Cary Nelson and Lawrence Grossberg, 271–313 (Urbana: University of Illinois Press, 1988).

26. See, for example, Janet Halley, *Split Decisions: How and Why to Take a Break from Feminism* (Princeton, NJ: Princeton University Press, 2006); Inderpal Grewal, *Transnational America: Feminisms, Diasporas, Neoliberalisms* (Durham, NC: Duke University Press, 2005); Agustín, *Sex at the Margins*.

27. Doezema, "Ouch!" 16; see also Wendy Brown, *States of Injury: Power and Freedom in Late Modernity* (Princeton, NJ: Princeton University Press, 1995).

28. Chyng Sun, "The Fallacies of Phantasies," in *Pornography: Driving the Demand in International Sex Trafficking*, ed. David E. Guinn (Los Angeles: Captive Daughters Media, 2007), 245.

29. Kristen Anderberg, "No More 'Porn Nights,'" in *Not for Sale: Feminists Resisting Prostitution and Pornography*, ed. Christine Stark and Rebecca Whisnant (North Melbourne, Australia: Spiniflex, 2004), 275–277.

30. See, for example, Linda Gordon, "Why Nineteenth-Century Feminists Did Not Support Birth Control and Twentieth-Century Feminists Do: Feminism, Reproduction and the Family," in *Rethinking the Family: Some Feminist Questions*, ed. Barrie Thorne and Marilyn Yalom, 40–52 (New York: Longman, 1982); Judith Walkowitz, *Prostitution in Victorian Society* (Cambridge: Cambridge University Press, 1980).

31. Kathleen Barry, *The Prostitution of Sexuality: The Global Exploitation of Women* (New York: NYU Press, 1995).

32. Bernstein, *Temporarily Yours*.

33. See, for example, Charlotte Bunch, "Lesbians in Revolt," in *We Are Everywhere: A Historical Sourcebook of Gay and Lesbian Politics*, ed. Mark Blasius and Shane Phelan, 420–424 (1972; repr., London: Routledge, 1997); Robin Morgan, "Lesbian and Feminism: Synonyms or Contradictions?" in *We Are Everywhere*, 424–435 (1973;

repr.); Alice Echols, *Daring to Be Bad: Radical Feminism in America, 1967–1975* (Minneapolis: University of Minnesota Press, 1989).

34. Horowitz, who is employed by the neoconservative think tank the Hudson Institute, was a pivotal figure in cementing the anti-trafficking coalition during the Bush presidency. See Allen D. Hertzke, *Freeing God's Children: The Unlikely Alliance for Global Human Rights* (Lanham, MD: Rowman and Littlefield, 2004).

35. Donna M. Hughes, "Combating Sex Trafficking: A Perpetrator-Focused Approach," *University of St. Thomas Law Journal* 6, no. 1 (2008): 28–53. Hughes serves as the Eleanor M. and Oscar M. Carlson Endowed Chair of Women's Studies at the University of Rhode Island and has issued multiple reports in national and international arenas on the "traffic in women." She is also a regular contributor to the conservative journal *The National Review*.

36. D. A. Clarke, "Prostitution for Everyone: Feminism, Globalisation, and the 'Sex' Industry," in *Not for Sale: Feminists Resisting Prostitution and Pornography*, ed. Christine Stark and Rebecca Whisnant (North Melbourne, Australia: Spiniflex, 2004), 149–206.

37. In her classic essay "The Traffic in Women," the feminist anthropologist Gayle Rubin drew upon the works of Marx and Engels, Claude Lévi-Strauss, and Jacques Lacan (in addition to a wealth of cross-cultural data) to argue that the linchpin of women's oppression resides in the social conventions of marriage and kinship (Gayle Rubin, "The Traffic in Women: Notes on the 'Political Economy' of Sex," in *Toward an Anthropology of Women*, ed. Rayna Reiter [New York: Monthly Review Press, 1975]).

38. See, for example, Morgan, "Lesbian and Feminism"; Kathleen Barry, *Female Sexual Slavery* (New York: NYU Press, 1979); Catharine A. MacKinnon, *Toward a Feminist Theory of the State* (Boston: Harvard University Press, 1989).

39. Inderpal Grewal, "'Security Moms' in the Early Twentieth-Century United States: The Gender of Security in Neoliberalism," *Women's Studies Quarterly* 34, nos. 1/2 (2006): 25–39.

40. Regarding anti-prostitution activists, see, for example, Josephine Ho, "From Anti-Trafficking to Social Discipline: Or, the Changing Role of 'Women's NGOS' in Taiwan," in *Trafficking and Prostitution Reconsidered*, ed. Kamala Kempadoo (Boulder, CO: Paradigm, 2005), 83–105; Leslie Ann Jeffrey, *Sex and Borders: Gender, National Identity, and Prostitution Policy in Thailand* (Honolulu: University of Hawaii Press, 2002). For transnational feminism, see Hester Eisenstein, *Feminism Seduced: How Global Elites Use Women's Labor and Ideas to Exploit the World* (Boulder, CO: Paradigm, 2009); Manisha Desai, "Transnationalism: The Face of Feminist Politics Post-Beijing," *International Social Science Journal* 57, no. 2 (2005): 319–330.

41. Demographic research has shown that whereas high educational attainment and the capacity for economic independence were once marital deterrents for women,

highly educated white women are now the most likely group to be married. See, for example, Steven P. Martin, "Trends in Marital Dissolution by Women's Education in the United States," *Demographic Research* 15, no. 20 (2006): 537–560; Joshua R. Goldstein and Catherine T. Kenney, "Marriage Delayed or Marriage Forgone: New Cohort Forecasts of First Marriage for U.S. Women," *American Sociological Review* 66, no. 4 (2001): 506–519.

42. Author's field notes, November 2006.

43. Other events at which strikingly similar stories were told include the CATW's "End Demand" conference at the UN's Commission on the Status of Women meetings on March 2, 2007, the CATW "Abolishing Sexual Slavery from Stockholm to Hunts Point" conference held at the New York City Bar Association on November 6, 2008, and the conference on "Sex Trafficking and the New Abolitionists," held at the Brooklyn Museum on December 13, 2008.

44. Although by some estimates trafficking for domestic work has been found to be more prevalent than trafficking into the sex sector (see, e.g., David Feingold, "Think Again: Human Trafficking," *Foreign Policy* 150 [September/October 2005]: 26–30), the former is more compatible with professional-class women's gendered interests in the home.

45. There is an abundance of critical feminist scholarship that demonstrates the contrary; see, for example, Bernstein, *Temporarily Yours*; Agustín, *Sex at the Margins*; Wendy Chapkis, *Live Sex Acts: Women Performing Erotic Labor* (New York: Routledge, 1997); Denise Brennan, *What's Love Got to Do with It? Transnational Desires and Sex Tourism in the Dominican Republic* (Durham, NC: Duke University Press, 2004).

46. Feingold, "Think Again"; Kempadoo, "Victims and Agents of Crime"; Kevin Bales, *Disposable People: New Slavery in the Global Economy* (Berkeley: University of California Press, 1999).

47. U.S. Department of Justice, "Characteristics of Suspected Human Trafficking Incidents, 2008–2010," 2011, http://bjs.ojp.usdoj.gov/content/pub/pdf/cshti0810.pdf.

48. Agustín has described the anxieties which circulate around trafficking in terms of displaced concerns about women "leaving home" for sex. *Sex at the Margins*. Here, I highlight feminists' concerns about men's, and specifically husbands', extra-domestic sexual pursuits.

49. About driving prostitution indoors, see Julia O'Connell Davidson, "'Sleeping with the Enemy'? Some Problems with Feminist Abolitionist Calls to Penalise Those Who Buy Commercial Sex," *Social Policy and Society* 2, no. 1 (2003): 1–9; Deborah Brock, *Making Work, Making Trouble: Prostitution as a Social Problem* (Toronto: University of Toronto Press, 1998); Bernstein, *Temporarily Yours*; Wacquant, *Punishing the Poor*.

50. Bernstein, *Temporarily Yours*.

51. Bernstein, *Temporarily Yours*; Barbara Hobson, "Women's Collective Agency, Power Resources and the Framing of Citizenship Rights," in *Extending Citizenship, Reconfiguring States*, ed. Michael Hanagan and Charles Tilly (Lanham, MD: Rowman and Littlefield, 1999), 149–178. Components of the Swedish criminalization model have since been adopted in countries ranging from Norway and Iceland to South Korea, the Philippines, and Chile. Although the Swedish law specifically criminalizes only the customers of prostitutes (and not sex workers themselves), transnational feminist activists and nation-states that claim the Swedish mantle have used it to widen the sphere of criminalization to encompass both sex workers and their clients (Bernstein, *Temporarily Yours*).

52. Lisa Duggan, *The Twilight of Equality? Neoliberalism, Cultural Politics and the Attack on Democracy* (Boston: Beacon, 2003), and Kate Bedford, *Developing Partnerships: Gender, Sexuality, and the Reformed World Bank* (Minneapolis: University of Minnesota Press, 2009).

53. Duggan, *The Twilight of Equality?*, 14.

54. Duggan, *The Twilight of Equality?*

55. On the spread of harsh criminal laws against sex offenders in Europe, see Georgia Harlem, "Unjust and Ineffective," *Economist*, August 8, 2009. On the heteronormative underpinnings of World Bank development policy, see Bedford, *Developing Partnerships*.

56. Bumiller, *In an Abusive State*, 136.

57. See also Grewal, "'Security Moms' in the Early Twentieth-Century United States"; Miller, "Sexuality, Violence against Women, and Human Rights."

58. Chuang, "Rescuing Trafficking from Ideological Capture"; Kempadoo, "Victims and Agents of Crime"; Ticktin, "Sexual Violence as the Language of Border Control"; Wendy Chapkis, "Soft Glove, Punishing Fist: The Trafficking Victims Protection Act," in *Regulating Sex: The Politics of Intimacy and Identity*, ed. Elizabeth Bernstein and Laurie Schaffner (London: Routledge, 2005), 51–66.

59. Chuang, "Rescuing Trafficking from Ideological Capture"; Saunders, "Traffic Violations"; Network of Sex Work Projects (NSWP), "Taking the Pledge (Video)," 2006, http://sexworkerspresent.blip.tv/file/181155/.

60. The International Justice Mission is the largest evangelical Christian anti-trafficking organization in the United States, with upward of eighty full-time paid staff members and operations in fourteen countries. Additional discussion of the International Justice Mission is provided in Bernstein, "The Sexual Politics of 'New Abolitionism'"; Bernstein, "Militarized Humanitarianism Meets Carceral Feminism"; and Noy Thrupkaew, "Beyond Rescue," *Nation*, October 26, 2009, http://www.thenation.com/article/beyond-rescue/.

61. Bumiller, *In an Abusive State*; Janet Halley, "Rape in Berlin: Reconsidering the Criminalization of Rape in the International Law of Armed Conflict," *Melbourne Journal of International Law* 9, no. 1 (2008): 78–124; Janet Halley, "Rape at Rome: Feminist Interventions in the Criminalization of Sex-Related Violence in Positive International Criminal Law," *Michigan Journal of International Law* 30, no. 1 (2008): 1–123; Grewal, " 'Security Moms' in the Early Twentieth-Century United States."

62. On the feminist pornography debates of the 1980s and 1990s, see Carole Vance, ed., *Pleasure and Danger: Exploring Female Sexuality* (London: Routledge & Kegan Paul Books, 1984); Vance, "Negotiating Sex and Gender in the Attorney General's Commission on Pornography"; and Duggan and Hunter, *Sex Wars*.

63. Author's field notes, December 3, 2008.

64. Trafficking Victims Protection Reauthorization Act of 2005, H.R. 972, 109 Cong. (enacted).

65. The 2000 Trafficking Victims Protection Act defines "sex trafficking" very broadly as "the recruitment, harboring, transportation, provision, or obtaining of a person for the purpose of a commercial sex act." Victims of Trafficking and Violence Protection Act of 2000, Pub. L. No. 106-386, 114 Stat. 1464.

66. See, for example, Denise Brennan, "Competing Claims of Victimhood? Foreign and Domestic Victims of Trafficking in the United States," in "Sexual Commerce and the Global Flows of Bodies, Desires and Social Policies," special edition, *Sexuality Research & Social Policy* 5, no. 4 (2008): 45–61. Since the passage of the 2000 Trafficking Victims Protection Act, the government has downgraded its estimates of U.S. transborder victims, from 50,000 to 14,500–17,000 people per year (U.S. Government Accountability Office (GAO), "Human Trafficking: Better Data, Strategy, and Reporting Needed to Enhance U.S. Antitrafficking Efforts Abroad" (GAO-06-825), 2006, http://www.gao.gov/new.items/d071034.pdf). In cases of "domestic trafficking," the force requirement is waived if the women in question are underage.

67. U.S. Department of Justice, "Characteristics of Suspected Human Trafficking Incidents, 2008–2010."

68. Chapkis, "Soft Glove, Punishing Fist"; Bernstein, *Temporarily Yours*; Melissa Ditmore, *The Use of Raids to Fight Trafficking in Persons* (New York: Urban Justice Center Sex Workers Project, 2009), http://sexworkersproject.org/downloads/swp-2009-raids-and-trafficking-report.pdf.

69. See also Sophie Day, "The Re-Emergence of 'Trafficking': Sex Work between Slavery and Freedom," *Journal of the Royal Anthropological Institute* 16 (2010): 816–834.

70. Epigraph quoted in Gottschalk, *The Prison and the Gallows*, 11.

71. Halley, *Split Decisions*, 21.

72. Simon, *Governing through Crime*.

73. In the case of anti-trafficking campaigns, such materially oriented strategies would likely include challenges to current international debt and lending policies, global commodity markets, and the economic development policies that create incentives for women to engage in risky migration and exploitative sexual labor in the first place.

| 11 |

California's Proposition 35 and the Trouble with Trafficking

In November 2012, California's sometimes-controversial voter initiative process led to the passage of a new law that sought — in very specific ways — to criminalize human trafficking. Civil rights advocates and activists for the rights of sex workers, prisoners, and people of color warned that California's Proposition 35, the CASE Act (Californians Against Sexual Exploitation), while claiming to target primarily human trafficking, would actually

> expand the definition of trafficking well beyond that currently recognized by global experts;
>
> increase prison sentences and sex offender registrations, including in some cases for the people the law claimed to protect;
>
> further criminalize sex workers' associates, including their partners and families;
>
> erode affected persons' online privacy through requirements to register their Internet accounts with law enforcement;
>
> channel fines to police agencies, sex work abolition agencies, and nonprofits associated with Homeland Security — limiting or eradicating entirely funds that would, under earlier anti-trafficking strategies, be available to support victims directly.

Organizations led by people of color publicly protested Proposition 35, raising profound concerns about the racism and xenophobia that lay at the heart of the initiative. These advocates described the ways the law would further criminalize young people in the sex trade and increase policing and deportation of immigrant communities.[1] They also warned that mandatory sentencing provisions, as well as sections of Proposition 35 that make it difficult for anyone charged under the act to mount an effective defense, would lead to devastating consequences for people without the resources needed to go to trial.[2] Organizations for the rights of prisoners warned that the act "fuel[ed] the growth of the prison system" by further criminalizing and targeting sex workers and increasing police power (and funding) to detain and interrogate people under the pretext of looking for trafficked minors.[3]

Funded by an Internet entrepreneur with political aspirations and riding a wave of anti-trafficking activism, the CASE Act is likely to spawn comparable attempts at law reform in other states. Our analysis and discussion of the law is based in sex worker rights and human rights advocacy. We are also deeply indebted to the critiques developed by organizations and coalitions that coalesced to say "No! on 35."[4] Carol Queen is trained as a sexologist and cofounded San Francisco's Center for Sex & Culture, which participated in educational events seeking to help voters and those who might be affected by the CASE Act better understand the proposed law's provisions. Penelope Saunders is an anthropologist and coordinator of the Best Practices Policy Project, an organization dedicated to the health and rights of sex workers, people in the sex trade, and related communities affected by anti-prostitution policies.

Covering the history of the law in California as well as the way anti-trafficking activism in the United States has trended toward a conflation of the notion of "trafficking" with the much larger category or phenomenon of prostitution (and sometimes other forms of sex work), we will give special attention to elements of the new law that further criminalize sexual and other conduct, support increased breaches of privacy and surveillance as government policy, and subvert civil rights through the CASE Act's use of the sex offender registry. In understanding these issues, we are also guided by the perspectives of leaders from communities of color and people affected by prisons and incarceration; prioritizing a "race and class analysis of policing" helps to show how the law will further criminalize and stigmatize immigrants, youth of color, and low-income LGBTQ people.[5]

The push for the passage of Proposition 35 — a money- and media-driven frenzy that deeply affected politics surrounding the proposed act — was the product of California's initiative system.[6] This system bypasses the legislative process and forgoes the need to educate or influence politicians. Instead, it relies on the individual voter, who is informed and influenced by advertising campaigns funded by various political advocacy groups. Millions of dollars are raised and spent each election cycle to do this; in 2012 alone, over $400 million was spent on California ballot initiative advocacy, including over $3 million spent on Proposition 35.[7]

Based on inflated numbers and junk science, the notion of trafficking sold by CASE Act supporters to the state's voters bore little resemblance to the United Nations' definition of human trafficking, with its focus on debt bondage, exploitation, and forced labor (of all kinds, not just sexual) — which California law has already criminalized.[8] Considering the sex-only definition of trafficking in relation to other sex panics, we see in particular a media largely unable or unwilling to dig deeply enough into partisan rhetoric to understand and elucidate potential social and legal problems associated with the misinformation it helps to foster. In the case of Proposition 35, as we will see, the media itself seems to have lit the flame *and* fueled the fire.

SEX WORK VERSUS TRAFFICKING — "WHITE SLAVERY" FOR A NEW CENTURY

Over the past two decades, sex trade prohibitionists and anti-prostitution activists working within the United States and internationally have not only sought to call attention to the ills of human trafficking for the purposes of what they term "sexual slavery," but also have persisted in eliding the differences between sex trafficking and sex *work* (e.g., prostitution, exotic dancing, and other forms of eroticized labor). By conflating these two phenomena, these activists stand at stark cross-purposes to those who seek to make sexual labor safer for its practitioners; organized both globally and regionally, activists for the rights of sex workers take a harm-reduction angle in seeing sex work as a form of labor, viewing it through an occupational health and safety lens. Influenced by the work of San Francisco prostitutes' rights activist Carol Leigh (also known as Scarlot Harlot), who coined the phrase "sex work" to reference the provision of sexual entertainment and erotic services for money, community representatives and organizations have worked to decriminalize prostitution; to dialogue with feminists who may have only heard sex work represented in "sexual exploitation and violence against women" terms; and to provide sex workers with the kind of support they actually need and demand.[9]

Even though advocates for the rights of sex workers can disagree on many tactics and outcomes, they do agree that criminalization is a great source of harm to sex workers. Many, therefore, pressure for law reform. As the harm-reduction coalition Sex Workers without Borders (Raleigh, North Carolina) puts it, "We believe that most social ills attributed to prostitution itself are actually caused by its criminalization; for example, 'sex trafficking' by definition is only possible within criminalized, underground, and unregulated industries. . . . Decriminalization is the only way to place individual agency back into the hands of sex workers."[10] California's activist sex workers (especially those in the San Francisco Bay Area, home to a robust and politicized cadre of sex worker activists since the founding of Call Off Your Old Tired Ethics [COYOTE] in 1973 and the establishment of the US PROStitutes Collective in 1982) have tried several times to decriminalize prostitution.[11] In 2004, Berkeley was the site of a pro-decriminalization ballot initiative fight, Measure Q, led by the late Robyn Few, founder of Sex Workers' Outreach Project (SWOP-USA), while decriminalization went on the San Francisco ballot in 2008 via Measure K.[12] (Although each generated much activism and networking with supporters, both ballot measures failed.)

The changes wrought by the rise of the term "sex work" and its conceptual importance to both the U.S. and international prostitutes' rights organizations are hard to overstate. What had been considered in largely sexual deviance and criminal justice terms could now be understood through an occupational health and safety lens and as a workers' rights issue.[13] Also central in the United States is the school of organizing, responding to police repression and criminalization, that has emerged from communities of color, service providers, prisoner's rights advocates and prison abolitionists, and harm reductionists.[14] These advocates have brought new approaches: raising questions about the limitations of focusing on the decriminalization of sex work as a primary goal, challenging the carceral tendencies inherent in much of the anti-trafficking discourse, and taking leadership on the impact of anti-trafficking policies on youth in the sex trade.[15]

The decades of activism and discourse that have given rise to a movement advocating for the rights of people in the sex trade, however, are barely acknowledged in much of the anti-trafficking movement. The more conservative forms of anti-trafficking work, which focus on the notions of "sex trafficking" and "abolishing prostitution," purport to have the best interest of "victims" in mind, but in fact these strategies and priorities bear precious little resemblance to those of the sex worker rights movement — which does not automatically think of sex workers as victims — nor do they have anything in common with activism led by communities of color to resist criminalization of those in the sex trade. In order to understand how deeply rooted many campaigns against trafficking are in histories of racism, classism, and xenophobia, we need to trace the impulse to address "trafficking in women and children" back to earlier panics about protecting "good women" from "white slavery" and the perils of sexual activity outside of protective social norms; this history has led to legal frameworks that still exist to this day. For example, the Mann Act, passed into law in the United States in 1910 as an anti-trafficking measure, made crossing state lines for purposes of prostitution (among other "immoral purposes," such as adultery) illegal.[16] Its official name is the White Slave Traffic Act, and it remains on the federal books.[17]

Some organizations engaged in anti-trafficking discourses, particularly those who operate on a global basis, embrace human rights from a contemporary social justice point of view. In 1996, one of us (Carol Queen) accompanied a group of San Francisco Bay Area sex worker activists to the Global Fund for Women's Circle Against Trafficking conference in Reno, Nevada, which "brought together international activists, law enforcement and legal professionals, social workers, government representatives, survivors and sex workers to examine the problem of sex trafficking both in the U.S. and abroad."[18] Our contingent raised concerns about the concept of "sex trafficking," arguing that it would lead to greater criminalization of sex worker communities. Another anti-trafficking organization was represented at the conference, one which didn't restrict its focus to sex trafficking only; the difference between their analysis and that of the sponsoring organization was notable. Advocates from this organization used a broad definition of trafficking in persons to address all forms of forced or coerced labor, and their representation of the issues did not rely on the alarmist sex-panic rhetoric used by so many other organizations at the meeting (including the sponsors). Since that time, however, the anti-sex-trafficking movement in the United States has exploded — the discourse about trafficking victims has become a significant lens through which well-meaning people in the mainstream understand prostitution, though many of these "understandings" are false.

Even though groups such as the Freedom Network continue to advocate for a broader, rights-based understand of human trafficking, more conservative anti-trafficking activists rally around their focus on "sex trafficking" today, grabbing much media attention and thereby generating public sympathy for their anti-sex-worker and carceral agendas.[19] They home in on issues relating to youth (represented through an emphasis on child and youth prostitution; the numbers they cite are almost certainly inflated); trafficking across international borders (in which hapless women and youth are brought to the United States from other countries and forced to work in brothels, massage parlors, and strip clubs; the number reported are once again almost certainly inflated); and "domestic trafficking" (leading to the policing of U.S. sex workers, people presumed to be "purchasers" of sexual services, and people profiled as prostitutes, such as transgender women of color).[20]

Trafficking numbers are hard to come by and overstated; the *Village Voice* and other publications have run articles and exposés on this issue in recent years.[21] More recently have come news reports that superstar anti-trafficking activist Somaly Mam falsified her tale of forced sex slavery and those of at least some other women associated with her foundation.[22] Some of the most enduring rallying cries to address "sex trafficking," such as the claim that "the average age of entry into prostitution is thirteen," have been debunked in efforts to return media attention to the things that both youth and people in the sex trade actually need to ensure their health and rights.[23] However, even in the face of earnest calls for evidence-based policy and journalism based on accurate and careful reporting, the tropes of "trafficking sensationalism" hold members of the media, politicians, and much of the general public in their thrall. Sensationalism in media coverage (encouraged by advocates wishing to gain public attention to "end sex trafficking") has a snowball effect: ever-more lurid tales of depravity fuel the sex panic, justifying layer upon layer of oppressive laws and policies. The CASE Act is part of this trend and, like many other anti-trafficking initiatives discussed here, elides the difference between noncoerced sex work and forced trafficking, removing sex workers' own agency and obfuscating what is really being policed.

HOW THE CASE ACT CAME TO BE

In California's initiative process, citizen activists, organizations, legislators acting on their own, or business interests can write proposed law and, if enough voters' signatures can be collected, get it on the ballot. The CASE Act began as Proposition 35, an initiative statute proposed by the nonprofit California Against Slavery and funded primarily by millionaire Chris Kelly, the former chief privacy officer for Facebook. Initiatives have become controversial among some California commentators because some have been tools deployed in the interests of radical social perspectives (like the notorious and homophobic Briggs Initiative in 1978 that would have barred gays and lesbians from teaching jobs and the Prop. 13 ballot measure that cut property taxes, drastically affecting state budgets from 1978 to the present day).[24] Others may enshrine into law the wishes and priorities of big business or other interest groups. As journalists Heather Tuggle and Zachary Stauffer put it, "What began as a progressive, grassroots movement has morphed into a multi-million dollar industry. The interest groups have changed and rather than simply lobbying government officials for support, they shell out millions hoping to lure voters to their various causes."[25]

Proposition 35 did have significant money and political interests behind it. Chris Kelly, who bankrolled the initiative, had run unsuccessfully for state attorney general against Kamala Harris in 2010. Promoting "tough-on-crime" approaches — including dramatic calls to "stamp out sex trafficking" — can be a way to burnish one's political reputation. An anti–Proposition 35 flyer distributed by California Coalition for Women Prisoners noted that the "CASE [Act] may be [Kelly's] bid to win elected office in the future. By using emotionally charged terms like slavery and trafficking, Prop 35 has won the endorsement of a wide range of politicians and groups across the state — no one wants to be accused of being for human trafficking."[26] Even commentary in support of the initiative spelled out the importance of Proposition 35 for Kelly's political future. "He will run for office again, though he's not sure when," wrote a senior editor in the *Sacramento Bee* in May 2012. "He knows, however, that promoting an initiative is not a bad idea for someone seeking to build name identification."[27]

Perhaps the key motivator behind the initiative was the nonprofit advocacy organization California Against Slavery, which for its part was founded not by a millionaire but by a citizen activist — one who was inspired by a TV show to work against trafficking. According to California Against Slavery's official website, Daphne Phung, the organization's founder and executive director, was prompted to action after watching MSNBC *Dateline*'s "Sex Slaves in America." "After grappling with how a just God and a free nation can allow such injustice," Phung had a revelation that "God uses people to change the world. And the idea of an initiative came about." As much as she was influenced by the idea of "sex slavery," her concern was especially strong on behalf of children: "To her, nothing robs a child's innocence and future as violently as the crime of human trafficking."[28] Phung was motivated by her faith, which appears to be evangelical, but the exact nature of her religious affiliation is not clear. Early on in her efforts to garner support for the idea of the initiative, she was embraced by groups such as the Unification Church in the Bay Area, who saw it as a key way to carry out Reverend In Jin Moon's plan to become involved in the issue of "human sex trafficking."[29]

Phung and Kelly were joined by Sharmin Bock, the head of the Human Exploitation and Trafficking Unit (HEAT) and Cold Case Units of the Alameda County DA's office, who is credited as being a coauthor of the initiative.[30] Like the former privacy officer of Facebook, Sharmin Bock also had political ambitions. In May 2011 she had entered the race for San Francisco district attorney in order to address the "lack of women citywide elected officials in San Francisco."[31] Bock has made it clear that the proposition drew on her expertise, which almost exclusively consisted of prosecution of "sex trafficking cases."[32] On the campaign trail in 2011, when asked how many cases of *labor* trafficking the HEAT unit had prosecuted, she responded, "This unit has done zero."[33]

Proposition 35 is clearly the product of this coalition and is tailored to address the religiosity of Phung and her concern for children, the electoral ambitions of Bock based on her expertise in "sex trafficking," and the "tough on sex crime in the Internet age" reputation needed by Kelly for his political future. The initiative redefined "human trafficking" in two ways to specifically address sexual and other conduct such as public indecency and prostitution.[34] The first of these two provisions could be very broadly applied to anyone who "deprives or violates the personal liberty of another" with the intent to violate one or more of twelve existing portions of the California Penal Code dealing with (among other things) prostitution or "illicit carnal connection with any man," living on the proceeds of prostitution, procuring, the engagement of minors in prostitution and pornography, any trafficking in "obscene matter," and "engaging or participating in, or sponsoring, obscene live conduct in public, with or without admission fee."[35] Because preexisting legal definitions of prostitution and obscenity in California were already vague and because "deprivation or violation of personal liberty" is defined expansively under Proposition 35, activities that were not previously criminalized or were misdemeanors would now be considered "human trafficking."[36] The initiative also introduced a new section with similarly broad reach that applied specifically to minors. The CASE Act substantially increased the penalties faced by those charged under the law, and — in line with the interests of the authors — specified much higher penalties for sex trafficking compared to any other kind.

VICTIM? PERPETRATOR? WHO WOULD BE
TARGETED UNDER CASE?

Organizers from many different communities already subject to policing and surveillance soon recognized the threat posed by Proposition 35. Of great concern to the community of activists working on sex workers' and trafficking victims' rights was that language in the proposed law could easily be turned against sex workers, and the act includes no guarantee against deportation when a noncitizen trafficking victim is "rescued." Sex workers could be charged for helping one another, and their partners, children, friends, and roommates could risk being pursued as "human traffickers" for living on the proceeds of prostitution.[37] Gloria Lockett, the executive director of CAL-PEP (California Prostitutes Education Project, a peer-run organization that primarily serves African American and Latino/a communities in Oakland), highlighted the impact of racism in the legal system at a panel discussion on Proposition 35 hosted by the agency, detailing how people of color are affected by pimping and prostitution arrests and how plea deals are manipulated to lead to their incarceration.[38]

Numerous organizations and commentators disambiguated the meaning of Proposition 35 in terms of its impact on minors and young adults. Black Women for Wellness, for example, explained in their 2012 voting guide that "an 18 year old who take[s] his/her partner out for dinner and a movie and then engages in sex could be seen as a trafficker. In addition, [Proposition 35] could punish anyone who associates with minor sex workers, even if their only intent was to buy him/her food or give [him/her] a ride to the store. Yes the odds of this seem rare, but knowing many communities of color relationships with law enforcement, it's not much of a reach to imagine a California in which this happens if [Proposition] 35 passes."[39] Alexandra Lutnick, a researcher focusing on young people's involvement in the sex trades, noted, "We've seen in other situations when that language ends up hurting the very folks we're trying to protect, and I don't feel that increased penalties [in Proposition 35] will actually make a dent. It's not doing anything to address the poverty that encourages young people to trade sex, racism, homophobia, these structural factors."[40] The US PROStitutes Collective analysis raised similar concerns, arguing that many youth engage in the sex trade because of the economic crisis and cuts in welfare, and Proposition 35 did not provide fiscal support for these young people; the assets seizures and fines that are written into the CASE Act would go instead to anti-trafficking NGOs and to law enforcement.[41]

RAISING MONEY THROUGH
FINES AND FORFEITURES

A closer examination of the flow of money and resources mandated by Proposition 35 reveals that the framework designed by Phung, Kelly, and Bock feeds law enforcement and an attendant nonprofit sector working in collusion with the prison-industrial complex and border control. Cynthia Chandler, an attorney with Justice Now, an organization working for the rights of prisoners, was one of the first legal advocates to analyze the initiative. Her reading of the proposed legal language revealed a tight relationship between law enforcement and the expansive way trafficking would be redefined. She found that Proposition 35 "mandates that all police in the field get anti-trafficking training, so it institutionalizes this view of commercial sex as trafficking into the police culture state-wide."[42] This becomes "culturally and economically significant" because all police departments would have to pay to have officers trained, resulting in a steady flow of funds to groups and institutions espousing the "sex trafficking" approach.

The economic impact of the initiative is, however, much more substantial than this. Proposition 35 requires that prosecuted traffickers pay up to $1.5 million in fines in addition to existing criminal fines.[43] The money would be divided up between unidentified governmental agencies and nongovernmental service providers, with "seventy percent of the fines . . . granted to public agencies and nonprofit corporations that provide shelter, counseling, or other direct services for trafficked victims" and "[t]hirty percent . . . granted to law enforcement and prosecution agencies in the jurisdiction in which the charges were filed to fund human trafficking prevention, witness protection, and rescue operations."[44] Prisoner rights advocate Chandler explained that this "specifically creates a mechanism whereby police departments will be funded through fines collected through crimes defined through this act. As such, it creates a mechanism whereby the state becomes financial[ly] dependent upon the maintenance of the legal schema created."[45] The California Coalition for Women Prisoners critique distilled the concerns of sex workers' and migrants' rights organizations by adding that this would also channel funds to "non-profit agencies that work hand-in-hand with law enforcement, ICE [US Immigration and Customs Enforcement] and Homeland Security, giving those agencies a vested interest in the fines that are charged to those convicted of trafficking."[46] Loyola law professor Kathleen Kim and her colleagues Kevin Kish and Cindy Liou (both of whom provide legal and other support to trafficked persons) noted that since none of these fines are earmarked for victims in terms of restitution or damages in a civil action, it marks a fundamental shift away from California's existing approach to human trafficking. "If all human traffickers were multi-millionaires," they argued, "this requirement would be of little concern. But most are not. The mandatory fine will therefore deplete or eliminate trafficker's assets that under current law go directly to the victims of forced labor. Prop 35, in its laudable determination to ensure that traffickers do not profit from their crimes, has the perverse effect of making traffickers 'judgment proof' and diverting money away from trafficking survivors."[47]

SEX OFFENDER REGISTRY AND INTERNET MONITORING

For many opponents, the most chilling element of the CASE Act was the way it would cast a too-wide net for "traffickers" via its vague language — targeting sex workers, people in the sex trade, transgender people, young people of color, and immigrants, as well as sex workers' partners, children, families, friends, and associates, and even harm-reduction service providers — who would then be forced to register as sex offenders for life. Sex offender registries are explored elsewhere in this volume in essays that lay out the lifelong effects of having to register as a sex offender, often including limits on where one is allowed to reside or work and public announcement of one's sex offender status.[48] Sex workers, people in the sex trade, and communities of people affected by anti-prostitution policies have long been subjected to sex offender registration statutes. For example, a woman in Tennessee who was charged with "aggravated prostitution" because of her HIV status has been placed on a registry, affecting where she can live and even her relationship with her own infant daughter — and she is hardly alone.[49] Once a person is placed on a sex offender registry, it is remarkably difficult to have one's name removed from it or to stop the practice via the courts. Even though community organizers successfully challenged the placement of people charged under the "Crimes Against Nature" statute on a registry in Louisiana, police continue to charge people under it and those already on the list are not removed as required by law.[50]

Proposition 35 proposed to extend section 290 of the Penal Code (the "Sex Offender Registration Act") to apply to its two newly defined forms of "human trafficking" pertaining to both adults and children.[51] Thus, anyone convicted under those sections would be required to register for the rest of their lives as sex offenders in the state of California. Since sex offender registration is applied retroactively to any case dating back to July 1, 1944, leading figures for the rights of sex workers, such as Naomi Akers (who was then director of the occupational health and safety clinic for sex workers and their families, the St. James Infirmary), came out publicly with their concern that they personally could be mandated to register as "sex offenders."[52] This outpouring of concern was not hyperbole; networks of sex workers and other organizations reported that their colleagues (sex workers, gay men, transgender people) had already been placed on the registry for other reasons. Proposition 35 gave the police "even more powers of surveillance" and prosecutors even more tools to extract plea bargains and other admissions from people who would be charged under the CASE Act and would fear the lifelong consequences of having to live as a "sex offender."[53]

Proposition 35 also sought to extend sex offender registration in other ways, by monitoring convicted persons' Internet usage for life, requiring those convicted to report all their "Internet identifiers" (email addresses, user names, and screen names) and the names of their Internet service providers (ISPs) to police and other authorities. This is the one provision of the law that has not taken effect (discussed later). Whatever the outcome of the constitutional challenge to this part of the CASE Act, advocates contend that these provisions are part of "the assault on the internet which began with the moralistic crusade against Craigslist and now Backpage, blaming the internet for promoting trafficking . . . [and] a dangerous precedent to allow such an invasion of privacy and law enforcement intrusion into the internet."[54]

CRACKS IN THE FAÇADE: LOSING SUPPORT FROM OPPONENTS OF TRAFFICKING

Elizabeth Bernstein has analyzed how new and diverse coalitions of "feminist activists, evangelical Christians, and bipartisan state officials" have "recently produced policy transformations on a scale unparalleled since the White Slavery scare of the last century."[55] While it is true that the expansion of policies against "sex trafficking" is relentless, in examining the case of the production and promotion of Proposition 35 in California, we note that local-level alliances in support of such policy agendas are much more frayed than they initially appear. Furthermore, mainstream media representations of the progress of Proposition 35 repeatedly mentioned that for a measure against trafficking, the initiative was "surprisingly controversial" — indicating that messages about the limitations of the initiative were chipping away at public perception that any law against trafficking must be a good law.[56] An analysis of how simplistic solutions for "sex trafficking" have, in fact, lost support is useful for ongoing advocacy in this arena. We also need to examine more closely the exact nature of the elements that sustained Proposition 35 if we seek to prevent these kinds of developments in the future.

In California many anti-trafficking advocates, including those from a law enforcement background, immediately saw the CASE Act for the poorly written law it was. One significant early opponent was John Vanek, retired lieutenant at the San Jose Police Department and manager of its Human Trafficking Task Force.[57] He joined with Perla Flores, program director of Solutions to Violence Services at Community Solutions, and Lynette Parker, an associate clinical professor of law at Santa Clara University School of Law — all were current or past board members for the South Bay Coalition to End Human Trafficking — to debunk the initiative in the media and via public appearances throughout the months of debate. They challenged the creation of a hierarchical binary between "sex trafficking" and labor-related human trafficking, the idea that "drastic increase in prison sentencing standards will prevent the incidence of trafficking, even though broad research refutes this theory," and many other elements of Proposition 35.[58]

The list of people and organizations opposing Proposition 35 is extensive and diverse.[59] Even stalwart "victim" advocates who believe that sex work damages participants in all cases, such as SAGE (Standing Against Global Exploitation), publicly rescinded support of the CASE Act, and Lois Lee, founder of Children of the Night, also registered her opposition to the initiative. It is perhaps no surprise that the American Civil Liberties Union (ACLU) and the Bay Area Freedom Socialist Party opposed Proposition 35, but so did the California Council of Churches and the California Association for Criminal Justice. And perhaps most significant was the groundswell of opposition from organizations led by people from communities of color — along with those led by immigrants and prisoners — whose clear critiques exposed the "anti-trafficking rhetoric of Prop. 35 and recognized it for the racism, sexism, and xenophobia that underlie the increased surveillance and criminalization of their communities."[60] Emi Koyama concludes that this "new, emerging alliance against criminalization of our people and communities in an increasingly multi-racial and queer/trans-friendly America" is a very hopeful sign "despite of the massive overreach of policing and criminalization advanced by the mainstream anti-trafficking movement."[61]

Given this significant pushback, what are the elements that continue to allow initiatives like Proposition 35 to emerge and flourish? Certain kinds of religious engagement remain a major motivator of these types of anti-trafficking measures, as Elizabeth Bernstein has shown, though it is not clear whether Daphne Phung sees herself as part of the "Justice Generation" (a new group of young, highly educated, and relatively affluent evangelicals).[62] Phung's determination to pass an anti-sex-trafficking law by whatever means necessary was certainly important, but she could not have sustained the efforts without a significant infusion of funds.[63] What stands out in the case of Proposition 35 is that social capital accrues to highly ambitious, often wealthy people who use "sex trafficking" to burnish their image and raise their public profile, particularly as they seek public office. This is why the campaign in support of Proposition 35 garnered such substantial financial backing from people like Chris Kelly; it is notable that those opposing Proposition 35 raised no funds at all. At this particular time, "investing" one's money in a campaign to "end sex trafficking" is one that will almost certainly pay social and political dividends — albeit often cynical ones. Another important element — perhaps essential in these days of public opinion driven by social media — is the "celebrity endorsement" that can garner even more media attention and drive public opinion. Jada Pinkett Smith signed on as an "actress and celebrity" and "a mom," driving home the Proposition 35 message — glamorously, with goody bags filled with wine and other luxury items — to women in the blogosphere and beyond.[64]

SEX PANIC ON THE BALLOT

As Melissa Gira Grant wrote in her *New York Times* op-ed about the Somaly Mam fraud accusations, "Ms. Mam's target audience of well-off Westerners, eager to do good, often knows little about the sex trade. It doesn't require much for them to imagine all women who sell sex as victims in need of rescue."[65] This is exactly why, despite many significant voices of opposition, the CASE Act prevailed on Election Day in 2012. Over 81 percent of California voters cast their ballots for Proposition 35.[66] The heavily funded, media-driven campaign to vote "yes on 35" succeeded, riding the wave of trafficking sensationalism and creating a new and highly problematic law.

All but one provision went into effect. The ACLU and the Electronic Frontier Foundation sued to block the provision that would require convicted persons to submit to lifetime online monitoring. Their suit challenges the constitutionality of the two newly enacted California Penal Code sections that require registered sex offenders to provide their Internet identifiers and ISPs to the police, because this will "irreparably harm" the plaintiffs' right to freedom of association and free speech.[67] To date, the other deeply problematic provisions of the CASE Act remain in effect.

Religious beliefs were indeed important in motivating the advocacy behind this legislation. Feminist debates were also present but were perhaps less central to the discourse than they have been in previous decades. We conclude this essay with the suggestion that the most unacknowledged yet important deciding factor in the initiative's success is the social capital that can be bought by "opposing sex trafficking." However, despite the seeming ease with which Proposition 35 passed, the United States is changing from the grass roots up, slowly but surely, to dismantle the culture of ignorance about sexuality and sex work. One day when it is no longer a "good investment" to pour one's money or reputation into poorly worded and oppressive anti-sex-trafficking legislation, we will look back on the connections made by communities of color, activists defending human rights, sex workers and other people in the sex trade, immigrants, prisoners, and queers, and we will recall when the seeds of the "sex trafficking" agenda's undoing were sown.

NOTES

We are most indebted to Carol Leigh for her website AgainstTheCaseAct.com, an excellent resource that collected not only the text of the law itself but also many statements and articles about the CASE Act, links to op-eds and newspapers that opposed it, and much more useful information. The website, however, is no longer available.

1. Emi Koyama, "Anti-Criminalization: Criminalization Happens on the Ground, Not in the Legislature," *Eminism*, November 27, 2012, http://eminism.org/blog/entry/362.

2. SWOP-NYC, "Black Women for Wellness Opposes Prop. 35," http://swop-nyc.org/wpress/2012/10/31/swop-nyc-signs-onto-black-women-for-wellnesss-opposition-letter-on-prop-35/, accessed September 29, 2014.

3. California Coalition for Women Prisoners, "Proposition 35 — A Dangerous Initiative," *No! on 35*, http://www.againstthecaseact.com/CCWP.html, accessed September 29, 2014.

4. *No! on 35*, http://www.againstthecaseact.com/, accessed September 29, 2014.

5. As described by Kelli Dorsey and Emi Koyama in a roundtable discussion about the passage of Proposition 35 convened by *In These Times*. Rebecca Burns, "The War

on Trafficking: Will California's Crackdown Do More Harm than Good?" *In These Times*, December 24, 2012, http://inthesetimes.com/article/14290/the_war_on _trafficking.

6. In the state of California new laws may be proposed via an initiative process in which groups collect signatures in order for a proposition to be placed on the ballot for a vote. *Ballotpedia*, "History of Initiative and Referendum in California," http:// ballotpedia.org/History_of_Initiative_and_Referendum_in_California, accessed October 1, 2014.

7. Reid Wilson, "Initiative Spending Booms Past $1 Billion as Corporations Sponsor their Own Proposals," *Washington Post*, November 8, 2013, http://www.washingtonpost .com/blogs/govbeat/wp/2013/11/08/initiative-spending-booms-past-1-billion -as-corporations-sponsor-their-own-proposals/; The "Yes on 35" campaign raised about $3.7 million as of November 3, 2012. *Ballotpedia*, "California Proposition 35, Ban on Human Trafficking and Sex Slavery (2012)," http://ballotpedia.org/California _Proposition_35,_Ban_on_Human_Trafficking_and_Sex_Slavery_(2012), accessed September 29, 2014.

8. In 2005 the California legislature passed AB 22 to address human trafficking. Kamala D. Harris, Attorney General, California Department of Justice, *The State of Human Trafficking in California* (California Department of Justice, 2012), http://oag .ca.gov/sites/all/files/agweb/pdfs/ht/human-trafficking-2012.pdf.

9. In 1992, Carol Queen attended the International AIDS Conference in Amsterdam, which, like most other annual HIV/AIDS conferences, also drew a sex workers' delegation, a kind of conference within a conference, since so many sex worker organizations around the globe received AIDS funding. Among the stories of international advocacy we heard there was that one of India's largest sex worker support organizations requested literacy support for its members and their children.

10. Harm Reduction Coalition, "Sex Workers without Borders," http://harm reduction.org/connect-locally/north-carolina/sex-workers-without-borders/, accessed September 29, 2014.

11. See Alexandra Lutnick and Deborah Cohan, "Criminalization, Legalization or Decriminalization of Sex Work: What Female Sex Workers Say in San Francisco, USA," *Reproductive Health Matters* 17 (2009): 38–46.

12. *Wikipedia*, s.v. "Robyn Few," http://en.wikipedia.org/wiki/Robyn_Few, accessed September 29, 2014; *Ballotpedia*, "San Francisco Decriminalization of Prostitution, Measure K (November 2008)," http://ballotpedia.org/San_Francisco_Decriminalization _of_Prostitution,_Measure_K_%28November_2008%29, accessed September 29, 2014.

13. Black Women for Wellness was part of efforts to circulate a sign-on letter detailing these concerns and advised California voters to reject Prop. 35 on these grounds; see Black Women for Wellness, 2012 *Propositions Voter Guide*, http://www.bwwla.org

/wp-content/uploads/2012/10/BWW-VoteGuide-PROPS.pdf, accessed September 29, 2014.

14. See Kari Lerum, Kiesha McCurtis, Penelope Saunders, and Stéphanie Wahab, "Using Human Rights to Hold the US Accountable for Its Anti-Sex Trafficking Agenda: The Universal Periodic Review and New Directions for US Policy," *Anti-Trafficking Review* 1 (2012): 93.

15. INCITE! Women of Color Against Violence, "No Simple Solutions: State Violence and the Sex Trades," *INCITE! Blog*, April 22, 2011, http://inciteblog.wordpress .com/2011/04/22/no-simple-solutions-state-violence-and-the-sex-trades.

16. Eric Werner, "The Long Colorful History of the Mann Act," *National Public Radio*, March 11, 2008, http://www.npr.org/templates/story/story.php?storyId =88104308.

17. The Mann Act, 18 U.S.C.A. § 2421 et seq., http://uscode.house.gov/view.xhtml ?req=granuleid:USC-prelim-title18-section2421&num=0&edition=prelim, accessed August 2, 2016.

18. Marta Druly, "Letters to the Editor," *San Francisco Chronicle*, April 13, 1997, http://www.sfgate.com/opinion/letterstoeditor/article/LETTERS-TO-THE -EDITOR-3126042.php; See also Global Fund for Women, Circle Against Sex Trafficking, *Sisters and Daughters Betrayed: The Sex Trade of Women and Girls, an International Conference on the Dynamics of Sexual Coercion, October 17–18, 1996, Reno, Nevada* (Palo Alto, CA: Global Fund for Women, 1997).

19. The Freedom Network explicitly rejects approaching trafficking as either a "sexual-moral problem" or as a "saving women and girls" issue. "Human Rights," *Freedom Network, USA*, http://freedomnetworkusa.org/about-us/human-rights-approach /, accessed September 30, 2014.

20. An example of organizations addressing "sex trafficking" involving children and youth is Girls Educational and Mentoring Services (GEMS). GEMS, "Very Young Girls," GEMS, http://www.gems-girls.org/get-involved/very-young-girls, accessed October 1, 2014. For analysis of the numbers of people affected by human trafficking, see Ann Jordan, *Fact or Fiction: What Do We Really Know about Human Trafficking* (Washington, D.C.: Program on Human Trafficking and Forced Labor, Center for Human Rights and Humanitarian Law, Washington College of Law, 2011). For international trafficking, see, for example, Polaris Project, "Sex Trafficking in the U.S.," *Polaris*, https://polarisproject.org/sex-trafficking, accessed August 2, 2016. For domestic trafficking, see Ryan Beck Turner, "Project ROSE and Oppression as 'Rescue,'" *Human Trafficking Center*, http://humantraffickingcenter.org/posts-by-htc-associates /project-rose-and-oppression-as-rescue/, accessed October 1, 2014.

21. Martin Cizmar, Ellis Conklin, and Kristen Hinman, "Real Men Get Their Facts Straight," *Village Voice*, June 29, 2011, http://www.villagevoice.com/2011-06

-29/news/real-men-get-their-facts-straight-sex-trafficking-ashton-kutcher-demi
-moore/; Kristen Hinman, "Lost Boys: New Research Demolishes the Stereotype
of the Underage Sex Worker — and Sparks an Outbreak of Denial among Child-Sex-
Trafficking Alarmists Nationwide," *Riverfront Times*, November 3, 2011, http://www
.riverfronttimes.com/2011-11-03/news/commercial-sexual-exploitation-of-children
-john-jay-college-ric-curtis-meredith-dank-underage-prostitution-sex-trafficking
-minors/.

22. Melissa Gira Grant, "The Price of a Sex-Slave Rescue Fantasy," *New York Times*,
May 29, 2014, http://www.nytimes.com/2014/05/30/opinion/the-price-of-a-sex
-slave-rescue-fantasy.html?_r=1.

23. Chris Hall, "Is One of the Most-Cited Statistics About Sex Work Wrong?" *The
Atlantic*, September 5, 2014, http://www.theatlantic.com/business/archive/2014/09
/is-one-of-the-most-cited-statistics-about-sex-work-wrong/379662/.

24. *Ballotpedia*, "California Proposition 6, the Briggs Initiative (1978),", http://
ballotpedia.org/California_Proposition_6,_the_Briggs_Initiative_%281978%29,
accessed September 29, 2014; *Ballotpedia*, "California Proposition 13 (1978)," https://
ballotpedia.org/California_Proposition_13_(1978), accessed August 3, 2016.

25. Heather Tuggle and Zachary Stauffer, "California Initiative Process Remains
Confounding and Controversial," *UC Berkeley Graduate School of Journalism*, October 31, 2006, http://journalism.berkeley.edu/projects/election2006/2006/10
/california_initiative_process.php.

26. California Coalition for Women Prisoners, "Proposition 35."

27. Dan Morain, "Human Trafficking — 'I'm Somebody's Daughter' — Voter Initiative in November Would Toughen Criminal Penalty for Pimps," *Sacramento Bee*,
May 13, 2012, E1.

28. Daphne Phung, "Who's Daphne?" *California Against Slavery*, http://california
againstslavery.org/about/founder/, accessed September 29, 2014.

29. UTS Alumni Association, "Catching Up: With Pat Detlefsen (UTS '83)," *Unification Theological Seminary Alumni Association*, December 15, 2011, http://www.utsalumni
.org/news/catching-up-with-pat-detlefsen-uts83-2896/#sthash.rU3H6GbF.dpuf;
Camy Tsukamoto, *Human Trafficking Activist Speaks at Bay Area Church to Urge Ballot Initiative*, December 21, 2011, http://www.tparents.org/Library/Unification/Talks
/Tsukamoto/Tsukamoto-111221.pdf.

30. Nancy O'Malley, *Alameda County District Attorney's Office, Biennial Report
2011–2012* (Oakland, CA: Alameda County, Office of the District Attorney, 2013), 43,
http://www.alcoda.org/files/DA_annual_report_2011-2012_V3_opt.pdf.

31. Brent Begin, "Sharmin Bock Kicks off San Francisco District Attorney Campaign
with Jackie Speier," *San Francisco Examiner*, May 17, 2011, http://www.sfexaminer.com

/sanfrancisco/sharmin-bock-kicks-off-san-francisco-district-attorney-campaign-with-jackie-speier/Content?oid=2175054.

32. Victoria Kim, "Anti-Sex-Trafficking Proposition 35 Is Surprisingly Controversial," *Los Angeles Times,* October 30, 2012, http://articles.latimes.com/2012/oct/30/local/la-me-prop35-20121031.

33. Jason Winshell, "A Candidate for S.F. Prosecutor Makes Human Trafficking an Issue in Campaign, Downplays Federal Help," *SF Public Press,* October 21, 2011, http://sfpublicpress.org/news/2011-10/a-candidate-for-sf-prosecutor-makes-human-trafficking-an-issue-in-campaign-downplays-fe#sthash.Q1TQ3ERG.dpuf.

34. Two new sections were to be added to Chapter 8, Section 236.1 of the Penal Code, reading "(b) Any person who deprives or violates the personal liberty of another with the intent to effect or maintain a violation of Section 266, 266h, 266i, 266j, 267, 311.1, 311.2, 311.3, 311.4, 311.5, 311.6, or 518 is guilty of human trafficking and shall be punished by imprisonment in the state prison for 8, 14, or 20 years and a fine of not more than five hundred thousand dollars ($500,000).

(c) Any person who causes, induces, or persuades, or attempts to cause, induce, or persuade, a person who is a minor at the time of commission of the offense to engage in a commercial sex act, with the intent to effect or maintain a violation of Section 266, 266h, 266i, 266j, 267, 311.1, 311.2, 311.3, 311.4, 311.5, 311.6, or 518 is guilty of human trafficking." "Proposition 35," *No! on 35,* http://againstthecaseact.com/CASEAct_InitiativeText.pdf, accessed October 2, 2014.

35. Under §6 of the CASE Act, "any person who deprives or violates the personal liberty of another with the intent to effect or maintain a violation of Section 266, 266h, 266i, 266j, 267, 311.1, 311.2, 311.3, 311.4, 311.5, 311.6, or 518 is guilty of human trafficking and shall be punished by imprisonment in the state prison for 8, 14, or 20 years and a fine of not more than five hundred thousand dollars ($500,000)." *California Legislative Information,* http://leginfo.legislature.ca.gov/faces/codes_displaySection.xhtml?lawCode=PEN&sectionNum=236.1, accessed September 29, 2014.

36. Greg Diamond, "I Despise Human Trafficking, but I Oppose the Badly Drafted Prop 35," *Orange Juice Blog,* July 31, 2012, http://www.orangejuiceblog.com/2012/07/i-despise-human-trafficking-but-i-oppose-the-badly-drafted-prop-35/.

37. Edith Kinney, "Prop. 35's Sex-Crimes Focus Too Narrow," *San Francisco Chronicle,* September 23, 2012, http://www.sfgate.com/opinion/openforum/article/Prop-35-s-sex-crimes-focus-too-narrow-3888247.php.

38. Carol Leigh, "Aliens Abducted Me and Forced Me to Vote for Prop 35," *Facebook,* October 21, 2012, https://www.facebook.com/notes/carol-leigh/aliens-abducted-me-and-forced-me-to-vote-for-prop-35/457905240918851.

39. Black Women for Wellness, *2012 Propositions Voter Guide.*

40. Carol Leigh, "Prop 35, Youth, Sex Trade and Sex Trafficking: Interview with Alexandra Lutnick, Researcher," *San Francisco Bay Area Independent Media Center*, November 2, 2012, https://www.indybay.org/newsitems/2012/11/02/18724988.php.

41. US PROStitutes Collective, "Briefing against the CASE Act/Proposition 35," *No! on 35*, http://www.againstthecaseact.com/Briefing-USPROS.html, accessed September 29, 2014.

42. Carol Leigh, "What Is Wrong with the Case Act (Preliminary Analysis by Cynthia Chandler)," *Facebook*, July 11, 2012, https://www.facebook.com/notes/carol-leigh/what-is-wrong-with-the-case-act/406785242697518.

43. Kathleen Kim, Kevin Kish, and Cindy Liou, "Don't Undermine Victims' Rights in Fighting Sex Trafficking," *Pacific Standard*, October 18, 2012, http://www.psmag.com/legal-affairs/prop-35-case-act-undermines-victims-rights-48314/, accessed October 2, 2014.

44. Sec. 8 of Proposition 35 added Sec. 236.4 to the penal code to create a mechanism so that "every fine imposed and collected pursuant to Section 236.1 and this section shall be deposited in the Victim-Witness Assistance Fund, to be administered by the California Emergency Management Agency (Cal EMA), to fund grants for services for victims of human trafficking." "Proposition 35," *No! on 35*, http://againstthecaseact.com/CASEAct_InitiativeText.pdf, accessed October 2, 2014.

45. Carol Leigh, "What Is Wrong with the Case Act (Preliminary Analysis by Cynthia Chandler)," *Facebook*, July 11, 2012, https://www.facebook.com/notes/carol-leigh/what-is-wrong-with-the-case-act/406785242697518.

46. California Coalition for Women Prisoners, "Proposition 35."

47. Kim, Kish, and Liou, "Don't Undermine Victims' Rights."

48. Melissa Gira Grant, "California's Prop 35: A Misguided Ballot Initiative Targeting the Wrong People for the Wrong Reasons," *RH Reality Check*, November 1, 2012, http://rhrealitycheck.org/article/2012/11/01/prop-35/; *Wikipedia*, s.v. "Sex Offender Registry," https://en.wikipedia.org/wiki/Sex_offender_registry, accessed October 2, 2014; Shouse California Law Group, "How Sex Offender Registration Works in California," *Shouse California Law Group Blog*, http://www.shouselaw.com/registration.html, accessed October 2, 2014.

49. Best Practices Policy Project, Desiree Alliance, and SWOP-NYC, *Human Rights Violations of Sex Workers, People in the Sex Trades, and People Profiled as Such* (Submission to the United Nations Universal Periodic Review of the United States of America), September 15, 2014, http://www.bestpracticespolicy.org/wp-content/uploads/2013/01/2014UPRReportBPPPDASWOPNYC1.pdf.

50. Best Practices Policy Project et al., *Human Rights Violations of Sex Workers*.

51. Title 9 of Crimes against the Person Involving Sexual Assault, and Crimes against Public Decency and Good Morals [261–368.5], *California Legislative Informa-*

tion, http://leginfo.legislature.ca.gov/faces/codes_displaySection.xhtml?lawCode =PEN&sectionNum=290, accessed October 2, 2014.

52. Gira Grant, "California's Prop 35: A Misguided Ballot Initiative."

53. US PROStitutes Collective, "Briefing against the CASE Act/Proposition 35."

54. US PROStitutes Collective, "Briefing against the CASE Act/Proposition 35."

55. Elizabeth Bernstein, "Sex, Trafficking, and the Politics of Freedom" (unpublished manuscript, 2012), 2, https://www.sss.ias.edu/files/papers/paper45.pdf, accessed September 29, 2014.

56. Kim, "Anti-Sex-Trafficking Proposition 35 Is Surprisingly Controversial."

57. Perla Flores, Lynette Parker, and John Vanek, "Prop 35: More Harm than Good for Victims of Human Trafficking," *San Jose Mercury News*, September 28, 2012, http://www.mercurynews.com/opinion/ci_21655248/perla-flores-lynette-parker -and-john-vanek-prop.

58. Flores et al., "Prop 35."

59. Vote No on Prop 35, "Organizations and Media Endorsements in Opposition to Prop 35," *No! on 35*, http://www.againstthecaseact.com/opposingprop35.html, accessed September 29, 2014.

60. Koyama, "Anti-Criminalization."

61. Koyama, "Anti-Criminalization."

62. Bernstein, "Sex, Trafficking, and the Politics of Freedom," 9.

63. Melissa Gira Grant reported that Phung's previous efforts on her own to introduce legislation on trafficking to the California state legislature had been rejected. It was not until she connected with Chris Kelly and his financing that she found a way to mount a bid to have an initiative on trafficking placed on the ballot. Gira Grant, "California's Prop 35: A Misguided Ballot Initiative."

64. Janis Brett Elspas, "Election 2012: Jada Pinkett Smith Says Vote Yes on Prop 35 Stop Human Trafficking in California," *Mommy Blog Expert*, November 5, 2012, http:// www.mommyblogexpert.com/2012/11/election-2012-jada-pinkett-smith-says.html.

65. Gira Grant, "The Price of a Sex-Slave Rescue Fantasy"; reportage about Somaly Mam's fabrications and resignation emerged in early 2014. Gerry Mullany, "Activist Resigns Amid Charges of Fabrication," *New York Times*, May 29, 2014, http://www .nytimes.com/2014/05/30/world/asia/anti-trafficking-activist-quits-amid-charges -stories-were-fabricated.html?mabReward=RI%3A9&action=click&contentCollection =Opinion&region=Footer&module=Recommendation&src=recg&pgtype=article, accessed October 2, 2014.

66. *Ballotpedia*, "California Proposition 35."

67. Robyn Hagan Cain, "ACLU, EFF Sue to Block Prop 35," *Findlaw*, November 12, 2012, http://blogs.findlaw.com/california_case_law/2012/11/aclu-eff-sue-to-block -prop-35.html.

PART IV

Making
HIV
a Crime

| 12 |

HIV: Prosecution or Prevention?

HIV Is Not a Crime

Iowan Nick Rhoades is HIV-positive and has had an undetectable viral load for many years, making it virtually impossible for him to sexually transmit the virus. When he had sex with a man he met online in 2008, he also used a condom. Despite these protective measures, Rhoades was prosecuted and convicted for not disclosing his HIV status to his partner before they had sex. He was sentenced to twenty-five years in prison and lifetime sex offender registration.[1] Willy Campbell is serving thirty-five years in Texas for spitting at a police officer; David Plunkett served over six years in a New York state prison before an appeals court ruled that saliva could not be considered a "deadly weapon" in New York State.[2] Monique Howell Moree was charged by the U.S. Army for failing to disclosure her HIV-positive status to a partner in South Carolina before having sex with him, even though the partner said he didn't want her charged and that she told him to use a condom.[3] Kerry Thomas is serving thirty years in Idaho, even though his accuser agrees that he always used a condom.[4]

All over the United States — and in much of the world — people living with HIV/AIDS (PLHIV) are facing criminal penalties for nondisclosure of their HIV status prior to having sex or for perceived or possible exposure to, or transmission of, HIV. About two-thirds of U.S. states have HIV-specific criminal statutes, laws that *only* apply to PLHIV.[5] Most people believe the law should apply equally to all and that creating different statutes for different parts of society based on immutable characteristics — whether it is gender, sexual orientation, race, physical ability, or genetic makeup — is a bad idea. Yet here we are doing exactly that, creating a viral underclass in the law with one group singled out for different treatment.

Sero Project, a network of PLHIV combating HIV criminalization, has documented more than 1,300 instances of charges filed under HIV-specific statutes.[6] But HIV criminalization isn't constrained by geography; in every state, regardless of whether there is an HIV-specific statute, PLHIV can and often do face more serious charges or harsher sentencing under regular criminal statutes than do HIV-negative individuals accused of the same crimes. Texas and New York do not have HIV-specific statutes, but as mentioned, have incarcerated PLHIV because they considered their saliva dangerous.

These statutes and prosecutions create an illusion of safety for those who do not have HIV or do not know their HIV status, putting the entire burden of HIV prevention on those who have been tested and know they have HIV. The statutes undercut the fundamental public health message that HIV prevention is a shared responsibility and that everyone should act in such a way as to maintain their own health and protect themselves from contracting HIV or other sexually transmitted infections.

Decades-long sentencing and required sex offender registration are not unusual punishments for HIV-related crimes in the United States, even though actual HIV transmission is seldom (less than 5 percent of cases) a factor in these prosecutions.[7] Many cases boil down to whether the PLHIV can prove they disclosed their status to their partners in advance of intimate physical contact; it doesn't matter whether there was even a risk of HIV transmission. People living with HIV charged under prostitution or assault statutes frequently face significantly more severe penalties solely because they have HIV. They sometimes face charges for spitting, scratching, or biting that are "pile-on" charges, driven by accusations made by law enforcement, first responders, or prison guards.

The first HIV criminalization laws in the United States were passed in the late 1980s and early '90s, largely in response to a provision of the Ryan White Care Act that required states, in order to qualify for funding, to demonstrate an ability to prosecute what was then labeled "intentional transmission."[8] At the time many considered *any* intimate contact with an HIV-positive person a life-threatening risk; contracting HIV was believed by many to be tantamount to a death sentence.

A second wave of statutes was enacted after the introduction of combination therapy in the mid-1990s, which fundamentally changed what an HIV-positive diagnosis meant.[9] What was once thought a death sentence had become a chronic but manageable long-term health condition.[10]

As it became understood that PLHIV were surviving much longer, the public's perception of PLHIV also changed. Rather than objects of pity facing a "death sentence," PLHIV became seen as viral vectors, potential infectors — an inherent threat to society. Living longer meant PLHIV would be around longer to infect others.

The criminal justice and public health systems began to define and treat PLHIV as a dangerous population, one that needed to be sought out, tracked down, tested, reported, listed, tagged, monitored, regulated, and, increasingly, criminalized.

While the statutes were used in the early years disproportionately often against heterosexual African American men (often in conjunction with other criminal charges), today they are used more broadly, typically in circumstances where there was no intent to harm, often when there was no other crime involved, and frequently for behaviors that pose no or little risk of HIV transmission.

Beyond the blatant injustice, HIV criminalization is also horrible public health policy, because it discourages people at risk from getting tested for HIV and makes those who do test positive less trustful of public health authorities.

To be liable for prosecution, one must get tested for HIV and know one's HIV status. Current HIV criminalization punishes this responsible behavior — getting tested — and privileges the ignorance of not knowing one's HIV status. Yet new cases of HIV are transmitted in disproportionate numbers by those who have not been tested and do not know they have it; those who do get tested and know they have HIV are far less likely to transmit HIV than those with HIV who do not know it.

Although the HIV-specific statutes were passed by state legislatures with the intent to reduce HIV transmission, the evidence increasingly shows that the statutes may be having the reverse effect.

The Sero Project's 2012 survey of more than 2,000 PLHIV in the United States revealed that at least 25 percent of the respondents knew one or more individuals who were afraid to get tested for fear of facing criminalization.[11] Research has shown that HIV criminalization makes those who do test positive for HIV less likely to cooperate with traditional disease prevention measures, like partner notification programs, or with treatment adherence programs. Most recently, a study found that HIV-negative gay men who knew they lived in a state with an HIV criminalization statute were more likely to engage in unprotected intercourse.[12]

Repeal of HIV criminalization statutes is necessary both to protect the rights of people with HIV and to reduce the transmission of HIV.

An individual who demonstrates a premeditated malicious intent to harm another person can be prosecuted under existing assault statutes, whether they use a gun, a baseball bat, their fists, or a virus. The HIV-specific statutes are unnecessary and, worse yet, they stigmatize people with HIV/AIDS, discourage people at risk from accessing testing and treatment services, and feed a public bloodlust for punishment. In short, they are worsening the epidemic.

The prevention of HIV — or preventing any sexually transmitted infection — is a shared responsibility, but that does not mean there is not harm inflicted when someone misleads another person and transmits an infectious disease. In those circumstances, the injured party may seek recourse in the civil courts or possibly through a restorative justice process.

In any case, incarceration of PLHIV does not necessarily prevent further HIV transmission, as there is significant HIV transmission within penal environments, where condoms are seldom available.[13]

Advocacy to repeal HIV-specific statutes, modernize public health statutes concerning perceived or possible exposure to, or transmission of, HIV and other infectious diseases, and educate law enforcement, prosecutors, and other actors in the criminal justice system has been under way for several years.

A network of survivors of HIV criminalization prosecutions, launched in 2010, has helped to educate and mobilize affected communities. This HIV criminalization reform advocacy has received support from public health professionals and policy leaders, including the Presidential Advisory Council on HIV/AIDS, the National Alliance of State and Territorial AIDS Directors, UN-AIDS, and the American Medical Association. The first national conference on HIV criminalization in the United States was held in June 2014 at Grinnell College in Grinnell, Iowa. Organized primarily by PLHIV — including participation by a dozen PLHIV who had been prosecuted for "HIV crimes" — the conference included participants from twenty-eight states. It focused on how HIV criminalization affects communities of color, transgender women, sex workers, and gay men. It also showed the impact of HIV criminalization on how members of those communities (and others) access HIV prevention, testing, and treatment and whether they decide to disclose their HIV status. Finally, the conference highlighted effective strategies for reform.

The only state, so far, to modernize their statute substantively in recent years has been Iowa, where the conference was held. After a four-year education and lobbying effort led by Nick Rhoades and other PLHIV in the state, the Iowa legislature repealed its HIV-specific statute in 2014. The legislature replaced it with a new statute that addressed several infectious diseases, required a higher standard of intent to harm, and established tiered punishments.[14] Similar efforts are under way in about a dozen states. A few weeks later, the Iowa Supreme Court overturned Rhoades's conviction and removed the sex offender registration requirement for all others previously convicted under the Iowa statute.

HIV criminalization is an extreme manifestation of stigma. That is particularly true of HIV-specific statutes that create a viral underclass in the law, establishing a different criminal law for one segment of society based on an immutable characteristic. Despite the biomedical advances in the treatment of HIV, HIV-related stigma remains stubborn, driven in significant part by HIV criminalization.

It is time we learned a basic lesson: HIV can be prevented or it can be prosecuted, but not both.

NOTES

1. "SERO Stories: Nick Rhoades," Sero, http://seroproject.com/video/nick-rhoades /#tabs1, accessed September 28, 2016.

2. On Campbell, see G. C. Kovach, "Prison for Man with HIV who spit on a Police Officer," *New York Times*, May 16, 2008, http://www.nytimes.com/2008/05/16/us /16spit.html?_r=0. On Plunkett, see R. Vreeland, "Full-Court Press on HIV Criminal Laws," POZ, July 20, 2012, https://www.poz.com/article/Schoettes-HIV-Plunkett -22698–2663.

3. "SERO Stories: Monique Moree," Sero, http://seroproject.com/video/monique -moree/#tabs1, accessed September 28, 2016.

4. "SERO Stories: Kerry Thomas," Sero, http://seroproject.com/video/kerry -thomas/#tabs1, accessed September 28, 2016.

5. J. Stan Lehman et al., "Prevalence and Public Health Implications of State Laws That Criminalize Potential HIV Exposure in the United States," AIDS Behavior 18, no. 6 (2014): 997–1006.

6. See Sero, "Protection Center," http://seroproject.com/protection-center/, accessed September 28, 2016.

7. Lehman et al., "Prevalence and Public Health Implications."

8. Ryan White Comprehensive AIDS Resources Emergency Act of 1990, P.L. 101–381, https://history.nih.gov/research/downloads/PL101–381.pdf.

9. S. G. Lee, "Criminal Law and HIV Testing: Empirical Analysis of How At-Risk Individuals Respond to the Law," *Yale Journal of Health Policy, Law, and Ethics* 14, no. 1 (2015): 194–238.

10. Michael Shernoff and Raymond A. Smith, "HIV Treatments: A History of Scientific Advance," The Body, July 2001, http://www.thebody.com/content/art30909 .html.

11. Sero Project, National Criminalization Survey Preliminary Results, July 25, 2012, http://seroproject.com/wp-content/uploads/2012/07/Sero-Preliminary-Data -Report_Final.pdf.

12. Keith J. Horvath, Craig Meyer, and B. R. Simon Rosser, "Men Who Have Sex with Men Who Believe that Their State Has a HIV Criminal Law Report Higher Condomless Anal Sex than Those Who Are Unsure of the Law in Their State," *AIDS and Behavior* (2016). doi:10.1007/s10461–016–1286–0

13. Ralf Jürgens, Manfred Nowak, and Marcus Day, "HIV and Incarceration: Prisons and Detention," *Journal of the International AIDS Society* (2011). doi: 10.1186/ 1758–2652–14–26

14. Miranda Leitsinger, "Iowa Scraps Harsh HIV Criminalization Law in Historic Vote," NBC News, May 1, 2014, http://www.nbcnews.com/news/us-news/iowa -scraps-harsh-hiv-criminalization-law-historic-vote-n94946.

| 13 |

HIV Monsters

Gay Men, Criminal Law, and the New Political Economy of HIV

In a routine analysis of HIV statistics for 2006, public health officials in the Netherlands noticed a significant increase in new HIV infections in the northern city of Groningen, which has a population of 185,000. While fourteen new infections were reported in 2005, twenty-five new infections were reported in 2006. Alarmed by what the numbers showed, local and national officials began an investigation to determine the cause of the new infections. Their inquiries turned up anecdotal reports that some gay men in Groningen had acquired HIV after being assaulted by sexual partners they had met at local bars or over the Internet. In January 2007, after a number of men came forward with similar stories, health officials persuaded one of the alleged victims to file a formal complaint with the local police, opening the door for a criminal investigation.[1]

Approximately four months later, on May 13, 2007, Groningen police arrested four HIV-positive men on charges of rape, premeditated severe assault, and possession of ecstasy and the "date rape" drug GHB. The police announced in a press conference two weeks later that three of those arrested had invited men to "sex parties," where the victims were drugged, raped (without the use of condoms), and injected with a mixture of HIV-infected blood drawn from the bodies of the accused. The arrested men had, according to the police, confessed to these behaviors, stating that their motive was the "kick" and "excitement" of the acts themselves. Though the story would later change, one of the men, at the time of his arrest, allegedly claimed that "our mission is to promote unprotected sex as it is the purest form of relationship. This hangup about condoms could be destroyed only when the virus is rampant and everyone reconciles himself to that."[2] The chief of police said the men believed that "the more HIV-infected people there were, the better their chances of unprotected sex."[3] A total of fourteen men ultimately identified themselves as victims. Over a year later, in November 2008, three men would ultimately stand trial and be found guilty of rape and of attempting to commit grievous bodily harm to others by injecting them with HIV-infected blood.

News of the arrests traveled quickly across the Netherlands and around the globe. Newspapers sported predictably sensational headlines: "Three Men Confess to HIV Injection Orgies"; "Gay Orgy Gang's HIV Rapes Stun Holland"; "Gay Gang Spread HIV at Sex Orgy"; and "Dutch Police Arrest 4 Men in Bizarre Sex-Crime Investigation."[4] Capitalizing on a public perception of gay culture as hypersexual, some journalists in the Dutch press used the incongruous term *seksfeesten* or "sex parties" to describe the incidents, while others painted a hyperbolic picture of a "gay gang" menacing the streets of Groningen.[5] Yet the most striking epithet used to describe the men was also the most simple. In the eyes of many, they became known simply as "HIV Monsters."[6] As such, the Groningen perpetrators quickly took their place in a pantheon of HIV "fiends" and "monsters" whose stories have, for two decades now, provided fodder for the popular press and fueled readers' appetites for stories of HIV-infected individuals who knowingly expose their sexual partners to the virus by failing to disclose their HIV status and sometimes forgoing the use of condoms. From the infamous case of Nushawn Williams in New York in 1997 to the highly publicized case of German pop singer Nadja Benaissa in 2010, sensational stories of deliberate HIV exposure continue to appear around the globe. The particular circumstances of the Groningen case made it especially easy for journalists, bloggers, and other commentators to demonize the perpetrators. Their case was far from a one-night stand gone wrong: their actions were premeditated, and the alleged infections were systematic, widespread, and achieved through extraordinarily violent means.

The events in Groningen are especially important, I think, to the sociopolitical history of HIV because they highlight HIV's political instrumentality, its use as a political weapon. By drugging, raping, and injecting their victims with HIV-infected blood, the Groningen perpetrators engaged in something more than a sexual act. They were seeking a social and political good — the "purest form of relationship" — exceeding whatever erotic "kick" they derived from their actions. If one takes the claims of the perpetrators at face value, it seems the primary purpose of using HIV as a weapon is not to punish or to harm but to liberate. The goal is to purify, to remedy, and to make sex whole again.

There is something particularly disturbing in the fact that an act so horrible as deliberately injecting another person with HIV-infected blood could appear to be a vehicle for liberation. Thus, HIV's place in a complex technological lineup is what captures my interest and signals the need for a deeper analysis of the virus's instrumentalization in the political sphere.

To understand HIV's incorporation into a symbolic field of political meaning, we must look beyond the personal motivations of the individual Groningen perpetrators to consider the broader historical and discursive frameworks that help animate HIV and transform it into a political tool. My argument, simply put, is that the significance of the events in Groningen stems not from the violence of the acts themselves but from the larger contexts of health policy, state security, and criminal law that have fundamentally changed the symbolic meanings of HIV over the past twenty years. To understand the events in Groningen, we must consider the actions of the perpetrators as well as the work of judges, lawyers, policy experts, state bureaucrats, police, public health officials, scientists, legislatures, politicians, nongovernmental organizations, and non-state actors whose actions pull HIV into the sphere of political life. It is not uncommon today to hear HIV/AIDS described as a threat to personal health, public health, state security, and global security, all at the same time. Collectively, these developments constitute what I call the new political economy of HIV.[7]

The term "political economy" helps to specify how HIV functions as more than a political symbol; the virus also serves as a vector for the exercise of state power and the invention of novel logics and techniques of government. These include the passage and enforcement of new laws criminalizing HIV transmission, mandating new partnerships between public health services and the police, establishing domestic and international policy goals, formally recognizing HIV/AIDS as a threat to international security, and new collaborations between government and NGOs to address the changing realities of the epidemic. Through public health laws, policy initiatives, domestic and international relief efforts, research sponsorship, medical services, drug regulations, the courts, and in many other ways, the state is heavily involved in the management of HIV. Infection with HIV virtually guarantees that a citizen will need to interact, either beneficently or coercively, with one or more state bureaucracies. If we wish to understand HIV's contemporary symbolic and political life, we must turn our attention to how governments have responded to HIV/AIDS in recent years and how they have invented new logics, laws, rationales, and techniques for managing the epidemic. In particular,

HIV criminalization — the emergence of HIV-specific statutes, case law, legal briefs, court opinions, and policy statements that make HIV transmission, exposure, or nondisclosure a crime — constitutes one of the most significant ways in which HIV has been integrated into state bureaucracies. I examine here a number of key events in HIV criminalization over a period of roughly fifteen years — from 1996, when antiretroviral drugs first became widely available, through 2011, when anti-criminalization advocates began to gain some ground. We see in this time the formation, in the Netherlands and in other Western countries, of a discursive "breach" or opening that facilitated HIV's uptake into the larger domain of political economy.

The Groningen case is certainly not the first case of criminal HIV transmission to make international headlines. A full decade prior to Groningen, the international media made a spectacle of Nushawn Williams, an HIV-positive African American man in Chautauqua County, New York. Initially arrested for drug possession, Williams later pled guilty to charges of statutory rape and reckless endangerment for having unprotected sex while knowing he was HIV-positive.[8] Recent data on worldwide prosecutions are still spotty, but the most reliable estimates indicate that hundreds of new convictions for criminal HIV transmission, exposure, and nondisclosure have been handed down since the Williams case first made headlines. Approximately sixty countries have won convictions, while at least that many countries have passed or are considering laws that specifically designate HIV transmission or exposure a criminal act. A report issued by the Global Network of People Living with HIV (GNP+) in July 2010 notes that "the number of people prosecuted and convicted [of criminal HIV transmission or exposure] is growing" and that countries are seeking convictions either through the use of existing laws related to assault or through new laws specifically focusing on HIV. In general, industrialized, developed countries with strong legal systems and well-established epidemics were the first to prosecute HIV-infected people under the criminal law. Northern Europe, the United States, Canada, Australia, and New Zealand are spearheading the global movement toward criminalization, though all regions of the globe are quickly following suit. In the past ten years alone, twenty-seven African countries have adopted HIV-specific criminal statutes. The United States currently leads other nations in the total number of convictions for HIV transmission or exposure, totaling over three hundred convictions to date.[9]

While efforts to criminalize HIV transmission ostensibly aim to reduce new infections, the GNP+ and others insist that "there is no evidence to show that laws that explicitly regulate the sexual conduct of people living with HIV significantly impact sexual conduct or moderate risk behaviors."[10] More specifically, laws do not seem "to impact disclosure" of HIV status nor, it appears, do they reduce the sexual transmission of HIV. In fact, advocates argue that criminalizing HIV transmission drives people into hiding by increasing stigma and fear of prosecution: this, in turn, drives people away from testing and treatment programs that have been scientifically proven to slow the spread of the epidemic.[11]

At their most extreme, criminal laws can be used to prosecute individuals for spreading HIV even when they are unaware of their HIV status, when their behaviors pose little or no risk of transmission, or when they have protected sex. In France, a man was convicted in early 2012 of infecting two other men with HIV in separate episodes in 2003 and 2005, even though the accused man did not have an HIV test until the court imposed one in 2007.[12] In the United States, at least twelve states have convicted individuals with HIV for spitting or biting, neither of which poses a risk of transmission. Additionally, laws in some U.S. states, such as Michigan and Arkansas, criminalize protected sex by HIV-positive people who do not disclose their status to their partners before engaging in a wide variety of behaviors defined as "sexual penetration." In Michigan, that wording was interpreted by a trial court as including the insertion of an uninfected man's nose into an infected woman's vagina.[13] Such laws defy the science of HIV prevention and undermine traditional safer-sex efforts by intimating that condom usage alone is not adequate protection against the risk of HIV infection. These examples suggest not only how state management of HIV has grown to include an expansive juridical apparatus but also how people living with HIV today must deal with an additional level of stress and uncertainty beyond the already significant medical and personal burdens that stem from infection.

In the Netherlands, prosecutions for criminal HIV transmission began in earnest in 2001. The five-year period between 2001 and 2005 saw as many as twelve HIV-related convictions.[14] This spike in prosecutions led to the formation of an advisory committee on AIDS Policy and Criminal Law. At the time the committee was formed, there was a rift in the Netherlands' governmental response to management of the HIV epidemic. While the police and the courts were forcefully ramping up their criminalization proceedings, many public health officials, policymakers, and community leaders in the field of HIV/AIDS prevention were shocked and appalled by what was happening. It seemed as if the police and the courts had taken on an authority that was not accorded to them under the law, particularly to the extent that they were sending HIV-positive people to jail for exposing others to HIV. The recent convictions were especially alarming because, as the committee noted in 2004, "in none of these cases was the virus actually transferred to the sexual partner in question."[15]

In the now infamous "Leeuwarden Case," police arrested a fifty-year-old, HIV-positive gay man in 2001 for having sex with two teenage male prostitutes, ages thirteen and sixteen. He did not disclose his HIV-positive status to the prostitutes, nor did he insist that they use condoms for oral or anal sex when they penetrated him. He was initially convicted of rape and attempted murder, though the Supreme Court ultimately — after more than five years of appeals — upheld only the rape conviction. In the initial court case, the counsel for the defense argued unsuccessfully that there was no proof of "conditional intent" to harm another person, since the specific sexual acts the man had committed — oral sex and receptive anal sex — did not pose a "significant risk" of transmitting the virus (and in fact the prostitutes were not infected). Despite expert testimony for the defense that the chances of acquiring HIV through condomless sex were, statistically speaking, small, the Court of First Instance in Leeuwarden ruled that "the term 'significant risk' is not an objective, absolute, determined by" statistics term, but "a legal-normative concept that is determined by the degree of social acceptability of the occurrence of certain consequences by performing certain actions." By failing to disclose his status, the court concluded, the defendant "necessarily consciously accepts the significant risk to the death of his victims."[16] In short, precedent set by this case opened an extended window — between the defendant's initial trial in 2001 and the final Supreme Court ruling in 2005 — that emboldened Dutch prosecutors to view any instance of condomless sex by an HIV-positive person as an act of premeditated attempted murder.

It is no coincidence that the majority of sexual assaults and HIV injections in the Groningen case occurred in 2005, at the very height of the HIV criminalization panic in the Netherlands. These highly publicized criminal proceedings created a hostile social climate for gay men living with HIV, including the Groningen perpetrators, in the years and months preceding the crimes. The frenzy surrounding criminal HIV transmission added another current of moral condemnation to the national wave of conservative backlash against Holland's liberal sexual culture that was taking place in the same period, which also saw rancorous public debate about legalized prostitution. The Leeuwarden judges' rejection of the expert scientific testimony brought by the defense helped intensify an already reactionary social climate by explicitly invoking norms of "social acceptability" over and against a well-established body of factual evidence about the probabilities of HIV transmission. Even if the actual statistical risk of HIV transmission is small or miniscule during acts of oral and receptive anal intercourse, especially when the HIV-positive person's viral load is low as a result of antiretroviral treatment, such "objective" truths have little standing, apparently, in the light of the "legal normative" definition of risk spontaneously offered by the court, in which the entirely "unacceptable" notion that someone infected with the virus might ever have unprotected sex eliminates any statistical distinctions and makes all forms of risk the same. In making this argument, the court quite ironically drew on normative or relative standards to create precisely what it was trying to avoid, an "objective, absolute" notion of risk. Circular logic such as this helped to create a social climate in which anyone who was sexually active and infected with HIV was already, in effect, a potential murderer.

People living with HIV/AIDS have always been stigmatized, but earlier forms of stigma were based explicitly on such identity markers as sexual orientation, gender, race, sexual history, and nationality. In the era of criminalization, these older forms have been augmented by a new kind of stigma that equates HIV infection with sexual irresponsibility and antisocial intentions. This stigma draws its power from a public morality that devalues those who are not seen as team players and whose actions can be regarded as selfish or willfully malicious. One sees this moral sensibility clearly in the Leeuwarden decision, when the judges note that the "[s]uspect sorely failed in his duty of care to prevent the spread of HIV and thus risked the lives of others" and "is therefore eligible for a prison sentence of considerable length."[17] The term "considerable" here is illuminating to the extent that it registers the crime's excessive nature, which makes it especially antisocial and extensively punishable.

We find similarly questionable moral reasoning in the Groningen case, where the judges make an explicit distinction between responsible and irresponsible forms of sexual citizenship. In deciding how many years the principal defendants would serve in prison, the court took into consideration the fact that the crimes committed "caused great public unrest . . . [e]specially in the gay community" and that coverage of the case had "damaged public opinion of homosexuals."[18] The court here draws a distinction between the perpetrators on the one hand and a nominal "gay community" on the other. The court even speaks on behalf of the "gay community," whose political aims and sexual interests are clearly separate from those of the men in Groningen and, presumably, better aligned with the legal and political interests of the state. In effect, the judges imposed on the perpetrators not only physical separation from mainstream society by placing them in jail but symbolic separation as well. In aligning its interests with those of the "gay community," the judges effectively excommunicated the perpetrators from socially respectable gay life, or what cultural theorist Jasbir Puar would call "homonational citizenship."[19]

Legal scholar Matthew Weait, in his book *Intimacy and Responsibility*, was the first to offer a theoretical framework for understanding how changing notions of responsibility have helped drive forward efforts to criminalize HIV transmission. Weait builds on the work of Anthony Giddens and Ulrich Beck, who argue that modern Western societies have embraced a paradigm of risk management as a method of conducting the governance of states and of everyday life. Whereas risk, in premodern times, might encompass events like natural disasters or, as it was thought, acts of divine retribution, today we live in a world in which risk is manufactured and made quantifiable by new technologies and new forms of expert knowledge. Risk now inheres in everything we do, from eating, investing, and driving a car to simply breathing. Risk is, simply put, ideological. It is "a discourse that is deployed for the legitimization of socio-economic policies and that pretends to certainty when such certainty does not, and cannot exist."[20] Health, in particular, is one of "the extravagant promises of modernity" that risk society frequently touts but ultimately fails to deliver, especially when a virus like HIV threatens the health of individuals as well as entire nations.

For Weait, people with HIV pose a particular threat to modern, Western societies in which the management of risk and health are paramount. "HIV positive people represent the paradigm Other of risk society," he argues, "and recklessness [represents] the paradigm fault. Those who are reckless with respect to HIV transmission are those who represent one of the most significant threats to our physical and ontological security."[21] One result of this way of thinking is that the "general population" becomes increasingly detached from the epidemic and feels *less* responsible for its progress; at the same time, those infected with the virus become, symbolically and materially, *more* responsible. There is a growing sense today that the state should exercise its authority to identify, monitor, and, when necessary, punish those who place others at risk of infection.

FIGURE 13.1. Courtroom sketch of defendant Michael Neal in Victorian County, Australia. Credit: Mick Connolly, *The Age*.

FIGURE 13.2. Courtroom sketch of defendant Andre Parenzee in South Australia. Credit: Tim Ide, Australian Broadcasting Corporation.

We are afraid of sexually active people with HIV because, in choosing to have sexual contact with others, they seem to abdicate their moral commitment to society and free themselves from care about the safety and health of their fellow citizens. They are selfish, reckless, and blinded by their own desires for sex, no matter the costs. It is not their being (as, say, homosexual) that is offensive but their intentions; their true disease is not of the body but of the will, in that they clearly intend to harm others in order to obtain pleasure for themselves. This invisible commonality connects the myriad faces of the "HIV monsters" we see prominently featured on the Internet and on television. This very invisibility accounts, perhaps, for the prominence of HIV monsters in our visual field, the startling proliferation of sketches, mug shots, and "most wanted" posters that accompany the sensational news stories (see figures 13.1–13.4).

Viewing these faces of HIV criminals over and over and over again becomes a sort of repetition compulsion, as if we might finally catch a glimpse of what lies beneath the skin and begin to read the true monstrosity — the antisocial intention — that remains terrifyingly illegible on the surface. Despite seeming to effect an uncanny return to the "Faces of AIDS" exhibits that have been used for decades to garner sympathy and support for people living with

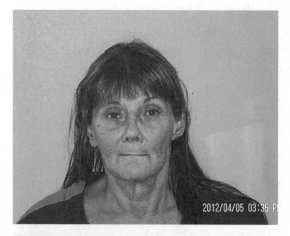

FIGURE 13.3. Police mug shot of defendant Valerie Lynn Johnson in Isabella County, Michigan. Credit: Isabella County Sheriff's Department.

FIGURE 13.4. Courtroom sketch of defendant Johnson Aziga in Hamilton County, Canada. Credit: Marianne Boucher, Citytv.

HIV/AIDS, these mug shots and sketches eschew the sympathetic appeals of earlier AIDS portraiture. They are a new genre of HIV/AIDS image that repeatedly entices viewers to see the true (inner) face of the HIV criminal, intensifying both the necessity and the impossibility of recognizing the HIV monster within. Unlike more sympathetic genres of HIV/AIDS portraiture, these images do not convey the message that those living with HIV are "just like us." Instead, they seem to evince the anger, panic, and mania that supposedly drive HIV criminals to inflict their illness on others. While their intentions, like HIV itself, remain invisible, these images compensate for that loss by making their subjects hypervisible.

A team of Canadian researchers led by Barry Adam observed changes in notions of personal responsibility in the wake of the infamous *Cuerrier* decision, in which the Canadian Supreme Court upheld the conviction of an HIV-positive man for aggravated assault for failing to disclose his HIV status to a sexual partner. The court's decision, according to Adam et al., "implicitly endors[es] a model of human behavior that holds that HIV-positive people can and should assume the responsibility of warning others of the potential for infection, and that prospective partners, once informed of that potential, will act appropriately to avoid infection."[22] This model "relies on a set of presumptions concerning individual responsibility [and] rational and contractual interaction" that are "consistent with dominant constructions of Western individualism" and, in particular, with "the paradigmatic subject of contemporary neo-liberalism" who conducts his or her affairs in an "actuarial" fashion.[23] One problem with such thinking is that few people, particularly where sex is concerned, actually behave this way; another is that the court in this instance effectively makes HIV disclosure, not condom usage or other safe-sex practices, the primary mode of HIV prevention. Whereas safe-sex campaigns rely on the assumption of mutual responsibility for HIV prevention, HIV criminalization laws and decisions like *Cuerrier* emphasize only the individual responsibility of the HIV-infected person.

Similar shifts were occurring in the Netherlands in the years immediately preceding the incidents in Groningen. The Executive Committee on AIDS Policy and Criminal Law reported in 2004 that "there is every chance that people without HIV will wrongly expect people living with HIV always to take their own responsibility for preventing infection."[24] The committee worried that safer sex would become "an individual rather than a joint responsibility, thus raising the risk of new infections," and noted that the "desire to exclude risks" on the part of the uninfected "is consistent with recent Western thinking on individual responsibility, liability and criminal law. Recent years have also seen (renewed) interest in ethical standards (including the taking of a tougher line on socially undesirable behaviour)." Like Adam et al., the Dutch committee was expressing concern about the power of contemporary jurisprudence to construct idealized legal subjects who, when HIV-negative, bear no responsibility for HIV transmission and, when HIV-positive, bear 100 percent of the blame. These contrasting responsibilities are symptoms of a broader ideological transformation in Western societies away from notions of collective responsibility for preventing HIV infection and other harms and toward increasing — and one is tempted here also to say *pathological* — responsibilization of individuals.

In the most extreme cases, people convicted of exposing others to HIV must endure restrictions on their personal freedom identical to those placed on rapists, child molesters, and other sex offenders. In the United States, the South Dakota legislature passed a law in 2008 that defines "intentional exposure to HIV infection by sexual intercourse as a sex crime subject to registry as a sex offender."[25] The law applies even in cases where sex is consensual; it makes no mention of informed consent regarding the risk of HIV transmission, leaving open the possibility that the state could label someone a sex offender even if both partners fully understood and accepted such risk. Another particularly egregious example of harsh sentencing is the case of Nick Rhoades, discussed by David Halperin and Sean Strub in this volume.[26] In an interview with Strub, Rhoades described the overwhelming stigma he faced due to his conviction:

> The severity of that punishment tells you how bad you are as a person, you know? "You're a class B felon, lifetime sex offender. You are a very, very, very bad person and you did a very, very, very bad thing," and so that's just, you know, programmed into you and, you know, you just, you go through the correctional system and everyone's telling you the same thing and you're just like, "I'm a very bad person, very bad person."[27]

Laws that treat instances of HIV nondisclosure, exposure, or transmission as sex crimes cast people with HIV as violent criminals. They create, in the words of Nick Rhoades, "bad person[s]" by reorganizing our fundamental assumptions about what it means to harbor a virus within our bodies. Infection becomes, under these new laws, less an accident and more an intention, the expression of an inner, predatory desire to harm another person. The laws in Iowa, Nebraska, and others like them create states of exception in which, for the first time in history, the transmission of a microbe is punished as a sexual crime.

Yet people infected with HIV are not the only ones who are experiencing a change in public perception: the virus, too, is undergoing a similar shift. Unlike some, HIV has never been just another microbe, but today it is seen increasingly as a weapon wielded by those who have willfully chosen to disregard human life. For example, in March 2003 the Dutch Supreme Court overturned the Leeuwarden murder conviction in what appeared to be a major victory for the defense. However, the court explicitly called for a retrial of the case under Article 300, Section 2 of the Dutch Criminal Code, which allows courts to impose fines and custodial sentences for acts of "singular physical abuse" which lead to "grievous bodily harm."[28] In their demand for retrial, the court drew upon Article 82, Paragraph 1 of the criminal code, which expands the legal definition of "grievous bodily harm" to include "illness that does not offer any chance of complete healing and will cause continuous disability for working or ... continuous disability to hold official functions."[29] In addition to its standing charge that the defendant tried "intentionally to deprive [the victim] of life," the prosecution during retrial added the alternative charge of "intentionally inflicting grievous bodily harm on [the victim]."[30] A lower court found the defendant guilty of the lesser charge on June 30, 2003.

Lowering the sentence from murder to aggravated assault was a pyrrhic victory for those infected with HIV. While the seemingly automatic assumption that anyone with HIV who engaged in unprotected sex was a murderer had been challenged, a far more insidious, if ostensibly less alarming, discursive and conceptual shift was under way. Whereas murder convictions have the effect of creating a stigma around entire persons, imbuing them with a murderous subjectivity, assault charges create stigma around HIV itself by formally classifying the virus as an instrument of harm under the law. In vacating the murder conviction, the Supreme Court shifted the focus of Dutch law from the person to the virus, the deadly weapon with which the defendant was said to have committed "grievous bodily harm." The prosecution in retrial effectively convinced the appeals court that the defendant, solely by having unprotected sex, had in fact committed a premeditated act of assault, "willfully," "intentionally," and "knowingly" using HIV as an instrument of harm. The judges were so convinced of this argument that, in delivering their guilty verdict, they took the liberty to note that, "[f]rom a social point of view, the defendant's behavior [is] totally unacceptable." They thereby helped give birth to a new crime of viral assault.

The transformation of HIV into a deadly weapon has been taking place on a much broader scale in many countries in a number of different arenas, including the popular press, political discourse, and even scholarly debates about HIV criminalization.[31] Legislators have been particularly willing to support laws that classify HIV as a deadly weapon, often going to the extreme, as a recent example from the state of Nebraska makes clear. In June 2011, the Nebraska legislature passed statute 28-934, which states that "[a]ny person who knowingly and intentionally strikes any public safety officer with any bodily fluid is guilty of assault with a bodily fluid against a public safety officer."[32] The law makes this a felony offense if the perpetrator knows the fluid is infected with HIV or hepatitis. The particular language used in the statute, especially the verb "strikes," contributes to the sense that bodily fluids, and the viruses contained in them, can be used as instruments of violence. One year earlier, on the eve of Nushawn Williams's scheduled release from prison,

New York state senator Cathy Young proposed an HIV criminalization bill aimed at protecting citizens from "deadly predator[s]" like Williams, who, she declared, was still a danger to society because, while he was in prison, he "threw his urine at another inmate."[33] Here, Young employs the same logic as the Nebraska law, suggesting, contrary to scientific fact, that urine from a person with HIV could become a deadly weapon simply by being hurled and coming into contact with someone else. She made this position explicit in a press release in April 2010, stating, "People who knowingly use HIV/AIDS as a deadly weapon by purposely exposing others to the disease should be severely punished."[34]

Leading bioethicist Udo Schuklenk has defended efforts to criminalize HIV transmission, arguing that HIV transmission laws do not unnecessarily stigmatize those who are brought to trial for breaking them: "If we punish people for transmitting HIV to their partners, who had no reason to assume that they were consenting to that risk when they had unsafe sex, what we criminalize is what people do with the virus, not the virus itself or even the people who happen to be infected."[35] Schuklenk argues that criminalizing HIV transmission will not lead to witch hunts and that, in theory, we should be able to separate infection with the virus from specific criminal, instrumental acts involving HIV. Yet in making "what people do" with HIV the ethical and legal grounds for criminal prosecution, Schuklenk draws upon the same predicative logic that Senator Young and the Nebraska law do, albeit in a far less rabid and more thoughtful manner. As far as HIV transmission is concerned, what people *do*, generally speaking, is have sex or inject drugs; transmission occurs in the context of other actions that make it possible for the virus to travel from one person to another. Yet Schuklenk gives the impression that the virus itself is an object that is willfully manipulated, like a gun, a knife, or a hammer.

I want to make it clear that I am not accusing Schuklenk or the judges in either the Groningen or the Leeuwarden case of being reactionary, moral zealots; rather, they are trying to the best of their abilities to establish legal and moral grounds on which to punish individuals who had, particularly in the Groningen case, inflicted tangible harm on others. Yet in consolidating that new ground, the judges in both cases, like the judges in many HIV criminalization cases around the globe, were moving into moral, legal, and political territory that had not been thoroughly considered by other branches of government, particularly the legislature and the Dutch Ministry of Health, Welfare, and Sport. The Supreme Court of the Netherlands would eventually comment on this fact in 2005, when it finally overturned the most serious convictions in the Leeuwarden case, by concluding its decision with an admonition to the lower courts that such decisions were a "task for the legislator to evaluate."[36] Indeed, the Dutch courts, like those in Canada, the United States, and many other countries, have gotten caught up in frenzies of policymaking, often at a pace that outstrips that of legislators. As Adam et al. remarked in 2008, "public policy, as manifested in the courts' and prosecutors' interpretation of the criminal law, is being made largely in an evidentiary vacuum."[37] The problems had, as we've already seen, become quite apparent years earlier in the Netherlands. As early as 2003, the director general of health for the Netherlands sent a letter to the minister of justice affirming the nation's safer-sex policy and the principle on which "the whole prevention policy is based," namely that disclosure "by no means absolves sexual partners from their own responsibility for protecting themselves."[38] The very fact that one senior government official had to remind another that people need to "protect themselves" in an epidemic is remarkable; yet it seems clear that in the period between 2001 and 2005 notions of shared responsibility were quickly losing ground to a new culture of blame. The director general's letter serves as a striking historical marker of just how out of control the situation in the Dutch courts had become. It suggests, as well, that high-level Dutch officials in the Ministry of Health, Welfare, and Sport were not working in unison with the Ministry of Justice; in fact, the two ministries seemed to have competing agendas as far as management of the HIV epidemic was concerned.

To get a sense of just how polarized the situation had become, it is useful to compare what was happening in the courts with sweeping reforms in Dutch public health laws that were taking place between 1998 and 2008, when the criminal prosecution of HIV transmission was accelerating. In the summer of 1998, the Dutch Parliament passed the Infectious Diseases Act, an omnibus piece of legislation that revamped the country's entire approach to the management, reporting, and treatment of infectious disease. An official explanatory memorandum of the law prepared by parliament outlined the major reasons for reform, noting that "scientific understanding in the field of infectious disease control" had changed drastically over the course of the twentieth century and that changes in Dutch society and citizens' lifestyles had eliminated the need for monitoring some diseases while creating a need to keep tabs on others. The most important reason cited for reform, however, was that the older infectious disease laws were out of step with current thinking about human rights, notably because they encouraged liberal exercise of the state's police power to quarantine individuals suspected of carrying disease. The older laws, according to the official summary, "provide[d] insufficient safeguards against coercive measures of government. The emphasis . . . [was] on isolation, and not only of the (presumed) carrier of an infectious disease but also of people in his vicinity. In addition, the law provide[d] no form of judicial review nor adequate legal protection tailored to the situation."[39] Further stressing the value of human rights and the protection of individual interests, lawmakers also noted that "coercive measures" and "targeted measures against individuals" are, as a rule, unnecessary when combating infectious diseases and that they should only be used as a last resort. "The cornerstone of the fight against infectious diseases," the new law affirmed, "remains the voluntary cooperation of the population." These ideas drastically diverge from the logics of epidemic management that would dominate the Dutch legal system in the years immediately following the law's passage.

In short, Dutch public health and infectious disease laws were becoming more progressive at precisely the same time that Dutch jurisprudence was becoming more repressive. The fundamental difference in these approaches, as the authors of the Dutch Infectious Diseases Act seem to have presciently understood, was between a liberal view of the state in which individual rights must be protected except in the most extreme instances and a more totalitarian view in which state interests trump those of private citizens. Conceptually speaking, something like a great schism existed between the Ministry of Justice and the Ministry of Health, Welfare, and Sport, and it was precisely within the opaque space of this breach that the country's most notorious HIV monsters emerged: not, I would argue, as freaks of nature, but as symptoms of the crises in HIV governmentality transpiring in the domains of law, public health policy, and state bureaucracies.

In its health policy, then, the Netherlands had explicitly tried to restrict the police powers of the state when dealing with infectious diseases and to preserve human rights by respecting the freedom of individuals infected with HIV. Dutch lawmakers had, in this regard, managed to avoid in their infectious disease legislation a serious problem that beset lawmakers in Switzerland, where public health legislation that created criminal penalties for maliciously infecting others with biological agents became the basis for criminal prosecutions of HIV exposure and transmission. The Swiss Epidemics Acts created Article 231 of the Swiss Penal Code, under which "anyone who intentionally spreads a dangerous transmittable human disease" is subject to fines or imprisonment. In theory, Article 231 was meant to address instances of bioter-

rorism, but it has been used predominantly — and with devastating consequences — against people living with HIV. As many critics of the law have
noted, applying Article 231 in this manner unnecessarily and dangerously
duplicates the provisions of Swiss Penal Code Article 122, which sanctions
"anyone who causes intentionally . . . grievous injury to a human being's body
or his/her physical or mental health."[40] In March 2012, as the Swiss Federal
Assembly considered reforms to the Epidemics Act, lawmakers introduced
legislation to revise Article 231 in order to clarify its focus on bioterrorism as
distinct from more general public health concerns. Green Party representative Alec von Graffenried explained that tremendous confusion in the Swiss
legal system resulted from the two laws and that "[t]he problem is that when
it comes to transmission of diseases there are always two levels. On the one
hand, there is the individual level, the individual health of the victim [in the
case of disease transmission]. . . . On the other hand, there is the disease control part of it. . . . Article 231 in its present form confuses these two levels.[41]
He added that the commission that drafted the article originally intended it
to cover "a highly criminal, if not even terroristic offense" that posed a broad
threat to public, as opposed to individual, health.

Van Graffenried's comments succinctly describe one of the most significant historical developments in the domain of HIV governmentality in the
early twenty-first century, one that characterizes the situation in Switzerland
and in many other developed countries, including the Netherlands and the
United States. The "confusion" he describes marks a particular moment in the
history of the HIV/AIDS epidemic when many Western governments began
to perceive HIV not only as a threat to individual citizens but as a danger to
the state as a whole. In the Swiss case, Article 231 inadvertently opened the
door to address HIV as a state security issue, allowing for unprecedented use
of the state's police power to target an epidemic disease as a terroristic threat
to national interests. This breach of the separation of powers between public
health and state security is precisely what Dutch legislators were trying to
avoid in their own Infectious Diseases Act. Yet despite the de jure separation
of police and public health powers in both countries, the de facto outcomes
for people living with HIV were the same. Both countries saw a sharp rise in
criminal HIV prosecutions, with those in Switzerland proceeding on the basis
of both infectious disease and assault laws, effecting a pernicious and nearly
invisible slippage that significantly altered the very meaning of HIV in the domain of state policy and politics. More than ever before, HIV was becoming
an enemy of the state.

The impetus for this shift in global attention to HIV as an issue of state security came from several different developments, including the attacks of September 11, 2001, which raised new fears about biological weapons, including HIV, being used by terrorists to attack first-world targets. Another source of concern was the particularly devastating spread of HIV and AIDS throughout sub-Saharan Africa. As researchers Colin McInnes and Susan Peterson have separately argued, the language of security has become a new form of orthodoxy in policy discussions of HIV/AIDS. McInnes writes that the "UN and its associated agencies have been amongst the most important players globally . . . not simply in raising AIDS awareness but in constructing HIV/AIDS as a national security problem which demanded international attention and action."[42] This "securitising move" has emerged not only through the implementation of international policy but also through the disciplinary response to the pandemic by political scientists and economists. Thus, the period between 1996 (when UNAIDS was created) and the year immediately following 9/11 (when an international policy consensus on HIV/AIDS began to take shape) is a defining era in the history of HIV/AIDS. In this period, policymakers established the broader governmental frameworks for how the pandemic would be managed and how it would be framed as an object of state interest. The move to "securitize" AIDS fundamentally alters how we see the virus and informs the techniques, rationalities, and resources we employ to contain it.

Nowhere has this "securitizing move" been more pronounced than in the United States, where prosecutors flagrantly invoke bioterrorism laws to prosecute HIV-infected individuals for exposing others to the virus. In Easton, Pennsylvania, a homeless, mentally ill man pleaded guilty to two counts of assault and one count of making terroristic threats after spitting and shaking his bleeding fist at police. In Michigan in 2009, Macomb County prosecutor Eric Smith brought bioterrorism charges against Daniel Allen, an HIV-positive gay man who allegedly bit his neighbor during an altercation. Michigan law makes it a crime to "manufacture, deliver, possess, transport, place, use, or release . . . a harmful biological substance or a harmful biological device" for an unlawful purpose, and Smith argued that Allen's saliva was just such a "harmful biological substance," despite the fact that HIV is not present in saliva.[43] The prosecutor hoped that the court would view Allen's saliva in the same way an earlier Michigan court, in 2007, viewed the blood of HIV-infected persons. In the 2007 case, the defendant had spit blood at a corrections officer, and the court ruled that bioterrorism charges were appropriate because blood, in the case of people infected with HIV, "is a substance produced by a human organism that contains a virus that can spread or cause disease in humans."[44] As the ACLU and other organizations argued in Allen's defense, saliva alone does not present a risk of infection, nor was the state's bioterrorism law ever intended to be used in cases like Allen's, in which there was no threat to state security. According to the state's official analysis of the law, published by the Michigan legislature, lawmakers passed the bioterrorism statute in 1998, "in the wake of the Oklahoma City federal building bombing — as well as an incident in which police in Lansing stopped a van driven by a Battle Creek man for a traffic violation only to discover weapons and a bomb."[45] The intent of the legislature was "to comprehensively revise and update the chapter of the penal code dealing with terrorist crimes involving bombs and other explosive devices" so as to include biological devices and other terroristic threats. The fact that prosecutors were using the law to seek harsher sentences for people with HIV involved in physical disputes with neighbors or corrections officers was like bringing a battleship into a bathtub.

The significance of these cases lies in their reframing of interpersonal violence as political violence. Because HIV appears as a threat not only to the health of individuals but also to the body of the state, it symbolically refigures the risks inherent in everyday life (the risk of getting in a fight or, say, of hooking up with someone) into political danger, giving rise to crises of state security in which the health of the state must be protected at all costs. Diseases such as leprosy, smallpox, syphilis, and the flu have long served as symbolic vectors for the expression of collective anxieties about national borders and cultural identity, but new in this era of HIV's intensive biopolitical management are the juridical and governmental logics that link HIV to national identity and specifically to concerns about state security, a problem that must be solved by ramping up state bureaucracies, intensifying controls over the body, and inventing new technologies of governance. The interesting thing about these developments is how the body itself is being remade in the image of the state. Its very fluids have been reclassified as "harmful biological substances." The body can now be said to "manufacture, deliver, possess, transport, place, use, or release" agents of destruction, as if it were a factory or machine, a sort of mobile laboratory and ticking bomb rolled into one. In this way, HIV serves as the point of entry for the state into the most mundane of interpersonal activities and into the invisible and mute interior of the body, where its silent and microscopic workings are made to speak, even to cry out, as its various humors are reborn as weapons of mass destruction.

The state's new, aggressive interest in HIV dovetails with an extremist and increasingly popular view of HIV-infected persons as dangerous disease carries who pose a threat to local communities. In some cases, people with HIV and violent sex offenders appear to be completely fungible in popular discourse, one standing in for the other amid calls to deprive those with HIV of their civil rights, including their right to privacy. Extremists are using the Internet to promote a form of crowdsourced, vigilante justice targeting sex offenders and so-called HIV predators. The website STDcarriers.com, for example, publishes the names and photographs of thousands of people worldwide who have tested positive for sexually transmitted infections or who have been prosecuted for criminal HIV transmission. The site bills itself as "the first public early warning alert system for identifying potential sources of sexually transmitted diseases" and offers viewers access to a database called "The International Sexually Transmitted Disease Carrier Registry" as well as to "the largest centralized list of people arrested for crimes involving criminal HIV exposure and transmission." These lists are drawn from public records, news stories, and submissions from users of the site. One subsection of the criminal HIV list maintained on the site is the "Biological Terror Watch List," which "showcases people who have used their bodies to weaponize the deadly virus and deploy it in hostilities against their fellow man." Anyone visiting the site will note that it bears, in certain areas, an uncanny resemblance to officially sponsored U.S. government public health sites like those of the Centers for Disease Control and Prevention. The site's home page displays a large banner announcing "Disease Control and Prevention Services," which sounds vaguely like an official government organization or public health service. A circular red, white, and blue logo, a riff on the official U.S. presidential seal, appears on several pages within the site, furthering the sense that the site is an official government "registry," similar to that used for sex offenders. The site presents information in ways that suggest an ideological agenda that affirms the need for protecting individual and national borders from unwanted outsiders. It is linked to a site with similar themes and graphics called the "Illegal Alien Report," which allows users to report suspected illegal alien activity based on "media reports as well as personal experience." The site further reminds readers that "STDs don't have borders." Thus, it ties criminalization to the moral work of nation building and social purification. Noting that "the government should have made a site like this years ago," the site's creators express a wish for greater government intervention into private affairs of sexuality and health, expressing no concern whatever for the civil rights of those whose names and pictures are published on the site, many accompanied by lurid banners and biohazard symbols that reduce the individuals depicted to abstract embodiments of pure danger.

STDcarriers.com provides a troubling vision of the effects of HIV criminalization taken to an extreme, but its fantasy of a larger role for the state in policing and punishing those who threaten the moral order is not a total fiction. The increasingly blurred lines between public health, criminal law, and state security that have contributed to the spike in HIV criminalization are unfortunately all too real. The site mirrors reality as well in its call to defend "the purity and essence of our natural fluids," a line it borrows from *Dr. Strangelove*. What's worth noting here is how closely this line resembles the purported claims of the Groningen perpetrators, who wanted "to promote unprotected sex as it is the purest form of relationship." These claims to social and sexual purity may come from opposite ends of the political spectrum, but they share a nostalgic wish for an imagined time and place that is somehow beyond HIV. The ideological extremism of both appears far removed from the complicated realities of life in an age of chronic and epidemic HIV infection. They also remind us how desires for social and sexual purity often go hand in hand, as they did under National Socialism, and how central these ideological formations are to the logics of state governance. In the case of the tragic events in Groningen, we would be wise to acknowledge the extent to which the perpetrators' desire for a post-HIV sexual utopia, as well as their "weaponization" of HIV, participates in a larger political economy of HIV and in the state's changing technological and bureaucratic management of HIV infection.

NOTES

1. Coverage of these events in the news media was widespread. For the original Dutch article that cites statistics from the local health service, see "Voor de kick met hiv injecteren," NRC Handelsblad, May 31, 2007, http://www.nrc.nl/binnenland /article1802288.ece/Voor_de_kick_met_hiv_injecteren.

2. "Gay Gang in Netherlands Lures, Rapes and Infects Fellow Homosexuals with HIV/AIDS," Medindia, June 5, 2007, http://www.medindia.net/news/Gay-Gang-in -Netherlands-Lures-Rapes-and-Infects-Fellow-Homosexuals-With-HIV-AIDS-21671 -1.htm.

3. "Dutch Police Arrest 4 Men in Bizarre Sex-Crime Investigation," *International Herald Tribune*, May 31, 2007. The original story is no longer available online, but a revised reprint is; see Andy Towle, "Dutch Arrest 4 for Gay Sex Party HIV Blood Injections," May 31, 2007, http://www.towleroad.com/2007/05/dutch_arrest_4_.html. See also "Dutch Shock over Gay HIV Rape Gang," ABC, June 1, 2007, http://www.abc.net.au/news/stories/2007/06/01/1939382.htm. For another summary, see Edwin J. Bernard, "Four Dutch Men Accused of 'Premeditated' Criminal HIV Transmission via Rape and Injection," Aidsmap, June 1, 2007. http://www.aidsmap.com/en/news/6D11E243-92B8-45E4-98B2-48A4774C70B4.asp.

4. "Three Men Confess to HIV Injection Orgies," News.com.au, June 1, 2007, http://www.news.com.au/three-men-confess-to-hiv-injection-orgies/story-e6frfkp9-1111113658903; "Gay Orgy Gang's HIV Rapes Stun Holland," *The Age*, June 2, 2007, http://www.theage.com.au/articles/2007/06/01/1180205513859.html; "Gay Gang Spread HIV at Sex Orgy," *Daily Telegraph*, October 16, 2008, http://www.dailytelegraph.com.au/news/world/gay-gang-spread-hiv-at-sex-orgy/story-e6frevo0-1111117766301; "Dutch Police Arrest 4 Men in Bizarre Sex-Crime Investigation," *International Herald Tribune*, May 31, 2007.

5. See "Voor de kick met hiv injecteren." For a representative example of how the term was used in press headlines, see "Homo's opzettelijk besmet met hiv op seksfeest," May 31, 2007, http://vorige.nrc.nl//binnenland/article1802288.ece/Voor_de_kick_met_hiv_injecteren.

6. " 'Mijn cliënt is geen hiv-monster,' " *De Telegraaf*, January 7, 2010, http://www.telegraaf.nl/binnenland/5735292/—Mijn_clint_is_geen_hiv-monster__.html. For a story that mentions the term's use in the media, see Rob Zijlstra, "Hiv en interview," January 4, 2009, http://robzijlstra.wordpress.com/2009/01/04/hiv/.

7. While the term "political economy" may describe a highly technical, quantitative branch of economics, Foucault significantly expanded the meaning of the phrase and claimed it for the humanities. In particular, Foucault describes his later work on sexuality as an "attempt to constitute the 'political economy' of a will to knowledge" about sex. See Michel Foucault, *The History of Sexuality*, Volume 1, *An Introduction*, trans. Robert Hurley (New York: Pantheon, 1978), 73.

8. Thomas Shevory, *Notorious HIV: The Media Spectacle of Nushawn Williams* (Minneapolis: University of Minnesota Press, 2004).

9. Global Network of People Living with HIV [GNP+], *The Global Criminalisation Scan Report 2010*, July 2010. Updated statistics are available online at http://criminalisation.gnpplus.net/. See also UNAIDS, *Criminalization of HIV Non-Disclosure, Exposure and Transmission: Background and Current Landscape*, February 2012, https://dl

.dropboxusercontent.com/u/1576514/BackgroundCurrentLandscapeCriminalisatio nHIV_9Feb2012.pdf.

10. GNP+, *The Global Criminalisation Scan Report 2010*, 3, 9.

11. While the small body of social scientific evidence to date does not definitely support the claim that criminal laws exacerbate the spread of HIV, there is some evidence suggesting that criminal laws work against public health efforts to slow HIV prevention. For a recent and relatively comprehensive overview of the best studies to date, see GNP+ and HIV Justice Network, *Advancing HIV Justice: A Progress Report on Achievements and Challenges in Global Advocacy against HIV Criminalization* (June 2013), 20–24, http://www.hivjustice.net/wp-content/uploads/2013/05/Advancing-HIV-Justice-June-2013.pdf.

12. The defendant was sentenced to two years in prison (the prosecutor had sought a prison sentence of three years), but his sentence was ultimately reduced to a fine and the wearing of an electronic bracelet for a year. See *Var-matin*, "Deux ans de prison pour avoir volontairement transmis le sida," February 17, 2012, http://www.varmatin.com/article/faits-divers/deux-ans-de-prison-pour-avoir-volontairement-transmis-le-sida.777954.html.

13. Trevor Hoppe, "From Sickness to Badness: The Criminalization of HIV in Michigan," *Social Science & Medicine* 101 (2014): 139–147.

14. For the most up-to-date statistics, see GNP+, *The Global Criminalisation Scan Report 2010*; UNAIDS, *Criminalization of HIV Non-Disclosure, Exposure and Transmission*; and GNP+ and HIV Justice Network, *Advancing HIV Justice*.

15. " 'Detention or Prevention?' A Report on the Impact of the Use of Criminal Law on Public Health and the Position of People Living with HIV," Executive Committee on Aids Policy & Criminal Law, March 1, 2004, p. 3, http://criminalisation.gnpplus.net/sites/default/files/detention_or_prevention(1).pdf.

16. "Supreme Court of the Netherlands, Criminal Division," *Journal of Criminal Law* 70 (2006): 485.

17. Trial Court of Leeuwarden, Netherlands (Rechtbank Leeuwarden), LJN: AB0355, Rechtbank Leeuwarden. Date of decision January 3, 2001. http://deeplink.rechtspraak.nl/uitspraak?id=ECLI:NL:RBLEE:2001:AB0355.

18. Rechtbank Groningen (Groningen Court), LJN: BG4169, 18/630120-07, subsection 5.0.14. Date of sentence November 12, 2008. http://zoeken.rechtspraak.nl/resultpage.aspx?snelzoeken=true&searchtype=ljn&ljn=BG4169&u_ljn=BG4169. Translations are my own.

19. Puar has called the ideological affinity between mainstream gay politics and exclusionary biopolitical imperatives "homonationalism." Noting that being gay, particularly in the global north, does not "necessarily contradict or undermine" heterosexual

privilege, she argues that emerging forms of homosexual citizenship "may support forms of heteronormativity and the class, racial and citizenship privileges they require." See Jasbir K. Puar, *Terrorist Assemblages: Homonationalism in Queer Times* (Durham, NC: Duke University Press, 2007), 9.

20. Matthew Weait, *Intimacy and Responsibility: The Criminalization of* HIV *Transmission* (New York: Routledge, 2007), 119.

21. Weait, *Intimacy and Responsibility*, 197.

22. Barry D. Adam et al., "Effects of the Criminalization of HIV Transmission in Cuerrier on Men Reporting Unprotected Sex with Men," *Canadian Journal of Law and Society* 22, nos. 1–2 (2008): 143.

23. Adam et al., "Effects of the Criminalization of HIV Transmission," 157.

24. See "'Detention or Prevention?'"

25. Legislative Assembly of the State of South Dakota, Senate Bill 65, Eighty-third session, 2008, http://sdlegislature.gov/sessions/2008/Bills/SB65P.htm.

26. "Introduction: The War on Sex" and chapter 12, "HIV: Prosecution or Prevention? HIV Is Not a Crime," respectively.

27. Sean Strub, "HIV Is Not a Crime," YouTube, November 30, 2011, https://www.youtube.com/watch?v=iB-6blJjbjc.

28. Supreme Court of the Netherlands (Hoge Raad der Nederlanden), LJN: AE9049. Date of decision: March 25, 2003; http://deeplink.rechtspraak.nl/uitspraak?id=ECLI:NL:HR:2003:AE9049.

29. GNP+, "Criminalisation of HIV Transmission in Europe: A Rapid Scan of the Laws and Rates of Prosecution for HIV Transmission within Signatory States of the European Convention of Human Rights," http://criminalisation.gnpplus.net /country/netherlands; accessed July 27, 2016.

30. Appeals Court of Arnhem, Netherlands (Gerechtshof Arnhem), LJN: AH8890. Date of decision: June 30, 2003; http://deeplink.rechtspraak.nl/uitspraak?id=ECLI:NL:GHARN:2003:AH8890.

31. See, for example, Trevor Hoppe's analysis in *Social Science & Medicine*, "From Sickness to Badness."

32. NEB. REV. STAT. § 28-934 (2013), http://nebraskalegislature.gov/laws/statutes .php?statute=28-934.

33. "Senator Moves to Keep HIV Predator in Jail," WIVB, http://www.wivb.com /dpp/news/crime/Sen-moves-to-keep-HIV-predator-in-jail, accessed May 5, 2010 (page no longer available).

34. Edwin J. Bernard, "US: Nushawn Williams "Poster Child" of Newly Proposed HIV-specific Law Faces a Lifetime of Civil Confinement (Update 2)," HIV Justice Network, July 20, 2010, http://www.hivjustice.net/news/us-nushawn-williams-poster

-child-of-newly-proposed-hiv-specific-law-faces-a-lifetime-of-civil-confinement-update-2/.

35. Udo Schuklenk, "Why Some HIV Transmissions Should be Punished," Hastings Center, October 31, 2008, http://www.thehastingscenter.org/why-some-hiv-transmissions-should-be-punished/.

36. Supreme Court of the Netherlands (Hoge Raad der Nederlanden), LJN: AR1860. Date of decision: January 18, 2005; http://deeplink.rechtspraak.nl/uitspraak?id=ECLI:NL:HR:2005:AR1860

37. Adam et al., "Effects of the Criminalization of HIV Transmission," 147.

38. "'Detention or Prevention?'"

39. *Tweede Kamer der Staten Generaal*, Number 3 (1996–1997). Bill number 25 336. ISSN 0921-7371, pp. 1–2. Translations are my own.

40. GNP+, "Criminalisation of HIV Transmission in Europe," http://criminalisation.gnpplus.net/country/switzerland, accessed July 27, 2016.

41. Edwin J. Bernard, "Switzerland: New Law on Epidemics Only Criminalising Intentional Transmission Passed in Lower House," HIV Justice Network, March 9, 2012. http://www.hivjustice.net/news/switzerland-new-law-on-epidemics-only-criminalising-intentional-transmission-passed-in-lower-house/#sthash.IX4Biu2K.dpuf.

42. Colin McInnes, "HIV/AIDS and National Security," in *AIDS and Governance*, ed. Nana K. Poku, Alan Whiteside, and Bjorg Sandkjaer (Aldershot, UK: Ashgate, 2007), 93–94.

43. Michigan Penal Code, Section 750.200i, http://legislature.mi.gov/doc.aspx?mcl-750-200i, accessed October 7, 2014.

44. Court of Appeals of Michigan, *People of the State of Michigan v. Antoine Deshaw ODOM*, Docket No. 267867. Decided August 9, 2007. http://caselaw.findlaw.com/mi-court-of-appeals/1259798.html#sthash.k2KyvHZr.dpuf.

45. "Terrorist Devices," House Legislative Analysis Section, State of Michigan, Senate Bills 443 and 997. Date of analysis May 19, 1998. https://www.legislature.mi.gov/documents/1997-1998/billanalysis/House/pdf/1997-HLA-0443-A.pdf.

HANS TAO-MING HUANG

| 14 |

HIV Care as Social Rehabilitation

Medical Governance, the AIDS Surveillance Industry,
and Therapeutic Citizenship in Neoliberal Taiwan

THE "AIDS BUDGET CRISIS"

In April 2014, Taiwan's Center for Disease Control (CDC) announced a draft bill to amend the HIV Control and Patients' Rights Protection Act (hereafter "HIV Control Act"), the regulative basis of the country's HIV policy. While the bill would lift draconian border restrictions on HIV-positive individuals, it would also fundamentally change HIV care and treatment in Taiwan. Since 1989, HIV care had been made freely available to HIV-positive citizens; the new plan would provide free care only for a period of two years from the date of the patient's HIV-positive diagnosis. According to the statute, during that time, "the patient's medical condition is expected to be stabilized."[1] After two years, the patient will be required to move on to a new treatment regime of "maintenance," which will require copayment through the National Health Insurance Program's chronic illness provisions.[2]

Over the years, expenditures on care and treatment for persons infected with HIV have been moved back and forth between a special CDC budget (intended mainly for disease prevention and subject to parliamentary approval) and the National Health Insurance Program (between 1998 and 2005, under the category of "catastrophic illness," which is exempted from copayment).[3] The move to make HIV patients pay, branded by the government as "normalizing HIV," came as a result of the so-called "AIDS budget crisis" of 2011, which ignited Taiwan's first treatment-based activism in the post-HAART (highly active antiretroviral treatment) era.

Due to the worsening of the state budget deficit, the CDC broke the news in 2011 that it would introduce a copayment scheme, creating a special fiscal measure modeled on the National Health Service (NHS) copayment scheme but not dispensed from the NHS itself. Angered by the CDC's abrupt decision and lack of communication, several key NGOs — spearheaded by the country's leading community-based HIV/AIDS organization on prevention and care, the Taiwan Lourdes Association — got together to form a coalition called Taiwan AIDS Action. The coalition was quick to attack the beguiling principle of "fairness" that the government was holding up. Activists asked why, even if HIV-positive patients were being asked to pay for their medical expenses, they should be excluded from the NHS. At the same time, people living with HIV united to form the Positive Alliance, the coalition's only organization run by people living with HIV. Members of the Positive Alliance rightly pointed out that people living with HIV, far from being "normalized," continued under the new scheme to be administered as a controlled population subject to lifelong state surveillance.[4]

Crucially, Taiwan AIDS Action framed the budget crisis as one of national security and called on the government to increase funding for prevention and treatment by adopting a comprehensive, top-down state response similar to the one in China. Meanwhile, they urged people living with HIV (who had previously been invisible due to the intense social stigma they faced) to become involved and to speak out for themselves. To this end, three rounds of public forums were held in different regions of the island nation. These conversations were largely dominated by frontline workers expressing their concerns about the negative impact the new policy might have on patient care, especially for the underprivileged.[5] In response to NGO agitation about the AIDS budget crisis, the CDC subsequently held a public hearing that was attended by the country's leading HIV experts. Professor Yi-ming Arthur Chen, a U.S.-trained epidemiologist central to HIV policymaking, contended that sustainable HIV care ought to be grounded in the NHS. Dr. Chen proposed a copayment plan analogous to that of liver care, which distinguishes between patients with acute infections (whose care is fully covered by the NHS) and those considered to have a chronic condition (who are charged copayments).[6] The two-phase plan for HIV care proposed in the draft bill appears to have followed his recommendation.

The treatment-based advocacy triggered by the budget crisis encapsulates a number of contradictions in the politics of AIDS in Taiwan. These contradictions are evident within the regulatory context established by the HIV Control Act during the past two decades. For one thing, free access to HIV care is not just a right but also an obligation imposed by the state. I contend that HIV treatment and care are integral to Taiwan's authoritarian regime of HIV control. This regime employs a number of public health strategies to achieve control, including name-based case reporting; tracking and contact tracing by local public health bureaus; border restrictions; mandatory HIV testing of targeted high-risk groups; forced quarantine (prior to 2007); and, above all, the criminalization of HIV nondisclosure, exposure, and transmission. These strident public health measures, coordinated with policing and the criminal justice system, form a punitive regime of name-based HIV state surveillance under which people on the national HIV registry are required to organize their lives.

Significantly, the HIV registry in Taiwan is predicated on the modern system of household registration (*hukou zhidu*), which was established under Japanese colonial rule. During the Cold War period, the system of household registration was deployed by the anti-communist regime of the ruling Kuomintang political party as a means of political and crime control under martial law (1949–1987). Household registration and census verification were an integral part of local police administration until 1990.[7] Because of this historical legacy, HIV control in Taiwan can be characterized as statist.[8] For instance, those registered by the state as HIV-positive must notify the local public health bureau if they intend to move to a new residence.[9] HIV stigma in Taiwan stems largely from this system of active state surveillance, which effectively treats people living with HIV as suspects.

In a gesture purported to align Taiwan's HIV Control Act with UNAIDS's international guidelines, human rights protections were added to the 2007 revamp of the act. Ironically, however, these provisions reinforced the regime of HIV state surveillance. Not only was the maximum penalty for the crime of HIV nondisclosure, exposure, and transmission raised from seven to twelve years, but the regime also began to extend its regulatory arms from the domain of public health to that of HIV care, thanks to the implementation of a certain hospital-based HIV case management (HCM) program in 2007. The program integrates "positive prevention" (that is, HIV prevention aimed at HIV-positive people) into HIV care, cultivating self-care by offering support, counseling, and health advice services that emphasize risk reduction and medical compliance.[10]

Notably, enrollment in the program requires the patient's consent (this "respect" for the subject greatly enhances the legitimacy of the program). However, unbeknownst to many, the revamped 2007 HIV Control Act requires case managers to submit updated patient information and treatment progress to the CDC. To date, around 40 percent of the HIV-positive population is managed under the program as its scale continues to expand.[11] Curiously, while AIDS service organizations do advise patients registered by the state as HIV-positive about how to deal with public health tracking and contact tracing, informational materials detailing this new form of medical surveillance specifically tailored to people living with HIV remain nonexistent to date.

This context of renewed HIV control raises serious questions about Taiwan AIDS Action's campaign and, specifically, its call for a comprehensive, top-down state response to HIV/AIDS. To begin with, what does it mean to demand maximal state intervention, when the Taiwanese version of "treatment as prevention" — under the overriding imperative of "positive-as-crime prevention" — has already been in place for some time and has intensified in recent years?[12] Furthermore, what is one to make of the NGO's reluctance to discuss the new form of state surveillance, even while they continue to speak in the name of people with HIV? What function does the rhetoric of HIV human rights serve in a therapeutic milieu in which medical surveillance looms large? Finally, given that the routes of HIV infection are associated with stigmatized sexual and/or drug-taking practices, how does all this relate to questions of criminal intimacy and sexual justice?

In this essay, I address these issues by showing what the technology of HIV case management does when it is welded onto a system of name-based state surveillance. By tracking the transformation of HIV surveillance and its constitutive effects, and by analyzing the state's treatment of HIV-positive gay men, I demonstrate how the apparatus of HIV care operates as a diffuse form of medical policing that joins with nonprofit organizing to assert control over a stigmatized population.

My aim in this essay is twofold. First, I aim to challenge the local AIDS service organizations for their unquestioning support of state surveillance. While small AIDS patient support groups began to emerge in the early 1990s under the aegis of prevention-based organizations set up by some U.S.-trained epidemiologists, it was not until early in the following decade that the local AIDS service industry gradually came into being and rapidly professionalized sexual health care.[13] Significantly, the mainstreaming of AIDS in Taiwan over the past decade has been embedded in a larger process of readjustments to liberal governance in the post–martial law era on the part of a developmental, authoritarian state supported by U.S. imperialism, a process in which nonprofit organizing plays a key part.[14] Critics such as Josephine Ho and Ning Yingbin have shown how, following the hegemonic ascendency of anti-prostitution state feminism in 1990s Taiwan, a new mode of "flat governance" — conjugated by NGOs, elite experts, and the state — gradually came to prevail in the areas of gender and sexuality. Mediated by global gender mainstreaming as well as the mandate of UN child protection, this mode of governance gave rise to new legislation that tightened sexual control in the name of gender equity and child protectionism.[15] Taiwan's nascent AIDS service industry came into formation within such a sex-negative milieu of "gender friendliness" (where the sociality of "friendliness," as a new structure of feeling, purportedly reduces stigma and cultivates a more enabling living environment for gendered/sexual minorities). In the meantime, transnational technologies of HIV care and prevention, facilitated by HIV experts and the NGOs they were running, began to take hold through the early twenty-first century. The only HIV-identity-based group in Taiwan, the Positive Alliance, emerged from the Taiwan Lourdes Association's empowerment program. By examining the pastoral power that Lourdes deploys in its cultivation of the "good" poz (HIV-positive person), I consider how "flat governance" unfolds under the regime of HIV surveillance and control.

Second, I aim to explain how the state regulates and controls citizens by doling out rights and responsibilities to the infected. To this end, I analyze the state's forcible maintenance of moral order in the realm of consumer society in late modernity. In his book *Pleasure Consuming Medicine: The Queer Politics of Drugs*, Kane Race cogently demonstrates that the consumption of illicit drugs represents an "excessive conformity" to the logic of consumerism in the amoral market, over which the state stakes its claim as a moral arbiter.[16] Under certain conditions, the neoliberal state makes an example of illicit drug users, usually through the spectacular display of police raids in the media, to proclaim its moral sovereignty — what Race refers to as an ideological politics of "sending a message."[17] Race's analysis of state power as paternalistic and authoritarian is useful for thinking about the policing of drugs and sex in Taiwan. Over the past decade, the Taiwanese state has been "making an example" of HIV-positive gay men who use recreational drugs. Indeed, the implementation of the hospital-based HCM was a response to the police raid of a gay sex party in 2004, which I examine in the following section. In order to understand how the local AIDS service industry aligns with the Taiwanese state's regulatory power, I juxtapose Positive Alliance and its exemplary status as the new normal with a recent high-profile criminal case involving unprotected sex between drug-using HIV-positive men.

In the early morning of January 17, 2004, undercover police infiltrated a residential apartment in Taipei, where a "home party" was taking place. (In Taiwanese gay culture, "home party" is a term used to refer to a gay sex party.)[18] Ninety-two gay men were arrested. Answering the police's call, the media arrived shortly thereafter and were allowed into the "crime scene" while it was still under investigation.

What ensued was unprecedented mass hysteria. Occurring just a few days before the lunar Chinese New Year — the festive season of family gathering — scenes of the police raid were broadcast on a loop through cable news channels for more than three weeks, showing shamed-faced, half-naked young men being ordered to crouch on the floor (see figure 14.1), as masked policemen searched through the promiscuous ruins of used condoms. A fresh wave of moral panic came just three days after the raid, which became known as the Nong-an home party incident, when police revealed that twenty-eight of the men had tested HIV-positive, including fourteen whose names were already listed on the state's name-based HIV registry. The media joined the CDC with a litany of diatribes, publicly decrying the men as irresponsible, dangerous individuals who had no sense of self-respect. They were supposed to have quit having sex for good after becoming seropositive, and now they were caught having orgies, taking drugs, and infecting others.

After a closed-door meeting with AIDS NGO representatives and HIV experts, the CDC decided to hand the twenty-eight gay men with HIV over for prosecution. Although months later the charges of HIV transmission for these men were dropped due to insufficient evidence, the intensification of sexual stigma had, regrettably, led one gay man to commit suicide. Still, the prosecution service took the trouble to state (obviously not wanting to send the wrong message) that dropping charges did not mean that "home parties" were not illegal, adding that "gay people should not have a twisted understanding of the Law."[19]

In fact, it was the state that twisted the law. In 2004, the HIV Control Act did not allow the governing body (the CDC) to divulge any patient information to a third party. But in taking the initiative to check their test results list against the police arrest records, the CDC violated this stipulation. Furthermore, the fourteen unlisted men discovered to be HIV-positive should never have been handed over for prosecution, because undiagnosed HIV infection

FIGURE 14.1. Police raid on Taipei "home party." Credit: Apple Daily.

fell, and continues to fall, outside the remit of the act. The incident set a key precedent: the CDC's unlawful actions were later made legal with a new round of legislation enacted in 2007. This revamp of the act allows medical confidentiality to be breached in the name of "prevention needs."[20] In other words, people on the HIV registry in post–martial law Taiwan live permanently under a state of emergency.

Significantly, when the state revamped the act in 2007, the law's mandatory testing guidelines now included a new category, known as "illicit drug users involved in group sex," which replaced the former category of "homosexuals." Practically, this means that, if you are a good homosexual, you can be exempted from the violence of having the state check up on you. But a new category of deviance — the sex/party subject — comes into being. Furthermore, anyone arrested at sex parties and found, after testing, to be HIV-negative is now subject to three months of tracking by local public health bureaus.[21]

Several months after the Nong-an home party incident, the CDC received alarming reports about a 77 percent spike in the prevalence of HIV among incarcerated injecting drug users. The sharp increase swiftly prompted the CDC to introduce a harm reduction policy, with Australian harm reduction experts, such as Alex Wodak, flown in to assist. These experts were to pilot schemes of clean needle exchanges, methadone treatment, and HIV screening/AIDS awareness, which began to operate in different parts of Taiwan from the second half of 2005. By 2006, the state's new harm reduction policy was officially implemented throughout the country.[22]

In his study of the harm reduction policy in Taiwan, the sociologist Chen Jiashin has shown that the policymaking body was composed of CDC officials, HIV experts, and NGO workers; he argues that the policy itself was a purely utilitarian move designed to protect the "general public" rather than to promote the well-being of injecting drug users (IDUs) themselves.[23] By medicalizing the IDUs as patients (rather than criminals) and by framing the deployment of harm reduction in terms of social rehabilitation, the Taiwanese government was able strategically to make a "low-key" intervention without appearing to contradict its overall prohibitionist drug policy.[24]

One of the profound effects of this harm reduction policy is the "high-key" reinforcement of drug prevention measures directed at the young. For example, the period beginning in 2006 saw the onset of an "HIV-positive public speaking" model for abstinence-based AIDS awareness education. This was a new global technology, in circulation in Asia since around 2000, that sought to reverse AIDS stereotypes and to involve people living with HIV in

HIV prevention.[25] This kind of "life-affirming" education, enacted on school and college campuses by such mainstream NGOs as the Taiwan AIDS Foundation and Harmony Home Association, typically stages rituals of confession, performed by an ex-addict or a reformed male homosexual, whose narrative of redemption serves as a cautionary tale for the young.[26]

It was this "drug-induced" sense of public health crisis that led the CDC to review its measures of HIV control. Longitudinal data on HIV populations was desperately needed, as the CDC came to realize.[27] In particular, the efficiency of HIV case management by local public health bureaus was called into question: public health nurses, seen as lacking in professional HIV-care training, were criticized as insensitive, intrusive, and deeply unpopular among people with HIV.[28] Looking to modernize and tighten HIV control, the Taiwan CDC followed the U.S. CDC's 2003 recommendations and guidelines on the integration of positive prevention into HIV care. As part of this new harm reduction policy, the CDC introduced another pilot program — tellingly called "Behaviour Therapy for Individuals with HIV" — that was carried out in three trials in HIV clinics in north, central, and south Taiwan from the second half of 2005. The programs initially enrolled more than 500 patients, and by 2007, the hospital-based HCM program was officially launched.

HCM AS MORAL QUARANTINE

Run by nursing experts and doctors who were to become the dominant figures in the HIV sector, the three trials laid out the key parameters for the new policy. The southern trial, administered by Dr. Ko Naiying, a U.S.-trained nursing expert, established the model for the current program. In this U.S.-based model, the case manager concocts a tailor-made counseling plan based on initial clinical assessments of the patient (determination of risk and screening for sexually transmitted infections [STIs]) and involving quarterly check-ins to monitor the patient's behavior and to see if it has been modified. In particular, the program targeted sexually active men and those using illicit drugs.[29] Ko noted that the introduction of this model marked a watershed moment in local HIV prevention, as it shifted the focus from risk groups/populations to risky individuals.[30] Thus, HCM in the clinical setting constitutes a key technology of biomedical individuation. As Kane Race points out, "the more identifiable and clinically calculable HIV disease has become at the level of the individual body, the more individual bodies have been rendered responsible for the risk of onward transmission."[31]

The northern trial, run by another nursing expert, Zhuang Ping, at Taipei City Hospital, had the largest number of enrolled patients. Boasting of her team's excellent quality of care (rated "five stars/hearts"), Zhuang underscored her soft approach, contending that the protection of confidentiality was paramount in fostering a "compliance-enabling" (rather than health-enabling) environment. Further, she accentuated the importance of building a client relationship that starts with anonymous voluntary testing and counseling, suggesting that further specifications of differences within and among each subgroup of patients are required to meet the challenge of "heart-to-heart" counseling.[32]

In contrast to the north's benevolent mode of "positive" intervention, the central trial had a harder edge to it. The administrator, Dr. Wang Renxian, regarded the reforming of HIV patients as the duty of medicine, employing STI testing as a device to verify the patient's reliability and recruiting a team of psychiatrists to rectify those he considered "deviant." Wang recommended that mandatory registration would be necessary for the purpose of long-term tracking and suggested that punitive measures be included in the state-funded program for disciplinary purposes.[33]

The trials all showed satisfactory results, especially among newly diagnosed cases, with participants reporting lower numbers of casual sex partners, greater use of condoms, and lower rates of substance use. The CDC clearly took note of these results, moving to amend the HIV Control Act halfway through the pilot scheme. Crucially, the 2007 revamp of the HIV Control Act incorporated a new mode of state surveillance stipulated by the 2004 revamp of the Communicable Disease Act in the wake of the state of emergency set off by SARS during 2002–2003. Under the post-SARS public health regime, medical institutions are now mandated to submit up-to-the-minute reports of patient treatment progress to health authorities, and it was this augmented state power that the CDC wanted to obtain in order to tighten its control over the drug-using HIV-positive population. Up until this time, the Communicable Disease Act only allowed the CDC to obtain patient data from the previous quarter, which contained basic information, such as CD4 counts and viral load. By contrast, the hospital-based HCM program was able to gather an individual's most recent medical and biographical information (attitude, values, habits, behavior modifications, etc.). Significantly, as HIV infection became a manageable condition in the era of antiretroviral treatment, the state adopted disease management strategies devised for emerging infectious diseases such as SARS. As such, HIV acquires the status of a highly contagious disease.[34] No wonder Dr. Wang of the central trial scheme refers to the HCM program as a "quarantine policy for chronic illness."[35]

What I find most objectionable about the program is its total lack of transparency. The consent form contains fewer than two lines, which read, "Having had it explained to me what this program is about, I hereby give my consent to join the program to receive counseling and health advice services." Given the positive outcome of the trials and the self-validating claims made by subsequent research about the efficacy of the program, HIV patients are urged to join the program, with promises about "enhancing the quality of life" or "receiving whole-person care."[36] Moreover, while the program claims to be voluntary, this is not always the case. Enrollment to the program is, for example, the precondition to getting access to second-line treatment — further evidence of the arbitrary power wielded by the CDC.[37]

At issue is how those enrolled in the program are treated and guided. If governmentality for Foucault is "the conduct of conduct"[38] — that is, a power relation that takes the form of leading others, with varying degrees of coercion, but nevertheless presumes the individual's capacity to act, to behave in certain ways so as to produce desired outcomes — then the question of ethics becomes paramount. For the majority of those diagnosed with HIV infection in Taiwan, the hospital-based HIV case manager is likely to be their first, and probably only, source of support. If the counseling in the HCM program were one kind of guidance among many available to HIV-positive people, then the support it offers to those isolated by the stigma around HIV would be valuable.[39] But as it stands, the program exploits the vulnerability of the newly diagnosed so as to "win their hearts."[40] Indeed, the HIV case manager, trained to be kind, must not reveal to the client that he or she is the agent of state surveillance, who "communicat[es], when appropriate, with the public health sector or the governing body," as a nursing textbook subtly puts it.[41]

The HIV state surveillance is now operationalized in a two-pronged system. The hospital-based HCM program is in charge of 70 percent of the poz population in medical care, while the public health sector takes care of the rest. Significantly, the CDC's one-window policy creates an apparatus of management that is both intimate (the HIV subject thinks he or she is under confidential care) and economically efficient (as it makes sense to have the primary point of contact and information gathering integrated into care).

The situation is perfect for the "good cop, bad cop" routine, where the hospital-based case manager plays good cop, while the public health nurse represents the bad cop. In this way, the HIV patient is lured into a make-believe world of love and security where he or she may be more likely to disclose information that has nothing to do with medical care and everything to do with social control.[42] Training manuals of the hospital-based HCM program provide ample examples of techniques for disarming the client ("displaying an open-minded attitude," for instance) and of gambit questions (such as "there are plenty of news reports about the gay sex party these days, do you agree with their description?"), which help the caregiver suss out the patient's history of sex and drug use.[43]

In order to conduct a liberal style of management, HIV case managers are trained to hide their aversion to forms of otherness that stand for social deviance. But no matter how empathic and nonjudgmental the case manager appears to be, his or her liberal guidance is necessarily grounded in systems of normative knowledge. In such a context, harm reduction, as currently deployed in this therapeutic setting, is operationalized as a technology of self-care that reduces the harm that the poz subject might do to society as a whole: it takes the form of reducing the number of sex partners and the frequency of drug taking, and avoiding the spaces associated with both (such as "home parties" or gay saunas). This liberal mode of governance proves to be more effective than the prohibitionist approach. By allowing the patient a degree of autonomy and by keeping him or her under observation, the case manager is able to change and reform him or her, in a benevolent way.

In the program, "safe sex" means sex only with condoms. This narrowly defined notion of safe sex corresponds to the new definition of risky sexual behavior in the 2007 revamp of the HIV Control Act, which designates any sexual contact without a latex barrier as dangerous.[44] Thus, condomless oral sex performed by a person with HIV is not viewed as "safe," nor is condomless sex between HIV-positive men with undetectable viral loads. In the "Notification on the Rights and Duties of Patients with HIV" (a new measure introduced by the CDC amid the AIDS budget crisis), condomized "safe sex" is prescribed not only as a responsibility (not to infect others) but also as a right: the right to be informed by public health nurses that unprotected sex could lead to reinfection, which would eventually exhaust the treatment options.[45] To this end, STI screening is used to monitor the patient's compliance with condom use, with secondary infections viewed as evidence of rule-breaking, and case managers are instructed to emphasize the harmful effects of condomless sex when counseling patients.[46]

In her study of syphilis prevalence among those enrolled in the HCM program, Dr. Ko Naiying urges case managers to aggressively target sexually active gay men with CD4 counts over 400 who use recreational drugs, as they are more likely to "relapse" after controlling their HIV infection.[47] Singling out this type of gay man for intervention has profound implications for the configurations of HIV subjecthood and individual responsibility within the punitive regime of name-based HIV state surveillance. (I will return to this point later in my discussion of the outlawing of poz-on-poz sex.) In the current program, if those sexually active gay men have achieved good compliance with HAART and can stay clean of STIs and/or drug use for two years, they can be classified as "stable cases." The socially rehabilitated patient can choose either to stay in the program (but it is not expected that case managers would offer much care, as their caseload is capped at 150, excluding the "stable cases") or to exit the program and be followed by the system of public health case management. In this regard, the two-year "transitional phase" proposed under the draft bill of the HIV Control Act that I described at the beginning of the essay can now be understood as a chrono-biopolitical project that imposes a period of moral quarantine for the purpose of social rehabilitation.

LOURDES'S POSITIVE EMPOWERMENT

With the HCM program becoming the nucleus of HIV control and surveillance, scheduled meetings on HIV case management involving the public health, medical care, and NGO sectors are routinely held in different regions of the country to tackle "special cases," thus enhancing the overall knowledge of individuals with HIV. While a new breed of public health case managers, emulating the HCM program, has recently emerged, NGOs' workers or volunteers have also been steadily absorbed into the program. Indeed, NGOs' experience and knowledge have proven invaluable for the institutionalization of medical surveillance. The training program of hospital-based HIV case managers routinely includes talks or lectures given by workers for NGOs. The Taiwan Lourdes Association plays a key part in the building of the HCM program.

Initially a small Catholic charity serving women and children, Lourdes changed direction in 1998. Its foray into the field of AIDS was marked mainly by a social work approach, a specialty that was just beginning to become established in Taiwan at the time. Lourdes had transformed itself into a leading NGO by about 2005 under the supervision of the United Way of Taiwan, filling the gap in HIV-related social services left by the Taiwanese state, which was unable to provide such services. Since then, it has been the key actor in mediating transnational technologies of HIV care and prevention, such as harm reduction and the positive empowerment program.[48] Lourdes positions itself as a community-based, rather than a faith-based, organization. Yet the community it claims to serve is one that it fabricated,[49] which not only dovetails with its own agenda of "soul governing" but also aligns with the HCM program.[50] Lourdes has chosen the educated class of gay men as its target of empowerment.

In his master's thesis, "From Support to Self-Help: My Action and Reflection with AIDS Support Group," Paul Hsu (currently the general secretary of Lourdes) employs the method of participatory action research (PAR) to reflect on his role as a social worker in supervising the country's first NGO-run support group, set up in 2000. In his account, intense social stigma around HIV not only hampers the recruitment of patients from HIV clinics but also highly constrains the cohesion and the development of the group itself.[51] Among the range of techniques drawn from the "psy" disciplines to which Hsu refers, "psychodrama" (a form of individual psychotherapy carried out, through role playing and dramatized self-presentation, in a group setting and designed to help clients to gain a deeper understanding of their lives) proves to be pivotal, as it enables Hsu to orientate the group toward the goal of spiritual growth. This is evidenced in a scene of psychodrama in action, illustrated by Hsu and colleagues. In this instance, a gay man, trying to come to terms with his own infection, is guided by the director (Hsu) to converse with God. God promises to give him an antidote to HIV if he is prepared to offer something of equivalent value in exchange.[52] This "something" comes to be interpreted as self-restraint, which is much needed for those already fallen from grace and seeking redemption. This ethic of self-discipline renders the HIV subject governable, facilitating the integration of the subject into the given moral order.

Out of those who availed themselves of such an ethical project emerged a subgroup called "New Life," which later became the prototype of the self-help seed group at Lourdes. Even though HIV stigma catalyzed the emergence of New Life, this driving force did not give rise to a collective consciousness that questioned the nature of social oppression around HIV/AIDS. What New Life discovered instead, partly through the technology of psychodrama, was the voice of the "inner child" within the self.[53] Impervious to the forces of history, culture, and politics, the "inner child," masquerading as the spiritual, turns out to be a given that is loaded with normative assumptions about what counts as a livable and meaningful life. This ahistorical and reified account of HIV stigma narrowly limits what is purported to be a self-critique of Hsu's own professionalism and its institutional power.

What emerged from New Life, then, is a new paradigm of empowerment that deploys the form of role modeling. To this end, talks given by senior members of New Life, as well as by HIV-positive professionals from abroad, have become a routine feature of Lourdes's capacity-building packages, such as the "Happy Life" biennial conference. In an empowerment workshop that I attended in 2012, three HIV-positive role models from abroad were even given the title of "international positive elite."[54] Crucially, as Lourdes became increasingly involved in training the new health professionals for the hospital-based HCM program, it also launched a new empowerment initiative called "the P Project" in 2010, from which Positive Alliance emerged. With its emphasis on positive outlook, positive emotions, and positive prevention, the project forged a new identity, Positi (帕斯堤). A transliteration of "Positive," this new name sought to displace the existing and much-spoiled identity term, "one who is infected with HIV" (感染者).[55] In this regard, Lourdes's conferral of "elite" status (with its "unknowing privilege" that comes from respectability) on self-empowered HIV-positive gay men not only crowns them with the neoliberal virtue of self-betterment but also erects, even as Lourdes disavows it, a new moral hierarchy among gay men living with HIV: they are now differentiated through their varying capacity and willingness to detach themselves from the stigma of HIV that is highly associated with sex and drug use.[56]

This gesture of de-stigmatization is articulated in part through the global gay rights discourse that affirms gay identity as the new normal. Guangge, a member of New Life and an employee of Lourdes, was chosen to be the new face of HIV. Addressing the 2011 Taiwan LGBT pride rally, an annual event claiming to be the largest of its kind in East Asia, he came out as HIV-positive and a former drug user, urging gay men to renounce the lifestyle of partying.[57] Similarly, Shihao, another key member of Positive Alliance, celebrates his spiritual rebirth in his HIV blog by way of repudiating his former self.[58] Meanwhile, Mathew, whose heartwarming story of family acceptance is the subject of the country's first documentary film on HIV/AIDS, was elected to be the winner of the Happy Life Award at Lourdes's 2013 Happy Life biennial conference.[59] The panel of judges was made up of three representatives from the local AIDS industry: Dr. Lo Yijun (an HIV doctor from the CDC), Zhuang Ping (the honcho of the hospital-based HCM program in Taipei), and Lourdes itself. Significantly, poz exemplarity comprises the following civic virtues that serve as the criteria of selection: 1) self-care and medical compliance; 2) self-empowerment; 3) cooperation and social participation; 4) capacity and innovation; 5) community work and rights advocacy.[60] Lourdes's biopolitical production of "happy life" thus performs a key disciplinary function in the making of therapeutic citizenship.

OUTLAWING POZ-ON-POZ SEX

Against the figure of the happy poz who receives the state's endorsement, the Taiwanese state made a cautionary example of an HIV-positive schoolteacher, Feng, who was arrested in late 2011 and charged with intentional transmission of HIV and with drug offenses. He was found guilty in September 2013 and sentenced to twelve years in prison, the most severe sentence for such offenses since they were outlawed by the HIV Control Act in 1990. This case embodies the violence of HIV care and surveillance.

In September 2011, an anonymous email was sent to Feng's school, accusing him of spreading HIV. The school's administration acted quickly, politely asking Feng to be tested for HIV in order to clear his name, which Feng refused to do. The school then secretly asked the police to follow Feng. Weeks later, the police obtained a search warrant and arrested Feng at his flat, on suspicion of illicit drug use, as he was reportedly having fun with a hookup. It was at this point that he was forced to undergo HIV testing.

When it emerged that Feng was already on the HIV registry, the media went into a frenzy over his arrest. His story fit neatly into the powerful cultural narrative of the evil HIV-positive gay man, recklessly infecting other "innocent" gay men. The media estimated there to be no fewer than one hundred victims in his wake. Without any concrete evidence, the prosecution held Feng in custody and vowed to put him in jail.[61] Feng's Internet history ultimately became the incriminating evidence needed to secure his indictment, alongside the testimony of thirteen former sexual partners who agreed to testify against him. The fact that Feng himself had been on antiretroviral treatment with an undetectable viral load, and that ten of the witnesses were also known by the state to be HIV-positive, did not matter. Nor did the fact that all of his partners consented to engage in condomless sex and use drugs with him.

In the state's view, Feng's crime lay mainly in exposing others to the risk of reinfection. Since 2005, the category of repeat offender (with a criminal record) in Taiwan's criminal justice system has been replaced by a harsher regime of punishment, in which each identical act of criminality, when committed repeatedly, is counted as a single count, meriting a separate penalty on its own. So Feng's sentence, for example, includes two penalties based on two occasions when he had unprotected "chem sex" with the same HIV-positive guy. This is the first time that poz-on-poz sex has been criminalized in Taiwan.[62] The judge went so far as to suggest, in his verdict, that the prosecution should pursue the ten positive witnesses.[63]

Zhuang Ping, the aforementioned nursing expert who is now in charge of Taipei City Hospital's HIV case management, testified as the prosecution's expert witness in Feng's trial, stating that the danger of reinfection was routinely emphasized in the health advice given to people undergoing HIV care. Even though what is scientifically known to date about reinfection is far from conclusive, Taiwan CDC enjoins that HIV-positive individuals must always use condoms — even with other HIV-positive partners.[64] Interestingly, Zhuang, hailed by the AIDS service industry as the "poz's guardian angel," actually managed to track Feng down to give him counseling before his arrest. Despite the bad press he had received, Zhuang said that she chose to stand by him. She couldn't bring herself to blame him for not having self-respect, Zhuang wrote on her Facebook note (open to the public), because his will had been "kidnapped" by his addiction to methamphetamine. What he needed was more love and aid, she said.[65]

Surely, love and aid could have taken the form of an expert intervention designed to contest Taiwan CDC's moralistic stance with regard to poz-on-poz sex. Surely, Zhuang must have known that the stakes of her expert testimony were high, not only for Feng himself but also for others undergoing medical care.[66] Yet by affirming the official position, the "poz's guardian angel" turned her back on Feng in her expert testimony, leaving him outside the gated community of compassion. In the wake of the verdict, Positive Alliance broke the AIDS industry's silence around Feng's case by issuing a statement, reserved in tone and appearing to be nonjudgmental, urging illicit drug users to adopt harm reduction practices while calling on people with HIV to enact universal protection by adhering unswervingly to condom use. Yet Positive Alliance could not even bring itself to acknowledge the fact that what was being outlawed in this case was poz-on-poz sex, a form of risk reduction recognized to be effective.[67]

CONCLUSION: BEYOND THE AIDS SURVEILLANCE INDUSTRY

A recent treatment campaign dramatizes the set of questions I pose to Taiwan's treatment activism. In December 2013, the Taiwan AIDS Society, a key establishment central to the institutionalization of the moral program that

I have described, launched a World AIDS Day campaign called "I-C.A.R.E." In the campaign, C.A.R.E. stands for "Compliance, Acceptance, Respect, and Employment." The campaign features Positive Alliance's Mathew, deploying the rhetoric of international AIDS human rights to adorn what is essentially a draconian regime of HIV control.[68] As Feng's case makes clear, the language of international AIDS human rights, which has recently been appropriated and depoliticized by the paradigm of "treatment as prevention" that now pervades the global scene, simply cannot address the specificity of HIV stigma in Taiwan.[69] Feng lost his job because of the media exposé. Civil society has turned a blind eye to the Taiwanese state's abuse of civil liberties. Feng was compliant with HIV medication, but his moral noncompliance — promiscuity, group sex, drug use, and barebacking — necessitated severe punishment. As HIV testing and treatment have been scaled up, militarized social control comes to be reactivated under the current regime of HIV surveillance. The state hunts down gay men through online entrapment and pursues sexual deviants through their sexual networks, as Feng learned the hard way. This means that if you are caught and test positive for drugs, a six-week compulsory rehabilitation in a detention center under the Drug Control Act is in order.[70] If you are also found to be already on the HIV registry, you could face the same fate as Feng. In this regard, the compliant, exemplary subject presumed in the I-C.A.R.E. campaign remains a sitting duck, because the Taiwanese state wants to see whether the HIV-positive individual has been successfully rehabilitated as a moral subject by HIV care.[71] Any moral relapse on his part can immediately turn him into a bad example.

Meanwhile, echoing the CDC's recent plan to "diversify" the culture of HIV case management, Lourdes's general secretary Paul Hsu has called on the government to increase the involvement of AIDS NGOs in building a network of HIV care together with the public health and medical sectors. While criticizing HIV surveillance and tracking on the part of public health, Hsu tactically avoids acknowledging the fact that a new form of medical surveillance has been operationalized through HIV care. Astonishingly, he concurs with the CDC's plan to incorporate the MSM (men who have sex with men) population into the hospital-based HCM program.[72] To this end, Lourdes has teamed up with other NGOs and Zhuang Ping to train a new breed of "buddy" volunteer to assume the role of para-HIV case manager, so as to "smooth over" the patients' resistance to medical care and compliance.

This new cadre of volunteer-qua-HIV case managers will also play an active role in the burgeoning culture of gay health centers. Supervised by the CDC, these NGO-run centers have proliferated throughout the island since

2010. Well versed in the neoliberal language of global gay equality and LGBT diversity, they share the same brand image of homonormative exemplarity, offering HIV/STI testing services that are linked to HIV clinics and hospitals.[73] Additionally, in conjunction with the hospital-based HCM program, Lourdes has recently launched a "harm-reduction" group therapy program for HIV-positive gay men, aiming to get them to quit taking (the wrong kind of) drugs.[74] What emerges, then, is a web of state-NGO co-governance that turns any risk subject into a "case" and subjects it to the benevolent gaze of HIV surveillance. To invoke the terms of the current global paradigm of "treatment as prevention," the modus operandi of HIV control in Taiwan can perhaps be characterized as "seek, test, treat, and retain in medical custody."[75]

Currently, local AIDS NGOs are still busying themselves with educating the public about the fact that HIV is not contagious, yet they have all embraced the state-inspired neoliberal project of self-care and medical surveillance that is premised on the logic of moral contagion. From the Nong-an home party incident to the criminalization of poz-on-poz sex in Feng's case, we see how gay men become demonized as folk devils before being sequestered by the apparatuses of HIV care and the law. Given that there is no such thing as confidentiality in HIV care, HIV-positive gay men who use illicit drugs are in a particularly precarious situation, where they can be easily scapegoated by the Taiwanese state under the sway of anti-sex and anti-drug populist sentiments.

It is curious that efforts to control and punish deviant HIV-positive subjects coincide with efforts to mobilize the AIDS surveillance industry to support the cause of gay marriage. Campaigns to secure same-sex marriage rights have reached new heights in the past two years. Is the current advocacy of HIV rights and LGBT rights in Taiwan premised upon the foreclosure of the deviant HIV subject? Must the "community" be cleaned up before it can seek legal recognition, as the "new MSM movement" promoted by the burgeoning culture of gay sexual health — with the old epidemiological term "MSM" being given a new spin as "Mitigate Stigma Myself" — suggests?[76]

Ironically, as the Christian Right in Taiwan mobilizes HIV stigma in its opposition to gay marriage, Lourdes and Positive Alliance can only respond by employing a language of harmony that leaves out the pressing question of institutional power.[77] The nonconfrontational position taken by AIDS NGOs in dealing with HIV stigma is congruent with the culture of compassion that currently prevails in mainstream Taiwan: members of the general public are now encouraged by the AIDS surveillance industry to cheer for people with HIV — "Go, go, my HIV-positive friend, you can do it!" In the climate of neomoralism, where individuals with HIV are responsibilized through a new mode of flat governance that is at once liberal and authoritarian, HIV control has come to operate in an increasingly individualizing and isolating way through moralized HIV care. The public cheering, in effect, functions as "compulsory happiness" for those who are not yet qualified by the new mode of therapeutic citizenship, a mode of citizenship that arises from the disciplining and punishing of deviant practices and pleasures.[78]

While HIV care is still free at the moment, people on the HIV registry are continually held for ransom by the Taiwanese state, as my contextualized analysis of the AIDS budget crisis has shown. Thus, rather than scratching the surface of neoliberal tolerance, Positive Alliance ends up making the general public feel good about themselves. Model positive individuals might be feeling happy about having a share in the happiness of the general public, but I see this act of sharing as one of self-purification.[79] Given the privation and indeed the sequestration of HIV experiences shaped by the biomedicalization of HIV surveillance, developing a politics that contests statist HIV control and the benevolent AIDS service/surveillance industry it spawns has become the most pressing challenge for queer survival in Taiwan today.

NOTES

This essay emerges from a three-year research project entitled "The Emotional Governance of a Stigmatized Disease: AIDS NGOs and the Cultural Politics of Shame" (NSC 100-2410-H-008-065-MY3), funded by the Ministry of Technology, Taiwan. Part of the writing was undertaken during my research leave in 2012 and 2013. I wish to express my gratitude to Top University Strategic Alliance of Taiwan for providing generous funding and to the Centre for the History of Science, Technology and Medicine at Imperial College London for hosting me. Many thanks are also due to Josephine Ho, Naifei Ding, and Trevor Hoppe, who have given me very helpful comments and suggestions at different stages of the writing. Needless to say, all the shortcomings are mine.

1. Taiwan CDC, "Draft Bill for the 2014 Amendment of the HIV Control and Patients Right Protection Act" 人類免疫缺乏病毒傳染防治及感染者權益保障條例部分條文修正草案總說明 (2014), http://www.cdc.gov.tw/downloadfile.aspx?fid=4B07C4726A5F554E.

2. Taiwan CDC, "Draft Bill for the 2014 Amendment of the HIV Control and Patients Right Protection Act" 人類免疫缺乏病毒傳染防治及感染者權益保障條例部分條文修正草案總說明.

3. Taiwan's National Health Insurance program was implemented in 1997. Following the introduction of the global cap system in 2000, private hospitals appointed by the CDC to provide HIV care began, it was alleged, to feel the strain of administering costly HIV medicine. After successful lobbying, led by the Taiwan Medical Association, which contended that HIV treatment is an integral part of communicable disease prevention and therefore should be paid for by the administration, the parliament amended the HIV Control Act to allocate the expenditure back to the CDC's budget in 2005.

4. Positive Alliance 帕斯堤聯盟, "Ten Myths on the Copayment of HIV Medical Care: A Response from Positive Alliance" 關於愛滋醫療部分負擔十大迷思，帕斯堤有話要說, September 27, 2012, http://positive31920.blogspot.co.uk/2012/09/blog-post.html/, accessed May 15, 2013.

5. For the coalition's statement and news coverage of the NGO response to the budget crisis, see http://aidsactions.blogspot.tw/.

6. CNA News 中央社, "NGOs Calling on HIV Medical Expenditure to Be Relocated Back to the NHS" 愛滋藥費支出 民團籲回歸健保, September 28, 2012, https://tw.news.yahoo.com/%E6%84%9B%E6%BB%8B%E8%97%A5%E8%B2%BB%E6%94%AF%E5%87%BA-%E6%Bo%91%E5%9C%98%E7%B1%B2%E5%9B%9E%E6%AD%B8%E5%81%A5%E4%BF%9D-101222451.html.

7. Z. Lin and H. Zeng 林宗弘、曾惠君, "The Politics of Household Registration: A Comparative Study between the System of Household Registration in China and Taiwan" 戶口的政治：中國大陸與台灣戶籍制度之歷史比較, China Studies 中國大陸研究 57, no. 1 (2014): 63–93.

8. Here the work of medical anthropologist Vinh-Kim Nguyen on HIV governmentality in West Africa can serve as a useful comparative framework to underscore my discussion of therapeutic citizenship in the East Asian context. Departing from the concept of "biological citizenship" developed by A. Petryna, *Life Exposed: Biological Citizens after Chernobyl* (Princeton, NJ: Princeton University Press, 2002), and by N. Rose and C. Novas, "Biological Citizenship," in *Global Assemblages: Technology, Politics, and Ethics as Anthropological Problems*, ed. A. Ong and S. J. Collier (Malden, MA: Blackwell Publishing, 2005), 439–463, Nguyen proposes "therapeutic citizenship" to underscore the precarious state of living with HIV/AIDS in places with poor public health infrastructures. In particular, he shows how biopolitics is exercised in West Africa not so much through state sovereignty as through a "mobile sovereignty" established by the neoimperial power of humanitarian aid and transnational NGO governance. V.-K. Nguyen, *The Republic of Therapy: Triage and Sovereignty in West Africa's Time of AIDS* (Durham, NC: Duke University Press, 2010). In Taiwan, the technique of HIV registry is patently statist, whereas a system of patient registration in West Africa had to be created in order to facilitate the operationalization of massive

treatment programs. V.-K. Nguyen, "Government-by-Exception: Enrolment and Experimentality in Mass HIV Treatment Programmes in Africa," *Social Theory & Health* 7 (2009): 196–217. Similar mechanisms of HIV surveillance premised on household registration are also found in China (T. Kang, "Reinventing the Self under Socialism," *Critical Asian Studies* 42, no. 2 [2012]: 283–308) and South Korea (B.-H. Cho, "HIV/AIDS Policy in South Korea," *International Studies of Education* 9 (2008): 37–39). As the system of household registration is closely tied up with the politics of family and marriage, a comparative study of HIV state surveillance among these East Asian countries would yield new insights on the materialization of sexual and therapeutic citizenship in the region.

9. If they fail to do so, they could face the prospect of their guarded secret of HIV infection (which is what, for most people, it remains) being divulged to their family, as public health nurses attempt to track them down at their previous addresses.

10. Instead of "adherence," I use "compliance" to underscore the abiding paternalism of medical authority in the Taiwanese context. On medical compliance, see K. Race, *Pleasure Consuming Medicine: The Queer Politics of Drugs* (Durham, NC: Duke University Press, 2009); E. Mykhalovskiy et al., "Compliance/Adherence, HIV and the Critique of Medical Power," *Social Theory & Health* 2 (2004): 315–340.

11. Taiwan CDC, "The 2013 Plan for Hospital-Based HIV Case Management Program" 102 年度愛滋病個案管理計畫, November 2012, http://www.cdc.gov.tw/public /Attachment/1111810352871.doc.

12. A 2004 study of Taiwan has been frequently cited by recent research to show the efficacy of "treatment as prevention." C. Fang et al., "Decreased HIV Transmission after a Policy of Providing Free Access to Highly Active Antiretroviral Therapy in Taiwan," *Journal of Infectious Diseases* 190, no. 1 (2004): 879–885. I thank Cindy Patton for this reference.

13. On the history of early AIDS organizing in Taiwan, see H. Huang 黃道明, "Mainstreaming the Red Ribbon: Sexual Governance and the NGO Culture of HIV Prevention in Taiwan" 紅絲帶主流化：台灣愛滋NGO防治文化與性治理, in *AIDS Governance and Local Actions* 愛滋治理與在地行動, ed. H. Huang (Zhongli: Center for the Study of Sexualities, National Central University 中央大學性／別研究室, 2012). Until about 2005, state HIV/AIDS prevention was relegated to an education unit at the Sexually Transmitted Diseases Clinic of Taipei City Hospital. C. Cai 蔡春美, "A Health Educator's Praxes of Knowledge and Reflections: Using AIDS to Nourish My Life 一位衛生教育工作者的實踐知識與反思: 用愛滋潤我的生命" (PhD thesis, Institute of Health Education, National Normal University, Taiwan, 2005), 36–37. Established in 1969 at the request of the U.S. government to protect the health of GIs coming to Taiwan for "Rest and Relaxation" during the Vietnamese war, the clinic currently retains the largest numbers of HIV patients in Taiwan.

14. K. H. Chen, *Asia as Methods: Toward Deimperialization* (Durham, NC: Duke University Press, 2009).

15. J. Ho, "Is Global Governance Bad for East Asian Queers?" GLQ: *A Journal of Lesbian and Gay Studies* 14, no. 4 (2008): 457–479; J. Ho, "Queer Existence under Global Governance: A Taiwan Exemplar," *Positions: East Asia Cultures Critique* 18, no. 2 (2010): 537–554; Y. Ning 甯應斌, "The Extreme Protectionist Prejudice: Technocratic Government through Child Welfare in the New Regulatory State of Taiwan" 極端保護觀：透過兒少保護的新管制國家與階級治理, *Taiwan: A Radical Quarterly of Social Sciences* 台灣社會研究季刊 83 (2011): 279–293.

16. Race, *Pleasure Consuming Medicine.*

17. Race, *Pleasure Consuming Medicine*, 59–79.

18. The underground gay rave club culture took off in Taiwan around the late 1990s when the party drug ecstasy became popular. Due to constant police raids on venues, clubbing underwent a sharp decline. This factor, combined with online cruising, gave rise to the urban phenomenon of "home party" gay subculture. C. Hung 洪啟明, "Gay Rave Culture and HIV Prevention: A Subcultural Intervention in Public Policy" (MA thesis, Department of English, National Central University, 2007). See J. Chang 張永靖, "Affective Ruptures, Queer (Op)Positionalities: Sex and Intimacy in Contemporary Taiwanese Literary Representations on Ecstasy" (MA thesis, Department of English, National Central University, 2010), for a very fine analysis of contemporary Taiwanese literary representations of the "home party."

19. Apple Daily 蘋果日報, "92 Gay Men Having Group Sex: 28 are Found with AIDS, 31 with Syphilis" 92 人雜交 28 人患愛滋 31 梅毒, January 21, 2004, http://www.appledaily.com.tw/appledaily/article/headline/20040121/660437/.

20. See Article 14 of the HIV Control Act. This is a classic Agambenian example of the normalization of the "state of exception." G. Agamben, *Homo Sacer: Sovereign Power and Bare Life* (Stanford, CA: Stanford University Press, 1998).

21. Taiwan CDC 行政院衛生署疾病管制局, *HIV Prevention in Taiwan: A Handbook* 台灣地區愛滋病防治工作手冊, 1st ed. (Taipei: Center for Disease Control 行政院衛生署疾病管制局, 2004), http://www2.cdc.gov.tw/public/Attachment/2112211572271.doc/.

22. Having successfully brought down the HIV infection rate among IDUs within two years, the intensive operations of harm reduction were gradually phased out, and the policy was integrated into the newly set up hospital-based HCM program (J.-S. Chen, "Studying Up Harm Reduction Policy: The Office as an Assemblage," *International Journal of Drug Policy* 22 (2011): 471.

23. Chen, "Studying Up Harm Reduction Policy"; J.-S. Chen, "Beyond Human Rights and Public Health: Citizenship Issues in Harm Reduction," *International Journal of Drug Policy* 22 (2011): 184–188.

24. What is interesting about Chen's study is that the CDC maneuvered public opinion with its timing of the press release and then made use of the responses it elicited from civil society (demanding the government take action) to increase its influence in cross-departmental negotiations with the police and the Department of Justice (Chen, "Studying Up Harm Reduction Policy," 473–476).

25. M. Finn and S. Sarangi, "Humanising HIV/AIDS and Its (Re)Stigmatising Effects: HIV Public 'Positive' Speaking in India," *Health: An Interdisciplinary Journal for the Social Study of Health, Illness and Medicine* 13, no. 1 (2009): 47–65.

26. Huang, "Mainstreaming the Red Ribbon," 93–98.

27. Y. Chen 陳宜民, "The Crisis of HIV Prevention in Taiwan" 我國愛滋防治的危機及轉機, 2004, http://www.ym.edu.tw/aids/aids/PPT/824.ppt/; Y. Chen 陳宜民, "HIV/AIDS Care Policy" 愛滋病的照護政策, 2004, http://www.ym.edu.tw/aids/aids/PPT/hiv-care.ppt/.

28. Chen, "HIV/AIDS Care Policy."

29. N. Y. Ko and W. Ko 柯乃熒、柯文謙, "Behaviour Therapy for Individuals with HIV: Pilot Program of Southern Taiwan" 愛滋病毒感染者行為治療醫療給付計畫—南區, 2005 Center for Disease Control Funding Program 行政院衛生署疾病管制局 94 年度補助計畫, Project Number: DOH94-DC-118, 2006.

30. Ko and Ko, "Behaviour Therapy for Individuals with HIV," 3.

31. K. Race, "Framing Responsibility: HIV, Biomedical Prevention and the Performativity of the Law," *Journal of Bioethical Inquiry* 9, no. 3 (2012): 329.

32. P. Zhuang and Y. Wang 莊苹、王永衛, "Behaviour Therapy for Individuals with HIV: Pilot Program of Northern Taiwan" 愛滋病毒感染者行為治療醫療給付計畫—北區. 2005 Center for Disease Control Funding Program 行政院衛生署疾病管制局 94 年度補助計畫, Project Number: DOH94-DC-116, 2006.

33. R. Wang 王任賢, "Behaviour Therapy for Individuals with HIV: Pilot Program of Central Taiwan" 中部地區愛滋病毒感染者行為治療計畫, 2005 Center for Disease Control Funding Program 行政院衛生署疾病管制局 94 年度補助計畫, Project Number: DOH94-DC-117, 2006.

34. On the politics of medical ontology, see A. Mol, "Ontological Politics: A Word and Some Questions," in *Actor Network Theory and After*, ed. J. Law and J. Hassard (London: Blackwell, 1999), 74–89; A. Mol, *The Body Multiple: Ontology in Medical Practice* (Durham, NC: Duke University Press, 2002).

35. See R. Wang 王任賢, "Case Management for Chronic and Communicable Disease" 慢性傳染病之個案管理, http://www.ccd.org.tw/upload/news/345/2upfile.pdf/, accessed May 15, 2013.

36. See B. Ji 紀秉宗, "Efficacy of Hospital-Based HIV Case Management Program" 愛滋病個案管理計畫效果研究 (MA thesis, Department of Health Promotion and Education, National Normal University 國立師範大學健康促進與教育學系在職進修碩士班

碩士論文, 2010); B. Ji et al. 紀秉宗等, "Hospital-Based HIV Case Management Program and the Analysis of Behavioral Modifications" 愛滋病個案管理師計畫與個案行為改變分析, *Epidemiology Bulletin* 疫情報導 26, no. 16 (2010): 222–227; Z. Qiu and C. Ting 邱珠敏、丁志音, "Effects of HIV Case Management Program on the Behavior and Health Outcomes of Clients" 「愛滋個案管理計畫」對個案行為及健康影響, *Journal of Taiwan Public Health* 台灣衛誌 29, no. 4 (2010): 299–313. See R. Grob, "The Heart of Patient-Centered Care," *Journal of Health Politics, Policy and Law* 38, no. 2 (2013): 547–565, for a critique of "patient-centered" care. When viewed from the point of view of the state's biopolitical objectives to produce useful individuals, such promises are not necessarily false.

37. Taiwan CDC, "The 2013 Plan for Hospital-Based HIV Case Management Program," 102 年度愛滋病個案管理計畫, 2012.

38. M. Foucault, "The Subject and Power," in *Michel Foucault: Beyond Structuralism and Hermeneutics*, ed. H. Dreyfus and P. Rabinow (Chicago: University of Chicago Press, 1982), 208–226.

39. In a cultural context where the authority of medicine remains largely unquestioned, the case manager is unlikely to encourage the patient to think about the workings of institutional power in the production of the social stigma around HIV/AIDS.

40. It is crucial to note that the scaling up of anonymous testing since 2007 has been well coordinated with the HCM program. Ji et al. 紀秉宗等, "Hospital-Based HIV Case Management Program and the Analysis of Behavioral Modifications" 愛滋病個案管理師計畫與個案行為改變分析.

41. Z. Shi 施鍾卿, "Case Management for Chronic Illness 慢性照護個案管理," in *Nursing Case Management: Essential Concepts and Practice* 護理個案管理導論, ed. Y. Liu et al. (Taipei: Huxing 華杏出版社, 2013), 200.

42. Because of their proximity to the patient, HIV case managers have taken on the task of contact tracing, which was previously assigned to the public health nurse. In the CDC's performance appraisal, the HIV case manager gets more points when he or she is able to track down the real identity of the patient's sexual contacts.

43. G. Lai 賴岡言, "Characteristics of HIV Positive Gay Men and the Key Points of Management," in *HIV Case Management: An E-Book* 愛滋病個案管理電子書, ed. Nurse AIDS Prevention Foundation 護理人員愛滋病防治基金會 (Taipei: Nurse AIDS Prevention Foundation 護理人員愛滋病防治基金會, 2009), 8; C. Cai 蔡春美, "On the Techniques of Sex and Self-Inspection" 談論「性」技巧與自我省察, in *HIV Case Management: An E-Book* 愛滋病個案管理電子書, ed. Nurse AIDS Prevention Foundation 護理人員愛滋病防治基金會 (Taipei: Nurse AIDS Prevention Foundation 護理人員愛滋病防治基金會, 2009), 4. Foucault underscores that the warrant of confidentiality is key to the production of sexuality: "We belong to a society which has ordered sex's difficult knowledge . . . around the slow surfacing of confidential statements."

M. Foucault, *The History of Sexuality*, Volume 1, *An Introduction* (London: Penguin, 1990), 63.

44. Taiwan CDC, "Definition of Risk Behavior" 危險性行為之範圍標準, 2008, http://www.praatw.org/right_1_cont.asp?id=5/.

45. HIV patients are issued with a special card for HIV medical care. From 2011 onward, this notification has to be read out by health officials at the local public health bureau before the card is given to the patient. Although the notification is not legally binding, it has to be signed, and this symbolic ritual subjects those on the HIV registry to the moral universe ordained by the Taiwanese state. Taiwan CDC, "Notification on the Rights and Duties of Patients with HIV" 領取全國醫療服務卡權利與義務告知書, 2011, https://www.e-services.taipei.gov.tw/eservicesFile/formfile/021107/40/%E9%A0%98%E5%8F%96%E5%85%A8%E5%9C%8B%E9%86%AB%E7%99%82%E6%9C%8D%E5%8B%99%E5%8D%A1%E6%AC%8A%E5%88%A9%E8%88%87%E7%BE%A9%E5%8B%99%E5%91%8A%E7%9F%A5%E6%9B%B8.pdf/.

46. C. Chen 陳昶勳, "HIV Prevalence and Prevention in Taiwan: An Update" 臺灣愛滋感染與防治現況, 2012, http://www.kmuh.org.tw/www/Tropical/20120507_台灣愛滋病防治政策與相關法令規定_陳組長.pdf/.

47. N. Y. Ko et al., "One-Year Follow-up of Relapse to Risky Behaviors and Incidence of Syphilis among Patients Enrolled in the HIV Case Management Program," *AIDS and Behavior* 15, no. 5 (2010): 1073.

48. Apart from translating booklets on treatment information published by I-Base, a U.K.-based treatment advocacy and information organization, Lourdes was also instrumental in mediating the harm reduction approach to HIV prevention in the middle of the first decade of the 2000s.

49. Vinh-Kim Nguyen has shown in his study of antiretroviral globalism that so-called "community-based organizations" (CBOs) in the Third World context are both an instrument and an effect of transnational HIV technologies. V.-K. Nguyen, "Antiretroviral Globalism, Biopolitics, and Therapeutic Citizenship," in *Global Assemblages: Technology, Politics, and Ethics as Anthropological Problems*, ed. A. Ong and S. J. Collier (Malden, MA: Blackwell, 2005), 124–144; Nguyen, *The Republic of Therapy*.

50. I take the phrase "soul governing" from N. Rose, *Governing the Soul: The Shaping of the Private Self* (London: Free Association Books, 1999).

51. P. Hsu 徐森杰, "From Support to Self-Help: My Action and Reflection with AIDS Support Group" 從支持到自助 — 我與愛滋感染者支持團體的行動與反思 (MA thesis, Suchow University, Institute of Social Work 東吳大學社會工作研究所碩士論文, Taipei, 2004).

52. P. Hsu et al. 徐森杰等, "People with HIV and Their Experience with Psychodrama" 愛滋病毒感染者心理劇經驗, *Chinese Group Psychotherapy* 中華團體心理治療 9, no. 2 (2003): 18–19.

53. Hsu et al., "People with HIV and Their Experience with Psychodrama" 愛滋病毒感染者心理劇經驗, 18.

54. Taiwan Lourdes Association, "Dialogues with International Poz Elites" 與國際帕司堤菁英對話, October 30, 2012, http://www.lourdes.org.tw/Activity_list_1.asp?id=124&menu1=3&menu2=18. These poz elites are Ken ("Rainbow China," Hong Kong), Joey (Hong Kong AIDS Foundation), and Laurindo Garcia ("B-Change," the Philippines).

55. See Taiwan Lourdes Association 露德協會, "On 'Positi'" 關於帕斯堤, http://www.lourdes.org.tw/onePage.asp?menu1=7&menu2=117/, accessed January 17, 2014.

56. See J. Chang 張永靖, "The Privilege of Coming Out: Homonormative AIDS Activism and Its Unknowing Stigmas" 出櫃的特權：正典同志愛滋運動及其未顯的污名, in *Law, Prevention and the Politics of Pleasure: AIDS Governance and Local Actions II 法律、防治與愉悅的政治：愛滋治理與在地行動> II*, ed. H. Huang (Zhongli: Center for the Study of Sexualities, National Central University 中央大學性／別研究室 [2014], 181–208), for a brilliant discussion of sexual stigma as a structure of "bad feelings," as that which is to be rejected by the "Good Poz" discourse in Taiwan. Importantly, Chang notes that those who are unable or who refuse to think positive thoughts come to be psychologized as "problem Poz": as such, they are construed as being in need of rescue.

57. On Guangge's speech, see Citizen News 公民新聞, "HIV Patient Out and Optimistic" 愛滋帶原者陽光開朗現身，樂觀面對, 2011, http://www.peopo.org/quendigay/post/92567/.

58. For Shihao's blog (called "Spiritual Food for Gay Men"), see http://gsoup1069.blogspot.tw/.

59. Happy Life international conference, Taipei, September 7–8, 2013, http://23711406.blogspot.tw/2013/09/2013.html/.

60. See Happy Life international conference, 2013.

61. H. Huang 黃道明, "On the Case of Feng" 評馮姓教師案, 2012, http://www.coolloud.org.tw/node/72175.

62. Trevor Hoppe points out that while the criminalization of poz-on-poz sex is rare worldwide, the cases are not well publicized (personal communication).

63. Taipei District Court 台北地方法院刑事判決, Criminal verdict no. 221 102 年度訴字第 221 號 (2013).

64. Chen 陳昶勳, "HIV Prevalence and Prevention in Taiwan: An Update" 臺灣愛滋感染與防治現況.

65. P. Zhuang 莊苹, "Who Cares if the Teacher Is Infected with HIV or Not: A Retake" 如今再看「管他老師有沒有感染」, September 20, 2012, http://www.facebook.com/notes/%E8%8E%8A%E8%8B%B9/%E7%AE%A1%E4%BB%96%E8%80%81

%E5%B8%AB%E6%9C%89%E6%B2%92%E6%9C%89%E6%84%9F%E6%9F%93/475315879168120.

66. Zhuang makes this clear in an article discussing, with specific reference to Feng's case, the negative impacts of HIV criminalization on public health. P. Zhuang 莊苹, "It's Too Harsh to Accuse Someone of Intentionally Transmitting HIV: A Medical Personnel's View on the Impact of the Criminalization of HIV on HIV Prevention" 說「蓄意」太沈重：一位醫事人員看待愛滋條例第 21 條對防疫之影響, *Persons with HIV/AIDS Rights Advocacy Association Bulletin* 權通訊 17 (2013): 2.

67. S. Kippax, "Effective HIV Prevention: The Indispensable Role of Social Science," *Journal of the International AIDS Society* 15, no. 2 (2012): 17357.

68. H. Huang 黃道明, "AIDS Human Rights and the Sequestration of Viral Sex" 愛滋人權下的性隔離, 2014, http://www.intermargins.net/Activity/2014/0103/pdf/.

69. As Cindy Patton ("Rights Language and HIV Treatment: Universal Care or Population Control?" *Rhetoric Society Quarterly* 41, no. 3 (2011): 250–266) points out in her critique of "treatment as prevention," this depoliticized language, based on populations rather than on individuals, not only massively glosses over the long-term side effects of HAART on different individual bodies but also buttresses the authoritarian desire to seek out those deviant bodies and to control them for the greater good of society.

70. I am conducting a research project on how a new regime of drug control came into formation shortly after the lifting of martial law.

71. I thank Ding Naifei for this point.

72. P. Hsu 徐森杰, "Diagnosing Taiwan's System of HIV Case Management: Outlooks of the Social, Medical and Public Health Models" 為台灣愛滋病個案管理制度把脈——談社會、醫療暨公衛個案管理模式之展望, *Community Development Bulletin* 社區發展季刊 137 (2012): 241–249.

73. Huang, "Mainstreaming the Red Ribbon," 106–129. Interestingly, Lourdes itself has spawned two gay health centers, and one of them has recently transformed itself into a registered NGO.

74. See Taiwan Lourdes Association, "Learning the Pleasure in/of 'Harm-Reduction' Group Therapy," March 29, 2013, http://www.lourdes.org.tw/list_1.asp?id=2322&menu1=3&menu2=120. Importantly, knowledge extracted from this group has recently become part of the training material provided to hospital-based HIV managers.

75. The model "seek, test, treat, and retain" (STTR) was proposed by the U.S. National Institute on Drug Abuse to target the drug-using population. See http://www.drugabuse.gov/researchers/research-resources/data-harmonization-projects/seek-test-treat-retain, accessed May 5, 2014.

76. This new take on MSM was proposed by public health expert Dr. Chih-Yin Ting. C. Ting 丁志音, "Overcoming Double Labelling: Gay Men Should Advocate the New MSM Movement" 突破雙重標籤化，同志應推廣新 MSM 運動, in *Getting to Know Tongzhi: 2009 Tongzhi Citizen Movement Handbook* 2009 年同志公民運動：認識同志手冊 (Taipei: Taipei City Government and Taiwan AIDS Foundation 台北市政府、紅絲帶基金會, 2009), 50–51.

77. Taiwan Lourdes Association 露德協會, "A Statement on the 'Heart-Broken Mother' Short Film" 露德聲明：關於心碎媽媽短片, 2013, http://www.coolloud.org.tw/node/76265/; Positive Alliance 帕斯堤聯盟, "A Statement on the 'Heart-Broken Mother' Short Film" 露德聲明：關於心碎媽媽短片, 2013, http://www.coolloud.org.tw/node/76266/.

78. See H. Love, "Compulsory Happiness and Queer Existence," *New Formation* 64, no. 1 (2007): 52–64, for the critique of the happy queer in neoliberal times.

79. I draw on Ahmed's critique of "sociable happiness" here. S. Ahmed, "Killing Joy: Feminism and the History of Happiness," *Signs* 35, no. 3 (2010): 571–592.

PART V

Resistance

MAURICE TOMLINSON

| 15 |

The New War on Sex

A Report from the Global Front Lines

Sex is political. Nowhere is this more apparent than in the worldwide struggle for the recognition of human rights for lesbian, gay, bisexual, Trans*, and intersex (LGBTI) people. Globally, between seventy-six and eighty countries (depending on whether you view criminalization as a matter of class or conduct) impose sanctions against same-gender intimacy and/or gender-nonconforming expression. Five of these countries impose the death penalty for homosexuality.

In 2014, the daughter of Cuban president Raúl Castro, Mariela Castro, reportedly became the first Cuban legislator ever to vote "no" in the history of the country's 612-seat post-revolution national assembly. The legislation up for consideration was a workers' rights bill that she felt did not go far enough to prevent discrimination against transgender workers or people with HIV. Despite the bill's passage without the broader provisions sought by Castro, Cuba still has the most extensive protections for LGBTI people in the northern Caribbean, with protections that rival those available in the United States.

Elsewhere in the Caribbean, legislative protections for LGBTI people are far more tenuous. In the Americas, anti-gay laws have been largely stripped from the books. The exception to this trend is the eleven independent Anglophone Caribbean countries that make up the Caribbean Community (CARICOM), where laws imposed during the period of colonization remain on the books. Meanwhile, territories still controlled by Britain, France, the Netherlands, and the United States have all abolished these archaic statutes. Ironically, for LGBTI citizens, Caribbean colonies are now freer than independent states.

In my own country of Jamaica, the anti-gay legislation is comparatively mild: "only" ten years in prison at hard labor. Even so, the human rights situation for homosexuals is quite complex. Research by the region's premier university, the University of the West Indies, found that well over 80 percent of Jamaicans self-identify as homophobic, and the country has recorded the most savage anti-gay attacks region-wide. Jamaica also has the highest HIV prevalence rate among men who have sex with men (MSM) in the Western Hemisphere, if not the world (33 percent). Homophobia has long been recognized as the reason for this disparity: MSM are simply driven underground, away from effective HIV prevention, treatment, care, and support interventions.

Jamaica's troubled reality for gays is emblematic of the situation in many parts of the world. The interplay among laws, religious morality, and neocolonial and geopolitical issues looms large in this debate. I will attempt to provide a very cursory perspective of how the "sex wars" are being fought from a global perspective, based primarily on my experience working on LGBTI and HIV issues in the Jamaican "trenches."

Essays in this collection largely deal with the regulation of sex in the West. This essay highlights the ongoing struggle for securing basic legal protections for LGBTI people globally, as this remains a pressing issue outside of the global north.

THE STATE OF LGBTI HUMAN RIGHTS GLOBALLY: THE GOOD, THE BAD, AND THE CONFUSING

For over forty years, modern-day anti-gay crusaders from the global north have been busy stoking the fires of international homophobia. These persons are mostly losers in their own countries' fierce culture wars and include Americans (e.g., Peter LaBarbera and Scott Lively), Britons (Paul Diamond and Andrea Minichiello Williams), and Canadians (Dr. Janet Epp Buckingham and Douglas Allen). Their impact has been most profound in states with long traditions of repressing minorities in response to, or as an excuse for, economic, social, and political challenges. The most notorious manifestation of this situation involves Scott Lively.

In 2009, Lively traveled to Uganda and conducted public conferences attended by local parliamentarians. During those sessions, Lively compared gays to Nazis and claimed that they were, among other things, actively recruiting children into a dangerous and deviant lifestyle. A few months later, a draconian anti-homosexuality bill was presented to the Ugandan Parliament that: 1) called for the death penalty for gays (which was subsequently amended to life imprisonment), 2) required parents and other caregivers to hand over their gay charges to the police or face imprisonment, and 3) mandated the extradition to Uganda of any citizen who engaged in homosexuality internationally. Even in draft form, the law unleashed a wave of unprecedented anti-gay violence in the country perpetrated by both state and non-state actors. One reason is that in the most popular Ugandan native language, there is no difference between a "bill" and a "law." For all intents and purposes, the legislation was already in force. Lively was subsequently ordered to stand trial in the United States under the Alien Tort Statute for harm done to Ugandan LGBTI people as a result of his actions in that country.

Uganda's president, Yoweri Museveni, initially went on public record to declare that the private lives of consenting adults did not concern him, and he questioned the need for the bill when it was eventually passed in 2013. However, President Museveni faced a robust and credible challenge to his reign of nearly three decades from the Speaker of the Ugandan Parliament, Rebecca Kadaga. In 2012, Kadaga, a lawyer, had promised the wildly popular bill to the Ugandan people as a "Christmas present" and managed to deliver on this promise a few months later.

In response to this political threat, the president abruptly changed course and resorted to some of the most virulently anti-gay rhetoric imaginable. He dropped his resistance to the bill's passage and publicly signed it into law. The "jail the gays" act was subsequently struck down by the country's constitutional court on a technicality (conveniently, during a state visit by the president of the United States — which happens to be Uganda's major donor — who was a vocal critic of the bill). However, as of this writing, the law is about to be reintroduced into the Ugandan Parliament. In the meantime, Uganda's sister African nation, the Gambia, has passed the original form of the bill.

The fact that global north religious fundamentalists have helped to foment hate against LGBTI people in the global south does not detract from the agency of local nationals to hate. While Scott Lively and others like him bear significant responsibility for these developments, neither Ugandan nor Gambian leaders are off the hook. Same-gender intimacy in precolonial Africa is a matter of anthropological record. However, many African leaders today object to same-gender attraction, arguing that it is a foreign practice. Such rhetoric is usually couched in religious morality.

Around the world, the struggle to recognize the human rights of LGBTI people takes many forms. The following examples illustrate the multifaceted state of the movement.

Turkey's president often uses popular anti-gay rhetoric in this largely Muslim society as a way to sustain his power base. However, the country is seen as a bastion of LGBTI equality in the Middle East, and Istanbul's annual gay pride parade rivals many in the major cities of the global north.

In Iran, the death penalty is imposed for same-gender intimacy — a penalty enforced as recently as July 2014, when two men were publicly hanged for sodomy. However, despite the country's violent reaction to homosexuality, more gender reassignment surgeries are performed in Iran than in almost any other country in the world; they trail only Thailand for the lead.

In the wake of Nelson Mandela's progressive coalition to overhaul dramatically his country's legal system, South Africa today has the most progressive anti-discrimination laws protecting LGBTI people in the world. Yet, despite these legal protections, so-called corrective rapes of lesbians intended to "cure" their homosexuality remain common. Homophobia is also rampant; the country's own high commissioner to Uganda was convicted of homophobic hate speech.

In Australia, the marriage-equality discussion hit a reef in the person of the arch-conservative Roman Catholic former prime minister Tony Abbott. Prime Minister Abbott staunchly refused to accept the views of the overwhelming majority of Australians who support same-gender marriage. Abbott's stance set his country at odds with its political contemporaries, including the United Kingdom and Canada. In those countries, marriage equality is accepted as a manifestation of conservative ideals. New Zealand has also recognized marriage equality, based on, and celebrated as, an Aboriginal tradition.

The Caribbean situation is similarly nuanced. Despite a reputation as a popular tourist destination, the region is home to the only two remaining countries in the Western Hemisphere that still ban the entry of homosexuals (Belize and Trinidad and Tobago). Barbados also has the most draconian anti-gay law in the region (life imprisonment for "buggery"). Despite less severe anti-gay criminal punishments (maximum of ten years imprisonment at hard labor), Jamaica is home to a greater amount of violence against LGBTI people than any other Caribbean country.

In India, there is perhaps the most glaring example of the apparent schizophrenia that defines the global LGBTI human rights movement. In a much-maligned decision, the country's Supreme Court decided to re-criminalize same-gender intimacy in January 2014. But just a few weeks later, the Court recognized full equality for Trans*-identified people. This represents the collision between imposed Victorian morality that criminalized same-gender intimacy and traditional Indian values that recognized gender-divergent individuals. In most LGBTI liberation struggles, sexual orientation usually received protection before gender identity and expression. India appears to be approaching the matter from the opposite direction.

VOICES OF JAMAICAN VICTIMS:
UNDERSTANDING THEIR REALITY

In discussions with Jamaican parliamentarians and opinion leaders, I am constantly amazed at their level of denial about human rights abuses against LGBTI people. This denial is largely responsible for their refusal to take definitive action to end homophobia. The only way to counter the delusion is hopefully through evidence. Therefore, I have tracked just a few of the anti-gay assaults that were reported by Jamaican media in one year.

It is important to note that Jamaican media has not been very supportive of the LGBTI liberation movement (for example, the major broadcasters refused to air an ad calling for respect of the rights of gays). Therefore, media reporting on these incidents must not be viewed as objective and in no way serves any interest of the LGBTI community.

Dwayne Jones was a Jamaican sixteen-year-old Trans* teen who had been evicted from her home at the age of fourteen. As with many other LGBTI youth from the lower socioeconomic strata, Dwayne was forced to live in abandoned buildings, as there is no dedicated shelter for LGBTI youth. Those homeless shelters that do exist are notoriously hostile toward LGBTI people.

Dwayne "squatted" with friends in an unoccupied house, and on the evening of June 21, 2013, she decided to attend a public street dance. Dwayne was dancing with one of her gay friends when a female member of her church recognized her and outed her biological gender to the crowd. A mob then set upon Dwayne, stabbing her, shooting her, and running over her body with a car before dumping her remains in a nearby ditch. After the murder, the dance continued while Dwayne's friends sought refuge in a nearby church.

The police found Dwayne's body the next morning. As of this writing, despite a town full of witnesses, no one has been arrested for her murder.

The story does not end there. The house where Dwayne's surviving friends resided was later firebombed. Again, no one was arrested. In fact, when the youngsters sought refuge in a police station, they were turned away by officers who feared that the station would itself become a target for mob attacks if it was seen to be harboring gay people. The fears of the officers were not unjustified. Earlier in the year, Jamaican media reported that a police officer was mobbed in downtown Kingston because he was accused of being gay. He had to be rescued by other officers, who fired shots into the air and teargas into the crowd. Again, no one was arrested.

Since Dwayne's gruesome murder, the attacks against gay Jamaicans have continued unabated. To give a sense of the perverse regularity of such crimes, the most egregious reported assaults include:

- August 1, 2013: A mob attacked the home of two gay men in St. Catherine. They too had to be rescued by police.

- August 10, 2013: A mob attacked a Trans* woman in St. Catherine. The police again had to rescue the individual.

- August 22, 2013: A mob attacked five allegedly gay men, who were trapped in their house in Green Mountain until police arrived and escorted them to safety.

- August 26, 2013: A mob surrounded two allegedly gay men who were involved in a minor traffic accident in Old Harbour, St. Catherine. A member of the mob said that homosexuality might be acceptable elsewhere but not in Old Harbour. The men had to flee to a nearby police station to escape harm.

- October 8, 2013: A mob firebombed the abandoned building in Montego Bay that was the former home of murdered teen Dwayne Jones and where her friends continued to live.

- June 14, 2014: A mob attacked a young man at a shopping mall in May Pen, Clarendon, because he was allegedly seen putting on lipstick.

These crimes are the direct result of violent anti-gay rhetoric that spews from the mouths of local leaders. In June 2014, there was a massive anti-gay rally in

Kingston with reportedly 25,000 people in attendance. Similar homophobic protests have been held in major cities across the island. Jamaica's homophobia has also caused regional ripples. On Sunday, August 24, 2014, religious groups on the island of St. Thomas in the U.S. Virgin Islands held an anti-gay march to protest proposed marriage-equality legislation. They cited the Jamaican anti-gay rally as their inspiration.

If these violent acts were intended in part to suppress LGBTI rights claims, they have sadly succeeded. In response to the startling upsurge in homophobic attacks and bigotry in Jamaican society, a young man who mounted a constitutional challenge to the country's anti-sodomy law terminated his claim on August 28, 2014. He cited threats to himself and his family. This case had attracted widespread national interest; over a dozen religious organizations had joined the case as interested parties in support of the government's defense of the country's 1864 statute imposed by British colonists.

CLASS WARFARE: FRIENDLY FIRE IN THE JAMAICAN LGBTI COMMUNITY

Jamaican gay men crudely categorize ourselves as falling into two distinct camps: "rich queens" or "scary queens." "Rich queens" (in which category I would fall) are middle- to upper-class gay men who are largely untouched by physical manifestations of homophobia. They can insulate themselves from the more aggressive forms of homophobia by living in gated communities and driving wherever they need to go by private car in order to avoid dangerous public transit. They can also choose to attend safe social events only. "Scary queens," on the other hand, are gay men from the lower socioeconomic strata who have had to develop intimidating personas as a means of survival. They bear the brunt of the attacks against LGBTI Jamaicans.

Of course, this divide is not unique to Jamaica: many struggles for LGBTI liberation are similarly organized around dichotomies of class and social status. For example, the struggles of poor African American Trans* women are rarely represented in the debate for marriage equality in the United States. Paraphrasing one meme: white Americans are fighting for the right to put a ring on a finger while black Trans* women are fighting to stay alive.

My own journey to become an LGBTI activist required crossing economic and social divides. My work with the Jamaican LGBTI community was initially behind the scenes. As a corporate lawyer, I assisted the major LGBTI and HIV groups on the island with statutory filings and the like but had no intention of being a visible face for the movement. This was in an attempt to preserve my privilege and to ensure my safety.

This privilege both shielded and blinded me from most of the physical abuse faced by Jamaican LGBTI people. Ignorant of these struggles, I instead chose to accept the social and psychological limitations of being a gay man in a homophobic society. For example, I was not "allowed" to be seen with a male partner for fear of inciting raised eyebrows, heckles, or even physical attacks. I was not "allowed" to discuss my same-gender relationships at work. And although I grew up in a very religious society and had a strong Christian faith, there were no inclusive spiritual congregations that I could join. Instead of viewing the victims of homophobic violence as a systematically oppressed group deserving of legal recognition and justice, I tended to view them with disgust and shame — the victims of their own actions. I was conditioned to think that "scary queens" were an embarrassment, impeding our progress as an LGBTI community.

Like many gay men in repressive and criminalized contexts, I eventually married a woman in a vain attempt to suppress my unwanted same-gender attraction. It should come as no surprise that the number of such relationships in homophobic cultures is often staggering. In the context of arranged marriages, such as those regularly organized in Indian society, the number of closeted LGBTI people stuck in unwanted, heterosexual marriages is likely even more inflated. It is not just the LGBTI person who suffers in these arrangements; many heterosexual partners and children are caught up in this maelstrom.

In my role as a legal advisor to LGBTI organizations, I was initially asked to develop a training program in human rights documentation and advocacy for LGBTI people. This was seen as crucial to ensuring greater visibility for the gay community, and leaders hoped that it would lead to a reduction in the level of homophobia. People fear what they do not know; this training program would help to educate people about a subject that most Jamaicans only understood through media reports.

Although I specialized in intellectual property and not in human rights law, I accepted the request to provide training for the LGBTI community. Few other local lawyers would undertake this task, fearing professional suicide. Even so, it was never my intention to become an activist. It wasn't until I began to listen regularly to stories of horrendous homophobic abuse that I converted into an advocate. How could I not?

These deeply upsetting stories forcefully made me aware that there was a systematic violence being largely ignored in Jamaican society. I filed reports on behalf of LGBTI people who were still bleeding from an attack. It was traumatic. However, nothing prepared me for the utterly soul-crushing experience of attempting to file these reports with local police officers who responded to victims' experiences with stoic homophobia. Officers regularly refused to accept reports because the victims, they claimed, were required to provide the names and addresses of their attackers!

On multiple occasions, I had to explain to a client who had been caught in a compromising position with another consenting adult that if he refused to pay a bribe to the police, then his story would inevitably be released to the vulgarly anti-gay tabloids. The press would effectively destroy their lives and the lives of their families, as well as their future employment prospects. Witnessing these human rights atrocities, and suddenly realizing my own vulnerability to them, prompted me to do what I find cathartic: writing.

I began with fairly innocuous letters to the editors of the major dailies in which I simply recounted stories of anti-gay violence. News of these homophobic attacks had gone largely unreported, and, when they were picked up, it was usually in a deliberately inflammatory and stigmatizing fashion; tabloid reports mostly vilified gays as freaks and dangers to society. By writing publicly about anti-gay violence, I thought I could appeal to the innate empathy of Jamaicans, who would then rise up en masse to denounce the human rights atrocities against the minority LGBTI population.

I was wrong. Instead, my actions unleashed an avalanche of hate against me and the gay community. People responded in vulgar tones to my letters and op-eds. One government official even went so far as to tell me that my call for an end to the killing of gays amounted to a request for "special rights" because "we kill straight people too." This stunning statement was made by an official responsible for working with youth. The obvious fact that heterosexual Jamaicans are not killed *because* they are straight completely escaped her.

I was similarly rebuffed when I recounted the variety of ways that LGBTI people are economically disadvantaged, on the grounds that a large number of Jamaicans are also poor (nearly 1.1 million out of a population of 3 million live below the poverty line). Sympathy — or, more correctly, empathy — was overridden by religious fundamentalists who strategically promoted fear: fear of HIV, fear of pedophilia, fear of the unknown. This juggernaut of hysteria was nearly impossible to overcome.

Parents resorted to tossing their LGBTI children out on the street as young as ten years old because they had been indoctrinated to believe that their children were a biblical abomination. "Harboring" gays was equated with courting destruction on the magnitude of the Haitian earthquake. In the minds of religious fundamentalists, there was only one responsible way to deal with LGBTI people: dispose of them.

Many homeless LGBTI kids resorted to living in abandoned buildings. Police intervened in some cases to evict them, while in other cases the buildings were torn down in order to prevent the youth from "re-infesting" them. Some of these youngsters were forced to live in the sewers of the capital. Many continue to sell sex to survive, and they are paid extra for condom-less sex. This increases their vulnerability to HIV, and most of their clients are men with girlfriends or wives waiting for them back at home.

THE BATTLE PLAN FOR SECURING LGBTI RIGHTS IN JAMAICA

As a first step to understanding the scale of the battle for LGBTI rights in Jamaica, an island-wide project was undertaken to document the human rights abuses against LGBTI people. This was done in partnership with local and international NGOs, such as J-FLAG and AIDS-Free World. The result was credible and robust information used to generate multiple reports for international and regional human rights organizations, such as the Inter-American Commission on Human Rights and the UN Universal Periodic Review.

A coalition of local, regional, and international organizations provided Jamaican LGBTI groups with advocacy training in advance of presentations at high-level meetings of the United Nations, the Organization of American States (OAS), and CARICOM. These presentations helped launch the first international agreements at the UN and OAS condemning violence on the basis of sexual orientation, gender identity, and gender expression.

The same coalition supported the development of LGBTI visibility campaigns, including public demonstrations, tolerance ads, and meetings with politicians and other opinion leaders. Performers and sponsors of popular anti-gay music were confronted, and in some cases boycotted, with the result that most of the record 200-plus homophobic songs for which Jamaica is infamous are no longer commercially produced.

Researchers also played an important role in developing two groundbreaking university studies into the levels and drivers of homophobia in Jamaican society. These studies confirmed the role of fundamentalist religion and popular music in forming and sustaining anti-gay views among all sectors of the society.

Police and other security services are central to the sexuality wars being waged around the globe. This is typical of all liberation struggles. Indeed, the LGBTI movements in the United States and Canada were ignited after communities became fed up with regular police raids on gay establishments. However, while activists in the global north have made significant progress in sensitizing the police to LGBTI concerns (or, at the very least, have legally prohibited cops from discriminating against them), such progress is largely unheard of in many other parts of the world. The organization AIDS-Free World attempted to change this by developing and implementing a police training specifically for the Caribbean. Incidentally, as many Caribbean police officers also serve as lay-pastors, these trainings provided for an unexpected opportunity to address religious homophobia directly at the source. While these trainings did not change things overnight, they did provide officers with appropriate information on LGBTI rights that will hopefully help to dismantle their deep-seated homophobic beliefs.

Jamaican politicians advised LGBTI activists in private conversations that, although they personally do not support anti-gay laws, they felt powerless to repeal them against the might of the fundamentalist churches. Hence, the prime minister's 2011 election promise to review the anti-sodomy law remains unfulfilled, and in 2014 she reversed herself by declaring that there would be no official timeline for such a review because the law does not affect the majority of Jamaicans who are poor (apparently she believes that all LGBTI people are well off).

Because of legislative inaction, activists decided that challenging anti-gay laws in court was the most practical way to end Jamaican and region-wide homophobia.

INCHING JAMAICA TOWARD LEGAL EQUALITY

In 2004, the Staff Orders for the Jamaican Civil Service were revised. Quietly and without fanfare, this update to the 1976 document expanded the protections of public servants to include the right to nondiscrimination on the basis of sexual orientation (section 13.1.9). This reform created an anomaly whereby government employees had more protections from discrimination than the general public they serve.

It was therefore reasonable to expect that, when the country adopted a new Charter of Fundamental Rights and Freedoms in 2011, the grounds for nondiscrimination in all sectors would have been expanded to include sexual orientation. Regrettably, the parliament caved to fear-mongering by fundamentalist evangelicals (some from the global north) and specifically excluded LGBTI people from protection.

With the legislature's failure to protect LGBTI citizens, activists took to the courts. Despite their being left out from the language of the statute, Jamaica's Constitutional Court ruled in 2013 that gay Jamaicans are still covered by the charter. In the case of *Tomlinson v. TVJ et al.*, which AIDS-Free World brought to challenge the refusal of local TV stations to air an ad promoting tolerance for gays that the organization had produced, the president of the court said,

> It is perhaps to be recognized that the claimant cannot seek redress for any allegations of discrimination on the grounds of his sexual orientation as the Charter does not afford that protection specifically. This may be viewed as a significant deficiency in this Charter but it is to be noted that the first paragraph of the Charter [which declares that the state and private individuals are obligated to uphold the fundamental rights and freedoms of all citizens] is comprehensive enough to point to a view that it be interpreted to embrace all rights and responsibilities of all Jamaicans. (para. 28)

Thus, although the court ruled against the right to air the ad, it nonetheless proved helpful by clarifying that the charter does in fact protect gays. The extent of this protection will certainly have to be tested in future cases, but this judicial statement is a very promising start. Sometimes you have to lose to win.

As a Jamaican national leading AIDS-Free World's anti-homophobia work in the Caribbean, I was required to travel extensively across the region. Among other things, I had to attend meetings with senior government officials and policymakers involved in the regional HIV/AIDS response. The Joint United Nations Programme on HIV/AIDS (UNAIDS) hosts many of these meetings at their regional head office in Trinidad; however, I am legally barred from entering that country.

The Immigration Act of the Republic of Trinidad and Tobago was last revised in 1995. Section 8 of the statute lists groups of persons who are deemed "prohibited classes." It may be surprising to learn that included in this list are "idiots, imbeciles, feeble-minded persons ... persons infected with any infectious disease ... persons who are dumb, blind or otherwise physically defective, or physically handicapped ... prostitutes, homosexuals ... chronic alcoholics ... persons who are addicted to the use of any drug."[1] Choosing to house the UNAIDS Caribbean regional office in a country where most vulnerable persons are barred from entering is therefore strange, to say the least. Immigration restrictions to Belize, last revised in 2000, are less discriminatory than their Trinidadian counterparts. However, Belize still bars entry to several vulnerable groups, including "any idiot or any person who is insane or mentally deficient or any person who is deaf and dumb or deaf and blind, or dumb and blind ... any prostitute or homosexual."[2] Belize and Trinidad and Tobago are the only countries in the Western Hemisphere that retain such travel restrictions.

Having traveled to Belize and Trinidad and Tobago in the past, I was unaware that I was breaking the law. However, I learned of the immigration restrictions while reviewing regional anti-gay laws. When UNAIDS subsequently invited me to attend a regional meeting with senior policymakers on how to address the stigma of vulnerable groups, I declined the invitation on the grounds that, as a lawyer, I cannot willfully break the law. I was later invited to deliver a human rights documentation and advocacy training for civil society groups in Belize. Again, I had no choice but to decline.

The travel ban on homosexuals is rarely invoked. However, in 2007, anti-gay church groups on the island of Tobago tried to get the government to enforce it against Sir Elton John. Sir Elton was scheduled to perform at a jazz and blues concert, but the religious leaders argued that his appearance would be illegal and would cause youngsters confused about their sexuality to become gay. The government of the island intervened to ensure Elton's appearance.

One of the rights guaranteed to citizens of the Caribbean Community (CARICOM) is freedom of movement.[3] Breaches of this right by a member state must be settled by the Caribbean Court of Justice (CCJ), which has the compulsory and exclusive jurisdiction on matters pertaining to the Caribbean Single Market and Economy (CSME).[4] In recognition of the very political nature of the CSME, citizens must first ask their home states to bring a claim on their behalf. Only if the state refuses can the national approach the CCJ for special leave to pursue the matter themselves. As an international court, the CCJ is only empowered to act when actual harm has occurred. Therefore, the preemptive jurisdiction of domestic courts does not apply. Since I had not been denied entry into Belize or Trinidad and Tobago, the harm claimed had to be based on other human rights infringements, such as my right to dignity.

Initially, AIDS-Free World asked the Jamaican government to take up the issue of the homophobic travel restrictions with the governments of Trinidad and Belize. Not surprisingly, the government flatly refused to do anything, arguing, *inter alia*, that the non-enforcement of the law against me rebutted any presumption of harm. Neither would the government pursue the claim with the CCJ or grant leave for a private action.

An application for special leave was therefore filed with the CCJ on May 31, 2013 (*Tomlinson v. Trinidad and Tobago and Belize*). Both Belize and Trinidad resisted the application, and at the hearing on November 12, 2013, the court heard from both governments that neither had any intention of enforcing the laws. However, when the court then inquired as to the need for these unenforced statutes, the senior counsel representing the Republic of Trinidad and Tobago indicated that the law was necessary to keep out *terrorists*.

When the court handed down its decision on May 8, it unanimously found that there was a presumption of prejudice and granted special leave to appeal. Specifically, the court said,

> In relation to homosexuals, there is indeed international case law, in particular jurisprudence of the European Court of Human Rights [*Norris v. Ireland* (1991) 13 EHRR 186 [33]] and the UN Human Rights Committee [*Toonen v. Australia*, Communication No. 488/1992, U.N. Doc CCPR/C/50/D/488/1992 (1994)], which suggests that under certain circumstances the mere existence of legislation, even if not enforced, may justify a natural or legal person to be considered a victim of a violation of his or her rights under an international human rights instrument. (para. 6)

After my claim was filed, the CCJ handed down its decision in another case regarding free movement in CARICOM, *Myrie v. Barbados*.[5] This case established the unqualified right of free movement of CARICOM nationals. My lawyers therefore applied and were granted permission to expand my immigration claim to reflect the fact that the immigration laws of Belize and Trinidad and Tobago could also violate my right to nondiscrimination on the grounds of nationality.[6] Simply put, CARICOM non-nationals of Belize and Trinidad can be denied entry to either country if they belong to the aforementioned prohibited classes, while citizens of the subject states are unimpeded from entering, even if they are, among other things, homosexuals.

A regional LGBTI group, Caribbean Forum for Liberation and Acceptance of Genders and Sexualities (CariFLAGS), which is headquartered in Trinidad, applied to be joined as an interested party to the claim. They argued that the law negatively impacts their advocacy work with other LGBTI groups across the region because they are unable to legally hold meetings in Trinidad with counterparts from across the Caribbean.

Ironically, a Trinidadian senior counsel and former judge of the Belize Court of Appeal, Douglas Mendes, presented the claim against the governments of Belize and Trinidad and Tobago, which was heard on March 17–18, 2015. The CCJ has reserved its judgment and was expected to hand down a decision before the end of 2015.

Although narrowly framed as a Caribbean case, if successful, the ruling will likely result in the complete repeal of the offending sections of the laws, directly benefiting citizens from every country in the world.

The fact that the region's highest court took judicial notice of the harmful impact of unenforced laws that discriminate against LGBTI people will also be significant in other Caribbean cases, which are challenging the British colonially imposed anti-sodomy laws. These include two petitions against the Jamaican anti-sodomy law, which are before the Inter-American Commission on Human Rights, and a challenge to the Belizean anti-sodomy law, which is before that country's Constitutional Court.

WHAT CAN THE GLOBAL NORTH DO?

For two years, I spent time in the United States as my husband pastored a congregation of the Metropolitan Community Church in Rochester, New York. This church was founded in Los Angeles by LGBTI Christians who were unable to find acceptance in their other faith traditions. While in the United States, I sensed that the bruising struggle for LGBTI liberation has triggered a level of "gay rights fatigue." Activists and allies I met wanted a break from campaigning for LGBTI causes. However, it is useful to remember that hate is not static and is in fact quite mobile. As nearly every country in the world has significant immigrant populations, they should take care to protect against the importation of harmful ideologies, including homophobia. This involves actively working to ensure that originating countries for U.S. emigrants accept the human rights of LGBTI people.

There is also a real threat that exported homophobia will embolden and empower previously diffident governments to support regressive international agreements that serve to whittle away at the advances made for LGBTI human rights globally. A growing chorus of "traditional family values" has been used by reactionary regimes to promote anti-gay instruments at the United Nations and the Organization of American States.

Global homophobia also negatively affects travel. As hysteria about homosexuality and gender nonconformity spreads, some visits abroad become more perilous. Even straight travelers are not safe if they are wrongly perceived to be LGBTI. In Jamaica, straight fathers report being hesitant to go to the beach with their adult male sons without a woman present. In Ugandan culture, the practice of innocent heterosexual male intimacy (hugging, holding hands, etc.) is now being questioned in the face of increasingly negative views of homosexuality.

Finally, some believe that addressing global homophobia should be an economic imperative. The "cost" of LGBTI refugees is considered, especially by fiscally conservative governments, to be an onerous charge on taxpayers. While this cynical perspective is less than commendable (e.g., it fails to take account of the real cost to refugees who have to abandon families, friends, social support, work, and assets to seek asylum), it is not an inconsequential concern. Whether the decision of northern states to fight global homophobia is based on human rights principles or pure economics, they do have a role to play.

Eager but ignorant allies have unnecessarily complicated LGBTI liberation movements around the world. What is particularly troubling is how unnecessary, even unforgivable, this ignorance is in the age of social media: Updates and advice on how to respond to local groups is never more than a mouse-click away. Yet spectacular missteps happen, even by diplomats who have access to intelligence briefs that really ought to make such faux pas unthinkable.

A case in point was the aggressive posture taken by the Canadian Foreign Minister toward the Ugandan delegation during a state visit to Toronto in 2012. The minister used the opportunity to upbraid the Ugandans for the anti-gay bill, which was then before their parliament. This action incited the Ugandan Speaker of the House, Rebecca Kadaga, to remind the Canadians that Uganda is not a colony of Canada and would decide the matter of the anti-gay law for itself.

As a result of the immense popularity generated by her standing up to a major global power, Speaker Kadaga was met with jubilant crowds upon her return to Kampala. She then lent her public support to the anti-gay bill, which was subsequently passed. The whole unfortunate affair could have been avoided. In that situation, Canada squandered the moral authority it had by not having been a colonial power. Instead, the country's neocolonial posturing inflamed nationalistic tendencies that were quickly exploited for political gain by local politicians engaged in a jostle for power.

Countries like the United States have an immense opportunity to influence in positive ways the tenor of the debate for global LGBTI rights, but only if they are willing to engage in constructive dialogue. The temptation to score cheap political points with pro-gay constituents at home must be resisted. One useful approach that supportive and now "decriminalized" countries could take would involve (1) acknowledging that they also had these horrid laws, which wreaked havoc on the lives of ordinary civilians; (2) admitting that it took time to get rid of the legislation in the face of very conservative forces (most of which are still present); and (3) plainly discussing the immense benefits reaped after consigning these laws to the dustbin of history. American and global north politicians can also offer to share frank strategies with legislative counterparts from the global south for addressing these problematic laws. This approach leaves the door open to real engagement, without sacrificing the universal human rights principles that sustain modern democracies. It would also forestall any suggestion of neocolonialism.

It is a mistake to think that leaders from countries with punitive anti-gay laws universally support them. Many do not, largely because (1) they have other national priorities; (2) they are more likely to have actually met LGBTI people than the majority of their compatriots; and (3) they are sensitive to how their policies and decisions are perceived internationally. Despite their potential misgivings, minorities serve as convenient scapegoats in times of social and economic distress. Throwing stigmatized minorities under the bus is a long-standing strategy politicians employ for shoring up their political power. In culture wars, it is arguable that the appearance of foreign support for minorities can foment a witch hunt.

There will inevitably be those leaders who — for reasons of political expediency, moral and philosophical bankruptcy, or malice — will hold fast to hateful rhetoric. Those individuals can and should be isolated from the world community until they conform. Individual sanctions (such as visa or other travel restrictions, or freezing their foreign assets) should then be imposed. The potency of such measures cannot be underestimated. For example, media reports indicate that Ugandan politicians were so concerned about how voting for the "jail the gays" bill would have affected their international standing that they had initially called for a secret ballot.

Global north allies also have many opportunities to provide effective support to LGBTI liberation in the global south, starting with educating themselves about the local realities. These allies should also ensure that their leaders are held accountable and respond appropriately.

More thoughtful financial decisions can also positively influence change for LGBTI people around the world. For example, travel choices could coincide with visiting societies that approach inclusiveness in a manner that you wish to support and encourage. But for such a choice to have an impact beyond the individual, it must be conveyed to leaders: They should know why tourists stay away. Silent boycotts are less effective.

That said, there is certainly a credible case to be made against the blunt instrument of travel boycotts. The presence of loving LGBTI people visiting an otherwise intolerant society may have the effect of causing locals to rethink their intolerant and bigoted views. This is one reason that my husband and I jointly conduct LGBTI sensitization training sessions for police; allowing officers to engage with a gay couple in a safe space has helped them to confront honestly their preconceived notions about homosexuality. Gay travel operators, such as Olivia Lesbian Travel, also schedule tours to states where homosexuality remains criminalized, and often these excursions incorporate social projects for underprivileged communities. Such initiatives have real impacts on changing hearts and minds.

The economic advocacy of gay tourism (valued at over US$200 billion annually) is not insignificant. To convey this point, I often relate a favorite anecdote from a Dominican craft vendor. In 2012, the country's cruise industry received international attention when an American gay couple was arrested on charges of having engaged in public sex in full view of the dock while their ship was in port. Many expected that the scandal spelled the end of gay cruises to Dominica. However, a poll of commercial interests involved in the cruise industry revealed that they were quite willing to welcome more gay cruises. In the words of one vendor, she was happy for gay tourists because they bought her entire stock of sarongs! Stereotypes sometimes have their place in advocacy.

Large multinational corporations (MNCs) also have an opportunity to influence the development of LGBTI human rights by exporting their values through, among other things, inclusive employment practices. Regrettably, it has been my experience that many MNCs doing business in the Caribbean prefer to adopt the lower standards of their host countries. Pressure to take a more active role in influencing local LGBTI realities has to come from nationals in their home countries.

Supporting local groups on the ground that are engaged in documenting and responding to human rights abuses against LGBTI people is also incredibly important, if complex to coordinate. Simply making monetary donations to these sources can seem disempowering, but there is actually very little evidence that LGBTI groups are engaged in mismanagement.

CONCLUSION

This review of the ongoing LGBTI liberation movement, with particular focus on the global south perspective, is not meant to be exhaustive. Such an undertaking would require entire books on thematic and geographical areas. It has been my experience that there are sufficient parallels between the battles in the global north and south to illustrate the critical issues and, more important, to highlight what steps can usefully be taken to address them. The victim narrative has not served the movement very well, so it is time for a solution-oriented framing. It is my hope that this chapter has provided some context for finding or pursuing those solutions.

As with all phobias, anti-gay sentiments will only end through education. There may be need for drastic interventions to open the space for such education to occur, and the tactical options available to accomplish this are many. These should only be used to grab the attention of politicians and opinion-shapers so as to focus their attention on solving the problem of homophobia. Prolonged and inappropriate use of these techniques will justifiably raise claims of neocolonialism.

It has been my experience that targeted sanctions against anti-LGBTI individuals are the most effective. These include travel and financial bans as well as pursuing civil and criminal sanctions for promoting and inciting homophobic violence.

A largely unproven and very risky weapon in this conflict of rights is a blanket travel ban. It has the potential to inflict extensive collateral damage on members of local LGBTI communities, resulting in severe economic dislocation and/or making LGBTI people easy scapegoats in local political disputes. This is especially true when other human rights atrocities fail to attract similar global responses. The threat of a boycott can often have more of an impact than the boycott itself. But in my view, the risks associated with blanket travel bans do not outweigh the benefits.

In the end, whatever approach taken must be decided in direct consultation with the local LGBTI communities, because it is they who will have to live with — and rebuild after — the fallout.

NOTES

1. Immigration Act of 1995. Trinidad and Tobago.
2. Belize Immigration Act, Cap 156, sec. 5.
3. Revised Treaty of Chaguaramas, 2001, art. 45, 46.
4. Revised Treaty of Chaguaramas, 2001, art. 211.
5. Myrie v. Barbados [2013], CCJ 3 (OJ).
6. Revised Treaty of Chaguaramas, 2011, art. 7.

| 16 |

Building a Movement for Justice

Doe v. Jindal *and the Campaign against Louisiana's* Crime Against Nature Statute

INTRODUCTION

Hiroke Doe is an African American transgender woman in her thirties who has lived in New Orleans her whole life.[1] She began to transition as a teen-ager, struggling for survival with scarce resources. In the late 1990s, she was arrested after she verbally agreed to engage in oral sex with an undercover po-lice officer in exchange for money. Just as thousands of people do every day in a hostile and alienating criminal justice system, Hiroke took a guilty plea, as-suming that she had been charged with a generic prostitution-related misde-meanor.[2] But when she later met with her parole officer pending release from prison, Hiroke learned that she had in fact been charged under an obscure (and nationally unparalleled) statute: Crime Against Nature by Solicitation (CANS).[3] To her horror, Hiroke learned that as a result of her conviction, she had to register as a sex offender for fifteen years, pay the state hundreds of dol-lars in registration fees, and comply with humiliating community notification requirements. What ensued was years of embarrassment, fear, and struggle.

The CANS statute was adopted in 1982 when, without precedent, Louisiana expanded its nearly 200-year-old Crime Against Nature statute criminalizing all oral and anal sex to encompass Crime Against Nature by *Solicitation* — that is, offering to engage in oral or anal sex for money.[4] Of course, existing pros-titution laws already criminalized the solicitation of oral, anal, *and* vaginal sex.[5] But by bringing solicitation under the purview of the antiquated Crime Against Nature statute, state lawmakers singled out prostitution cases involv-ing oral or anal sex for particularly harsh punishment. Unlike the generic prostitution statute, CANS was a felony; and unlike the generic prostitution statute, it required registration as a sex offender.[6] In other words, someone offering oral sex in exchange for money could be charged with misdemeanor prostitution; or, at the prosecutor's discretion, she could be charged with a felony under the CANS statute and, if convicted, be required to register as a sex offender.

For almost thirty years, Louisiana incarcerated hundreds of people like Hiroke for years at a time on the basis of allegations that they merely *offered* oral or anal sex for money, and required them to register as sex offenders for between fifteen years and the rest of their lives. The individuals targeted by this statute were frequently struggling with poverty and lack of access to decent housing, services, and employment. Once they were convicted of a felony and labeled as a sex offender, these struggles became utterly debilitating.[7]

As part of a litigation team that would challenge the constitutionality of the CANS statute in *Doe v. Jindal*, I first met Hiroke, and many others affected by this law, in 2011.[8] They wanted to know why African American women (including a significant number of transgender women) and gay men were so frequently being charged with CANS.[9] They wanted to know how they were supposed to secure employment or safe and decent housing when their driver's licenses prominently featured the words "sex offender" in bright-orange letters. And they wanted to know exactly how the state expected them to afford the hundreds of dollars in fees required under the Registry Law.[10]

These questions quickly coalesced into a powerful campaign against the CANS law. Led by a fearless group of community members and organizations (most prominently, Women with a Vision), the campaign mobilized advocacy, lobbying, litigation, public education, and a press strategy to challenge the discriminatory effects of the CANS statute. In two short years, despite the state's concerted effort to defend the law, a coalition of community advocates, lawyers, and activists systematically and comprehensively stripped the law of its most pernicious effects. Though the statute remains on the books (along with Louisiana's generic noncommercial Crime Against Nature statute), the campaign fundamentally altered how, and to what ends, the state can mobilize the statute.

From my perspective as a social justice lawyer, this two-year campaign was an invaluable lesson in the power of social justice movements and the role lawyers can and should play in the service of those movements. For 200 years, Louisiana's archaic Crime Against Nature law has, in one iteration or another, been used to mete out harsh and discriminatory punishment against anyone seen to engage in non-normative sex. As a result of this campaign, a closing chapter in that sorry history has been written. In this essay, I first provide a brief overview of the history of Louisiana's Crime Against Nature statute. I then describe the contours of the anti-CANS campaign. Finally, I conclude by considering some of the possibilities and limitations of contemporary equal protection doctrine as illustrated by the legal challenge to the CANS statute.

PECCATUM ILLUD HORRIBILE: A HISTORY OF LOUISIANA'S CRIME AGAINST NATURE STATUTE

Generally speaking, the history of Louisiana's Crime Against Nature statute (as opposed to the Crime Against Nature *by Solicitation* statute, which became the focal point of the campaign described here) mirrors that of sodomy laws across the United States. Louisiana's first criminal code was enacted in 1805 and included a provision criminalizing what was described as "abominable and detestable Crime [A]gainst Nature, committed with mankind or beast."[11] As in most jurisdictions at the time, the precise conduct that constituted a Crime Against Nature did not appear on the face of the statute, but American courts and commentators in the nineteenth century uniformly followed English precedent in interpreting it to prohibit anal sexual intercourse with a man, woman, or animal.[12]

These sodomy laws were initially animated by religious and social prohibitions on nonprocreative sexual activity — irrespective of the sex, marital status, or consent of the participants.[13] As Nan Hunter has explained, "[t]he crime of sodomy originated in ecclesiastical regulation of a range of nonmarital, nonprocreative sexual practices. Nonprocreation was the central offense and the core of the crime. . . . The 'crime against nature' to which that phrase refers was not, as is often assumed today, a crime against heterosexuality, but a crime against procreation."[14] Indeed, the Supreme Court recognized in *Lawrence v. Texas* that "early American sodomy laws were not directed at homosexuals as such but instead sought to prohibit nonprocreative sexual activity more generally."[15]

Courts repeatedly upheld the Crime Against Nature statute against constitutional challenge but seemed reluctant to describe specifically what exactly a "crime against nature" entailed. In 1882, for example, the Supreme Court of Louisiana rejected a vagueness challenge brought by a criminal defendant being prosecuted under the statute, stating, "[t]he euphemism by which the law describes *peccatum illud horribile*, does not, in our opinion, leave its meaning doubtful or obscure."[16] If Louisianans did not understand the phrase "crime against nature," then the Latin phrase *peccatum illud horribile inter Christianos non nominandum* was apparently sufficient to put them on notice as to which sex acts to avoid.[17] To the extent that any doubts about the activities prohibited by the statute lingered, the Louisiana legislature amended it in 1896 to explicitly outlaw oral sex.[18]

Although the legislature continued to tinker with the Crime Against Nature law in the mid-twentieth century (actually reducing the penalties associated with a conviction under the statute), this was the beginning of a discernible shift in how the Crime Against Nature law was applied in Louisiana and across the country.[19] As sexual norms liberalized, heterosexual conduct began to be legally insulated by a cloak of privacy. In the landmark 1965 case *Griswold v. Connecticut*, the Supreme Court ruled that married couples have a constitutional right to use contraception, asking, "[w]ould we allow the police to search the sacred precincts of marital bedrooms for telltale signs of the use of contraceptives? The very idea is repulsive to the notions of privacy surrounding the marriage relationship."[20] The Supreme Court unambiguously announced, in other words, that state surveillance of consensual heterosexual activity, procreative or not, would be anathema to the sanctity of heterosexual marriage.[21] While sodomy laws were rarely used to prosecute private, consensual, heterosexual activity to begin with, the notion that these laws applied to such activity began to erode.

But rather than fade into obscurity, a second wave of sodomy laws began to emerge across the country in and after the 1960s that specifically focused on criminalizing homosexuality. The contemporaneous legislative expression of what has been described as an "antihomosexual kulturkampf," these laws "were a development of the last third of the twentieth century and reflect [a] historically unprecedented concern to classify and penalize homosexuals as a subordinate class of citizens."[22] Some laws criminalized only same-sex activity, such as the Texas law that was eventually declared unconstitutional in *Lawrence*.[23] Others, like Louisiana's Crime Against Nature statute, remained facially neutral. But sodomy became increasingly understood as a euphemism for homosexuality, and, as Nan Hunter has pointed out, "[n]ew social understandings . . . converted sodomy into a code word for homosexuality, regardless of the statutory definition."[24] In short, sodomy laws were, by the latter third of the twentieth century, unambiguously motivated by animus against homosexuality.[25]

In keeping with this national trend, Louisiana's Crime Against Nature statute also began to be applied and expanded in new ways. In 1962, the legislature enacted the Aggravated Crime Against Nature statute, defined as an act of sodomy combined with force, with the victim's inability to consent, or with an individual under the age of seventeen.[26] Rape and sexual assault laws already criminalized this conduct, making the new statute redundant from the outset. The fact that these generally applicable laws were deemed insufficient suggests a heightened sense of moral panic about sodomy, which was, at this stage, irrevocably associated with homosexuality.

Louisiana's Crime Against Nature statute remained in force until 2003, when the U.S. Supreme Court held in *Lawrence v. Texas* that the liberty principles protected by the due process clause gave consenting adults the right to engage in sodomy in private.[27] Though the Louisiana Supreme Court has never had an opportunity to squarely strike down the provision of the Crime Against Nature statute that criminalized private, consensual oral and anal sex, it has acknowledged that *Lawrence* has rendered it unconstitutional.[28] Yet, unlike most sodomy laws elsewhere in the country, the history of Louisiana's Crime Against Nature statute does not end here.

In 1982, without national precedent, the Louisiana legislature added to the Crime Against Nature statute for the first time since the 1890s. The new Crime Against Nature *by Solicitation* provision outlawed the "solicitation by a human being of another with the intent to engage in any unnatural carnal copulation for compensation."[29] A century of case law interpreting the Crime Against Nature statute defined "unnatural carnal copulation" as oral or anal sex.[30] Of course, Louisiana had long outlawed the exchange of oral, vaginal, or anal sex for money through its prostitution laws.[31] Despite the fact that the conduct prohibited under the new CANS statute was already illegal, Louisiana gave its law enforcement officers a powerful new tool: a discrete statute separate from existing prostitution laws that specifically singled out cases involving oral and anal sex.

In other words, since 1982, police and prosecutors in Louisiana have had unfettered discretion in choosing how to charge and prosecute a person who agrees to engage in oral and anal sex for money: either through the solicitation provision of the prostitution statute or through the CANS statute. The two statutes target identical conduct. The element of intent is also identical. The only difference between the activity targeted in the two statutes is that "prostitution" also encompasses solicitation of vaginal intercourse.

Why would the state adopt a redundant statute and expand its sodomy law for the first time in almost a century? The answer lies in a comparison of the penalties imposed under the two laws. While prostitution was categorized as a misdemeanor, punishable by a fine of no more than $500 and/or a maximum term of imprisonment of six months, CANS was categorized as a felony, punishable by up to *five years* in prison.[32] Additionally, in what became the central issue in *Doe v. Jindal*, a single CANS conviction required mandatory registration as a sex offender for fifteen years, while prostitution convictions do not; two CANS convictions required lifetime sex offender registration.[33] Whereas exactly the same conduct was treated more leniently elsewhere in the criminal code, what the Louisiana Supreme Court called the "loathsome and disgusting" acts singled out by CANS were to be treated differently because of their association with homosexuality, with law enforcement officers free to decide exactly when and for whom they would deploy this powerful tool.[34]

"THE DISCRIMINATION IS JUST ONGOING AND ONGOING AND ONGOING"

Before *Lawrence*, sodomy statutes were relatively rarely enforced across the country, and their power was arguably largely symbolic.[35] By contrast, one of the remarkable things about Louisiana's CANS statute is its widespread use. Prosecutors were not reluctant to mobilize this unparalleled and powerful tool: by mid-2012, nearly 900 people across the state were registered as sex offenders simply as a result of a CANS conviction.[36] The majority of these individuals were convicted in the first decade of the century.[37] These figures vastly outpace the use of sodomy laws in other states, suggesting that the expansion of the Crime Against Nature statute to include solicitation facilitated an increase in anti-sodomy prosecutions in Louisiana.[38]

Despite its frequent use, CANS was not evenly applied. Approximately 75 percent of the individuals registered as sex offenders in Louisiana as a result of a CANS conviction were women; approximately 65 percent were African American; and the majority were in New Orleans.[39] In February 2011, when *Doe v. Jindal* was filed, there were 812 registered sex offenders in Orleans Parish, of whom 292 were registered solely because of a CANS conviction.[40] This means that an astonishing 36 percent of all registered sex offenders in the jurisdiction were there simply because they were prosecuted under the state's sodomy law. Of these 292 individuals, 219 (or 75 percent) were women, and 230 of them (or 79 percent) were African American.[41] A total of 97 percent of all women on the registry in Orleans Parish were listed as a result of a CANS conviction.[42] Thus, a statute that was adopted for purposes of expressing moral distaste for nonprocreative sex acts historically associated with homo-sexuality ended up being used primarily to prosecute African American women.

Those convicted of CANS paid dearly for a prosecutor's arbitrary charging decision. First, the sentences served by those convicted of CANS are shock-ing. Ian Doe, a plaintiff in *Doe v. Jindal*, is a gay man in his thirties who was forced to leave home at the age of thirteen when his family discovered he was gay. He served four years in state prison for a single CANS conviction.[43] There, like many other people particularly vulnerable to sexual assault in prison because of their sexual orientation or gender expression, he was raped by a prison guard and contracted HIV.[44] Becca and Eve Doe, also plaintiffs in the case, were each sentenced to forty months' imprisonment with hard labor as a result of their first CANS convictions.[45]

Compounding the effects of such harsh prison terms and the devastat-ing economic impact of a felony conviction, those convicted of CANS were forced to register as sex offenders upon their release from prison and to com-ply with the Registry Law's onerous and myriad requirements.[46] Individuals like Audrey Doe, an African American grandmother in her mid-fifties who was convicted of CANS on multiple occasions while she was struggling with poverty, substance abuse, and mental health issues, spent hundreds of dollars on annual registration fees, the cost of printing and mailing notification post-cards to neighbors, and the fees for placing announcements in the newspaper disclosing her registration as a sex offender (expenses that accrue every time one moves).[47] Carla Doe, an African American woman in her mid-forties, was required to pay hundreds of dollars to comply with community notification requirements after she moved to escape a physically abusive common-law husband.[48]

Sex offender registration also erected significant barriers between people and much-needed employment, services, and housing. All registered sex of-fenders in Louisiana are forced to carry identification cards that included the words "sex offender" in bright-orange letters.[49] Both Becca and Carla de-scribed how, every time they applied for a job that required them to show a driver's license or identification card, they were denied employment on the spot.[50] And as Ian explained, "because of this charge I can't get a decent job now, I can't do anything. . . . I've been everywhere trying to get employment. The minute they find out I'm a registered sex offender, they tell me, 'no thank you,' or [that] they'll call me back, or they'll get back with me, and they never do."[51]

Housing providers were equally hostile. Diane Doe was repeatedly told by housing agencies that she was ineligible for subsidized housing because of her registration as a sex offender, leaving her trapped in an abusive relationship and worried that she would never be able to secure housing if she had to escape her husband.[52] Ian was asked to leave a homeless shelter when staff discovered that he was a registered sex offender.[53] So too were service providers reluctant to help. Eve, a forty-year-old transgender woman, has battled drug addiction for years. When she attempted to obtain treatment, three separate organizations providing substance abuse services denied her treatment because of her status as a registered sex offender.[54] She attempted to get temporary housing at a nonprofit agency but was refused placement for the same reason.[55] She explains,

> Trying to get my life back in order, it is seemingly impossible because I'm unable to access any kind of help that I need to find any normalcy to guide my life back on the right track. . . . I have tried numerous times to get into drug treatment facilities and the doors were slammed in my face because I was a sex offender. . . . I'm also HIV positive and there are times when I struggle because of joblessness and homelessness. I'm not allowed to access the housing programs because of the stigma of being a sex offender. I've sought out help for the last thirteen years. . . . [B]eing transgendered puts even more stigma on it because we're already looked on as social outcasts. The discrimination is just ongoing and ongoing and ongoing.[56]

If the obligations imposed by the Registry Law were not sufficiently brutal, the systematic marginalization resulting from registration impacted the lives of those convicted of CANS just as profoundly. During evacuation from New Orleans prior to Hurricane Gustav in 2008, Diane evacuated separately from her children and other family members because she knew that the law required her to show her ID stating that she was a registered sex offender at emergency shelters, and she did not want her seventy-seven-year-old grandmother to learn of her status.[57] Indeed, current protocols forbid registered sex offenders who need publicly run emergency shelter from remaining with their children and families in the event of an evacuation.[58]

The public exposure that sex offender registration imposes left many feeling unsafe and vulnerable. Audrey lived in fear that people in her neighborhood would physically harm her whenever she was required to send out community notifications. In 2008, after circulating such notifications, rocks were thrown through her windows.[59] At one point, a stranger came to Becca's residence looking for sex, indicating that he had seen her photograph "on the internet."[60]

Most people affected by this law reported that, aside from all the ways in which registration as a sex offender made their lives so much harder as a practical matter, they suffered considerable depression, humiliation, and alienation as a result of their legal status. Fiona Doe, an African American transgender woman in her thirties, spoke of her feelings of depression in the face of having to register as a sex offender for the rest of her life.[61] She felt constantly aware that her neighbors and other community members perceived her as a danger to themselves and specifically to their children.[62] Hiroke Doe learned to avoid situations in which she had to use her identification card so that she did not have to expose herself as a registered sex offender.[63]

As the impact of this law became more and more unbearable, those most affected began to ask questions. Ian, reflecting on his struggles as a young person and his subsequent registration as a sex offender after being convicted of CANS, put it this way:

> What happened when I was 13 years old and everyone knew I was on the streets and homeless? The crime was committed there. What happened when I went to prison and caught HIV? The crime was committed there. And this was all behind saying "fifty dollars" [in exchange for sex].[64]

And as these voices grew into a chorus, a movement began to emerge.

THE CAMPAIGN AGAINST CANS: A COMMUNITY-BASED APPROACH TO SOCIAL JUSTICE

The campaign to dismantle the devastating effects of the CANS statute found its genesis at a community organization called Women with a Vision (WWAV). This group is a New Orleans–based grassroots organization that works to "improve the lives of marginalized women, their families, and communities by addressing the social conditions that hinder their health and well-being," using a combination of "advocacy, health education, supportive services, and community-based participatory research."[65] In the months after Hurricane Katrina, WWAV began to notice that more and more women seeking their services were struggling with the stigma of sex offender registration as a result of a CANS conviction. More of their clients were being forced to register, and more of them were, for the first time, being forced to comply with some of the more onerous aspects of registration, such as community notification. Amassing information about how a CANS conviction affected their clients' ability to access employment, housing, treatment, social services, and health care, WWAV built a campaign they called NO Justice.[66] The campaign had three principal and mutually reinforcing facets: community-based legislative advocacy, movement lawyering, and a media and public education strategy.[67] In an extraordinarily short period of time, it would systematically reconfigure the legal infrastructure around the CANS statute.

The legislative campaign sought to untether the sex offender registration requirement from the CANS statute by educating sympathetic lawmakers about who was being affected by this charge and how. The legislative advocacy focused on the stories of the women and members of the LGBT community who were being disproportionately targeted and affected by the CANS statute. First, members of the campaign — including Deon Haywood from WWAV and lawyers from the *Doe v. Jindal* team — met with State Representative Charmaine Marchand Stiaes, highlighting these stories and explaining both the injustice and unconstitutionality of how the CANS statute was operating. The team then met with other legislators and state officials, and appeared at public hearings, to explain in unflinching detail how a 200-year-old sodomy statute was being used so destructively a decade into the twenty-first century.

In the face of those stories and that effort, the unimaginable happened. In just two sessions, the Louisiana legislature systematically dismantled the differential treatment meted out under the CANS statute. First, in 2010, a first CANS conviction was demoted to a misdemeanor and the statute was amended so that a first conviction no longer required sex offender registration.[68] Then, in 2011, Representative Marchand Stiaes sponsored a bill that would eliminate *all* differences between how CANS and prostitution convictions were treated for those convicted after August 15, 2011.[69] After members of the NO Justice campaign testified before criminal justice subcommittees in both the House and Senate, the legislature equalized all penalties with the prostitution statute and eliminated the sex offender registration requirement completely.[70] As a result, all penalties associated with the CANS statute are now identical to those associated with a prostitution conviction.

The NO Justice campaign understood, however, that struggles for social justice — particularly around issues as thorny and unpopular as this one — call for multifaceted approaches. And so, simultaneous with this legislative campaign was a litigation strategy. The NO Justice coalition, including community groups such as WWAV, Voice of the Ex-Offender (VOTE), and the Women's Health & Justice Initiative, met with a team of lawyers and described what was happening in and around New Orleans as a result of the CANS statute. The legal team then performed extensive legal research and presented the NO Justice coalition with its legal options. After the coalition decided independently that litigation should be part of its campaign, the legal team filed *Doe v. Jindal* in the federal district court for the Eastern District of Louisiana in February 2011.[71] Because none of the 2010 and 2011 legislative amendments were retroactive, they left behind those convicted prior to August 15, 2011.[72] The legislative victory did nothing, in other words, to mitigate the havoc wreaked by the CANS statute on the lives of those against whom it had been wielded for years, demonstrating that no single strategy can guarantee total victory. These individuals became the focus of the litigation.

Though other claims were raised,[73] the lawsuit hinged on an equal protection claim. Axiomatic under equal protection jurisprudence is the admonition "that States must treat like cases alike," unless (under rational basis review) there is a legitimate rationale for doing otherwise.[74] This principle, plaintiffs argued, applied squarely to those convicted of CANS: because these individuals were identically situated to those convicted of prostitution, but they alone were forced to register as sex offenders, the Equal Protection Clause was offended.[75] First, there was no doubt that individuals convicted under these two statutes were identically situated; the statutes shared the same elements, punished the same conduct, and required the same showing of intent (see table 16.1).

Further, there was no doubt that individuals convicted under the two statutes were being treated differently: those convicted of CANS were required to register as sex offenders, while those convicted of prostitution were not. And finally, plaintiffs argued, there could be no possible legitimate rationale for this differential treatment.

In making this argument, plaintiffs relied not on *Lawrence v. Texas* but on *Eisenstadt v. Baird*, another landmark Supreme Court case.[76] In *Eisenstadt*, the Supreme Court struck down a Massachusetts law that prohibited the distribution of contraception to unmarried people, even though married people were allowed access to contraception.[77] The Court rejected various purported governmental rationales for treating married and unmarried individuals differently, holding that "whatever the rights of the individual to access to contraceptives may be, the rights must be the same for the unmarried and the

Table 16.1. *Comparison of Criminal Elements in Louisiana Prostitution and* CANS *Statutes*

	PROSTITUTION — SOLICITATION La. Rev. Stat. § 14:82(A)(2)	CANS La. Rev. Stat. § 14:89.2(A)
ELEMENT NO. 1	Solicitation by one person of another	Solicitation of one human being of another
ELEMENT NO. 2	With the intent to engage in indiscriminate sexual intercourse (oral, anal, or vaginal intercourse)	With the intent to engage in unnatural carnal copulation (oral or anal intercourse)
ELEMENT NO. 3	For compensation	For compensation

married alike."[78] In language that would ultimately prove critical in *Doe v. Jindal*, the Court explained, "In each case the evil, as perceived by the State, would be identical, and the underinclusion would be invidious."[79]

In other words, where the state, for whatever reason, had not asserted an interest in prohibiting married persons from using contraception, it could not, consistent with the Equal Protection Clause, assert such an interest with respect to unmarried people. As the Supreme Court concluded,

> [N]othing opens the door to arbitrary action so effectively as to allow [government] officials to pick and choose only a few to whom they will apply legislation and thus to escape the political retribution that might be visited upon them if larger numbers were affected. Courts can take no better measure to assure that laws will be just than to require that laws be equal in operation.[80]

The *Doe v. Jindal* plaintiffs argued that the logic in *Eisenstadt* squarely applied to them and articulated why their constitutional rights were being violated. Given that the CANS and prostitution statutes were identical in all material respects, there was no discernible or defensible reason why the government was allowed to single out those convicted of CANS for such harsh treatment. Given that both statutes targeted exactly the same so-called evil, it could not assert an interest in registering some but not identically situated others as sex offenders.

The State of Louisiana struggled to counter this argument. The CANS statute, it claimed, applied not just to oral and anal sex but also to acts of bestiality, thus differentiating it from prostitution.[81] This argument, the Court ruled, following the plaintiffs' lead, "defies credulity. Its absurdity is betrayed by the statutory text, the Louisiana Supreme Court's pronouncements, and common sense."[82] The state then argued that even though the elements of the statutes were the same, perhaps there was a legitimate rationale for only requiring those convicted of CANS to register. The state claimed that its interests in public safety, health, and welfare justified the sex offender requirement prompted by a CANS conviction.[83] But if these interests did not require those convicted of prostitution to register as sex offenders, plaintiffs countered, why should the materially identical CANS statute trigger such interests? How did someone convicted of CANS threaten public safety, health, and welfare such that this drastic measure was necessary, whereas someone convicted of prostitution did not?

In March 2012, the Court agreed and granted plaintiffs summary judgment. Adopting the plaintiffs' argument almost entirely, the Court noted that the state had

> fail[ed] to credibly serve up even one unique legitimating governmental interest that can rationally explain the registration requirement imposed on those convicted of Crime Against Nature by Solicitation. The Court is left with no other conclusion but that the relationship between the classification is so shallow as to render the distinction wholly arbitrary.[84]

The Court declared that requiring those convicted of CANS to register as sex offenders was unconstitutional, ordered the state to cease and desist from continuing to register people convicted of CANS, and struck the plaintiffs from the registry.[85]

The equal protection theory that prevailed in this case turned on a fairly dry, textualist analysis. The legal argument deliberately avoided a substantive (or normative) analysis of what purposes sex offender registration schemes purportedly serve, and whether a CANS conviction warranted sex offender registration. Instead, the argument hinged on a clinical comparison of the CANS and prostitution statutes and the strict application of canonical equal protection principles. But there were intangible aspects of the litigation that both humanized the issue before the Court and highlighted the injustice of what was happening to those affected by the CANS statute. First, though the complaint filed in the case laid out the allegations necessary for the equal protection theory, it also detailed the devastating effects of a CANS conviction on the plaintiffs' lives, humanizing the issue and laying bare what was at stake. And second, the courtroom hearings in the case (on the state's motion to dismiss, and then the plaintiffs' motion for summary judgment) were widely attended by community members, students, advocates, individuals affected by this law, and members of the media. Packing the courtroom is a long-standing feature of civil rights lawyering. Though it will not sway an independent-minded judge, it serves other important functions. It signals widespread community concern about social justice issues. It allows those usually excluded or, at best, marginalized by the legal process to claim ownership over what happens in court in their name. Here, it forced the state to stand up before the people and defend its practices — practices that are ostensibly in the public interest and paid for with tax dollars. These intangibles, and "the dramatic impact of packing a courtroom with neighbors and organizational members," is not to be underestimated.[86]

Finally, the NO Justice campaign engaged in a media battle to complement its efforts in the legislative and judicial arenas. Individuals affected by the law, advocates from WWAV, and the attorneys involved in the litigation educated journalists about why this was such a crucial legal issue. On the day the case was filed, three of the plaintiffs gave anonymous statements on a teleconference with members of the press, telling their stories as no lawyer or legal pleadings could ever hope to do.[87] Ian, Hiroke, and Eve explained in devastating detail the abuse, humiliation, and systematic marginalization they had experienced simply because the state had arbitrarily chosen to charge them with CANS.[88] These efforts culminated in sympathetic coverage of the campaign and lawsuit in both the local and national press, in the form of articles, blog posts, and op-eds.[89] Crucially, an editorial appeared in the *Times-Picayune* that condemned the irrationality of the sex offender registration requirement associated with a CANS conviction, just as the legislature was preparing to vote on the 2011 amendments to the CANS statute.[90] Though also intangible, these efforts facilitated laying out the fundamental justice considerations at the core of a thorny issue, for the public and for lawmakers alike.

THE LIMITS OF EQUAL PROTECTION DOCTRINE

In the end, the central legal theory in *Doe v. Jindal* focused on the dry question of whether CANS complied with bedrock equal protection principles, and not on what was intuitively so troubling, from a social justice perspective, about Louisiana's law. It did not turn on questioning the wisdom, as a matter of public policy, of requiring individuals who have been so systematically deprived of social and material capital to register as sex offenders, further hampering their ability to access resources they need. Nor did it turn on an analysis of how a statute, passed in the context of virulent homophobia in the early 1980s, came to be predominantly wielded against African American women. This is partially because these constitute some of the real-world complexities that are ill-suited, at this historical juncture, to equal protection litigation. Equal protection cases are notoriously difficult to win, requiring a showing that a particular legislative scheme that disproportionately impacts a particular group — African Americans, say, or women — was animated by illicit intent (i.e., a base desire to harm that group).[91] This is already difficult enough to prove as a general matter; it would have been nearly impossible in this context, where the CANS statute was adopted and then enforced in ways that involve sometimes overlapping and sometimes distinct discriminatory purposes.

From the litigation perspective, it was a fortunate anomaly that the prostitution and CANS statutes mirrored one another so precisely but had such disparate consequences. This combination of textual symmetry and outcome asymmetry allowed us to craft a legal analysis based purely on the text of the statutes at hand and gave the Court a path to avoid public policy questions about the wisdom of sex offender registration (questions courts have been deeply hesitant to address) or an analysis of the complex ways in which racism, misogyny, class oppression, transphobia, and homophobia converged around the CANS statute. In this sense, *Doe v. Jindal* illustrates both the possibilities and the limitations of equal protection doctrine. Out of an extraordinarily complicated set of historical facts came a very simple legal theory and principle: the text of A (the CANS statute) is exactly like the text of B (the prostitution statute) and must therefore be treated in the same way.

Joseph Fischel, an assistant professor at Yale, has critiqued the NO Justice campaign, and the legal challenge to the CANS scheme, for valorizing our clients at the expense of others who have been forced to register as sex offenders.[92] Fischel argues that the "normatively superior" concept of consent was mobilized by activists and lawyers to sanitize those convicted of CANS and implicitly condemn others convicted of other sex offenses:

> Arguments by both activists and lawyers advocating the repeal of CAN registration requirements often revolve around consent as a morally

compelling metric; since the exchange of oral and anal sex for compensation is consensual, *so the argument goes*, it should not be a sex offense. Women With A Vision, the main local organization spearheading the declassification campaign, the CCR [Center for Constitutional Rights], which filed suit on behalf of the nine anonymous plaintiffs, and the amicus brief, filed by LGBT advocacy groups, repeatedly emphasize that the crime against nature statute is the only registerable offense that does not involve "force, coercion, use of a weapon, lack of consent, or a minor victim," which are all, rhetorically speaking, equally proof positive of nonconsent.[93]

Leaving aside the question of whether or not consent is a useful or desirable vehicle with which to regulate sex, the rhetorical sleight of hand implicit in the "so the argument goes" clause in this quotation is telling, revealing a fundamental misunderstanding of the equal protection theory in this case. At no point, in fact, did this litigation mobilize consent to make a normative argument about who should and should not be registered as sex offenders. (As Fischel eventually acknowledges thirty pages later, the concept of consent "is not, in the final juridical moment, the litigation strategy that succeeds in taking [plaintiffs] off the Registry."[94]) The legal theory in Doe v. Jindal was agnostic about what — if anything — *should* be categorized as a registerable sex offense and instead focused on what *is* categorized as such. Because the CANS and prostitution statutes shared exactly the same elements (in legal parlance, the same *actus reus* and *mens rea*), yet one resulted in sex offender registration while the other did not, formal equality principles had been violated. Fischel is correct that the Doe v. Jindal complaint did point out that all other statutes that trigger sex offender registration requirements included an element of force, coercion, use of a weapon, lack of consent, or a minor victim. But that point simply closed the analytical circle: looked at in terms of the elements that need to be proved in order to sustain a conviction, A (the CANS statute) is like B (the prostitution statute) but not like C (offense involving other elements of proof); thus A must be treated like B but not like C. The litigation remained deliberately silent about the status of category C — precisely because of a desire to avoid endorsing sex offender registration schemes or their utility (which, for the record, I oppose).

Fischel posits that, by seeking to remove almost 900 people from the sex offender registry, but not challenging the entire sex offender registry scheme, "those regulations are in turn relegitimized for all remaining sex offenders."[95]

Following this logic, so too might challenging the constitutionality of solitary confinement (an issue I also litigate at the Center for Constitutional Rights) be taken as a relegitimization of all other forms of incarceration. Frankly, no litigation strategy can withstand this critique. The NAACP Legal Defense Fund began its legal challenge to school segregation by challenging racial discrimination in graduate schools, focusing on the distinctive burdens discrimination places on the professional development of graduate students;[96] surely their approach was not intended to valorize discrimination in grade schools (which, of course, was later addressed by *Brown v. Board of Education*). The death penalty bar has successfully abolished the execution of people with intellectual disabilities and juveniles in the United States;[97] even while those cases focused on the unique status of these individuals to make the argument that evolving standards of decency prohibit their execution, they cannot reasonably be viewed as an endorsement of the state killing adults without disabilities. Cases like *Doe v. Jindal* must be understood in terms of where litigation, as opposed to other forms of political organizing or advocacy, can make meaningful interventions and where it cannot — or, otherwise put, what is ripe for legal challenge and what is not. *Doe v. Jindal* did not assert "the illegitimacy of so [*sic*] regulations for women convicted of CAN based on the fact that these women do not harm, rape, or commit violent acts."[98] Cognizant of its own limitations, the litigation theory purposefully steered clear of a normative assessment of the sex offender scheme writ large, or its appropriateness, opting instead for a rigid textual analysis that allowed a federal judge to issue a ruling that would result in the removal of almost 900 people from Louisiana's sex offender registry — an unprecedented outcome. Arguably, by building a record about the burdens associated with the sex offender registries, and proving that the state has deployed these burdens in arbitrary ways, the litigation actually opens up space for future challenges to other sex offender registries rather than shutting them down.

CONCLUSION: LESSONS LEARNED FROM THE NO JUSTICE CAMPAIGN

Within two years, three things happened that at the outset of the NO Justice campaign had seemed unimaginable. First, the legislature eradicated the most obviously and formally inequitable and discriminatory aspects of the CANS statute. Second, a federal court declared that the sex offender registration requirement associated with a CANS conviction offended the federal

Constitution, ordered the *Doe v. Jindal* plaintiffs removed from the sex of-fender registry, and instructed the state to cease and desist from placing any individuals convicted of CANS on the registry. And third, what began as a relatively obscure and uncomfortable issue became a rallying cry for advocates and community groups across Louisiana and indeed the country.

Of course, the story did not end there. Months after *Doe v. Jindal* was decided, Louisiana had still not purged its sex offender registry of hundreds of people who were there simply because of a CANS conviction, taking the position that the lawsuit benefited only the nine named plaintiffs — never mind that the Court unambiguously declared the practice unconstitutional across the board. And so, in June 2012, CCR, along with its co-counsel, filed a follow-up suit, *Doe v. Caldwell*, to force the state to extend the relief won in *Doe v. Jindal* to the hundreds of others who are identically situated.[99] After some legal wrangling, that case settled, leading to the removal of 870 people from the registry in June 2013.

The criminal justice system in Louisiana, just as across the country, continues to treat prostitution in irrational, draconian, and counterproductive ways. A national conversation is needed to end the vicious cycle of criminalization, incarceration, and marginalization that monopolizes policies around sex work. These are complex issues that were beyond the scope of the campaign against the CANS statute. The CANS statute, meanwhile, remains on the books, even if it is treated the same way as a prostitution conviction. In fact, in 2014, the Louisiana legislature voted by an astonishing 66–27 *against* removing Crime Against Nature (which outlaws all oral and anal sex committed by anyone in Louisiana under any circumstances, let alone in exchange for compensation) from the state's criminal code, even though that law is patently unconstitutional under *Lawrence*.[100] This is sobering context that puts into perspective the challenges of getting the CANS statute (which adds prostitution into the mix) fully repealed.

But what the NO Justice campaign did achieve was a significant change in how Louisiana polices, charges, prosecutes, and regulates prostitution. No longer can prosecutors wield the threat of a felony charge in order to pressure defendants to plead guilty to lesser (though still deeply consequential) prostitution-related charges without exercising their right to trial. No longer can police threaten to charge individuals with a felony that requires sex offender registration rather than a misdemeanor that does not, in order to extort sex (a practice that was reportedly rampant when CANS prosecutions were in full effect). And no longer are almost 900 people convicted of solicitation-related offenses subjected to the debilitating effects of sex offender registration.

Doe v. Jindal demonstrated the power and possibilities of movement-based lawyering. It gave voice to nine individuals who were willing to step forward and challenge this law in the most intimidating of settings: a federal court. But it followed the leadership of a courageous community group that decided enough was enough, and embedded itself within a larger social justice movement. No lawsuit, advocacy campaign, or editorial can single-handedly dismantle decades of injustice, no matter how dedicated those involved in these efforts may be. It takes a concerted and coordinated approach that taps into the resources and perspectives of a diverse group of committed individuals and organizations to engineer this kind of victory. It takes organizing, campaigning, lobbying, educating, and litigating to do this work, and these efforts must be mutually accountable and reinforcing in order to be effective. But, most important, communities must themselves articulate and define the struggles they face, and guide and shape the strategies used to tackle these issues. When all this comes together, power will occasionally yield to justice.

NOTES

1. The names used in this article are the same pseudonyms used in the Complaint filed in Doe v. Jindal, in order to maintain the plaintiffs' privacy. *See* Complaint at 1 n.1, Doe v. Jindal, 851 F. Supp. 2d 995 (E.D. La. 2012) (No. 11-388). The plaintiffs picked their own pseudonyms.

2. *See* LA. REV. STAT. ANN. § 14:82 (2012); *see also infra* note 31 and accompanying text.

3. LA REV. STAT. § 14:89.2(A) (2012).

4. *See* discussion *infra* Part B. The Crime Against Nature statute was a generic sodomy statute that outlawed engaging in oral or anal sex. As discussed below, such laws were common in the nineteenth and twentieth centuries and were declared unconstitutional by Lawrence v. Texas, 539 U.S. 558 (2003).

5. LA. REV. STAT. ANN. § 14:89.2(A) (2012).

6. *See Doe*, 851 F. Supp. 2d at 1003 ("The record also confirms that each plaintiff is required to register as a result of a Crime Against Nature by Solicitation conviction[.]").

7. *See infra* notes 51 and 56.

8. *Doe*, 851 F. Supp. 2d at 997–98.

9. *See* discussion *infra* Part C.

10. *See* LA. REV. STAT. ANN. § 15:542(D) (2012) (detailing fees associated with sex offender registration).

11. 1805 La. Acts 50.

12. George Painter, *The Sensibilities of Our Forefathers: The History of Sodomy Laws in the United States, Louisiana,* Glapn.org (last updated Aug. 10, 2004), http://www.glapn.org/sodomylaws/sensibilities/louisiana.htm.

13. Nan Hunter, *Life After Hardwick,* 27 HARV. C.R.-C.L. L. REV. 531, 533 (1992).

14. Nan Hunter, *Life After Hardwick,* 27 HARV. C.R.-C.L. L. REV. 531, 533 (1992).

15. *Lawrence,* 539 U.S. at 568.

16. State v. Williams, 34 La. Ann. 87, 88 (1882).

17. The phrase *"peccatum illud horribile, inter Christianos non nominandum"* was commonly used in legal treatises and in legislative debate at the time, and translates as "that horrible crime not to be named among Christians." *See* 4 SIR WILLIAM BLACKSTONE, COMMENTARIES ON THE LAWS OF ENGLAND 215 (1769).

18. 1896 La. Acts 69, § 1. The revised statute read, "Whoever shall be convicted of the detestable and abominable Crime against Nature committed with mankind or with beast with the sexual organs, or with the mouth, shall suffer imprisonment at hard labor for not less than two years and not more than ten years." State v. Vicknair, 52 La. Ann. 1921, 1925 (1900).

19. *See* Painter, *supra* note 12. (In 1942, the Louisiana Criminal Code was comprehensively revised, and the Crime Against Nature statute was amended. The text of the statute read, "Crime against Nature is the unnatural carnal copulation by a human being with another of the same or opposite sex or with an animal. Emission is not necessary, and, when committed by a human being with another, the use of the genital organ of one of the offenders of whatever sex is sufficient to constitute the crime." The maximum penalty was reduced from ten to five years, and a fine of up to $2,000 was added. The two-year minimum sentence remained, but the hard labor provision was made optional.)

20. Griswold v. Connecticut, 381 U.S. 479, 485–86 (1965).

21. *See id.*

22. Regarding "antihomosexual kulturkampf," *see* WILLIAM N. ESKRIDGE JR., DISHONORABLE PASSIONS: SODOMY LAWS IN AMERICA 1861–2003, 73–108 (2008). Brief of Professors of History George Chauncey, Nancy F. Cott, et al. as Amici Curiae in Support of Petitioners, Lawrence v. Texas, 539 U.S. 558 (2003) (No. 02-102), 2003 WL 152350, at *3.

23. TEX. PENAL CODE ANN. §21.06(a) (2003). (Texas struck down *Lawrence* providing, "A person commits an offense if he engages in deviate sexual intercourse with another individual of the same sex.")

24. Hunter, *supra* note 13, at 542; *see also Lawrence*, 539 U.S. at 578 (recognizing the irrelevance of the facial neutrality of some sodomy laws when it described sodomy as "sexual practices common to a homosexual lifestyle").

25. *See, e.g., Lawrence*, 539 U.S. at 570.

26. 1962 La. Acts. 60 § 1.

27. *Lawrence*, 539 U.S. at 558.

28. *See* State v. Thomas, 891 So. 2d 1233, 1235 (La. 2005) ("The Supreme Court majority recognized 'an emerging awareness that liberty gives substantial protection to adult persons in deciding how to conduct their private matters pertaining to sex' . . . [basing its decision] on the liberty interest found in a substantive component of the Due Process Clause of the Fourteenth Amendment to the Unites States Constitution.") (citing *Lawrence*, 539 U.S. at 572).

29. H.R. 853, 1982 Reg. Sess. 703 (La. 1982); *see also* State v. Forrest, 439 So. 2d 404, 407 (La. 1983). LA REV. STAT. § 14:89.2(A) (2012). The wording of the statute has changed slightly over the years, but the conduct targeted and element of intent have remained the same.

30. *See, e.g.,* State v. Smith, 766 So. 2d 501, 504–05 (La. 2000); State v. Murry, 136 La. 253, 257–59 (1914); State v. Long, 133 La. 580, 582–83 (1913); State v. Vicknair, 52 La. Ann. 1921, 1925 (1900).

31. *See* LA. REV. STAT. ANN. § 14:82(A)(2)–(B) (2012) (The solicitation provision of Louisiana's prostitution statute outlaws "[t]he solicitation by one person of another with the intent to engage in indiscriminate sexual intercourse with the latter for compensation." The statute defines "sexual intercourse" as "anal, oral, or vaginal sexual intercourse.").

32. *See* LA. REV. STAT. ANN. § 14:82(C)(1) (2012). *See* LA. REV. STAT. ANN. § 14:89(B) (2012). Until August 15, 2010, a first CANS conviction was treated as a felony offense, punishable by a term of imprisonment of up to five years, with or without hard labor, and/or a fine of not more than $2,000.

33. *See* LA. REV. STAT. ANN. § 15:541(24)(a) (2012); *see also* Doe v. Jindal, 851 F. Supp. 2d 995, 1006 (E.D. La. 2012) (stating, "examination of the two statutes reflects that [the state] treat[s] differently identically-situated individuals, because plaintiffs are required to register as sex offenders simply because they were convicted of Crime Against Nature by Solicitation, rather than solicitation of Prostitution (conduct chargeable by and covered under either statute)).

34. The Louisiana Supreme Court described sodomy as "loathsome and disgusting" in State v. Bonnano, 163 So. 2d 72, 74 (La. 1964).

35. The implications of this symbolic power should not, however, be underestimated. Indeed, the fact that the Supreme Court in Bowers initially upheld sodomy statutes regulating homosexual sex allowed conservative jurists to reason that, if

homosexual sex could be criminalized, there was a legitimate rationale for anti-LGBT animus in other contexts. Writing in dissent in Romer v. Evans, the 1996 Supreme Court decision holding that a state constitutional amendment in Colorado preventing protected status based upon homosexuality or bisexuality violated the equal protection clause, Justice Scalia observed, "In holding that homosexuality cannot be singled out for disfavorable treatment, the Court contradicts [the *Bowers*] decision, unchallenged here, pronounced only 10 years ago, and places the prestige of this institution behind the proposition that opposition to homosexuality is as reprehensible as racial or religious bias.... If it is constitutionally permissible for a State to make homosexual conduct criminal, surely it is constitutionally permissible for a State to enact other laws merely disfavoring homosexual conduct." Romer v. Evans, 517 U.S. 620, 636, 641 (1996) (Scalia, J., dissenting). And as the Supreme Court recognized in *Lawrence*, "[Bowers's] continuance as precedent demeans the lives of homosexual persons.... The State cannot demean their existence or control their destiny by making their private sexual conduct a crime." Lawrence v. Texas, 539 U.S. 558, 575, 578 (2003).

36. Complaint at ¶ 53, Doe v. Caldwell, No. 12-1670, 2012 WL 6674415 (E.D. La. June 27, 2012).

37. Ctr. for Constitutional Rights, Breakdown of Cans Convictions by Year (2011) (on file with author).

38. *Lawrence*, 539 U.S. at 581 (noting that prosecutions under the Texas sodomy law at issue in *Lawrence* were "rare").

39. Ctr. for Constitutional Rights, Breakdown of Cans Convictions by Sex and Race (2012) (on file with author). Complaint at ¶ 122, Doe v. Jindal, 851 F. Supp. 2d 995 (E.D. La. 2012) (No. 11-388).

40. Complaint at ¶ 122, Doe v. Jindal, 851 F. Supp. 2d 995.

41. *Id.* at ¶¶ 123, 125.

42. *Id.* at ¶ 124.

43. *Id.* at ¶ 179.

44. *See generally* Just Detention Int'l, A Call for Change: Protecting the Rights of LGBTQ Detainees (2009), http://justdetention.org/wp-content /uploads/2015/10/Call-for-Change-Protecting-the-Rights-of-LGBTQ-Detainees .pdf (Sexual orientation is the single most predictive characteristic of who is targeted for sexual assault in detention.). *Multimedia Audio Feature: Plaintiff Ian Doe Relates His Experience* (Feb. 16, 2011), http://ccrjustice.org/home/get-involved/tools-resources /fact-sheets-and-faqs/louisiana-s-crime-against-nature-law-modern [hereinafter *Ian Statement*].

45. Complaint at ¶¶ 139, 157, Doe v. Jindal, 851 F. Supp. 2d 995 (E.D. La. 2012) (No. 11-388).

46. Registration as a sex offender requires, among other mandated acts and prohibitions, the payment of annual registration fees (LA. REV. STAT. ANN. § 15:542(D) (2012)), extensive community notification obligations (LA. REV. STAT. ANN. § 15:542.1 (2012)), inclusion of the words "sex offender" in bright-orange capital letters on one's driver's license or state-issued identification card (LA. REV. STAT. ANN. § 40:1321(J)(1) (2008)), and adherence to separate evacuation protocols in the event of a state emergency (LA. REV. STAT. ANN. § 15:543.2 (2012)). Failure to comply with registration requirements carries significant penalties, including incarceration for periods of up to twenty years at hard labor — without the possibility of parole, probation, or suspension of sentence. *See* LA. REV. STAT. ANN. § 15:542(A) (2012).

47. Complaint at ¶ 133, *Doe*, 851 F. Supp. 2d 995.

48. *Id.* at ¶ 147.

49. LA. REV. STAT. ANN. § 40:1321(J)(1) (2008).

50. Complaint at ¶¶ 143, 148, *Doe*, 851 F. Supp. 2d 995.

51. *Ian Statement, supra* note 44.

52. Complaint at ¶ 152, *Doe*, 851 F. Supp. 2d 995.

53. *Id.* at ¶ 182.

54. *Id.* at ¶ 160.

55. *Id.*

56. *Multimedia Audio Feature: Plaintiff Eve Doe Relates Her Experience* (Feb. 16, 2011), http://ccrjustice.org/home/get-involved/tools-resources/fact-sheets-and-faqs /louisiana-s-crime-against-nature-law-modern [hereinafter *Eve Statement*].

57. Complaint at ¶ 153, *Doe*, 851 F. Supp. 2d 995.

58. *See* DEP'T OF SOC. SERV., DSS ESF-6 PROTOCOLS FOR EVACUATING AND SHELTERING REGISTERED SEX OFFENDERS (UNIQUE POPULATION) (2009).

59. Complaint at ¶ 134, *Doe*, 851 F. Supp. 2d 995.

60. *Id.* at ¶ 141.

61. *Id.* at ¶ 167.

62. *Id.*

63. *Id.* at ¶ 177.

64. *Ian Statement, supra* note 44.

65. WOMEN WITH A VISION, *Mission*, http://wwav-no.org/about/mission (last visited May 20, 2014).

66. WOMEN WITH A VISION, *NO Justice*, http://wwav-no.org/no-justice (last visited July 26, 2016).

67. WOMEN WITH A VISION, *NO Justice*, http://wwav-no.org/no-justice (last visited July 26, 2016).

68. S. 381, 2010 Reg. Sess., Act 882 (La. 2010).

69. *Compare* LA. REV. STAT. ANN. § 14:82(C) (2012), *with* H.R. 141, 2011 Reg. Sess., Act 223 (La. 2011).

70. H.R. 141, 2011 Reg. Sess., Act 223 (La. 2011).

71. Complaint, Doe v. Jindal, 851 F. Supp. 2d 995 (E.D. La. 2012) (No. 11-388).

72. *See* H.R. 141, 2011 Reg. Sess., Act 223 (La. 2011).

73. Complaint at ¶¶ 190–207, *Doe*, 851 F. Supp. 2d 995 (raising substantive due process, procedural due process, and Eighth Amendment claims).

74. Vacco v. Quill, 521 U.S. 793, 799 (1997) (citing Plyer v. Doe, 457 U.S. 202, 216 (1982)).

75. *See supra* note 71.

76. Eisenstadt v. Baird, 405 U.S. 438 (1972).

77. *Id.* at 440–41, 443.

78. *Id.* at 453.

79. *Id.* at 454.

80. *Id.* (quoting Railway Express Agency v. New York, 336 U.S. 106, 112–13 (1949) (Jackson, J., concurring)).

81. Order and Reasons at 23, Doe v. Jindal, 851 F. Supp. 2d 995 (E.D. La. 2012) (No. 11-388).

82. *Id.*

83. *Doe*, 851 F. Supp. 2d at 1007, 1008–09.

84. *Id.* at 1009.

85. Judgment, *Doe*, 851 F. Supp. 2d 995.

86. Quote from Charles Elsesser, *Community Lawyering — The Role of Lawyers in the Social Justice Movement*, 14 LOY. J. PUB. INT. L. 375, 393 (2013).

87. *See Ian Statement, supra* note 44.

88. *Id.*

89. *See, e.g.*, Trymaine Lee, *Sex Crime in New Orleans, Separate and Unequal*, HUFFINGTON POST, May 6, 2011, http://www.huffingtonpost.com/2011/05/06/new-orleans-sex-crime-felony_n_858180.html; Alexis Agathocleous, *Eight Years After Lawrence, Sodomy Laws Are Alive and Kicking*, BILERICO, Feb. 16, 2011, http://www.bilerico.com/2011/02/eight_years_after_lawrence_sodomy_laws_are_alive_a.php; Jarvis DeBerry, Op-Ed, *Sex Offender Label for Streetwalkers Is Misplaced*, TIMES PICAYUNE, Aug. 12, 2011, http://www.nola.com/opinions/index.ssf/2011/08/sex_offender_label_for_streetw.html.

90. Editorial, *These Two Sex Crimes Should Be Treated the Same*, TIMES-PICAYUNE, May 30, 2011, http://www.nola.com/opinions/index.ssf/2011/05/these_two_sex_crimes_should_be.html.

91. *See, e.g.*, Village of Arlington Heights v. Metropolitan Housing Development Corp, 429 U.S. 252 (1977).

92. *See generally,* Joseph Fischel, *Against Nature, Against Consent: A Sexual Politics of Debility,* 24 DIFFERENCES 55 (2013).

93. *Id.* at 60 (emphasis added).

94. *Id.* at 90.

95. *Id.* at 73.

96. Sweatt v. Painter, 339 U.S. 629 (1950).

97. Atkins v. Virginia, 536 U.S. 304 (2002) (holding that executing mentally retarded individuals violates the Eighth Amendment's ban on cruel and unusual punishments); Roper v. Simmons, 543 U.S. 551 (2005) (holding that it is unconstitutional to impose capital punishment for crimes committed while under the age of eighteen).

98. *Id.* note 95.

99. Complaint at ¶ 53, Doe v. Caldwell, No. 12-1670, 2012 WL 6674415 (E.D. La. Jun. 27, 2012).

100. H.B. 12, 2014 Reg. Sess. (La. 2014), http://www.legis.la.gov/legis/BillInfo .aspx?s=14RS&b=HB12&sbi=y.

AMBER HOLLIBAUGH

| 17 |

Bringing Sex to the
Table of Justice

The following remarks were given at the Sex and Justice Conference held at the University of Michigan in October 2012. I first heard about the idea for this conference from Trevor Hoppe, who contacted me more than a year before to discuss the idea of such a conference. At the time I thought it was an extraordinary idea — an actual academic conference on sex and justice? How wonderful, I thought, that someone actually wanted to do such a thing. And it wasn't even my suggestion. Also involved in creating this conference and thinking through its importance was David Halperin. I was interested.

I was in for a surprise. So many organizers did extraordinary work to make the conference possible. And their extraordinary work, in turn, brought together a unique group of thinkers and activists very unlike any that had come together before in the academy. This was a very different construct — a different conversation would be had. That fact allowed certain dynamics and issues to emerge that otherwise would not have. Sex work and queerness and sexual predator registries and poverty and the criminalized world of HIV and AIDS — all were invited to come together, listen, and talk.

Most activists and academics attend too many conferences. While those events may be useful, they are not always necessary. But this conference was significant, courageous, utterly necessary, and fundamentally frightening. By its very nature, a conference focusing on sex and justice recognizes and addresses particular kinds of vulnerabilities associated with desire, identity, sexuality, and the state. These issues are extremely complicated. Generally, the ways that these issues are policed are not discussed openly. Often these issues are contemplated individually and separately because of the silos of our identities or the stigmas connected to say, our HIV status or being a prostitute, and we remain alone and apart from one another. Such is the loneliness of the individual in the face of the state's terrifying power to control, to compartmentalize, to silence.

And this, too, is a particularly terrifying time in our country. It is terrifying because political society is moving increasingly to the right, and not incrementally so but in leaps and bounds. This is happening in ways that present us with very little ability to resist. And that is an important part of the agenda of the Right: to push, at a very speedy tempo, toward politics that are increasingly conservative, and doing it so loudly, so self-righteously, that fewer and fewer progressive voices — let alone *radical* voices — are heard at all.

The impact is felt everywhere. I have felt it. Ironically — after forty or more years of very radical activism — I find myself defending things I never thought were adequate in the first place! It is infuriating to fight about reproductive justice, Social Security, Medicaid, food stamps, public housing, unions. And it is, yes, absolutely terrifying.

Thus, the very idea of a conference on sex and justice came to me as a relief. But I understood immediately, too, that it would be a challenge. That is because it had the potential to truly address *this* moment in history — and what it means within the context of a radical vision for human freedom. The promise of the conference: to begin revving up the tempo of resistance ourselves — maybe even more quickly than the Right; to refuse to listen to naysayers; to refuse to give in to the timidity of liberals; to make the commitment to bring such a group together *now*. This would enable us to at least begin to analyze, together, the way the state currently controls and is attempting to exert even more control over sexuality. We need to face this. It doesn't help to always position our discourse around the silos of gender, or sexual orientation, or class, or race. It doesn't help to leave the discourse to academics — no matter how progressive they may be individually. Sexual freedom is a fundamental, an essential, freedom, and, oddly enough, the ultimate protector of human privacy, vulnerability, autonomy.

Focusing on sexual liberation — and the ways in which, at this moment in history, it is so terribly threatened by the political Right and the state — allows us to do something different. We can have a different kind of conversation about the terrible dangers we're facing. It is not just that sexuality is threatened; it is that, in the face of global economic oppression, global political terror, and the negation of so many human freedoms by those in power, a conversation about real sexual liberation becomes an indispensable conversation about radical social change and the possibility of human freedom.

However, there is a high price to pay. There is great difficulty in trying to build a progressive movement to address issues of sex, desire, pleasure, and possibility, at a point in history when increasing conservatism makes it more and more difficult to talk about sex in *any* context. Because the global market is making people pay a terrible price for desire. It is making people pay a terrible price for speaking, and living, complex sexual truth.

To this discussion, each of us brings our own history. My own particular history is that I am a person who often didn't really fit into the movements to which I felt the most committed. This has been a lifelong sorrow for me, because I've actually loved the movements I have been a part of. The civil rights movement, the radical Left, the women's movement, the gay liberation movement, the AIDS activist movement — all fundamentally transformed me. In many ways, they saved my life. But they were also quick to disown me when I disclosed the truth of my life — of being embedded in poverty and of being mixed race, of being a sex worker, of being a high-femme lesbian. My own list of differences was long. So I have always been profoundly disturbed at how vulnerable and marginalized I felt within these movements even as I fundamentally needed to be a part of them.

It was long ago, when I found myself a scholarship student attending a ruling-class high school — where I was flunking — that a professor said to me, "You're not failing here because you're stupid; you're failing because you were never meant to be here. You were never *meant* to succeed." And he gave me *The Communist Manifesto*. I will thank him to the end of my life. That piece of literature gave me — for the very first time — a realization that my parents and I weren't at fault for being throwaway people. I realized that the kind of impoverished, mixed-race, socially despised background I had come from was not my fault and it *was not unique.*

But there is a terrible silence that surrounds poverty and race, just as there is a deadening silence surrounding sexuality, difference, desire — and the deep-rooted human urge for freedom, for all kinds of nourishing, positive, life-giving freedoms. *And silence is what distorts these things — not the things themselves.*

So, because of my own complex history, I insist on this: if we are going to build a movement *for* sex and justice, we need to ask very problematic questions about *who we are bringing to the table.* Who are we really inviting to have a piece of the pie? And that has been a problem in *all* equality and radical justice movements — and in so much political organizing. Organizations that represent vulnerable and marginalized people are already fighting a terrible uphill battle. It isn't an accident that liberation movements of all sorts bring *only certain people* to the table and hide certain other ones.

For a long time, I directed the organization Queers for Economic Justice (QEJ). What QEJ confronted, and what many of us doing work around class, race, poverty, sexuality, and social justice continue to confront, is that our own organizations represent the "wrong kinds of people" in the larger movements we're supposed to be a part of. The people represented by QEJ are *not* the kind of people that the Human Rights Campaign (HRC) wants to bring to their media events.

This is very clear, for example, in communities dealing with incarceration and addiction, especially when they combine with the wrong kinds of queers: queer stone butches and aggressors, kick-ass high-femme lesbian hookers, bi queers and HIV-positive folks and transgender folks and queer and addicted folks who are trying to get into a family shelter so they can stay together as a couple, tired of riding the subway for the last week and having their sex in an alley—too poor, too queer, too of color, too undocumented. QEJ dealt with a population of poor people that nobody wants to name, that nobody wants to represent, and with issues *nobody* wants to take on.

The reason is that, in addition to acknowledging imprisonment, poverty, and racism, QEJ demanded that these movements acknowledge and represent sexual difference and expression and a desire for erotic freedom and liberation: inside juvie halls and detention centers and high-security prisons and outside in homeless shelters and Walmart stockrooms and in senior nursing homes. Because in all these lockdown places we see a blatant microcosm of the ways in which this country operates, the way it controls and disfigures justice, the way it controls and disfigures people's bodies and minds.

If we dare to look at organizations like the Excluded Workers Congress, the Texas Four, sex-worker organizing, those who organize against the criminalization of HIV, and those who are fighting to end prisons, we realize that these groups represent people with layered and complicated lives: people who must be defended around the reality of those lives, the choices they've made or were forced to make, and what they have done because of and in spite of those choices. These people are not victims. They are not simple. And they are not considered the "right kind" of people.

There are so many complex explanations for who we are in the context of sex and gender, class, race, difference. But if you don't even address these complex realities, then who and what are you talking about? But if you build movements that do address this human complexity, you actually build movements in a different *way*.

If we truly base our movements around these complex issues affecting sex and justice, we start from a different place. We ask different questions. We engage politically in different ways, because we have decided to build movements that can deal with the real complexities of the lives of the people we're talking about. A movement that can name things like the dangers inherent in capitalism, can talk about economic disparity, and can *not* give up talking about sex!

Sex is often framed within the context of innocence and its loss. But daring to go beyond that framework is enormously dangerous. Because if we tell the truth about our silenced desires, the actual truth about our lives — if we tell the truth about who we really are, and what we really do, or want to do, or try not to do — we will *never* be able to claim innocence. Because the living reality of our own histories is many-layered with sharp-edged sexual actualities — ones that are messy and compromised, stupid and dangerous, and at the same moments, often these experiences and choices have been the most important explorations of who we are, what we desire, what we cannot afford. So the notion of sexual innocence and its value to us as a sexual culture is a dangerous *idea*, and as we build a political movement that never gives up sex for freedom, we have to confront the danger and the violence the idea of sexual innocence inevitably brings.

Now, I've been an organizer for a long time, and what I've seen over and over again is that most of the movements I've been a part of have moved as far away from sex as possible! Because they think that ignoring sex is the only way to win equality or fight for liberation. "I'll be a homo — but not a homo*sexual*. I'll be a woman — but without a *vagina*. I'll be a person living in poverty — but without a *race or a body*."

Look: You cannot build movements that actually bring people together if you force people to omit crucial parts of their lives, lie about their histories, deny their most profound longings, skirt the truth.

You cannot build movements that actually bring people together if you refuse to recognize and articulate the *real* stories of our lives — the ways in which sex and justice, the state and the human longing for freedom intersect, clash, form, deform, and inform us.

And you never will be able to defend sex — including complicated sex — if you can't begin to defend the possibility of sex and the foundation it creates for *hope*.

I've seen so many of our important movements retreat from that. They've become terrified to take that on politically: to make it a seminal part of their agenda.

But in beginning to do this work now — inviting sex to the table, and all of the messy and brilliant and dangerous issues that raises, and insisting that sex sit there alongside justice — we may finally take it on. We may finally take on the desires of human minds and what we do with our human bodies — and demand the right to have that: to practice desire, to name it, defend it, without apology.

And what does it mean for us, at this historical time, to begin a different kind of conversation about the possibility of hope and desire in the face of terrible despair? Because we *are* in a state of despair. The majority of people in this country are desperate about their own survival, terrified that tomorrow will be even worse than today; the majority of people are too exhausted to fight. They don't have the tools to create resistance — and they cannot imagine the possibility of it. But as a progressive organizer, my job is to help create the *possibility of resistance* in a moment that is so frightening for so many people.

At the same time, however, *this is actually a moment in which I believe we have more ability to speak than we've had in many, many years.* When I talk about capitalism now, people don't roll their eyes as if I've just fallen off a cabbage truck direct from the Soviet Union. They're eager to tell me their stories about what's happened to them over the last decade. When I talk about sexuality and the criminalization of sex work, and of people with HIV, when I talk about the way communities of color and communities of poverty are policed and controlled, and our children stopped and frisked — the kinds of *shit* and despotism going on all around this country — people step up. They don't step back.

This is a moment, an opportunity for us all, to open up the conversation about sex and justice. And this conference will begin to construct the possibility of that conversation — *if* we understand that this needs to be the first step, not the last one.

We have a movement to build! A movement of intellectuals, and academics, and activists, and organizers who are *not* separate from one another in the ways that really count — and who *all* want to include those who have never been invited to *anyone's* table. A movement that doesn't operate as though the rest of us are mere cogs in a movement's wheel.

And at the same time we organize for action, we must build a movement that isn't *anti*-intellectual, that values and understands the necessity of thinking through in detail and moving forward with a fierce intelligence along different paths of resistance. A movement that, for example, uses legal strategies. A movement that cultivates allies and friends who understand the state and its use of power. We can begin to build movements like the effort in Louisiana to repeal the state's Crime Against Nature law, which became much more comprehensive and inclusive than anyone anticipated at the beginning.

Our job is to truly learn from our own history — and then create something new. This is not the 1930s, not the '60s or the '80s. This is a new moment. This is a moment to *fiercely* organize.

Sex and justice create the engine for organizing. Sex and justice, the human desire for freedom and fairness, are issues we can use to break down the walls by which identity, sexuality, class, and race become isolated, to organize in a way that celebrates desire, that excludes no one. We *can* build a response, and an *effective* resistance, if we actually do the work *together*.

And we can begin to say, again: *Yes.*

TREVOR HOPPE

Afterword

How You Can Get Involved

We hope that readers will come away from this volume feeling a sense of injustice and anger — but we also hope those emotions find an outlet in political engagement rather than cynicism. Although we will not end the war on sex tomorrow, we strongly believe that positive change is possible.

Recent developments reveal that positive change is already in motion. Petitions and sympathetic news stories circulated nationally in summer 2015 in support of convicted sex offender Zach Anderson, who was arrested when he was nineteen for having sex with a fourteen-year-old girl who told him she was seventeen. Meanwhile in Massachusetts, their state's highest court struck down a local ordinance forbidding sex offenders from living within 1,000 feet of a school or park — arguing that "the days are long since past when whole communities of persons, such as Native Americans and Japanese-Americans may be lawfully banished from our midst."[1] Despite objections from celebrities such as Lena Dunham and Meryl Streep, Amnesty International announced on August 18, 2015, that the organization has "chosen to advocate for the decriminalization of all aspects of consensual adult sex."[2]

These victories demonstrate that resistance in the war on sex is not futile. To help readers navigate the current political landscape, we thought it would be helpful to provide a list of organizations working around the country on the issues raised in this volume. As the contributions to this volume focus primarily on the United States, we limit the scope of this addendum to the United States. We realize that this list will quickly become outdated, but we nonetheless felt it was important to provide these resources to readers eager to learn more and get involved.

Note that this list is not meant to be exhaustive. We have done our best to include formal organizations that work specifically on the set of issues described in this volume. For the sake of brevity, we have excluded allied organizations that are doing important work but whose missions are much broader in scope (e.g., ACLU, Lambda Legal, the Center for Constitutional Rights, etc.).

HIV CRIMINALIZATION REFORM

Center for HIV Law & Policy, hivlawandpolicy.org

HIV Prevention Justice Alliance, preventionjustice.org

The Sero Project, seroproject.com

SEX OFFENDER LEGAL REFORM

National

Reform Sex Offender Laws (RSOL) (many state affiliates), nationalrsol.org

Sex Offender Solutions & Education Network (SOSEN), sosen.org

The Center for Sexual Justice, centerforsexualjustice.org

The National Center for Reason and Justice (NCRJ), ncrj.org

USA FAIR — usafair.org

Women Against Registry, womenagainstregistry.org

State

Arkansas Time After Time, arkansastimeaftertime.org

California RSOL, californiarsol.org

Colorado Advocates for Change, advocates4change.org

Colorado Coalition for Sex Offense Restoration, csor-home.org

Connecticut Voices, connecticut-voices.org

Florida Action Committee, floridaactioncommittee.org

Illinois Voices for Reform, ilvoices.com

Kentucky Citizens and Families for Reform, kycfr.org

Maryland Families Advocating Intelligent Registries, fairregistry.org

Michigan Citizens for Justice, micitizensforjustice.com

Michigan Coalition for a Useful Registry, coalitionur.org

Nebraskans Unafraid, nebraskarsol.com

New Hampshire Citizens for Criminal Justice Reform, ccjrnh.org

New Mexico Liberty and Justice Coalition, libjusco.net

Oklahoma RSOL, ok-rsol.org

Oregon Voices, www.oregonvoices.org

Texas Voices for Reason and Justice, texasvoices.org

SEX CRIME POLICY REFORM

CautionClick, cautionclick.com

CURE-SORT, cure-sort.org

Woodhull Sexual Freedom Foundation, woodhullalliance.org

SEX WORK LEGAL REFORM

Global

English Collective of Prostitutes, prostitutescollective.net

International Union of Sex Workers, iusw.org

National

Best Practices Policy Project (BPPP), bestpracticespolicy.org

Desiree Alliance, desireealliance.org

HOOK, hookonline.org

Sex Workers Outreach Project (many local chapters), swopusa.org

Sex Workers Project, sexworkersproject.org

State and Local

HIPS (Washington, D.C.), hips.org

Project SAFE Philadelphia, projectsafephilly.org

Red Umbrella Project (NY), redumbrellaproject.org

Sex Workers Action New York (SWANK), swop-nyc.org

Women with a Vision New Orleans, wwav-no.org

NOTES

1. John Doe & others v. City of Lynn, No. SJC-11822, 472 Mass. 521 (2015), p. 16.
2. Catherine Murphy, "Sex Workers' Rights Are Human Rights," Amnesty International, August 15, 2008, https://www.amnesty.org/en/latest/news/2015/08/sex-workers-rights-are-human-rights/

Contributors

ALEXIS AGATHOCLEOUS is the deputy legal director of the Center for Constitutional Rights (CCR), where he litigates cases challenging mass incarceration and abusive practices in the criminal justice system. He is currently counsel for plaintiffs in a class action challenging prolonged solitary confinement at California's notorious Pelican Bay State Prison.

ELIZABETH BERNSTEIN is associate professor of sociology at Barnard College. She is coeditor of *Regulating Sex: The Politics of Intimacy and Identity* (2005) and the author of *Temporarily Yours: Intimacy, Authenticity, and the Commerce of Sex* (2007).

J. WALLACE BORCHERT is dedicated to making prison systems transparent. He is a critical prisons and punishment scholar, a former prisoner himself, and a fierce advocate for social justice. He expects to receive his PhD in sociology from the University of Michigan at Ann Arbor in June 2016.

MARY ANNE CASE is Arnold I. Shure Professor of Law at the University of Chicago Law School. Her scholarship to date has concentrated on the regulation of sex, gender, sexuality, religion, and the family, and on the early history of feminism.

OWEN DANIEL-MCCARTER is a transgender attorney, educator, and advocate. He is the executive director of the Illinois Safe Schools Alliance, where he supports gender inclusivity in schools, LGBT-affirming curriculum, bullying prevention, and restorative school discipline practices. Owen attended the City University of New York School of Law and has been licensed to practice law in Illinois since 2007. He is a founding collective member of the Transformative Justice Law Project, the former legal director of the TransLife Center, and a former adjunct faculty at DePaul University in Chicago.

SCOTT DE ORIO is a doctoral candidate in history and women's studies at the University of Michigan in Ann Arbor. His dissertation, entitled "The Invention of Bad Gay Sex," examines the transformation of sex offender laws in the larger context of U.S. sexual politics in the second half of the twentieth century and shows how those laws affected gay people in particular.

DAVID M. HALPERIN is the W. H. Auden Distinguished University Professor of the History and Theory of Sexuality at the University of Michigan. He is the author and editor of a dozen books, including *How to Be Gay* (2012), *What Do Gay Men Want?* (2007), *Gay Shame* (2009), and *Saint Foucault* (1995).

AMBER HOLLIBAUGH is an activist whose movement politics date back to Freedom Summer in 1964. She is the author of *My Dangerous Desires: A Queer Girl Dreaming Her Way Home* (2000) and former executive director of Queers for Economic Justice.

TREVOR HOPPE is assistant professor of sociology at the University at Albany, SUNY. His research examines how institutions of medicine, law, and public health interface to control sex. His book, *Punishing Disease* (forthcoming), examines laws that make it a crime for HIV-positive people to have sex without first disclosing their HIV status.

HANS TAO-MING HUANG is associate professor at the Center for the Study of Sexualities, Department of English at National Central University, Taiwan. He is the author of *Queer Politics and Sexual Modernity in Taiwan* (2011). Most recently his work has focused on HIV care and drug control in transnational settings.

REGINA KUNZEL is the Doris Stevens Chair and Professor of History and Gender and Sexuality Studies at Princeton University. Her most recent book is *Criminal Intimacy: Prison and the Uneven History of Modern American Sexuality* (2008). She is currently working on a project exploring the encounter of LGBT/queer people with psychiatry and psychoanalysis in the mid-twentieth-century United States.

ROGER N. LANCASTER is the author of *Sex Panic and the Punitive State* (2011) and other award-winning books that try to understand how sexual mores, racial hierarchies, and class predicaments interact in a volatile world. He is professor of anthropology and cultural studies at George Mason University.

JUDITH LEVINE is a journalist and 2015 Soros Justice Media Fellow, writing on sex offender laws and the people they affect, and transformative justice approaches to sexual violence. She is the author of four books, including *Harmful to Minors: The Perils of Protecting Children from Sex* (2002), and thousands of articles in mainstream publications.

LAURA MANSNERUS is a journalist and lawyer who was a reporter and editor at the *New York Times* for twenty years. She was also a fellow of the Open Society Foundations, which supported research for this article.

ERICA R. MEINERS is the Bernard J. Brommel Distinguished Research Professor at Northeastern Illinois University and is a 2015 Soros Justice Media Fellow. She is the author of several books, including *For the Children? Protecting Innocence in a Carceral State* (2016), and is involved in range of ongoing justice mobilizations against state violence.

R. NOLL is a doctoral student in political theory and anthropology at the University of Chicago.

MELISSA PETRO is a freelance writer and writing instructor living in New York City. She has written for *New York Magazine, Pacific Standard Magazine, Marie Claire, Cosmopolitan, New Inquiry, Salon, Daily Beast,* and many other publications. She was a finalist for the PEN/Fusion Emerging Writers Prize in 2015.

CAROL QUEEN cofounded the Center for Sex and Culture in San Francisco. She is a writer and cultural sexologist with a PhD in human sexuality and a noted essayist whose work has appeared in dozens of anthologies. She is the author of several books, including *Real Live Nude Girl: Chronicles of Sex-Positive Culture* (1997).

PENELOPE SAUNDERS is director of the Best Practices Policy Project. She is also a member of the Desiree Alliance and SWOP-NYC, and participates in many local, regional, and international actions for the rights of sex workers and related communities, including trans and queer communities.

SEAN STRUB is a New York–based writer and AIDS activist who serves as executive director of the Sero Project (seroproject.com). He founded POZ magazine and is the author of *Body Counts: A Memoir of Politics, Sex, AIDS, and Survival* (2014).

MAURICE TOMLINSON is a Jamaican lawyer, LGBTI activist, and educator. For nearly twenty years, he has been working with a variety of local and international agencies to combat homophobia and HIV across the Caribbean. In 2012, he received the inaugural David Kato Vision and Voice Award.

GREGORY TOMSO is chair of the Department of English at the University of West Florida. His research interests include HIV, sexuality, and legal/scientific discourse.

Index

Abbott, Tony, 412

Abortion and the Politics of Motherhood (Luker), 302

abortion laws, 5, 6; Vatican and, 211, 212, 213, 214, 218, 219, 224n33. *See also* reproductive rights

abstinence-based education, 219, 385–86

abuse: cycle of, 100; definitions, 98–99. *See also* children and youth, violent crimes against; family abuse; sexual violence, abuse, and assault

accusation, 104; of San Antonio Four, 126–28, 137, 156, 159; of violent crimes against children, 98–99, 126–27, 136–37, 142, 156, 164n3. *See also* innocence

Ackerman, Alissa, 148

activism. *See* anti-trafficking activism; LGBTQI rights activism; prison abolition activism

actuarial logic in risk assessment, 89, 100, 113, 269, 279

Adam, Barry, 362–63, 367

Adam Walsh Child Protection and Safety Act (2006), 86–87, 90, 138, 146, 153, 276–77

administrative regulation, 32–34, 37

administrative segregation. *See* solitary confinement

Adorno, Theodor, 96

Advocate (magazine), 254, 255

affirmative consent standard, 32–34, 58n60. *See also* consensual sex; consent

Africa, 35–36, 217, 218, 398n8; Uganda, 46, 410–12, 424–26

African Americans, 101, 103, 298, 457, 459; Black feminists, 130, 131, 143–44; CANS and, 13, 429, 430, 434–35, 437, 443; children, 153; HIV criminalization and, 349, 350; human trafficking and, 43, 311, 312, 331, 333, 337; incarceration and, 69, 82, 145, 148, 170n77, 180, 181, 185; Prop 35 and, 323, 324, 326–27, 331, 333, 335; rape and, 29, 79, 83–84, 146, 151; restorative justice activism, 162–63; on sex offender registries, 12, 145, 147–52, 155–56, 170n77, 170n79, 434–35, 437; transpeople of color, 12, 15, 179, 181–82, 415, 429. *See also* race; white people; women of color

Against Our Will: Men, Women and Rape (Brownmiller), 133–34

Agamben, Giorgio, 97

Agathocleous, Alexis, 13

age of consent, 98, 100–101, 112, 172n96, 180; lowering, 133–34, 157; NAMBLA and, 134–35; statutory rape, 89, 106–7, 131–32, 154, 166n21, 356, 461. *See also* children and youth; children and youth, tried and/or convicted as sex offenders; consensual sex; consent

Aggravated Crime Against Nature statute (Louisiana), 433

AIDS. *See* HIV/AIDS

AIDS-Free World (Jamaican NGO), 418, 419, 420

Akers, Naomi, 334

Alabama, 250

Alaska, 14, 148–49

Alaskan Natives, 148–49

Alexander, Michelle, 131, 145

Alien Tort Statute, 411

Allen, Daniel, 370–71

alternatives question, 72, 184–88. *See also* prison abolition activism

American Association of University Women (AAUW), 306

American Civil Liberties Union (ACLU), 30, 258, 335, 336–37, 371; Gay Rights Chapter, 252, 256, 259

American Friends Service Committee (AFSC), 198–99

American Indians, 148–49

American Law Institute, 34, 252

American Medical Association (AMA), 350

American Psychiatric Association (APA), 239, 276

America's Most Wanted (television show), 86, 112

Amnesty International, 46, 461

anal sex: CANS and, 144, 429–30, 431, 433, 440–41, 444, 447n4; decriminalization, 5, 256, 257, 433; HIV crimes, 358–59; by minor-age sex offenders, 99, 154; rape, 152, 154, 358; sexual misconduct rules, 193. *See also* homosexuality; *Lawrence v. Texas*; Miller Law; sodomy laws

Anatrella, Tony, 212

Anderberg, Kristen, 303

Anderson, Zach, 51n13, 461

Ann Klein Forensic Center, 281

Antioch College, 32

anti-prison activism. *See* prison abolition activism

Anti-Prostitution Loyalty Oath (APLO) or Pledge, 35–37

anti-trafficking activism, sex trafficking and prostitution/sex work conflated, 41–46, 167n40, 325–328; criminalization of sex workers perpetuated, 41–43, 44–45; economic interests, 35–36, 310, 342n44; historical origins, 299, 311, 330; HTIC and,

42–43; PEPFAR and, 35, 60n83; Prop 35 and, 324, 335

anti-trafficking activism targeting trafficking other than sex, 319n44, 325, 330; definitions of trafficking, 44–45, 299, 327, 335. *See also* human trafficking

anti-trafficking activism targeting sex trafficking exclusively, 45; "demand" focus, 297–98, 303, 304, 307–8, 310; domestic, 311–12, 313, 321n66, 328; economic interests, 35–36, 323, 332–33; family values narrative, 30, 298, 300, 301–9, 313–14, 314, 319n48; feminists and conservative Christians partnered in, 299–304, 310, 313–14, 320n60, 329–30, 334, 336; Internet and, 7, 323, 334, 337; opposition to, 323–24, 331, 334–36; race and, 302–3, 305, 306, 311–12, 323, 327, 331; sensationalism and fictionalized, composite cases, 306–7, 319n43, 328, 336–37; sex offender registration and, 323, 324, 333–34, 337; social capital and political reputation, 329, 330, 336, 337; Sweden and, 308, 320n51; victim focus, 297–98, 300–301, 326, 335, 336; white slavery, 101, 300, 327, 334. *See also* Californians Against Sexual Exploitation; carceral feminism; sex trafficking

anti-violence movement, 138–41, 147, 155; restorative justice and, 161, 162; women of color and, 143–44, 151. *See also* feminists and feminism

Aristotle, 97

Arizona, 22–23, 250

Arkansas, 40, 357

Arkles, Gabriel, 41

Arnebergh, Roger, 255

arrests. *See* incarceration; mass incarceration

Atkins v. Virginia (2002), 453n97

Atlantic (magazine), 16

attentiveness, 187–88

Australia, 361, 412

Aziga, Johnson, 362

Baran, Bernard, 136–37

Barbados, 412

Barnard College, 136, 167n40

Baudrillard, Jean, 108

Bauman, Zygmunt, 204

Beck, Ulrich, 360

Bedford, Kate, 308, 309

Beijing World Conference on Women
(1995), 311

Belize, 412, 421–23

Benaissa, Nadja, 354

Benedict XVI, pope, 212, 216–17, 223n26

Bentham, Jeremy, 95

Berger, Morton R., 22–23

Berliner, Lucy, 141

Bernstein, Elizabeth, 30–31, 45–46, 79, 130,
334, 336

Bernstein, Robin, 153

biological determinism, 143, 214–16.
See also gender essentialism

bio-power, 96–97, 98, 101

black people. *See* African Americans

Black Women for Wellness, 331

Blair, Jerry, 259

Blast, Synthia China, 184

Bloomberg, Michael, 293

Bock, Sharmin, 330, 332

Body Politic (newspaper), 132

Borchert, Jay, 41

Boston, 133–34

Bowers v. Hardwick (1986), 450n35

Bowles, Samuel, 70

Bowman, Karl, 236

Bradley, Tom, 255–56

Brazil, 36

Breyer, Stephen, 275–76

Briggs Initiative, 133, 328–29

Britain, 14, 224n31, 409, 410, 412

Brown, Wendy, 76

Brown, Willie, 256

Brown bill, 256, 257

Brownmiller, Susan, 133–34

Bryant, Anita, 132, 136, 219

Bumiller, Elizabeth, 141–42

Bumiller, Kristin, 76–77, 298, 309–10

Bureau of Justice Statistics, 154, 203, 280

Burgess, Ann, 142

Bush, George W., 35

Byrne, Garrett, 131

California, 82, 149, 191; ballot initiatives,
324–25, 326, 328–29, 338n6; Briggs
Initiative, 133, 328–29; civil commitment,
242n7; consent law, 32; criminal registry,
20, 94; LAPD, 252–53, 255, 257; vagrancy
law, 251, 264n10. *See also* Californians
Against Sexual Exploitation; lewd or
dissolute conduct law (CA); sex offender
registry (CA)

California Against Slavery, 328, 329–30

California Coalition for Women Prisoners,
329, 332

Californians Against Sexual Exploitation
(CASE Act, Prop 35), 45–46, 323–25,
328–37; ballot initiative system and, 324–25;
Bock and, 330, 332; California Against
Slavery and, 328, 329–30; endorsement of,
328–30, 336, 337; funding and economic
impact of, 331, 332–33, 336, 342n44; Kelly
and, 328–29, 330, 332, 343n63; law enforcement and, 332–33, 334; minors and,
330, 331; opposition, 323–24, 331, 334–36;
Phung and, 329–30, 332, 336, 343n63;
provisions of, 330, 331–33, 336–37, 341n35,
342n44; race and, 323, 324, 326–27, 331,
333, 335; sex offender registry and, 323,
324, 333–34, 337; surveillance and, 323, 331,
333–34, 337; targets of, 331–33.
See also anti-trafficking activism

California Penal Code, 330, 333, 337, 341n34

California Prostitutes Education Project
(CAL-PEP), 331

California Supreme Court, 100, 248, 257,
258, 260

Call Off Your Old Tired Ethics (COYOTE), 326

Campbell, Willy, 23–24, 55n43, 347

Canada, 243n18, 362–63, 410, 412, 419, 424–25

Canadian Supreme Court, 362–363

CANS. See Crime Against Nature by Solicitation law

capital punishment. See death penalty

Caplow, Theodore, 312

carceral feminism, 30–31, 48, 79–81, 119n43, 130–31, 297–14; conservative Christians and, 299–304, 310, 313–14, 320n60, 329–30, 334, 336; family values and, 30, 300, 301–9; securitization and, 303, 305–6, 308; women's human rights and, 309–12, 313

carceral society, U.S. as, 10, 70–95, 109–15, 186; "affective" carceral state, 131; carceral feminism and, 30, 79–81, 119n43, 130–31; child safety zones, 91–93, 111; economic interests, 70, 71, 81; limits of, 81–83; medicalization and, 231–41; sex offender laws and, 83–84, 86–93, 111, 112, 231–41, 261; victimization and, 72–81. See also incarceration; mass incarceration; society of continuous control; victims and victimization

care work, 307, 309, 319n44

Caribbean Community (CARICOM), 46; Belize, 412, 421–23; free movement legislation, 420–23; Jamaica, 409–10, 412–20, 422, 423, 424; Trinidad and Tobago, 412, 420–23

Caribbean Court of Justice (CCJ), 421–22

Caribbean Forum for Liberation and Acceptance of Genders and Sexualities (CariFLAGS), 423

Caribbean Single Market and Economy (CSME), 421

Carpenter, Dale, 195

CASE. See Californians Against Sexual Exploitation

Case, Mary Anne, 29

Castonguay, Leopold, 38

castration, 90, 100, 129

Castro, Mariela, 409

Castro, Raúl, 409

CautionClick.com, 160

Center for Disease Control (CDC, Taiwan), 378–79, 383–86, 394, 395, 401n24. See also HIV/AIDS prevention, care, and treatment (Taiwan); Taiwan

Center for Gender and Sexuality Law (Columbia Law School), 40, 41

Center for Health and Gender Equity, 36

Center for Sex & Culture (San Francisco), 324

Centers for Disease Control and Prevention (U.S.), 372, 386

Chandler, Cynthia, 332

Chatelle, Bob, 137

Chauncey, George, 230

Chelf, Frank, 233, 243n29

Chen, Yi-ming Arthur, 379

Chen Jiashin, 385, 401n24

child abuse. See children and youth, violent crimes against; family abuse

child molestation. See children and youth, violent crimes against

child molestation laws. See sex offender laws

child molester image, 132, 249, 253

child pornography, 3, 5, 14, 83, 106, 330; Densen-Gerber and, 132, 142, 166n23; images classified as, 132, 157, 171n86, 172n100; penalties for, 22–24, 105, 158, 160; race and, 150, 151; sexting as, 15–18, 52n25, 107, 142, 175; SVP laws, 270, 276, 277. See also pornography

children and youth: consensual sex among, 98, 153, 180; innocence of, 85, 99, 106, 153, 285; legal definitions of, 98, 135; LGBTQI, 133, 135–36, 177, 179, 418; NAMBLA and, 133–35, 157; normative sexual behavior, 15, 154; Prop 35 and, 330, 331; sex panic effect on, 157–58; sex trafficking victims,

42, 328, 329, 341n34; sexual agency of, 7, 133, 154, 272; in solitary confinement, 40; statutory rape, 89, 106–7, 131–32, 154, 157, 166n21, 256, 461; victims' rights movement and, 141. *See also* age of consent; pedophiles and pedophilia

children and youth, tried and/or convicted as sex offenders, 14–18, 88–89, 183–84; age of consent and, 157, 172n96; LGBTQI youth, 179; minimum age for registry listing, 14–15, 129, 138, 153; offenses of, 15–18, 52n23, 52n25, 99, 153–54, 175; as over-represented on registry, 179–80; for sexting with minors, 15–18, 52n25, 175; surveillance of, 174, 180. *See also* sex offender demographics; sex offender registries; sex offenders

children and youth, violent crimes against, 3, 86–90, 171n83; accusations of, 98–99, 126–27, 136–37, 142, 156, 164n3; anti-gay, 413–14; daycare abuse panic, 136–37, 142, 143, 146, 164n3; definitions of, 98–99; homosexuality and, 101, 132, 133, 137, 142, 232, 237, 250, 259–61; lewd or dissolute conduct laws and, 247–49, 252, 258, 259–61; media attention, 86–87, 230, 232, 268–69, 271, 273–74; Miller Law and, 230, 232, 237; by minors, 15, 88–89; murder, 86–87, 88, 90, 132, 133, 164n3, 268, 273–74, 413–14; penalties for, 99, 112, 137, 269, 285; predictors of, 151, 249; prison abolition activism and, 185, 187; reporting, 151, 163; San Antonio Four, 126–28, 137, 156; by strangers, 88, 175, 249, 263n5, 285; SVP laws and, 268–69, 271, 273–74, 276–77, 285; vigilante violence after, 129, 271; Walsh Act (2006), 86–87, 90, 138, 146, 153, 276–77; Wetterling Act and, 86–87, 137–38, 146, 261. *See also* family abuse; International Megan's Law; sex offenders; sex offenders, violent; sexual violence, abuse, and assault

Children's Institute International, 154
child safety zones, 91–93, 104, 174, 461
China, 379, 398n8
Christianity: anti-gay activism and violence in Caribbean and, 410–11, 415, 419, 420; anti-trafficking activism, feminists and, 299–304, 310, 313–14, 320n60, 329–30, 334, 336; CANS and, 431–32, 448n17; Metropolitan Community Church, 423; in Taiwan, 391, 396. *See also* Vatican, gender and
Chronicle of Higher Education, 34
Circles of Support and Accountability (COSAS), 160–61
Citizens Committee to Outlaw Entrapment (CCOE), 250
citizens' rights, 147, 159–60
City University of New York (CUNY), 281
civil commitment, 24–28, 276–84; court proceedings for, 269, 276–80, 282–84; facilities for, 24, 26–27, 281; historical origins of, 24–26, 240, 242n7, 271; homosexuality and, 25, 30; Miller Law and, 229, 230, 233, 234; in Minnesota, 27, 56n48, 231, 232, 242n7, 278; in New Jersey, 170n79, 281–84; for nonsexual crimes, 273; number of people in, 26, 91, 278, 281; opposition to, 276; race and, 149, 152, 170n79; Supreme Court and, 24, 27, 90, 165n12, 269; SVP laws and, 269–70, 280. *See also* incarceration
civil commitment, treatment and, 26, 241, 269, 273, 280, 283; Miller Law and, 229, 230, 233, 234, 235; punishment distinction, 24, 90–91
civilizing process, 96, 112
civil law, 32, 34–35, 37
civil liberty laws, 48, 272
civil rights activism, 29, 442
Clinton, Bill, 80, 86, 174, 273
Clinton, Hillary, 11
Clinton administration, 81

Coalition Against Trafficking in Women (CATW), 303, 305, 307–8

Coalition for Public Safety, 11

Coleman, Thomas, 255, 258

collateral consequences, 72, 82, 98, 128, 160, 171n85, 181

college campuses, 171n83; affirmative consent standard, 32–34, 58n60; student/professor relationships, 21–22, 34

colonialism, 217, 218, 224n31, 409, 425

Columbia Law School, 40, 41

Combahee River Collective, 143

Commission on the Status of Women meetings, 307

Communicable Disease Act, 387

community-based organizations (CBOs), 391, 403n49

community notification of sex offender residency, 14, 174, 175, 240, 333; CANS and, 435, 436–37, 438, 451n46; race and, 149–51, 155, 169n71. See also residential restrictions

complementarity, 213

Comstock, Graydon Earl, 276–77

condom use and contraception, access to, 5, 6, 211, 218, 219, 432, 439–40. See also reproductive rights

condom use and contraception, HIV and, 366; disclosure and, 347, 363; in the Netherlands, 353–54, 356, 357, 358, 363, 367; in prison, 350; Rhoades and, 23, 347; scientific evidence, 357, 363; sex workers and, 36, 418; in Taiwan, 387, 389, 393, 394

consensual sex, 182, 230, 241, 461; among inmates, 40–41, 177–78, 192–93, 196–98, 203–5; among minors, 98, 153, 180; anti-gay legislation and, 411, 417; CANS and, 443–44; HIV and, 364, 393

consent, 133, 172n96, 443–44; affirmative consent standard, 32–34. See also age of consent

"Consenting Adult Homosexual and the Law, The" (UCLA Law Review study), 255

conservative politics, 31, 114, 174, 455; anti-trafficking activism, feminists and, 299–304, 310, 313–14, 320n60, 329–30, 334, 336; feminist history with, 80–81, 139–41; sex offender registry (CA) and, 248–49, 260; victims' rights movement and, 73–74, 77. See also liberal politics

contraception. See condom use and contraception

Cook County Jail, 185

Copening, Cormega Zyon, 16–17

Copilow, Barry, 255

Corrigan, Rose, 139

courts: California Supreme Court, 100, 248, 257, 258, 260; Canadian Supreme Court, 362–63; civil commitment legal proceedings, 269, 276–80, 282–84; Kansas Supreme Court, 275; Louisiana Supreme Court, 433, 434, 441, 449n34; prisoner access to, 202–3. See also U.S. Supreme Court

Cox, Laverne, 184

Craigslist, 38, 291, 295, 334

Crane, Michael T., 275–76

crime, nonsexual, 150, 151, 152, 272–73, 282; penalties for, 19, 22, 82–83, 145; recidivism rates, 280; SVP laws and, 284–85. See also murder

Crime Against Nature by Solicitation law (CANS, Louisiana), 144, 433–47, 449n29; African American women and, 13, 429, 430, 434–35, 437, 443; campaign against, 333, 430–31, 437–45; community notification and, 435, 436–37, 438, 451n46; Doe v. Jindal, 429–30, 434–35, 439–40, 442–47, 447n1; penalties for, 429–30, 433–34, 435, 438, 449n33; prostitution statute, compared, 429–30, 433–34, 438–41, 443–44, 446–47, 449n31; provisions of, 440; sex offender registry and, 429–30, 434, 435,

437–41, 444, 446, 447; WWAV and, 430, 437–39, 444

Crime Against Nature statute (Louisiana), 430, 431–34, 447n4, 448n17, 448n18, 448n19; addition of *Solicitation* to, 13, 429, 433–34

Crime and Justice (Caplow and Simon), 312

crime prevention. *See* prevention of offenses

crimes of survival, 44, 178

criminal justice, 78–79, 81–83, 160–64, 233–35, 243n21, 278; crime reduction, 66–70; reform, 10–11, 69–81, 174, 198–99. *See also* incarceration; mass incarceration

criminal registries, 19–20, 93–94, 129. *See also* HIV/AIDS registries; sex offender registries

Critical Resistance, 162, 176

cruises, 426

cruising, 237, 247, 249, 251–53, 261, 400n18

Cuba, 409. *See also* Caribbean Community

Cuerrier case (1998, Canada), 362–63

Daily News, 293, 295

Daily Show with Jon Stewart (television show), 100

Dateline (television show), 329

Davis, Angela, 70–71, 153

Davis, Edward "Ed," 252–53

Davis, Richard Allen, 273

daycare abuse panic, 136–37, 142, 143, 146, 164n3; San Antonio Four, 126–28, 137, 156, 159

death penalty, 80, 445, 453n97; for homosexuality, 409, 411, 412

debility, 129

Debord, Guy, 93

Delaware, 148

Deleuze, Gilles, 95

Densen-Gerber, Judianne, 132, 140, 142, 166n23

Denson, Brianna, 16–17

D'Entremont, Jim, 137

Department for Aging and Disability Services (Kansas), 26

Department of Public Safety (Texas), 14

detention without trial. *See* civil commitment

Diagnostic and Statistical Manual of Mental Disorders (DSM), 236, 245n54, 279

Dialectic of Enlightenment (Horkheimer and Adorno), 96

Diaz, Javier, 92

difference feminists, 131

disciplinary regime, 72, 94–95, 109, 111. *See also* Foucault, Michel

Discipline and Punish (Foucault), 72

discrimination, 68; Jamaican anti-gay legislation and, 419–20; PREA and, 39–41; Title IX and, 34, 57n55. *See also* gender discrimination

dispersed intimacies, 182–83

District of Columbia, 90, 132. *See also* Miller Law

divorce, 35. *See also* marriage

Dobbs, Bill, 127

Dodd, Westley Alan, 273

Doe, Hiroke, 429–30, 437, 442, 447n1

Doe, Ian, 435, 436, 442

Doe v. Caldwell (2012, Louisiana), 446

Doe v. Jindal (2012, Louisiana), 429–30, 434–35, 439–40, 442–47, 447n1. *See also* Crime Against Nature by Solicitation law

Doezema, Jo, 303

domestic violence, 34, 35, 162, 163, 172n103; feminism and, 79, 80, 139. *See also* family abuse

dominance feminism, 133–34

Dominican Republic, 426

Donovan, E. H. Duncan, 259

"Don't Ask, Don't Tell," 205–6

drug crimes and policy, 17, 69; penalties for, 82, 85, 128, 145, 148; as victimless crimes, 262n1; War on Drugs, 2, 11, 116n9, 128, 145, 154, 160, 174 drug offenders: race and, 148, 151; recidivism, 88; treatment for, 42, 395, 436

drug offenders, HIV crimes and, 381; in the Netherlands, 353–54, 356; in Taiwan, 382–86, 387, 389–90, 392, 395, 396, 400n18, 400n22

Du Bois, W. E. B., 196

Duggan, Lisa, 44, 248, 308, 309

Dunham, Lena, 105, 461

Dutch Supreme Court, 358, 364–65, 366–67

Dworkin, Andrea, 134

Economist (magazine), 93

education, 155, 176; about CANS, 430, 438, 442, 447; abstinence-based, 219, 385–86; anti-discriminatory, for law enforcement, 350; HIV, 386, 396, 399n13; LGBTQI people in Caribbean and, 416, 426, 427; marriage and, 318n41; Prop 35 and, 324; sex education, 6, 135, 219, 385–86; Title IX and, 34, 57n55; Vatican and, 218–19; while incarcerated, 80, 82, 194

educational institutions. *See* college campuses

Education Amendments Act (1972), 34

Eighth Amendment, 24, 129, 453n97

Eisenstadt v. Baird (1972), 439–40

Elders, Jocelynn, 219

Electronic Frontier Foundation, 336–37

electronic tracking. *See* surveillance, electronic

Elias, Norbert, 96

employment: care work, 307, 309, 319n44; sex offender registry as barrier to, 14, 90, 128, 174, 182, 430, 435, 437, 438; termination or denial of, 37–39, 291, 294, 295–96, 395, 435; unemployment, 70, 291. *See also* sex work

equality feminists, 131

Equality Now (NGO), 306

equal protection doctrine, 439–44

escort services, 3, 50n3. *See also* sex work

Europe and European Union, 10; age of consent in, 89; Britain, 14, 224n31, 409, 410, 412; France, 218–19, 223n26, 298–99, 357, 375n12, 409; gender and, 217; the Netherlands, 46, 157, 172n98, 353–60, 363–69, 409

ex-convicts, 72, 110–11, 128, 170n77; community notification of residency, 149–51, 155, 169n71, 174, 175, 240; electronic monitoring of, 93–94, 95, 97, 122n73; reintegration of, 94, 160–61, 177. *See also* parole

Executive Committee on AIDS Policy and Criminal Law (the Netherlands), 363

exoneration, 127, 137, 146, 151, 156, 172n94, 184. *See also* innocence

fabricated crimes, 156

Faculty of Arts and Sciences (FAS) (Harvard), 21

Fag Rag, 132

Faludi, Susan, 83

family, 78, 127, 249, 259, 262; anti-gay violence and, 133, 415, 435; of registered sex offenders, 159, 161, 436; sex work and, 36, 44, 45, 298, 314n3, 323

family abuse, 137; domestic violence, 34, 35, 79, 80, 139, 162, 163, 172n103; gay rights activism and, 259, 262; incest, 134, 140, 142, 147, 151, 155; race and, 151; Static-99 risk points, 150; *vs.* strangers, 88, 175, 249, 263n5, 282, 285; SVPs and, 282. *See also* children and youth, violent crimes against; sexual violence, abuse, and assault; strangers, crime by

family court, 35

family values: anti-trafficking and, 30, 298, 300, 301–9, 313–14, 319n48; global homophobia and, 424; homonormative politics, 248; Vatican and, 211, 214, 215, 217, 218, 223n26

the Farm, 253–54

Father-Daughter Incest (Herman), 134

fathers, 35
Federal Bureau of Investigation (FBI), 66
Federal Bureau of Prisons, 39, 193
Federal Inmate Handbook, 193
federal policy, 32, 35–37
female migrants, 45, 310
feminists and feminism, 30–31, 48, 75–76,
    262n2; affirmative consent standard and,
    33; anti-violence movement, 138–41,
    143–44, 147, 155, 161, 162; child protection
    culture and, 105–6; conservative politics,
    history of pairing with, 80–81, 139–41;
    divisions within, 131; domestic violence
    and, 79, 80, 139; dominance feminism,
    133–34; fear and, 141–43; NAMBLA and,
    133–35, 157; prison abolition and, 129–30;
    race and, 143–44, 298–99; radical, 213–14,
    300, 303–4, 305, 316n14; Vatican and, 213,
    214, 216–17, 224n31; women of color, 130,
    131, 143–44. *See also* anti-trafficking
    activism; carceral feminism
Feng (HIV-positive teacher in Taiwan),
    393–94, 395, 396, 405n66
Few, Robyn, 326
Filler, Daniel M., 149–50, 152, 155
Fischel, Joseph, 129, 138, 443–44
Fleissig, Audrey G., 27
Flores, Perla, 335
Florida, 22, 55n39, 92–93, 104, 132–33; crimi-
    nal registry in, 19, 94, 129
Foley, Mark, 100
Ford, Daniel, 137
48 Hours (television show), 274
Foucault, Michel, 117n26, 123n95, 234, 374n7,
    388, 402n43; disciplinary regime, 72, 94–95,
    109, 111; power and, 96–97, 98, 103, 109, 388
Foucha, Terry, 272–73
Foucha v. Louisiana (1992), 272–73, 275
France, 218–19, 223n26, 298–99, 357, 375n12,
    409
Francis, pope, 212, 217, 218, 224n31
Frank, Donovan, 27

Frank, Thomas, 302
Free Baran defense committee, 137
Freedman, Estelle, 230
Freedom Network, 327, 339n19
Freedom of Information Act (FOIA), 192
freedom of speech, 294

Gacy, John Wayne, 133
Gagnon, Julie, 38
Galatians (book of), 213, 221n10
Gambia, 411
Garcia, Jose, 195
Garland, David, 71, 117n22, 301, 310, 312, 313,
    314; on sex offender recidivism, 89
Gay Activists Alliance (GAA), 133
Gay Community News (GCN), 134, 135, 136
Gay Liberation Front (GLF), 253–54
gay people. *See* homosexuality; LGBTQI
    prisoners; LGBTQI rights activism; sexual
    orientation and gender identity
gay rights activism. *See* LGBTQI rights
    activism
Gay Youth, 135
generationFIVE, 162, 186
gender, 176; definitions of, 211, 214–15, 220n2,
    222n18; as identity disorder in DSM,
    245n54; in India, 413; male sexuality,
    313; presentation of, 192, 194, 198–200,
    264n14; reassignment surgery, 412; sexual
    misconduct violations and, 178–81, 192;
    in Sweden, 308. *See also* sexual orienta-
    tion and gender identity; transpeople;
    Vatican, gender and; women
"gender agenda," 214–15, 216–17, 222n16
gender discrimination, 12, 132–33, 215, 409,
    419–20; PREA and, 39–41; Title IX and,
    34, 57n55; while incarcerated, 182–83, 192.
    See also discrimination
gender essentialism, 130–31, 133–34, 135–36;
    anti-violence movement and, 138; restor-
    ative justice and, 162; Vatican and, 211,
    213–14, 216

gender flux, 313

gender of security, 305

Gender: The Deconstruction of Women, Analysis of the Gender Perspective in Preparation for the Fourth World Conference on Women (O'Leary), 212

Georgia, 51n19

Giddens, Anthony, 360

Gingrich, Newt, 174

Global Fund for Women's Circle Against Trafficking, 327

Global Network of People Living with HIV (GNP+), 356–57

Goffman, Alice, 103

Goffman, Erving, 239–40

Goldberg, Whoopi, 31

Gonzales, Jose, 37–38

Goodmark, Leigh, 133

Gottschalk, Marie, 79, 80, 83, 174, 175, 298

Government Accountability Office (GAO), 18

governmentality, 97–98, 99–102; Foucault and, 388; HIV law and, 368, 369, 388, 398n8; Prop 35 and, 324. *See also* carceral society, U.S. as; society of continuous control

Graffenried, Alec von, 369

Gramsci, Antonio, 67

Grant, Melissa Gira, 336, 343n63

Greenhouse, Linda, 23

Grewal, Inderpal, 305, 306, 310

Grisham, John, 105

Griswold v. Connecticut (1965), 5, 432

Groningen, the Netherlands, 353–56, 359–60, 366, 373

Growing Up Gay (Michigan publication), 136

Guantánamo Bay, 285

Guevara-Vilca, Daniel Enrique, 22, 55n39

Halley, Janet, 33, 217, 310

Halperin, David, 211, 364, 454

Hannon, Gerald, 132

Hannon, Michael, 247

Harcourt, Bernard, 10, 110

harm, language of, 161–62, 183–84, 186, 247, 325–26

harm, sex conflated with, 3–4, 15, 21, 23, 47, 106, 154; HIV and, 349, 358, 364–65; lewd or dissolute conduct law and, 252, 255, 256

harm reduction policy (Taiwan), 385–86, 400n22

Harris, Kamala, 329

Harvard University, 21, 57n55

Hay, Harry, 237

Haywood, Deon, 438

HCM. *See* HIV case management (HCM) programs (Taiwan)

Hendricks, Leroy, 273, 275

Herman, Judith Lewis, 134, 140

Heston, Charlton, 217, 223n26

Hispanics, 82, 149, 150. *See also* race

HIV/AIDS: perception of virus, 364; political economy of, 355, 356, 374n7; reinfection, 389, 393–94; as state security issue, 355, 369–72; testing mandates, 357, 380, 385, 393, 396, 405n75

HIV/AIDS, people living with (PLWHA), 347–51, 378; early portraiture and mug shots/composite sketches, 361–62; in Jamaica, 410, 418; prevention onus on, 348, 349–50, 363, 367, 380–82, 386, 392, 395–96, 405n69; prisoners, 207n2, 350; on sex offender registries, 23, 333, 347, 348, 351, 364; sex work and, 36, 37, 338n9, 418; stigmatization of, 359, 364–65, 366, 372, 391, 392, 436; viral load levels, 347, 359, 389, 393

HIV/AIDS criminalization, 347–51, 357, 372; governmentality and, 368, 369, 388, 398n8; sentencing for, 23–24, 364–65, 375n12, 393–94

HIV/AIDS criminalization (the Netherlands), 353–60, 363–69; AIDS Policy and Criminal Law committee, 357–58; condom use and, 353–54, 356, 357, 358, 363, 367; Groningen case, 353–56, 359–60, 366, 373; Leeuwarden case, 358–59, 364–65, 366, 367

HIV/AIDS criminalization, disclosure and, 348, 357; *Cuerrier* case, 362–63; Leeuwarden case and, 358–59; Rhoades case, 23, 347, 351, 364; in Taiwan, 380, 399n9

HIV/AIDS criminalization, transmission and, 20, 178, 189n15, 347, 353–54, 360–61; anal sex and, 358–59; bodily fluid projectiles, 23–24, 55n43, 348, 357, 365–66, 370–71; consensual sex and, 364, 393; Leeuwarden Case and, 358–59, 364–65, 366, 367; number of prosecutions and convictions, 356; scientific evidence ignored in, 357, 358–59, 366; Swiss Epidemics Act, 368–69; in Taiwan, 380, 383, 393–94, 396

HIV/AIDS prevention, 357, 375n11, 398n3, 410; onus on PLWHA, 348, 349–50, 363, 367; PEPFAR and, 35–37

HIV/AIDS prevention, care, and treatment (Taiwan), 30, 37, 378–97, 399n13; Feng case and, 396; harm reduction policy, 385–86, 389, 391, 394, 401n24, 403n48; Lourdes and, 379, 382, 390–93, 395, 403n48, 405n73; onus on PLWHA, 380–82, 386, 392, 395–96, 405n69; Positive Alliance, 379, 382, 392, 394–97; public health practitioners and, 388–89, 402n42; "seek, test, treat, and retain in medical custody," 396, 405n75; "treatment as prevention" model, 380–81, 399n12, 405n69. *See also* HIV case management (HCM) programs (Taiwan)

HIV/AIDS registries: STDcarriers.com, 20, 94, 372–73; in Taiwan, 37, 380, 383–85, 393–94, 397, 398n8, 399n9

HIV case management (HCM) programs (Taiwan), 380, 386–90, 400n22, 402n39, 402n42, 403n45; Lourdes and, 392, 395;

Positive Alliance, 379, 382, 392, 394–97; Zhuang and, 387, 394, 395, 405n66

HIV Control and Patients' Rights Protection Act (HIV Control Act, Taiwan), 378, 393–94; HCM programs and, 380, 386–90, 400n22, 402n39, 402n42, 403n45; provisions and amendments, 380–81, 383–86, 387, 389, 399n9

HIV Monsters, 354, 361–62. *See also* HIV/AIDS criminalization (the Netherlands)

Ho, Josephine, 381–82

Hoffman, Amy, 135

Hollibaugh, Amber, 9, 29, 455, 456–57

homelessness, 91–92, 182, 413

homonationalism, 46–47, 360, 375n19

homonormative politics, 248. *See also* family values

Homophile Effort for Legal Protection (HELP), 252, 253

homophobia, 13, 41, 100–101, 126–27, 412, 423–24; in Jamaica, 410, 413–15, 417, 418–19

homosexuality, 3, 5–6; anti-gay violence, 133, 412–15, 435; anti-sickness resolution, 25, 238–40, 245n54; Briggs Initiative and, 133, 328–29; children, violent crimes and, 101, 132, 133, 137, 142, 232, 237, 250, 259–61; civil commitment and, 25, 30; closeted, 416; coming out, 133; criminalization of, 409, 410–11, 412; cruising, 237, 247, 249, 251–53, 261, 400n18; "curing," 154, 236; in DSM, 236, 245n54; Groningen case and, 359–60; HCM programs and, 389–90; lesbians and lesbianism, 127, 136, 137, 143–44, 412; Mattachine society and, 237–40, 250, 252; Miller Law and, 230, 232–33; MSM, 395, 396, 410; police entrapment and, 104, 106, 250–51, 258–59, 263n9; registries of, 137; sex offender stereotypes, 84–85, 232–33, 236–40, 243n34, 252–53, 259; sexual misconduct rules, 20–21, 178–81, 192–98, 204–6, 207n2; solitary

homosexuality (*continued*)
confinement and, 40–41, 178, 193,
194–95, 196–98, 207n2; SVPs and, 282;
in Taiwan, 382–86, 391, 400n18; teaching and, 132–33, 137, 328–29; travel ban,
420–24, 426, 427; Vatican and, 211, 213,
214, 216, 220n1; of youth, 133, 135–36,
177, 179, 418. *See also Lawrence v. Texas*;
lewd or dissolute conduct law (CA);
LGBTQI prisoners; LGBTQI rights activ-
ism; sexual psychopath diagnosis and
legislation
Hoover, J. Edgar, 66, 271
Hoppe, Trevor, 8, 454
Horkheimer, Max, 96
Horowitz, Michael, 304, 318n34
household registration (Taiwan), 380, 398n8.
See also HIV/AIDS registries
Hsu, Paul, 391, 395
Huang, Hans Tao-Ming, 30, 37, 46
Huffington Post, 37–38, 291, 295
Hughes, Donna, 304
Human Exploitation and Trafficking Unit
(HEAT) and Cold Case Units (Alameda
County), 330
human rights, 27, 42, 367–68; women's
human rights, 309–12, 313. *See also*
LGBTQI rights activism
Human Rights Campaign (HRC), 30,
457
Human Rights Watch, 14, 51n19, 171n85,
183–84
human trafficking: definition of, 7, 45, 299,
323, 325, 330, 341n34; investigations and
statistics, 311–12; PEPFAR and, 35–36;
race and, 43, 311, 312, 331, 333, 337. *See also*
anti-trafficking activism, sex trafficking
and prostitution/sex work conflated;
Californians Against Sexual Exploitation;
sex trafficking; sex work
Human Trafficking Intervention Courts
(HTICS), 42–43, 44

Human Trafficking Intervention Initiative
(New York), 41–45
Humphreys, Laud, 255
Hunt, Kaitlyn, 179
Hunter, Nan, 431, 432
Hurricane Katrina, 436, 437
hymens, 126

I-C.A.R.E. (Taiwan), 395
Idaho, 40, 347
identity politics, 12, 39; of PLWHA, 359;
Vatican and, 215–16
Illinois, 133, 163–64, 189n15, 242n7; sex offender laws in, 137, 175, 182
Illinois Department of Corrections (IDOC),
178
immigrants and immigration, 82, 182, 372,
420–23
Immigration and Customs Enforcement
(ICE), 18, 332
incapacitation, 72, 109–10, 113, 154
incarceration, 10–11; alternatives question, 72, 184–88; consensual sex among
inmates, 40–41, 177–78, 192–93, 196–98,
203–5; education while incarcerated, 80,
82, 194; HIV and, 207n2, 350; PREA and,
39–41, 207n2; prisoner access to courts,
202–3; prison jurisprudence, 178–81,
193, 200–206; race and, 69, 82, 145, 148,
170n77, 180, 181, 185; sexual misconduct
rules, 20–21, 178–81, 192–98, 204–6. *See
also* civil commitment; LGBTQI prisoners; mass incarceration; parole; prison
abolition activism; sentencing; solitary
confinement
incarceration rates, 68–71, 83, 115n7, 149,
185; peaks/declines, 8, 72, 82, 273–74; for
transpeople of color, 181–82
incest, 134, 140, 142, 147, 151, 155. *See also*
family abuse
INCITE! Women of Color Against Violence,
162

indecent exposure charges, 20–21

indefinite confinement. *See* civil commitment

India, 413, 416

Indiana Department of Corrections, 194

Infectious Diseases Act (1998, the Netherlands), 367–68, 369

initiative system (California), 324–25, 328–29, 338n6

injecting drug users (IDUs), 366, 385. *See also* drug offenders

innocence: carceral feminism and, 79–81; of children, 85, 99, 106, 153, 285; exoneration, 127, 137, 146, 151, 156, 172n94, 184; protection of, 74–75, 99, 106, 284–85; of San Antonio Four, 126–28, 137, 156, 159; wrongful convictions, 29, 128, 184, 284–85. *See also* victims and victimization

Innocence Project of Texas, 127

In re Reed (1983, California), 260

Inter-American Commission on Human Rights, 418, 423

intercourse, vaginal, 134, 433–34, 449n31. *See also* anal sex; oral sex

International AIDS Conference (1992, Amsterdam), 338n9

International Colloquium on the Complementarity between Man and Woman ("Humanum Conference"), 212–13

International Gay and Lesbian Human Rights Commission (IGLHRC), 215

International Justice Mission 310, 320n60

International Megan's Law to Prevent Child Exploitation and Other Sexual Crimes through Advanced Notification of Traveling Sex Offenders, 17–18, 87. *See also* children and youth, violent crimes against; Megan's Law; sex offender registries

Internet, 138, 393; anti-trafficking activism and, 7, 323, 334, 337; social media, 104–5, 336, 424

Intimacy and Responsibility (Weait), 360

Iowa, 23, 92, 347, 350–51, 364

Iowa Department of Corrections, 193

Irvine, Janice, 105–6

Jacoby, Russell, 75

Jamaica, 409–10, 412–20, 422, 423, 424; anti-gay violence victims, 412–15; LGBTQI rights activism in, 415–20. *See also* Caribbean Community

Janus, Eric, 279, 284, 285

Jayadev, Arjun, 70

Jenkins, Philip, 73

Jenness, Valerie, 200

Jennings, Dale, 250–51

Jessica's Law, 146

J-FLAG (Jamaican NGO), 418

John, Elton, 421

John Jay College of Criminal Justice (CUNY), 281

Johnson, Lyndon, 2

Johnson, Toni Cavanaugh, 154

Johnson, Valerie Lynn, 362

Joint Legislative Committee for Revision of the Penal Code, 256

Jones, Dwayne, 413–14

Judge, Peter Thomas, 256

Justice Now, 332

K6G unit, 191

Kagada, Rebecca, 411, 424–25

Kaiser, Matt, 33

Kameny, Frank, 238–39

Kaminer, Wendy, 33–34, 141

Kanka, Megan, 86. *See also* International Megan's Law

Kansas, 26, 40–41, 269–70, 274–75

Kansas Supreme Court, 275

Kansas v. Crane (2002), 275–76, 279

Kansas v. Hendricks (1997), 24, 27, 165n12, 269–70, 275, 277, 281, 284–85

Karpman, Benjamin, 232, 236, 243n34

Kelly, Beth, 135

Kelly, Chris, 328–29, 332, 343n63

Kennedy, Anthony, 27, 40, 206, 224n35, 277

Killing the Black Body: Race, Reproduction, and the Meaning of Liberty (Roberts), 162

Kim, Kathleen, 332–33

Kim, Mimi, 162

Kincaid, James, 106

King, Martin Luther, Jr., 137, 164

Kinsey, Alfred, 267n52

Kipnis, Laura, 34

Kish, Kevin, 332–33

Klass, Polly, 273

Ko Naiying, 386, 389–90

Korematsu v. United States (1944), 284–85

Koyama, Emi, 335–36

Kunzel, Regina, 24–25

Kuomintang political party (Taiwan), 380

Lady Gaga, 31

Lampedusa, Frank, 38

Lancaster, Roger, 10, 19–20, 31, 146–47, 149, 271

Lancet, The, 36–37

Latin America, 218

Latinos, 82, 149, 150. *See also* race

law enforcement, 69, 110, 324; CANS and, 446–47; employment of, 70; homophobia in, 419, 426; in Jamaica, 413–14, 417; of lewd conduct law (CA), 250–57; Nong-an home party incident, 382–86, 396; police entrapment, 104, 106–7, 153–54, 250–51, 258–59, 263n9; Prop 35 and, 332–33, 334; sex work patrons and, 307–8

Lawrence, John, 195

Lawrence v. Texas (2003), 5, 100, 144, 431, 432, 433, 448n23; sexual misconduct rules and, 192, 195, 197, 204, 205, 206. *See also* sodomy laws

Lee, Angela, 298

Lee, Lois, 335

Leeuwarden case, 358–59, 364–65, 366, 367

Leigh, Carol (Scarlot Harlot), 325

Lesbian Feminist Liberation (LFL), 134

lesbians and lesbianism, 127, 136, 137, 143–44, 412. *See also* homosexuality; LGBTQI rights activism; sexual orientation and gender identity

Letter to the Bishops of the Catholic Church on the Collaboration of M[a]n and Wom[a]n in the Church and in the World (Ratzinger), 212, 214, 221n4

Levine, Judith, 14, 19, 31, 48, 99, 105–6

lewd or dissolute conduct law (California), 249–62, 264n14; children, violent crimes and, 247–49, 252, 258, 259–61; cruising and, 237, 247, 249, 251–53, 261; language of, 251, 264n10; legal definitions, 257; police entrapment, 250–51; punishment for, 260–61; reforming, 25–26, 250, 252–57, 258–59, 261; sex offender registration and, 257–60. *See also* homosexuality; sex offender registry (CA)

Lexicon: Ambiguous and Debatable Terms Regarding Family Life and Ethical Questions (Pontifical Council for the Family), 212

LGBTQI people. *See* homosexuality

LGBTQI prisoners, 191–206; criminalization of consensual sex, 40–41, 177–78, 192–93, 196–98, 203–5; punished for being victims of rape and sexual assault, 203–4, 207n6; rape by prison guards, 435; sexual misconduct rules, 40–41, 177–81, 192–98, 204–6; solitary confinement and, 40–41, 178, 193, 194–95, 196–98, 207n2; transpeople targeted, 178, 181–82, 198–200. *See also* incarceration

LGBTQI rights activism, 132, 174–88, 415–28; age of consent and, 133, 157–58; antisickness resolution, 25, 238–40, 245n54; Baran case and, 136–37; conservative turn in, 248–49, 260; homonationalism and, 46–47, 375n19; in Jamaica, 415–20; lewd conduct law (CA), reform of, 25–26, 250, 252–57, 258–59, 261; Mattachine Society, 237–40, 250, 252; Michaels case and, 137, 172n100; military and, 138, 205–6; NAMBLA and, 133–36, 157; political reputation and, 424–26; prison abolition and, 29, 144, 175, 178, 189n13; race and, 177; same-sex marriage and, 8, 9, 29–30, 138, 241, 248; San Antonio Four, 126–28, 137, 156, 159; sex offender registry (CA) and, 55n45, 247–49, 258–61; sexual psychopath legislation and, 231, 238; travel ban, 420–24, 426, 427; Vatican as model for, 211, 213–16, 218–20. See also homosexuality; *Lawrence v. Texas*; sexual psychopath diagnosis and legislation

LGBTQI rights activism, distancing from sex offenders, 25, 29–30, 130–38, 241, 245n56; anti-sickness resolution, 238–40, 245n54; prison abolition and, 129–30; "worst of the worst" rhetoric, 158, 164, 175–76, 187, 270, 282. See also sexual psychopath diagnosis and legislation

LGBTQI youth, 133, 135–36, 177, 179, 418

Lianos, Michalis, 103

liberal politics, 31, 74–76, 80–81; anti-trafficking activism and, 304; homonationalism and, 46–47; progressive politics, 127, 129–31, 133–35; sex offender registry (CA) and, 248–49, 260; society of continuous control and, 65–66, 114; victims' rights movement and, 73–74, 77. See also conservative politics

Limón, Javier, 126

Liou, Cindy, 332–33

Lippman, Jonathan, 42

Lively, Scott, 410–11

Lockett, Gloria, 331

Longmore, Paul K., 240

Lopez, Eric, 20–21

Los Angeles County Jail, 191

Los Angeles Police Department (LAPD), 252–53, 255, 257

Louisiana, 13, 14, 89, 175, 272–73. See also Crime Against Nature by Solicitation law

Louisiana Supreme Court, 433, 434, 441, 449n34

Lourdes (Taiwan), 379, 382, 390–93, 395, 403n48, 405n73

Lowenthal, Bonnie, 33–34

Lo Yijun, 393

Luker, Kristin, 302

MacFarlane, Kee, 142, 154

MacKinnon, George, 232, 233, 234–35, 243n29

Mam, Somaly, 328, 336

Mandela, Nelson, 412

Mann Act (1910), 327

Mansnerus, Laura, 24, 25, 27–28, 30

marriage, 30, 308; anti-trafficking activism and, 303–4, 305–6, 309, 318n41; of closeted LGBTQI people, 416; contraception rights and, 5, 432, 439–40; Parents United and, 140; spousal rape, 5. See also same-sex marriage

Marshall, Thurgood, 272

Martin, Lloyd, 132, 140, 166n23

Martinez, Stephanie Limón, 127

Marx, Karl, 70

Massachusetts, 40, 242n7, 282, 439, 461; sex offender laws in, 92, 131–32, 166n21

mass incarceration, 11, 128, 174, 175; decline in, 82, 94, 109; race and, 73, 84, 131, 145; "reserve army of labor," 70; U.S. ranking in, 68–69. See also carceral feminism; incarceration; prison abolition activism

mass incarceration, factors in, 69–81, 84, 116n9; carceral feminism, 79–81; economic, 70; enforcement, 69, 70; fear, rise in, 73; neoliberalism, 70, 103–5;

mass incarceration (*continued*)
sentencing, harshness, 69, 83; victims'
rights movement, 72–75
masturbation, 220
Mathiesen, Thomas, 95
Mattachine Society, 237–40, 250, 252
Mayhugh, Kristie, 126
McCarter, Owen Daniel, 15, 176, 178–79, 183,
184–86
McInnes, Colin, 370
McMartin trials, 154
media coverage: ballot initiatives (CA),
324–25; CANS, 442; HIV in the Netherlands, 353–54, 361, 373n1; HIV in Taiwan,
383, 393; Jamaican anti-gay violence, 413,
417; at odds with crime statistics, 273;
Petro, 291, 293–96; Prop 35, 325, 334–35,
336; rape convictions by people of color,
146; San Antonio Four, 159; sex trafficking, 327–28, 329; sexualized imagery,
304–5; victims *vs.* accused, 127; violent
crimes against children, 86–87, 230, 232,
268–69, 273–74; youth "sex offenders,"
179
medicalization. *See* sex offenders, medicalization of
Meese Commission on Pornography, 140,
300
Megan's Law. *See* International Megan's
Law
Megan's Law (1996 amendment to Wetterling Act), 86–87, 88, 128, 146, 155, 263n5;
passing of, 240, 261; race and, 150; 2016
amendment restricting international
travel, 17–18, 87. *See also* children and
youth, violent crimes against; sex offender registries
Meiners, Erica R., 15, 129–30, 131, 166n16, 176,
177; on harm, 183–84, 186
men: care work by, 309; child care and, 35;
dominance feminism and, 133–34; feminist, 307; male sexuality, 313; NAMBLA

and, 133–36, 157; SVP laws and, 268, 271.
See also gender; women
Mendes, Douglas, 423
"Men Loving Boys Loving Men" (Hannon),
132
mental health, 185, 239, 269–70, 437. *See
also* civil commitment; Sexually Violent
Predator (SVP) laws
men who have sex with men (MSM), 395,
396, 410. *See also* homosexuality
Metropolitan Community Church, 423
Metzl, Jonathan, 239–40
Michaels, Margaret Kelly, 137, 172n100
Michaels, Walter Benn, 68
Michigan, 41, 92, 242n7, 357, 370–71
Michigan Department of Corrections
(MDOC), 194–95, 196–200
military, 138, 205–6
Milk, Harvey, 133
Miller, Arthur Lewis, 229, 242n11
Miller Law (Public Law 615, Washington,
D.C.), 229–40; homosexuality and, 230,
232–33; Mattachine Society and, 237–40;
provisions of, 229–30, 236, 241n3; as pur-
portedly humane, 233–34, 239; as seldom
used, 237, 244n40, 244n41. *See also* sex
offender laws
Ministry of Health, Welfare, and Sport
(the Netherlands), 366, 367–68
Ministry of Justice (the Netherlands),
367–68
Minnesota, 148, 271, 274; civil commitment
in, 27, 56n48, 231, 232, 242n7, 278
Minnesota Sex Offender Program, 27
minors. *See* children and youth
Missouri, 26, 27
Moldova, 47
Molnar, Mary Sue, 159
Montana, 149
Moody, Jeremy and Christine, 129
Moon, In Jin, 330
moral hierarchies, 68, 98–99

moral panics, 65, 101, 108, 154–59, 270; Nong-an home party incident and, 383; victimization and, 75. *See also* sex panics

Moral Penal Code, 252

Moree, Monique Howell, 347

Moscone, George, 256

mothers, 35, 164n3; "security mom," 305–6

Ms. magazine, 142

Mulligan, Lark, 176

murder, 22; anti-gay violence in Jamaica, 413–14, 417; of children and youth, 86–87, 88, 90, 132, 133, 164n3, 268, 273–74, 413–14; HIV transmission penalized as, 359, 364–65; of sex offenders by vigilantes, 129. *See also* crime, nonsexual

Museveni, Yoweri, 411

Myrie v. Barbados (2012, CCJ), 422

NAMBLA (North American Man/Boy Love Association), 133–36, 157

Nares, Gilbert, 37

Nathan, Debbie, 128, 140

Nation, The, 44, 152

National Alliance of State and Territorial AIDS Directors, 350

National Association for the Advancement of Colored People (NAACP) Legal Defense Fund, 445

National Center for Lesbian Rights, 30

National Center for Reason and Justice (NCRJ), 127, 137

National Coalition for Children's Justice, 132

National Committee for Sexual Civil Liberties (NCSCL), 252, 256, 257, 258

National Former Prisoner Survey, 203

National Health Insurance Program (Taiwan), 378–79, 398n3

National Incident-Based Reporting System (DOJ), 15, 52n23

National Institute of Justice, 281

National LGBTQ Task Force, 30

National Organization for Women (NOW), 157–58, 259, 306

National Registry of Exonerations, 156, 172n94

NationInside.org, 144–45

Native Hawaiian Islanders, 149

Nazis, castration by, 100

Neal, Michael, 361

Nebraska, 149, 364, 365–66

neoliberalism, 163, 298, 308–9, 312, 382; mass incarceration and, 70, 103–5; neoliberal penality, 10, 123n95; responsibility constructions and HIV, 362–63. *See also* carceral feminism; carceral society, U.S. as; governmentality; society of continuous control

the Netherlands, 46; age of consent in, 157, 172n97; colonies controlled by, 409; Groningen case, 353–56, 359–60, 366, 373; Leeuwarden case, 358–59, 364–65, 366, 367; public health law reform in, 367–68. *See also* HIV/AIDS criminalization (the Netherlands)

Nevada, 20–21, 94, 250

New Hampshire, 278

New Jersey, 157–58, 170n79, 281–84; sex offenders in, 86, 88, 99, 145, 148

New Jim Crow, The (Alexander), 131, 145

New Life, 391–92

New Mexico, 20, 93–94

New Orleans, 144, 429, 434, 436, 437, 439. *See also* Crime Against Nature by Solicitation law

New York Police Department (NYPD), 3

New York Post, 38, 291, 293, 294

New York State, 32, 56n48, 82, 297, 300, 366; Human Trafficking Intervention Initiative, 41–45; NAMBLA and, 134–35; sex offender registry, 148, 174

New York Times, 22, 23, 99, 336

New Zealand, 412

Nguyen, Vinh-Kim, 398n8, 403n49

Nietzsche, Friedrich, 65

Nixon, Richard, 1–2, 67, 73

NO Justice campaign, 438–42, 445–47. *See also* Crime Against Nature by Solicitation law

Noll, R., 15, 176–77, 182–83

Nong-an home party incident (Taiwan), 382–86, 396

nongovernmental organizations (NGOS), 35–36, 300; anti-trafficking, 303, 306, 310; in Jamaica, 418, 419, 420; in Taiwan, 379, 381, 382, 385, 390–93, 395–96

North American Man/Boy Love Association (NAMBLA), 133–36, 157

North Carolina, 16–17, 89, 148

Northcutt, Stevan T., 22

North Dakota, 149

Not for Sale (Anderberg), 303

NOW (National Organization for Women), 157–58, 159, 306

Obama, Barack, 11, 18, 40, 87

Obama administration, 82

Obamacare, 163

O'Connor, Sandra Day, 201–2

O'Hara, Joseph, 232, 243n21

Ohi, Kevin, 101

Ohio, 250

Oklahoma, 14

O'Leary, Dale, 212

Olivia Lesbian Travel, 426

Oprah, 112

oral sex, 144, 256, 429–30, 432, 433, 448n18. *See also* anal sex; Miller Law

Orange Is the New Black (Netflix series), 184

Organization of American States (OAS), 418

Organization of the Islamic Conference, 212

organizing and protests, 326, 454–60; centrality of sex and justice, 458–60; for and by marginalized people, 456–58. *See also* anti-trafficking activism; LGBTQI rights activism; prison abolition activism

Orio, Scott De, 25–26

Otto, Darrell, 127

Overholser, Winfred, 233, 234, 236, 237

Pacific Islanders, 149

Pannel, Ronald Thaxton, 254

panopticism, 95, 113

paraphilias, 279

Parents and Friends of Gays, 259

Parents United, 140

Parenzee, Andre, 361

Parker, Charles and Gretchen, 129

Parker, Lynette, 335

parole, 18, 24, 78, 86, 170n77; life without possibility of, 22, 158; number of people on, 72, 94, 128, 165n6; surveillance and, 94, 122n73, 268; violation of, 69, 193, 194, 199. *See also* ex-convicts

participatory action research (PAR), 391

Patterson, Orlando, 93

pedophiles and pedophilia, 132, 158–59, 240, 279; conflated with sex offenders, 131, 174; homophobia and, 100–101; race and, 84–85, 146–47. *See also* children and youth

Peluso, Richard, 131–32, 166n21

penal Keynesianism, 70

penalties. *See* sentencing

Pennsylvania, 15, 52n25, 154, 370

people living with HIV/AIDS. *See* HIV/AIDS, people living with

people of color. *See* African Americans; race; women of color

People v. Mills (1978, California), 258

PEPFAR (President's Emergency Plan for AIDS Relief), 35–37, 60n83

personality disorders, 279

Personal Responsibility and Work Opportunity Act (PROWA), 80

Petersilia, Joan, 67

Peterson, Susan, 370

Petro, Melissa, 37–38, 291–96

Peyser, Andrea, 291

Pheterson, Gail, 301

Phung, Daphne, 329–30, 332, 336, 343n63

Pines, Burt, 255

Ping Zhuang, 393

Planned Parenthood, 6

Platania, John, 254

Plato, 79

plea bargaining, 16–17, 78, 170n77, 182, 250, 283; CANS and, 429, 446; legal counsel regarding, 128; lewd or dissolute conduct law and, 254, 258, 261; Prop 35 and, 331, 334. *See also* sentencing

Pleasure Consuming Medicine: The Queer Politics of Drugs (Race), 382

Plunkett, David, 347

PLWHA. *See* HIV/AIDS, people living with

Poland, 217, 223n30

police. *See* law enforcement

police entrapment, 104, 106–7, 153–54, 250–51, 258–59, 263n9

political economy, 355–56, 374n7

pornography, 5, 7, 38–39, 76, 303, 310–11; Meese Commission on, 140, 300; WAP and, 136, 140, 168n40. *See also* child pornography

Pornography: Driving the Demand in International Sex Trafficking (Guinn et al.), 303

Positive Alliance (Taiwan), 379, 382, 392, 394–97

"Postscript on the Societies of Control" (Deleuze), 95

poverty, 44, 126, 145, 298, 331; CANS and, 430, 435; as predictor of child abuse, 151

power, 112, 133–34, 135; Foucault and, 96–97, 98, 103, 109, 388

PREA (Prison Rape Elimination Act), 39–41, 207n2

predators. *See* Sexually Violent Predator (SVP) laws; sexually violent predators

Presidential Advisory Council on HIV/AIDS, 350

President's Emergency Plan for AIDS Relief (PEPFAR), 35–37, 60n83

prevention of HIV/AIDS. *See* HIV/AIDS prevention; HIV/AIDS prevention, care, and treatment (Taiwan)

prevention of offenses, 3–4, 15, 48; PREA and, 39–41; restorative justice and, 160–64. *See also* anti-trafficking activism; civil commitment; prison abolition activism; risk assessment; sex offender registries; surveillance

"primitive law," 96, 122n78

prison. *See* incarceration; mass incarceration

prison abolition activism, 10–11, 128–30; alternatives question, 184–88; Critical Resistance, 162, 176; incarceration rates, 70–71; LGBTQI rights activism and, 29, 144, 175, 178, 189n13; NationInside.org, 144–45; restorative justice and, 161. *See also* incarceration; mass incarceration

prisoners. *See* LGBTQI prisoners

prison jurisprudence, 178–81, 193, 200–206

Prison Litigation Reform Act (PLRA, 1996), 202–3, 204

Prison Rape Elimination Act (PREA), 39–41, 207n2

privacy, 74, 111–12, 256, 324, 432, 433; lewd or dissolute conduct law (CA) and, 251–52, 253; loss of, 323, 334. *See also* surveillance

privatization of justice, 77–78

privilege, 415

progressive politics, 127, 129–31, 133–35. *See also* conservative politics; liberal politics

Project Lambda, 136

Prop 35. *See* Californians Against Sexual Exploitation

prostitution. *See* sex work

prostitution statute, Louisiana, 429–30, 433–34, 438–41, 443–44, 446–47, 449n31. *See also* Crime Against Nature by Solicitation law protector role, 83, 84, 119n51

Pryor, Don, 257

Pryor v. Municipal Court (1979, California), 257

psychiatry. *See* sex offenders, medicalization of

psychodrama, 391–92

psychopath category, 235–36. *See also* sexual psychopath diagnosis and legislation

Puar, Jasbir, 360, 375n19

public employment, 37–39

Public Law 615. *See* Miller Law

public sex, 144, 251–52

punishment, 4, 129, 248, 259; incapacitation and, 72, 109–10, 113, 154; Miller Law and, 233–35; *vs.* rehabilitation, 101, 109, 241; restorative justice and, 160–64; treatment distinction, 24, 90–91. *See also* LGBTQI prisoners; rehabilitation; solitary confinement

punitive state, 66, 71, 103, 124n96. *See also* carceral society, U.S. as; society of continuous control

punitive turn in penal policy. *See* carceral society, U.S. as; mass incarceration, factors in

Queen, Carol, 45–46, 324, 338n9

queer, use of term, 177, 178

queer criminals, human rights of, 114, 127–30, 136–38, 144, 157, 187; Miller Law and, 232; vulnerability and, 179–82. *See also* LGBTQI rights activism

queer disavowal. *See* LGBTQI rights activism, distancing from sex offenders

queer rights activism. *See* LGBTQI rights activism

Queers for Economic Justice (QEJ), 457

queer theory, 46, 65, 68, 248; sex offender laws and, 93, 121n72, 249, 261–62. *See also* LGBTQI rights activism

Quinn, Pat, 164

race, 8–9, 43, 67, 177; anti-trafficking activism and, 302–3, 305, 306, 311–12, 323, 327, 331; CANS and, 13, 429, 430, 434–35, 437, 443; civil commitment and, 149, 152, 170n79; community notification and, 149–51, 155, 169n71; feminism and, 143–44, 298–99; incarceration rates, 69, 149, 181–82; Latinos, 82, 149, 150; mass incarceration and, 73, 84, 131, 145; pedophilia and, 84–85, 146–47; Prop 35 and, 323, 324, 326–27, 331, 333, 335; rape and, 29, 79, 83–84, 146, 151; sentencing disparities, 82, 170n77; sex offender registries' demographics, 84–85, 131, 145–52; sexual psychopath stereotypes, 84–85; transpeople of color, 12, 15, 179, 181–82, 415. *See also* African Americans; white people; women of color

Race, Kane, 382, 386

Racial Innocence (Bernstein), 153

radical feminism, 213–14, 300, 303–4, 305, 316n14

radical movements, 68, 77, 131, 132, 135, 162, 455–56

Ramirez, Elizabeth, 126

rape: anal sex and, 152, 154, 358; anti-violence movement and, 138–40; CANS and, 433; carceral feminism and, 79–80, 119n43; children convicted of, 154; on college campuses, 171n83; definition, 152, 171n81; dominance feminism and, 133–34; HIV transmission and, 353–54, 356, 358–59; of inmates by prison guards, 435; innocence and, 153; Leeuwarden Case and, 358–59; of lesbians to "cure" homosexuality, 412; PREA and, 39–41, 207n2; prisoners punished for being victims of, 203–4, 207n6; race and, 29, 79, 83–84, 146, 151; rape shield laws, 79–80, 139; reported cases, rates of, 152, 171n81; sex offender registry (CA) and, 247–48, 261; spousal, 5; statutory, 89, 106–7, 131–32, 154, 157,

166n21, 256, 461. *See also* sexual violence, abuse, and assault

Rapping, Elayne, 75

rational law, 78–79

Ratzinger, Joseph, 212, 213, 219, 221n4

Ratzinger Report, The, 212, 213

Ray, Audacia, 44

Reagan, Ronald, 77, 141

Reagan administration, 81

recidivism, 51n18, 82, 160–61, 230, 280–81; actuarial logic in risk assessment, 89, 100, 113, 269, 279; sex offender registries contributing to, 155, 171n91; Static-99 and, 30, 57n54, 100, 150, 169n71; of violent sex offenders, 30, 88, 91, 152

recreational *vs.* relational sex ethic, 304–6

Red Umbrella Project (RUP), 43, 44

Reed, Allen Eugene, 260

Reform Sex Offender Laws (RSOL), 130, 144, 159–60, 183

rehabilitation, 69, 72, 74, 77, 82, 88; drug use and, 42, 395, 436; Miller Law and, 233–34; *vs.* punishment, 101, 109, 241; rehabilitative turn, 201; social, 385, 390. *See also* civil commitment, treatment and; punishment

Rehnquist, William, 281

religion. *See* Christianity; Vatican, gender and

Rentboy.com, 3, 30, 50n3

reproductive failure, 306–7

reproductive rights: abortion laws, 5, 6; contraception, 5–6, 211, 432, 439–40; Vatican and, 211, 212, 213, 214, 218, 219, 224n33. *See also* condom use and contraception

residential restrictions, 14, 90, 91–93, 104, 174, 175, 333, 436; repeal of, 461. *See also* community notification of sex offender residency

responsibilization, 363, 367

restorative justice, 160–64

Reynolds, Lauri Jo, 164

Rhoades, Nick, 23, 347, 351, 364

Richardson, H. L., 258

Richie, Beth E., 129

Right on Crime, 174

risk assessment: actuarial logic in, 89, 100, 113, 269, 279; HIV transmission and, 357, 358–59, 360–61, 366; sex offender registries and, 89–90; sexual psychopaths and, 230; Static-99, 30, 57n54, 100, 150, 169n71

Rivera, Cassandra, 126

Roberts, Dorothy, 162

Roberts, John, 147

Roberts, Richard, 107

Roberts, Rodney, 283–84

Robinson, Paul, 78

Rofes, Eric, 136

Roger Williams University study, 150–52

Romer v. Evans (1996), 450n35

Roper v. Simmons (2005), 453n97

Rosenbloom, Rachel, 215

Rosin, Hanna, 16

RSOL. *See* Reform Sex Offender Laws

Rubin, Gayle, ix, 13, 87–88, 99, 136, 318n37

Ruffin v. Commonwealth (1871), 201

Russia, 46, 217

Rustin, Bayard, 137

R. v. Cuerrier (1998, Canada), 362–63

Ryan White Care Act (1990), 348

Sachs, Sidney, 237–38

safer sex, 347, 357, 363, 367, 389. *See also* condom use and contraception

SAGE (Standing Against Global Exploitation), 335

Saint Elizabeths Hospital, 229, 230, 232, 233, 234, 244n40. *See also* civil commitment

same-sex marriage, 5–6; in Australia, 412; in Jamaica, 415; LGBTQI rights activism and, 8, 9, 29–30, 138, 241, 248; in Taiwan, 30, 396; Vatican and, 211, 212, 218, 223n22. *See also* marriage

San Antonio Four, 126–28, 137, 156, 159

San Diego Law Review, 259–60

San Francisco, 256, 325–26

San Francisco Mental Health Advisory Board, Subcommittee on Homosexual Activity and the Law, 258–59

SARS, 387

satanic ritual abuse, 128, 142, 154, 164n3

Satan's Silence: Ritual Abuse and the Making of a Modern American Witch Hunt (Nathan and Snedeker), 128

Saunders, Penelope, 45–46, 324

"Save Our Children" campaign, 132, 136

Scalia, Antonin, 450n35

Schuklenk, Udo, 366

seamless garment activism, 218, 220, 224n33

securitization, 66, 97, 105; carceral feminism and, 303, 305–6, 308; HIV law and, 370–72

segregation, administrative. See solitary confinement

segregation, school, 445

self-help movements, 75–76

sentencing, 22–28, 73, 99, 174, 269; for child pornography possession, 22–24, 105, 158, 160; civil commitment and, 24–27; harshness of, 7, 22–24, 69, 83; for HIV crimes, 23–24, 364–65, 375n12, 393–94; for homosexuality, 409–10, 412; life, 22, 137, 158, 269; for nonsexual crime, 19, 22, 82–83, 145; Prop 35 and, 323–24; race and, 82, 170n77. See also plea bargaining

Sentencing Commission, 160

September 11, 2001, 97, 285, 370

Sero Project, 348, 349–50

sex, definitions of, 98, 100, 106, 214, 220n2, 262; HIV law and, 357; sexual contact, 34, 58n60

sex acts, outlawed. See Crime Against Nature by Solicitation law; Lawrence v. Texas; lewd or dissolute conduct law (CA); Miller Law; sodomy laws

Sex and Justice Conference (2012), 454–56, 459

sex crime laws. See sex offender laws

sex education, 6, 135, 219, 385–86. See also education

Sex Handbook, The: Information and Help for Minors, 272

sex offender demographics, 88–89, 153; homosexuality stereotypes, 84–85, 232–33, 236–40, 243n34, 252–53, 259; race, 84–85, 131, 145–52. See also children and youth, tried and/or convicted as sex offenders

sex offender laws, 35, 86–93, 101–3; Adam Walsh Act, 86–87, 90, 138, 146, 150, 153, 276–77; as anxiety-producing, 105–9; collateral consequences, 72, 82, 98, 128, 160, 171n85, 181; as ineffective, 129, 130; offenses covered under, 89–92, 107, 144, 153–54, 175; reluctance to reform, 83–84, 129–30, 144–45, 159–60, 166n17, 183; residential restrictions, 14, 90, 91–93, 104, 174, 175, 333, 436; as social control model, 86, 93–94, 284–85; statutes of limitations in, 112; Wetterling Act, 86–87, 137–38, 146, 261. See also civil commitment; community notification of sex offender residency; International Megan's Law; lewd or dissolute conduct law (CA); Miller Law; sex offender registries

Sex Offender Management, Treatment, and Civil Commitment (Mercado et al.), 281–82

sex offender registration and notification (SORN) laws. See community notification of sex offender residency; sex offender laws; sex offender registries; sex offender registries, repercussions of

sex offender registries, 7–8, 13–22, 80, 165n6, 259–60; calls to dismantle, 156, 162, 184, 186, 249, 261–62, 444–45; CANS and, 429–30, 434, 435, 437–41, 444, 446, 447; criminal registries based on model of, 19–20, 93–94, 129; as ineffective, 155–56,

159, 171n91, 175; initial laws for, 86–87, 137–38, 249–50, 273–74; number of people on, 8, 13, 51n19, 52n22, 89, 128, 165n6, 174; PLWHA on, 23, 333, 347, 348, 351, 364; Prop 35 and, 323, 324, 333–34; race and, 12, 145, 147–52, 155–56, 170n77, 170n79, 434–35, 437; removal of people from, 333, 446; retroactive application, 55n45, 334; risk assessment and, 89–90; RSOL and, 130, 144, 159–60, 183; Walsh Act and, 86–87, 90, 138. *See also* children and youth, tried and/or convicted as sex offenders; community notification of sex offender residency; International Megan's Law

sex offender registries, repercussions of, 177, 258; banishment from society, 71, 96, 110–11, 159; barrier to services and employment, 14, 90, 128, 174, 182, 430, 435, 437, 438; CANS and, 435, 437–38; castration, 90, 129; collateral consequences, 72, 82, 98, 128, 160, 171n85, 181; emotional distress, 155–56, 159, 183, 364, 437; fees, 429, 430, 435, 451n46; ID mandates, 14, 145, 175, 430, 435, 437, 451n46; privacy issues, 323, 334; prohibited social contact, 127, 129; residential restrictions, 14, 90, 91–93, 104, 174, 175, 333, 436, 461; travel bans, 18, 87; vigilante violence, 129. *See also* community notification of sex offender residency

sex offender registry (California), 25–26, 100, 149, 254, 257–62; calls to dismantle, 248, 259; enactment of, 249–50; mandates of, 55n45, 91–92; Prop 35 and, 323, 324, 333–34, 337; victimless crimes and, 26, 247–49, 258, 262n1. *See also* California; lewd or dissolute conduct law (CA)

sex offenders, 13–21, 97–99, 177–79; banishment from society, 71, 96, 110–11, 159; conflated with pedophiles, 131, 174; family of, 159, 161, 436; incurability claims, 100,

111, 160, 236, 273; motives of, 185–86; political mobilization of, 130, 144, 159–64, 166n17, 183; vigilante violence against, 129. *See also* children and youth, tried and/or convicted as sex offenders; Crime Against Nature by Solicitation law; lewd or dissolute conduct law (CA); Miller Law; recidivism; sex offender registries; sex offenders, medicalization of; sex offenders, violent; sex offenders, violent *vs.* nonviolent; surveillance; worst of the worst

sex offenders, medicalization of, 229–30, 231–41, 243n18, 269; homosexuality, anti-sickness resolution, 25, 238–40, 245n54. *See also* civil commitment; sexual psychopath diagnosis and legislation

sex offenders, violent, 86–87, 99, 262; civil commitment for, 26, 30, 91, 152, 283–84; HIV and, 20, 364, 372; recidivism of, 30, 88, 91, 152; SVP laws and, 268, 270, 271–77, 280–85, 287n29. *See also* children and youth, violent crimes against; sexual violence, abuse, and assault

sex offenders, violent *vs.* nonviolent, 87–88, 112, 250, 271, 281–82; rate disparity, 14, 51n19, 89–90, 110; Static-99 and, 150; victimless crimes, 247, 258, 259–60

sex offenders, wrongfully accused. *See* innocence

sex offenses. *See* sexual violence, abuse, and assault

Sex Panic and the Punitive State (Lancaster), 146–47

sex panics, 87–88, 90, 96, 108, 109; anti-trafficking activism and, 300, 327; emotional effect, 156, 157–58; sexual psychopaths and, 230, 231–32; U.S. Supreme Court and, 270–77. *See also* moral panics

"sex rings," 142, 154

sex sting operations. *See* police entrapment

sexting, 15–18, 52n25, 107, 142, 175. *See also* children and youth, tried and/or convicted as sex offenders

Sexton, Lori, 200

sex trafficking, 101, 311, 335; children as victims in, 42, 328, 329, 341n34; definition of, 321n65, 326; media coverage, 327–28, 329; PEPFAR and, 35–36; travel bans, 112, 310. *See also* anti-trafficking activism; anti-trafficking activism, sex trafficking and prostitution/sex work conflated; Californians Against Sexual Exploitation; human trafficking; sex work

sexual abuse. *See* sexual violence, abuse, and assault

sexual assault. *See* sexual violence, abuse, and assault

"Sexual Child Abuse: A Contemporary Family Problem" (ACLU Gay Rights Chapter and NOW), 259

sexual deviance, 25, 152, 182, 233, 385; named conditions of, 98, 123n83, 279. *See also* lewd or dissolute conduct law (CA); sodomy laws

sexual freedom, 12, 21–22, 48, 76, 211, 455; feminism and, 131, 157–58; historical liberalization, 4–6, 272; Netherlands law and, 157, 172n97

Sexually Violent Predator (SVP) laws, 268, 271–77, 280–85; child pornography and, 270, 276, 277; criticism, 274–75; in New Jersey, 281–84; number of people held under, 277, 287n29. *See also* children and youth, violent crimes against; sex offenders, violent; sex offenders, violent vs. nonviolent

sexually violent predators, 146, 178, 182, 268, 269, 274; differences between other sex offenders and, 281–82. *See also* sex offenders

sexual misconduct rules, 20–21, 40–41, 178–81, 192–98; punishment for infrac-

tions, 193, 194–95, 196–98, 204–6. *See also* incarceration; *Lawrence v. Texas*; LGBTQI prisoners

Sexual Offense Prevention Policy (Antioch College), 32

sexual orientation and gender identity (SOGI), 132–33, 211; lesbians and lesbianism, 127, 136, 137, 143–44; LGBTQI youth, 133, 135–36, 177, 179, 418; male sexuality, 313. *See also* gender; homosexuality; LGBTQI prisoners; LGBTQI rights activism; transpeople

sexual psychopath diagnosis and legislation, 25, 26, 229–39, 243n34, 271; historical statistics, 231–32, 237, 242n7, 244n40, 250; medicalization and, 231–37; "psychopath" terminology, 235–36; race and, 84–85; repeal of, 272; social and legal effects of, 233–34, 237–38, 243n18; without criminality, 234–35, 238, 239. *See also* civil commitment; Miller Law; sex offenders, medicalization of

sexual violence, abuse, and assault: affirmative consent standard, 32–33; definitions of, 34, 98–99, 174–75; motives for, 185–86; PREA and, 39–41; preventing, 3, 4, 185–87; reporting, 151, 163, 171n81; *vs.* victimless crimes, 26, 247–49, 252, 253, 258, 262n1, 272. *See also* children and youth, violent crimes against; family abuse; prevention of offenses; rape; sex offenders, violent; sex offenders, violent *vs.* nonviolent; sexual misconduct rules; victims and victimization

sex work, 3, 7, 31, 50n3; California Penal Code, 330, 333, 341n34; contraception and, 36, 418; decriminalization, 37, 46, 299, 325–26; "demand" for services, 297–98, 303, 304, 307–8, 310; deportation and, 331; family of sex workers, 36, 44, 45, 298, 314n3, 323; HIV and, 36, 37, 338n9, 418; Mann Act and, 327; motivation for engaging in, 43–44, 178, 292, 314n3, 322n73; PEPFAR and, 35–37; Petro and, 37–38, 291–96; prostitution statute (Louisiana), 429–30, 433–34, 438–41, 443–44, 446–47, 449n31; "Swedish Plan," 308, 320n51; workers' rights, 299, 325–26, 338n9. *See also* anti-trafficking activism, sex trafficking and prostitution/sex work conflated; Californians Against Sexual Exploitation; Crime Against Nature by Solicitation law

Sex Workers' Outreach Project (SWOP-USA), 326

Sex Workers without Borders, 326

Shapiro, Bruce, 77

Shay, Giovanna, 203

Shulevitz, Judith, 33–34

silo effect, 29, 216, 219, 454–55

Silverglate, Harvey, 106

Simon, Jonathan, 74, 301, 305, 310, 312, 313, 314

Sixth Amendment, 71, 141, 171n79

Smith, Chris, 18, 35

Smith, Eric, 370

Smith, Jada Pinkett, 336

Smith v. Doe (2003), 14, 51n18

Snedeker, Mike, 128, 140

Snitow, Ann, 131

social capital, 337, 419, 425

social class, 143, 302, 305. *See also* poverty

social control systems, 84–115; banishment in, 71, 110–11; crime reduction and, 66–70; punishment-based, 109; rehabilitation-based, 109; sex offender laws as model, 86, 93–94, 284–85; sex offenders' place in, 97–99; SVP laws and, 268–69; synopticism and, 95–99, 113. *See also* carceral feminism; carceral society, U.S. as; HIV/AIDS prevention, care, and treatment (Taiwan); society of continuous control

socialism, 74

social media, 104–5, 336, 424. *See also* Internet

Society for Individual Rights, 256

society of continuous control, 65–66, 93–115; as anxiety-producing, 105–8; governmentality and, 99–102; neoliberalism and, 103–4; police entrapment and, 104; retrogression and, 101–2; spectacularization in, 113; statutes of limitations in, 112; synopticism in, 95–99, 113; terrorism and, 111; zones of safety in, 111–12. *See also* carceral society, U.S. as

Society of the Spectacle, The (Debord), 93

sodomy laws, 5, 229, 256, 434, 449n34; in Belize, 423; *Bowers v. Hardwick*, 449n35; CANS and, 144, 431–33, 435, 448n17; in Jamaica, 415, 419, 423. *See also* anal sex; *Lawrence v. Texas*; lewd or dissolute conduct law (CA); Miller Law; sexual misconduct rules

solitary confinement, 203, 208n9, 445; LGBTQI prisoners in, 40–41, 178, 193, 194–95, 196–98, 207n2; trans prisoners in, 199, 200. *See also* incarceration

SORN laws. *See* sex offender laws

South Africa, 412

South Bay Coalition to End Human Trafficking, 335

South Carolina, 129

sovereign power, 96–97, 112

Spade, Dean, 40

Spitzer, Elliot, 297, 314n2

Spivak, Gayatri, 302

States of Injury (Brown), 76

Static-99, 30, 57n54, 100, 150, 169n71

statutes of limitations, 112

statutory rape, 89, 131–32, 154, 157, 166n21, 356; age falsification and, 106–7, 461. *See also* children and youth, tried and/or convicted as sex offenders; children and youth, violent crimes against; rape

Stauffer, Zachary, 329

STDcarriers.com, 20, 94, 372–73
Stein, Arlene, 302
Steinem, Gloria, 142
Stiaes, Marchand, 438
stigmatization, 154, 155–56, 178, 239–40, 261, 457; of PLWHA, 359, 364–65, 366, 372, 391, 392, 436
STI testing, 389, 402n40; mandatory HIV, 357, 380, 385, 393, 396, 405n75
Stokes, Stephen, 17
Stormfront.org, 158–59
Stranger Next Door, The (Stein), 302
strangers, crime by, 141–42, 150, 180, 282, 302; children and, 88, 175, 249, 263n5, 285. *See also* family abuse
Strangio, Chase, 41
Streep, Meryl, 461
stripping, 291–92
Strub, Sean, 23, 364
student/professor relationships, 21–22, 34
Sun, Chyng, 303
surveillance, 93–99, 110; as anxiety-producing, 105–9; by citizens, 95, 112–13, 154; of incarcerated transpeople, 198–200; of minors convicted as sex offenders, 174, 180; of parolees, 94, 122n73, 268; Prop 35 and, 324, 331, 333–34, 337; synopticism and, 95–99, 112–13; travel bans, 87, 112. *See also* sex offender registries
surveillance, electronic, 92, 93–94, 104, 105, 375n12; costs of, 71, 114–15; intended to facilitate rehabilitation, 122n73; lifelong mandates, 51n19, 90, 91; number of monitored people, 19, 93; synopticism in, 95, 97
surveillance, HIV law and (Taiwain), 379, 380–81, 395; HCM programs and, 386–90, 402n42; HIV Control Act revamp (2007), 387; HIV registries, 37, 380, 383–85, 393–94, 397, 398n8, 399n9; name-based, 380, 381; Nong-an home party incident and, 382–86

SVP laws. *See* Sexually Violent Predator (SVP) laws
Sweden, 308, 320n51
Swiss Epidemics Act (2012), 368–69
Switzerland, 368
synopticism, 95–99, 112–13

Taiwan, 30, 46; CDC, 378–79, 383–86, 394, 395, 401n24; harm reduction policy in, 385–86, 400n22; HIV registry in, 37, 380, 383–85, 393–94, 397, 398n8, 399n9; National Health Insurance Program, 378–79, 398n3; Nong-an home party incident, 382–86, 396. *See also* HIV/AIDS prevention, care, and treatment (Taiwan); HIV case management (HCM) programs (Taiwan); HIV Control and Patients' Rights Protection Act
Taiwan AIDS Action, 379, 381
Taiwan AIDS Foundation, 386
Taiwan AIDS Society, 394–95
Taiwan Lourdes Association, 379, 382, 390–93, 395, 403n48, 405n73
Tamms supermax prison, 163–64
Tangents (magazine), 247
teachers and professors: Briggs Initiative and, 133, 328–29; "hooker teacher" scandal and, 37–38, 291–96; relationships with students, 21–22, 34
Tearoom Trade: Impersonal Sex in Public Places (Humphreys), 255
terrorism, 97, 111, 285, 369, 370–71, 422
Texas, 14, 20, 94, 195; San Antonio Four, 126–28, 137, 156, 159. *See also Lawrence v. Texas*
Texas Homosexual Conduct Law, 195
Texas Voices for Reason and Justice, 159
Thailand, 412
"Thinking Sex" (Rubin), ix, 13
Thomas, Clarence, 206, 275, 277
Thomas, Kerry, 347
Ticktin, Miriam, 298–99

Time magazine, 33, 58n60

Timmendequas, Jesse, 273

Title IX of Education Amendments Act, 34, 57n55

Tomlinson, Maurice, 9, 46, 415–20

Tomlinson v. Trinidad and Tobago and Belize (2013), 422

Tomlinson v. TVJ et al. (Jamaica), 420

Tomso, Gregory, 20, 46, 94

Tonry, Michael, 67

Toronto, Canada, 132

"Tracing a Radical Feminist Vision from the 1970s to the Present" (Pheterson), 301

trafficking. *See* anti-trafficking activism; human trafficking; sex trafficking

Transformative Justice Law Project of Illinois (TJLP), 176

Transgender Law Center, 30

transpeople, 40–41, 184, 219, 413–14; of color, 12, 15, 179, 181–82, 415, 429; sexual misconduct violations, 178, 181–82, 198–200; stigmatization, 178, 436. *See also* gender; LGBTQI prisoners; LGBTQI rights activism; sexual orientation and gender identity

travel bans, 3, 18, 87, 112, 420–24, 426, 427

treatment. *See* civil commitment; civil commitment, treatment and; HIV/AIDS prevention, care, and treatment (Taiwan); rehabilitation

Trinidad and Tobago, 412, 420–23

Truthout (website), 42

Tuggle, Heather, 329

Turkey, 412

Turner v. Safley (1987), 202, 209n26

UCLA *Law Review*, 255

Uganda, 46, 410–12, 424–26

Umansky, Lauri, 240

UNAIDS, 350, 370, 380, 420–21

unemployment, 70, 291. *See also* employment

United Kingdom, 412; Britain, 14, 224n31, 409, 410, 412

United Nations, 222n16, 300, 307, 325, 418; UNAIDS, 350, 370, 380, 420–21

United States, 2–3, 409, 419, 425; age of consent in, 89; domestic trafficking activism, 311–12, 313, 321n66, 328; historical crime rates, 66–72; September 11 and, 97, 285, 370; PEPFAR and, 35–37. *See also* carceral society, U.S. as; society of continuous control

U.S. Centers for Disease Control and Prevention (CDC), 23–24

U.S. Congress, 11, 39, 80, 132, 276; Megan's Law and, 17–18, 240; Miller Law and, 230, 231–32, 234, 235, 242n11; PEPFAR and, 35–36

U.S. Constitution, 4–5, 6, 14, 74, 78; Eighth Amendment, 24, 129, 453n97; Prop 35 and, 334, 337; protections of, for prisoners, 201–2, 203, 209n26; Sixth Amendment, 71, 141, 171n79, 171n79; SVP laws and, 268, 270, 271–77, 280–85, 287n29. *See also* civil commitment; Crime Against Nature by Solicitation law; *Lawrence v. Texas*; lewd or dissolute conduct law (CA); Miller Law; U.S. Supreme Court

U.S. Department of Homeland Security, 3, 332

U.S. Department of Justice, 3, 15

U.S. Sentencing Commission, 50n8, 82

U.S. Supreme Court, 5–6, 8, 41, 270–77, 433, 449n29; *Atkins v. Virginia*, 453n97; *Bowers v. Hardwick*, 449n35; civil commitment and, 90, 165n12, 269; *Eisenstadt v. Baird*, 439–40; *Foucha v. Louisiana*, 272–73, 275; *Griswold v. Connecticut*, 432; *Kansas v. Crane*, 275–76, 279; *Kansas v. Hendricks*, 24, 27, 165n12, 269–70, 275, 277, 281, 284–85; *Korematsu v. United States*, 284–85; PEPFAR and, 35–36; prison jurisprudence and, 201–2; *Romer v. Evans* and, 450n35;

U.S. Supreme Court (*continued*)
Roper v. Simmons, 453n97; *Ruffin v. Commonwealth*, 201; same-sex marriage and, 218, 224n35; sentencing and, 22–23; sex offender registries and, 14, 51n18, 129; *Smith v. Doe*, 14, 51n18; *Turner v. Safley*, 202, 209n26; *United States v. Comstock*, 276–77. See also *Lawrence v. Texas*
U.S. Trafficking Victims Protection Act (TVPRA), 311
United States v. Comstock (2010), 276–77
University of the West Indies, 410
unprotected sex. See condom use and contraception
Up Against a Wall: Rape Reform and the Failure of Success (Corrigan), 139
Urban Institute, 44
USA Today, 107, 108
US PROStitutes Collective, 326, 331
Utah, 7

Vance, Carole, 42, 76
Vanek, John, 335
Vasquez, Anna, 126
Vatican, gender and, 211–20; biological determinism and, 214–16; complementarity and, 213; definition objections, 211, 214–15, 220n2, 222n18; education and, 218–19; feminism and, 213, 214, 216–17, 224n31; "gender agenda," 214–15, 216–17, 222n16; "gender theory," 211, 213, 214, 217; seamless garment activism, 218, 220, 224n33. See also Christianity; gender
Vermont, 51n19, 242n7
victimless crimes, 26, 247–49, 252, 253, 258, 262n1, 272
victims and victimization, 10, 72–81, 203–4; age and power imbalance, 135; anti-gay violence in Jamaica and, 416–17; anti-trafficking activism and, 297–98, 300–301, 326, 335, 336; anti-violence movement and, 147; commodification, 75–76;

innocence and, 74–75, 79–81, 85; media attention, 127; support groups, 77, 79; victims' bill of rights, 77, 78; victims' rights movement, 72–75, 77, 79–80, 141. See also carceral feminism; carceral society, U.S. as; innocence
vigilante activity, 20, 93, 104, 129, 271; by anti-trafficking activists, 310; HIV criminalization and, 372–73; in Jamaica, 413–14
Violence Against Women Act (VAWA) (1994), 80, 144
Violent Crime Control and Law Enforcement Act (1994), 80
violent crimes. See anti-violence movement; children and youth, violent crimes against; crime, nonsexual; sex offenders, violent; sex offenders, violent *vs.* nonviolent; sexual violence, abuse, and assault
Virginia, 52n25
Virilio, Paul, 102
Voice of the Ex-Offender (VOTE), 439

Wacquant, Loïc, 124n96, 308, 309, 310, 314; mass incarceration and, 70; on rise of carceral state, 301, 312, 313
Walsh, Adam, 86
Walsh, John, 86
Walsh Act (2006), 86–87, 90, 138, 146, 153, 276–77
Wang Renxian, 387, 388
WAP. See Women Against Pornography
war, terminology of, 2–3
Warner, Michael, 240
War on Crime, 2
War on Drugs, 2, 11, 116n9, 128, 145, 154, 160, 174
Washington, D.C., 90, 132. See also Miller Law
Washington Post, 174
Washington State, 274
Watergate scandal, 108
Weait, Matthew, 360

welfare services, 77, 80, 163; public health law reform (the Netherlands), 367–68

welfare state, 308–9, 313

West Virginia, 41

Wetterling, Jacob, 86

Wetterling Act (1994), 86–87, 137–38, 146, 261

What's the Matter with Kansas? (Frank), 302

White, William Alanson, 235–36

white people, 29, 79, 82, 319n41; anti-trafficking activism and, 302–3, 306, 307. *See also* African Americans; race

white slavery, 101, 300, 327, 334

White Slave Traffic Act (Mann Act, 1910), 327

Williams, Nushawn, 354, 356–57, 365–66

Wisconsin, 52n25, 56n48, 242n7, 274, 278

Wodak, Alex, 385

women: dominance feminism and, 133–34; lesbians and lesbianism, 127, 136, 137, 143–44, 412; mothers, 35, 164n3, 305–6; NAMBLA and, 134–35; ordination of, 213; sex panic effect on, 156; treatment units for, 177–78. *See also* carceral feminism; feminists and feminism; gender

Women Against Pornography (WAP), 136, 140, 168n40

women of color, 15, 298; CANS and, 13, 429, 430, 434–35, 437, 443; criminalization as response to reported sexual violence against, 130, 151; opposition to mainstream feminist movement by, 130, 131, 143–44; rape law reform and, 157–58; restorative justice and, 162; sexual misconduct rules and, 179, 180. *See also* African Americans; race

Women's Health & Justice Initiative, 439

women's rights, 5, 211, 215, 309–12, 313. *See also* anti-trafficking activism; feminists and feminism

Women with a Vision (WWAV), 430, 437–39, 444

workers' rights, sex work and, 299, 325–26, 338n9

worst of the worst: disavowal of, 175, 176; incarceration of, 91, 158, 164, 187, 270, 278, 282

Yingbin, Ning, 381–82

Young, Cathy, 366

Yung, Corey, 284, 285

Zhuang Ping, 387, 394, 395, 405n66

Zimring, Franklin, 67